CRITICAL
STRATEGIES
for Academic Writing

CASES, ASSIGNMENTS, and READINGS

CRITICAL STRATEGIES
for Academic Writing

CASES, ASSIGNMENTS, and READINGS

MALCOLM KINIRY
Rutgers University–Newark

MIKE ROSE
*University of California,
Los Angeles*

Bedford Books of *St. Martin's Press · Boston*

To our students and colleagues in the Veterans Special Educational Program and the Freshman Preparatory Program.

And to Ruth Kiniry and Susan Dolan, Rose Newby and Bill Newby

For Bedford Books

Publisher: Charles H. Christensen
Associate Publisher: Joan E. Feinberg
Managing Editor: Elizabeth M. Schaaf
Developmental Editor: Ellen Darion
Production Editor: Mary Lou Wilshaw

Copyeditor: Barbara G. Flanagan
Text Design: Claire Seng-Niemoeller
Cover Design: Visual Dialogue
Cover Art: Corbusier Centre I, Zurich
  photographed by Jenny Okun

Library of Congress Catalog Card Number: 88–70426

Manufactured in the United States of America

4   3   2   1   0

f   e   d   c   b

For information, write: St. Martin's Press, Inc.
175 Fifth Avenue, New York, NY 10010

Editorial Offices: Bedford Books of St. Martin's Press
29 Winchester Street, Boston, MA 02116

ISBN: 0–312–00342–0

Acknowledgments

George D. Abell. Excerpt from *Exploration of the Universe,* 3rd edition, by George D. Abell, copyright © 1975 by Holt, Rinehart and Winston, Inc., reprinted by permission of the publisher.
Franklin Pierce Adams. Excerpt from *FPA Book of Quotations* by Franklin Pierce Adams. Copyright 1952 by Funk & Wagnalls Company; copyright © renewed 1980 by Anthony, Timothy, Jonathan and Persephone Adams. Reprinted by permission of Harper & Row, Publishers, Inc.
James L. Adams. Conceptual Blockbusting, © 1986, Addison-Wesley Publishing Co., Inc., Read-ing, Massachusetts. Reprinted with permission of the publisher.
Paula Gunn Allen. From *The Sacred Hoop.* Copyright © 1986 by Paula Gunn Allen. Reprinted by permission of Beacon Press.

Acknowledgments and copyrights are continued at the back of the book on pages 726–735, which constitute an extension of the copyright page.

Preface for Instructors

THE RATIONALE FOR THE BOOK

The labels vary — critical thinking, academic discourse, higher-order cognition — but the fundamental issue seems to be the same. A high percentage of college students — from those entering community college to those enrolled in upper-division university courses — have trouble when they must generate concise definitions or summarize a scholarly discussion, when they need to detail a laboratory procedure, explain a method, or evaluate a taxonomy, when they're asked to compare two theories, analyze a text, or argue a position. Though some policymakers are beginning to label such activities "the new basics," these are, in fact, very sophisticated cognitive-rhetorical activities — that is, activities that involve the complex interplay of thinking and writing. We forget, sometimes, how hard it is to learn how to do them. They require immersion in certain kinds of language use — ongoing practice, modeling, and successive approximation in settings where teachers have the training, time, and reasonable class load to comment and advise. We see the freshman composition course as a central place to focus on these thinking-writing activities, which we're calling here critical strategies. Such a course provides an opportunity for students not only to improve their ability to summarize, explain, and analyze but to step outside of such procedures and consider their nature and purpose. *Critical Strategies* is our attempt to provide an approach and a set of materials that can contribute to such a process.

To affirm the need for a curriculum focused on critical strategies is not to deny that students define and classify and analyze continually in their day-to-day lives. These are basic human activities. But many students have not had extended opportunity to engage in the particular kind of systematic defining and classifying and analyzing that occur in academic contexts, have not done so with academic materials in ways that are complex and exploratory rather than formulaic, have not had multiple opportunities to reflect on the very intellectual activity they're engaged in, have not been encouraged to complicate thinking and writing. This lack of experience will significantly limit them, of course, because the kinds of strategies they must command are not straightforward, mechanical routines but heuristic, generative, and flexible — they resist easy procedure.

Unfortunately, the most familiar embodiments of such critical strategies are the formulaic approaches and static models students find in traditional English textbooks. The dynamic act of comparing, for example, is reduced to two or three compare/contrast essay patterns or is represented in a fixed way through models to imitate, where the messy, interactive *work* of comparing is long since past and students have before them the closed and polished comparison essay. While we rely on familiar chapter headings — i.e., comparing, analyzing[1] — our book does not function traditionally. What we try to do is create conditions that encourage students to employ critical strategies flexibly and in combination, inviting them to engage problematic materials and seize interpretive opportunities, experimenting with and reevaluating the thinking and writing they do. Our goal is the development of a performative competence, a sense of how to take on certain kinds of intellectual work rather than merely to search for the correct form, the right answer.

THE CONTEXT OF THE BOOK

Our curriculum began nearly twenty years ago in a preparatory course for adults entering college, but it has been influenced in more recent years by insights and procedures gained from two movements: English for specific (or academic) purposes — work emerging primarily from the applied linguistics and ESL camps — and writing across the curriculum. One exceptionally useful by-product of the English for academic purposes research has been the attempt to determine the kinds of writing tasks actually required of college students.[2]

---

[1] To avoid a confusion of static modes with dynamic processes, we tried to come up with a different labeling system for the strategies. We thought about following Mina Shaughnessy's lead and labeling by functional descriptions: For example, "This Is What Happened" instead of "Serializing" or "This Is Like (or Unlike) This" instead of "Comparing." But the functional descriptions got cumbersome as we got into increasingly complex activities ("Analyzing" became "This Is How Phenomena Change in Meaning as One Shifts Perspectives"). We thought, as well, about creating a new set of terms that would stress the heuristic nature of the strategies. But this resulted in a foreign terminology that created more problems than it solved. We decided, then, to stay with more familiar terms but to make them participles to indicate action, to modify and explain their varied nature in the introductions and assignments, and to use them in ways that illustrate their strategic, rhetorical flexibility.

[2] See, for example, Brent Bridgeman and Sybil B. Carlson, "Survey of Academic Writing Tasks," *Written Communication* 1 (April 1984): 247–80; and Daniel Horowitz, "Essay Examination Prompts and the Teaching of Academic Writing." *English for Specific Purposes*, v. 5 (1986), pp. 107–20. These fine-grained analyses divide academic writing tasks into more categories than we did. Bridgeman and Carlson's, for instance, breaks down assignments requiring comparing into "compare and contrast" and "compare and contrast plus take a position." Such analyses might also classify activities in different ways. Horowitz, for example, lists both "cause/result" and "similarities and differences" under the general heading "Display Familiarity with the Relationship between/among Concepts"; in our scheme, trying to establish cause and result is included in "Serializing" while considering similarities and differences comes under "Comparing."

An early survey conducted by one of us was influenced by this research, and it revealed — as have other such surveys — that students are commonly called on to define, summarize, compare, and analyze.[3] And as the courses we taught and the programs we managed took us increasingly across disciplinary boundaries, we had opportunity to examine the contexts of written language use in the academy, and what we found was complementary with and given a public discourse by the writing-across-the-curriculum discussions emerging at our conferences and in our journals.

The tremendous value of these movements has been to increase teachers' awareness of the specialized reading and writing demands of various disciplines and, more theoretically, to move them to examine communities of discourse within the academy. One potential liability of these movements has been their tendency to represent writing instruction in a fairly service-oriented, product-directed way, that is, to assist students in learning the forms and conventions of sociology, biology, literature, and so on. Such instruction is valuable and sorely needed, and at places in *Critical Strategies* we try to provide it. But our sense is that, at least in some settings, it is not adequately critical and self-examining. It teaches, say, how to summarize material for a literature review but doesn't create the conditions for students to consider the act of summarizing. So while we see our book as oriented toward cross-curricular needs, we try not to imprison writers within those needs. Our attempt is to develop a curriculum that equips students to write well in college but is not simply functional in its orientation — a book that encourages critical reflection, that is intellectually unpredictable and vital.

THE BOOK'S ORGANIZATION

It is very hard, perhaps impossible, to teach complex intellectual processes through static print alone.[4] What we have tried to do is to create a kind of sourcebook of discussions, cases, examples, readings, and assignments that can help establish the conditions to foster academic thinking and writing. Each strategy is treated in a separate chapter that begins with an introduction and is followed by a series of assignments. And each of these chapter introductions opens with an overview ("General Considerations") of the nature

---

We felt that dividing tasks into so many subcategories would make our book too difficult to use — though within discussions and assignments we try to reflect the variability represented by such subcategories. We were also reluctant, for the reasons stated earlier, to classify tasks in new ways. Though a more original classification scheme would have solved some problems, we finally felt that it would make the book too unfamiliar and, perhaps, less useful.

[3] Mike Rose, "When Faculty Talk about Writing." *College English* 41 (November 1979): 272–79; and "Remedial Writing Courses: A Critique and a Proposal," *College English* 45 (February 1983): 109–28. For further discussion and application, see Malcolm Kiniry and Ellen Strenski, "Sequencing Expository Writing: A Recursive Approach," *College Composition and Communication* 36 (May 1985): 191–202.

[4] See, for example, Mike Rose, "Speculations on Process Knowledge and the Textbook's Static Page," *College Composition and Communication* 34 (May 1983): 208–13.

and purpose of the strategy and its use in academic reading and writing. This overview is followed by one or more extended illustrations ("Cases") of the way one can use the strategy to think through an issue. By weaving questions and writing opportunities within these illustrative discussions, we invite readers to participate in a range of interpretive decisions, to consider the effects of varying contexts on such decisions, and to reflect upon how a particular strategy may prove inadequate. Ultimately, we hope to get students to think in fresh ways about critical strategies that, in their experience, might have been reduced to fixed models that cut short thoughtful engagement with problems. We want students to engage these strategies — use them in multiple ways, question them, turn them back on themselves.

Each chapter introduction is followed by a series of assignments, and here we are influenced by current research on the development of expertise. In an attempt to promote mastery of complex cognitive-rhetorical tasks, we provide multiple opportunities to use a strategy, with a variety of materials, arranged in a general order of increasing difficulty. Let us illustrate this pattern by focusing on four of the *defining* assignments from Chapter 1.

We begin "Defining" with an assignment that requires students to consider the ways in which familiar words can gain specialized meaning in particular disciplinary contexts. One such word is *performance.* We ask students to define its meanings in common speech and then ask them to determine and discuss Erving Goffman's use of *performance* in a brief passage from *The Presentation of Self in Everyday Life.* A middle assignment in "Defining" builds on the Goffman assignment (and others like it) by asking students to examine the range of meanings a word acquires in common and specialized use. We provide a list of sentences that contain the word *light* and ask students to operate like lexicographers and create definitions for each category of meaning that emerges in the sentences. This leads to a consideration of variation in meaning and the way meaning becomes established in dictionaries. A later assignment offers an account of the eugenics movement to encourage students to consider the inadequacies of typical dictionary definitions and to construct definitions that gain in meaning through the use of descriptive historical context. And in one of the last assignments we use an article on environmental policy to encourage students to consider the politics of defining: the way a particular definition — say of *protection, restoration,* or *management* — is determined by social and political forces. The amount and kind of writing students are asked to do builds as well: the first assignment requires no more than a paragraph; the last one is essay length.

The earlier assignments in a given chapter tend to be shorter and more focused than later assignments, and we encourage teachers and students to see these earlier assignments as *first passes* through a strategy — ones that can be used as rehearsals, done in rough draft or in journals, assessed as the teacher walks around the classroom. Following these "First Passes" come longer, more ambitious assignments and — in keeping with the nature of *Critical Strategies* as a sourcebook of materials — we offer a variety of *options* for teachers and students to choose from. The materials contained in "Options," as with those in "First Passes," represent a range of disciplines — from biology to sociology — and can be assigned in a variety of disciplinary, thematic, or strategic sequences and also can be connected to research projects involving primary or secondary sources. We intend the materials in *Critical Strategies,* then, to contribute to a dynamic classroom in which students are continually discussing tables, texts, and primary data, writing about them, revising that writing, and presenting what they've written.

The second half of *Critical Strategies* is devoted to academic argument and consists of a general introduction and four miniature libraries for the development of sustained projects. The four collections cover cross-cultural explorations of gender roles, historical-literary considerations of a Hawthorne short story, the dispute over the origins and treatment of schizophrenia, and an investigation of the comic — thereby representing social sciences, humanities, and life sciences. In general, each of the four chapters begins with cases, primary materials, or overviews and is followed by theoretical and critical materials. A set of preliminary questions comes after the cases and primary materials, and a fuller set of questions comes at the end of the theoretical and critical texts. In various ways the questions invite students to apply and combine the critical strategies they've encountered in Chapters 1 through 6 — providing, thereby, an integrative and cumulative thrust to *Critical Strategies.* Having said that, however, let us also stress that *Critical Strategies* is not neatly linear. In the introductions, assignments, and, particularly, the teacher's manual, interrelations are drawn, and teachers are encouraged to make this book their own, drawing connections and creating assignments that fit the needs of their particular classes and institutions.

ACKNOWLEDGMENTS

The materials at the heart of this project have had a long and varied life and we would like to thank the many people who have been involved with them. We begin by thanking the students who have used these materials, particularly those in the Veterans Special Educational Program and the Freshman Preparatory Program. We thank, as well, our colleagues at UCLA who have taught with us and helped us critique and develop assignments: Jennifer Bradley, Bill Creasy, Bob Cullen, Pat Donohue, Diane Dugaw, Carol Edwards, George Gadda, Pat Gilmore, Cheryl Giuliano, Mike Gustin, Bonnie Lisle, Faye Peitzman, Ellen Quandahl, Jeff Skoblow, Ellen Strenski, and David Ward. While coordinator of the Freshman Preparatory Program, Gary Colombo was particularly generous in class-testing readings and assignments. Early on Phill Volland, David Fein, Jonathan Losk, and Barbara Belfer assisted us in gathering cross-curricular readings. Along the way, we received helpful suggestions from a number of tutors: Suzanne Gottschang, Sandra Jones, Celia Naylor, Rose Shalom, and Rika Uto. During the final stages we have appreciated the support, at Rutgers University-Newark, of Patricia Gartenberg, Katheryn Bethea, Barbara Gross, Robert White, and Kathy Zambias.

We have been particularly fortunate, through the last three years of this project, to have had the research assistance of William Richey. His work has been of remarkable quality; some sections of the book would not have taken their current shape without him. We thank him for his energy and resourcefulness.

At key points in the development of the ideas contained herein, Charles Cooper, Frank D'Angelo, and Linda Flower offered support, and, early on, Carol L. Edwards, Kris Gutierrez, Lucia Z. Knoles, Richard L. Larson, Madge Manfred, Donald McQuade, Barbra S. Morris, Ellen Quandahl, and Louise Smith provided comprehensive reviews. We are especially indebted to David Bartholomae, Patricia Bizzell, Bruce Herzberg, and David A. Jolliffe, who reviewed the manuscript both early and late — their help was invaluable. Let us also mention that Chapter 8, "Women and Power," benefited from the advice of Karen Rowe, past Director of the UCLA Center for the Study of Women. We were fortunate to have so much intelligence and good will focused on our work.

We are grateful to the people at Bedford Books for the time they gave us — the remarkable competence, the patience, the careful attention to detail. We thank Chuck Christensen who has helped us to envision, and to reenvision, this project as a book. Joan Feinberg encouraged us throughout the book's history — keenly, warmly, tactfully, persistently. Elizabeth Schaaf and Claire Seng-Niemoeller brought the project to its final stages — and here special mention is due Barbara Flanagan for masterful copyediting and Mary Lou Wilshaw for her skills and equanimity in seeing the book through production. Jane Betz, Constance Mayer, and Sarah Royston also provided a great deal of assistance. Ellen Darion, our developmental editor, allowed us to monopolize her professional life: She shaped the book day by day, helped us work out text and assignments, and gave us far more thoughtful assistance than we deserved.

Contents

CHAPTER FIVE · Comparing   206

CHAPTER SIX · Analyzing 286

PART TWO
Readings for Academic Argument: A Sourcebook   371

CHAPTER SEVEN · Sustaining Academic Argument: General Considerations   373

CHAPTER EIGHT · Women and Power: Perspectives from Anthropology   408

Framing the Issues   408

■ *Complicating the Issues* 415

CHAPTER NINE · Nathaniel Hawthorne's *Young Goodman Brown:* Historical Imagining 494

■ *Framing the Issues* 494

■ *Complicating the Issues* 506

CHAPTER ELEVEN · What's Funny? Investigating the Comic   664

PART ONE

Critical Strategies:
Cases and Assignments

CHAPTER 1

Defining

General Considerations

If you think of definition as only a passive or mechanical act — copying out words you've looked up in a dictionary or giving back short, memorized answers from notes and textbooks — you'll need to revise your thinking. It's true that at times, particularly exam times, you will find yourself plugging in ready-made definitions, as on an economics exam when you are asked to define terms such as *fixed cost, inelastic demand,* and *substitution effect.* But definition involves far more than committing crisp glossary definitions to memory. Defining is a continuous process, crucial to receptive reading and persuasive writing; and it is fundamental to the critical thinking encouraged in all college courses.

To define something is to look at it more clearly. We speak of something as well defined when we can perceive its boundaries against a background. Biology students, for example, quickly learn to define the nucleus of a cell by its central location, its distinct coloration, and the membrane that separates it from the rest of the cell's cytoplasm. In an American history course, you begin to define the office of secretary of state as you learn what the secretary's powers and responsibilities are and how those powers and responsibilities are limited by the structure of the government as a whole. If you go further, you will probably see that your general understanding of what the secretary of state does needs to be modified to account for how the job has changed over time. Further still, you might conclude that no two secretaries of state handled the office in exactly the same way: Henry Kissinger defined his role in the Nixon administration much differently than did George Schultz in the Reagan administration. Defining is seldom a matter of understanding an idea in isolation — it calls for seeing and understanding relationships.

As pieces of writing, too, definitions seldom occur in isolation. They are used in coordination with other strategies. Asked on a biology exam to describe the stages of photosynthesis, you might decide to begin with an overview definition before going on to describe the process sequentially. For a political science term paper, "The Influence of Interest Groups in U.S. Politics," you might decide to organize your essay as a classification of the various types of U.S. interest groups and precede that classification with a definition establishing what all the types have in common. In an essay comparing the thought of two social philosophers, you might arrive at a pivotal point where a definition helps you to make a distinction crucial to your comparison: "For Marx, then, unlike Weber, the concept of 'surplus value' is central to understanding the operation of modern economies. Marx sees surplus value as. . . ." In an interpretive essay for a literature class, you might produce a summary of a novel's key events and follow with a definition that refocuses attention on an aspect of the novel that the rest of your paper will go on to analyze. Asked in an education class to write a position paper for or against bilingual programs in elementary schools, you might find yourself defining a number of terms along the way as they become necessary for your argumentative purpose.

Definitions are flexible. They can expand, contract, or shift in emphasis, all according to the uses to which they are put. They are also powerful. When we look at complex problems, definitions help to shape what we see and don't see. Consider a term like *adolescence*. Take a moment and write out your definition of the word. Then compare your definition with someone else's. How might you expect your definition or a classmate's to be different from a parent's or a teacher's? How do you think a biologist's definition might differ from a psychologist's? How might the uses various people make of this term help account for their different emphases in defining it?

The early assignments in this chapter ask you to formulate definitions in response to short but difficult readings. They ask you to reflect on how we define when we read as well as when we write. The later assignments, based on lengthier readings, pose problems meant to further challenge and extend your sense of what is at stake in defining.

Cases

DEFINING ACADEMIC WORDS: THE CASE OF MODEL

As readers, we do most of our defining on the run. As we encounter new words, or familiar words used in new ways, we struggle with them as best we can, forming hesitant, even semiconscious, conclusions about what they mean. If we're attentive, we notice that some of these words are more important than others and that some reoccur as we move from one subject to another. Paying special attention to such terms can help develop a useful vocabulary for thinking and writing critically.

We can illustrate this process by trying to build a definition of an academic term you're likely to encounter frequently, the word *model*. Most of us start with some familiar sense of the word, and then at some point in our reading we realize that our definition needs revising. For instance, we think of a model as a person whose job is displaying clothes. Or we might think of a model as a small-scale replica, like a model airplane. We may feel puzzled, when we think about it, by the apparent disparity between these two uses of the word. But neither use prepares us to make sense of a passage like this one:

> Why does the market model still attract academic economists, Galbraith asks, in the radically different conditions of today? First, because the intellectual framework with which a profession is familiar exerts a powerful hold over the minds of its members, even when changing conditions make it less applicable. It provides them with familiar concepts and assumptions to bring to bear on contemporary issues. Second, in the age of technology and technique, the simplifying assumptions of the market model provide a base from which mathematical models can be constructed and refined; the form of the model is nicely adapted to the style of thought preferred by social scientists.
> — Michael H. Best and William E. Connolly,
> *The Politicized Economy*

Evidently, in the way economists use the term, a model isn't as tangible as a person or a replica. It's something that can be "applied," something involving an "intellectual framework," and something that, for some people at least, involves mathematics. Do you feel at sea? Try writing a definition that makes some connection between this new use of the term and your earlier ones.

If you feel bewildered by the model in the economics passage, you'll probably feel a little relieved by the following passage, which describes a science writer's visit to the lab of a famous chemist.

> On the tables were models. They were surprisingly large, and at
> first difficult to take in; they were responsible for the room's impression

1

of clutter. We went over to one. It was built, like the others, within a cubical frame of steel straps that defined the edges, about four feet long. The floor of the cube was thick, unpainted plywood. From that, within the cube, a jungle sprang up of thin metal rods. Looping through these like creepers were several lengths of flexible, plastic-coated cable, red or white. The rods only provided support. The trick was to ignore them totally, though they obscured almost everything else, and concentrate on where the colored cables led.

2   This model before us, Perutz said, was a single molecule of hemoglobin of horse in its oxygen-carrying state. The living hemoglobin molecule, human or horse, was made of 574 amino acids, in four chains, ten thousand atoms strong, and totalling 64,500 times the weight of a single hydrogen atom, or about 4,000 times the weight of a single atom of oxygen. That was all required to transport just four molecules of oxygen each made of two atoms. At those ratios, the breath of life requires about 280 million hemoglobin molecules in each red blood cell, and there are about 160 trillion red blood cells in a pint of blood.

3   Perutz picked up a pointer to trace the twisting, swooping paths of the four chains in the model — two identical chains termed "alpha," another identical pair called "beta." These were constructed out of thousands of short, straight bits of brass wire socketed together at angles, each bit precisely in scale with the length of a chemical bond, and the sockets where the wires intersected showing the positions of principal atoms. The tracery was clamped at hundreds of places to the supporting rods. The red cords and white ones, Perutz said, were not the real structure but only aids to the eye, Ariadne threads tracing beta and alpha chains.

> — Horace Freeland Judson, *The Eighth Day of Creation:*
> *Makers of the Revolution in Biology*

Here we have a model that we think we recognize. It's not so different from the model airplane. Of course, we'd have to modify our notion that a model is a "small-scale replica," since Perutz's hemoglobin model is vastly larger than a hemoglobin molecule. We might be tempted to reduce our definition to a synonym — a model is a replica — but when we look back at the passage we may suddenly feel reluctant to say even that. For notice that Perutz's model is *not* a replica if by replica we mean an exact, proportionate image of how something looks. His model is dominated by metal rods that have no equivalent in the structure of the actual hemoglobin molecule and by red and white cables that represent alpha and beta chains not as they are but only as "aids to the eye." Perutz's model is not so much a replica of how the hemoglobin molecule "looks" as a sort of visualized description of how its parts must be related. When understood, it can help to tell something about how hemoglobin carries oxygen in the bloodstream.

What does this latest recognition do to our effort to join the hemoglobin and the airplane in a single definition? The new emphasis might lead us to this reformulation:

```
A model is a simplified image of how something looks or
works.
```

We've said "looks or works" to cover ourselves. One word fits the airplane, the other the molecule. It may not be the best definition, but it's one we can live with, at least until we have to think about the word again. But what if we're reminded of the economics passage we left behind? Or what if a new piece of reading, like the following excerpt from a sociology text, reminds us of our earlier difficulty?

> The *concentric zone model* . . . presents the city as a set of circles, each one ringing the smaller one within it. At the center is the business district, where property values favor the income-earning uses of land. The only residents there are transients living in rundown hotels. The next zone, ringing the center, is the home of wholesale businesses and light industry. Third is a zone in transition. Formerly containing decent housing, it has been blighted by the encroachment of the business center. As its residential desirability declines and as housing is neglected by owners who anticipate selling their property to business or factory interests, this area becomes the home of the poor and minorities. Next is a zone of middle-class homes. These in turn are encircled by an outer ring of upper-class homes.
>
> — Peter I. Rose, Myron Glazer, and Penina Migdal Glazer,
> *Sociology: Inquiring into Society*

Here again we find the emphasis on a model as something imaginary, something theoretical, something that some experts favor and others criticize. When we think of the definition we've built around the airplane and the hemoglobin molecule, we find to our surprise that that definition is still useful. The emphasis on "how it works" — in this case how a city develops — leads us toward an even fuller and clearer definition. Instead of simply settling for a one-sentence statement, we can go on to explain and illustrate what we mean:

```
A model is a simplified image of how something
looks or works or develops.  Chemists construct models
to describe the structures of molecules, economists to
describe how an economy functions, and sociologists to
describe the patterns in which cities have developed.
Models are not necessarily replicas of what exists;
they are educated guesses about how things are, how
they have come to be, or how they will behave.
```

What we have been doing with the word *model* is similar, in a way, to what dictionary makers do. You may have the impression that a dictionary is essentially a grammar book — that it authoritatively tells you the permissible meanings of words. Actually, dictionaries are compilations of what words have meant and are likely still to mean. A dictionary's authority comes only from its accuracy in categorizing and describing how particular words have been used. Its descriptions are always incomplete because the meanings of words keep shifting as they are used in new situations or as some meanings of words come into new or sharper prominence. Look back at the definition we've constructed for the word *model*. Now look at the following entry in the *Random House College Dictionary*, published in 1975:

> **mod·el** (mod/ºl), *n., adj., v.,* -eled, -el·ing or (*esp. Brit.*) -elled, -el·ling. —*n.* 1. a standard or example for imitation or comparison. 2. a representation, generally in miniature, to show the structure or serve as a copy of something. 3. an image in clay, wax, or the like, to be reproduced in more durable material. 4. a person or thing that serves as a subject for an artist, sculptor, writer, etc. 5. a person, esp. an attractive young woman, whose profession is posing with, wearing, using, or demonstrating a product for purposes of display or advertising. 6. a pattern or mode of structure or formation. 7. a typical form or style. —*adj.* 8. serving as a model: *a model apartment.* 9. worthy of serving as a model; exemplary: *a model student.*

Do any of these definitions much resemble ours? Perhaps the sixth entry comes closest; "a pattern or mode of structure or formation" is so general that it probably includes our definition. But what emphasis is missing? Would any of the definitions you see here help you to decipher the word we met in the economics or sociology texts?

Our point is not that dictionaries can't be trusted. They are useful tools for helping us work out meanings; and they can be particularly helpful in showing how the meanings of a word may vary and how those meanings may change over time (some of the exercises in this chapter ask you to think about words historically). But the real burden of defining will fall on you — on your powers of inference as a reader and your powers of management as a writer.

A SAMPLING OF DEFINING STRATEGIES

What are some of the defining strategies available to you as a writer? One is to make use of the form of **classifying** you see in dictionaries, which begins by placing words in categories. When we say that a *soliloquy* is "a type of speech" or that *acculturation* refers to "social interaction" or that *Brown v. Board of Education* is "a Supreme Court decision," we've begun to define those terms. Having established a meaningful general category, we then go on to offer particulars:

    A soliloquy is a speech delivered by a theatrical char-
    acter who is alone on the stage.

Acculturation is a social interaction in which a subordinate group adjusts its behavior to conform to that of
a dominant group.

Brown v. the Board of Education is the Supreme Court
decision that in 1954 made segregated public school
systems illegal.

This two-part strategy of discovering a category and then filling in particulars, sometimes called "formal definition," is useful not only in presenting
definitions but in thinking them through. It offers a flexible way to alter our
wording as our thinking changes. We can play with the general category,
sharpening or broadening it; or we can experiment with the particulars, adding,
deleting, or substituting features. Imagine, for example, that you keep running
up against the term *refugee* in a course on contemporary political issues. You
try writing out a definition:

A refugee is a person who has come to the United States
from another country.

Once you've written out a rough definition like this one, you can start to
rethink it, looking for ways to make it more accurate or more helpful. Here
the general category "person" seems too general to be helpful, and the
particular phrase "has come to the United States" seems imprecise and misleading (don't other countries have refugees?). You might improve the last
part of the definition with more careful phrasing, but you might also realize
that there is a single word — *immigrant* — that you can substitute for the
category "person," thus making the last part of the definition unnecessary:

A refugee is an immigrant....

Are all refugees immigrants? Yes, you think so. Are all immigrants refugees?
If you don't think so, you can try to construct a definition that gets more
specific:

A refugee is an immigrant who ...

In looking back over your reading, you might notice that refugees seem to
be people who are not merely leaving their countries but anxiously fleeing
from them. As you think about that, you might notice that the word *refugee*
contains the word *refuge,* a place of safety. You fill in the definition a little
more:

A refugee is an immigrant who flees from one country,
seeking safety in another.

This definition is more satisfying and might hold up well. But you might try quarreling with it a bit. See if you can find ways in which it might be tightened. If you think there's something missing, try to pinpoint what it is. In this case, you might object that the definition fits smugglers and tax dodgers. Further, you might notice that *refugee* usually seems to carry with it the connotation of fear. You modify your definition to read:

> Refugees are immigrants fleeing the political condi-
> tions in one country and seeking safety in another.

This revised definition seems stronger and clearer still, and it would probably serve you well if you ever had to define the term in a general way. But in the context of a course about contemporary politics — and, in fact, in the context of any political discussion — a pointed and probing set of questions might push you a little further: "What's at stake in this definition?" "To whom does it matter?" "How would this definition be used?" If you return to your reading with such questions in mind, you may find yourself alert to important disagreements. In the case of *refugee,* the problem of definition can be crucial, for those people defined by the U.S. government as refugees are often allowed to stay in this country while other immigrants face much tighter restrictions. Are people fleeing from Cuba defined as refugees? From El Salvador? From Mexico? From Iran? From the Soviet Union? How might the official definition of what a refugee is differ in practice from the one we've worked out in theory? What social and political factors will affect the definition? Pursuing the implications of this effort at definition might lead you beyond your two-part definition to a more extended essay about the problem of defining what a refugee is.

We have been demonstrating another defining strategy — using **examples.** The general statement "A model is a simplified image" seems vague until you illustrate it with the hemoglobin molecule or with an example of an economic prediction. Well-chosen examples invariably clarify and solidify definitions that otherwise would be lifelessly abstract. However, one problem in using an example to tie down a definition is that a specific example is often so powerful that it colors the entire definition, becoming in effect more than just an example. If we were given only the hemoglobin molecule as an example, what misimpression about models might we come away with?

Consider the following passage, a definition of the term *gland,* by the science writer Isaac Asimov. In modern times the word *gland,* says Asimov, came to mean "any organ that had the prime function of producing a fluid secretion." He then elaborates:

> The most noticeable glands are large organs such as the liver and pancreas. Each of these produces quantities of fluid which are discharged into the upper reaches of the small intestine through special ducts.
> — Isaac Asimov, *The Human Brain*

Notice how the formal definition (a *gland* is an organ that produces a fluid secretion) is followed immediately by specific examples. And notice how vividly Asimov puts the examples to work. If you think of what you know about glands, however, what misimpression would these sentences give if they were allowed to stand alone? Most of the body's glands are in fact quite small. Left alone, the examples of the liver and the pancreas could be misleading. But Asimov has seen this potential problem. His wording "most noticeable" signals that there are also less noticeable glands. And here's how he fills out his definition:

> Other smaller glands also discharge their secretions into various sections of the alimentary canal. The six salivary glands discharge saliva into the mouth by way of ducts. There are myriads of tiny glands in the lining of the stomach and the small intestine, producing gastric juice in the first case and intestinal juice in the second.

Where one kind of example would have been misleading, several leave us with a stronger, surer sense of both the limit and the range of the term *gland* (actually Asimov is not finished; he goes on to add to the examples he has mentioned thus far, further clarifying the definition). Sometimes a single example will do the job well; at other times you'll find it helpful to use several. In all cases, you'll want to make sure that your specific examples effectively illustrate your general statements.

Besides helping you to present definitions clearly and vividly, examples help you to think through definitions as you try to reformulate them. As we constructed our definition of *refugee,* it helped us at one stage to ask whether smugglers fit our definition, and at a later stage to wonder whether — and why — the United States would be more apt to define as refugees immigrants from Cuba than immigrants from El Salvador. By calling up specific examples in this way, you can keep probing and readjusting your general definitions. Examples — particularly examples that you invent for yourself — can also help you to check your understanding of new terms. For instance, you may have learned that an *opportunity cost* can be defined as "an estimated measurement of goods and services that are sacrificed in order to obtain other goods and services." As a way of testing your understanding of that abstract statement, you might try illustrating it in terms more familiar to you:

```
Besides what my family and I are paying to send me to
college, I am sacrificing the money I would have been
making if I stayed on at my summer job. So in addition
to the money I'm paying in fees and tuition, there is
the $6.00 an hour that I would have had the opportunity
to make if I hadn't decided to go to college.
```

You won't always be able to illustrate academic concepts with examples from your own experience (you should be willing to search more widely for examples), but your best examples often will come from areas you already know well.

A third defining strategy is to **create subtopics.** When faced in an art history course with a broad topic such as "What is impressionism?" you might use a formal definition to get you started: "*Impressionism* refers to the movement among French painters of the 1870s who experimented with ways to represent the effects of light." Having specific examples of artists — Pissarro, Monet, Renoir — would help too. But to produce an effective essay, you would want to do more than combine an opening generalization with an illustrated list. Creating meaningful subtopics is one way to let your definition structure your essay. With the impressionists, you might decide that each artist you choose to write about used a different means of experimentation, and these types of experimentation then could become your subtopics. Or you might choose to organize your essay with subtopics like these:

> One characteristic of the impressionists is their choice of everyday subjects....
>
> The impressionists also experimented with color....
>
> Each impressionist devised ways to express the flickering movement of light....

Such definitions work not so much by enclosing a term within careful boundaries as by opening up its parts to further definition.

Another fertile defining strategy is to look at the idea that you are trying to define **as part of a larger process.** We all have a tendency when constructing definitions to think in frozen time, as though things were standing still. But often you can define something more clearly and fully by seeing it as a functioning part of some ongoing process. It is not inaccurate in a physiology course to define an *axon* as "a long tubular structure in a nerve cell." But a better definition would clarify its function: "An *axon* is a tubular structure that carries an electrical impulse through a nerve cell." Better still, a definition might fill in more context:

> An axon is a tubular structure that carries an electrical impulse from dendrites, branched receptors at the base of a nerve cell, and then transmits it to the cell's extremities, the terminal boutons, where it must cross a synapse to the next nerve cell.

Here one definition leads to others, and in the process we become aware of more that we need to know. In this way, defining can help you to recognize incompleteness in your thinking and push you on to ask further questions.

This strategy of looking at something as part of a process can at times help you redefine terms that otherwise might seem dead ends. Consider the term *thirst*. Most of us would define *thirst,* in a practical way, as "the desire for liquids." And once we've said that, we might assume that there's not much more to say. Seen as part of a process, however, the idea opens up to a broader perspective. Notice how nutrition expert Jane Brody defines *thirst* in the context of the body's regulation of fluids:

> Our tissues swim in a salty sea — a vestige, perhaps, of our aquatic 1
> evolution. The more salt in that sea, the more water is needed to dilute
> it to maintain the proper concentration of sodium. Sodium and its equally
> essential companion chloride (the combining form of chlorine) are the
> principal regulators of the balance of water and dissolved substances
> outside cells. You'll recall . . . that this is the job potassium does within
> cells. These three minerals — called electrolytes — also regulate the
> balance of acids and bases in body fluids and cells. If the balance of water
> and electrolytes or acids and bases is disturbed, normal metabolic func-
> tions may grind to a near halt.
>
> Eating something salty makes you thirsty because when salt is added 2
> to the body, extra water is needed to dilute it. Bartenders cash in on
> this fact of human physiology by offering salty nuts and pretzels gratis
> to patrons. It's good for business. And if you lose water through sweating,
> the increased concentration of salt in your blood also stimulates thirst.
> The "purpose" of thirst is to keep the body functioning properly by
> maintaining the concentration of salt within a certain narrow range.
>
> — Jane E. Brody, *Jane Brody's Nutrition Book*

Perhaps the most versatile defining strategy is the use of **comparisons.** With a comparison we can show one thing against another, sometimes high-lighting resemblances and sometimes differences. Actually, comparisons are implied in almost any definition, including all those we've worked with so far. "A *gland* is an organ that secretes fluid" implies that glands are unlike other organs, such as the heart and lungs, which do not secrete fluids. Definitions can get sharper as such comparisons become explicit. And discovering good comparisons can make definitions convincing.

Sometimes comparisons are of opposites. We can define and explain *monotheism* by opposing it to *polytheism.* At other times comparisons are of complements — we need one term to define the meaning of another. In Marxist political theory, for example, it would be difficult to define *bourgeoisie* without defining *proletariat.* But the most frequent use of comparison is to distinguish between terms that otherwise might be confused or thought iden-tical. An effective definition leaves us with a better sense of both terms. For most of us, for instance, the term *cruise missile* means little more than the term *ballistic missile* or the term *missile* alone. The term gains definition when we are told, "Unlike ballistic missiles, which are designed to climb at a high trajectory over great distances and plunge steeply toward their targets, cruise missiles are designed to fly much more horizontally, close to the earth and over a smaller range."

Let us illustrate how comparison can be used in developing a more extended definition. Suppose that you are asked on a political science examination to discuss the *coup d'état* as a political action. Comparisons can help you to think through the definition as well as to shape it. You might begin with the observation that a *coup* is "the takeover of a national government." A quick comparison of other "takeovers" convinces you that you haven't produced an effective definition yet — this one could apply equally to a revolution, an occupation by a foreign nation, a civil war, and even perhaps to the change of administration after a presidential election. Once you've narrowed the definition more effectively — "A *coup* is a violent takeover of a nation's government by a portion of that nation's military" — you can put comparisons to further use in clarifying and developing the essay itself.

> A coup d'état is an armed takeover of a nation's
> government by a portion of that nation's military.
> Unlike a more broadly based revolt or insurrection, a
> coup is usually the result of a rapid action by a few
> highly placed soldiers. Unlike a civil war, which in-
> volves all segments of a society over some length of
> time, a coup d'état, if successful, is over almost in-
> stantaneously. Like some political assassinations, a
> coup usually aims to topple only the head of state,
> leaving the rest of the country's administrative struc-
> ture intact. While a genuine revolution depends on the
> widespread dissatisfaction and participation of the
> populace, a coup depends only on public indifference.

To clarify and extend some of your comparative points, you would probably want to interweave some illustrative examples, which themselves might be compared. Which better fits the definition of a *coup,* for example, the removal of Ferdinand Marcos as president of the Philippines in 1986 or the unseating during that same year of president-for-life Jean Claude Duvalier in Haiti?

Sometimes comparisons define by pointing to underlying similarities, and sometimes they define by moving beyond apparent similarities to make finer distinctions. Ordinarily we use the words *precise* and *accurate* interchangeably. In a physics course, however, where matters of measurement are crucial, the words are meaningfully distinguished. Here's how physicist Yardley Beers defines them in relation to errors:

> When a given measurement is repeated, the resulting values, in general, do not agree exactly. The causes of the disagreement between the individual values must also be causes of their differing from the "true" value. Errors resulting from these causes are called *random* errors. . . . If, on the other hand, all of the individual values are in error by the same amount, the errors are called *systematic* or *constant* errors. For example, all the measurements made with a portion of a steel tape which includes a kink will appear to be too large by an amount equal to the loss in length resulting from the kink. . . . If an experiment has small random errors, it is said to have high *precision*. . . . If an experiment has small systematic errors, it is said to have high *accuracy*.
> — Yardley Beers, *Introduction to the Theory of Error*

It's worth stressing one special form of comparison — the analogy. Analogies are extended comparisons that lay out a whole set of correspondences between the things being compared. An urban planner might try to define the operation of a highway system by comparing it to the circulation of blood in the body. A literature student might explain dramatic tragedy by comparing its movement to that of the passing seasons. Writers use analogies to give readers helpful overviews, manageable ways to grasp complex subjects. Consider how mathematician Norbert Wiener defines the human nervous system with an analogy to a computer:

> The nervous system and the automatic machine are fundamentally alike in that they are devices which make decisions on the basis of decisions they have made in the past. The simplest mechanical devices will make decisions between two alternatives, such as the closing or opening of a switch. In the nervous system, the individual nerve fiber also decides between carrying an impulse or not. In both the machine and the nerve, there is a specific apparatus for making future decisions depend on past decisions, and in the nervous system a large part of this task is done at those extremely complicated points called "synapses" where a number of incoming nerve fibers connect with a single outgoing nerve fiber. In many cases it is possible to state the basis of these decisions as a threshold of action of the synapse, or in other words, by telling how many incoming fibers should fire in order that the outgoing fibers may fire.
> This is the basis of at least part of the analogy between machines and living organisms.
> — Norbert Wiener, *The Human Use of Human Beings*

As a defining strategy, developing an analogy can help you to think freshly and to write persuasively. But because analogies are almost always comparisons of two complex systems that are dissimilar in some fundamental way, you also need to regard analogies skeptically. Even when they have proved useful, most analogies can be criticized. Look at what biologist Francis Crick does with the brain-machine comparison:

> Unfortunately the analogy between a computer and the brain, although it is useful in some ways, is apt to be misleading. In a computer information is processed at a rapid pulse rate and serially. In the brain the rate is much lower, but the information can be handled on millions of channels in parallel. The components of a modern computer are very reliable, but removing one or two of them can upset an entire computation. In comparison the neurons of the brain are somewhat unreliable, but the deletion of quite a few of them is unlikely to lead to any appreciable difference in behavior. A computer works on a strict binary code. The brain seems to rely on less precise methods of signaling. Against this it probably adjusts the number and efficiency of its synapses in complex and subtle ways to adapt its operation to experience. Hence it is not surprising to find that although a computer can accurately and rapidly do long and intricate arithmetical calculations, a task at which human beings are rather poor, human beings can recognize patterns in ways no contemporary computer can begin to approach.
>
> — Francis H. C. Crick, "Thinking About the Brain"

But notice that even while Crick is tearing down the analogy, the comparison is also helping him to articulate, and thus define, his own view of the brain.

As an exercise in building and unbuilding analogies, think back to what you know about *coups d'état*. Try developing, then criticizing, these two analogies: (1) a *coup d'état* is like surgery; (2) a *coup d'état* is like a corporate takeover. Which works better?

DEFINING AS PERSPECTIVE: A CASE FROM PSYCHOLOGY

As one last illustration of the power and flexibility of definition, let us imagine a difficult college writing assignment, an interpretive essay about a book written by Sigmund Freud. Freud wrote *An Analysis of a Case of Hysteria* in 1905, several years after treating "Dora," the eighteen-year-old patient whose case he describes in the book. Dora's father, a well-to-do manufacturer, brought her to see Freud, somewhat against her will, on the basis of several symptoms — including general fatigue, despondency, a halfhearted suicide attempt, and a recent fainting spell. In addition, she had recently claimed that a family friend, Herr K, had sexually approached her. Freud does not give us her case history all at once but parcels it out in the sequence in which he himself received it. Let us summarize some of the most important details.

Since early childhood, Dora had a very strong attachment to her father; only recently had relations between them become strained. Toward her mother, whom she regarded as a foolish woman obsessed by housework, she felt only contempt. She had an older brother whom she regarded warmly.

She also had a long, affectionate relationship with Herr K and his wife. At some point in her childhood, however, Dora realized that her father was having an affair with Frau K, a fact that helped explain much about her father's long absences and the two families' mutual vacations. Despite his long-standing affair with Frau K, Dora's father very much doubted that Herr K had attempted to seduce his daughter. Early in his diagnosis, Freud decided that the seduction attempt probably did occur, but he came to regard it as only the most recent trauma in an illness that had deeper psychological roots in Dora's childhood, some of which he proceeded to uncover.

Let's assume that we've decided to approach the essay through a definition of the key term in the book's title, *hysteria*. We might begin, as we did with *model*, with our own commonsense understanding of the word. Written out in a formal structure, it might look like this:

```
Hysteria is an emotional state characterized by loud,
out-of-control behavior.
```

But this definition doesn't really suit what we know about Dora. Dora's behavior, at least in her office visits with Freud, wasn't particularly loud or out of control; nor had she behaved that way toward others. Her behavior seemed only sullen and uncooperative. We might question our choice of category, too. Dora was not simply in an "emotional state"; she was experiencing real physical symptoms that must be taken into account.

If we go to the section of Freud's book where he identifies those symptoms of Dora's that he regards as typical of hysterics, we could produce a revised definition:

```
Hysteria is an illness characterized by shortness of
breath, a persistent cough, loss of voice, migraines,
unsociability, depression, and fatigue.
```

This definition is much more specific, but why does it still feel dissatisfying? Perhaps it's *too* specific. We doubt that someone would have to experience all of these symptoms to be considered a hysteric. But it also seems an overreaction to our earlier "emotional state" category — this definition mentions only physical symptoms. And when we return to look more closely at Freud's text, we see that he himself is not satisfied to list this array of symptoms that he has inherited from other medical descriptions. When we realize that Freud is concerned with Dora's physical symptoms primarily as clues to her emotional disturbance, our definition can shift again:

```
Hysteria is a mental illness characterized by physical
symptoms with unknown emotional causes.
```

If we were writing our essay for a psychology course, we probably would be reading Freud in the context of psychology vocabulary and could take advantage of the greater precision that such vocabulary offers. For instance, we may have learned that the word *neurosis* is used by many psychologists to differentiate an illness like Dora's from the more severe and disabling illnesses called *psychoses*. We may have learned that the single word *psychosomatic* is sometimes used to describe physical symptoms of emotional origin. When we feel comfortably in control of such terms, they become part of our thinking:

```
Hysteria is a neurosis characterized by psychosomatic
symptoms.
```

Our definition has been getting more confident, but if we have been thinking actively, we may still feel some misgivings. Have we gone too far? Not far enough? Does this definition distinguish hysteria from other neuroses? Will our definition satisfy a psychology teacher? These misgivings are worth listening to, but they should probably take a back seat to an overriding question: To what use are we putting our definition? In other words, how is it going to help us write about Freud? Reminding ourselves that we want to write an essay not about hysteria itself but about Freud's treatment of it, we think of a further modification. We can sidestep the problem of having to define the term in a way that suits all psychologists:

```
For Freud, hysteria is a neurosis characterized by psy-
chosomatic symptoms.
```

Or, with tougher editing:

```
For Freud, hysteria is a psychosomatic neurosis.
```

Even more important, for all the care we've taken in arriving at this single sentence, we need to remember that such a sentence can serve only as a jumping-off point. Our definition should be clarified further as we explain and elaborate and, eventually, as we call Dora to testify:

```
    For Freud, hysteria is a psychosomatic neurosis.
It expresses itself in behavior and physical symptoms
that are disguised expressions of deep conflicts and
anxieties.  These feelings are usually sexual, and
they usually stem from childhood experiences.  To dis-
cover the sources of hysteria, Freud felt he must trace
```

```
present symptoms back to their most recent causes and
from there back to their original sources in childhood
experience.
        In the case of Dora....
```

The essay you see emerging here would probably then go on to recount the story of Freud's gradual analysis of Dora, describing stage by stage Freud's efforts to uncover links between Dora's symptoms and the psychological events behind them. As writers, we take on the role of guide, using our opening definition as a sort of base of operations, the perspective on which the rest of our essay depends.

Such an essay would more than satisfy most college writing assignments. Yet we still could do more, particularly if we were willing to think critically about how Freud's own perspective helped to define his view of Dora. Our essay might benefit from our knowing that there are theoretical perspectives toward mental illness different from the one offered by Freud. With a little searching, we might also discover that the term *hysteria* is no longer in clinical use, even among psychoanalysts. Thinking skeptically, we might note that much in Freud's manner of investigation seems to take as given what he is also out to prove. Dora, we might say, was treated as hysterical by definition. Reflections like these might encourage us to reconsider our entire essay, or at least to make room within it to accommodate this critical perspective:

```
        The label hysteria is no longer used by practicing
psychologists, perhaps because earlier psychologists,
including Freud, applied it far too freely, particu-
larly to women.  Freud was convinced from the outset
that Dora's neurosis was entirely her own and could be
treated only by a painful examination of her childhood.
Today a family therapist would not insist on going so
far back.  No doubt Dora was neurotic, but the defini-
tion of her neurosis should be broadened to include
those around her.  Her father, her mother, Herr K, and
Frau K all bear some responsibility for the group
neurosis they perpetuated.
```

As thinkers and as writers, we don't see well without defining what we're viewing. But our definitions, in turn, do much to influence what we subsequently see. That's a good reason for questioning and then requestioning our definitions, for considering the contexts in which we create them and the purposes we ask them to serve.

Assignments: First Passes

1. Revising Definitions: Some Academic Paragraphs

In academic readings, words sometimes trick us by their familiarity. A word we commonly use or easily recognize may be used by a writer in a somewhat special way. If we don't recognize the specialized meaning, we're apt to read imprecisely, never getting a good grip on what we're reading.

Each of the following passages makes specialized use of a word you probably know already. Before reading each passage, write out your general sense of what the word means. Then after you've read the passage, note any differences you see between your initial sense of the word and the way the writer seems to be using it. Briefly describe those differences.

a. Write out your initial sense of what the term *qualified* means. Then, after reading the following passage, write out a second definition and compare the two.

> The average man in the West takes science and medicine for granted, not only as activities likely on the whole to benefit him, but as the necessary accompaniments of civilized life. Indeed, for many people civilization itself would be defined primarily in terms of achievements in science and medicine. If this point of view is not to be absurdly naive, it must be qualified by a realization that it is not universally valid by any means. There have been great civilizations, like the Inca, for example, which lacked any real science and practiced only a somewhat rudimentary medicine. On the other hand, there have been societies which, despite the highest skills in science and medicine, have hardly deserved the title "civilized" — like the Nazi regime of 1933–45.
> — R. M. Savory, *Introduction to Islamic Civilization*

b. What would you say the word *disinterested* means? Write out a definition. Then write out a revised definition based on the following passage.

> For Kant it is of the very essence of morality that it be disinterested. A good act done to please somebody or to gain an advantage or to secure a reward from God would cease thereby to be good; it would fall to the level of mere expediency. An action should be done because the doer sees for himself that it is right, that it is his duty. Or one may say that the moral imperative is categorical and not hypothetical. That is to say, it does not run: "If you want society to prosper or your own property to be secure, then do not steal," but simply: "Thou shalt not steal!" It comes to us as a law requiring unconditional obedience. We do not make it but find it; yet as rational beings we obey it because we impose it upon ourselves. The command of an external authority, be it God himself, is binding on us only as it wins the recognition of our conscience.
> — E. L. Allen, *From Plato to Nietzsche*

c. In ordinary speech, what are *accommodations?* Write out a definition of *accommodation* that takes into account the following passage. Do you see any bridge between the meaning of *accommodations* in ordinary speech and the meaning of *accommodation* in Dallek's passage on Lyndon Johnson?

> By the time Johnson came to the White House, the country had become congealed into large units in which accommodation and conformity were more likely to make a man's career than individual initiative. This change in the culture did not, however, throw Johnson into sharp conflict with national trends. Having grown up in a household where he had learned to avoid passionate and emotional divisions over issues, he was also a superb consensus politician skilled at pasting over differences and knitting together opposing forces. Thus, powerful impulses toward individualism and conformity resided in him side by side. But, facing a world in which the latter was now more valued than the former, he found ways to rationalize his own and the country's accommodation to this change.
> — Robert Dallek, *The American Style of Foreign Policy*

d. In *The Presentation of Self in Everyday Life* sociologist Erving Goffman, to serve his analytical purposes, redefines many terms that we tend to use fairly narrowly. Define what we usually mean by the word *region* and then look at how he defines it.

Something similarly odd seems to be going on with the word *performance* in this passage, though we are not provided with Goffman's definition. Using the context of this passage, including the examples he offers, explain what Goffman seems to mean by *performance* and how his use differs from our usual sense of the word.

> A region may be defined as any place that is bounded to some degree 1
> by barriers to perception. Regions vary, of course, in the degree to which they are bounded and according to the media of communication in which the barriers to perception occur. Thus thick glass panels, such as are found in broadcasting control rooms, can isolate a region aurally but not visually, while an office bounded by beaverboard partitions is closed off in the opposite way.
>
> In our Anglo-American society — a relatively indoor one — when a 2
> performance is given it is usually given in a highly bounded region, to which boundaries with respect to time are often added. The impression and understanding fostered by the performance will tend to saturate the region and time span, so that any individual located in this space-time manifold will be in a position to observe the performance and be guided by the definition of the situation which the performance fosters.
>
> Often a performance will involve only one focus of visual attention 3
> on the part of performer and audience, as, for example, when a political speech is presented in a hall or when a patient is talking to a doctor in the latter's consulting room. However, many performances involve, as constituent parts, separate knots or clusters of verbal interaction. Thus

a cocktail party typically involves several conversational subgroups which
constantly shift in size and membership. Similarly, the show maintained
on the floor of a shop typically involves several foci of verbal interaction,
each composed of attendant-customer pairs.

— Erving Goffman, *The Presentation of Self in Everyday Life*

2. Developing a Definition from Contexts: The Term *Mechanism*

As readers we gain a better sense of definition as we come across the
same word in differing contexts. Gradually we develop a sense of how the
word can be used, sometimes learning that a word is more restricted than
we first thought and sometimes discovering that it is more flexible. Often we
can speed up this process of acquisition simply by thinking more curiously
and deliberately about words that we notice recurring. As a word is used in
new contexts, what remains the same?

Try out this defining strategy with the word *mechanism* in the following
three passages. Write one short paragraph defining and illustrating the word,
making sure that your definition adequately fits all three situations.

The scheme of making a human being through technology belongs
to thousands of years of mythology and alchemy, but Turing and his
followers have given it a new twist. In Greek mythology, in the story
of Pygmalion and Galatea, the artifact, the perfect ivory statue, came to
life to join its human creator. In the seventeenth and eighteenth centuries,
some followers of Descartes first suggested crossing in the other direction, arguing, with La Mettrie, that men were no more than clockwork
mechanisms.

— J. David Bolter, *Turing's Man: Western Culture in the Computer Age*

In fact, each of Darwin's books played its part in the grand and
coherent scheme of his life's work — demonstrating the fact of evolution
and defending natural selection as its primary mechanism. Darwin did not
study orchids solely for their own sake. Michael Ghiselin, a California
biologist who finally took the trouble to read all of Darwin's books (see
his *Triumph of the Darwinian Method*), has correctly identified the treatise
on orchids as an important episode in Darwin's campaign for evolution.

Darwin begins his orchid book with an important evolutionary premise: continued self-fertilization is a poor strategy for long-term survival,
since offspring carry only the genes of their single parent, and populations
do not maintain enough variation for evolutionary flexibility in the face of
environmental change. Thus, plants bearing flowers with both male and
female parts usually evolve mechanisms to ensure cross-pollination. Orchids have formed an alliance with insects. They have evolved an astonishing variety of "contrivances" to attract insects, guarantee that sticky

pollen adheres to their visitor, and ensure that the attached pollen comes in contact with female parts of the next orchid visited by the insect.

— Stephen Jay Gould, *The Panda's Thumb*

Retrospective interpretation involves the mechanisms by which re-actors come to view deviators or suspected deviators "in a totally new light." Undoubtedly the most glaring examples are found in such public "status-degradation ceremonies" as the criminal trial. Sociologists have long been aware of the social-psychological processes by which an individual perceived one day as simply John Doe can (as a result of conviction at trial or even of having been held as a suspect) become "a murderer" or "a rapist" the next.

— Edwin M. Schur, *Labeling Deviant Behavior*

3. Defining a Process: *Hypertension*

Here in a somewhat fuller form is a passage we've already quoted in this chapter, Jane Brody's definition of *thirst* as part of a biological process. Before rereading it, write out your own definition of the term *hypertension*. Then after rereading the passage, define *hypertension* more fully by describing it as part of a process.

Of course, sodium is a vital constituent of the human body. Our tissues swim in a salty sea — a vestige, perhaps, of our aquatic evolution. The more salt in that sea, the more water is needed to dilute it to maintain the proper concentration of sodium. Sodium and its equally essential companion chloride (the combining form of chlorine) are the principal regulators of the balance of water and dissolved substances outside cells. You'll recall . . . that this is the job potassium does within cells. These three minerals — called electrolytes — also regulate the balance of acids and bases in body fluids and cells. If the balance of water and electrolytes or acids and bases is disturbed, normal metabolic functions may grind to a near halt. 1

Eating something salty makes you thirsty because when salt is added to the body, extra water is needed to dilute it. Bartenders cash in on this fact of human physiology by offering salty nuts and pretzels gratis to patrons. It's good for business. And if you lose water through sweating, the increased concentration of salt in your blood also stimulates thirst. The "purpose" of thirst is to keep the body functioning properly by maintaining the concentration of salt within a certain narrow range. 2

The body's machinery for keeping a normal level of sodium in its fluids is the *kidneys*. When the body has too much sodium, the kidneys dump it out into the urine and excrete it. When the body needs sodium, the kidneys reabsorb it from urine and pump it back into the blood. Unfortunately, in a significant percentage of people, perhaps as a result of having to dump excess sodium for years, this machinery fails to operate properly and the kidneys don't get rid of enough sodium. The retained 3 sodium holds water, and the volume of blood rises. The blood vessels become water-logged and more sensitive to nerve stimulation that causes them to contract. Since more blood now has to pass through the same ever-narrower channels, the blood pressure increases. The heart rate also increases because the heart has more blood to pump around the body. This in turn sets up a vicious cycle in which the blood vessels contract to reduce the blood flow. The pressure then rises even further until you have hypertension.

— Jane E. Brody, *Jane Brody's Nutrition Book*

4. Distinguishing Between Terms: Some Near-Synonyms

Some terms can best be clarified by defining them in relation to other terms. One frequent strategy is to define a word in comparison to a near-synonym. The two words may be sufficiently alike for some purposes, but in other situations they may carry different connotations, important distinctions in meaning. For example, the words *prejudiced* and *biased* are nearly indistinguishable in many situations: We use both words to accuse someone of having an unreasonable or preconceived opinion. Yet while *prejudice* almost always carries negative overtones, as in the phrase "racial prejudice," *bias* sometimes functions more neutrally to describe a prevailing tendency or slant. A book review describing a sociologist's "urban bias" may not be saying anything strongly critical, just describing a direction in which someone leans.

From the following list, choose a pair of terms and write a short paragraph distinguishing one term from the other. Make clear how the two terms may be used interchangeably in some contexts while in others their connotations can be quite different.

rebellion/revolution	observe/witness
useful/utilitarian	spread/proliferate
elastic/resilient	solitude/isolation
pulverize/slaughter	part/segment
collection/accumulation	work/labor

5. Dictionary Thinking: Definitions of *Light*

This assignment asks you to work along the lines that compilers of dictionaries do — taking a collection of sentences that show the range of a word's actual use and then sorting the examples into distinct categories and creating brief definitions to describe the examples in each category.

The following sentences all use the word *light*. Sort the uses into categories and then describe the categories using selected sentences as illustrations. Present your categories either in the form of a dictionarylike list of uses, with illustrative examples, or in the form of a short essay that explains and illustrates your categories.

1. Light and lust are deadly enemies.
2. All colours depend on light.
3. Beyond a certain intensity . . . light ceases to be light, and becomes mere pain.
4. Light, both solar and terrestrial, is a sensation occasioned by rays emanating from luminous bodies.
5. We have strong reason to conclude that light itself, including radiant heat (and other radiations if any), is an electromagnetic disturbance in the form of waves.
6. He had . . . an eye without light, a voice without charm.
7. Almost all patients lie with their faces turned to the light exactly as plants always make their way towards the light.
8. I have received great light from him, and hope for much more.
9. That which is called life in Christ the Word, was called Light in us.
10. Joan of Arc, a light of ancient France.
11. The lights and shades, whose well-accorded strife,
    Gives all the strength and colour of our life.
12. Italian masters universally make the horizon the chief light of their picture.
13. If a house or wall is erected so near to mine that it stops my ancient lights . . . I may enter my neighbor's land, and peaceably pull it down.
14. If a house is sold with all the lights belonging to it, and it is intended to build upon the adjoining ground . . . so as to interfere with the lights, the right to build in that manner should be expressly reserved.
15. He swore that I should not leave him till his purse was as light as eleven-pence.
16. The best water is clear, transparent, and light.
17. To travel in America one must travel light.
18. Making light of what ought to be serious.
19. Jude found the room full of soldiers and light women.
20. Light reading does not do when the heart is really heavy.
21. And so when I couldn't stand it no longer, I lit out.

— *Oxford English Dictionary*

Assignments: Options

6. A History of Science Option: Eugenics

Some ideas can best be defined by describing how they have been used in the past and how their present meanings have developed. In the following passage, notice how Ted Howard and Jeremy Rifkin, without offering a one-sentence definition, clarify the concept of *eugenics* by summarizing its history. Also notice that they offer this historical account from their own strong point of view. After reading it, try summarizing their summary. What does the term *eugenics* mean today, and how did we arrive at that meaning?

From *Who Should Play God?*
TED HOWARD AND JEREMY RIFKIN

Eugenics is not a new idea. Writing in *The Republic*, Plato asserted that "the best of both sexes ought to be brought together as often as possible and the worst as seldom as possible and that the former unions ought to be reared and that of the latter abandoned, if the flock is to attain to first-rate excellence."   1

Caesar was so interested in improving the stock of Rome's best family lines that he offered a thousand sesterces to every "Roman" mother for each child. Augustus later offered two thousand, but to no avail. The birthrate among the rich continued to decline.   2

The recognized father of modern-day eugenics was Sir Francis Galton. A cousin of Charles Darwin's, Galton was very much influenced by the publication of *Origin of Species*. Galton believed that Darwin's theory of evolution and the survival of the fittest also applied to the human species, so he set out to construct a theory which interpreted human social actions and behavior on the basis of his biological origins. In his book *Hereditary Genius*, Galton laid down much of the theory that was to be later used by so-called Social Darwinists to rationalize the worst abuses of unrestrained capitalism and racism in America. . . .   3

In *Hereditary Genius* Galton concludes that the modern European (of which he considered himself the best of the lot) possesses much greater natural ability than do those of "lower" races. He then speculates as to the potential of a eugenics program. "There is nothing either in the history of domestic animals or in that of evolution to make us doubt that a race of sane men may be formed, who shall be as much superior mentally and morally to the modern Europeans, as the modern European is to the lowest of the Negro races." Galton sums up his hopes for humankind's future by asserting that just as it is easy "to obtain by careful selection a permanent breed of dogs or horses gifted with peculiar powers . . . so it would be quite practical to produce a highly gifted race of men" by similar means.   4

One man who read Galton's thesis, and decided it was time to put the theory into practice, was utopian socialist John Humphrey Noyes, the founder of the Oneida Colony in New York State. "Every race horse, every straight backed bull, every premium pig," said Noyes, "tells us what we can do and what we must do for man." In 1869, Noyes had fifty-three women and thirty-eight men sign a pledge to participate in an experiment to breed healthy perfectionists by "matching those most advanced in health and perfection." The women pledged that they would "become martyrs to science," and with that the first American experiments in eugenics began.   5

From his theory of eugenics, Galton concocted a new view of charity, one that would be later taken up by American eugenics reformers in their campaign to purify the racial stock of the nation. Charity, said Galton, should "help the strong rather than the weak, and the man of tomorrow rather than the man of today; let knowledge and foresight control the blind emotions and impetuous instincts." So convinced was Galton of the wisdom of applying his theory to human beings that he regretted that "there exists a sentiment for the most part quite unreasonable against the gradual extinction of an inferior race." 6

Just a few short years after Galton constructed his theories, new discoveries in genetics provided just enough meager evidence (later proven erroneous) to construct the thinnest "scientific" rationales for a eugenics movement. And that was all that many people needed to hop on board the eugenics bandwagon in America. . . . 7

By 1915, most of the leading educators already agreed with Irving Fisher, the well-known Yale economist, that "eugenics is incomparably the greatest concern of the human race." It's not surprising, then, that by 1928 over three fourths of all the colleges and universities in America were teaching eugenics courses. Their teachers were men like Earnest A. Hooton of Harvard, who preached that "crime is the resultant of the impact of environment upon low grade human organisms." "The solution to the crime problem," he told Harvard undergraduates, is the "extirpation of the physically, mentally and morally unfit or (if that seems too harsh) their complete segregation in a socially aseptic environment." 8

The eugenics creed also found willing adherents within the media. The *New York Times* helped fan the eugenics hysteria with statements like "labor disturbances are brought about by foreigners" and "demonstrations are always mobs composed of foreign scum, beer smelling Germans, ignorant Bohemians, uncouth Poles and wild-eyed Russians." 9

It might interest today's subscribers to the prestigious left-liberal magazines the *Nation* and the *New Republic* that the founders of both publications were crusaders for eugenics reform. Edwin Laurence Godkin, founder of the *Nation*, believed that only those of superior biological stock should run the affairs of the country, and Herbert David Croly of the *New Republic* was convinced that blacks "were a race possessed of moral and intellectual qualities inferior to those of the white man." 10

Imagine, if you will, a President of the U.S. writing in *Good Housekeeping* (a favorite forum of Presidents) that "there are racial considerations too grave to be brushed aside for any sentimental reasons." According to President Coolidge, biological laws tell us that certain divergent people will not mix or blend. Coolidge concludes that the Nordics propagate themselves successfully, "while with other races, the outcome shows deterioration on both sides." 11

Even some of America's great heroes succumbed to the eugenics fever. Alexander Graham Bell was one of them. Speaking before the American Breeders Association in Washington in 1908, Bell remarked: "We have learned to apply the laws of heredity so as to modify and improve our breeds of domestic animals. Can the knowledge and expe- 12 rience so gained be available to man, so as to enable him to improve the species to which he himself belongs?" Bell believed that "students of genetics possess the knowledge . . . to improve the race" and that education of the public was necessary to gain acceptance for eugenics policies.

Many modern-day feminists will be chagrined to learn that Margaret   **13**
Sanger, a leader in the fight for birth-control programs, was a true believer in the biological superiority and inferiority of different groups. In some of the toughest-sounding words to ever come out of the eugenics movement, Sanger remarked that "it is a curious but neglected fact that the very types which in all kindness should be obliterated from the human stock, have been permitted to reproduce themselves and to perpetuate their group, succored by the policy of indiscriminate charity of warm hearts uncontrolled by cool heads." Sanger had her own solution to the problem of human biological contamination of society and better breeding: "There is only one reply to a request for a higher birth rate among the intelligent and that is to ask the government to first take the burden of the insane and feebleminded from your back. . . . Sterilization," said Sanger, "is the solution."

The eugenics ideology became so pervasive between 1900 and 1930   **14**
that some historians even attempted to rewrite world history from a eugenics perspective. Thus, David Starr Jordan, president of Stanford University, claimed that Rome's decline resulted from its frequent military conquests, in which its best blood was sent out to battle and scattered throughout the empire. This left Rome to the stable boys, slaves, and camp followers, whose poor biological stock multiplied and populated the city with an inferior genetic species. Ironically, this kind of eugenics analysis of history led many like Jordan to become pacifists, on the grounds that war would take away and destroy the best blood of the nation.

It was this obsessive concern with the blood of the nation that so   **15**
animated the eugenicists. Jordan best summed up the attitude of the supporters of eugenics when he declared that "the blood of the nation determines its history . . . the history of a nation determines its blood." To Jordan and his cohorts, "the survival of the fittest in the struggle for existence is the primal cause of race progress and race changes." Just a few years later, a house painter from Munich was to echo that exact same sentiment from his jail cell in Germany as he put the final touches on a work which he entitled *Mein Kampf.*

Even the success of the fledgling Boy Scout movement in America   **16**
was attributable to some degree to the interest in eugenics. As a matter of fact, David Starr Jordan served as the vice-president of the Boy Scouts of America in those early days. Jordan and his colleagues believed that the Scout program could help rear the "eugenic new man."

One of the most bizarre twists in the eugenics movement was Fitter   **17**
Family Contests, run by the American Eugenics Society. Blue ribbons were presented at county and state fairs all over the Midwest to those families that could produce the best family pedigrees. Families were judged on their physical and mental qualities, right alongside pigs and cows.

The acceptance of eugenics by much of the general public as a scientifically sound theory was due in large part to the early and enthusiastic support of eugenics by some of America's most prominent scientists. The scientists legitimized the theory of eugenics in the public mind, although in the end they largely refused to accept any responsibility for the consequences that flowed from its application. The story of its ruthless application represents one of the darkest pages in American history.

18

7. A Language Option: Word Histories

The Oxford English Dictionary (*O.E.D.*) provides not only standard definitions but etymological information — that is, information about the origins of words — along with illustrations of how words have been used in the past. By using the *O.E.D.*, we often can learn something about the paths by which a word has come to have its present meanings and something about meanings buried just below the surface of words.

This assignment asks you to compose an essay that defines a word by drawing on the historical information provided by its *O.E.D.* entry. First consider the example of a short essay composed from the information about the word *assassin*. Then choose *one* of the entries that follow as the basis of your own essay. To help you interpret the information provided in the *O.E.D.* entries, we've also appended selected entries from its "List of Abbreviations, Signs, Etc."

O.E.D. ENTRY

ESSAY CONSTRUCTED
FROM THE ENTRY

assassin (ə'sæsɪn). Also **7 assassine, -asin(e, -acine.** [a. F. *assassin*, or ad. It. *assassino*: cf. also Pr. *assassin*, Pg. *assassino*, Sp. *asesino*, med.L. *assassinus* (OF. forms were *assacin, asescin, asisim, hasisin, hassissin, haussasin,* etc.; med.L. (pl.) *assessini, ascisini,* etc.), ad. Arab. *hashshāshīn* and *hashīshiyyīn,* pl. of *hashshāsh* and *hashīshiyy,* lit. 'a hashish-eater, one addicted to hashish,' both forms being applied in Arabic to the Ismāʿīli sectarians, who used to intoxicate themselves with hashish or hemp, when preparing to dispatch some king or public man. The OF. variants, (pl.) *assacis, hassisis, haississis,* med.L. *assasi, haussasi,* med.Gr. χασίσιοι, point to the Arabic singular, but the form finally established in the European languages arises from the Arab. plural, as in *Bedouin*; cf. also It. *cherubino, serafino,* F. and earlier Eng. *cherubin, seraphin* (sing.). Naturally the plural was first in use, in the historical sense, and occurred in Eng. in the Lat. or It. form before *assassin* was naturalized: the latter was still accented 'assassin by Oldham in 1679.]

1. *lit.* A hashish-eater. *Hist.* (in *pl.*) Certain Moslem fanatics in the time of the Crusades, who were sent forth by their sheikh, the 'Old

Assassin crept into English most directly from the French assassin and Italian assassino. The word originates from the Arabic Hashshasin, a plural form of a word meaning "hashish-eater, one addicted to hashish." More specifically, the term applied to a specific Moslem sect, whose members "used to intoxicate themselves with hashish or hemp, when preparing to dispatch some king or public man." The word may have passed into European languages at the time of the

Man of the Mountains,' to murder the Christian leaders.

[c **1237** R. WENDOVER *Flores Hist.* (1841) II. II. 246 Hos tam Saraceni quam Christiani Assissinos appellant.] **1603** KNOLLES *Hist. Turks* (1638) 120 This messenger..was.. one of the Assasines, a company of most desperat and dangerous men among the Mahometans. **1611** SPEED *Hist. Gt. Brit.* IX. x. 5 That bloudy Sect of Sarazens, called Assassini, who, without feare of torments, vndertake..the murther of any eminent Prince, impugning their irreligion. *c* **1860** J. WOLFF, The assassins, who are otherwise called the People of the Man of the Mountain, before they attacked an enemy, would intoxicate themselves with a powder made of hemp-leaves, out of which they prepared an inebriating electuary, called *hashish*.

2. Hence: One who undertakes to put another to death by treacherous violence. The term retains so much of its original application as to be used chiefly of the murderer of a public personage, who is generally hired or devoted to the deed, and aims purely at the death of his victim.

[*a* **1259** M. PARIS *Angl. Hist. Maj.* (1589) 459 Qui tandem confessus est, se missum illuc, vt Regem more assessinorum occideret, à VVillielmo de Marisco.] **1531** *Dial. Laws Eng.* II. xli. (1638) 133 Hee is an Ascisinus [*printed* Ascismus] that will slay men for money at the instance of every man that will move him to it, and such a man may lawfully be slaine..by every private person. **1621** BURTON *Anat. Mel.* I. iii. I. iii, Men of all others fit to be assassins. **1679** OLDHAM *Sat. Jesuits* (1686) 7 Think on that matchless Assassin, whose name We with just pride can make our happy claim. **1702** ROWE *Tamerlane* III. i. 1330 When bold Assassines take thy Name upon 'em. **1778** WOLCOTT (P. Pindar) *To Reviewers* Wks. 1812 I. 5 That stabbed like brave assassins in the dark. **1855** MACAULAY *Hist. Eng.* IV. xxi. 668 Barclay's assassins were hunted like wolves by the whole population.

3. *fig.* or *transf.*

1736 THOMSON *Liberty* V. 385 The hir'd assassins of the Commonweal. **1824** DIBDIN *Libr. Comp.* 744 Lord Byron was the assassin of his own fame.

4. *attrib.* and in *comb.*, as *assassin-like*; **assassin bug**, a predaceous insect of the family Reduviidæ.

1895 J. H. & A. B. COMSTOCK *Man. Stud. Insects* xiv. 137 Family Reduviidæ..There are many bugs which destroy their fellows, but the members of this family are so preeminently predaceous that we call them the Assassin-bugs. **1937** *Discovery* Dec. 368/2 A..cheerful brute occurs in North America, where it is known as the 'big bed bug' and the assassin bug. **1667** MILTON *P.L.* XI. 219 Who, to surprize One man, Assassin-like, had levied Warr, Warr unproclam'd. *a* **1846** B. R. HAYDON *Autobiogr.* (1927) vii. 104 On this principle I have acted in not making the assassins so assassin-like as perhaps they were. **1847** DISRAELI *Tancred* IV. ix. (1871) 305 He caught in his hand the assassin spear.

Crusades, when certain Moslem sheikhs selected fanatics to murder Christian leaders. A historian named Speed in his History of Great Britain (1611) refers to "that bloudy Sect of Sarazens, called Assassini, who, without feare of torments, undertake ... the murther of any eminent Prince." Hence, the word has come to mean anyone who "undertakes to put another to death by treacherous violence," but particularly when the victim is a public figure and when the assassin either has been hired to do the job or does it out of devotion. The word still suggests someone who is not in his right mind, often someone who is considered a beast. Thus another historian speaks of assassins being hunted down "like wolves." Sometimes the word has been used in a figurative way, as when a man named Dibdin said that Lord Byron was "the assassin of his own fame." You could say that Dibdin was practicing character assassination.

List of Abbreviations, Signs, Etc.

Some abbreviations listed here in italics are also in certain cases printed in roman type, and vice versa.

a. (in Etym.)	adoption of, adopted from	*adv.*	adverb
a (as *a* 1850)	*ante,* "before," "not later than"	*Amer.*	American
		Anat.	(as label) in Anatomy;
a.	adjective		(in titles) *Anatomy, -ical*
A.D.	*Anno Domini*	*attrib.*	attributive, -ly
ad. (in Etym.)	adaptation of	*Autobiogr.*	(in titles) *Autobiography, -ical*
adj.	adjective		
		Bull.	(in titles) *Bulletin*

List of Abbreviations, Signs, Etc. (*continued*)

c (as *c* 1700)	*circa*, "about"	lang.	language
Cf., cf.	*confer*, "compare"	lit.	literal, -ly
comb.	combined, -ing	*Lit.*	Literary
compar.	comparative	*Mag.*	(in titles) *Magazine*
Devel.	(in titles) *Development,* -al	*Man.*	(in titles) *Manual*
dial.	dialect, -al	*Math.*	(as label) in Mathematics; (in titles) *Mathematics,* -al
Dict.	Dictionary; *spec.*, the *Oxford English Dictionary*	med. L.	medieval Latin
Eng.	England, English	*Myst.*	(in titles) *Mystery*
Engin.	in Engineering	*Obs., obs.*	obsolete
etc.	et cetera	orig.	origin, -al, -ally
etym.	etymology	Pg.	Portuguese
Exam.	(in titles) *Examination*	*Philol.*	(as label) in Philology; (in titles) *Philology, -ical*
f.	feminine		
f. (in Etym.)	formed on	*phr.*	phrase
f. (in subordinate entries)	form of	pl., plur.	plural
		ppl. a., pple. adj.	participial adjective
F.	French	Pr.	Provençal
fig.	figurative, -ly	*Princ.*	(in titles) *Principle, -s*
G.	German	*R.*	(in titles) *Royal*
Geol.	(as label) in Geology; (in titles) *Geology, -ical*	refl.	reflexive
		Res.	(in titles) *Research*
Ger.	German	*sb.*	substantive
Gr.	Greek	*sc.*	*scilicet*, "understand" or "supply"
Gram.	(as label) in Grammar; (in titles) *Grammar, -tical*	sing.	singular
		Soc.	(in titles) *Society*
Hist.	(as label) in History; (in titles) *History, -ical*	Sp.	Spanish
		Stud.	(in titles) *Studies*
hist.	historical	Suppl.	Supplement
Ibid.	*Ibidem*, "in the same book or passage"	s.v.	*sub voce*, "under the word"
intr.	intransitive	*Trans.*	(in titles) *Transactions*
It.	Italian	*transf.*	transferred sense
Jrnl.	(in titles) *Journal*	*Univ.*	(in titles) *University*
L.	Latin	*v.*, vb.	verb

SIGNS AND OTHER CONVENTIONS

BEFORE A WORD OR SENSE

† = obsolete
‖ = not naturalized, alien
¶ = catachrestic and erroneous uses

IN THE ETYMOLOGIES

* indicates a word or form not actually found, but of which the existence is inferred
: − = normal development of

IN THE LISTING OF FORMS

1 = before 1100
2 = 12th c. (1100 to 1200)
3 = 13th c. (1200 to 1300), etc.
5–7 = 15th to 17th century
20 = 20th century

The printing of a word in SMALL CAPITALS indicates that further information will be found under the word so referred to.
. . indicates an omitted part of a quotation.
~ (in a quotation) indicates a hyphen doubtfully present in the original; (in other text) indicates a hyphen inserted only for the sake of a line-break.

a. Write an essay defining *chauvinism* by drawing on historical information.

chauvinism ('ʃəʊvɪnɪz(ə)m). Also **Chauvinism**. [a. F. *chauvinisme*, orig. 'idolatrie napoléonienne' La Rousse; from the surname of a veteran soldier of the First Republic and Empire, Nicolas *Chauvin* of Rochefort, whose demonstrative patriotism and loyalty were celebrated, and at length ridiculed, by his comrades. After the fall of Napoleon, applied in ridicule to old soldiers of the Empire, who professed a sort of idolatrous admiration for his person and acts. Especially popularized as the name of one of the characters in Cogniard's famous vaudeville, *La Cocarde Tricolore*, 1831 ('je suis français, je suis Chauvin'); and now applied to any one smitten with an absurd patriotism, and enthusiasm for national glory and military ascendancy.]

a. Exaggerated patriotism of a bellicose sort; blind enthusiasm for national glory or military ascendancy; the French quality which finds its parallel in British 'Jingoism'.

1870 *Pall Mall G.* 17 Sept. 10 What the French may have contributed to the progress of culture within the last twenty years is nothing in comparison to the dangers caused within the same space of time by Chauvinism. **1882** *Spectator* 16 Sept. 1186 Throughout Southern Europe, including France, the journalists are much more inclined to chauvinism than the people are. **1883** *American* VII. 156 Educated men are supposed to see the difference between patriotism and Chauvinism.

b. Excessive loyalty to or belief in the superiority of one's own kind of cause, and prejudice against others. Freq. with defining adj., as *cultural, scientific,* etc. *chauvinism. male chauvinism*: see MALE *sb.*[2] 4.

1955 *Bull. Atomic Sci.* Apr. 142/3 Even though scientists did not go as far as to confuse scientific knowledge with national ideological doctrine, they did, nonetheless, often make it a point of patriotic honor to practice a certain kind of scientific nationalism and almost indeed a scientific chauvinism. **1968** *Voice of Women's Lib. Movement* June 8 The chauvinism .. they met came from individuals and was not built into the institution itself. **1970** K. MILLETT *Sexual Politics* (1971) II. iv. 208 At times there is a curious tone of 'female chauvinism'. **1973** C. SAGAN *Cosmic Connection* (1974) xxiv. 180 Contact with another intelligent species on a planet of some other star .. may help us to cast off our .. human chauvinism. **1975** *New Left Rev.* Nov.–Dec. 48 Bachelard's neglect .. cannot be ascribed to cultural chauvinism alone. **1984** *N.Y. Times* 15 Jan. 23/1 Freedom from sexism .. must include a commitment to freedom from national chauvinism; class and ethnic bias; anti-Semitism; [etc.].

So **'chauvinist** *sb.* and *a.,* **chauvi'nistic** *a.,* **chauvi'nistically** *adv.*

1870 *Pall Mall G.* 3 Oct. 10 'Là où Rhin nous quitte, le danger commence,' said Lavalée in his chauvinistic work on the frontiers of France. **1877** WALLACE *Russia* xxvi. 411 Among the extreme chauvinists. **1883** D. C. BOULGER in *Fortn. Rev., China & For. Powers*, The most chauvinist of Manchu statesmen. **1885** *Athenæum* 17 Oct. 504/3 The curious Chauvinistic character taken by German patriotism. **1968** *Ramparts* May 12/3 Paternalism, male ego and all the rest of the chauvinist bag are out of place today. **1970** *Univ. Leeds Rev.* May 65 There will be in one's country and its life a mixture of good and ill, and .. if the good were not present or were exiguous by comparison with the ill, then one could not love it, except chauvinistically. **1973** C. SAGAN *Cosmic Connection* (1974) vi. 47 A carbon chauvinist holds that biological systems elsewhere in the universe will be constructed out of carbon compounds, as is on this planet. **1975** *N.Y. Sunday News* 29 June 18 Linda Wolfe's new book .. may cause some chauvinistic husbands to sit bolt upright in their easy chairs. **1977** *Rolling Stone* 21 Apr. 6/3 First, her treatment of Edmund—female chauvinist! **1983** *N.Y. Times* 20 Nov. VI. 75/3 What Giacomo Casanova chauvinistically called 'the Italian style'—and what the Americans call the French kiss.

b. Write an essay defining *cybernetics* by drawing on historical information.

cybernetics (saɪbə'nɛtɪks). [f. Gr. κυβερνήτης steersman, f. κυβερνᾶν to steer (see GOVERN *v.*) + -ICS.] The theory or study of communication and control in living organisms or machines. Hence (as back-formation) **cyber'netic** *a.,* pertaining or relating to cybernetics. So **cyberne'tician, cyber'neticist**, one who is skilled in cybernetics.

Used in Fr. form *cybernétique* (= the art of governing) by A.-M. Ampère *Essai sur la Philos. des Sciences*, 1834.
1948 N. WIENER *Cybernetics* 19 We have decided to call the entire field of control and communication theory, whether in the machine or in the animal, by the name Cybernetics. **1951** *Jrnl. R. Aeronaut. Soc.* Oct. 624/2 All these machines represent developments in that part of what has been called the cybernetic revolution which is gradually taking over those operations in the fields of numbers, quantities, and data that are strictly clerical or mechanical. **1952** *Science News* XXIII. 77 The cyberneticists approach the problem of neural activity from a purely functional angle, and seek to model the activity of the brain as a whole on the electronic devices of modern communications systems and servo-mechanisms. **1958** *Listener* 18 Sept. 413 The claim of cybernetics is that we can treat organisms *as if* they were machines, in the sense that the same methods of synthesis and analysis can be applied to both. **1959** *Times* 11 May 6/6 Cybernetics is the study of man in relation to his particular job or machine with special reference to mental processes and control mechanisms. **1961** *Times Lit. Suppl.* 6 Jan. 2/4 It is all right for cyberneticians to make machines like men. **1961** J. WILSON *Reason & Morals* ii. 113 If men are machines, at least their behaviour suggests that they are cybernetic or self-regulating machines. **1962** *Listener* 1 Nov. 718/1 Cybernetics, as the people who practise cybernetics would appear to call themselves, can build a larynx with which an injured man can speak. *Ibid.* 718/2 In education, too, cybernetics begins to intrude as electronic teaching machines make good the lack of human teachers. **1968** *Brit. Med. Bull.* XXIV. 197/2 The integration of cells, organs, and systems .. appears to be done on a cybernetic basis with feed-back processes .. clearly interwoven at all levels. **1970** *Nature* 12 Sept. 1167/1 The cyberneticist's approach to the concepts of psychology is not, however, in evidence here.

c. Write an essay defining *evolve* by drawing on historical information.

evolve (ɪ'vɒlv), *v.* [ad. L. *ēvolvĕ-re* to roll out, unroll, f. *ē* out + *volvĕre* to roll.]

1. *trans.* To unfold, unroll (something that is wrapped up); to open out, expand. Almost always *fig.*

a **1641**, **1647** [see EVOLVED *ppl. a.*] **1677** HALE *Prim. Orig. Man.* I. i. 31 This little active Principle as the Body increaseth .. evolveth, diffuseth and expandeth if not his Substantial Existence, yet his Energy and Virtue. **1835** I. TAYLOR *Spir. Despot.* ii. 54 If we wish to see .. the Voluntary Principle fully evolved and ripened under a summer heat.

1839-40 W. IRVING *Wolfert's R.* (1855) 67 Mr. Glencoe.. would stimulate and evolve the powers of his mind. **1855** H. REED *Lect. Eng. Lit.* vi. (1878) 188 Their condensed wisdom may be evolved for new applications.

†**b.** *lit.* To unwind (a thread, also a curved line). *Obs. rare.*

1730-6 BAILEY (folio), *Evolute*, the first curve supposed to be opened, or evolved, which being opened describes other curves. **1796** HUTTON *Math. Dict.*, *Evolute*..is any curve supposed to be evolved or opened, by..beginning to evolve or unwind the thread from the other end, keeping the part evolved, or wound off, tight stretched. **1811** —— *Course Math.* II. 334 If AE, BF, etc. be any positions of the thread, in evolving or unwinding; it follows, etc.

2. To disengage from wrappings, disclose gradually to view; to disentangle; to set forth in orderly sequence. (Only with reference to immaterial objects, though often consciously *fig.* from the physical sense).

1664 H. MORE *Myst. Iniq.* xvii. 63, I have not yet evolved all the intangling superstitions that may be wrapt up. **1737** THOMSON *To Memory of Ld. Talbot* 144 He thro' the Maze of Falsehood urg'd it [the Truth] on, Till, at the last evolv'd, it full appear'd. **1744** AKENSIDE *Ep. to Curio*, Time.. Evolves their secrets, and their guilt proclaims. **1773** MONBODDO *Lang.* I. I. viii. 101 With so many various forms and substances, that it is difficult to evolve them and shew them by themselves. **1852** LD. COCKBURN *Jeffrey* I. 189 Jeffrey's..whole opinions and tastes were evolved in these articles. **1858** SEARS *Athan.* III. ix. 325 The outlines of Paul's system of Pneumatology..have been sufficiently evolved in the preceding pages.

3. *Math.* To extract (the root of a number or quantity). Cf. EVOLUTION 4 b.

1810 HUTTON *Course Math.* I. 202 To Evolve or Extract the Roots of Surd Quantities.

4. To give off, emit, as a product of chemical, vital, or other internal action; to liberate or disengage from a state of chemical combination.

1800 *Med. Jrnl.* III. 125 The expectorated fluid..may.. evolve fetor. **1806** DAVY in *Phil. Trans.* XCVII. 9 The fixed alkali is not generated, but evolved, either from the solid materials employed, or from saline matter in the water. **1822** IMISON *Sc. & Art* II. 63 The chlorine will be evolved. **1844-57** G. BIRD *Urin. Deposits* (ed. 5) 80 Nitrogen and carbon evolved from the system..in the form of urea and uric acid. **1869** PHILLIPS *Vesuv.* iii. 69 In September the vapours evolved from Vesuvius grew to be considerable.

5. To bring out (what exists implicitly or potentially): *e.g.* to educe (order from confusion, light from darkness, etc.); to deduce (a conclusion, law, or principle) from the data in which it is involved; to develop (a notion) as the result of reflection or analysis; to work out (a theory or system) out of pre-existing materials.

1831 CARLYLE *Sart. Res.* (1858) 47 An English Editor, endeavouring to evolve printed Creation out of a German

printed and written Chaos. **1851** HUSSEY *Papal Power* iii. 172 New claims of authority..were gradually evolved from the doctrine of the Supremacy. **1859** MILL *Liberty* (1865) 30 Other ethics than any which can be evolved from exclusively Christian sources. **1864** BOWEN *Logic* viii. 262 The particular instances are first stated as facts, and then the law they constitute is evolved. **1874** SAYCE *Compar. Philol.* vii. 296 The idea of a subject-pronoun was evolved last of all. **1883** Mrs. PLUNKETT in *Harper's Mag.* Jan. 241/2, I evolved a satin-covered heart-shaped Christmas leaf.

6. Of circumstances, conditions, or processes: To give rise to, produce by way of natural consequence.

1851 LONGF. *Gold. Leg.* I. *Castle Vaultsberg*, The new diseases that human life Evolves in its progress. **1866** HUXLEY *Phys.* x. (1872) 236 The simple sensations which are thus evolved. **1868** HELPS *Realmah* xvii. (1876) 476 New felicities—evolved in each representation. **1879** *Spectator* 7 June 719 That habits of gregariousness tend eventually to evolve a morality.

7. To develop by natural processes from a more rudimentary to a more highly organized condition; to originate (animal or vegetable species) by gradual modification from earlier forms; in wider sense, to produce or modify by 'evolution'. (See EVOLUTION 6-9). Chiefly in *pass.* without reference to an agent.

1832 LYELL *Princ. Geol.* II. i. 14 The orang-outang, having been evolved out of a monad, is made slowly to attain the attributes and dignity of man. **1837** SIR F. PALGRAVE *Merch. & Friar* (1844) 204 Was the first Ichthyosaurus gradually evolved from some embryo substance? **1849** MURCHISON *Siluria* ii. (1867) 23 Lying upon them, and therefore evolved after them, other strata succeed. **1873** H. SPENCER *Study Sociol.* v. 102 Societies are evolved in structure and function as in growth. **1881** SOLLAS in *Science Gossip* No. 202. 217 The organism..was evolved in the course of ages from some simpler form of life. **1884** E. P. ROE in *Harper's Mag.* Apr. 737/2 If God..chooses to evolve His universe, why shouldn't He?

8. *intr.* for *refl.* in various of the above senses: To open out, expand; to come gradually into view; to arise by way of natural or logical consequence; to be developed by 'evolution'.

1799 S. TURNER *Anglo-Sax.* (1836) I. IV. iv. 288 When great political exigencies evolve..they are usually as much distinguished by the rise of sublime characters. **1800** A. CARLYLE *Autobiog.* 488 The excellence of that character which gradually evolved on his admiring countrymen. **1827** G. S. FABER *Sacred Cal. Proph.* (1844) I. 201 Then come the days of blessedness, which both Daniel and John describe as evolving..in the course of the present visible sub-lunary world. **1849** C. BRONTË *Shirley* v. 57 May feel ripe to evolve in foliage. **1863** W. PHILLIPS *Speeches* ix. 235 Everything else will evolve from it. **1879** H. SPENCER *Data of Ethics* §104. 269 How does mechanical science evolve from these experiences? **1881** *Student* II. 35 A tree evolves in obedience to his [God's] laws.

---

d. Write an essay defining *technology* by drawing on historical information.

technology (tɛk'nɒlədʒɪ). [ad. Gr. τεχνολογία systematic treatment (of grammar, etc.), f. τέχνη art, craft: see -LOGY. So F. *technologie* (1812 in Hatz.-Darm.).]

1. a. A discourse or treatise on an art or arts; the scientific study of the practical or industrial arts.

1615 BUCK *Third Univ. Eng.* xlviii, An apt close of this general Technologie. **1628** VENNER *Baths of Bathe* 9 Heere I cannot but lay open Baths Technologie. **1706** PHILLIPS (ed. Kersey), *Technology*, a Description of Arts, especially the Mechanical. **1802-12** BENTHAM *Ration. Judic. Evid.* (1827) I. 19 Questions in technology in all its branches. **1881** P. GEDDES in *Nature* 29 Sept. 524/2 Of economic physics, geology, botany, and zoology, of technology and the fine arts. **1882** *Mechanical World* 4 Mar. 130/1 The Department of Applied Science and Technology.

b. *transf.* Practical arts collectively.

1859 R. F. BURTON *Centr. Afr.* in *Jrnl. Geog. Soc.* XXIX.

437 Little valued in European technology it [the chakazi, or 'jackass' copal] is exported to Bombay, where it is converted into an inferior varnish. **1864** —— *Dahome* II. 202 His technology consists of weaving, cutting canoes, making rude weapons, and in some places practising a rude metallurgy. **1949** in W. A. Visser t' Hooft *First Assembly World Council of Churches* 75 There is no inescapable necessity for society to succumb to undirected developments of technology. **1958** J. K. GALBRAITH *Affluent Society* ix. 99 Improvements in technology..are the result of investment in the highly organized scientific and engineering knowledge and skills. **1971** *Daily Tel.* (Colour Suppl.) 10 Dec. 18/2 In the production of millions of children a year, it is not surprising that occasionally nature's complex technology should break down to produce an imbalance of hormones with masculinisation of the female foetus or feminisation of the male. **1975** *Ecologist* V. 120/1 Guiding technological development effectively is not a matter of being for or against technology, which is the form the discussion usually assumes.

c. With *a* and *pl*. A particular practical or industrial art.

1957 *Technology* Apr. 56/1 It [*sc.* Chemical Engineering] is now recognized as one of the four primary technologies, alongside civil, mechanical, and electrical engineering. **1960** *Electronic Engin.* Mar. 148/1 Electronic data-processing for business is a young technology. **1969** *Listener* 5 June 778/1 To compare one technology with another. **1979** *Computers in Shell* (Shell Internat. Petroleum Co.) 2 Highly complex problems involving the many technologies needed within the energy and associated industries.

d. high-technology applied *attrib.* to a firm, industry, etc., that produces or utilizes highly advanced and specialized technology, or to the products of such a firm. Also (unhyphened) as *sb. phr.* Similarly **low-technology**. Cf. *high tech* s.v. TECH³ 1.

1964 S. M. MILLER in I. L. Horowitz *New Sociology* 292 The youthful poor possess limited or outmoded skills and inadequate credentials in a high-technology, certificate-demanding economy. **1970** *Physics Bull.* Apr. 146/1 'High technology' industries demand huge capital and R and D investments. **1972** *Nature* 28 Jan. 183/2 In high technology . . errors in estimates of development cost are more serious in their effects. **1973** *Newsweek* 18 June 92/2 As their old, low-technology industries wilt under the pressure of mounting labor costs. **1981** *Times* 14 May 1/7 Export licences are required for a variety of high technology goods including computers, electronic equipment, chemicals, metals and building equipment.

2. The terminology of a particular art or subject; technical nomenclature.

1658 SIR T. BROWNE *Gard. Cyrus* v. 70 The mother of Life and Fountain of souls in Cabalisticall Technology is called Binah. **1793** W. TAYLOR in *Monthly Rev.* XI. 563 The

port-customs, the technology, and the maritime laws, all wear marks of this original character. **1802-12** BENTHAM *Ration. Judic. Evid.* (1827) IV. 252 An engine, called, in the technology of that day, *fork*. **1862** *Morn. Star* 21 May, Aluminium, and its alloy with copper—which the manufacturers, with a slight laxity of technology, denominate bronze.

†**3.** = Gr. τεχνολογία: see etym. *Obs. rare*⁻¹.

1683 TWELLS *Exam. Gram.* Pref. 17 There were not any further Essays made in Technology, for above Fourscore years; but all men acquiesced in the Common Grammar.

4. Special Combs.: **technology assessment**, the assessment of the effects on society of new technology; **technology transfer**, the transfer of new technology or advanced technological information from the developed to the less developed countries of the world.

1966 *Inquiries, Legislation, Policy Stud. Subcomm. Sci., Res., & Devel.* (U.S. Congress: House: Comm. Sci. & Astronaut.) 27 We must be cognizant of what technology is doing to us—the bad as well as the good. Toward this end we would consider the exploration of legislation to establish a Technology Assessment Board—with the somewhat appropriate acronym TAB, since this would be its function. **1979** *Bull. Amer. Acad. Arts & Sci.* Mar. 21 Unanswered questions are threatening to leave technology assessment a mere intellectual pastime. **1969** *Listener* 24 July 106/3 This seems to show that Africa can use western techniques to her advantage, but only so long as the different cultural, intellectual and material contexts are kept firmly in mind when the technology-transfer is being planned. **1978** *Internat. Relations Dict.* (U.S. Dept. State Library) 40/2 *Technology transfer* has been defined as 'the transfer of knowledge generated and developed in one place to another, where it is used to achieve some practical end.'

8. A Social Science Option: Politics and Ecology

The following passage by Alston Chase is part of an article that appeared in the *Atlantic* in July 1987. After thinking about the article, write an essay that discusses how environmental issues become matters of political definition. Among the concepts you might consider are *National Park, National Park Service, protection, management, restoration,* and *ecosystem.* In what ways might the definitions of such terms vary? Who tries to do the defining? What determines which definitions prevail?

From *How to Save Our National Parks*
ALSTON CHASE

What our national parks need, more than protection, is restoration. If the parks are to be preserved, they must first be restored to a semblance of ecological balance. Restoration of the land, moreover, is not a utopian ideal but a developing science. The task of restoration ecology is like searching for and then assembling parts of a puzzle to make a picture. Ecologists find isolated communities of native genetic types and carefully transplant representative individuals of these species to preserves that are reconstructed to replicate their original habitat.   1

Many promising examples of ecological restoration are visible today. Throughout the Midwest and the West wetlands and grasslands prairies have been nursed back to life. The University of Wisconsin Arboretum, for example, was founded in 1934 for this specific purpose. "Our idea,"   2 wrote its first director, Aldo Leopold, "is to reconstruct . . . a sample of original Wisconsin — a sample of what Dane County looked like when our ancestors arrived here during the 1840s." Today the arboretum has been reasonably successful in restoring about a third of its 1,280 acres of wetlands, forest, and prairie.

Reclamation, however, can never be complete. We cannot suppose 3 that even after a relatively successful restoration parks could be left alone. We cannot bring extinct species back to life, nor can we reproduce all the conditons that prevailed before the coming of the white man. Animals that evolved in ecosystems the size of half a continent cannot be expected to survive unaided in the relatively tiny areas we call national parks, any more than Indians can be expected to live as hunter-gatherers on the postage-stamp-sized reservations to which they are now consigned.

The habitat of scavengers like condors and grizzly bears, for example, 4 cannot be completely reclaimed. In pre-Columbian times these species depended heavily on natural deaths in abundant and widespread animal species such as bison and spawning salmon, and also on carrion left by Indians and predators. Yet the animal world will never be as fecund or widely dispersed as it once was, nor will Indians and predators be playing their ecological role to the extent they once did. So if we wish to preserve scavengers, we may have to find substitutes for the food sources on which they once depended.

Restoration therefore leads to a kind of management we might call 5 sustenance ecology. In national parks this process would go forward in four steps. First would come the collection of what scientists call baseline data — information gathered by historians, anthropologists, archaeologists, and biologists which would tell us what the parks were like in pre-Columbian times. Second would be an inventory of changes in the park's wildlife population, noting what species had been lost and what exotic species had been introduced. Third would be the removal of exotic species and the reintroduction of native plants and animals now missing. And fourth, ecologists would make and implement strategies to compensate for conditons that prevailed in pre-Columbian times but cannot be recovered. Such strategies might include, for example, providing carrion for scavengers, culling game herds, and burning forests and grasslands to replace lost Indian hunting and fire practices.

Protectionism in its ordinary form neither allows for any human use 6 of wilderness nor offers any plan for reversing the changes in the wilderness that our civilization has already introduced. Sustenance ecology does both. It is a philosophy specifically for parks, dedicated to reestablishing and sustaining ecological equilibrium in lands that receive a reasonable amount of public use.

Restoring and sustaining our national parks is not a new idea. As 7 early as the 1930s thoughtful wildlife ecologists and rangers were aware of the limitations of protectionism. Yet the policies of protection were still prevailing when, in 1962, President John F. Kennedy's Secretary of the Interior, Stewart Udall, created a committee known as the Advisory Board on Wildlife Management and directed the committee to address wildlife problems then afflicting the national park system. The conclusions of this committee — which was chaired by A. Starker Leopold, a professor of zoology at the University of California, and the son of Aldo — were far-reaching, containing both the outline of a philosophy of wildlife management and a statement of purpose for national-parks preservation.

"As a primary goal [of park management]," the committee stated, **8** "we would recommend that the biotic associations within each park be maintained, or where necessary recreated, as nearly as possible in the condition that prevailed when the area was first visited by the white man. A national park should represent a vignette of primitive America."

Yet most of the parks, the Leopold committee noted, had changed **9** dramatically since the white man first came on the scene.

> Many of our national parks — in fact most of them — went through periods of indiscriminate logging, burning, livestock grazing, hunting and predator control. Then they entered the park system and shifted abruptly to a regime of equally unnatural protection from lightning fires, from insect outbreaks, absence of natural controls of ungulates, and in some areas elimination of normal fluctuations in water levels. Exotic vertebrates, insects, plants, and plant diseases have inadvertently been introduced. And of course lastly there is the factor of human use — of roads and trampling and camp grounds and pack stock. The resultant biotic associations in many of our parks are artifacts, pure and simple. They represent a complex ecologic history but they do not necessarily represent primitive America.
>
> Restoring the primitive scene is not done easily nor can it be done completely. . . . Yet if the goal cannot be fully achieved it can be approached. A reasonable illusion of primitive America could be recreated, using the utmost in skill, judgment, and ecologic sensitivity. This, in our opinion, should be the objective of every national park and monument.

The Leopold report was made official Park Service policy by the **10** Department of the Interior in 1963. In 1968 the Park Service published policies for management of natural areas (in a publication known as the Green Book) that it claimed incorporated the recommendations of the Leopold report. These policies, in slightly revised form, are still in force.

Yet, surprisingly, little restoration was attempted following publication **11** of the Green Book. Few base-line studies were ever undertaken; almost no historical, archaeological, or anthropological research was done in parks classified as natural zones; native-species restoration — of wolves, in particular — was stalled, and proliferating exotic species, rather than being removed, were for many years ignored.

In truth, the Park Service was unable to implement the Leopold **12** report. When Udall accepted the committee's recommendations, the National Park Service research program was almost nonexistent. A study of Park Service science done that year by the National Academy of Sciences reported that "for the year 1962 the research staff (including the Chief Naturalist and field men in natural history) was limited to 10 people and . . . the Service budget for natural history research was $28,000 — about the cost of one campground comfort station."

Unfortunately, attempts to strengthen Park Service resource man- **13** agement and research met with considerable resistance from the ranger corps, which saw development of a professional cadre of scientists and resource managers as a threat to its control of the Service. The only way reformers could increase the science budget was to put research and resource management under the supervision of the rangers, which is what they did.

Government research in the national parks, the Service decided, would be "mission-oriented." That was interpreted to mean that the role of scientists was to provide "service to the superintendents." Scientists in the major national parks reported to the superintendents, were graded by the superintendents, could do only research approved by the superintendents, and had every incentive to publish only those findings that pleased the superintendents. Similarly, resource managers reported to the chief rangers, whose primary function was visitor protection.

Funding for research by university scientists was increased substantially, but such work remained under the control of the rangers. Funds were awarded by contract between the National Park Service or its contracting agencies and the individual researcher or his institution. Decisions regarding who was to receive a contract were either delegated to the field level — that is, to the superintendent or his supervisor of research — or made by university-based "cooperative park-study units," on which park administrators or district headquarters often had considerable influence.

Further, each of the Park Service regional headquarters (their number has grown from six in 1968 to ten today) was given control of research and resource management in its region. The major parks were to a large degree autonomous. In these ways superintendents and regional directors acquired nearly total control over scientific activity. Being untrained in ecology, they had little appreciation for the kind of base-line research that was needed to accomplish restoration.

Through the delegation of such powers to the regions and superintendents, the Service was decentralized, preventing any coordinated scientific undertaking. Park studies tended to be short-term and politically directed. Both the flow of information and the chain of accountability between the parks and Washington were broken. Results of research that might reflect badly on a park administration could be — and often were — prevented by the superintendent from leaving the park.

The balkanization of the Park Service was further encouraged by the national park system reorganization of 1964, which divided the parks into three categories: natural, historical, and recreational. The emphasis built into this functional separation effectively discouraged the kind of sustained interdisciplinary research that true restoration ecology required.

While mission-oriented biological research continued in natural zones like Yellowstone, historical research — which the Leopold report had said was "the first step" in restoration — was almost never undertaken.

Through this evolution the Park Service, while spending more and more money on research, was making little of the effort necessary to save the park system. To make matters worse, the retrograde nature of this trend was obscured by describing park policy in a new and attractive way: its goal, the Park Service decided, should be to "perpetuate the natural ecosystems."

Ecosystems management was supposedly the translation into policy   21
of the Leopold report. Yet the committee explicitly declared that parks are *not* ecosystems: "Few of the world's parks," the report stated, quoting a 1962 report from the First World Conference on National Parks, "are large enough to be in fact self-regulatory ecological units." Nevertheless, by 1968 the Park Service was calling our parks "natural, comparatively self-contained ecosystems." What the Leopold report in 1963 regarded as a challenge — the creation of vignettes of primitive America — the Park Service in 1968 took as a given, though it had done no restoration work at all. By defining intact ecosystems into existence, the Park Service created a rationale for continuing its policy of protection. If parks were intact ecosystems, then restoration was unnecessary. Nature could be left to take its course. Nor was scientific research required. Parks could be run by people trained as policemen. That this is a kind of voodoo ecology is not lost on professional biologists. Bruce A. Wilcox, the director of the Center of Conservation Biology, at Stanford University, explained last year, "A laissez-faire approach to management is simply not tenable any longer."

9. A Philosophy Option: Defining Ethics

How we define something often depends on the perspective from which we approach it and the assumptions we hold about it. Perspective, then, is a crucial thing to know about our own and other people's analytical thinking. Consider the term *ethics*. What are ethics, and how did we get them? After reading the following passage by Peter Singer, explain in a substantial paragraph how the definition of *ethics* might differ for an eighteenth-century orthodox Christian, for a political philosopher like Rousseau, and for a modern scientist.

From *The Expanding Circle*
PETER SINGER

Human beings are social animals. We were social before we were human.   1
The French philosopher Jean-Jacques Rousseau once wrote that in the state of nature human beings had "no fixed home, no need of one another; they met perhaps twice in their lives, without knowing each other and without speaking." Rousseau was wrong. Fossil finds show that five million years ago our ancestor, the half-human, half-ape creature known to anthropologists as *Australopithecus africanus,* lived in groups, as our nearest living relatives — the gorillas and chimpanzees — still do. As *Australopithecus* evolved into the first truly human being, *Homo habilis,* and then into our own species, *Homo sapiens,* we remained social beings.

In rejecting Rousseau's fantasy of isolation as the original or natural condition of human existence, we must also reject his account of the origin of ethics, and that of the school of social contract theorists to which he belonged. The social contract theory of ethics held that our rules of right and wrong sprang from some distant Foundation Day on which previously independent rational human beings came together to hammer out a basis for setting up the first human society. Two hundred years ago this seemed a plausible alternative to the then orthodox idea that morality represented the decrees of a divine lawgiver. It attracted some of the sharpest and most skeptical thinkers in Western social philosophy. If, however, we now know that we have lived in groups longer than we have been rational human beings, we can also be sure that we restrained our behavior toward our fellows before we were rational human beings. Social life requires some degree of restraint. A social grouping cannot stay together if its members make frequent and unrestrained attacks on one another. Just when a pattern of restraint toward other members of the group becomes a social ethic is hard to say; but ethics probably began in these pre-human patterns of behavior rather than in the deliberate choices of fully fledged, rational human beings.

10. A Social Science Option: A Historical Analogy

Here is a passage written by the French cultural critic Michel Foucault about social behavior during a time of plague in the seventeenth-century town of Vincennes. Although it is a very detailed description of actual procedures taken to keep the disease from spreading, Foucault also seems to have in mind some sort of analogy or comparison. After rereading the passage and considering the title of Foucault's book, *Discipline and Punish*, take a guess at the analogy he is trying to draw and then defend your guess by developing the comparison as explicitly as you can.

From *Discipline and Punish*
MICHEL FOUCAULT

First, a strict spatial partitioning: the closing of the town and its outlying districts, a prohibition to leave the town on pain of death, the killing of all stray animals; the division of the town into distinct quarters, each governed by an intendant. Each street is placed under the authority of a syndic, who keeps it under surveillance; if he leaves the street, he will be condemned to death. On the appointed day, everyone is ordered to stay indoors: it is forbidden to leave on pain of death. The syndic himself comes to lock the door of each house from the outside; he takes the key with him and hands it over to the intendant of the quarter; the intendant keeps it until the end of the quarantine. Each family will have made its own provisions; but, for bread and wine, small wooden canals are set up between the street and the interior of the houses, thus allowing each person to receive his ration without communicating with the suppliers and other residents; meat, fish, and herbs will be hoisted up into the houses with pulleys and baskets. If it is absolutely necessary to leave the house, it will be done in turn, avoiding any meeting. Only the intendants, syndics, and guards will move about the streets and also, between the infected houses, from one corpse to another, the "crows," who can be left to die: these are "people of little substance who carry the sick, bury the dead, clean and do many vile and abject offices." It is a segmented, immobile, frozen space. Each individual is fixed in his place. And, if he moves, he does so at the risk of his life, contagion, or punishment.

Inspection functions ceaselessly. The gaze is alert everywhere: "A considerable body of militia, commanded by good officers and men of substance," guards at the gates, at the town hall and in every quarter to ensure the prompt obedience of the people and the most absolute authority of the magistrates, "as also to observe all disorder, theft and extortion." At each of the town gates there will be an observation post; at the end of each street sentinels. Every day, the intendant visits the quarter in his charge, inquires whether the syndics have carried out their tasks, whether the inhabitants have anything to complain of; they "observe their actions." Every day, too, the syndic goes into the street for which he is responsible; stops before each house: gets all the inhabitants to appear at the windows (those who live overlooking the courtyard will be allocated a window looking onto the street at which no one but they may show themselves); he calls each of them by name; informs himself as to the state of each and every one of them — "in which respect the inhabitants will be compelled to speak the truth under pain of death"; if someone does not appear at the window, the syndic must ask why: "In this way he will find out easily enough whether dead or sick are being concealed." Everyone locked up in his cage, everyone at his window, answering to his name and showing himself when asked — it is the great review of the living and the dead.

This surveillance is based on a system of permanent registration: reports from the syndics to the intendants, from the intendants to the magistrates or mayor. At the beginning of the "lock up," the role of each of the inhabitants present in the town is laid down, one by one; this document bears "the name, age, sex of everyone, notwithstanding his condition": a copy is sent to the intendant of the quarter, another to the office of the town hall, another to enable the syndic to make his daily roll call. Everything that may be observed during the course of the visits — deaths, illnesses, complaints, irregularities — is noted down and transmitted to the intendants and magistrates. The magistrates have complete control over medical treatment; they have appointed a physician in charge; no other practitioner may treat, no apothecary prepare medicine, no confessor visit a sick person without having received from him a written note "to prevent anyone from concealing and dealing with those sick of the contagion, unknown to the magistrates." The registration of the pathological must be constantly centralized. The relation of each individual to his disease and to his death passes through the representatives of power, the registration they make of it, the decisions they take on it.

Five or six days after the beginning of the quarantine, the process of purifying the houses one by one is begun. All the inhabitants are made to leave; in each room "the furniture and goods" are raised from the ground or suspended from the air; perfume is poured around the room; after carefully sealing the windows, doors, and even the keyholes with wax, the perfume is set alight. Finally, the entire house is closed while the perfume is consumed; those who have carried out the work are searched, as they were on entry, "in the presence of the residents of the house, to see that they did not have something on their persons as they left that they did not have on entering." Four hours later, the residents are allowed to re-enter their homes. 4

CHAPTER 2

Serializing

General Considerations

Serializing refers to expository writing ordered sequentially: "First . . . Next . . . Then . . . Finally. . . ." When we read a serial presentation we are guided partly by how well the writer controls our sense of passing time. Academic writers serialize when they need to pay close attention to the steps of a procedure or the sequence of events or the relationships between effects and their possible causes. Many college assignments call directly for serializing; but many others, without specifying so, also lend themselves to serial approaches. Learning to recognize these opportunities can help you become more flexible as a thinker and expand your repertoire as a writer.

Examination questions often require you to order material sequentially. Consider the following assortment:

Describe how sand dunes are formed. (From a geology class)

Illustrate the principle of linguistic diffusion. (From a linguistics class)

Explain the process of amending the U.S. Constitution. (From a political science class)

How are etchings produced? (From an art history class)

Such questions call for the recollection of course material, usually in the same form you have read or listened to it. They reward accuracy, clarity, and a careful attention to the transitions from one step to another. But they do not require much critical thinking. Similarly, a paper topic that calls for a serial presentation sometimes seems simply to be requesting a rehash of course material:

> Trace the history of antitrust legislation from the turn of the century through the Truman administration.

But sometimes a question such as this one is designed to make you rethink the course material, with an eye for seeing new patterns and making new connections. You may know something about individual antitrust acts, but looking at them as a series may put you in a position to make informed generalizations.

The questions we've quoted so far demand serializing. But there are other questions — many questions actually — where you can discover the opportunity to serialize. Look over this imposing set of paper topics, for example:

1. What made *Brown v. Board of Education* a landmark decision of the Supreme Court?
2. In Plato's *Republic* how does Socrates answer Thrasymachos's argument that injustice is more profitable than justice?
3. In *Huckleberry Finn*, why does Huck decide "All right, then, I'll go to hell"?

Questions like these can sometimes leave a writer floundering, without a strong sense of how to proceed or with only a few sentences' worth to say. It helps to see that the "What," "How," and "Why" are disguising opportunities to proceed sequentially. One way to take on the question about the Supreme Court case is to see *Brown v. Board of Education* as the climax in a sequence of legal actions. An essay on the topic might be structured like this:

> The decision in <u>Brown v. Board of Education</u> did not appear out of thin air. It was the climax of years of tugging back and forth between branches of the state and federal governments....
>
> After the Civil War, the 13th, 14th, and 15th Amendments extended the full protection of the law to all citizens regardless of race. These provisions, however, applied only in theory. In practice....
>
> With the passage of Jim Crow laws in the following decades, state governments were able further to restrict the gains....

> Then in <u>Plessy v. Ferguson</u> (1896), the policy of
> "separate but equal" was firmly established....
>
> In the years that followed, the Supreme Court be-
> gan to move away from <u>Plessy v. Ferguson</u> in a series of
> decisions that questioned whether equal facilities were
> maintained....
>
> Finally, in 1954, the Court ruled in <u>Brown v.</u>
> <u>Board of Education</u> that separate facilities were "in-
> herently unequal."...

Similarly, the question about Plato's *Republic* lends itself to a stage-by-stage approach:

> In responding to Thrasymachos, Socrates first ar-
> gues that a tyrant is the least happy of men because he
> is driven by excess....
>
> Then he develops a second argument about the supe-
> riority of seeking wisdom....
>
> Then Socrates offers a third argument....
>
> Finally Socrates turns to the question of whether
> justice is something valuable in and of itself....

And a similar sequential strategy could be used in answering the question about *Huckleberry Finn*:

> At the outset of the novel Huck is presented as a
> clever but unreflective boy. With Tom Sawyer he plays
> happily at the game of robbers, content to follow the
> lead of his friend....
>
> Huck soon finds himself having to make difficult
> choices. When life with Pap becomes unbearable, he
> plans to escape....
>
> Then when he finds himself on the river with Jim
> the runaway slave, he takes on more responsibility....
>
> At the Phelps place, he faces his strongest crisis
> of conscience. Local "morality" tells him he should
> turn Jim in. But his own conscience, of which he has
> only recently become aware, tells him the opposite....

Serial presentations like these are vehicles for independent thinking. They allow you — in fact, they force you — to make interpretive judgments, decisions about how items, events, or stages relate to one another, about their relative importance and their position in an overall sequence. Thus serializing, like defining, is more than a mechanical operation or a pat form for giving back information. Serializing, like defining and the other strategies we present in this book, can work not only as the overarching strategy for organizing a piece of writing (as in the preceding example) but also in co-ordination with other strategies. You might use serializing to illustrate a definition: The best way to support a definition of the word *etymology* (the origin and historical development of a word), for instance, might be to illustrate the shifting meanings of a particular word as it has changed over time. You might use a serial presentation in service of comparison: In a political science essay about flexibility and inflexibility in U.S. government you might compare how relatively easy it is to pass a bill through Congress and how difficult it is to amend the Constitution. You might use serializing in support of classi-fication: For a marketing class you might write a term paper classifying small businesses on the basis of how they respond to first opportunities for ex-pansion. Or you might use a serial account as a component of an argument: A persuasive essay on tighter controls over food processing might include a serial account of the production of hot dogs.

The assignments in this chapter move from those that require fairly straightforward reassembling of information to those that invite complex in-terpretive judgments. All the assignments call for intelligent decision making. To illustrate some of the varieties of serial decisions, let's look in a little more detail at a range of occasions to use a serializing strategy.

Cases

PRESENTING A PROCEDURE: A CASE FROM BIOLOGY

Most lab reports in science classes include a methods section that describes the procedures used in an experiment or field observation. Sometimes, par-ticularly when the procedures are merely those outlined in a lab manual, writing up a methods section involves little more than translating instructional language ("Take two samples and expose them to two hours of direct sun-light") into report language ("The two samples were then exposed to two hours of direct sunlight"). But usually you need to do much more. When you hold some responsibility for choosing and describing your own procedures, your decisions about serializing can make a great difference.

Consider the following example, a Methods and Materials section from a biology lab report. Biology reports consist of four main parts: an Introduction, which acquaints readers with the general problem being investigated and the specific hypothesis being tested; a Methods and Materials section, which describes how the experiment was conducted; a Results section, which reports the data obtained; and a Discussion section, which interprets the results. The particular experiment we consider here investigated whether differing levels of salinity affected the fertilization abilities of sea urchin sperm (the term *gametes* in the report refers to both sperm and eggs). This Methods and Materials section is fairly technical, but read it through once, trying to get a general idea and ignoring terms that are foreign to you. Then, with the general idea in mind, read it once more, doing your best to understand the technical language in context.

METHODS AND MATERIALS

Gametes of *Strongylocentrotus purpuratus* were obtained by injecting 2 ml of 0.5M KCl into the perivisceral cavities of male and female urchins. This muscle stimulant forced the release of gametes through the gonopores of the animal at the aboral surface. Sperm were collected undiluted by inverting the male over a petri dish. A beaker was filled with 40 ml of chilled seawater, and the eggs were collected by inverting the female over the beaker.   1

Five concentrations of seawater — 60%, 80%, 100%, 120%, and 140% — were prepared, either by the dilution of natural seawater with tap water or the addition of concentrated Instant Ocean (Aquarium Systems, Mentor, Ohio). Slides were prepared by applying Vaseline jelly to the slide in a circular pattern to raise the cover slip, thus protecting the gametes and forming a seal to prevent evaporation and desiccation. 10 ml quantities of the five concentrations were prepared and placed in separate test tubes and set in an ice bath. One drop of the concentrated sperm was placed in each test tube. The solution was mixed thoroughly and allowed to sit for five minutes. One drop of the egg solution was placed by pipette onto each of the five slides. Then one drop of the sperm solution from the 60% salinity seawater was added to the egg solution. After a minute, when all the fertilization that could be expected to occur would have occurred, each solution was examined through a microscope at 100X magnification. Percent fertilization was determined by comparing the total number of eggs in a central area of the slide to the total number of eggs that had formed fertilization membranes.   2

This procedure was repeated for each salinity. Then at five-minute intervals the entire procedure was repeated to see whether the influence of the various salinities increased over time. Seven trials were conducted over a total period of forty minutes.   3

We find this description hard to follow. Some of our difficulty may be caused by the technical features of the experiment, but the problem also lies in the writing itself. Try rereading it once more to see if you can get a clearer idea of what went on in the experiment. Could the writer have done more to help us? Can you locate trouble spots where readers are apt to get confused? Mark them.

The following is a second version of the Methods and Materials section, revised with readers more in mind. Go through the two versions with an eye to the way each organizes material and offers guides to the reader; pinpoint places in the second version that seem clearer than corresponding places in the first. What do you think the writer's key decisions were in reshaping this material? Do you find the second version a clear improvement, or are there some features you prefer about the first?

METHODS AND MATERIALS

To test the fertilization success of sea urchin sperm at varying concentrations of salinity, five solutions of seawater were prepared — at 60%, 80%, 100%, 120%, and 140% salinity. The 60% and 80% solutions were obtained by diluting seawater with tap water, and the 120% and 140% solutions were obtained by adding a saline concentrate (Instant Ocean from Aquarium Systems, Mentor, Ohio). 10 ml of the five salinities were then poured into separate test tubes and set in an ice bath, ready for the addition of sperm. Next, to receive the eggs, seven sets of slides were prepared — five slides per set — by forming circular receptacles of Vaseline on each slide.   1

Gametes of *Strongylocentrotus purpuratus* were obtained by injecting 2 ml of 0.5 KCl, a muscle stimulant, into the perivisceral cavities of male and female urchins. The eggs were collected by inverting a female over a beaker containing 40 ml of chilled seawater. Sperm were collected undiluted by inverting a male over a petri dish. Then a drop of sperm was added to each of the five test tubes containing the seawater and allowed to mix in solution for five minutes. In the meantime a drop of egg solution was placed with a pipette into the Vaseline circle on each of the first five slides. To each drop of egg solution a drop of sperm solution was added from one of the five concentrations.   2

When a minute had elapsed (enough time for maximum fertilization) each slide was examined at 100X magnification, and percentages of fertilization were calculated by comparing the total number of eggs in a sector to the number that had formed a fertilization membrane. To test whether the salinity level affected the sperm's fertilization success over time, the sperm and egg solutions were mixed again, and percentages calculated, at five-minute intervals over a period of forty minutes.   3

SERIALIZING AS INTERPRETIVE STRATEGY: TWO CASES FROM LITERATURE

Serializing is always an option in writing about literature. Your experience of reading a literary work over time can be used to help structure what you find to say about it: "As the novel opens. . . . Then a new issue arises. . . . The turning point comes when. . . ." The risk of this approach is that you will simply retell what happens rather than examining what happens in an interpretive way. But subordinated to some central question or concern, serializing can help you both in structuring essays and in working out ideas.

We've suggested here and in the *Huckleberry Finn* example how you might employ serializing to begin thinking critically about a piece of fiction. Plays too are well approached sequentially. Since plays are written to be performed in consecutive scenes, serial accounts of how scenes build on one another can be a particularly effective way of thinking about and writing about drama. One effective interpretive device is to look at a sequence of scenes and examine how they work in coordination. Another strategy is to try grasping an entire play, like a piece of music, in terms of a few basic movements. What do the first scenes accomplish? How does our interest get heightened? How is the action resolved? Are there strong turning points? How are we left at the end? A few questions like these can often lead to a simple but persuasive overview of a play's rhythm or pattern, a set of actions developing in several phases. Here's how one student got herself off to a good start in an essay about Shakespeare's *Hamlet.*

> Editors divide Hamlet into five acts. But when we imagine the play acted, this five-part structure disappears. We're aware only of the passage of scenes, some happening quickly and others more slowly. I see the action of Hamlet consisting of three movements. During the first we watch the rising outrage of Hamlet as he learns of his father's murder and watches his mother with Claudius. This movement climaxes with the rapid events in the confrontation scene between Hamlet and his mother. The second group of scenes, the middle movement of the play, occurs after Hamlet has left for England. Much happens during this phase of the play: Fortinbras appears, Ophelia runs mad and drowns herself, Laertes returns home to find his father and sister dead, Horatio receives a letter from Hamlet. But these scenes do not seem to build in power like the earlier ones. It's hard to grasp where events are heading or where to invest our feelings. With Hamlet's arrival back on stage, the play's third and final movement begins, and from the graveyard scene on, the action intensifies toward its bloody conclusion.
>
> In this essay I'd like to look more closely at the portion of the play I've called the second movement.

```
In these scenes is Shakespeare simply taking care of
plot business, or is he doing something more?...
```

This looks like the start of a very good essay. Perhaps the writer will go on to consider the middle scenes in the sequence they occur. In the meantime, look how she has put serializing to use in the opening paragraph by boldly dividing the play into three phases. This interpretive decision could be challenged by her English teacher, but by asking us to consider the play this way, she is able to seize a problem worth investigating. She'll need to find something persuasive or interesting to say about the scenes she has decided to focus on, but she's got us set up for her delivery.

You'll also find that serializing can work well in writing about poetry. Most critical writing about poetry serializes to some extent, but serializing is particularly prevalent in writing about short poems. In fact, one variety of poetry interpretation — explication — consists entirely of line-by-line commentary meant to guide a reader carefully through a poem. But you can also treat a poem sequentially without committing yourself to interpreting every line. One helpful strategy is to view a poem, like the student viewed *Hamlet*, as something experienced in stages. The stages can be temporal or geographical — the speaker moving from one time or place to another — or the stages can be psychological, different degrees or levels of awareness that develop in the speaker or in the reader. Consider the poem "And Your Soul Shall Dance" by the contemporary American poet Garrett Kaoru Hongo.

And Your Soul Shall Dance
for Wakako Yamauchi

Walking to school beside fields
of tomatoes and summer squash,
alone and humming a Japanese love song,
you've concealed a copy of *Photoplay*   4
between your algebra and English texts.
Your knee socks, saddle shoes, plaid dress,
and blouse, long-sleeved and white
with ruffles down the front,   8
come from a Sears catalogue
and neatly complement your new Toni curls.
All of this sets you apart from the landscape:
flat valley grooved with irrigation ditches,   12
a tractor grinding through alkaline earth,
the short stands of windbreak eucalyptus
shuttering the desert wind
from a small cluster of wooden shacks   16
where your mother hangs the wash.
You want to go somewhere.

Somewhere far away from all the dust
and sorting machines and acres of lettuce.   20
Someplace where you might be kissed
by someone with smooth, artistic hands.
When you turn into the schoolyard,
the flagpole gleams like a knife blade in the sun,   24
and classmates scatter like chickens,
shooed by the storm brooding on your horizon.

One way of taking on "And Your Soul Shall Dance," which seems to address a Japanese-American schoolgirl, is to discuss the psychological adjustments you find yourself making as you move through the poem. After thinking about those adjustments, come up with a thesis that describes or characterizes those adjustments and then use your serial response to the poem to support your claim. If you like, you can try using the following transitional signposts to help you to map out an interpretation.

```
    The first five lines of Garrett Hongo's "And
Your Soul Shall Dance" focus on a Japanese-American
schoolgirl....
    And lines 6 through 10 further develop....
    With lines 11 through 17, the focus widens....
    And, then, suddenly, with line 18, the readers are
given access....
    Finally, as the girl enters the schoolyard in the
last four lines, there's the ominous recognition....
```

FORMULATING HISTORICAL ACCOUNTS: CASES FROM HISTORY AND POLITICAL SCIENCE

Most historical accounts employ serializing. In fact, looked at superficially, some historical accounts seem simply to be the serial retelling of events. But the "simply" in the previous sentence is deceptive. The first question is What constitutes an event? And in sequencing several events into a single account, other troubling questions arise: what to include, what to omit, and how to shape what is included. To consider the problems you may encounter in trying to construct meaningful sequences of events, look at the following chronology pertaining to the Iran-U.S. crisis of 1979–1981. Then as an exercise, write a short serial account based on the list.

1. The shah leaves Iran (Jan. 16, 1979).
2. Khomeini returns from exile as head of revolutionary government (Jan. 31, 1979).

3. American hostages are seized at the U.S. embassy in Teheran (Nov. 4, 1979).
4. President Carter suspends Iranian oil imports to the United States (Nov. 12, 1979).
5. The shah dies of cancer in Egypt (July 27, 1980).
6. Iran's conflicts with Iraq escalate to open war when Iraq attacks Iranian airfields and oil refineries (Sept. 22 and 23, 1980).
7. The American hostages are released (Jan. 20, 1981), the same day that Ronald Reagan is inaugurated as president of the United States.

Here is one student's attempt at a narrative of these events:

```
     Two weeks after the shah left Iran in early 1979,
Khomeini returned as head of a revolutionary govern-
ment.  On November 4, American hostages were seized at
the U.S. embassy in Teheran.  A week later President
Carter suspended Iranian oil imports.  In July 1980 the
shah died of cancer in Egypt.  In September Iraq at-
tacked Iranian airfields and oil refineries, escalating
their border conflict to outright war.  The following
January the hostages were released on the day that Ron-
ald Reagan was inaugurated as U.S. president.
```

Why do we find this account unsatisfying? Why the mention of the shah's cancer? For that matter, why stress the U.S. suspension of oil imports? Do the events make any pattern? The writer has made few decisions about what to include and what to leave out, and the paragraph as a whole reads disjointedly.

Notice how hard the writer has tried to stay with all the facts as presented in the list, as though determined not to fall from objectivity into interpretation. Part of the problem may be the sketchiness of the information available. Events like Khomeini's return and the Iraqi attack are themselves outcomes of complex processes, events we risk oversimplifying unless we know more. But notice, too, that interpretations are impossible to avoid. Sometimes the mere positioning of sentences implies an interpretation, in this case a relationship of cause and effect. Look at the first two sentences. Taken together, they imply that the hostages were seized with the cooperation of the Iranian government — an interpretation. Now look at the last two sentences. What do they imply about the release of the hostages?

Since interpretations are unavoidable, it is better to take charge of them. Viewed a little more selectively, the Iranian events, for example, could be presented in a more coherent sequence:

> Two weeks after the departure of the shah in Janu-
> ary 1979, the Khomeini government assumed control of
> Iran. That government had been in power less than a
> year when the American hostages were seized in Novem-
> ber. With government approval, the hostages remained
> captives for the next fourteen months, despite U.S.
> economic reprisals and long after the death of the
> shah. The hostages were finally released on January
> 20, 1981, only after a war with Iraq had begun to
> preoccupy Iran.

If we had more information to work with, our interpretation might get
even bolder. Any of these sentences, for example, might serve as the opening
for an effective serial interpretation:

> The hostage taking in Iran played an important
> part in stabilizing the new government....
> The U.S. role in the hostage crisis was a futile
> one....
> The resolution of the hostage crisis, like its be-
> ginning, had more to do with inter-Arab relations than
> with U.S. foreign policy....
> The taking and the release of the hostages re-
> sulted in political gains both for the Khomeini govern-
> ment and the Reagan administration....

We offer another example of the interpretive pressure placed on historical
accounts. Imagine that for a political science class you are asked to write a
short essay explaining the data in Table 1 on the next page (from *Sociology:
Inquiring into Society* by Peter I. Rose, Myron Glazer, and Penina Migdal
Glazer). If you took the most cautious serial approach to this information,
you would have to settle for something like this:

> From 1890 to 1979, the number of women in the ci-
> vilian labor force increased from 3.7 million to 43.5
> million. From 1890 to 1900 the number climbed by 1.3
> million. In the period from 1900 to 1920, it grew an-
> other 3.2 million to a total of 8.2 million....

But an essay like this does little more than translate lines from the chart into
sentences. An instructor would have had more in mind in asking for your

TABLE 1. Women in the Civilian Labor Force, 1890–1979

YEAR	NUMBER (MILLIONS)
1890	3.7
1900	5.0
1920	8.2
1930	10.4
1940	13.8
1945	19.2
1947	16.7
1950	18.4
1955	20.6
1960	23.2
1965	26.2
1970	31.5
1975	37.1
1979	43.5

SOURCE: United States Department of Labor, Bureau of Labor Statistics.

commentary. You might try getting speculative, using your general knowledge to help you move sequentially through the data, highlighting the features that seem most significant to you. One student, for example, decided to use something he knew about World War II — that the movement of troops overseas depleted the labor force at home:

> The big shift in women's working patterns began during the years of World War II. Until then the number of women in the civilian labor force had been rising, but only at the rate of about 210,000 jobs per year. Then in the five-year period from 1940 to 1945, when many men left their jobs to go to war, another 5.4 million women joined the labor force, their numbers reaching a peak of 19.2 million in 1945. Women's employment fell off a little when men returned to their civilian jobs after the war, but many women by then had become a permanent part of the work force. There followed another period of steady growth as young working women were joined by mothers of the baby boom era....

An instructor will almost always prefer an interpretive response like this one to a flat restatement of undifferentiated facts — so long as your inferences make sense. If you feel yourself speculating on something you know too little about, look for ways of qualifying or restricting your interpretations as you make them. Here, for example, after a short serial treatment of the data, the writer turns back to look critically at its limitations:

> This table shows a steady growth in the number of women workers throughout this century. Two periods in particular stand out. The first is the years of World War II, when women joined the civilian work force in large numbers, compensating for the men who went to war. The second is the period of the 1970s when the total number of working women increased at the rate of 1.3 million per year, more than double the number during the 1950s and 1960s. How do we explain this dramatic increase in the 1970s, and what does it tell us about changes in our society?
>
> To answer these questions convincingly, we would need to know more. Does the rise in women's employment simply correspond to the rising number of total jobs, or do women fill an increasing percentage of the total labor market? Do the figures include part-time jobs? And what kinds of jobs?...

Serial strategies, then, are helpful whenever you want to convey a process or set of procedures, the flow of events, or the development of awareness over time. They serve not only to convey information but to raise questions. Some assignments call for serializing; others gain by it. In some essays, serial presentations can be embedded within larger structures. In others, they can provide the larger structures, serving as containers for the rest of what you find to say. In all cases writing serially should engage your interpretive intelligence.

Assignments: First Passes

1. Explaining a Cyclical Movement: Earth's Water Cycle

This passage about the water exchange among land, air, and ocean was written by the geographers William F. Marsh and Jeff Dozier. After reading their commentary, write a paragraph describing the phases of the hydrologic cycle.

> We begin our discussions of water by introducing the "hydrologic   1
> cycle." This is an idealized model of the land-ocean-atmosphere water

exchange, or cycle, which includes evaporation from the sea, movement of water vapor over the land, condensation, precipitation, surface runoff, subsurface runoff, and so on. In reality, the flow of water from atmosphere to land, land to atmosphere, and land to oceans is complex and irregular over time and geographical space. This fact is not widely appreciated, however, because of the acceptance of a "standard" hydrologic cycle which has become more or less a norm of modern academic thought. Since this hydrologic cycle is a fundamental concept in natural science today, it is appropriate here to outline briefly its origins so that we may better understand its meaning and scientific utility. . . .

Humans have long puzzled over the origins of rainfall, rivers, streams, springs, and their interrelations, but our understanding of the true nature of the hydrologic cycle is comparatively recent. Prior to the sixteenth century, it was generally believed that water discharged by springs and streams could not be derived from the rain, for two reasons: 2

1. Rainfall was thought to be inadequate in quantity;
2. The earth was thought to be too impervious to permit penetration of water very far below the surface.

The ancients did, however, recognize that the oceans did not fill up   3
and that rivers continued to flow. They recognized then that somehow the water got from the sea into the rivers and in the process lost its salt content. The Bible says:

> All the rivers run into the sea, yet the sea is not full; unto the place from whence the rivers come thither they return again. (Ecclesiastes 1:7)

Generally the removal of salt was attributed to various processes of either filtration or distillation. The elevation of the water above sea level was ascribed to vaporization; subsequent underground condensation, to rock pressure, to suction of the wind, to a vacuum produced by the flow of springs, and other processes.

The recognition of the role of infiltration in supplying water to springs   4
and rivers began in the sixteenth century. Leonardo da Vinci, an exceptional genius who was in charge of canals in the Milan area, is generally credited with one of the earliest accurate descriptions of the hydrologic cycle:

> Whence we may conclude that the water goes from the rivers to the sea and from the sea to the rivers, thus constantly circulating and returning, and that all the sea and rivers have passed through the mouth of the Nile an infinite number of times. . . . The conclusion is that the saltness of the sea must proceed from the many springs of water which, as they penetrate the earth, find mines of salt, and these they dissolve in part and carry with them to the ocean and other seas, whence the clouds, the begetters of rivers, never carry it up." (John P. Richter, *Literary Works of Leonardo da Vinci*)

In the seventeenth century the French scientist Pierre Perrault mea-   5
sured rainfall for three years in the drainage basin of the Seine River above a point in the province of Burgundy. He computed that the total volume of the rainfall was six times the river flow. Although his measurements were crude, he was able to disprove the fallacy that the rain

was inadequate to supply the flow in rivers. Edmund Halley, the English scientist after whom Halley's comet was named, made estimates of evaporation from the Mediterranean Sea and demonstrated that it was as great as the flow of all rivers into the Mediterranean.

This was a period in history of energetic dialogue between Christian theologians and natural scientists, and new ideas about nature were carefully scrutinized by the Church. Although the theory of the hydrologic cycle was initially rejected by theologians, the modern geographer Yi-Fu Tuan tells us that the theory gained favor when it became clear that it could be used to support the doctrine of the Divine plan of nature. This doctrine held that the earth was created by God expressly as the home of humans and that all of its processes were parts of a great ordered scheme with humans at its center. In early versions of the hydrologic cycle, natural theologians saw verification by science of a portion of the Divine plan of nature. Eventually they adopted and idealized the model, and over the course of the past several centuries a more or less standard hydrologic cycle evolved. This model appears in academic texts today in a form little changed from that, for example, presented by theologians such as John Ray in the seventeenth century.

— William F. Marsh and Jeff Dozier, *Landscape: An Introduction to Physical Geography*

2. Working with a Figure: Barter Economies

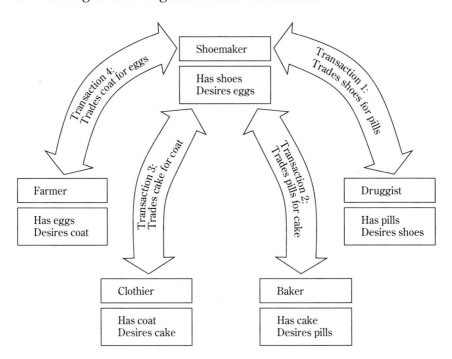

FIGURE 1.   A Barter System of Exchange

Introductory economics textbooks often point out that today's complex economies have replaced bartering, a far older system of direct trade. In *Microeconomics* Lewis Solmon uses the figure on page 56 (Figure 1) to illustrate the unwieldiness of a barter system. To underscore the point, draft a serial account of how Solmon's shoemaker gets the desired eggs. Then, making use of what you've written, write a short essay explaining why barter systems are usually replaced by systems employing money.

3. Working with Text and Figures: Endocytosis and Exocytosis

To read a biology textbook is to struggle with sequences. Most biological facts mean little in isolation but must be understood in relation to larger processes. Editors of introductory biology texts, aware that their readers may feel swamped by new information, often provide illustrations to support their explanations. As a learner you can sometimes spend as much time profitably reading the illustrations as reading sentences. Some illustrations are themselves provided with substantial captions so that a reader is free to work back and forth among two written explanations *and* an illustration.

Here we present an excerpt from a biology textbook describing the complementary processes of endocytosis and exocytosis. After consulting all three sources of information, write a paragraph describing what happens to a food particle digested by a cell.

After you've written your explanatory paragraph, write a second paragraph raising further questions about these processes. Because the passage is meant only to introduce the subject, it leaves much unexplained. What could use more explaining?

Finally, write a third paragraph about which information you thought best communicated by text and which by illustration. Try speculating on textbooks' limitations in presenting dynamic processes.

ENDOCYTOSIS AND EXOCYTOSIS

Other types of transport processes involve vacuoles that are formed 1 from or that fuse with the cell membrane. In *endocytosis* (Figure 2a), material to be taken into the cell attaches to special areas on the cell membrane and induces the membrane to bulge inward, producing a little pouch or vacuole enclosing the substance. This vacuole is released into the cytoplasm. The process can also work in reverse (Figure 2b). For example, many substances are exported from cells in vesicles or vacuoles formed by the Golgi bodies. The vacuoles move to the surface of the cell. When the vacuole reaches the cell surface, its membrane fuses with the membrane of the cell, thus expelling its contents to the outside. This process is *exocytosis*.

As you can see by studying Figure 2, the surface of the membrane 2 facing the interior of a vacuole is equivalent to the surface facing the

Endocytosis   Exocytosis

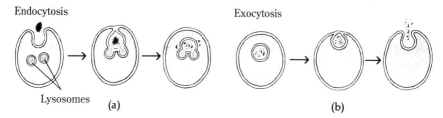

Lysosomes   (a)   (b)

FIGURE 2.   (a) *Endocytosis*. Material to be taken into the cell is enveloped in a
portion of the cell membrane, which pinches off to become a separate vacuole. If
the material is a food item, lysosomes fuse with the vacuole, spilling their digestive
enzymes into it. (b) *Exocytosis*. Material is transported out of the cell as the vacuole membrane fuses with the cell membrane. This process is used for the secretion of substances synthesized by the cell for export, as well as for the elimination
of the indigestible remains in a food vacuole.

exterior of the cell; similarly, the surface of the vacuole membrane facing
the cytoplasm is equivalent to the cytoplasmic surface of the cell membrane. Material needed for expansion of the cell membrane as a cell
grows is thought to be transported, ready-made, from the Golgi bodies
to the membrane by a process similar to exocytosis. There is also evidence that the portions of the cell membrane used in forming endocytotic
vacuoles are returned to the membrane in exocytosis, thus recycling the
membrane lipids and proteins.

When the substance to be taken into the cell in endocytosis is a solid,   3
such as a bacterial cell, the process is usually called *phagocytosis,* from
the Greek word *phage,* "to eat." Many one-celled organisms, such as
amoebas, feed in this way, and white blood cells in our own bloodstreams
engulf bacteria and other invaders in phagocytic vacuoles. Often lysosomes fuse with these vacuoles, emptying their enzymes into them and
so digesting or destroying their contents.

The taking in of dissolved molecules, as distinct from particulate   4
matter, is sometimes given the special name of *pinocytosis,* although it
is the same in principle as phagocytosis. Pinocytosis occurs not only in
single-celled organisms but also in multicellular animals. One type of cell
in which it has been frequently observed is the human egg cell. As the
egg cell matures in the ovary of the female, it is surrounded by "nurse
cells," which apparently transmit nutrients to the egg cell, which takes
them in by pinocytosis.

— Helena Curtis, *Biology*

4. Serializing Tabular Information: The Nuclear Arms Race

Table 2 compares the nuclear arsenals of the United States and the Soviet
Union. Write a paragraph, or several paragraphs, serially interpreting these
data. Before writing, you might try experimenting with your point of view.
First, try looking at the table as neutrally and unemotionally as possible. Then

TABLE 2. The U.S.–Soviet Strategic Arms Race

	ICBMS		SLBMS		BOMBERS		TOTAL STRATEGIC DELIVERY VEHICLES		TOTAL WARHEADS		TOTAL MEGATONS[1]	
	US	USSR	US	USSR	US	USSR	US	USSR	US	USSR	US	USSR
1990[2]	1,350	1,700	720	1,300	450	200	2,550	3,200	18,000	20,000	7,100	13,000
1985[2]	1,052	1,500	664	1,100	348	140	2,064	2,740	13,300	10,000	4,200	9,200
1982	1,052	1,400	632	950	348	140	2,032	2,490	11,000	8,000	4,100	7,100
1980	1,054	1,400	640	950	348	140	2,042	2,490	10,000	6,000	4,000	5,700
1978	1,054	1,400	656	810	348	140	2,058	2,350	9,800	5,200	3,800	5,400
1976	1,054	1,500	656	750	390	140	2,100	2,390	9,400	3,200	3,700	4,500
1974	1,054	1,600	656	640	470	140	2,180	2,380	8,400	2,400	3,800	4,200
1972	1,054	1,500	656	450	520	140	2,230	2,090	5,800	2,100	4,100	4,000
1970	1,054	1,300	656	240	520	140	2,230	1,680	3,900	1,800	4,300	3,100
1968	1,054	850	656	40	650	155	2,360	1,045	4,500	850	5,100	2,300
1966	1,054	250	592	30	750	155	2,396	435	5,000	550	5,600	1,200
1964	800	200	336	20	1,280	155	2,416	375	6,800	500	7,500	1,000
1962	80	40	144	20	1,650	155	1,874	290	7,400	400	8,000	800
1960	20	a few	32	15	1,650	130	1,702	150	6,500	300	7,200	600

[1] The figures shown are for "equivalent megatons," the most commonly used measure of aggregate explosive power. It is obtained by taking the square root of weapon yields above one megaton and the cube root of weapon yields below one megaton.
[2] Assumes no SALT Treaty limiting strategic offensive weapons. The numbers shown are extrapolations of official U.S. estimates provided in congressional testimony on the SALT II Treaty.
SOURCE: Ground Zero, *Nuclear War: What's in It for You?* (New York: Pocket Books, 1982), p. 266.

try looking at it from the points of view of someone in the U.S. or Soviet military. Of someone committed to the idea that "mutual assured destruction" is the best way of preventing nuclear war. Of someone worried that increasing arsenals makes nuclear war more likely. (ICBMs are intercontinental ballistic missiles, which can fly from the United States to the Soviet Union or vice versa. SLBMs are submarine-launched ballistic missiles, also long range.)

5. The History of an Idea: Evolution

Most of us associate the theory of evolution with Charles Darwin. But actually Darwin's conception of evolution can be seen as one stage (probably the crucial stage) in the development of the general evolutionary theory that most scientists share today. After reading the following account, write a short chronological description of the development of evolutionary theory. This passage was written to provide some scientific background for readers of science fiction.

In 1859, Charles Darwin (1809–1882) published *The Origin of Species by Means of Natural Selection.* This work described how an animal species would develop slowly, through many generations, as the forces of the environment gradually selected for certain survival traits. . . . Darwin called this process of development "Natural Selection." (The term "evolution," as well as the associated phrase "survival of the fittest," was actually coined by the philosopher Herbert Spencer.) Darwin did not know how the traits were transmitted, nor did he know how they changed, but his theory had two strong points which we still accept today. First, he saw that an animal had to "fit" its environment. He discovered, for example, a flower with an eleven inch throat and predicted that there must exist a moth with an eleven inch tongue to pollinate it. Four years later the moth was discovered. Second, he saw that traits were *born* into individuals, and natural selection was really a process by which certain individuals reproduced more than others.   1

This second point stood in direct contradiction to the accepted theory of Darwin's day, which was based on the work of the French naturalist Lamarck. He had suggested that traits were caused by the environment, rather than born into the individual. For example, giraffes, by continually stretching to reach leaves at treetops, get longer necks. A stretched neck parent passes his stretched neck on to his children. This theory has since been definitely disproved. No matter how many generations of laboratory rats have their tails cut off, the offspring of the amputees are still born with tails. What Darwin was arguing was that if a survival advantage inhered in tail-lessness, then *should* a tail-less rat develop (however that might happen), its offspring would breed more successfully than those of tailed rats. In the laboratory, the tail has no advantage.   2

Lamarckian evolution would have died with the nineteenth century, but for the Russian Revolution (1917). Stalin installed as President of the Soviet Academy of Sciences a man named Lysenko who arranged to support all research tending to validate Lamarckian evolution while squashing all research tending to validate Darwinian evolution. Since the   3 early Soviet government supposed that human nature would be changed by life under the dictatorship of the proletariat, thus allowing the withering away of the dictatorship, Lamarckian theories, which implied quite rapid evolution in response to rapid changes in environment, were politically useful. Even in the West, some writers of science fiction accepted Lamarckian evolution as a story premise because of sympathy with Lysenko's political aims. After Stalin's death in 1953, this came to an end and Darwinian evolution has been universally accepted by scientists.

In 1869, Gregor Mendel, an Austrian monk, published the results of **4** his experiments in crossbreeding garden plants. He laid down the basic laws of inheritance. He argued that there were hereditary "factors" (which today we call "genes") which control plant color, size, and so on. He also discovered the notions of dominance and recessiveness by which gene function sometimes does not appear in the individual yet can reappear in a future generation. However, although this supplied the answer to the question of how the Darwinian traits were transmitted, this answer, by a quirk of publication, remained unknown for a generation. Mendel had presented his results in an obscure Bavarian scientific journal and it wasn't until they were rediscovered in 1899 by Bateson that they became widely known. . . .

It was left to Hugo De Vries, a Dutch botanist, to suggest in 1900 **5** how genes change. Darwin had suggested that natural selection allowed for the slow accumulation of infinitesimally small variations in hereditary traits. It was quite clear to him that two breeds of dog could be made to breed true or to interbreed, thus creating a new type of individual. Unfortunately, it was also true that the offspring of members of this new type often reverted to the original breeds. In addition, many animals which could interbreed, like donkeys and horses, produced sterile offspring, like mules. And further, most animals, even those closely related like sheep and goats, clearly couldn't interbreed at all. If the changes that were always going on in the origin of one species from the next were infinitesimal, then there should exist an overlapping series of species the members of which could interbreed with near neighbors, but not with distant ones. This clearly was not the case. De Vries suggested that the reason for this was that changes in hereditary factors were not infinitesimal but were quite substantial. Somehow, the genes made a discontinuous change, which he called a mutation. Today we think of evolution as the process by which species develop through the heritable mutation of genetic information yielding a survival advantage in a given environment.

— Robert Scholes and Eric Rabkin, *Science Fiction:*
History, Science, Vision

6. Serializing a Contemporary Event: A Political Crisis

Choose a political event, preferably something of international interest, that has been in the news recently. Restricting yourself to what you've heard and seen in newscasts, write a paragraph describing the actions leading to the event.

Then consult a daily newspaper or weekly newsmagazine for a fuller account of the event, particularly of its historical background. Revise the paragraph you've written, putting your account of the event into a larger sequence of events.

Assignments: Options

7. A Psychology Option: Procedures in Problem Solving

We present two puzzles to solve. The object of the assignment is to watch your own problem-solving strategies in action and then to write a short serial description of how you went about solving, or trying to solve, one of the puzzles.

a. Without lifting your pencil from the page, draw no more than four straight lines that cross through all nine dots.

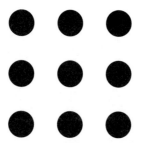

— James L. Adams, *Conceptual Blockbusting*

b. Place four paper matches on top of the four matches that form the "cocktail glass" in the following figure. The problem is to move two matches, and only two, to new positions so that the glass is re-formed in a different position and the cherry is *outside* the glass.

— Martin Gardner, *Mathematical Magic Show*

8. A Literature Option: Interpreting a Poem Sequentially

Here is a poem written by Emily Dickinson (1830–1886). In a short essay, interpret the poem by guiding a reader serially through it. You might want to look again at the discussion of the poem by Garrett Hongo on page 49.

I started Early — Took my Dog —
EMILY DICKINSON

I started Early — Took my Dog —
And visited the Sea —
The Mermaids in the Basement
Came out to look at me —   4

And Frigates — in the Upper Floor
Extended Hempen Hands —
Presuming Me to be a Mouse —
Aground — upon the Sands —   8

But no Man moved Me — till the Tide
Went past my simple Shoe —
And past my Apron — and my Belt
And past my Bodice — too —   12

And made as He would eat me up —
As wholly as a Dew
Upon a Dandelion's Sleeve —
And then — I started — too —   16

And He — He followed — close behind —
I felt His Silver Heel
Upon my Ankle — Then my Shoes
Would overflow with Pearl —   20

Until We met the Solid Town —
No One He seemed to know —
And bowing — with a Mighty look —
At me — The Sea withdrew —   24

9. A Literature Option: Interpreting a Poem Sequentially

Here is the poem "Death, Etc." by Linda Hogan (b. 1947). In a short essay, interpret this poem by guiding a reader serially through it. Or, after looking back at the Dickinson poem above, write an essay comparing the movement of the two poems.

Death, Etc.

LINDA HOGAN

Señorita, he said, come dance with me,
come kiss me.
He wore a suede jacket.
I let him hold me in his arms.   **4**
Praiseworthy types often wear suede jackets.
I did, I held that man death in my arms,
Señor death and me out under the moon
dancing and the stars lighting up my face,   **8**
but his — all bones!

He put his cool hand
down my hip.
No, I said.   **12**

You can tell the bones nothing, sí?
I know yours.
They want me
to see them naked.   **16**
He put his hand inside my dress.

I am a taxpayer,
I tell him,
you can't do that to me.   **20**

You've slept with the doomed, he said.
You come from those found
only by the buzzing of flies.
I know your cuentos.° Go ahead,   **24**
bless yourself, but you are already puffy
around the eyes and your knees creak.
It's a wonder I still want you.
Will you have some guacamole?   **28**

I've seen the beds you visited, I said.
You don't make good corners
and you leave them a mess.

Will you have wild rice with butter and lime?   **32**
Just forget what I said about your knees.
Señorita, I will call you up
and don't think to give me the wrong number.
I always find the women whose souls live   **36**
in their fingernails.

cuentos: Stories.

Señorita, he said in his deepest voice,
I know the men you've been seeing.
They think with their genitals   40
and make love with their brains.

I stopped to think about that one
and held him a little tighter.

10. A Science Option: The End of the Universe

This speculative essay by physicist James S. Trefil was written for *Smithsonian* magazine as the second of two parts. In Part 1, Trefil had sketched and discussed current theories about the origins of the universe. Here he turns to theories about its end. After reading the article, answer one of the following questions.

a. What are the possible fates of the universe, according to Trefil? Briefly describe these possibilities in separate serial paragraphs.
b. Trefil's subject is vast and hard to connect to our lives. But he helps us to envision cosmic events by creating useful metaphors. Write an essay that takes a reader through the article, treating each new major metaphor as a separate stage of Trefil's presentation and discussing how each metaphor adds to the reader's understanding of the way(s) the universe will end.
c. On the whole, do you think Trefil feels that the universe will end "in fire" or "in ice"? Defend your position by presenting serially the cases for the closed and open universes.

How the Universe Will End
JAMES S. TREFIL

In most lines of work, it is far easier to know the past than to predict   1
the future: Ask any Monday-morning quarterback. But when it comes to
talking about the ultimate fate of the Universe, the rule does not hold.
Looking backward in time to the Big Bang, as we did last month in Part
One of this series, involves the development of complex new theories
about the behavior of matter in very unusual environments. Tracing the
future of the Universe from the present onward is not nearly so hard;
we do not need any new way of looking at the world. All that we really
need to plot out our future are a few good measurements.

This does not mean that we can sit down today and outline the future   2
course of the Universe with anything like certainty. There are still too
many things we do not know about the way the Universe is put together.

But we do know exactly what information we need to fill in our knowledge, and we have a pretty good idea of how to go about getting it.

Perhaps the best way to think of our present situation is to imagine   3
a train coming into a switchyard. All of the switches are set before the train arrives, so that its path is completely determined. Some switches we can see, others we cannot. There is no ambiguity if we can see the setting of the switch: We can say with confidence that some possible futures will not materialize and others will. At the unseen switches, however, there is no such certainty. We know the train will take one of the tracks leading out, but we have no idea which one. The unseen switches are true decision points in the future, and what happens when we arrive at them determines the entire subsequent course of events.

When we think about the future of the Universe, we can see our   4
"track" many billions of years into the future, but after that there are decision points to be dealt with and possible fates to consider. The goal of science is to reduce the ambiguity at the decision points and find the true road that will be followed.

Just as we have no trouble predicting the path of the train as it enters   5
the switchyard, we have a pretty good idea about the short-term fate of the Universe. We expect that the galaxies will continue to separate and stars will continue to form and evolve for many billions of years. The Universe is now about 15 billion years old, and the Earth and sun a little less than five. In another five billion years the sun will have used up all the hydrogen it can. The sun will then swell monstrously into what astronomers call a "red giant," and the Earth will be swallowed up.

Ten billion years is a typical lifetime for a star the size of the sun;   6
smaller stars, of which there are more, live longer. Depending chiefly on the mass of the star, the end product can be a white dwarf, a very dense star about the size of a planet (this will be the fate of the sun); a neutron star, an extremely dense object only a few miles across; or a black hole, an object with a gravitational field so strong that no light can escape. It might also self-destruct completely, returning its material to the galaxy. But whatever the end product of stellar evolution, each star uses up a certain amount of raw material. In 40 or 50 billion years, then, we expect that star formation will have slowed down considerably from what we see now. Stars will continue to go out: first the bright ones (which burn up their fuel most profligately, and therefore can die within a few million years), then more sedate stars like the sun. By this point in the future, our own galaxy may be a rather dull place, made up primarily of unspectacular stars much smaller than the sun.

Of course, when we talk of the future of the Universe, the fate of   7
any single galaxy is not terribly important. Conversely, because other galaxies form a completely insignificant part of the spectacle of the night sky, what happens to distant galaxies will have little effect on what is observed from the Earth. Nevertheless, we do know that other galaxies are receding from us because of the Universe's expansion, and we believe that this expansion has been going on for roughly 15 billion years. It will surely continue to go on for comparable times into the future. The question that must be asked is whether the expansion will someday slow

down and reverse itself, or whether it will continue forever. This question is the first (and most important) decision point we must face.

If a ball is thrown upward from the surface of the Earth, we know **8** that eventually it will slow down, stop, and reverse its direction because of the gravitational attraction of the Earth. If the ball were thrown fast enough (more than about seven miles a second), however, we know that it would not fall back, but would sail off into space instead. Whether the ball will fall back to the ground, then, depends on two things: how fast it is moving and how hard the Earth is pulling on it. The force of gravity exerted by the Earth, in turn, depends on how much matter it contains.

We can think of the present expansion of the Universe in the same **9** way. A given galaxy is now receding from us at a particular velocity, a velocity which we can measure. Whether it will ever stop and start falling back toward us depends on how much of a gravitational attraction the rest of the Universe exerts on it. If there is enough matter to exert a strong enough force, we can expect that the outward-rushing Universe will someday start to contract. If there is not enough matter, then the expansion may slow down, but it will never stop.

In the terminology of the cosmologists, a universe with enough matter **10** to reverse the expansion is "closed," while a universe which has less than this critical amount is "open." (A universe with exactly the critical amount is also considered to be open and will end pretty much the same way.) The first decision point, then, is marked by the fundamental question: "Is the Universe open or closed?"

At first glance it might seem strange that we do not know enough **11** to answer this fundamental question. After all, our telescopes are capable of detecting galaxies ten billion light years away (one light year is approximately six trillion miles). Why can't we just add up all the matter we see and have our answer?

It turns out that if we took all the stars and galaxies and spread their **12** matter out uniformly through space, we would find about one hydrogen atom in a volume that could be carried by a dump truck. (This may seem like a very thin distribution of matter, but remember that there is a lot of just plain emptiness out there.) If we wanted to close the Universe, we would need a lot more than this: at least one to three atoms per cubic yard. If we count only the luminous matter we can see we have only a few percent of the amount needed to close the Universe. We seem forced to conclude that the Universe is open.

But this statement is premature, for it depends on the assumption **13** that we can see all the matter there is. We know this is not always true. For example, someone looking at the solar system from another star would see the sun because it is luminous, but he probably would not see any of the other bodies we know are here: planets, asteroids, comets, and so on. In the case of the solar system this is probably not too important, because all of these bodies add up to only a tiny fraction of the mass of the sun. But in looking at galaxies the situation may very well be different. It may be that a large percentage of the matter in a galaxy is not visible to someone looking at it through a telescope. If the matter we see does not close the Universe, then perhaps the matter we do not see will be enough to do the job.

UNSEEN MATTER IN THE GALAXIES?

At least two lines of evidence suggest that there might be a lot of matter, the existence of which we can deduce from its effects on other bodies. One line comes from studies of galaxies themselves, the other from studies of clusters of galaxies. Galaxies like the Milky Way and our neighbor Andromeda are shaped like spirals and rotate around their centers. The sun, for example, makes a grand circuit around the Milky Way every 200 million years or so. This rotation is complex, with different parts of the galaxy going around at different speeds. We are sure, however, that we understand the way matter should behave when it is at the outermost edges of the system. Just as the outer planets like Jupiter and Saturn move more slowly in their orbits than the Earth, so too should matter in the outer fringe of a galaxy exhibit gradual slowing down as the distance from the center increases. We say that the rotation should become Keplerian (named for Johannes Kepler, who discovered the true nature of planetary motion).   **14**

When we speak of the "outer fringes" of a galaxy in this context, we are talking about tenuous material, mostly hydrogen atoms, that does not emit light and is not visible to the naked eye or an optical telescope. It does, however, emit radio waves which allow us to detect its presence and determine its speed of rotation. Radio maps reveal that in most galaxies, this hydrogen gas is rotating faster than would be expected unless there were still more matter involved.   **15**

The only way this puzzling fact can be explained is to assume that there *is* still more matter (and therefore mass) in addition to the hydrogen that we can detect with our radio telescopes. Many galaxies, then, have an extensive halo of "invisible" matter . . . , a halo which could very well contain even more material than the stars themselves.   **16**

What the galactic halos teach us is that we should not be too hasty in declaring the Universe to be open. Even though we can directly see only a small percentage of the matter required to reverse the Universal expansion, we believe there is a great deal of matter in the Universe that we cannot see. If we assume that most galaxies have halos, then we should multiply the amount of visible matter by a number between two and ten to get a rough idea of how much mass is really out there. Of course, doing so does not get us to the critical amount of mass by a long shot, but this episode does make us wonder whether there are not other unseen masses waiting to be discovered.   **17**

Another candidate for unseen matter arises from studies of clusters of galaxies — concentrations that can contain a thousand or more galaxies. A few of these clusters seem to be in a kind of equilibrium. Think of adding hot water to a partially full bathtub. For a while the area where you add the water will be hotter than the rest of the tub, but eventually everything will even out and you will be left with a uniform temperature throughout. At this point we say that the water has reached what is known as thermal equilibrium.   **18**

Now if you put your hand into a tub of water and found that the   19
temperature was pretty evenly distributed, you would be justified in
assuming that the water had been in the tub long enough for any initial
unevenness in the temperature to be smoothed out. When astronomers
look at clusters of galaxies, they see strong evidence that a different
type of equilibrium has been established, leading them to conclude that
the system has been together long enough for this to occur.

In a few spots in the Universe, such as the Coma cluster, we have   20
the paradoxical situation that a cluster is in equilibrium even though it
does not seem to contain enough visible mass to hold everything together.
Adding mass for galactic halos and diffuse background light does not solve
this problem (although it makes the discrepancy less acute). Conclusion:
There is additional unseen mass in that cluster of galaxies. In Coma, for
example, the actual mass of the system must be 10 or 20 times that of
the matter we observe in the galaxies. Adding this extra intergalactic
mass to clusters still will not give us enough to close the Universe, but
it brings us nearer.

A similar conclusion can be reached by looking at the Universe as it   21
existed three minutes after the Big Bang, the time when nuclei were
formed. By measuring abundances of light nuclei *now,* we can deduce
the density of nuclear matter *then.* The result: If we count only nuclei,
the Universe is open.

Such is the current state of our knowledge about the first decision   22
point in the future of the Universe. The amount of luminous matter that
we know about is not the amount needed to reverse the expansion, but
we already have two sources of unseen additional matter that were
hitherto unexpected. Whether we will keep adding new unseen matter
in bits and pieces until we achieve the critical amount or whether we
now know about most of the matter in the Universe is an open question.

A few years ago, for example, it appeared that the neutrino, a particle   23
presumed since its theoretical prediction and then its actual discovery to
have no mass, might have a small mass after all. Cosmologists have
speculated that if such were the case, there might be enough invisible
mass in the form of neutrinos to close the Universe. When experiments
in the United States and the Soviet Union seemed to indicate that the
neutrino did indeed have mass, the excitement spilled over into the news
media. After all, we have reason to believe that there are as many
neutrinos in the Universe as there are photons (the particles that are
light and other radiation), and so if neutrinos had mass, there are so
many of them that they might indeed add up to enough to close the
Universe. Unfortunately, a new generation of experiments has weakened
the evidence, and the question of what, if anything, will provide the
unseen mass remains unanswered.

This sort of on-again, off-again sequence is typical of the history of   24
this problem, so it probably makes sense to agree that while at present
it looks as if the Universe is open, there is enough uncertainty to leave
the closed future a strong possibility. The fact that the question is yet
to be answered, however, does not mean that it is unanswerable. We
could acquire the knowledge necessary to determine whether the Universe is open or closed in many ways, from measuring the deceleration

of distant galaxies to developing a better understanding of the problem of unseen mass. At the moment, however, neither our observational nor theoretical capabilities are up to the job.

EXPLORING ALL THE POSSIBILITIES

We have no choice, then, but to follow each possible outcome of the 25 first decision point and see where it leads. Let us begin by assuming that nature has chosen to hide 90 percent or so of the mass and that the Universe is actually closed. In this case we are in for a spectacular future. For another 40 or 50 billion years the Universe will continue to expand, but ever more slowly. Then, like the ball falling back to Earth, the expansion will reverse at some point — 50 billion years is a reasonable guess — and a great contraction will begin. Instead of a universe where light from distant galaxies is shifted toward the red (indicating that the source is receding from us), we will find such light is blue-shifted.

Eighty or a hundred billion years from now the Earth and the sun 26 will be long dead. The galaxies will be decidedly less luminous than they are now, with populations of white dwarfs, neutron stars, and other faint objects. As the contraction progresses, galaxies move closer together and the cosmic background radiation begins to shift toward the visible part of the spectrum. . . . The sky will eventually blaze with light. By this time, the Universe will have contracted to a thousandth or less of its present size. The stars and planets themselves will dissolve into a Universal sea of hot material, and atoms and molecules will dissociate into their constituent nuclei and electrons. From this point on, the stages of the Big Bang that we described last month will simply play backwards — nuclei dissociating into quarks . . . and so on — until we are back to the original state in which it is thought the Big Bang occurred.

This scenario leads inevitably to the most fascinating question of all. 27 Will the Universal contraction (which cosmologists half-jokingly call the "Big Crunch") be followed by another expansion (the "Big Bounce")? In other words, will the Universe arise phoenixlike from its ashes and repeat the entire cycle? The picture of a universe which is reborn every hundred billion years or so is very attractive to some people. The main advantage of an eternally oscillating universe is that the questions "Why did it all start? Where did it all come from?" simply do not have to be asked. The Universe always *was* and always *will be*. A hundred billion years from now the Universe may again consist of a large collection of separating galaxies. And perhaps there will be another version of you reading another version of this magazine.

It is a fascinating thought, but before we go too far into speculation, 28 I should warn you that there are some serious problems with this picture. At least a few theorists argue that unless some of the basic laws of physics change during part of the cycle, the average disorder of the Universe might have to increase during each bounce, so that eventually the system would have to run down. And, of course, the whole idea of oscillations depends on the presence of enough mass to close the Universe and initiate the Big Crunch. Our present information seems to favor a quite different future.

So let us go back to our first decision point and look at the other option, the case in which there simply is not enough matter around to stop the expansion.

Scientists used to think that the universal tendency of every system to run down would eventually result in a universe in which everything had come into equilibrium at the same low temperature. This was called the "heat death" of the Universe. But this cannot happen in an eternally expanding system, because the components become too isolated to interact, so some thought has to be given to what will actually take place. Freeman J. Dyson, one of the most inventive minds in the fraternity of theoretical physicists, has explored the possible future course of the Universe. He did so not only because of the intrinsic interest of the problem, but also to examine a much deeper question: Could life survive in an open universe? Besides, a closed universe gives him a feeling of claustrophobia.

Because the expected lifetime of an open universe is infinite, we will have to think about very long times indeed if we are to follow the twists and turns of this possible future. Scientists like to write large numbers in what is called exponential notation. For example, the number 10^3 should be interpreted as a one followed by three zeros, or 1,000. The Universe is now roughly ten billion years old, a number with ten zeros that we would render as 10^{10} years. The life cycle of a closed universe is often taken to be around a hundred billion, or 10^{11}, years. Each time the power of ten is increased by one unit, the number being represented increases tenfold.

When we talk about looking into the future, it is tempting to imagine watching a film being run at a uniform speed. Another way to think about it — one that will give a better feeling for the immense time scales involved — is to imagine that the film speed is multiplied by ten when the power of ten goes up one digit. Thus, if we imagine that we are watching such a film being run at the rate of ten billion years every minute, then right now we are a little less than two minutes into the story following the Big Bang. Eight minutes from now we will be seeing the Universe when it is 100 billion (or 10^{11}) years old. The power of ten has gone up one digit, so at that point the film speed increases by ten. The next ten minutes will take us to a trillion (10^{12}) years, at which point the speed again increases by ten, so that time is going by at the rate of a trillion years a minute, and so on. Adopting this way of looking at things is the only way we can even begin to imagine the immense time scales involved in working out the death of the Universe.

THE OPENING STAGES OF AN OPEN UNIVERSE

If the Universe is open, the only change in the expansion will be a slowing down. The process of star formation may be winding down in the next 100 billion years or so, as we have already seen. The burning-out process would go on for a long time. Small, slow-burning stars could last as long as 10^{14} years, giving a pale illumination to the sky. As these stars cool off, other kinds of dissipation begin to become important. Some stars will evaporate from the outer regions of the galaxy in a time scale of 10^{19} years, while the densely packed stars in the galactic center may collapse together into a large black hole. When the Universe is a billion times older than it is now, corresponding to nine changes in film speed, we will see an ever thinner sea of background radiation in which an occasional black hole is embedded. Scattered around among these landmarks in nothingness will be the solid remains of the evaporated stars and such debris as has escaped capture up to this point. The Universe will keep this aspect through 12 more increases in film speed until the next point, which occurs at about 10^{31} years.

At this point we have to ask about the fate of the remnant solid **34** matter. According to current theories, the protons that make up all matter are unstable, and have a lifetime of roughly 10^{31} years. If the proton is indeed unstable on this very long scale, then by the time the film gets near to this point matter will be disintegrating fast enough to be visibly disappearing in our cosmic version of time-lapse photography.

If, on the other hand, matter is stable, nothing of this sort will have **35** happened by 10^{31} years. The Universe will go on expanding and cooling off. Occasionally some of the miscellaneous solid material will fall into a black hole, producing radiation as it does so. A hypothetical astronomer observing the Universe would be getting very bored, because this state of affairs would persist until 10^{65} years had passed.

With the film now running at about 10^{65} years per minute, an important **36** process is starting to take place among the black holes the size of, say, our sun. We think of black holes as bodies so dense that nothing can ever escape their gravitational pull, yet on long time scales it turns out that this is not quite accurate. Black holes will lose appreciable energy through thermal radiation. In a sense, the black hole is like the ember of a fire, giving off radiation to its surroundings. When the film is running at 10^{65} years per minute, a black hole will start radiating substantial energy, getting brighter and brighter as it does so. In one minute of film time, the black hole will brighten the sky and then disappear, its only monument an addition to the expanding sea of radiation. As the film runs on, speeding up every ten minutes, larger and larger black holes will undergo the same process and evaporate themselves away. For the next 35 changes in film speed, this is what we would see, an expanding universe with occasional fireworks as a black hole dies. This process goes on until all black holes are gone, and by the time it is over the film will be running at the speed of 10^{100} years per minute.

If the protons have decayed, this is the end of our story, because **37** there is nothing left in the Universe to produce any real change. If the proton does not decay, however, the disappearance of the black holes still leaves us with some solid matter to watch. The film now runs for ten days, until each minute corresponds to 10^{1500} years. Just writing the zeros in this number would require a full typewritten page! On this time scale matter turns to iron, the most stable nucleus. As we watch the film, then, we will see whatever solid material is left transform itself into iron. On still longer time scales — scales so long that we might have to watch our film for longer than the lifetime of the Earth — these iron spheres would transform into black holes, which would eventually evaporate.

This means that at some distant time in the future, the Universe **38** will probably be a cold, thin sea of radiation, with perhaps a few forlorn particles. Undaunted by this bleak prospect, Freeman Dyson argues that life could evolve away from flesh and blood — possibly into clouds of electrically charged particles — and outlast the stars and galaxies themselves while the Universe cools.

The great debate over whether the Universe is open or closed comes **39** down to the question of whether it will all end in fire or in ice, whether everything will fall back in on itself only to repeat the cycle, or whether the last bits of matter and radiation will disappear into a darkness that expands forever.

This is, in a sense, the last, the ultimate, question of science. The **40** cosmic switch has already been thrown; the answer, though unknown, is already ordained, and Man cannot influence the outcome. But simply to discover it would be a triumph of the human intellect.

11. An Economics Option: Business Cycles

In *Beyond Boom and Crash*, the economist Robert L. Heilbroner describes modern business cycles. Writing in the late 1970s during a period of economic sluggishness following the oil crisis of 1973 (when members of OPEC drastically increased petroleum prices), Heilbroner urges that we see such downturns as part of a pattern. In an introductory section, he briefly compares the recession in the 1970s to the depression of the 1930s (a recession is a sharp slowdown in the growth of business activity but not as severe as a depression). He comments that "in both cases the system itself seems to be the cause of trouble." He closes his introductory section with several questions that lead directly to the sections presented here: Why did the economy get overstrained? Why didn't the economic growth in force since the 1950s quickly reassert itself? Do such events give us reason to fear that the entire economy of the West is in danger?

When you have read Heilbroner's explanation, answer one of the following questions.

a. According to Heilbroner, how does the economy grow? Briefly describe the key phases in a complete cycle.
b. In a short essay define the term *recession* by accounting for it as part of a larger economic cycle.
c. Using Heilbroner's discussion as a starting point, write an essay describing

the success or failure of a business currently in the financial news. Identify your sources of information.

From *Beyond Boom and Crash*
ROBERT L. HEILBRONER

Such questions take us backstage to consider how capitalism as a system   1
generates economic growth in the first place. Here I find it useful to adopt a view of the economy first described by Marx. Marx depicts the process much as a businessman would — namely, as the complicated way in which money makes money and business capital expands.

Marx pictures this as a great accumulation "circuit" that can be divided   2
into three distinct phases or stages. In the first phase, businessmen hire labor and buy the raw or semifinished goods needed to start up production. In other words, they turn their money capital into labor power and supplies of various kinds. Moreover, if their business is to grow, they must turn ever *more* money into labor power and materials. Generalized to include the entire system, this means that a growing economy requires the hiring of more and more labor, and the buying of larger and larger quantities of materials, not only to turn out more consumable goods, but also to build new plant and equipment, the process economists call investment.

This initial phase of Marx's "circuit" of accumulation immediately   3
identifies two potential sources of crisis. The first is the crucial role played by businessmen's expectations. If capitalists do not anticipate growth — if the state of business confidence is poor — they will not invest in additional plant and equipment, and may not even seek to convert all their existing cash into payrolls and supplies. That is a problem to which we will return later, for expectations obviously play a critical role in determining the pace of advance or in determining whether there will be *any* advance.

But a second obstacle, of no less importance, also resides in the first   4
stage. Money will not even begin its tortuous journey through the system if a labor force cannot be hired, or if supplies of materials or plant and equipment are not available. When workers strike, capitalist growth comes to a total halt, at least insofar as that particular portion of the economy is concerned. For the system as a whole this stoppage may be trivial, as when a small local union goes on strike, but it can also bring to a halt a very large section of industry.

Of course it is not only a strike that can paralyze the initial phase   5
in which money seeks to "become" labor power and materials. If workers are unwilling to work at the wages that employers want to pay, the circuit is interrupted as effectively as if there were a strike. Or if needed inputs are unavailable or too expensive, the circuit is cut just as effectively as by the high price of labor. The OPEC oil shock was precisely such an event — a blow to the first phase of the accumulation process sufficiently severe to bring about a marked reduction in the scale of activity in every industrial nation.

Let us suppose, however, that money capital is successfully con- 6
verted into payrolls and stocks of materials and equipment. This now
brings us to the second phase of the production process as Marx describes
it — a part of the circuit located entirely within the factory rather than
in the marketplace. Here no money is directly involved. Rather, the
money that has been turned into labor power, raw materials, and other
necessities for production is now further turned into the finished products
that will emerge from the factory gate. Labor energies, and the physical
and chemical properties of the materials and equipment with which labor
works, now make steel out of iron, gasoline out of petroleum, cloth out
of yarn.

And here again a set of potential obstacles to the accumulation process 7
must be surmounted. Labor must perform its task efficiently and in a
disciplined fashion. The engineering processes must function smoothly.
Raw materials must be of proper grade and kind. Obviously the difficulties
encountered in this second phase of the circuit are of a different nature
than those of the first. Interruptions to labor discipline, such as absenteeism, sabotage, "work-to-rule" slowdowns, vandalism, or indifference
will damage the process by which money, embodied in labor power and
materials, becomes transformed into salable outputs. The morale problems that have plagued American and European factories in recent years,
of which the obstreperous Lordstown plant of General Motors was for
a time a national symbol, are illustrations of the interruptions we encounter
in the second stage. So are disruptions to the flow of production when
raw materials are below grade, or goods in process defective, or plant
and machinery inadequate. To the extent that the ability of a company
to sell its products is damaged by a reputation for poor workmanship,
the ability of that company to recoup its money capital is hurt as severely
as if a strike had shut its plants. Generalized to a sufficient degree (as
in the automobile industry, where poor engineering and sloppy work have
forced the recall of millions of cars), the problems of the second phase
of the circuit of accumulation can threaten the profitability of an entire
industry.

Finally, there is the third phase, the one most familiar to businessmen 8
and economists alike. This is the phase in which capital, now embodied
in a finished good, must complete its metamorphosis back into money.
The metamorphosis takes place by selling the good, an act that commands
the principal attention of the business world, although we can now see
that selling is only the last, and not necessarily the most critical, of the
links in the chain.

The obstacles faced in this third stage are again of a different kind 9
than those of the previous ones. Changes in buyers' wants or needs,
whether the consequence of changes in fashion or technology, can reduce
the value of output to a fraction of its expected worth. Events over which
an individual business has no control — indeed, events over which the
collective business world, or the nation-state itself, [has] no control —
can cause markets to disappear into thin air, or on occasion can create
profitable sales opportunities out of equally thin air. Thus the process of
completing the circle of capital accumulation by selling the output of

business is always attended by anxiety and uncertainty. In one way or another it is essential that the last loop of the process be closed if business is to recoup its original money outlays, but closing that loop is often difficult and sometimes impossible.

Thus three separate obstacle courses must be negotiated if capital, **10** in the form of money, is to return to its original hands, ready for still another round of metamorphoses. In view of the complexity and the dangers of these successive stages, our first reaction is to wonder how the process can ever be completed at all. Rather than accounting for the recurrent fact of crises — that is, of breakdowns somewhere in the system — the burden seems shifted: How, we ask, can such a labyrinthine journey hope to be safely undertaken, not once, but again and again, as part of the "mechanism" of the system?

The answer lies in becoming aware that the mechanism is not some **11** kind of tutelary deity that smiles over the capitalist process, but is lodged in the living, breathing — often very hard breathing — bodies of millions of persons whose full-time endeavor is to *make* the process work. For example, the initial process by which money is turned into labor power and materials is successfully concluded only because workers and their union leaders are as eager to come to terms with employers as employers are with them. The labor market in which hiring takes place is motivated by pressures of need as well as greed, of aspiration as well as defeat. Labor and capital come together as iron filings to the pole of a magnet, each "particle" of labor drawn to an employer, and the "pole" of capital drawn to the mass of workers. So too, similar efforts bring together the suppliers of raw materials and equipment with the firms who must spend money to procure them. Purchasing agents, brokers, executives of both buying and selling concerns, all spend their energies in finding supplies of materials of the right kind and price so that production may begin.

The same outpouring of energy seeks to assure the completion of **12** the production stage, where labor and materials are joined to create goods for sale. This is the domain of the foreman, the efficiency expert, the personnel manager, and the production boss. Here is where Ph.D.'s trained in psychology seek to remove obstacles of behavior, while other Ph.D.'s, trained in engineering and business management, seek to remove those of space, time, and organization; where union shop stewards and local managers work to prevent grievances from exploding into disruptions to the work process, and safety engineers install precautionary devices to prevent accidents from slowing or stopping production lines; where statistical sampling procedures detect variations in the quality of output before it is too late, and computer printouts inform men in shirtsleeves whether the rivers of subassemblies are advancing in proper coordination. Thus, like the metamorphosis of money into labor power and goods, the interaction of labor power with goods takes place not by the workings of a mysterious "mechanism," but because it is the object of the intense concern, attention, expertise, and will of millions of individuals.

The same is true again when we reach the final stage in which **13** commodities turn back into money, like frogs into princes. This time, of course, the process takes place as the consequence of an army of persons concerned with selling — copywriters, television actors with stentorian voices, models with pretty faces, merchandisers with clever ideas, ordinary sales clerks behind counters. At the same time, this crucial final closure of the total circuit is also expedited by two other extremely important groups who anxiously superintend the process at a remove. One consists of the financial institutions — banks, finance companies, savings and loan associations — who help complete the closure (as they also help business initiate it in the first phase) by lending buyers money. Second is the government, watching anxiously over the confused process in which all three loops of the capital-regeneration process are inextricably intertwined. Although the government intervenes at many points in all three stages, its main attention is fixed on the buying power of the households and businesses who must create princes by waving the magic wand of money. By its fiscal and monetary policies — that is, by raising and lowering expenditures and taxes, or by adjusting the supply of money — the government tries mightily to assure that the wand is waved and the process brought to a successful termination, prior to its instant recommencement. Thus, at the apex of the economy, as at its base, the economy "works" because an enormous fraction of the total life energies and intelligence of society is devoted to making it work.

When we look at the process of capitalist growth in this fashion, the **14** question changes once more: How can the process *fail* to work? When so much energy and intelligence, drive and adaptation go into the various subprocesses that constitute the whole, how can the accumulation process falter?

One reason, of course, is that the actors who strive so earnestly **15** can make mistakes. If they are small mistakes, they cancel out, one person's shortfall balanced by another's windfall. From time to time very large mistakes are made, and huge enterprises go under because they cannot begin production, or because they are unable to discipline the work process, or through a failure of marketing. Then the Edsel fails, or the Pennsylvania Railroad goes bankrupt, or the Lockheed Company totters.

But as these instances illustrate, even giant failures do not create **16** more than temporary pauses in the ongoing accumulation process of the entire economy. A more likely candidate for the role of villain is mistaken or wrong-headed action taken by the government itself. In the 1930s, for example, the Federal Reserve Board deliberately tightened the money supply, making it difficult for banks to resume their lending operations, because the Board was obsessed with a fear of inflation,° despite the fact that a quarter of the work force was unemployed. In so doing it was probably the single most important contributory element in the persistent failure of the economy to resume its forward momentum.

inflation: A period of rapidly rising prices in most sectors of the economy.

In more recent years recessions have actually been deliberately in-   **17**
itiated in Washington, the fear of inflation taking precedence over a concern for unemployment — the difference being that the Federal Reserve
in the 1930s knew not what it wrought, whereas the Administration in
1974 knew very well what it was doing. In similar fashion, a considerable
part of the explanation for the poor performance of the American (and
most European) economies after "oil shock" was the imposition of conscious monetary restraints by governments seeking to put a halt to
inflation, even at the expense of recession, or indeed by the very means
of an engineered recession.

We shall subsequently have more to say about the role of government   **18**
in managing or mismanaging inflation, but the answer to our question
does not lie in the upsetting presence of "mistakes" or deliberate re-
cessionary policy. Capitalist economies have encountered regular crises
long before governments were meddling in the economic process, and
the collapses of giant firms, usually in finance, generally took place as a
consequence, rather than as a direct cause, of recessions. Thus we shall
have to search elsewhere for explanations of the recurrence of crisis.
Indeed, we shall have to see if we cannot find causes for crisis that are
the outgrowth of the very success of capitalist growth.

One such endemic "counterprocess" is relatively easy to locate. It   **19**
is the inherent spoiling effect of a period of boom on the labor and materials
markets of the first phase of the accumulation process. For the more
successful is this first phase — the more steadily money becomes transformed into labor power and goods — the more do the prices of labor
and materials tend to rise. As Adam Smith already saw, the accumulation
of wealth bids up the price of labor, and as David Ricardo added, it also
raises the price of any other commodity whose supply cannot be quickly
increased, or whose supply can be increased only at higher cost.

Thus the successful completion of the first stage tends to tighten   **20**
loose markets — for labor, materials, space, money — because the
growing demand for the factors of production tends to raise their prices.
As every businessman knows, booms jack up costs. Rising costs in turn
squeeze business income. As the pressure against profits mounts, the
general enthusiasm of the early days of the boom gives way to a growing
unease about labor's "demands" and raw materials' prices.

As the squeeze intensifies, the willingness or the ability to go on   **21**
producing declines. Businesses cancel plans for expansion as too expensive. They decide to hang on to their money rather than to risk it in the
accumulation process. The process begins to falter. A recession is at
hand.

There is, I must emphasize, nothing mechanical or certain about this.   **22**
A tight labor market may be relieved if cheap labor can be imported from
abroad, or if automation can be quickly introduced. A rise in materials'
prices may simply lead to the use of substitutes or the rapid exploitation
of new sources of supply. Credit shortages can be eased by government
policy. Or the business outlook may remain buoyant, despite a rise in
costs, because businessmen are convinced that "they" won't allow a
recession to occur. In a word, expansion can continue in the face of rising

costs, or rising costs may themselves set into motion corrective processes that temper the rise in wages and prices. (Adam Smith pointed out that a rise in wages would enable more of the child labor force to stay alive, thereby offsetting the increased demand for labor by an increased supply of it.)

So there is nothing in the self-spoiling propensities of a successful boom that is certain to abort the overall circuit of capital accumulation. Rather, a *potential* for disruption lies in the tendency of a boom to raise prices and thereby to constrict profits. Whether such a potential constriction *actually* takes place hinges on innumerable circumstances and cannot be predicted. It is enough to recognize that it could. **23**

A second source of disruption, likewise rooted in the success of the accumulation process, lies within the second phase, where labor power and materials are combined to create salable commodities. Here the problem has nothing to do with money. It is to be found in the difficulty of maintaining a smooth flow of production during an extended period of prosperity. **24**

In turn, this difficulty rests on the nature of the labor process within industrial capitalism (and, indeed, within the forms of industrial socialism that are heirs to this labor process). Industrial labor requires an extraordinary amount of discipline. This is because labor under capitalism is systematically reduced to what Marx called "detail labor" — the performance of operations that have no significance in themselves, but are important only as units of a larger whole. Industrial production requires the steady, coordinated, dependable performance of tasks each one of which has little or no meaning, aesthetic satisfaction, tradition, art, pleasure, or completion. Compared with the work of artisans, or even of peasant farmers, the work of men and women in factories and offices is fragmented, pointless, empty of intrinsic meaning, however much money it may earn for its protagonist. (This is probably what Marx meant when he said that the worker under capitalism became ever more "impoverished," whether his wage was high or low.) **25**

To perform this labor with the machinelike regularity on which the production process as a whole depends requires that men and women submit to a routine that few do not find irksome. In the main the great majority of working people *do* submit, partly from the need to earn a living, partly from the social pressure to conform, partly from the absence of any imaginable alternative. But the irksomeness of the work process, like a hair shirt, is never lost to consciousness. And when prosperity continues, and the bargaining position and economic security of working people improve, the necessary discipline becomes harder to obtain. Absenteeism increases. Unions demand and get more job perks. Wildcat strikes break out over trifles. The authority of foremen diminishes. The issue of "work satisfaction" comes to the fore. **26**

It is clear that a very large potential for the interruption of capitalist accumulation resides in the lurking indiscipline of the labor process. General strikes are unknown in this country, but are all too familiar abroad, where they have on occasion paralyzed England, France, Italy, Austria, **27** the Netherlands, Sweden, and other nations. Even in countries that lack a unified and militant labor force, the problem of indiscipline is an ever present threat to the smooth regeneration of capital. Moreover, the threat of indiscipline worsens as the general prosperity of the work force improves, and bright prospects for employment elsewhere encourage labor to express its dissatisfactions. Consequently, we find efforts to lessen the irksomeness of labor by breaking up the monotony of assembly lines, as in the famous Volvo team system first tried in Sweden and now being used in a number of firms elsewhere; or to instill a sense of self-respect through trim uniforms, piped-in music, "personalized" cubicles, special training for foremen in the dynamics of group psychology, company sports, outings, and morale-building activities. The effort to overcome the problem of labor indiscipline is probably most fully expressed in Japanese firms that begin the day with mass calisthenics and singing, and that provide lessons in flower arranging for their female employees, as well as guaranteeing lifetime employment (after a relatively short apprenticeship), provided that the employee does not give "cause" for dismissal.

28 A third, separate source of potential difficulty, also generated by the boom itself, lies in the last of the three phases of the accumulation process, where commodities must be converted into money. Here the difficulty is simply stated. It is that production tends to glut markets. Goods come off assembly lines faster than consumers can absorb them. Inventories pile up. Eventually, production has to be cut back.

29 Every businessman knows that gluts can spoil individual markets. The great question — one that has been debated in economics for a century and a half — is whether there can be "general gluts," gluts for everything. Most economists today say no, that total demand is for all intents and purposes limitless and insatiable, spreading out from necessities toward infinite luxuries.

30 The problem of the third phase, however, is not one of spoiling total demand. It is rather that an economy that has enjoyed a boom may find it very difficult to rearrange production to suit the changing patterns of demand as *particular* markets get filled up. Production processes that are city blocks long and months "deep" are not easily switched off or turned around. Gluts for products such as automobiles or ships or planes or export crops lead to pockets of unused labor and equipment that cannot be rapidly redeployed to meet other possible demands. These pockets become centers of depression whose infectious power is very great.

31 In addition, there is the larger problem of matching demand against supply, not just in one market or another, but in terms of the total amount of purchasing power generated back in phase one and the total value of goods produced in phase two. Here the question is not one of glut, but one of a balance between buying power and *expected* revenues. Perhaps all the existing output can be sold, but if it must be unloaded at prices less favorable than were originally hoped for, the expectations that drive the accumulation process will receive a setback. It is also true that if goods are sold at prices greater than those originally hoped for, business will receive a very strong stimulus. Thus the matching of buying power, on the one hand, and expected revenues on the other, holds out the

possibility of disappointments that can lead to reduced production, or of windfalls that can lead to increased prices. In the phrase of Sir Roy Harrod, the eminent English economist who first formulated the difficulties of achieving "balanced growth," capitalism walks a "knife edge" between recession on one side and inflation on the other.

Thus the third phase of the overall process of capitalist reproduction and growth is a center of constant tragedy and near-tragedy, as well as of triumph or lucking-out. Gluts, or mismatches between supply and demand, are the stuff of everyday market life, as the business pages of any newspaper will testify, and a vast amount of effort goes into seeking to avert or rescue such gluts through sales, write-downs, write-offs, promotions, and the like. On a larger scale, the mismatch of whole sectors of outputs, such as crops or raw materials or housing, may lead to government intervention to prevent disasters from spreading. And, not least, the fiscal and monetary authorities are constantly scanning the economic scene for indications of mismatches between the volume of production and the volume of money incomes. . . . 32

The difficulties of the third phase, like those of the first two, do not dictate an "inevitable" breakdown. It would be better to say that gluts, either for particular sectors or on a larger scale, are the principal reason for shortcircuits in this last of the three distinguishable stages of accumulation. They result in what Marx called "realization crises" — failures to "realize" the capital tied up in commodities because they cannot be sold at profitable prices. 33

The above is not, of course, anything like a full description of the causes of economic crisis, much less a systematic tracing through the interconnections by which crises exert their effects. But it must be clear that the susceptibility to crisis lies directly within the process of capitalist expansion itself. It is the success of the system — its solution to the problem of converting money into goods and labor, and then reconverting the resultant production into new money, that increases the tension of the accumulative process. The tension is eventually snapped by a change in expectations or behavior, or in physical or social realities, somewhere along the length path of money making. Crisis thus appears to be not so much an exceptional occurrence as an event whose appearance is to be expected, although one never quite knows where or when. The system is crisis-prone not because it cannot make its subcircuits operate, but because the very act of successfully operating them creates tensions that make the economy vulnerable to breakdown. 34

12. A Cultural History Option: Reevaluating Historical Accounts

The following selection, written by Jane Tompkins, an English professor, recounts an intellectual journey. Write an essay serially describing that journey, making sure to let your account serve a point that you want to make about Tompkins's description of her experience.

"Indians": Textualism, Morality, and the Problem of History

JANE TOMPKINS

When I was growing up in New York City, my parents used to take me 1
to an event in Inwood Park at which Indians — real American Indians
dressed in feathers and blankets — could be seen and touched by children
like me. This event was always a disappointment. It was more fun to
imagine that you *were* an Indian in one of the caves in Inwood Park than
to shake the hand of an old man in a headdress who was not overwhelmed
at the opportunity of meeting you. After staring at the Indians for a while,
we would take a walk in the woods where the caves were, and once I
asked my mother if the remains of a fire I had seen in one of them might
have been left by the original inhabitants. After that, wandering up some
stone steps cut into the side of the hill, I imagined I was a princess in
a rude castle. My Indians, like my princesses, were creatures totally of
the imagination, and I did not care to have any real exemplars interfering
with what I already knew.

I already knew about Indians from having read about them in school. 2
Over and over we were told the story of how Peter Minuit had bought
Manhattan Island from the Indians for twenty-four dollars' worth of glass
beads. And it was a story we didn't mind hearing because it gave us the
rare pleasure of having someone to feel superior to, since the poor Indians
had not known (as we eight-year-olds did) how valuable a piece of property
Manhattan Island would become. Generally, much was made of the Indian
presence in Manhattan; a poem in one of our readers began: "Where we
walk to school today / Indian children used to play," and we were encouraged to write poetry on this topic ourselves. So I had a fairly rich
relationship with Indians before I ever met the unprepossessing people
in Inwood Park. I felt that I had a lot in common with them. They, too,
liked animals (they were often named after animals); they, too, made
mistakes — they liked the brightly colored trinkets of little value that
the white men were always offering them; they were handsome, warlike,
and brave and had led an exciting, romantic life in the forest long ago,
a life such as I dreamed of leading myself. I felt lucky to be living in one
of the places where they had definitely been. Never mind where they
were or what they were doing now.

My story stands for the relationship most non-Indians have to the 3
people who first populated this continent, a relationship characterized by
narcissistic fantasies of freedom and adventure, of a life lived closer to
nature and to spirit than the life we lead now. As Vine Deloria, Jr. has
pointed out, the American Indian Movement in the early seventies couldn't
get people to pay attention to what was happening to Indians who were
alive in the present, so powerful was this country's infatuation with people
who wore loincloths, lived in tepees, and roamed the plains and forests
long ago. The present essay, like these fantasies, doesn't have much to
do with actual Indians, though its subject matter is the histories of European-Indian relations in seventeenth-century New England. In a sense,
my encounter with Indians as an adult doing "research" replicates the

childhood one, for while I started out to learn about Indians, I ended up preoccupied with a problem of my own.

This essay enacts a particular instance of the challenge post-structuralism poses to the study of history. In simpler language, it concerns the difference that point of view makes when people are giving accounts of events, whether at first or second hand. The problem is that if all accounts of events are determined through and through by the observer's frame of reference, then one will never know, in any given case, what really happened. 4

I encountered this problem in concrete terms while preparing to teach a course in colonial American literature. I'd set out to learn what I could about the Puritans' relations with American Indians. All I wanted was a general idea of what had happened between the English settlers and the natives in seventeenth-century New England; post-structuralism and its dilemmas were the furthest thing from my mind. I began, more or less automatically, with Perry Miller, who hardly mentions the Indians at all, then proceeded to the work of historians who had dealt exclusively with the European-Indian encounter. At first, it was a question of deciding which of these authors to believe, for it quickly became apparent that there was no unanimity on the subject. As I read on, however, I discovered that the problem was more complicated than deciding whose version of events was correct. Some of the conflicting accounts were not simply contradictory, they were completely incommensurable, in that their assumptions about what counted as a valid approach to the subject, and what the subject itself was, diverged in fundamental ways. Faced with an array of mutually irreconcilable points of view, points of view which determined what was being discussed as well as the terms of the discussion, I decided to turn to primary sources for clarification, only to discover that the primary sources reproduced the problem all over again. I found myself, in other words, in an epistemological quandary, not only unable to decide among conflicting versions of events but also unable to believe that any such decision could, in principle, be made. It was a moral quandary as well. Knowledge of what really happened when the Europeans and the Indians first met seemed particularly important, since the result of that encounter was virtual genocide. This was the kind of past "mistake" which, presumably, we studied history in order to avoid repeating. If studying history couldn't put us in touch with actual events and their causes, then what was to prevent such atrocities from happening again? 5

For a while, I remained at this impasse. But through analyzing the process by which I had reached it, I eventually arrived at an understanding which seemed to offer a way out. This essay records the concrete experience of meeting and solving the difficulty I have just described (as an abstract problem, I thought I had solved it long ago). My purpose is not to throw new light on antifoundationalist epistemology — the solution I reached is not a new one — but to dramatize and expose the troubles antifoundationalism gets you into when you meet it, so to speak, in the road. 6

My research began with Perry Miller. Early in the preface to *Errand into the Wilderness*, while explaining how he came to write his history of 7 the New England mind, Miller writes a sentence that stopped me dead. He says that what fascinated him as a young man about his country's history was "the massive narrative of the movement of European culture into the vacant wilderness of America." "Vacant?" Miller, writing in 1956, doesn't pause over the word "vacant," but to people who read his preface thirty years later, the word is shocking. In what circumstances could someone proposing to write a history of colonial New England *not* take account of the Indian presence there?

The rest of Miller's preface supplies an answer to this question, if   **8** one takes the trouble to piece together its details. Miller explains that as a young man, jealous of older compatriots who had had the luck to fight in World War I, he had gone to Africa in search of adventure. "The adventures that Africa afforded," he writes, "were tawdry enough, but it became the setting for a sudden epiphany" (p. vii). "It was given to me," he writes, "disconsolate on the edge of a jungle of central Africa, to have thrust upon me the mission of expounding what I took to be the innermost propulsion of the United States, while supervising, in that barbaric tropic, the unloading of drums of case oil flowing out of the inexhaustible wilderness of America" (p. viii). Miller's picture of himself on the banks of the Congo furnishes a key to the kind of history he will write and to his mental image of a vacant wilderness; it explains why it was just here, under precisely these conditions, that he should have had his epiphany.

The fuel drums stand, in Miller's mind, for the popular misconception   **9** of what this country is about. They are "tangible symbols of [America's] appalling power," a power that everyone but Miller takes for the ultimate reality (p. ix). To Miller, "the mind of man is the basic factor in human history," and he will plead, all unaccommodated as he is among the fuel drums, for the intellect — the intellect for which his fellow historians, with their chapters on "stoves or bathtubs, or tax laws," "the Wilmot Proviso" and "the chain store," "have so little respect" (pp. viii, ix). His preface seethes with a hatred of the merely physical and mechanical, and this hatred, which is really a form of moral outrage, explains not only the contempt with which he mentions the stoves and bathtubs but also the nature of his experience in Africa and its relationship to the "massive narrative" he will write.

Miller's experiences in Africa are "tawdry," his tropic is barbaric   **10** because the jungle he stands on the edge of means nothing to him, no more, indeed something less, than the case oil. It is the nothingness of Africa that precipitates his vision. It is the barbarity of the "dark continent," the obvious (but superficial) parallelism between the jungle at Matadi and America's "vacant wilderness" that releases in Miller the desire to define and vindicate his country's cultural identity. To the young Miller, colonial Africa and colonial America are — but for the history he will bring to light — mirror images of one another. And what he fails to see in the one landscape is the same thing he overlooks in the other: the human beings who people it. As Miller stood with his back to the jungle, thinking about the role of mind in human history, his failure to see that the land into which European culture had moved was not vacant but already occupied by a varied and numerous population is of a piece with his failure, in his portrait of himself at Matadi, to notice *who* was carrying the fuel drums he was supervising the unloading of.

The point is crucial because it suggests that what is invisible to the 11 historian in his own historical moment remains invisible when he turns his gaze to the past. It isn't that Miller didn't "see" the black men, in a literal sense, any more than it's the case that when he looked back he didn't "see" the Indians, in the sense of not realizing they were there. Rather, it's that neither the Indians nor the blacks *counted* for him, in a fundamental way. The way in which Indians can be seen but not counted is illustrated by an entry in Governor John Winthrop's journal, three hundred years before, when he recorded that there had been a great storm with high winds "yet through God's great mercy it did no hurt, but only killed one Indian with the fall of a tree." The juxtaposition suggests that Miller shared with Winthrop a certain colonial point of view, a point of view from which Indians, though present, do not finally matter.

A book entitled *New England Frontier: Puritans and Indians, 1620–* 12 *1675*, written by Alden Vaughan and published in 1965, promised to rectify Miller's omission. In the outpouring of work on the European-Indian encounter that began in the early sixties, this book is the first major landmark, and to a neophyte it seems definitive. Vaughan acknowledges the absence of Indian sources and emphasizes his use of materials which catch the Puritans "off guard." His announced conclusion that "the New England Puritans followed a remarkably humane, considerate, and just policy in their dealings with the Indians" seems supported by the scope, documentation, and methodicalness of his project (p. vii). The author's fair-mindedness and equanimity seem everywhere apparent, so that when he asserts "the history of interracial relations from the arrival of the Pilgrims to the outbreak of King Philip's War is a credit to the integrity of both peoples," one is positively reassured (p. viii).

But these impressions do not survive an admission that comes late 13 in the book, when, in the course of explaining why works like Helen Hunt Jackson's *Century of Dishonor* had spread misconceptions about Puritan treatment of the Indians, Vaughan finally lays his own cards on the table.

> The root of the misunderstanding [about Puritans and Indians] . . . lie[s] in a failure to recognize the nature of the two societies that met in seventeenth century New England. One was unified, visionary, disciplined, and dynamic. The other was divided, self-satisfied, undisciplined, and static. It would be unreasonable to expect that such societies could live side by side indefinitely with no penetration of the more fragmented and passive by the more consolidated and active. What resulted, then, was not — as many have held — a clash of dissimilar ways of life, but rather the expansion of one into the areas in which the other was lacking. (p. 323)

From our present vantage point, these remarks seem culturally biased 14 to an incredible degree, not to mention inaccurate: Was Puritan society unified? If so, how does one account for its internal dissensions and obsessive need to cast out deviants? Is "unity" necessarily a positive culture trait? From what standpoint can one say that American Indians were neither disciplined nor visionary, when both these characteristics loom so large in the ethnographies? Is it an accident that ways of describing cultural strength and weakness coincide with gender stereotypes — active/passive, and so on? Why is one culture said to "penetrate" the other? Why is the "other" described in terms of "lack"?

Vaughan's fundamental categories of apprehension and judgment will   **15** not withstand even the most cursory inspection. For what looked like evenhandedness when he was writing *New England Frontier* does not look that way anymore. In his introduction to *New Directions in American Intellectual History*, John Higham writes that by the end of the sixties

> the entire conceptual foundation on which [this sort of work] rested [had] crumbled away. . . . Simultaneously, in sociology, anthropology, and history, two working assumptions . . . came under withering attack: first, the assumption that societies tend to be integrated, and second, that a shared culture maintains that integration. . . . By the late 1960s all claims issued in the name of an "American mind" . . . were subject to drastic skepticism.

"Clearly," Higham continues, "the sociocultural upheaval of the sixties created the occasion" for this reaction. Vaughan's book, it seemed, could only have been written before the events of the sixties had sensitized scholars to questions of race and ethnicity. It came as no surprise, therefore, that ten years later there appeared a study of European-Indian relations which reflected the new awareness of social issues the sixties had engendered. And it offered an entirely different picture of the European-Indian encounter.

Francis Jennings's *The Invasion of America* (1975) rips wide open   **16** the idea that the Puritans were humane and considerate in their dealings with the Indians. In Jennings's account, even more massively documented than Vaughan's, the early settlers lied to the Indians, stole from them, murdered them, scalped them, captured them, tortured them, raped them, sold them into slavery, confiscated their land, destroyed their crops, burned their homes, scattered their possessions, gave them alcohol, underminded their systems of belief, and infected them with diseases that wiped out ninety percent of their numbers within the first hundred years after contact.

Jennings mounts an all-out attack on the essential decency of the   **17** Puritan leadership and their apologists in the twentieth century. The Pequot War, which previous historians had described as an attempt on the part of Massachusetts Bay to protect itself from the fiercest of the New England tribes, becomes, in Jennings's painstakingly researched account, a deliberate war of extermination, waged by whites against Indians. It starts with trumped-up charges, is carried on through a series of increasingly bloody reprisals, and ends in the massacre of scores of Indian men, women, and children, all so that Massachusetts Bay could gain political and economic control of the southern Connecticut Valley. When one reads this and then turns over the page and sees a reproduction of the Bay Colony seal, which depicts an Indian from whose mouth issue the words "Come over and help us," the effect is shattering.

But even so powerful an argument as Jennings's did not remain   **18** unshaken by subsequent work. Reading on, I discovered that if the events of the sixties had revolutionized the study of European-Indian relations, the events of the seventies produced yet another transformation. The American Indian Movement, and in particular the founding of the Native American Rights Fund in 1971 to finance Indian litigation and a court decision in 1975 which gave the tribes the right to seek redress for past injustices in federal court, created a climate within which historians began to focus on the Indians themselves. "Almost simultaneously," writes James Axtell, "frontier and colonial historians began to discover the necessity of considering the American natives as real determinants of history and the utility of ethnohistory as a way of ensuring parity of focus and impartiality of judgment." In Miller, Indians had been simply beneath notice; in Vaughan, they belonged to an inferior culture; and in Jennings, they were the more or less innocent prey of power-hungry whites. But in the most original and provocative of the ethnohistories, Calvin Martin's *Keepers of the Game*, Indians became complicated, purposeful human beings, whose lives were spiritually motivated to a high degree. Their relationship to the animals they hunted, to the natural environment, and to the whites with whom they traded became intelligible within a system of beliefs that formed the basis for an entirely new perspective on the European-Indian encounter.

Within the broader question of why European contact had such a   19
devastating effect on the Indians, Martin's specific aim is to determine why Indians participated in the fur trade which ultimately led them to the brink of annihilation. The standard answer to this question had always been that once the Indian was introduced to European guns, copper kettles, woolen blankets, and the like, he literally couldn't keep his hands off them. In order to acquire these coveted items, he decimated the animal populations on which his survival depended. In short, the Indian's motivation in participating in the fur trade was assumed to be the same as the white European's — a desire to accumulate material goods. In direct opposition to this thesis, Martin argues that the reason why Indians ruthlessly exploited their own resources had nothing to do with supply and demand, but stemmed rather from a breakdown of the cosmic world-view that tied them to the game they killed in a spiritual relationship of parity and mutual obligation.

The hunt, according to Martin, was conceived not primarily as a   20
physical activity but as a spiritual quest, in which the spirit of the hunter must overmaster the spirit of the game animal before the kill can take place. The animal, in effect, *allows* itself to be found and killed, once the hunter has mastered its spirit. The hunter prepared himself through rituals of fasting, sweating, or dreaming which reveal the identity of his prey and where he can find it. The physical act of killing is the least important element in the process. Once the animal is killed, eaten, and its parts used for clothing or implements, its remains must be disposed of in ritually prescribed fashion, or the game boss, the "keeper" of that species, will not permit more animals to be killed. The relationship between Indians and animals, then, is contractual; each side must hold up its end of the bargain, or no further transactions can occur.

What happened, according to Martin, was that as a result of diseases   21 introduced into the animal population by Europeans, the game suddenly disappeared, began to act in inexplicable ways, or sickened and died in plain view, and communicated their diseases to the Indians. The Indians, consequently, believed that their compact with the animals had been broken and that the keepers of the game, the tutelary spirits of each animal species whom they had been so careful to propitiate, had betrayed them. And when missionization, wars with the Europeans, and displacement from their tribal lands had further weakened Indian society and its belief structure, the Indians, no longer restrained by religious sanctions, in effect, turned on the animals in a holy war of revenge.

Whether or not Martin's specific claim about the "holy war" was correct, his analysis made it clear to me that, given the Indians' understanding of economic, religious, and physical processes, an Indian account of what transpired when the European settlers arrived here would look nothing like our own. Their (potential, unwritten) history of the conflict could bear only a marginal resemblance to Eurocentric views. I began to think that the key to understanding European-Indian relations was to see them as an encounter between wholly disparate cultures, and that therefore either defending or attacking the colonists was beside the point since, given the cultural disparity between the two groups, conflict was inevitable and in large part a product of mutual misunderstanding. **22**

But three years after Martin's book appeared, Shepard Krech III edited a collection of seven essays called *Indians, Animals, and the Fur Trade*, attacking Martin's entire project. Here the authors argued that we don't need an ideological or religious explanation for the fur trade. As Charles Hudson writes, **23**

> The Southeastern Indians slaughtered deer (and were prompted to enslave and kill each other) because of their position on the outer fringes of an expanding modern world-system. . . . In the modern world-system there is a core region which establishes *economic* relations with its colonial periphery. . . . If the Indians could not produce commodities, they were on the road to cultural extinction. . . . To maximize his chances for survival, an eighteenth-century Southeastern Indian had to . . . live in the interior, out of range of European cattle, forestry, and agriculture. . . . He had to produce a commodity which was valuable enough to earn him some protection from English slavers.

Though we are talking here about Southeastern Indians, rather than the subarctic and Northeastern tribes Martin studied, what really accounts for these divergent explanations of why Indians slaughtered the game are the assumptions that underlie them. Martin believes that the Indians acted on the basis of perceptions made available to them by their own cosmology; that is, he explains their behavior as the Indians themselves would have explained it (insofar as he can), using a logic and a set of values that are not Eurocentric but derived from within Amerindian culture. Hudson, on the other hand, insists that the Indians' own beliefs are irrelevant to an explanation of how they acted, which can only be understood, as far as he is concerned, in the terms of a Western materialist economic and political analysis. Martin and Hudson, in short, don't agree on what counts as an explanation, and this disagreement sheds light on **24** the preceding accounts as well. From this standpoint, we can see that Vaughan, who thought that the Puritans were superior to the Indians, and Jennings, who thought the reverse, are both, like Hudson, using Eurocentric criteria of description and evaluation. While all three critics (Vaughan, Jennings, and Hudson) acknowledge that Indians and Europeans behave differently from one another, the behavior differs, as it were, within the order of the same: all three assume, though only Hudson makes the assumption explicit, that an understanding of relations between the Europeans and the Indians must be elaborated in European terms. In Martin's analysis, however, what we have are not only two different sets of behavior but two incommensurable ways of describing and assigning meaning to events. This difference at the level of explanation calls into question the possibility of obtaining any theory-independent account of interaction between Indians and Europeans.

At this point, dismayed and confused by the wildly divergent views 25 of colonial history the twentieth-century historians had provided, I decided to look at some primary materials. I thought, perhaps, if I looked at some firsthand accounts and at some scholars looking at those accounts, it would be possible to decide which experts were right and which were wrong by comparing their views with the evidence. Captivity narratives seemed a good place to begin, since it was logical to suppose that the records left by whites who had been captured by Indians would furnish the sort of firsthand information I wanted.

I began with two fascinating essays based on these materials written 26 by the ethnohistorian James Axtell, "The White Indians of Colonial America" and "The Scholastic Philosophy of the Wilderness." These essays suggest that it would have been a privilege to be captured by North American Indians and taken off to Canada to dwell in a wigwam for the rest of one's life. Axtell's reconstruction of the process by which Indians taught European captives to feel comfortable in the wilderness, first taking their shoes away and giving them moccasins, carrying the children on their backs, sharing the scanty food supply equally, ceremonially cleansing them of their old identities, giving them Indian clothes and jewelry, assiduously teaching them the Indian language, finally adopting them into their families, and even visiting them after many years if, as sometimes happened, they were restored to white society — all of this creates a compelling portrait of Indian culture and helps to explain the extraordinary attraction that Indian culture apparently exercised over Europeans.

But, as I had by now come to expect, this beguiling portrait of the 27 Indians' superior humanity is called into question by other writings on Indian captivity — for example, Norman Heard's *White into Red*, whose summation of the comparative treatment of captive children east and west of the Mississippi seems to contradict some of Axtell's conclusions:

> The treatment of captive children seems to have been similar in initial stages. . . . Most children were treated brutally at the time of capture. Babies and toddlers usually were killed immediately and other small children would be dispatched during the rapid retreat to the Indian villages if they cried, failed to keep the pace, or otherwise indicated a lack of fortitude

needed to become a worthy member of the tribe. Upon reaching the village, the child might face such ordeals as running the gauntlet or dancing in the center of a throng of threatening Indians. The prisoner might be so seriously injured at this time that he would no longer be acceptable for adoption.

One account which Heard reprints is particularly arresting. A young girl captured by the Comanches who had not been adopted into a family but used as a slave had been peculiarly mistreated. When they wanted to wake her up the family she belonged to would take a burning brand from the fire and touch it to her nose. When she was returned to her parents, the flesh of her nose was completely burned away, exposing the bone.   28

Since the pictures drawn by Heard and Axtell were in certain respects irreconcilable, it made sense to turn to a firsthand account to see how the Indians treated their captives in a particular instance. Mary Rowlandson's "The Soveraignty and Goodness of God," published in Boston around 1680, suggested itself because it was so widely read and had set the pattern for later narratives. Rowlandson interprets her captivity as God's punishment on her for failing to keep the Sabbath properly on several occasions. She sees everything that happens to her as a sign from God. When the Indians are kind to her, she attributes her good fortune to divine Providence; when they are cruel, she blames her captors. But beyond the question of how Rowlandson interprets events is the question of what she saw in the first place and what she considered worth reporting. The following passage, with its abrupt shifts of focus and peculiar emphases, makes it hard to see her testimony as evidence of anything other than the Puritan point of view: 29

> Then my heart began to fail: and I fell weeping, which was the first time to my remembrance, that I wept before them. Although I had met with so much Affliction, and my heart was many times ready to break, yet could I not shed one tear in their sight: but rather had been all this while in a maze, and like one astonished: but now I may say as, Psal. 137.1. *By the Rivers of Babylon, there we sate down; yea, we wept when we remembered Zion.* There one of them asked me, why I wept, I could hardly tell what to say: yet I answered, they would kill me: No, said he, none will hurt you. Then came one of them and gave me two spoon-fulls of Meal to comfort me, and another gave me half a pint of Pease; which was more worth than many Bushels at another time. Then I went to see King Philip, he bade me come in and sit down, and asked me whether I woold smoke it (a usual Complement nowadayes among Saints and Sinners) but this no way suited me. For though I had formerly used Tobacco, yet I had left it ever since I was first taken. It seems to be a Bait, the Devil layes to make men loose their precious time: I remember with shame, how formerly, when I had taken two or three pipes, I was presently ready for another, such a bewitching thing it is: But I thank God, he has now given me power over it; surely there are many who may be better imployed than to ly sucking a stinking Tobacco-pipe.

Anyone who has ever tried to give up smoking has to sympathize with Rowlandson, but it is nonetheless remarkable, first, that a passage which begins with her weeping openly in front of her captors, and comparing herself to Israel in Babylon, should end with her railing against   30 the vice of tobacco; and, second, that it has not a word to say about King Philip, the leader of the Indians who captured her and mastermind of the campaign that devastated the white population of the English colonies. The fact that Rowlandson has just been introduced to the chief of chiefs makes hardly any impression on her at all. What excites her is a moral issue which was being hotly debated in the seventeenth century: to smoke or not to smoke (Puritans frowned on it, apparently, because it wasted time and presented a fire hazard). What seem to us the peculiar emphases in Rowlandson's relation are not the result of her having *screened out* evidence she couldn't handle, but of her way of constructing the world. She saw what her seventeenth-century English Separatist background made visible. It is when one realizes that the biases of twen-tieth-century historians like Vaughan or Axtell cannot be corrected for simply by consulting the primary materials, since the primary materials are constructed according to *their* authors' biases, that one begins to envy Miller his vision at Matadi. Not for what he didn't see — the Indian and the black — but for his epistemological confidence.

Since captivity narratives made a poor source of evidence for the nature of European-Indian relations in early New England because they were so relentlessly pietistic, my hope was that a better source of evi-dence might be writings designed simply to tell Englishmen what the American natives were like. These authors could be presumed to be less severely biased, since they hadn't seen their loved ones killed by Indians or been made to endure the hardships of captivity, and because they weren't writing propaganda calculated to prove that God had delivered his chosen people from the hands of Satan's emissaries.   31

The problem was that these texts were written with aims no less specific than those of the captivity narratives, though the aims were of a different sort. Here is a passage from William Wood's *New England's Prospect*, published in London in 1634.   32

> To enter into a serious discourse concerning the natural conditions of these Indians might procure admiration from the people of any civilized nations, in regard of their civility and good natures. . . . These Indians are of affable, courteous and well disposed natures, ready to communicate the best of their wealth to the mutual good of one another; . . . so . . . per-spicuous is their love . . . that they are as willing to part with a mite in poverty as treasure in plenty. . . . If it were possible to recount the courte-sies they have showed the English, since their first arrival in those parts, it would not only steady belief, that they are a loving people, but also win the love of those that never saw them, and wipe off that needless fear that is too deeply rooted in the conceits of many who think them envious and of such rancorous and inhumane dispositions, that they will one day make an end of their English inmates.

However, in a pamphlet published twenty-one years earlier, Alex-ander Whitaker of Virginia has this to say of the natives: 33

> These naked slaves . . . serve the divell for feare, after a most base manner, sacrificing sometimes (as I have heere heard) their own Children to him. . . . They live naked in bodie, as if their shame of their sinne deserved no

covering: Their names are as naked as their bodie: They esteem it a virtue to lie, deceive and steale as their master the divell teacheth to them.

According to Robert Berkhofer in *The White Man's Indian*, these 34 divergent reports can be explained by looking at the authors' motives. A favorable report like Wood's, intended to encourage new emigrants to America, naturally represented Indians as loving and courteous, civilized and generous, in order to allay the fears of prospective colonists. Whitaker, on the other hand, a minister who wishes to convince his readers that the Indians are in need of conversion, paints them as benighted agents of the devil. Berkhofer's commentary constantly implies that white men were to blame for having represented the Indians in the image of their own desires and needs. But the evidence supplied by Rowlandson's narrative, and by the accounts left by early reporters such as Wood and Whitaker, suggests something rather different. Though it is probably true that in certain cases Europeans did consciously tamper with the evidence, in most cases there is no reason to suppose that they did not record faithfully what they saw. And what they saw was not an illusion, was not determined by selfish motives in any narrow sense, but was there by virtue of a *way* of seeing which they could no more consciously manipulate than they could choose not to have been born. At this point, it seemed to me, the ethnocentric bias of the firsthand observers invited an investigation of the cultural situation they spoke from. Karen Kupperman's *Settling with the Indians* (1980) supplied just such an analysis.

Kupperman argues that Englishmen inevitably looked at Indians in 35 exactly the same way that they looked at other Englishmen. For instance, if they looked down on Indians and saw them as people to be exploited, it was not because of racial prejudice or antique notions about savagery, it was because they looked down on ordinary English men and women and saw them as subjects for exploitation as well. According to Kupperman, what concerned these writers most when they described the Indians were the insignia of social class, of rank, and of prestige. Indian faces are virtually never described in the earliest accounts, but clothes and hairstyles, tattoos and jewelry, posture and skin color are. "Early modern Englishmen believed that people can create their own identity, and that therefore one communicates to the world through signals such as dress and other forms of decoration who one is, what group or category one belongs to.

Kupperman's book marks a watershed in writings on European-Indian 36 relations, for it reverses the strategy employed by Martin two years before. Whereas Martin had performed an ethnographic analysis of Indian cosmology in order to explain, from within, the Indians' motives for engaging in the fur trade, Kupperman performs an ethnographic study of seventeenth-century England in order to explain, from within, what motivated Englishmen's behavior. The sympathy and understanding that Martin, Axtell, and others extend to the Indians are extended in Kupperman's work to the English themselves. Rather than giving an account of "what happened" between Indians and Europeans, like Martin, she reconstructs the worldview that gave the experience of one group its content. With her study, scholarship on European-Indian relations comes full circle.

It may well seem to you at this point that, given the tremendous 37 variation among the historical accounts, I had no choice but to end in relativism. If the experience of encountering conflicting versions of the "same" events suggests anything certain it is that the attitude a historian takes up in relation to a given event, the way in which he or she judges and even describes "it" — and the "it" has to go in quotation marks because, depending on the perspective, that event either did or did not occur — this stance, these judgments and descriptions are a function of the historian's position in relation to the subject. Miller, standing on the banks of the Congo, couldn't see the black men he was supervising because of his background, his assumptions, values, experiences, goals. Jennings, intent on exposing the distortions introduced into the historical record by Vaughan and his predecessors stretching all the way back to Winthrop, couldn't see that Winthrop and his peers were not racists but only Englishmen who looked at other cultures in the way their own culture had taught them to see one another. The historian can never escape the limitations of his or her own position in history and so inevitably gives an account that is an extension of the circumstances from which it springs. But it seems to me that when one is confronted with this particular succession of stories, cultural and historical relativism is not a position that one can comfortably assume. The phenomena to which these histories testify — conquest, massacre, and genocide, on the one hand; torture, slavery, and murder on the other — cry out for judgment. When faced with claims and counterclaims of this magnitude one feels obligated to reach an understanding of what actually did occur. The dilemma posed by the study of European-Indian relations in early America is that the highly charged nature of the materials demands a moral decisiveness which the succession of conflicting accounts effectively precludes. That is the dilemma I found myself in at the end of this course of reading, and which I eventually came to resolve as follows.

After a while it began to seem to me that there was something wrong 38 with the way I had formulated the problem. The statement that the materials on European-Indian relations were so highly charged that they demanded moral judgment, but that the judgment couldn't be made be-cause all possible descriptions of what happened were biased, seemed to contain an internal contradiction. The statement implied that in order to make a moral judgment about something, you have to know something else first — namely, the facts of the case you're being called upon to judge. My complaint was that their perspectival nature would disqualify any facts I might encounter and that therefore I couldn't judge. But to say as I did that the materials I had read were "highly charged" and therefore demanded judgment suggests both that I was reacting to some-thing real — to some facts — *and* that I had judged them. Perhaps I wasn't so much in the lurch morally or epistemologically as I had thought. If you — or I — react with horror to the story of the girl captured and enslaved by Comanches who touched a firebrand to her nose every time they wanted to wake her up, it's because we read this as a story about cruelty and suffering, and not as a story about the conventions of prisoner exchange or the economics of Comanche life. The *seeing* of the story as a cause for alarm rather than as a droll anecdote or a piece of curious information is evidence of values we already hold, of judgments already made, of facts already perceived as facts.

My problem presupposed that I couldn't judge because I didn't know **39** what the facts were. All I had, or could have, was a series of different perspectives, and so nothing that would count as an authoritative source on which moral judgments could be based. But, as I have just shown, I did judge, and that is because, as I now think, I did have some facts. I seemed to accept as facts that ninety percent of the native American population of New England died after the first hundred years of contact, that tribes in eastern Canada and the northeastern United States had a compact with the game they killed, that Comanches had subjected a captive girl to casual cruelty, that King Philip smoked a pipe, and so on. It was only where different versions of the same event came into conflict that I doubted the text was a record of something real. And even then, there was no question about certain major catastrophes. I believed that four hundred Pequots were killed near Saybrook, that Winthrop was the Governor of the Massachusetts Bay Colony when it happened, and so on. My sense that certain events, such as the Pequot War, did occur in no way reflected the indecisiveness that overtook me when I tried to choose among the various historical versions. In fact, the need I felt to make up my mind was impelled by the conviction that certain things *had* happened that shouldn't have happened. Hence it was never the case that "what happened" was completely unknowable or unavailable. It's rather that in the process of reading so many different approaches to the same phenomenon I became aware of the difference in the attitudes that informed these approaches. This awareness of the interests motivating each version cast suspicion over everything, in retrospect, and I ended by claiming that there was nothing I could know. This, I now see, was never really the case. But how did it happen?

Someone else, confronted with the same materials, could have de- **40** cided that one of these historical accounts was correct. Still another person might have decided that more evidence was needed in order to decide among them. Why did I conclude that none of the accounts was accurate because they were all produced from some particular angle of vision? Presumably there was something in my background that enabled me to see the problem in this way. That something, very likely, was post-structuralist theory. I let my discovery that Vaughan was a product of the fifties, Jennings of the sixties, Rowlandson of a Puritan worldview, and so on lead me to the conclusion that all facts are theory dependent because that conclusion was already a thinkable one for me. My inability to come up with a true account was not the product of being situated nowhere; it was the product of certitude that existed *somewhere else,* namely, in contemporary literary theory. Hence, the level at which my indecision came into play was a function of particular beliefs I held. I was never in a position of epistemological indeterminacy, I was never *en* *abyme.* The idea that all accounts are perspectival seemed to give me a superior standpoint from which to view all the versions of "what happened," and to regard with sympathetic condescension any person so old-fashioned and benighted as to believe that there really was some way of arriving at the truth. But this skeptical standpoint was just as firm as any other. The fact that it was also seriously disabling — it prevented me from coming to any conclusion about what I had read — did not render it any less definite.

At this point something is beginning to show itself that has up to **41** now been hidden. The notion that all facts are only facts within a perspective has the effect of emptying statements of their content. Once I had Miller and Vaughan and Jennings, Martin and Hudson, Axtell and Heard, Rowlandson and Wood and Whitaker, and Kupperman; I had Europeans and Indians, ships and canoes, wigwams and log cabins, bows and arrows and muskets, wigs and tattoos, whisky and corn, rivers and forts, treaties and battles, fire and blood — and then suddenly all I had was a metastatement about perspectives. The effect of bringing perspectivism to bear on history was to wipe out completely the subject matter of history. And it follows that bringing perspectivism to bear in this way on any subject matter would have a similar effect; everything is wiped out and you are left with nothing but a single idea — perspectivism itself.

But — and it is a crucial but — all this is true only if you believe **42** that there is an alternative. As long as you think that there are or should be facts that exist outside of any perspective, then the notion that facts are perspectival will have this disappearing effect on whatever it touches. But if you are convinced that the alternative does not exist, that there really are no facts except as they are embedded in some particular way of seeing the world, then the argument that a set of facts derives from some particular worldview is no longer an argument against that set of facts. If all facts share this characteristic, to say that any one fact is perspectival doesn't change its factual nature in the slightest. It merely reiterates it.

This doesn't mean that you have to accept just anybody's facts. You **43** can show that what someone else asserts to be a fact is false. But it does mean that you can't argue that someone else's facts are not facts *because they are only the product of a perspective,* since this will be true of the facts that you perceive as well. What this means then is that arguments about "what happened" have to proceed much as they did before post-structuralism broke in with all its talk about language-based reality and culturally produced knowledge. Reasons must be given, evidence adduced, authorities cited, analogies drawn. Being aware that all facts are motivated, believing that people are always operating inside some particular interpretive framework or other is a pertinent argument when what is under discussion is the way beliefs are grounded. But it doesn't give one any leverage on the facts of a particular case.

What this means for the problem I've been addressing is that I must **44** piece together the story of European-Indian relations as best I can, believing this version up to a point, that version not at all, another almost entirely, according to what seems reasonable and plausible, given every-thing else that I know. And this, as I've shown, is what I was already doing in the back of my mind without realizing it, because there was nothing else I *could* do. If the accounts don't fit together neatly, that is not a reason for rejecting them all in favor of a metadiscourse about epistemology; on the contrary, one encounters contradictory facts and divergent points of view in practically every phase of life, from deciding whom to marry to choosing the right brand of cat food, and one decides as best one can given the evidence available. It is only the nature of the academic situation which makes it appear that one can linger on the threshold of decision in the name of an epistemological principle. What has really happened in such a case is that the subject of debate has changed from the question of what happened in a particular instance to the question of how knowledge is arrived at. The absence of pressure to decide what happened creates the possibility for this change of venue.

The change of venue, however, is itself an action taken. In diverting 45 attention from the original problem and placing it where Miller did, on "the mind of man," it once again ignores what happened and still is happening to American Indians. The moral problem that confronts me now is not that I can never have any facts to go on, but that the work I do is not directed toward solving the kinds of problems that studying the history of European-Indian relations has awakened me to.

CHAPTER 3

Classifying

General Considerations

To classify is to sort into categories. "Is it animal, vegetable, or mineral?" goes one of our most comprehensive — though not often useful — classification systems. Classifying occurs all the time: when we call one person a friend and another an acquaintance, when we describe one movie as realistic and another as fantasy, when we refer to our hometowns as rural, suburban, or urban. In a sense, all words are categories, grouping particular experiences or ideas in general terms that we can differentiate from other general terms.

In academic situations we are constantly exposed to categories. Only recently you may have found yourself categorized as a freshman, a high school graduate, a commuter, a math major, or a minority student. The English class for which you are reading this paragraph is itself part of a system of categories: there are broad categories of subject areas (humanities, for instance), of disciplines (sociology), of specializations (chemical engineering). Particular courses are regarded as categories ("The Eighteenth Century"), and often they organize their material in further categories (poetry, fiction, drama). Textbooks, too, are often organized as classifications, and so are the chapters within textbooks. And you'll find many college lectures organized by category — they are the ones for which it's possible to take neatly outlined notes.

Thinking critically in academic situations means being willing to evaluate and even resist other people's categories. Sometimes it also means formulating categories of your own. To be honest, you could probably go through an entire collegiate career without seriously reexamining or challenging the categories imposed upon you. The question to ask yourself is, why would you want to be so passive? As a student you will frequently find yourself on the receiving end of other people's categories, and it's crucial to recognize that these categories are not statements of fact but acts of interpretation.

As an experiment, take a few moments now to create a classification system. The topic: remembering. Try brainstorming on this topic for a while, coming up with different kinds of memories that you've had or different ways you seem to remember past events. The more varied the better. Then try sorting your examples into categories. Think some more to see if you can extend or subdivide the categories. What kinds of remembering do you say there are?

Here is how the authors of a psychology textbook have classified the subject of remembering. How does their treatment compare with yours?

All learning implies retaining, for if nothing were left over from previous experience, nothing would be learned. We think and reason largely with remembered facts; the very continuity of our self-perceptions depends upon the continuity of our memories. We are able to deal with the concept of time as no other animal can, relating the present to the past and making predictions about the future, because of the strength, flexibility, and availability of our memories. 1

One way of remembering is to recollect or *redintegrate* an event and the circumstances surrounding it, as when you remember going with a date to your first dance. The word *recollect* is from ordinary vocabulary; *redintegrate* is a technical word meaning to reintegrate or to reestablish an earlier experience on the basis of partial cues. For example, you redintegrate that first dance only if something "reminds" you of it. The stimuli to redintegration are in a literal sense souvenirs, remembrances or reminders of a total, personal experience that occurred at a given time in the past. In your recollection you conjure up the band playing the popular songs of that time, the cool breeze as you stepped outside, perhaps your aching feet when you finally got home. Such redintegrative memories are often quite detailed and complete, but they need not be. They are distinguished from other kinds of remembering because they reconstruct a past occasion from your personal autobiography, with its setting in time and place. 2

Many signs of earlier experience lack this reconstruction of the past. For example, you may *recall* a poem by reciting it, even if you do not remember the circumstances under which you learned it. You can remember how to ride a bicycle or sing a song without any direct reference to the past. Remembering through recall is easier to measure than the redintegration of earlier experiences, and it is the kind usually studied in the laboratory. 3

Another kind of remembering is the indication of memory merely by **4** *recognizing* someone or something as familiar. "That tune is familiar. What is it?" "Someone I used to know had a copy of that picture on the wall, but I can't place it now." Finally, you may show that you once learned something by now *relearning* it more rapidly than you could if there were no retention of the earlier learning.

Redintegration, recall, recognition, and relearning all give evidence **5** of memory, but each of these terms implies a different aspect of remembering.

— Ernest R. Hilgard, Richard C. Atkinson, and
Rita L. Atkinson, *Introduction to Psychology,* 5th ed.

Do you find the psychologists' system thorough and persuasive? Does it account for all the examples you came up with earlier? Do you like your own classification better?

It's important to learn to think critically about categories. That implies being able to look at categories not as natural parts of the world but as human constructions, groupings and divisions created by some people to shape and influence the thinking of others. Sometimes, particularly when we are encountering a subject for the first time, we seem to have little choice but to accept material according to the categories in which we receive it. We have no critical distance, no awareness of other possible ways to organize the information. By devising your own classification of remembering before reading the one by Hilgard, Atkinson, and Atkinson, you may have achieved some such distance. Let us offer a few further strategies. They take the form of questions with which to probe classifications you encounter.

First, you can ask **on what basis the categories are being differentiated.** Effective categories have some unifying underlying principle to make the system coherent. In the excerpt from the psychology textbook, the kinds of remembering are distinguished according to the completeness with which a person retains past experience. When you thought about this topic, you may have used a basic principle other than degree of retention. For instance, you may have thought of your own memories in emotional terms, devising categories such as "intensely pleasing," "mildly pleasing," "neutral," "unpleasant," and "intensely unpleasant." Memories grouped at opposite, incompatible ends of your system might well be grouped within a single category of the psychologists' system because the memories happen to be remembered in a full, redintegrated way. That doesn't mean your system of categories isn't effective or meaningful, just that the two systems are structured on different underlying principles.

Another question to help you think critically is to ask **whether the categories are meant to be absolute or only approximate.** Are they meant to neatly and definitively divide all possibilities into specific categories, or is there deliberately some overlap, imprecision, or flexibility in the system? Many classifications, particularly those of the either/or type, are meant to be absolute: living or nonliving, moving or at rest, accepted or rejected, under budget or over budget. Similarly, just as playing cards are absolutely either spades, clubs, hearts, or diamonds, votes in an American presidential election can be categorized absolutely as Democrat, Republican, or other. Sometimes, however, even the most clear-cut system does not work as absolutely as we might think. Neither living nor nonliving, for example, quite fits the viruses, which some biologists think of as alive and others as not.

Many classification systems are not intended to provide absolute categories. Differences among categories are matters of emphasis and degree. The psychologists' classification of remembering is an example of such a system. One category shades into another along a continuum of possibilities. A redintegrated memory wouldn't be confused with relearning, but there could be instances where it would be hard to say if a particular memory is an example of redintegration or recall. That blurring of the edges of categories wouldn't bother the authors, for they do not intend that their classification allow us to place every example of remembering precisely within a category; they merely want their system to reflect how varied remembering can be. Understanding how rigid or flexible a system of categories is meant to be can put us in a good position to judge how well it works.

Another question to ask is **whether the classification system is meant to be all-inclusive.** Is it meant to include all possible instances? Many classifications do not attempt inclusiveness. A chapter of a biology textbook beginning with the sentence "There are three major types of plant hormones that have been discovered thus far" admits with the words *major* and *thus far* that other categories may exist. So too when a lecturer in a political science course begins, "Let's look today at several types of parliamentary government," she implies that there are other types the class won't be hearing about. Some classifications, by contrast, are meant to be inclusive. For example, literature anthologies are sometimes organized into the categories poetry, drama, fiction, and nonfiction prose. This system covers all the literary possibilities, partly because nonfiction prose is a catch-all category that can include essays, letters, newspaper articles, diaries, and so on. In biology the categories called kingdoms were devised to be such a system, but the system has had to change as new evidence has complicated the picture. In the eighteenth century it seemed perfectly reasonable to divide living things into plants and animals, but the discovery of the microscope made it clear that some microorganisms could fit either category, and other microorganisms — bacteria — had a cellular structure radically different from that of both plants and animals. Today the prevailing system of classification uses five categories: plants, animals, fungi, bacteria, and protists. Not all biologists accept this system, however, partly because it too may not be inclusive.

A classification presented as inclusive makes a stronger claim than one presented as merely helpful or interesting. It's a good mental habit to test classification systems that make strong claims by inventing examples of your own. Does the system really work as a method of dividing up the territory? See if you can come up with problem cases, examples that the existing categories are unable to handle. Take a look back at the psychologists' clas-sification of remembering, and then look again at your own. Did you think of any examples that their system couldn't comfortably handle? Can you think of any now? Do you think the authors intend that their system be complete? Where would they account for the remembering of a troubling image from a nightmare? What about the experience of misremembering? The experience of *déjà-vu?* What about the kind of remembering that we do when we piece together a story for the first time — say, when someone asks you which events in your life influenced you to come to college? Do any of these types of remembering cause wrinkles in the system? Perhaps some do not qualify as memories, and perhaps others can fit somewhere along the continuum. What do you think? Is theirs a successfully inclusive system?

Perhaps the most helpful critical question of all is this one: **Of what use is the classification?** What does it enable us to do or see? What is gained by using it? If we were to examine the textbook that includes the psychologists' classification, we would see that the authors have a purpose beyond impressing us with their thoroughness. The chapter that follows their introduction on remembering is mostly about the research that has been done on the type of remembering they label recall. By setting the research in the context of all kinds of remembering, they let us see both the nature of the research and its limitations. No one yet knows enough about the workings of the mind to study recollection and redintegration in a precise way, but recall is largely a measurable ability. Experiments can be constructed and variables introduced. Other psychologists, the authors will go on to show, have learned a good deal about this kind of remembering. Their classification system allows us to look at that knowledge against a wider backdrop, the more complex context provided by their discussion of the other types of remembering.

Besides being useful in its own terms, classification complements most of the other academic strategies we present in this book. As we stressed in Chapter 1, classifying is one of the means by which we can arrive at definitions. When we can begin to classify abstract terms such as *political authority, epics,* or *phosphates* into more specific kinds of political authority, epics, and phos-phates, we begin to grasp a surer sense of the larger terms themselves. Classification can also be useful in summarizing. By noticing that a particular article is organized into clear subdivisions, for example, we can make effective decisions about how to summarize it — perhaps by giving each section a roughly equivalent emphasis or perhaps by summarizing each section in a parallel sentence. Classification also aids analysis, often by suggesting an appropriate framework from which to begin analyzing. Asked to analyze an essay by the political columnist George Will, we might begin by recognizing that Will writes from a conservative point of view. The "conservative" cat-egory alerts us to features of his essay that we might not have noticed otherwise (but it also might close our eyes to other features — we need to be provisional and flexible in trying out analytical categories). Classifying can also aid argument. Categorizing an opposing point of view, for example, is often a good way to stress its limitations.

Above all, classification enables comparison. Sometimes the comparisons are across categories. Having established that Cuba's economic system is Communist and Japan's capitalist, a writer can go on to look at how the two economic systems control the way the two countries conduct international trade. At other times the comparisons are within categories. Having decided that both cacti and fir trees are temperature-adapted, a naturalist can go on to compare how adaptations to extreme heat in the cactus compare with adaptations to extreme cold in the fir tree. Having categorized both Edgar Allan Poe and Stephen King as horror writers, a student could go on to compare the qualities of horror in the two writers' work.

The classification assignments in this chapter are of two types. One type asks you to take someone else's classification system and thoughtfully apply it. The other asks you to generate a classification system of your own. In your undergraduate courses, you'll find the first type of assignment much more frequent than the second. You'll also find that applying someone else's categories isn't difficult when the system itself is easy to grasp. But when the system is complex, such assignments put pressure on your abilities to read, interpret, and explain. The second type of assignment, creating categories, gives you a chance to assert your intellectual independence. In many courses, such assignments never appear. The construction of categories seldom is required of you; rather, it's an opportunity to be seized. In the two following cases, we offer an example of each type of assignment.

Cases

APPLYING CATEGORIES: A CASE FROM SOCIOLOGY

Imagine that for a sociology course you are asked to read an article by Talcott Parsons entitled "Social Systems." In one section of the article Parsons offers a classification of social organizations. Later in the term you are asked to write a short essay demonstrating your understanding of Parsons's system of categories.

Taken out of its full context, here is the most relevant portion of Parsons's article, the section in which he offers his classification of social organizations.

CLASSIFICATION OF TYPES OF ORGANIZATION

Organizations are of course always part of a larger social structure   1
of the society in which they occur. There is necessarily a certain variability among organizations which is a function of this wider societal matrix; an American organization is never quite like a British one even though they are nearly cognate in function. Discounting this type of variability, however, organizations may in the first instance be classified in terms of the *type of goal or function* about which they are organized. . . .

Seen in these terms the principal broad types of organization are: 2

1. *Organizations oriented to economic production.* The type case in   3
this category is the business firm. Production should be understood in
the full economic sense as "adding value"; it is by no means confined to
physical production, e.g., manufacturing. It has been emphasized several
times that every organization contributes in some way to every primary
function (if it is well integrated in the society); hence we can speak only
of economic *primacy,* never of an organization as being exclusively economic. This applies also to the other categories.

2. *Organizations oriented to political goals,* that is, to the attainment   4
of valued goals and to the generation and allocation of power in the society.
This category includes most organs of government, but in a society like
ours, various other organizations are involved. The allocation of purchasing power through credit creation is an exercise of power in this
sense; hence a good part of the banking system should be treated as
residing in primarily political organizations. More generally, it seems
legitimate to speak of incorporation as an allocation of power in a political
sense; hence the corporate aspect of formal organizations generally is a
political aspect.

3. *Integrative organizations.* These are organizations which on the   5
societal level contribute primarily to efficiency, not effectiveness. They
concern the adjustment of conflicts and the direction of motivation to the
fulfillment of institutionalized expectations. A substantial part of the functions of the courts and of the legal profession should be classed here.
Political parties, whose function is the mobilization of support for those
responsible for government operations, belong in this category, and, to
a certain extent, "interest groups" belong here, too. Finally, those organizations that are primarily mechanisms of social control in the narrower
sense, for example hospitals, are mainly integrative.

4. *Pattern-maintenance organizations.* The principal cases centering   6
here are those with primarily "cultural," "educational," and "expressive"
functions. Perhaps the most clear-cut organizational examples are
churches and schools. (Pattern maintenance is not here conceived to
preclude creativity; hence research is included.) The arts so far as they
give rise to organization also belong here. Kinship groups are ordinarily
not primarily organizations in our technical sense, but in a society so
highly differentiated as our own the nuclear family approaches more
closely the characteristics of an organization than in other societies. As
such it clearly belongs in the pattern-maintenance category.

Here is a possible assignment based on the reading.

Explain Talcott Parsons's classification of social organizations and
show how he would apply it to the following organizations.

the Republican Party

the Postal Service

a labor union

a professional athletic team
a college athletic team
a public high school
a private high school
a poker club
a street gang
a police department
the John Birch Society
an alumni organization
the American Medical Association (AMA)
the Federal Reserve Bank
the Environmental Protection Agency (EPA)
a mental institution
an insurance company
a health maintenance organization (HMO)

This assignment stretches a student's ability to make sense of Parsons, a notoriously difficult writer. A sociology teacher would probably reward students simply for demonstrating that they have done the reading thoughtfully, whether or not they sorted out the organizations exactly as Parsons would.

With a difficult piece of reading like this one, it's often a good idea to try putting into your own words what you think you understand, while also admitting, at least to yourself, what you don't. The act of writing out both sets of ideas may help you clarify them. Let's follow an imaginary student trying this strategy. As he wrestles his way through paraphrasing the categories, he makes points and raises questions, some of which will find their way into his eventual essay.

```
     Organizations oriented to economic production.  No
problem with this one.  Parsons is talking about busi-
nesses.  Not just businesses that "add value" by pro-
ducing things, but businesses that provide services
too.  The emphasis is on organizations that add some-
thing of value to the economy.
     Organizations oriented to political goals.  This
one sounds straightforward, but I have trouble with
it.  I think I understand what Parsons means by "the
generation and allocation of power," but I don't see
what he means by saying these organizations are ori-
ented toward "the attainment of valued goals."  How is
```

that different from the economic category? I'm also
surprised by his bank example. I think of banks as
businesses, but he thinks of them as political. But
maybe I see what he means. Banks decide who gets how
much and when. They allocate. They pull the strings
that determine who gets what.

Integrative organizations. These seem to be organizations that help other organizations, and society
as a whole, function smoothly. I don't get what he
means by saying they're "efficient, but not effective"
though. To integrate means to put together in a well-
coordinated way, so integrative organizations coordinate things, perhaps without adding any value besides
coordination. The example of lawyers and the legal
system bothered me at first, until I thought of lawyers
as go-betweens. Lawyers are always between opposing
interests. By determining outcomes of these conflicts,
lawyers help the system as a whole to operate.

Pattern-maintenance organizations. These are organizations with educational and cultural purposes. I
think these look distinct enough. Except that I don't
understand the label itself. Why "pattern maintenance"?
I guess the emphasis is on how these organizations preserve a society's status quo through education and culture. People in the PTA tend to perpetuate the school
system as it is. People in an Italian-American Society
tend to build solidarity that can be passed down among
Italian-Americans. I see how churches are a particularly clear example, preserving particular religious
values from generation to generation.

Having worked through the categories in this way, our student is better
prepared to use the categories to think about the organizations in the assignment question. Let's follow this student through the next stage of his
thinking as he tries to figure out how to group the examples themselves. In
his notes he probes — developing details, raising questions, trying out more
than one category per organization. Here's a sampling of his notes.

Republican Party. Integrative. Parsons says
so. Strange, though. Why aren't political parties
"political"? Maybe because they simply serve as pipe-
lines for politicians. It's only the elected officials
who exercise power; the parties only provide the "raw
material" in a fairly efficient way.

Postal Service. Integrative. It helps keep other
organizations running, especially businesses, but also
the government. Lately it has become privately operated, a sort of corporation, but I still don't think it
fits the business category.

Professional athletic team. Pattern maintenance? I think of teams as part of culture. But pro
sports are also businesses, maybe mainly businesses. I
see the next category is "college athletic teams." I
suppose I'm expected to place them in different categories. Well, the more I think about it, the stronger
the business angle seems. Pro teams certainly add
value--consumers pay plenty.

A public high school. There's another pairing
here, with private high school. I suppose it depends
on which high schools we have in mind. My high school
did a good job. I suppose Parsons sees it as pattern
maintenance, but I see that it could be called integrative too. It starts the sorting out process for people's professional roles, their jobs. "Efficiently"?
That might be going too far. I'm pretty sure that Parsons would say that the main function of schools is to
pass on cultural values, to keep those patterns in
place.

Federal Reserve Bank. Clearly political. The
biggest bank of all. It controls how much goes where
and when.

Environmental Protection Agency. Another big
branch of government. It's supposed to protect the environment for us all and so could be called pattern
maintenance. But I think Parsons would call it political. From what I've heard of it lately, it hasn't done
all that much protecting anyway. The question of how
much gets protected and which polluters get leaned on
is very political.

Mental institution. Definitely pattern maintenance. It takes troublesome people off the streets--
though with all the homeless that may also be a political question. Helps keep the rest of us in line,
fulfilling our social functions. Wait a minute, maybe
that makes it "integrative." I'm starting to lose my
grip on these categories again.

Insurance company. I wish I knew more about how
these work. They're businesses and in some sense "add
value," but they're also like banks in their power to
throw money around. They could also be seen as integrative like the lawyers. Maybe I'll have to give over
a section of my essay to the organizations that do not
seem to fall within a single function.

HMO. These are like hospitals, which Parsons
calls integrative. This will give me a chance to contrast the AMA. I think I'm starting to see what Parsons means by efficient, rather than effective. HMOs
seem a good way of getting people medical help quickly
and adequately. But they're not necessarily the most
effective or satisfying way.

This sort of note taking might have gone on mentally, without the writing.
But writing out these ideas gives the writer more opportunity to retain and
evaluate them. Notice that this student sometimes changes his mind or makes
a discovery in the act of writing a note. He also composes some sentences
and phrases that will find their way into the essay he ultimately writes.

As a next step, the student uses lists to sort the examples into Parsons's categories.

ECONOMIC	POLITICAL	INTEGRATIVE	PATTERN MAINTENANCE
Professional team	Labor union?	Rep. Party	College team
	AMA	Postal Service	Public school
	Federal Reserve	Labor union?	Private school?
	EPA	Private school?	Street gang?
		Police dept.	John Birch Soc.
		Mental instit.?	Alumni org.
Insurance Co.?	Insurance Co.?	Insurance Co.?	Mental instit.?
		HMO	

Notice that in sorting the organizations into lists, the writer has made liberal use of question marks to indicate placements he is particularly unsure about. His classifications are still provisional as he approaches the job of actually writing the essay. Although it's an advantage to know where an essay is going, there are also advantages in leaving room for more decisions and rethinking.

Looking over the number of uncertain placements and thinking about his uncertain interpretation of the categories themselves, this particular student faces a hard decision. Should he simply go for it, making the calls as best he sees them and leaving it at that? Or should he write the essay in a way that admits his hesitations about the placements? Before going further, he decides to ask himself some of the critical questions about classification schemes: Is this system meant to be absolute? Of what use is it? He quickly sees that Parsons doesn't mean it to be absolute. He decides that one of its uses is to help us become aware of the social organizations we take for granted and the various ways in which they influence our lives. Parsons also wants to suggest that some institutions are deceptive: They don't necessarily do what we think they do. The student decides that Parsons's system is deliberately an imprecise one and that Parsons intends the overlap between categories. He decides to stress a sentence in Parsons's entry on economic organizations: "Every organization contributes in some way to every primary function." That statement gives the student some leeway. He needs only to establish a "primary" function, and where he cannot see one, maybe he can say so. This decision enables the student to put his many hesitations to work for him.

The following is one of the later drafts of the student's essay in response to the assignment on pages 103–104. What do you think of it?

According to Talcott Parsons, our most important social organizations can be classified into four types. These types he calls "organizations oriented to economic production," "organizations oriented to political

goals," "integrative organizations," and "pattern-
maintenance organizations." By the economic type he
means businesses, organizations that exist because they
"add value," economic value, to the social system as a
whole. By the political type he means organizations
that exert power and determine who benefits from that
power. By integrative organizations he seems to mean
organizations that are concerned primarily neither with
economics nor with political power but with helping the
society as a whole, including the other organizations,
function smoothly. Finally, pattern-maintenance organizations have to do with preserving culture. They
function mainly to keep new members of society behaving
in the same general ways as the established members.
Parsons doesn't see his categories as mutually exclusive. Most complex organizations fulfill several functions, but he thinks it's worth seeing which goals are
most important to which organizations. Although I'm
not sure I can follow every turn in Parsons's argument,
I do think his system is a useful one for examining the
institutions that influence our lives, sometimes in
ways we don't realize.

Among the organizations I have been asked to classify, Parsons would find few that are oriented primarily for economic production. The insurance company is
one possibility, but I think it could as easily belong
to one of the other categories, and I'll discuss it
later. The purest example of an economic organization,
oddly enough, is a professional sports team. An economic function is to add value, not necessarily goods,
and a professional athletic team does that by providing
something for which people are willing to pay. We
could argue that professional teams are also pattern-
maintaining. Families pass down their Green Bay Packer
tickets from generation to generation, and people in
Chicago are always asking, "Do the Cubs have a chance

this year?" But I think that as organizations their
cultural function is dominated by their economic one.

Quite a few of the organizations on the list are
political in Parsons's terms, but not as many as we
might at first think. The Federal Reserve Bank is a
strong political force. When it makes credit easier or
harder to come by, its influence is felt by people all
over the country. Here we can see the difference between what Parsons calls political and what he calls
economic. The Federal Reserve, like other banks,
doesn't add value, it distributes value by "allocating"
it. That's power. Other governmental departments, including the Environmental Protection Agency, have the
same role. Even if in theory that agency's role is to
protect the entire public, in practice it protects some
more than others. During most of the 1980s that agency,
in a sense, allocated more power to businesses by not
enforcing much environmental legislation. Again, that's
politics. I'd include the American Medical Association
and the bigger labor unions on this list of power allo-
cators, though someone else might argue that they do
not directly exert power but only seek to influence
those who do. That's one of the main differences between Parsons's second and third categories. Political
institutions allocate power directly, whereas integrative organizations make it possible for power to be distributed efficiently.

Most of the organizations on the list can be seen
as mainly integrative or pattern-maintaining. The integrative ones include organizations like the Postal
Service and the police department, which help keep various other segments of society either running smoothly
or in check. An HMO is another good example of an integrative organization, and it illustrates what Parsons
means in saying that integrative organizations are efficient but not necessarily effective. People insist

on health care, and HMOs have developed as the most efficient way to get it to them, though that is not to
say that the medical care they offer is the best care.

The Republican Party, it's interesting to notice,
would also be classified by Parsons as integrative,
even though they think of themselves as political. By
calling political parties integrative, he seems to mean
that political parties themselves don't distribute
power, just juggle various of their members into position to get it if elected. This seems to me a somewhat
shaky point though. Aren't those preparing for power
also participating in power, and don't the elected politicians function also as party members?

Among the pattern-maintenance organizations Talcott Parsons would also place public and private
schools, alumni organizations, college athletic teams,
and (probably) mental institutions. All of these are
primarily involved in preserving the status quo, that
is, in keeping cultural arrangements essentially the
way they are from one year or one generation to the
next. This category is quite flexible, though, and
most of the organizations we place in it tend to tilt
toward one of the other functions. Thus college sports
are also businesses; public high schools have a major
integrative function (sorting students toward their
eventual social positions and roles); and mental institutions, besides maintaining cultural patterns, are
also integrative and, in some way, businesses. Certainly for families that send troublesome members to
them, they "add value," and the families pay highly
for it.

The greatest value of Parsons's system is that it
helps us to see that an organization fulfills several
functions and that sometimes its apparent functions are
not its most important. His classification, I want to
point out, works primarily for large, important insti-

tutions, ones that affect us all. Thus I don't think
the John Birch Society, which is primarily a cultural
nuisance, or poker clubs, which are mainly a way of
circulating money among the same men week after week,
are major organizations in any of the four senses. On
the other hand, something like an insurance company
seems so hard for me to understand that I suspect it
fulfills all the functions. It's a business because it
adds a value that people are willing to pay for. But
it's also political, in that where and how an insurance
company distributes its funds can make other things
happen or not happen. And insurance companies are integrative in the same way that the legal profession is
--they manage conflict between other groups. And the
insurance business does a lot to maintain at least the
impression of continuity, as the images of umbrellas
and fire hats seem to tell us. "You're in good hands
with Allstate." Some organizations' functions seem so
mixed that even Parsons might not want to try untan-
gling them.

CREATING CATEGORIES: A CASE FROM PUBLIC HEALTH

As the previous example has demonstrated, applying someone else's classification system can demand interpretation, judgment, and decision making.
These same abilities are called on when you develop categories on your own,
but more pressure is placed on inventing than receiving.

As an example of this second sort of classifying, imagine yourself in a
public health class that has stressed issues of public responsibility in national
health care. As a final assignment at the end of the course, you are asked
to classify the diseases on the following list. Some of the diseases you have
read about in the course; others you only vaguely know as names. Rather
than launching into lengthy research on the various diseases, you decide that
your first step is to look them all up in a scientific dictionary, hoping that an
effective way of grouping and dividing the diseases will occur to you. Do you
see any possible drawbacks to this strategy?

Here is the actual wording of the assignment, followed by a compilation of the diseases with short definitions taken from the scientific dictionary.

In light of the public health issues discussed in this course, develop a meaningful classification for the following diseases.

African sleeping sickness [MED] A disease of man confined to tropical Africa, caused by the protozoans *Trypanosoma gambiense* or *T. rhodesiense;* symptoms include local reaction at the site of the bite, fever, enlargement of adjacent lymph nodes, skin rash, edema, and during the late phase, somnolence and emaciation. Also known as African trypanosomiasis; maladie du sommeil; sleeping sickness.

Alzheimer's disease [MED] A type of presenile dementia associated with sclerosis of the cerebral cortex.

arteriolosclerosis [MED] Thickening of the lining of arterioles, usually due to hyalinization or fibromuscular hyperplasia.

cancer [MED] Any malignant neoplasm, including carcinoma and sarcoma.

cirrhosis [MED] A progressive, inflammatory disease of the liver characterized by a real or apparent increase in the proportion of hepatic connective tissue.

cystic fibrosis [MED] A hereditary disease of the pancreas transmitted as an autosomal recessive; involves obstructive lesions, atrophy, and fibrosis of the pancreas and lungs, and the production of mucus of high viscosity. Also known as mucoviscidosis.

diabetes [MED] Any of various abnormal conditions characterized by excessive urinary output, thirst, and hunger; usually refers to diabetes mellitus.

elephantiasis [MED] A parasitic disease of man caused by the filarial nematode *Wuchereria bancrofti;* characterized by cutaneous and subcutaneous tissue enlargement due to lymphatic obstruction.

gonorrhea [MED] A bacterial infection of man caused by the gonococcus (*Neisseria gonorrhoeae*) which invades the mucous membrane of the urogenital tract.

kwashiorkor [MED] A nutritional deficiency disease in infants and young children, mainly in the tropics, caused primarily by a diet low in proteins and rich in carbohydrates. Also known as nutritional dystrophy.

leukemia [MED] Any of several diseases of the hemopoietic system characterized by uncontrolled leukocyte proliferation. Also known as leukocythemia.

malaria [MED] A group of human febrile diseases with a chronic relapsing course caused by hemosporidian blood parasites of the genus *Plasmodium,* transmitted by the bite of the *Anopheles* mosquito.

multiple sclerosis [MED] A degenerative disease of the nervous system of unknown cause in which there is demyelination followed by gliosis.

parkinsonism [MED] A clinical state characterized by tremor at a rate of three to eight tremors per second, with "pill-rolling" movements of the thumb common, muscular rigidity, dyskinesia, hypokinesia, and reduction in number of spontaneous and autonomic movements; produces a masked facies, disturbances of posture, gait, balance, speech, swallowing, and muscular strength. Also known as paralysis agitans; Parkinson's disease.

pertussis [MED] An infectious inflammatory bacterial disease of the air passages, caused by *Hemophilus pertussis* and characterized by explosive coughing ending in a whooping inspiration. Also known as whooping cough.

plague [MED] An infectious bacterial disease of rodents and humans caused by *Pasteurella pestis,* transmitted to humans by the bite of an infected flea (*Xenopsylla cheopis*) or by inhalation. Also known as black death; bubonic plague.

poliomyelitis [MED] An acute infectious viral disease which in its most serious form involves the central nervous system and, by destruction of motor neurons in the spinal cord, produces flaccid paralysis. Also known as Heine-Medin disease; infantile paralysis.

rickets [MED] A disorder of calcium and phosphorus metabolism affecting bony structures, due to vitamin D deficiency.

rubella [MED] An infectious virus disease of humans characterized by coldlike symptoms, fever, and transient, generalized pale-pink rash; its occurrence in early pregnancy is associated with congenital abnormalities. Also known as epidemic roseola; French measles; German measles; röteln.

scarlet fever [MED] An acute, contagious bacterial disease caused by *Streptococcus hemolyticus;* characterized by a papular, or rough, bright-red rash over the body, with fever, sore throat, headache, and vomiting occurring 2–3 days after contact with a carrier.

sickle-cell anemia [MED] A chronic, hereditary hemolytic and thrombotic disorder in which hypoxia causes the erythrocyte to assume a sickle shape; occurs in individuals homozygous for sickle-cell hemoglobin trait.

smallpox [MED] An acute, infectious, viral disease characterized by severe systemic involvement and a single crop of skin lesions which proceeds through macular, papular, vesicular, and pustular stages. Also known as variola.

syphilis [MED] An infectious disease caused by the spirochete *Treponema pallidum,* transmitted principally by sexual intercourse.

trichinosis [MED] Infection by the nematode *Trichinella spiralis* following ingestion of encysted larvae in raw or partially cooked pork; characterized by eosinophilia, nausea, fever, diarrhea, stiffness and painful swelling of muscles, and facial edema.

tuberculosis [MED] A chronic infectious disease of humans and animals primarily involving the lungs caused by the tubercle bacillus, *Mycobacterium tuberculosis,* or by *M. bovis.* Also known as consumption; phthisis.

— McGraw-Hill Dictionary of Scientific and Technical Terms

How might you try to classify these diseases? Try brainstorming a list of possible ideas on which you might base a classification. Write out your list.

One of the first ideas to occur to most people is to classify the diseases on the basis of their *causes*. Here's a sketch of categories you might establish after a quick run through the list.

PROTOZOA	NEMATODES	BACTERIA	PARASITES	VIRUSES	HEREDITY
African sleeping sickness	elephan- tiasis	gonorrhea plague scarlet fever syphilis tuberculosis pertussis	malaria	poliomy- elitis rubella smallpox	cystic fibrosis sickle-cell anemia

DIETARY DEFICIENCIES	DETERIORATION	INFLAMMATION	OTHER	UNKNOWN
kwashiorkor rickets	Alzheimer's disease arteriolosclerosis parkinsonism multiple sclerosis	cirrhosis	diabetes	cancer leukemia

This scheme helps a little; it gives some order to the list. But the categories seem unwieldy, don't they? Some seem imprecise; more important, there are simply too many categories. Because not enough diseases are combined, the categories do not seem to lend themselves well to generalizations. One strategy is to try to merge some of the causes in more general terms. A revised set of categories might look like this:

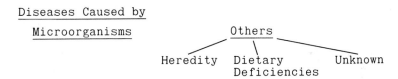

Or perhaps a two-way scheme like this one could handle various subcategories:

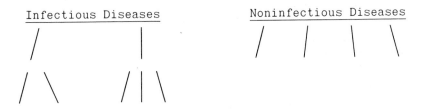

Do either of these possibilities seem more promising to you? Do you see other sorts of simpler groupings on the basis of cause?

Using some system like those we just devised, we can imagine beginning the essay:

Human diseases can be classified into three (or two, or four) main types....

Before launching into such an essay, however, we would do well to step back and reevaluate where we are heading. Notice how the classification of diseases has become an end in itself, divorced from the question and the issues of the public health class. We might want to reexamine our earlier decisions: for example, our silent assumption to regard all of these diseases as equals. Similarly, we might start to question our early decision to base our classification on our list of medical definitions. (Where did that decision lead us?) Look back at your own list of possible bases for classification. Do any of them seem more promising? Or any from the following list?

<u>Possible Bases for Classifying Diseases</u>

```
Causes
Treatments
Prevalence (which affect the most people?)
Severity
Organs & systems affected
Recurring or acute
Contagiousness
Future threat
Distribution
Expense
Research opportunities
Curability
```

To use one of these possible bases effectively, you would need to draw on whatever you had learned about the importance of the diseases in the public health course — and that is probably the intent of the question. With these considerations in mind, you might reshuffle your categories this way:

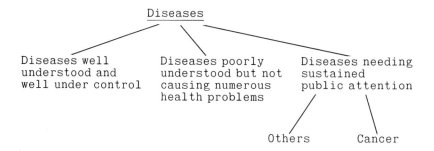

In what ways, given the question and the course, does this last classification seem to have advantages over the earlier ones? What might the opening paragraph of this student's essay look like? Without making yourself into a public health expert, but simply drawing on your general knowledge and a few of the facts from the definitions, try drafting that opening paragraph.

A readiness to think critically about classifying can enrich your academic writing. In most situations we are neither completely dependent on nor completely free of categories constructed by other people. In learning to recognize, apply, and modify the categories of other writers, we learn to participate in their ways of thinking. And in learning to develop categories of our own we begin to find ways to affect the thinking of others.

Assignments: First Passes

1. Applying Categories: Children's Scribbles

In the following passage, Howard Gardner summarizes some of the work of Rhoda Kellogg, who has extensively studied children's drawing and art. After reading this summary to establish meaningful categories, look over the examples of children's scribbles on page 118 (all were done by children two to three years old). Draft a short essay that classifies and comments on the drawings in relation to Kellogg's categories.

Let us run through the "progress of drawing" as described by Kellogg. 1 By the age of two or two and a half, children begin to realize (or "draw out") various forms that have been latent in their scribbles. . . . Circular scribbles smooth out to become recognizable, discrete circles; or, heightening in angularity, they become rectangular or triangular. Indeed, with each apparent repetition, the form becomes slightly clearer, more differentiated from other forms. . . . The first circles can hardly be differentiated from a series of wavy lines; subsequent forms are distinguished by their extreme oval or elliptical qualities. By the same token, early squares may resemble circles, or the more angular scribbles of the first year; but with succeeding practice the lines become increasingly parallel or perpendicular to one another, [and] angles are sharpened. . . .

It is usually only a matter of months before the child begins to 2 rehearse on the same page a number of these forms. Much as the older child practices letters of the alphabet or words in a primer, the three-year-old runs through his vocabulary of forms, making first a square, then a triangle, then a patch filled with color, then a series of dots, and so on, for many hours at a stretch. Virtual juxtaposition of forms occurs after a while and then, either gradually or suddenly, the child comes to superimpose the forms on one another. Kellogg refers to these superimposed patterns — the circle filled with lines, the triangle set in a circle, the square embedded in a triangle — as combines.

— Howard Gardner, *Artful Scribbles*

1.

2.

3.

4.

5.

6.

7.

8.

9.

2. Applying Categories: Creation Stories

Religious scholars Charles Doria and Harris Lenowitz have compiled and studied ancient stories describing the creation of the world. Some of these accounts are passed along in the Judeo-Christian Bible, and others have survived as independent texts. In putting together an anthology of these stories, Doria and Lenowitz faced the problem of how to organize their material. As a first step they created tne two-way classification system described in the following passage.

After reading the passage, try using this system to classify the creation stories that follow. If the categories seem to fit well, write a short essay explaining the authors' categories and illustrating how they apply. If you run into difficulties or come up with objections, explain those difficulties and objections in a short critical essay.

1   The main groupings for this anthology are *creation through word* and *elemental creation*. These seemed the ones our material suggested, not our willful imposition. We observed secondary categories of nationality, language, history, and so forth inside the two main groupings in hopes of making the typology as informative as possible. These categories seem to hold up about as well as any, and, more importantly, do least damage to the stories and even tell us something about the creation story itself, over and beyond narrative summaries of individual tales.

2   By *creation through word* we mean that situation where the god(s) makes any sound — a cough, chuckle, hiss, whatever they emit as separate from themselves — their first emanation. This sound seeks a response; finding it, worlds come into being and take shape, forming basically the name of the god(s). We chose to begin with this grouping not only because it is the one that all poets and storytellers mime in their essential activity, but because through word the first intelligible separation occurs between the maker and the made; cases in which the word serves as the demiurge, the spirit in service of the god's intelligence. It is interesting that Wisdom, appointed the job of creation in one Jewish tradition, says she issued from the mouth of El the Most High before proceeding to her assigned task.

3   Our second grouping we called *elemental creation* because we noticed how the very things of these worlds (they are usually fire, air, earth, and water) tend to make themselves in various ways and directions, sometimes with, sometimes without the help of gods. The elements themselves in these old stories are animate and divine, the powers of the sensate world. They survive, among other places, in the djinns of Islam. Only a later, more skeptical age stripped them of their numinous presence, converting them into the elements of the scientist's table.

— Charles Doria and Harris Lenowitz, *Origins: Creation Texts from the Ancient Mediterranean*

a. This story appears in the *Theogony* of Hesiod, a Greek poet of the eighth century B.C. The translation is by Dorothea Wender.

Chaos was first of all, but next appeared
Broad-bosomed Earth, sure standing-place for all

The gods who live on snowy Olympus' peak,
And misty Tartarus, in a recess   4
Of broad-pathed earth, and Love, most beautiful
Of all the deathless gods. He makes men weak,
He overpowers the clever mind, and tames
The spirit in the breasts of men and gods.   8
From Chaos came black Night and Erebos.
And Night in turn gave birth to Day and Space
Whom she conceived in love to Erebos.
And Earth bore starry Heaven, first, to be   12
An equal to herself, to cover her
All over, and to be a resting-place,
Always secure, for all the blessed gods.
Then she brought forth long hills, the lovely homes   16
Of goddesses, the Nymphs who live among
The mountain clefts. Then, without pleasant love,
She bore the barren sea with its swollen waves,
Pontus. And then she lay with Heaven, and bore   20
Deep-whirling Oceanus and Koios; then
Kreius, Iapetos, Hyperion,
Theia, Rhea, Themis, Mnemosyne,
Lovely Tethys, and Phoebe, golden-crowned.   24

b. Here is the familiar biblical version of creation as it appears in the King James Bible, Genesis 1:1–31.

1 In the beginning God created the heaven and the earth.

2 And the earth was without form, and void; and darkness *was* upon the face of the deep. And the Spirit of God moved upon the face of the waters.

3 And God said, Let there be light: and there was light.

4 And God saw the light, that *it was* good: and God divided the light from the darkness.

5 And God called the light Day, and the darkness he called Night. And the evening and the morning were the first day.

6 And God said, Let there be a firmament in the midst of the waters, and let it divide the waters from the waters.

7 And God made the firmament, and divided the waters which *were* under the firmament from the waters which *were* above the firmament: and it was so.

8 And God called the firmament Heaven. And the evening and the morning were the second day.

9 And God said, Let the waters under the heaven be gathered together unto one place, and let the dry *land* appear: and it was so.

10 And God called the dry *land* Earth; and the gathering together of the waters called he Seas: and God saw that *it was* good.

11 And God said, Let the earth bring forth grass, the herb yielding seed, *and* the fruit tree yielding fruit after his kind, whose seed *is* in itself, upon the earth: and it was so.

12 And the earth brought forth grass, *and* herb yielding seed after

his kind, and the tree yielding fruit, whose seed *was* in itself, after his kind: and God saw that *it was* good.

13 And the evening and the morning were the third day.

14 And God said, Let there be lights in the firmament of the heaven to divide the day from the night; and let them be for signs, and for seasons, and for days, and years:

15 And let them be for lights in the firmament of the heaven to give light upon the earth: and it was so.

16 And God made two great lights; the greater light to rule the day, and the lesser light to rule the night: *he made* the stars also.

17 And God set them in the firmament of the heaven to give light upon the earth.

18 And to rule over the day and over the night, and to divide the light from the darkness: and God saw that *it was* good.

19 And the evening and the morning were the fourth day.

20 And God said, Let the waters bring forth abundantly the moving creature that hath life, and fowl *that* may fly above the earth in the open firmament of heaven.

21 And God created great whales, and every living creature that moveth, which the waters brought forth abundantly, after their kind, and every winged fowl after his kind: and God saw that *it was* good.

22 And God blessed them, saying, Be fruitful, and multiply, and fill the waters in the seas, and let fowl multiply in the earth.

23 And the evening and the morning were the fifth day.

24 And God said, Let the earth bring forth the living creature after his kind, cattle, and creeping thing, and beast of the earth after his kind: and it was so.

25 And God made the beast of the earth after his kind, and cattle after their kind, and every thing that creepeth upon the earth after his kind: and God saw that *it was* good.

26 And God said, Let us make man in our image, after our likeness: and let them have dominion over the fish of the sea, and over the fowl of the air, and over the cattle, and over all the earth, and over every creeping thing that creepeth upon the earth.

27 So God created man in his *own* image, in the image of God created he him; male and female created he them.

28 And God blessed them, and God said unto them, Be fruitful, and multiply, and replenish the earth, and subdue it: and have dominion over the fish of the sea, and over the fowl of the air, and over every living thing that moveth upon the earth.

29 And God said, Behold, I have given you every herb bearing seed, which *is* upon the face of all the earth, and every tree, in the which *is* the fruit of a tree yielding seed; to you it shall be for meat.

30 And to every beast of the earth, and to every fowl of the air, and to every thing that creepeth upon the earth, wherein *there is* life, *I have given* every green herb for meat: and it was so.

31 And God saw every thing that he had made, and, behold, *it was* very good. And the evening and the morning were the sixth day.

c. This story is taken from *The Birds* by Aristophanes, a Greek dramatist

of the fifth century B.C. The chorus is a convention of Greek drama, and
this particular chorus is made up of birds. This translation is by Gilbert
Murray.

CHORUS

Leader

O Humans, ye natures so dimly alive, like leaves that
    blossom and fade,
Ye little-achievers, creations of clay, impermanent
    tribes of the shade,
Ephemeral, wingless, much-suffering mortals, Men!
    Men that are shapes of a dream,
To Us, the immortal, surrender your minds, Us ever
    alive and a-gleam;   4
Us, dwellers in heaven, eternally young, whose
    mysteries never shall die,
Till ye learn from our teaching the ultimate truths,
    the secrets of stars and of sky,
The Being of Birds, the Becoming of Gods, Streams,
    Chaos and Erebos; so
You can bid the astronomers shut up their shops, for
    you and you only will know.   8
There was Chaos at first, and Erebos black, and Night,
    and the Void profound,
No Earth, no Air, no Heaven; when, lo, in the realm
    of the Dark without bound,
In a vortex of winds the Primordial Egg was engendered
    by black-winged Night;
And out of the Egg, as the seasons revolved, sprang
    Eros, the world's delight.   12
His back soft-gleaming with feathers of gold, his
    heart like a whirlwind storm.
And he with Chaos the winged and dark, being mixed
    in the Void without form,
Begat the original nestlings of us, and guided them up
    to the sun.
The Immortals had never existed at all till Eros made
    all things one.   16
For at last, as one kind with another combined, came
    the Earth and the circling Sea,
And the Sky, and the heavenly race of the Gods ever-
    living; but eldest are we,
And foremost of all happy dwellers in heaven; and
    verily all things declare
We are children of Love, for we fly as He flies, and
    when true lovers meet, we are there.   20

  d. This passage is taken from an African creation story of the Bakuba people
     in Zaire, collected in modern times and translated by Jan Knappert.

Darkness was over the earth which was nothing but water. Mbombo,   1
the white giant, ruled over this chaos. One day he felt a terrible pain in
his stomach, and vomited the sun, the moon, and the stars. The sun
shone fiercely and the water steamed up in clouds. Gradually, the dry
hills appeared. Mbombo vomited again, this time trees came out of his
stomach, and animals, and people, and many other things: the first woman,
the leopard, the eagle, the falling star, the anvil, the monkey Fumu, the
first man, the firmament, the razor, medicine, and lighting. Nchienge,
the woman of the waters, lived in the East. She had a son, Woto, and
a daughter, Labama. Woto, the first king of the Bushongo (Bakuba) moved
westward with his children and dyed their skins black. He also changed
their language by laying a medicine on their tongues. Later his people
blamed him for marrying his sister, and he withdrew with his followers
and founded the nation of the Baluba. He changed their language by
means of an incision in their tongues.

They settled in the desert. Woto blew his horn and lo! there, out   2
of the barren sand, rose many trees, a whole forest, which still stands
today near Salamudimu.

3. Creating Categories: Metaphors About Writing

Writing researcher Barbara Tomlinson has studied the comparisons (usually metaphors) professional writers use when they talk about their writing.
The following statements appear in her book *The Buried Life of the Mind:
Writers' Metaphors for Their Writing Processes.* Read them closely and develop
a classification scheme to identify the different ways these writers talk about
the act of writing, the different kinds of comparisons they make. Write a
short essay presenting your scheme. As a second option, ask your classmates
for metaphors they would use to describe their own writing and develop a
classification scheme for those metaphors.

1. It must be like chiseling a sculpture; if the sculptor does too fine a
   work too soon on what's big, heavy, gross work, then it's out of
   balance somewhere.

   — William Goyen

2. While I'm finishing a book it's a bit like tying a lot of knots that keep
   slipping and you're just impatient to get it done.

   — Nelson Algren

3. Finally, when I got within twenty pages of the end, I realized that
   I still hadn't delivered this [section]. I had a lot of threads, and I'd
   overlooked this one. . . . Putting in [that section] was like setting in
   a sleeve.

   — Joan Didion

4. "Consumer's Report" [the title of a poem] . . . was a breech-birth.
   The first thing to protrude was its bottom stanza. Then I had to
   urge forth the rest of it.

   — X. J. Kennedy

5. I always felt as if I were not writing the book myself, but rather as if I were serving as a subject for some intelligence which had decided to use me to write the book.

— Norman Mailer

6. It wasn't a matter of rewriting but simply of tightening up all the bolts.

— Marguerite Yourcenar

7. Barnacles growing on a wreck or rock. . . . Things attach themselves to wrecks. Strange fish find your wreck or rock to be a good feeding place; after a while you've got a situation with possibilities.

— Donald Barthelme

8. Someone takes over and you just copy out what is being said.

— Henry Miller

9. Each book is worked over several times. I like to compare my method with that of painters centuries ago, proceeding, as it were, from layer to layer.

— Albert Moravia

10. Details, ideas: like so many free-floating metal shavings in want of a magnet.

— James Baker Hall

11. I'm more an oil painter now. More deliberate. A good deal less certain.

— Gore Vidal

12. I literally give birth to the ideas which wiggle in me wanting to come out.

— Abelardo Delgado

13. You work at it long enough, and it becomes so impersonal and so much an object that you're working on . . . it's like a car you've been trying to get to run, an old Hupmobile.

— Fred Chappell

14. The construction gave me some trouble, and I let in a hemstitch here, a gusset there.

— Lawrence Durrell

15. It just takes a little — a tiny seed. Then it takes root, and it grows.
— Katherine Anne Porter

16. I like to do first drafts at night, when I'm tired, and then do the surgical work in the morning when I'm sharp.

— Alex Haley

17. I type draft after draft almost obsessively until that first soft clay shapes itself into the poem it has to become.

— Laura Chester

18. All I know is that at a very early stage in the novel's development I get this urge to collect bits of straw and fluff, and to eat pebbles.
— Vladimir Nabokov

4. Creating Categories: Conceptions of Genius

Following is a list of quotations collected by Franklin P. Adams in the *FPA Book of Quotations*. They illustrate ways in which people have spoken about the idea of "genius." Try classifying the uses of this term as if you were trying to compile a set of definitions for a dictionary (see Assignment 5 in Chapter 1, p. 24). Use your categories and examples to come to some conclusions about what people say about "genius." Write up your conclusions in a short essay.

1. Doing easily what others find difficult is talent; doing what is impossible for talent is genius.
   — Henri-Frederic Amiel

2. Genius is mainly an affair of energy.
   — Matthew Arnold

3. I have known no man of genius who had not to pay, in some affliction or defect either physical or spiritual, for what the gods had given him.
   — Max Beerbohm

4. Genius is nothing but a greater aptitude for patience.
   — Georges-Louis Leclerc de Buffon

5. Talent may be in time forgiven, but genius never!
   — George Gordon, Lord Byron

6. Time, place, and action may with pains be wrought;
   But genius must be born, and never can be taught.
   — John Dryden

7. Genius is one percent inspiration and ninety-nine percent perspiration.
   — Thomas Alva Edison

8. Every man of genius sees the world at a different angle from his fellows, and there is his tragedy.
   — Havelock Ellis

9. When Nature has work to be done, she creates genius to do it.
   — Ralph Waldo Emerson

10. Genius is the power of lighting one's own fire.
    — John Foster

11. For precocity some great price is always demanded sooner or later in life.
    — Margaret Fuller

12. The first and last thing required of genius is the love of truth.
    — Johann Wolfgang Goethe

13. A person of genius should marry a person of character.
    Genius does not herd with genius.
    — Oliver Wendell Holmes

14. Genius is an infinite capacity for taking pains.

> — Jane Ellice Hopkins

15. Genius is the ability to act rightly without precedent — the power to do the right thing the first time.

> — Elbert Hubbard

16. Genius is a promontory jutting out into the infinite.

> — Victor Hugo

17. The true Genius is a mind of large general powers, accidentally determined to some particular direction.

> — Samuel Johnson

18. Genius begins great works; labor alone finishes them.

> — Joseph Joubert

19. At least once a year, everyone is a genius.

> — Georg Christoph Lichtenberg

20. The appearance of a single great genius is more than equivalent to the birth of a hundred mediocrities.

> — Cesare Lombroso

21. There is no work of genius which has not delighted mankind, no word of genius to which the human soul has not, sooner or later, resounded.

> — James Russell Lowell

22. To have genius we must put up with the inconvenience of genius, a thing the world will never do; it wants geniuses, but would like them just like other people.

> — George Moore

23. One science only will genius fit;
So vast is art, so narrow human wit.

> — Alexander Pope

24. The lamp of genius burns quicker than the lamp of life.

> — Johann Christoph Friedrich von Schiller

25. There is no great genius without a touch of dementia.

> — Seneca

26. The poets' scrolls will outlive the monuments of stone.
Genius survives; all else is claimed by death.

> — Edmund Spenser

27. If it were not for my respect of human opinion, I would not open my window to see the Bay of Naples the first time, while I would go five hundred leagues to talk to a man of genius.

> — Madame de Staël

28. There is a certain characteristic common to all those whom we call geniuses. Each of them has a consciousness of being a man apart.

> — Miguel de Unamuno

29. The public is wonderfully tolerant. It forgives everything except genius.

— Oscar Wilde

5. Creating Categories from Observations: Body Language Among College Students

This exercise gives you nothing to work with beyond your own observations. Put yourself in the position of an anthropologist trying to gather data about a culture he or she has set out to observe as objectively as possible. In this case, the culture is that of a college campus. The behavior you have set out to observe is body language. After talking over this term with your friends and classmates, set aside some times and places for observing varieties of body language detectable on campus. You might situate yourself at a single spot on campus and take notes of what you observe. But beware: The selection of a single spot may limit the sorts of behavior to which you have access. Such a strategy might give your observations a particular focus, however, and you can let that focus be apparent in your title, for example, "Body Language Among Students En-Route to Class."

When you are satisfied that your observations have led you to some interesting distinctions and a good range of behavior, write an essay classifying the body language you have observed.

Assignments: Options

6. An Economics Option: Economic Perspectives

In the following passage economics writer Leonard Silk offers a two-part classification for helping us understand the points of view of various economists. After carefully reading Silk's piece, apply his classification to the six passages that follow. Write a short essay explaining your decisions.

In a separate paragraph, speculate about what is gained and what is lost in applying a scheme like Silk's to the work of Friedman, Thurow, and the other economists here. In other words, what does the classifying add to our reading and what does it take away?

Why Experts Don't Agree
LEONARD SILK

That economists of repute, secure tenure, and sound character do not agree suggests a deeper problem. Most commonly it is the problem of perception. Different people look at the same data and see different things.

1

Admittedly, some observers are born optimists while others are doom-and-gloomsters. But differences in psychological makeup are not at the heart of the problem. Rather, it is the vision, the image, the overall conception of what that mysterious entity called "the economy" really is that shapes the analysis and policy recommendations of different economists.

Some envision the economy as a set of flexible prices, wages, rents,   2
interest rates, moving up and down, bidding resources to their most profitable uses, as buyers and sellers assiduously pursue their self-interest; these true believers will conclude that interference by the state in that complex process will only gum up the works — cause goods to be produced inefficiently, create gluts and shortages, aggravate unemployment, aggravate inflation, and drag down the growth of the economy.

But others see the economy as predominantly a set of powerful   3
economic institutions — great corporations, highly concentrated industries, strong labor unions, big agribusiness, foreign cartels (of which the most powerful is the Organization of Petroleum Exporting Countries), and political blocs capable of turning the federal budget and national tax, credit, tariff, and other policies to their own interests; such economists believe it is madness to think that the "free market" can do the job of producing stable growth, when there is no free market, and stability was lacking even when there was.

Those in the first category vigorously oppose controls, those in the   4
second argue that they have become essential, like them or not.

But what is the true nature of this economy? That is the fundamental   5
question behind the confused debate over national policy now going on. Those who would prescribe for its ills should be asked to describe the model that haunts their dreams and their position papers.

From *Free to Choose*
MILTON AND ROSE FRIEDMAN

The fecundity of freedom is demonstrated most dramatically and clearly   1
in agriculture. When the Declaration of Independence was enacted, fewer than 3 million persons of European and African origin (i.e., omitting the native Indians) occupied a narrow fringe along the eastern coast. Agriculture was the main economic activity. It took nineteen out of twenty workers to feed the country's inhabitants and provide a surplus for export in exchange for foreign goods. Today it takes fewer than one out of twenty workers to feed the 220 million inhabitants and provide a surplus that makes the United States the largest single exporter of food in the world.

What produced this miracle? Clearly not central direction by gov-   2
ernment — nations like Russia and its satellites, mainland China, Yugoslavia, and India that today rely on central direction employ from one-quarter to one-half of their workers in agriculture, yet frequently rely on

U.S. agriculture to avoid mass starvation. During most of the period of rapid agricultural expansion in the United States the government played a negligible role. Land was made available — but it was land that had been unproductive before. After the middle of the nineteenth century land-grant colleges were established, and they disseminated information and technology through governmentally financed extension services. Unquestionably, however, the main source of the agricultural revolution was private initiative operating in a free market open to all — the shame of slavery only excepted. And the most rapid growth came after slavery was abolished. The millions of immigrants from all over the world were free to work for themselves, as independent farmers or businessmen, or to work for others, at terms mutually agreed. They were free to experiment with new techniques — at their risk if the experiment failed, and to their profit if it succeeded. They got little assistance from government. Even more important, they encountered little interference from government.

3   Government started playing a major role in agriculture during and after the Great Depression of the 1930s. It acted primarily to restrict output in order to keep prices artificially high.

4   The growth of agricultural productivity depended on the accompanying industrial revolution that freedom stimulated. Thence came the new machines that revolutionized agriculture. Conversely, the industrial revolution depended on the availability of the manpower released by the agricultural revolution. Industry and agriculture marched hand in hand.

From *The Zero-Sum Society*
LESTER C. THUROW

1   When viewed together, the problems of the 1980s share both a common set of causes and a common set of cures. Energy, growth, and inflation are interrelated on many fronts. Without growing energy supplies, economic growth is difficult, and rapidly rising energy prices provide a powerful inflationary force. Inflation leads to public policies that produce idle capacity and severely retard growth.

2   To adjust to a rapidly changing pattern of energy supplies, the energy industry needs to be deregulated. But eliminating regulations, protection, and subsidies is also one of the essential ingredients in any successful program for stimulating economic growth. Because of its value elsewhere in the economy and because it involves the fewest net costs, the elimination of regulations, protection, and subsidies becomes the preferred route to controlling inflation. Upward price shocks are deliberately counterbalanced with planned downward price shocks.

3   Solving our energy and growth problems demands that government gets more heavily involved in the economy's major investment decisions. Massive investments in alternative energy sources will not occur without government involvement, and investment funds need to be more rapidly

channeled from our sunset to sunrise industries. To compete we need the national equivalent of a corporate investment committee. Major investment decisions have become too important to be left to the private market alone, but a way must be found to incorporate private corporate planning into this process in a nonadversary way. Japan Inc. needs to be met with U.S.A. Inc.

From *The Coming Boom*
HERMAN KAHN

In our own country the free market system normally operates well without   1
additional guidance from the central government. Adjustments and innovations normally come about more or less spontaneously — i.e., by planners operating in a decentralized fashion. In principle, a wise government can improve both the choice and rapidity of adjustment or innovations by intelligent, sensible, and skillful intervention — if only by making information available and using indicative planning. There is a problem however, since in a relatively mature economy like that of the United States, with a high level of modernization and with the invisible hand of the market operating, the easy and obvious tasks are usually accomplished effortlessly and well by the decentralized planning system. If the government tries to intervene, it has to do so very competently or else it usually does not help the situation. But there is one special situation when economic policy set by the government does seem to work reasonably well. This occurs when the following three requirements are met:

— the economy is behind, so a reasonably clear idea of where one wants to go is furnished by examining more advanced economies;

— the government is sufficiently powerful and disciplined that it can resist pressures to dissipate its resources in propping up failing industries and subsidizing politically attractive but economically unattractive programs; and

— the government experts and decision makers are and appear competent and knowledgeable (appearance is important so that the businessmen will respect them and accept their information and indicative planning).

None but the last requirement holds for most advanced capitalist   2
nations today.

When the people making adjustments are not very knowledgeable or   3
skillful, the intervention can be destructive, or at least more counterproductive than productive. To reiterate, the basic standard for government intervention should be that the burden of proof of need of intervention be on the government. Unless it makes a very good case, it should not become involved. If there is a basic and distorting underlying

problem (e.g., the current inflation), the government must act to correct it. In that case, no decentralized planning system can do it alone. Nor can a decentralized system do a good job of internalizing external costs and benefits. In addition, when the operation of "the invisible hand of the market" has been distorted by acts of government (usually by unwise regulations and badly designed taxes) it will require acts of government to correct them. And, of course, the government must do those things which only a government can do, e.g., defense, law enforcement, foreign policy.

From *Ecology as Politics*
ANDRÉ GORZ

With needs determined by a series of institutions, professions, prescriptions, and rights, the citizen is invited to behave primarily as a consumer, a customer, a client who is legally entitled to a series of services, facilities, and forms of assistance. The citizen no longer consumes those goods and services which correspond to the autonomous needs which he or she feels, but those which correspond to the heteronomous needs attributed to him or her by the professional experts of specialized institutions.   1

The divergences between contending political parties are mainly over the character and extent of institutional treatment to be meted out for institutionally defined needs. In politics, too, citizens are treated as consumers of policies devised and implemented for them by those "in charge": They can choose between political parties in the same way they can choose between different brands of detergent. Let an individual refuse this choice and he or she will be dismissed as "apathetic." Discouraged from doing anything by or for themselves, deterred from associating with others in order to create — according to their own preferences — their own way of working, of housing themselves, of producing, moving about, consuming, living, people are encouraged instead to seek new forms of assistance, "from above," to fill up the last spaces left open to their own initiative.   2

Against this fundamental tendency, the limited "self-management" of municipalities or factories is helpless to withstand or counteract the increasing hegemony of the state. What is required at the same time is that the size, functioning, and organization of communities and institutions be opened up to provide new spaces for free action which permit self-regulation to bear upon the *what* and not only the *how*.   3

Local self-management of centrally regulated units is an absurdity, or at least a mystification. Such "self-management" is necessarily instituted by the system or by the state itself, and hence has lost its autonomy even before it has gained it. It can in no way obviate or even significantly modify the hazards and constraints inherent in large systems, whose very scale and complexity require the coordination and external regulation of their various units.   4

Self-management is meaningless in a concentrated and specialized   5
economy. Large cities which have specialized in the production of a single
commodity, such as steel or tires, are dependent on business cycles and
market fluctuations beyond their influence or control. Demands for local
self-determination and/or worker management of factories are vacuous
where big business corporations, or even worse, a single specialized
subsidiary, are the sole employers and by far the main taxpayers.

From *The Economics of Public Issues*
DOUGLASS C. NORTH AND ROGER LeROY MILLER

When the supply of a product is reduced without a concomitant reduction   1
in demand, the predicted result is a rise in price. In other words, when
the supply curve shifts in, unaccompanied by an equal shift inward of the
demand curve, the price rises. But, immediately after the reduction in
supply in 1973, the price of petroleum products in the United States was
not allowed to rise because of the price controls then in effect. We
experienced actual shortages, queuing, and numerous "out of gas" signs
because of those controls. When they were lifted in the spring of 1974,
lines at gas stations quickly disappeared. But price controls on U.S. crude
oil, together with a maze of regulations and controls on refineries, have
kept the U.S. price of oil below the world price. This is one reason why
U.S. consumption has not fallen. The controls on so-called old oil in the
United States have discouraged its production. Simultaneously, the artificially low prices have caused increased consumption which, coupled
with reduced U.S. production, has increased the demand for imported
oil.

What does the future hold? The answer can be found by looking at   2
the supply response to the new higher price of world oil. The long-run
price elasticity of supply seems to be very great indeed. Let's take just
a few examples.

Since the end of 1973, worldwide crude oil production has amounted   3
to about 90 billion barrels. New proven reserve *additions* have exceeded
110 billion barrels; thus, a decade after the big scarcity threat of 1973–
1974, new proven reserves are being added faster than production. In
other words, the world's proven reserve inventory continues to increase.
Also consider the fact that, up until World War II, U.S. oil production
accounted for 70 percent of the world production of oil, even though it
had at that time only about 12 percent of the recoverable conventional
crude oil proven reserves in the world. Since World War II, the United
States has still accounted for over one-third of cumulative production.
That means that the rest of the world hasn't done much yet with the oil
that it has in the ground. To date, less than 10 percent of the non-U.S.
conventional oil-resource proven reserves has been produced. The higher
price of oil has already elicited big finds in the North Sea, off the coast
of Greece, and off the coast of Mexico. If history is any indication of the

future, we will continue to see increased worldwide output because of the now higher prices of oil.

From *Small Is Beautiful*
E. F. SCHUMACHER

It used to be said that O.P.E.C. — the Organization of Petroleum Exporting Countries — would never amount to anything, because Arabs could never agree with each other, let alone with non-Arabs; today it is clear that O.P.E.C. is the greatest cartel-monopoly the world has ever seen. It used to be said that the oil exporting countries *depended* on the oil importing countries just as much as the latter depended on the former; today it is clear that this is based on nothing but wishful thinking, because the need of the oil consumers is so great and their demand so inelastic that the oil exporting countries, acting in unison, can in fact raise their revenues by the simple device of curtailing output. There are still people who say that if oil prices rose too much (whatever that may mean) oil would price itself out of the market; but it is perfectly obvious that there is no ready substitute for oil to take its place on a quantitatively significant scale, so that oil, in fact, cannot price itself out of the market.

1

The oil producing countries, meanwhile, are beginning to realize that money alone cannot build new sources of livelihood for their populations. To build them needs, in addition to money, immense efforts and a great deal of time. Oil is a "wasting asset," and the faster it is allowed to waste, the shorter is the time available for the development of a new basis of economic existence. The conclusions are obvious: it is in the real longer-term interest of *both* the oil exporting *and* the oil importing countries that the "life-span" of oil should be prolonged as much as possible. The former need time to develop alternative sources of livelihood and the latter need time to adjust their oil-dependent economies to a situation — which is absolutely certain to arise within the lifetime of most people living today — when oil will be scarce and very dear. The greatest danger to both is a continuation of rapid growth in oil production and consumption throughout the world. Catastrophic developments on the oil front could be avoided only if the *basic harmony of the long-term interests of both groups of countries* came to be fully realized and concerted action were taken to stabilize and gradually reduce the annual flow of oil into consumption.

2

7. An Anthropology Option: Little Communities

In his study *The Little Community*, anthropologist Robert Redfield employs categories to help him define what he means by a "little community." The following passage appears in his opening chapter. Read it several times and then go on to read the five descriptions that follow. Each description is a short summary that we have constructed from studies done by anthropologists and sociologists.

Write an essay classifying the communities on the basis of Redfield's model. Consider how closely you think each of the communities accords with the categories established by Redfield. Also consider which of the categories seem most important and why. Above all, consider how to give your own essay a purpose. In our large, interconnected, industrialized society, of what use is it to study little communities?

From *The Little Community*
ROBERT REDFIELD

The small community has been the very predominant form of human living throughout the history of mankind. The city is a few thousand years old, and while isolated homesteads appeared in early times, it was probably not until the settlement of the New World that they made their "first appearance on a large scale." To Tocqueville, the village or township was "the only association . . . so perfectly natural that wherever a number of men are collected it seems to constitute itself." One estimate is that today three-quarters of the human race still live in villages. . . .   1

In the development of systematic investigation of human life the small community has come to provide a commonly recognized unit of subject matter. Anthropologists have done most of their field work in little communities, and no small part of empirical sociology derives from the investigation of villages, small towns, and urban neighborhoods. . . .   2

What, then, do we mean more particularly by a little community? I put forward, first, the quality of distinctiveness: Where the community begins and where it ends is apparent. The distinctiveness is apparent to the outside observer and is expressed in the group-consciousness of the people of the community.   3

Second, the community we are here concerned with is small, so small that either it itself is the unit of personal observation or else, being somewhat larger and yet homogeneous, it provides in some part of it a unit of personal observation fully representative of the whole. A compact community of four thousand people in Indian Latin-America can be studied by making direct personal acquaintance with one section of it.   4

Third, the community to which we are to look in these chapters is homogeneous. Activities and states of mind are much alike for all persons in corresponding sex and age positions; and the career of one generation repeats that of the preceding. So understood, homogeneous is equivalent to "slow-changing."   5

As a fourth defining quality it may be said that the community we have here in mind is self-sufficient and provides for all or most of the activities and needs of the people in it. The little community is a cradle-to-the-grave arrangement. A club, a clique, even a family, is sectional or segmental contrasted with the integral little community.   6

These qualities — distinctiveness, smallness, homogeneity, and all-providing self-sufficiency — define a type of human community that is realized in high degree in the particular bands and villages to be mentioned in these chapters.   7

Summaries of Studies on Community

HUALCAN, PERU, 1952

Hualcan is a mountain village in Peru. It has been described by   1
anthropologist William Stein, who visited it in the 1950s and wrote about
it in his book *Life in the Highlands of Peru.*

In 1952 Hualcan had 740 residents, all Indians and all dependent on   2
farming. Although most families had small plots of their own, many residents relied on farm work at nearby estates. They were seldom paid in
wages, but in crops or grazing rights. According to Stein, two-thirds of
the parents of children born in Hualcan during 1951 were born there
themselves.

The main economic units in Hualcan are extended families. Few   3
families consist only of husband, wife, and children. A newly married
couple lives with the parents of one of them; or sometimes the families
of brothers and sisters live together as a single household. Each household
pools its resources under the leadership of a senior male, who assumes
responsibility for all of that household's economic decisions — from purchases and labor contracts to fines, bribes, and community contributions.

A large portion of the community's time and resources go into re-   4
ligious festivals. There are six major festivals and numerous minor ones.
Each festival is run by a *mayordomo* (steward). It is considered a great
honor to be chosen *mayordomo* for one of the festivals, but in return the
mayordomo must convert a sizable portion of his family's wealth to the
expenses of the festival. It's an honor no one can refuse, one that only
the older senior men have the resources to meet. The most prestigious
role is that of *mayordomo* of the festivity of St. Ursula, saint of the
harvest.

After having been *mayordomo,* a villager can be appointed to the   5
commission of *varyok,* six men who are in effect the ruling political body
of the town. They decide on public projects, collect taxes, and listen to
disputes. Technically, the highest-ranking official in Hualcan is an officer
stationed there by the Peruvian government, which does not officially
recognize the *varyok.* But this official must yield to the real power of the
varyok.

Although families seem to function independently economically, the   6
system of religious festivals subordinates individual wealth to community
purposes. And tying political power to these same religious celebrations
ensures a gradual rise to political power of men committed to community
traditions.

SPRINGDALE, NEW YORK, 1958

In *Small Town and Mass Society,* Arthur J. Vidich and Joseph Bens-   1
man describe the town of Springdale as it existed in 1958. A small town
in upstate New York, Springdale is within a short drive of several small
cities and within relatively easy reach of New York City and Washington,
D.C. In 1958 it had about 2,500 residents. Many of those residents were

farmers, and many of its businesses were farm-related. The town's largest single business was a sawmill owned and operated by two local families.

The stream that runs through the center of town originally split the community into two distinct neighborhoods, with separate shopping centers and even separate fire companies. But by 1958 there were few signs of the social tensions once felt between the two areas. Though no longer important as a boundary, the stream itself remained important enough to the community that a few years earlier the townspeople collectively contributed to reconstructing its dam.

2

The social life of the community revolved around churches, schools, and private homes. Local organizations included the Masons, the American Legion, the Grange, the local fire brigades, weekly book clubs, a community club, 4-H, and booster groups. Residents of Springdale spoke of themselves as "just plain folks" (p. 29) and saw their town as a place where "everybody knows everybody" (p. 30) and "where you can say hello to anybody" (p. 30). People passing on the street would regularly stop to exchange greetings; in fact, people not stopping would be regarded as snobs. Springdalers were very aware of the nearby cities and seemed very proud to think of themselves as rural people.

3

Much of the town's economy revolved around farming. Many of the town's small businesses depended on the trade of farmers, and many of the farmers, in turn, relied on stable grain prices. Small fluctuations in milk prices could be felt throughout the community. When fixed agricultural costs rose, the town's general economy suffered.

4

Next to farming, the closest thing to a major enterprise in Springdale, according to Vidich and Bensman, was the community school, employing about sixty people. Located in the center of town, it was also viewed as the social and moral hub of the community, and its tax support was seen by most residents as an investment in the town's future.

5

According to Vidich and Bensman, one-fourth of the adults living in Springdale in 1958 were born there. Some of them had not lived in Springdale continuously, however. One-third of the town's population arrived during the years between 1940 and 1952.

6

THE VICE LORDS, CHICAGO, 1967

R. Lincoln Keiser closely studied the Vice Lords, a group of street gangs inhabiting Chicago's major black ghettos (*The Vice Lords: Warriors of the Streets*). Keiser characterized the Vice Lords' social organization as a "federation," each branch "with its own name, set of officers, and territory" (pp. vii, 12). Most groups also had female auxiliaries. The number of branches kept shifting as old groups dissolved and new ones came into being. Keiser estimated that the size of the Vice Lords in the late 1960s varied between 600 and 3,000.

1

In his study, Keiser described the oldest branch of the Vice Lords, the City Lords. The City Lords were formed in 1958 at the Illinois State Training School for Boys in St. Charles, Illinois. It had a seven-man group of officers, including not only president, vice-president, and secretary-

2

treasurer, but "supreme war counselor, war counselor, gun keeper, and sergeant-at-arms" (p. 17). The center of the City Lords' territory became 16th and Lawndale. The precise boundaries of that territory were hard to define. As Keiser puts it, a Vice Lord's territory "is that part of Chicago in which there is little chance that a Vice Lord will be attacked by an enemy group but a significantly larger chance that a member of an enemy club will be attacked by a group of Vice Lords" (p. 22).

Violent exchanges with other street gangs are frequent. Sometimes they occur by chance, while at other times they occur when Vice Lords deliberately enter enemy territory or when they perceive an invasion into their own. Despite the constant violence, membership in the group is also perceived as a defense against violence. Young boys often see membership in the group as a way to prevent being harassed by older boys. The Vice Lords replenish their numbers by recruiting such boys. A young boy entering the brotherhood usually must go through a trial period, during which time an older member is assigned to watch out for him. Bonds usually form quickly, and there is a strong sense of group unity.

Despite the group's solidarity, membership is also very fluid among the older members. Keiser estimates the 1967 membership of the City Lords to be about 150, though he admits that an accurate number was hard to estimate, even for the City Lords themselves:

> A person may get a job, start supporting a family, and cease to take part in most Vice Lord activities. Occasionally, however, he may come out on the corner, drink wine, and shoot craps with other Vice Lords. While he is on the corner he acts like and is treated by others as a Vice Lord. . . . Further, an individual himself may claim to be a part of the group in one instance but deny he is a member at other times. (p. 20)

THE IKS, UGANDA, 1967

The Iks are a small tribe of hunter-gatherers described by Colin Turnbull in his book *The Mountain People.* Turnbull visited the tribe between 1964 and 1967, soon after the once nomadic tribe had been restricted by the Ugandan government to a mountainous region near the Kenyan border.

The Iks observed by Turnbull lived clustered in isolated villages. They foraged for food, but without the ability to move from place to place, they had to undergo great scarcities during some times of the year. When food was available, they consumed it immediately. The Iks made no attempt to share food with one another. Even little children had to compete for food, with the weaker children often dying.

Turnbull observed little social cooperation among the Iks. Husbands often beat their wives and discarded them casually whenever they wished. Most young women became prostitutes as a way of feeding themselves. Both men and women seemed to age very quickly, and old people were not tolerated for very long. When no longer self-sufficient they often were turned out of their homes to die. The Iks acknowledged few family bonds.

An Ik village consisted of a cluster of thatched huts, surrounded and [4] interpenetrated by a dense maze of brush. The largest village visited by Turnbull, "village Number Five," comprised thirty such huts. The village was without any central clearing or meeting place. Moving from hut to hut through the tangle of surrounding brush was very difficult, but each hut had a narrow crawl space leading to an outer edge of the compound. According to Turnbull, no villager had any need to see fellow villagers, and whole days passed without human interaction. Most villagers were distrustful of one another and particularly antagonistic toward their closest neighbors. Turnbull quotes a characteristic greeting and reply: "Brinji Ngag." . . . "Bera Ngag" ("Give me food." . . . "There is no food").

The Iks practiced no agriculture, and they were no longer successful [5] hunters — though in the past they had flourished by hunting cooperatively. The Iks did have some income: they let Ugandan cattle thieves hide cattle within their thickets. Indirectly cattle raids became their major economic activity, something quite irritating to the young and struggling Ugandan government, a government otherwise indifferent toward them.

THE HUTTERITES, JASPER, CANADA, 1967

The Hutterites are a religious sect that colonized Jasper, Saskatch- [1] ewan, emigrating from South Dakota during the 1950s and early 1960s. By the mid-1960s six separate Hutterite colonies existed in the Jasper region, representing about 8 percent of Jasper's total population. This account of their lifestyle is drawn from *Hutterite Brethren* by John W. Bennett.

The Hutterites are Anabaptists and can point to a five-hundred-year [2] tradition of religious harassment. Their religious beliefs and practices are not unlike those of other Protestant groups; what makes them different is their commitment to communal living and their rejection of the society around them.

The Hutterites colonize by buying up farmland. A settlement stops [3] growing and divides when it reaches a size of about 150 people. According to Bennett, a colony any larger than this "becomes difficult to manage by means of the intimate forms of social control used by the Hutterites, and difficult to support on the amount of land usually available" (p. 55). When a new colony starts up, it is located far enough away from estab- lished colonies to appease fears among other Jasper residents that the Hutterites are trying to buy up the entire district. The various colonies, though self-sustaining, do maintain social and economic contact with one another.

The Hutterites live by agriculture. Because of their thorough com- [4] mitment to rural life, their culture seems to have a peasant quality. They have a deep respect for traditional craftmanship and for conservative education. Yet they are not entirely resistant to modern developments, showing themselves quite willing, for example, to take advantage of advances in farm machinery.

The Hutterites antagonize other residents of Jasper by having little [5] or nothing to do with them. Their only contact with the town is their use of it for delivering, shipping, and receiving mail. Although the Hutterites do some buying and selling with the outside world, their economy does not seem to rely on such trade. When shortages occur, the Hutterites manage to get by on their reserves.

The Hutterites preach self-help and avoidance of worldly corruption.   6
They practice adult baptism. They associate only with other Hutterites, and they regard all those who do not practice communal living as fallen Christians. And they consider all who are not Christians heathen.

8. A Literature Option: Introductory Strategies of Fiction Writers

Each of the following paragraphs is the opening of a contemporary American novel or short story. Read them through, making notes on differences in content, style, point of view, tone, or any other characteristic that interests you. Then, as a way to consider the various strategies fiction writers can use to open their work, experiment with different ways to classify these paragraphs. Select the approach you like best, and write an essay explaining and illustrating your system.

Selected Opening Paragraphs from Works of Fiction

In December, 1954, Henry Soames would hardly have said his life was just beginning. His heart was bad, business at the Stop-Off had never been worse, he was close to a nervous breakdown.
— John Gardner, *Nickel Mountain*

The first time I saw Brenda she asked me to hold her glasses. Then she stepped out to the edge of the diving board and looked foggily into the pool; it could have been drained, myopic Brenda would never have known it. She dove beautifully, and a moment later she was swimming back to the side of the pool, her head of short-clipped auburn hair held up, straight ahead of her, as though it were a rose on a long stem. She glided to the edge and then was beside me. "Thank you," she said, her eyes watery though not from the water. She extended a hand for her glasses but did not put them on until she turned and headed away. I watched her move off. Her hands suddenly appeared behind her. She caught the bottom of her suit between thumb and index finger and flicked what flesh had been showing back where it belonged. My blood jumped.
— Philip Roth, *Goodbye, Columbus*

The telephone rang, and Richard Maple, who had stayed home from work this Friday because of a cold, answered it: "Hello?" The person at the other end of the line hung up. Richard went into the bedroom, where Joan was making the bed, and said, "Your lover just called."
— John Updike, "Your Lover Just Called"

Brewster Place was the bastard child of several clandestine meetings between the alderman of the sixth district and the managing director of Unico Realty Company. The latter needed to remove the police chief of the sixth district because he was too honest to take bribes and so had persisted in harassing the gambling houses the director owned. In turn, the alderman wanted the realty company to build their new shopping center on his cousin's property in the northern section of town. They came together, propositioned, bargained, and slowly worked out the consummation of their respective desires. As an afterthought, they agreed to erect four double-housing units on some worthless land in the badly crowded district. This would help to abate the expected protests from the Irish community over the police chief's dismissal; and since the city would underwrite the costs, and the alderman could use the construction to support his bid for mayor in the next election, it would importune neither man. And so in a damp, smoke-filled room, Brewster Place was conceived.

— Gloria Naylor, *The Women of Brewster Place*

"All happy families are more or less dissimilar; all unhappy ones are more or less alike," says a great Russian writer in the beginning of a famous novel (*Anna Arkadievitch Karenina,* transfigured into English by R. G. Stonelower, Mount Tabor Ltd., 1880). That pronouncement has little if any relation to the story to be unfolded now, a family chronicle, the first part of which is, perhaps, closer to another Tolstoy work, *Detstvo i Otrochestvo* (*Childhood and Fatherland,* Pontius Press, 1858).

— Vladimir Nabokov, *Ada*

Two weeks before Christmas, Ellen called me and said, "Faith, I'm dying." That week I was dying too.

— Grace Paley, "Living"

Sometimes Sonny felt like he was the only human creature in the town. It was a bad feeling, and it usually came on him in the mornings early, when the streets were completely empty, the way they were one Saturday morning in late November. The night before Sonny had played his last game of football for Thalia High School, but it wasn't that that made him feel so strange and alone. It was just the look of the town.

— Larry McMurtry, *The Last Picture Show*

Idi, my very best friend here in Senegal, was suffering from a very strange eye malady. He didn't know precisely what had caused his usually quick, pebble eyes to swell, yellow, tear, and itch so. He'd gone to both doctors and *marabous* and they didn't know either. "All that I can say," said Idi, "is that my eye sickness remind me very much of my Uncle Moustapha's eye sickness." And at that he proceeded to tell me the story of his Uncle Moustapha M'Baye's eye "sickness":

— Reginald McKnight, "Uncle Moustapha's Eclipse"

In 1903 an Indian named Chowt followed a pack of rats through Dume Canyon, north of Santa Monica. To Chowt, the wind-scarred canyon was not Dume Canyon (a white-man name) but was called Huyat, something white people would have laughed at had they known its meaning.

— Opal Lee Popkes, "Zuma Chowt's Cave"

All this happened, more or less. The war parts, anyway, are pretty much true. One guy I knew really *was* shot in Dresden for taking a teapot that wasn't his. Another guy I knew really *did* threaten to have his personal enemies killed by hired gunmen after the war. And so on. I've changed all the names.

— Kurt Vonnegut, *Slaughterhouse Five*

I was a desperate man. Quarterly, I got that crawly feeling in my wafer-thin stomach. During these fasting days, I had the temper of a Greek mountain dog. It was hard to maintain a smile; everyone seemed to jet toward the goal of The Great Society, while I remained in the outhouse, penniless, without "connections." Pretty girls, credit cards, charge account, Hart Schaffner & Marx suits, fine shoes, Dobbs hats, XK-E Jaguars, and more pretty girls cluttered my butterscotch-colored dreams. Lord — I'd work like a slave, but how to acquire an acquisitional gimmick? Mercy — something had to fall from the tree of fortune! Tom-toms were signaling to my frustrated brain; the message: I had to make it.

— Charles Wright, *The Wig*

A light snow was falling as the train from Mexico City pulled into Ciudad Juárez. A film of ice had formed on the wooden sidewalks, and the unpaved streets were deep in mud where the wagons and automobiles had sludged through. A man got off the train and elbowed his way through the crowd that inevitably gathered at the arrival of a train from the capital. Ten years earlier, as a young man of eighteen, he had come to this same city in not so quiet a fashion. Then he had been a cavalry officer in Villa's army that took Juárez, northern lifeline to the United States, from the forces of the government. A few months later, he had returned with the great General to retake the city after it had been sold out to the enemy by the army Villa had left there to protect it.

— José Antonio Villarreal, *Pocho*

Rhoda woke up dreaming. In the dream she was crushing the skulls of Jody's sheepdogs. Or else she was crushing the skulls of Jody's sisters. Or else she was crushing Jody's skull. Jody was the husband she was leaving. Crunch, crunch, crunch went the skulls between her hands, beneath her heels.

— Ellen Gilchrist, "The Lower Garden District Free
Gravity Mule Blight or Rhoda, a Fable"

The thick ticking of the tin clock stopped. Mendel, dozing in the dark, awoke in fright. The pain returned as he listened. He drew on his cold embittered clothing, and wasted minutes sitting at the edge of the bed.

— Bernard Malamud, "Idiots First"

Hale Hardy went to college because he couldn't think of anything better to do, and he quit because he couldn't see any reason to stay. He lasted one and a half years. He did not exactly quit; he was thrown out. When that happened he went to visit his sister Mary, who was living with another girl, Paula, who was being supported by some dude. Hale didn't know the dude's name, or why he was supporting her, or why his sister was living there. He just went.

> — Ann Beattie, "Hale Hardy and the Amazing Animal Woman"

In front of one of the most palatial hotels in the world, a very young man was accustomed to sit on a bench which, when the light fell in a certain way, shone like gold.

> — James Purdy, *Malcolm*

Con Tinh Tan sits in the waiting room. She avoids looking directly at the other patients. The Americans. She can see them partially reflected in the mirror that is the back pane of the fish tank. She can look past the underwater flash of lionfish, saltwater angels, yellow tangs, rock beauties, sea robins, past a ceramic replica of the Golden Gate Bridge, to watch the Americans, sitting and waiting.

> — John Sayles, "Tan"

Folks. This here is the story of the Loop Garoo Kid. A cowboy so bad he made a working posse of spells phone in sick. A bullwhacker so unfeeling he left the print of winged mice on hides of crawling women. A desperado so onery he made the Pope cry and the most powerful of cattlemen shed his head to the Executioner's swine.

> — Ishmael Reed, *Yellow Back Radio Broke-Down*

There are very few Japanese residing in Las Vegas proper, that glittering city which represents, probably, the ultimate rebellion against the Puritan origins of this singular country. A few Japanese families farm on the outskirts, but I can't imagine what they grow there in that arid land where, as far as the eye can see from a Greyhound bus (and a Scenicruiser it was, at that), there are only sand, bare mountains, sagebrush, and more sand. Sometimes the families come into town for shopping; sometimes they come for a feast of Chinese food, because the Japanese regard Chinese cuisine as the height of gourmandism, to be partaken of on special occasions, as after a wedding or a funeral.

> — Hisaye Yamamoto, "Las Vegas Charley"

Sandy's husband had been on the sofa ever since he'd been terminated three months ago. That day, three months ago, he'd come home looking pale and scared and with all of his work things in a box. "Happy Valentine's Day," he said to Sandy and put a heart-shaped box of candy and a bottle of Jim Beam on the kitchen table. He took off his cap and laid that on the table, too. "I got canned today. Hey, what do you think's going to happen to us now?"

> — Raymond Carver, "Preservation"

A summer wind, soaring just before it died, blew the dusk and the first scattered lights of downtown Brooklyn against the shut windows of the classroom, but Professor Max Berman — B.A., 1919, M.A., 1921, New York; Docteur de l'Université, 1930, Paris — alone in the room, did not bother to open the windows to the cooling wind. The heat and airlessness of the room, the perspiration inching its way like an ant around his starched collar were discomforts he enjoyed; they obscured his larger discomfort: the anxiety which chafed his heart and tugged his left eyelid so that he seemed to be winking, roguishly, behind his glasses.

— Paule Marshall, "Brooklyn"

A screaming comes across the sky. It has happened before, but there is nothing to compare it to now.

— Thomas Pynchon, *Gravity's Rainbow*

I was sitting before my third or fourth Jellybean — which is anisette, grain alcohol, a lit match, and a small, wet explosion in the brain. On my left sat Gerry Nanapush of the Chippewa Tribe. On my right sat Dot Adare of the has-been, of the never-was, of the what's-in-front-of-me people. Still in her belly and tensed in its fluids coiled the child of their union, the child we were waiting for, the child whose name we were making a strenuous and lengthy search for in a cramped and littered bar at the very edge of that Dakota town.

— Louise Erdrich, "Scales"

I knew I had made a mistake when the iced tea came with a spoon sticking out of it. I was in the Skelly truck stop restaurant in Alma, Arkansas. It's got a sign that says HOME COOKING and a glass case full of slabs of coconut pie and chocolate pie with real dilapidated meringue on them and a couple of flies crawling around on the inside of the glass.

— Lewis Nordan, "Sugar Among the Freaks"

Nobody's hands were quite like Mamma's. They were narrow with long thin fingers, and thumbs that bent out at the ends. The nails were scarred with nicks from the cutting of Salmon. In fish time they had rims of black, which had faded by winter till they were their usual pink-brown color. The hands acted as if they knew just what they were doing. When Mamma rested they folded, one on top of the other, and it seemed as if they were sleeping, but they were always ready to jump up. When they did, the turned-out thumbs gave them a busy air. The skin of her hands was both soft and rough. She thought about Mamma's hands coming toward her and Michael, usually holding things. It made her drowsy and comfortable.

— Mary TallMountain, "Naaholooyah"

9. A Literature Option: Introductory Strategies of Nonfiction Writers

Each of the following paragraphs is the opening of a nonfiction book or essay. Read them, making notes on differences in style, person, tone, or any other characteristic that interests you. Then, as a way to consider the various strategies writers can use to open their work, experiment with different ways to classify these paragraphs. Select the approach you like best, and write an essay explaining and illustrating your system.

For a longer essay, you might compare the opening strategies of nonfiction writers with those of fiction writers. Look back at Assignment 8. Can the two sets of paragraphs be classified in similar ways? Do the techniques of fiction and nonfiction writers differ? Do you find the distinction between fiction and nonfiction techniques useful or problematic — or both?

Selected Opening Paragraphs from Works of Nonfiction

This is a book about the ways in which the developing child perceives the world around him, and about his growing ability to make sense of what he perceives.
— T. G. R. Bower, *The Perceptual World of the Child*

The giraffe is the only species without a voice. We share with the dolphin identifiable laughter. We recognize and give integrity to the language of the apes, baboons, orangutans, and other primates though we cannot translate it. We understand and appreciate the growls and howls of the wolves, hyenas, lions, tigers, our own pet dogs and cats. Yet human beings are the only species with codifiable language.
— Nikki Giovanni, "The Women's Alliance"

Our interest here is community organization. It has also variously been termed community planning, community relations, planned change, and community work. Others have preferred terms such as neighborhood work, social action, intergroup work, and community practice. Under whatever label, we will be dealing with intervention at the community level oriented toward improving or changing community institutions and solving community problems. This activity is performed by professionals from many disciplines — social work, public health, adult education, public administration, city planning, and community mental health — as well as by citizen volunteers in civic associations and social action groups.
— Fred M. Cox, John L. Erlich, Jack Rothman, and John E. Tropman (Eds.), *Strategies of Community Organization*

Eddie Mason opened his eyes. The long window was a ghost of gray winter light. He reached for his cigarettes. Through the first puff of smoke he stared at the cold dawn and tried to remember why today was supposed to be so special. He said out loud, "Damn!"
— Ben H. Bagdikian, *Caged: Eight Prisoners and Their Keepers*

I undertook the writing of this book in a mood of anxiety and with a sense of urgency. Affirmative-action programs, adopted in the face of adverse public opinion, seemed to operate in a conspiracy of silence on the part of public officials, whose behavior defied their responsibility to defend their actions publicly. The field of public discourse had been left largely to opponents of affirmative action, who, in their arguments, had preempted the appeal to the ideals of justice and equality. Moreover, when the argument against affirmative action was not met with silence, it was often countered by evasion. Were the weightiest arguments really on that side of the issue?

> — John C. Livingston, *Fair Game? Inequality and*
> *Affirmative Action*

What do the codes used for sending messages back from spacecraft have in common with genes on a molecule of DNA? How is it that the second law of thermodynamics, a physicist's discovery, is related to communication, so that we can speak of the "entropy" of a musical score, or a page of text, or a conversation? Why are knotty problems in the mathematical theory of probability connected with the way we express ourselves in speech and writing? The answer to all these questions is "information," and the very fact that a single concept can link so many diverse ideas is an indication of its great generality and power.

> — Jeremy Campbell, *Grammatical Man*

In 1600, Elizabethan England had good reason to sing the praises of the art of arithmetic. The century just brought to a close had been characterized by continual expansion. Marked population growth, monetary inflation, and overseas discoveries stretched the boundaries of thought and custom in ways that called to mind size, number, and measure. Certainly it was an indulgence in hyperbole for the author of the paean to arithmetic, Thomas Hill, to single out counting as the essence of humanity, the skill that distinguished man from the beasts. But the exaggeration served to emphasize the paramount importance of arithmetic in a country rapidly becoming a center of commercial capitalism.

> — Patricia Cline Cohen, *A Calculating People:*
> *The Spread of Numeracy in Early America*

In the spring of 1975 I traveled the Dakotas with a band of UCLA students and my four-year-old daughter. The university let me teach an on-the-road seminar with a base at Jamestown College in Jamestown, North Dakota. We lived roughly equidistant from five reservations in North Dakota, between rural mid-America and the open plains, small towns and Indian tribal grounds. We talked with Native Americans, primarily Sioux, Chippewa, Mandan, Arikara, and Hidatsa, and with white farmers, ranchers, and merchants who lived near them. *The Good Red Road* is an ethnographic narrative taken from this field experience and from subsequent visits. The number of people present at gatherings and their names have been altered to tell the story.

> — Kenneth Lincoln with Al Logan Slagle, *The Good*
> *Red Road: Passages into Native America*

A quiet early morning fog shrouds rolling hills blanketed by pine-green stands of timber, patched with fields of red clay. As the sun rises

and burns off the fog, the blue sky is feathered with smoke let go from chimney stacks of textile mills: this is the Piedmont of the Carolinas.
— Shirley Brice Heath, *Ways with Words*

Writing groups, the partner method, helping circles, collaborative writing, response groups, team writing, writing laboratories, teacherless writing classes, group inquiry technique, the round table, class criticism, editing sessions, writing teams, workshops, peer tutoring, the socialized method, mutual improvement sessions, intensive peer review — the phenomenon has nearly as many names as people who employ it. The name, of course, matters less than what it describes, which is writers responding to one another's work. Writing groups, as I choose to call them, operate both within and outside schools. Specifics, like the names, vary. Groups range in size from three to more than forty. When writing groups meet in classroom, some instructors structure tasks and provide explicit direction, while others avoid interfering with student commentary. Some groups exchange written drafts and receive verbal or written comments, while some read aloud and receive oral response. Some shift the procedure to suit the material (reading long essays or poems and listening to shorter prose selections, for example). Groups observe differing codes for response. Some intervene directly in members' writing — helping generate ideas or telling the writer what to do next — while others restrict responses to what has already been written.
— Anne Ruggles Gere, *Writing Groups: History,*
Theory, and Implications

"Where are our intellectuals?" In his 1921 book, *America and the Young Intellectual*, Harold Stearns (1891–1943), a chronicler of his generation, asked this question. He found them fleeing to Europe, an act he supported and soon followed, joining what became the most celebrated of American intellectual groupings, the lost generation.
— Russell Jacoby, *The Last Intellectuals:*
American Culture in the Age of Academe

"Would you be able to tell me how you, Anne, see all of this?" Dr. Carol Nadelson's voice was gentle, almost not audible. Anne Munson, a somewhat plump girl of almost seventeen, stared at the psychiatrist, her blue-gray eyes preternaturally widened. She pushed her harlequin-framed eyeglasses slightly down on the bridge of her pug-nose, shrugged slightly: "I don't know." Her voice was puzzled and childlike. "This just isn't my day, I guess." The patient was wearing a blue velveteen bathrobe that zipped up the front and seemed overly heavy for this strangely warm, almost hot, early April morning.
— Maggie Scarf, *Unfinished Business: Pressure*
Points in the Lives of Women

In the Northern Latitudes the dawn comes early. Even as the bombers were turning away from the city, the first rays of light were coming up in the east. In the stillness of the morning, great pillars of black smoke towered over the districts of Pankow, Weissensee, and Lichtenberg. On the low clouds it was difficult to separate the soft glow of daylight from the reflections of the fires that blazed in bomb-battered Berlin.

— Cornelius Ryan, *The Last Battle*

Emma Lazarus, who wrote those lines inscribed on the base of the Statue of Liberty ("Give me your tired, your poor . . . Your huddled masses, yearning to breathe free"), was the first Jew whom Ralph Waldo Emerson ever met. Emerson's daughter Ellen, an old Sunday-school teacher, noted how astonishing it was "to get a real unconverted Jew (who had no objections to calling herself one, and talked freely about 'our Church' and 'we Jews'), and to hear how Old Testament sounds to her, and find she has been brought up to keep the Law, and the Feast of the Passover, and the day of Atonement. The interior view was more interesting than I could have imagined. She says her family are outlawed now, they no longer keep the Law, but Christian institutions don't interest her either."

— Alfred Kazin, "The Jew as Modern American Writer"

Philosophers usually write their books for other philosophers, and express parenthetical hopes that the book will prove useful to students and lay readers as well. Such hopes are usually vain. In hopeful contrast, I have written this book primarily and explicitly for people who are not professionals in philosophy, or in artificial intelligence, or in the neurosciences. It is the imagination of the general reader, and of the student, that I am here aiming to capture. I do indeed have subsidiary hopes that this compact volume will prove useful, as a comprehensive summary and source book, to my professional colleagues and to advanced graduate students. But I did not write this book for them. I have written it for newcomers to the philosophy of mind.

— Paul M. Churchland, *Matter and Consciousness*

The not-for-profit are different from you and me. Tennis courts, a swimming pool, a baseball diamond, a croquet lawn, a private hotel, 400 acres of woods and rolling hills, cavorting deer, a resident flock of Canada geese — I'm loving every minute here at the Educational Testing Service, the great untaxed, unregulated, unblinking eye of the American meritocracy.

— David Owen, *None of the Above: Behind the Myth of Scholastic Aptitude*

This [first] chapter will focus on the historical response of those researchers and scientists who have studied both the process of aging and the social conditions of the aged. The literature of gerontology — the study of all the aspects of aging — is relatively new; most of it has been produced since the turn of the century.

— Jack Levin and William C. Levin, *Ageism: Prejudice and Discrimination Against the Elderly*

The study of human beings using language is notoriously suspect because it must be conducted by human beings using language. The field of discourse is thus bedeviled by circularities and loopholes, the dangers of which can be avoided only by taking stock, from the outset, of guiding principles and theoretical foundations. It will not be enough to produce or stipulate a "workable" definition of rhetoric and then to proceed from these, thus using rhetoric to study rhetoric. Our first task is to discover and articulate larger frameworks which will provide bases for adequate definition.

> — Walter H. Beale, *A Pragmatic Theory of Rhetoric*

When I was small, my mother often told me that animals, insects, and plants are to be treated with the kind of respect one customarily accords to high-status adults. "Life is a circle, and everything has its place in it," she would say. That's how I met the sacred hoop, which has been an integral part of my life, though I didn't know to call it that until the early 1970s when I read John G. Neihardt's rendering of the life story of Oglala Lakota Holy Man Black Elk in *Black Elk Speaks.*

> — Paula Gunn Allen, *The Sacred Hoop: Recovering the Feminine in American Indian Traditions*

Between 1948 and 1952, tens of thousands of mutilating brain operations were performed on mentally ill men and women in countries around the world, from Portugal, where prefrontal leucotomy was introduced in 1935, to the United States, where under the name of "lobotomy" the procedure was widely used on patients from all walks of life. From our present perspective, these operations — referred to collectively as "psychosurgery" — seem unbelievably primitive and crude. After drilling two or more holes in a patient's skull, a surgeon inserted into the brain any of various instruments — some resembling an apple corer, a butter spreader, or an ice pick — and, often without being able to see what he was cutting, destroyed parts of the brain. In spite of the huge amount of psychosurgery done during the peak of its popularity, by 1960 this practice was drastically curtailed. Not only had chlorpromazine and other psychoactive drugs provided a simple and inexpensive alternative, but it had also been discovered that these operations were leaving in their wake many seriously brain-damaged people. Today lobotomy has largely fallen into disrepute and is now considered an evolutionary throwback, akin more to the early practice of trepanning the skull to allow the demons to escape than to modern medicine.

> — Elliot S. Valenstein, *Great and Desperate Cures: The Rise and Decline of Psychosurgery and Other Radical Treatments for Mental Illness*

The purpose of this book is to draw attention to the mbira, a uniquely African contribution to the world of music. Although it is one of the most well-established and popular melodic instruments in black Africa, the mbira has rarely received the attention in the West that it deserves. Many Westerners have the limited view that African music consists entirely of drumming. They are unaware that the melodic traditions of African music are rich and varied, having as important a history and as profound a meaning in certain cultures as the magnificent drumming ensembles have in others.

— Paul F. Berliner, *The Soul of Mbira*

For centuries Americans have seen domestic architecture as a way of encouraging certain kinds of family and social life. Diverse contingents have asserted that our private architecture has a distinctly public side, and that domestic environments can reinforce certain character traits, promote family stability, and assure a good society. Those who sought a new social order, whether they were radical orators or enterprising capitalists, have argued that American culture was malleable, in part because the physical environment of previous generations was less of a constraint than it had been in other countries. They contended that new models for housing, even more than improved factories or institutional buildings, would provide the proper setting for a great nation. Others who sought to resist radical change or assimilation have also looked to the home as a reminder of their own cultural traditions and as a protected realm for private family life, presumably outside the larger society. As a consequence, Americans have been quite self-conscious about where they live and where their fellow citizens live as well.

— Gwendolyn Wright, *Building the Dream: A Social History of Housing in America*

The decade of the 1970s was a critical period for ethnic minorities and women in the United States. The intellectual and political atmosphere of this period made these groups more introspective, leading them to examine critically their own history and culture. The result was an out-pouring of writing, both creative and analytical, which offered a new way of seeing what had always been there. For the first time in the history of people of Mexican descent in the United States, a significant body of written literature emerged. To be sure, Spanish-speaking people in the United States had written and published before the mid-1960s. In the contemporary period, however, a literary expression has emerged from working-class Mexican-Chicano communities. Since the 1960s such writings have been designated as Chicano literature, including works by a modern generation of Chicano authors in various classifications: poetry, novel, dramatic play, essay, and short story. Although continuous with the literary expression, usually transmitted orally, which previously existed in Mexican-Chicano communities, these contemporary writings have had a different perspective: the modern generation of Chicano authors has exhibited a political, social, and cultural self-consciousness.

— Marta Ester Sanchez, *Contemporary Chicana Poetry: A Critical Approach to an Emerging Literature*

Realistic observers of their northern province, the Spaniards always spoke of "The Californias" — Baja California and Alta California; Lower California and Upper California; New California and Old California. Later, still more Californias, more regional entities, were distinctly etched: the

Mother Lode Country, known to the natives as Superior California; the Delta district; the Redwood Empire; the great Central Valley; and the Desert Country. While most of these regions and sub-regions are clearly delineated, none is more sharply defined, geographically and socially, than the area now known as Southern California.

> — Carey McWilliams, *Southern California:*
> *An Island on the Land*

Living well is a challenge. Brian Palmer, a successful businessman, lives in a comfortable San Jose suburb and works as a top-level manager in a large corporation. He is justifiably proud of his rapid rise in the corporation, but he is even prouder of the profound change he has made recently in his idea of success. "My value system," he says, "has changed a little bit as the result of a divorce and reexamining life values. Two years ago, confronted with the work load I have right now, I would stay in the office and work until midnight, come home, go to bed, get up at six, and go back in and work until midnight, until such time as it got done. Now I just kind of flip the bird and walk out. My family life is more important to me than that, and the work will wait, I have learned." A new marriage and a houseful of children have become the center of Brian's life. But such new values were won only after painful difficulties.

> — Robert N. Bellah et al., *Habits of the Heart:*
> *Individualism and Commitment in American Life*

This book tries to explain how minds work. How can intelligence emerge from nonintelligence? To answer that, we'll show that you can build a mind from many little parts, each mindless by itself.

> — Marvin Minsky, *The Society of Mind*

In 1966 the National Congress of American Indians wanted to give an award to the then director of the Office of Economic Opportunity, R. Sargent Shriver. The N.C.A.I. had printed a special form which noted the achievements of the person receiving the award and stated that the award was for meritorious service to the Indian people. At the bottom of the form were several blanks under which the words "President," "Vice-president," and "Secretary" were printed. On the evening on which the award was to be made, the officers of the N.C.A.I. were gathered in the organization's offices, filling in the blanks with Shriver's name where it was appropriate. When they came to the blank for the President's name, one of the officers was stopped cold. "Is this our president who is to sign here," he inquired, "or theirs?"

> — Vine Deloria, Jr., *Behind the Trail of Broken Treaties*

The incest taboo is universal in human culture. Though it varies from one culture to another, it is generally considered by anthropologists to be the foundation of all kinship structures. Lévi-Strauss describes it as the basic social contract; Mead says its purpose is the preservation of the human social order. All cultures, including our own, regard violations of the taboo with horror and dread. Death has not been considered too extreme a punishment in many societies. In our laws, some states punish incest by up to twenty years' imprisonment.

— Judith Herman and Lisa Hirschman, "Father-Daughter Incest"

10. An Art Option: Images of the Human Form

Develop a system for classifying the human images that follow, all works of art produced in the 1920s. Explain your classification system in an essay. Make sure to find a meaningful basis of classifying that allows you to make interesting points about the works of art.

As a postscript to your essay, write an additional paragraph or two, reflecting on how this effort of classifying has affected how you look at these works of art. Is something lost as well as gained?

▓ *Selected Illustrations from Art of the 1920s*

George Grosz. *Republican Automatons.* 1920. Watercolor, 23⅝ × 18⅝". Collection, The Museum of Modern Art, New York. Advisory Committee Fund.

Above: Edward Hopper. *Night Shadows.* 1921. Etching, printed in black, 6¹⁵⁄₁₆ × 8³⁄₁₆″. Collection, The Museum of Modern Art, New York. Gift of Abby Aldrich Rockefeller. *Right:* Erich Heckel. *Self-Portrait (Portrait of a Man).* 1919. Woodcut, printed in color, 18³⁄₁₆ × 12¾″. Collection, The Museum of Modern Art, New York. Purchase.

Left: Fernand Leger. *A Skater* for the ballet *Skating Rink.* 1922. Watercolor and pencil, 12⅜ × 9½". Collection, The Museum of Modern Art, New York. W. Alton Jones Foundation Fund. *Below:* Edvard Munch. *Three Girls on the Bridge.* 1918. Woodcut, printed in color, comp.: 19¾ × 17⅟₁₆" (irregular). Collection, The Museum of Modern Art, New York. Purchase.

Top: Glenn O. Coleman. *Minetta Lane.* 1928. Lithograph, printed in black, 11¼ × 11″. Collection, The Museum of Modern Art, New York. Gift of Abby Aldrich Rockefeller. *Bottom:* Dod Proctor. *Morning.* 1926. Tate Gallery, London/Art Resource, New York.

Left: Henri Matisse. French, 1869–1954. *The Persian.* 1929. Lithograph, 17½ × 11⅜″. Courtesy, Museum of Fine Arts, Boston. *Below:* Georg Scholz. *Daily Paper.* 1922. Lithograph, printed in black, 7⅞ × 8⅝″. Collection, The Museum of Modern Art, New York. Purchase.

Right: Alfred Henry Maurer. *Standing Female Nude.* c. 1927–28. Casein on gesso on composition board, $21^{13}/_{16}$ × $18^{1}/_{4}''$. Collection, University Art Museum, University of Minnesota, Minneapolis. Gift of Ione and Hudson Walker. *Below right:* Georges Rouault. *Miserere: A Lady* (Trial proof). 1922. Aquatint over heliogravure, printed in black, 24 × $17^{1}/_{4}''$. Collection, The Museum of Modern Art, New York. Purchase. *Far right:* Max Beckmann. *In the Hotel (Hotel Lobby).* 1924. Woodcut, printed in black, $19^{1}/_{2}$ × $19^{5}/_{8}''$. Collection, The Museum of Modern Art, New York. Purchase. *Below far right:* Arshile Gorky. *The Artist and His Mother.* 1926–29. Oil on canvas. 60 × 50″. Collection of the Whitney Museum of American Art. Gift of Julien Levy for Maro and Natasha Gorky in memory of their father.

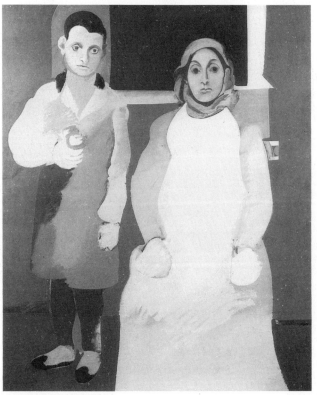

Right: Pablo Picasso. *Four Dancers.* 1925. Pen and ink, 13⅞ × 10". Collection, The Museum of Modern Art, New York. Gift of Abby Aldrich Rockefeller. *Below right:* Marc Chagall. *Before the Easel,* plate 18 from *Mein Leben,* by Marc Chagall. Berlin, Paul Cassirer, 1923. Etching and drypoint, printed in black, plate: 9¾ × 7½". Collection, The Museum of Modern Art, New York. The Louis E. Stern Collection.

CHAPTER 4

Summarizing

General Considerations

Academic experience is full of summarizing. Open a social science textbook. Chances are that each of its chapters begins or ends with a summary of the chapter's contents. Locate a scientific article. Probably it is prefaced with an especially careful form of summary, an abstract. Look up a book review. More than likely it contains a paragraph or two summarizing the book under discussion. Most college lectures are summaries — they aim to condense and sometimes simplify complex information into something readily grasped by listeners. Even many textbooks themselves can be seen as summaries: Each statement in a biology textbook, for example, is a generalization founded on the published research of scientists.

Summaries are condensed presentations of material appearing elsewhere in fuller forms. As a student you will be exposed to summaries again and again. Sometimes you also will be asked to write summaries, as when you must provide an abstract for an experiment performed in chemistry lab or when an instruction on an American history exam says, "Summarize Frederick Jackson Turner's thesis about the American frontier." At other times you may be expected to summarize without explicitly being told to do so. Deceptively wide-open exam questions such as "What are the causes of World War I?" or "How do dominant cultures typically treat religious minorities?" can be thinly disguised requests to condense and present long stretches of information from a textbook or lecture notes.

Assignments like these last ones contribute to the misimpression that summarizing is essentially a passive undertaking calling for accuracy perhaps, but little more. But like the rest of the strategies we present in this book, summarizing also can be an instrument of active, creative thinking and writing. Used well, summaries can engage our judgments, our critical thinking, and our interpretive intelligence.

The assignments and essay options in this chapter ask for focused summaries of specific texts. But you'll want to keep in mind that summaries most often work in coordination with other strategies. An essay defining what anthropologists mean by "participant observation" might summarize one anthropologist's account of her experience to illustrate the concept. In a history essay about the Napoleonic Wars, you might follow a sequential account of important battles with a summary paragraph clarifying the pattern of Napoleon's rise and fall. A psychology paper classifying personality types might be subdivided into summaries of several psychologists' descriptions of particular types. A comparison for an economics class of the role of the national banking system before and after the Great Depression might interweave a scholar's description of the earlier system with another's description of the later one. An analysis of a novel for an English literature course might contain in its early paragraphs a brief summary of the crucial events of the novel. An argumentative essay for an ethics class might summarize opposing arguments before going on to make a case for stronger gun-control laws.

Cases

ABSTRACTING PATTERNS: A CASE FROM PSYCHOLOGY

Writing summaries depends on being able to recognize, connect, and represent generalizations — abstractions. We offer as an example a short passage and a summary constructed from it. The passage, about alcoholism, is taken from a psychology textbook.

> Despite public concern over the increasing use of marijuana and hard drugs, alcohol is still the most widely used and abused drug in this country. It is estimated that some 9 million people in the United States are alcoholics or problem drinkers, and alcohol consumption appears to be steadily increasing. The cost in terms of lost productivity and medical care for alcohol-related illnesses is staggering. Other social consequences include increased crime (homicides and child abuse are both related to

alcohol use), family discord, deaths and injuries on the highway, and suicide.

The stereotype of an alcoholic — the skid-row drunk — constitutes   2
only a small proportion of the individuals who have serious drinking problems. The depressed housewife who takes a few drinks to get through the day and a few more to gear up for a social evening, the businessman who needs a three-martini lunch to make it through the afternoon, the overworked physician who keeps a bottle in her desk drawer, and the high-school student who drinks more and more to gain acceptance from peers are all on their way to becoming alcoholics. There are various definitions of alcoholism, but almost all of them include the *inability to abstain* (the feeling that you cannot get through the day without a drink) and/or a *lack of control* (an inability to stop after one or two drinks). . . .

An individual can progress from social drinking to alcoholism in many   3
ways. One survey of alcoholics describes the following four stages.

1. *Prealcoholic stage.* Individual drinks socially and on occasion heavily to relieve tension and forget about problems. Heavy drinking becomes more frequent, and in times of crisis, the person resorts more and more to the bolstering effects of alcohol.
2. *Prodromal stage.* Drinking becomes furtive and may be accompanied by "blackouts," during which the person remains conscious and relatively coherent but later cannot recall events. The individual becomes preoccupied with drinking and feels guilty about it but worries about when and where she or he will have the next drink.
3. *Crucial stage.* All control is lost; once the person starts drinking, he or she continues until sick or stuporous. Social adjustment deteriorates, and the drinking becomes evident to family, friends, and employers. The person starts drinking in the morning, neglects his or her diet, and may go on the first "bender" — several days of continuous drinking. Abstinence is still possible (the individual may go for several weeks or even months without drinking), but once he or she takes a drink, the whole pattern begins again. This is called the "crucial" stage because unless the individual seeks help, she or he is in danger of becoming a chronic alcoholic.
4. *Chronic stage.* Drinking is continual; the individual lives only to drink. The body has become so accustomed to alcohol that the person may suffer withdrawal symptoms without it. Malnutrition and alcohol have produced numerous physiological disorders. The person has lost all concern for physical appearance, self-esteem, family, friends, and social status. This is the stage of the skid-row drunk.

Not all elements of these stages have been corroborated. Some   4
alcoholics seldom get drunk but consume enough alcohol each day to maintain a certain level of relaxation, and some never experience blackouts. Nevertheless, the general progression from stage to stage is typical of many alcoholics.

— Rita L. Atkinson, Richard C. Atkinson, and Ernest R. Hilgard,
Introduction to Psychology, 8th ed.

In attempting to represent this passage in a summary, we notice immediately that the bulk of the passage is given over to describing the four stages of alcoholism. It is likely that we can let the four stages that structure the reading structure our summary too:

prealcoholic stage

prodromal stage

crucial stage

chronic stage

We might even attempt to capture the structure in a single sentence:

```
According to Atkinson, Atkinson, and Hilgard in Intro-
duction to Psychology (1983), alcoholism can be de-
scribed in four stages: the prealcoholic stage during
which a person drinks to relieve tension, the prodromal
stage during which the person becomes preoccupied with
drinking, the crucial stage during which the person
loses control but is still capable of abstaining, and
the chronic stage during which the person lives only to
drink.
```

We composed this summary sentence by working up a lead-in phrase to identify the book and authors, establishing the topic, and then filling in the four stages, describing each in a few words. Along the way, we made a few adjustments in wording, and we had to settle on a phrasing strategy for keeping the four entries parallel.

Notice that as a summary is constructed, the material becomes more *abstract*. In this instance, details about each stage of alcoholism drop from sight. A summary can expand or contract to suit a writer's purpose. Any piece can be summarized in a single sentence; the question is always how much detail we are willing to do without. Here a less abstract summary would force us to choose which other points are important enough to include. Should we say that most definitions of alcoholism include something about the lack of control? Should we work in the statistic about nine million Americans? Should we acknowledge the authors' qualifying statement that "not all elements of these stages have been corroborated"? As you look back over the summary we offered as an example, reevaluate it: Do you see any ways in which, without sacrificing much conciseness, our summary can be strengthened?

PROBING A TEXT:
A CASE FROM SOCIOLOGY

Summarizing calls for the ability to see connections between general, more abstract points and the specific points supporting and complicating them. It also means seeing how those generalizations are related one to another. The more readily we can see a pattern in the general sentences of a piece, the easier it is to summarize and the more confident we feel in our accuracy.

All summaries to some extent involve interpretive decisions. We can illustrate this a little better by looking at another example. Once again, we've chosen a very structured piece (it's organized as a classification), a passage written by a sociologist about the purposes of imprisonment.

1 Lying somewhere between total annihilation of the offender on the one hand and warning or forgiveness on the other, imprisonment is generally viewed as the appropriate consequence of most serious crimes. The issue is put more bluntly by prisoners themselves in their aphorism "If you can't pull the time, don't pull the crime," but the thought is much the same.

2 Yet why is imprisonment appropriate? On what grounds is imprisonment justified? It is a cliché of modern penology that placing the offender in prison is for the purposes of punishment, deterrence, and reform. There is a beguiling neatness and simplicity about this three-pronged aim, but it requires examination. . . .

3 The idea of punishment as the purpose of imprisonment is plain enough — the person who has committed a wrong or hurt must suffer in return. The State, through its agent the prison, is entitled if not morally obligated to hurt the individual who has broken the criminal law, since a crime is by definition a wrong committed against the State. Imprisonment should be punishment, not only by depriving the individual of his liberty, but also by imposing painful conditions under which the prisoner must live within the walls.

4 Now it is true that there are few persons directly concerned with handling the offender who will advance this view of the prison's purpose as baldly as we have stated it here. Penologists, prison psychiatrists, prison administrators, judges — all are far more apt to claim that we do not place the criminal in prison to secure retribution but to accomplish better things. Yet there is some reason to doubt that this denial of punishment as a legitimate aim of imprisonment accurately reflects the opinions of the general public. However harsh an insistence on retribution may appear to be, it cannot be ignored as a social force shaping the nature of the penal institution, whether in the form of community reactions to accusations of "coddling" prisoners or the construction of budgets by the state legislators.

5 The idea of deterrence as the aim of imprisonment is somewhat more complicated, for the argument contains three parts which need to be treated separately. First, it is claimed that for those who have been imprisoned the experience is (or should be) sufficiently distasteful to

convince them that crime had best be avoided in the future. This decision to forgo crime is not expected to come from a change in the attitudes and values concerning the wrongness of crime. Rather, it supposedly flows from a sharpened awareness of the penalties attached to wrongdoing. Second, it is argued that imprisonment is important as a deterrent not for the individual who has committed a crime and who has been placed in prison but for the great mass of citizens who totter on the edge. The image of the prison is supposed to check errant impulses, and again it is fear rather than morality which is expected to guide the individual in his action. Third, there is the assertion that the deterrent effect of imprisonment is largely a matter of keeping known criminals temporarily out of circulation and the major aim of imprisonment is to keep offenders within the walls where they cannot prey on the free community, at least for the moment.

Like those who argue for imprisonment as retribution, the adherents of imprisonment as deterrence tend to support those policies which would make life in prison painful, with the possible exception of those who argue for simple custody alone. They are faced with a moral dilemma when it comes to justifying punishment for the criminal in order to deter the noncriminal, for as Morris Cohen has pointed out, we feel uneasiness in hurting Peter to keep Paul honest. A more serious problem, however, is presented by the fact that the view of imprisonment as deterrence is based on a hypothetical, complicated cause-and-effect relationship. Does the prison experience actually induce the criminal to refrain from wrongdoing through fear of another period in custody? Does the image of the prison, for those who have never been within its walls, really check the potential criminal in mid-act? Affirmative answers to these questions must be secured before the use of imprisonment for the purpose of deterrence is rationally justified and this has proven to be no easy task. The usual procedure has been to make the common-sense assumption that men are rarely so good by either nature or training that they will always conform to the law without the threat of the pains of imprisonment in the background. For those who are too humanitarian to claim vengeance as the goal of confinement and too cynical, perhaps, to hope for real reform in the majority of cases, the objective of deterrence offers a comfortable compromise.

When we turn to the idea of imprisonment as reform, it is clear that there are few who will quarrel with such a desirable goal — the disputes center on how it can be accomplished, if at all. In seeking to use imprisonment for the rehabilitation of the offender, the aim is to eradicate those causes of crime which lie within the individual and imprisonment is commonly regarded as a device to hold the patient still long enough so that this can be achieved.

Unfortunately, the advocates of confinement as a method of achieving rehabilitation of the criminal have often found themselves in the position of calling for an operation where the target of the scalpel remains unknown. In recent years, with the rise of sociological and psychological interpretations of human behavior, the search for causal factors underlying criminality has grown more sophisticated but the answer remains almost as elusive as before. Yet in spite of the confusion in this area, there are many students of the problem who believe that the reformation of the offender requires a profound change in the individual's personality and that this change can be won only by surrounding the prisoner with a "permissive" or "supportive" social atmosphere. For those devoted to a psychiatric view of criminal behavior, psychotherapy in individual or group sessions is often advanced as the most hopeful procedure; for those with a more sociological bent, self-government, meaningful work, and education are frequently claimed as minimal steps in the direction of reformation. Both factions — divergent though they may be in their theoretical arguments — are apt to agree that the punishing features of imprisonment should be reduced or eliminated if efforts at rehabilitation are to be effective.

> — Gresham M. Sykes, *The Society of Captives: A Study of a Maximum Security Prison*

Recognizing how a piece of writing is organized helps us summarize it. In the case of this sociological essay, that means seeing the categories (punishment, deterrence, reform) that organize the passage from the end of the second paragraph to the end of the excerpt. Another key is to find some comfortable way of mapping out the main points so that we can see their relationships. The more complex the text we are trying to summarize, the more we may need to construct a rough text of our own as go-between, a set of notes from which we can work more easily than from the text itself. One such intermediary text is an outline. Outlines aren't always useful in writing summaries, but they can be very helpful when the text seems subdivided into balancing parts.

When we see in the essay about imprisonment that paragraphs 3 and 4 are about punishment, 5 and 6 about deterrence, and 7 and 8 about reform, a tentative outline begins to form (even if we're not sure what to do about paragraphs 1 and 2):

Purposes of Imprisonment

A. Punishment

B. Deterrence

C. Reform

As we look more closely, having noticed that there are two paragraphs for each purpose, we suspect that each set works in a similar way. We can say at least that in each pairing the first paragraph (3, 5, and 7) establishes one of the purposes while the second goes on to do something else. What that something else is we're not sure. But we can play with some possibilities. Does each of the follow-up paragraphs raise objections? Or is each second paragraph about how the motive of punishment, deterrence, or reform has helped to shape prison policy? Or perhaps the relations between paragraphs are not so parallel after all (maybe the follow-up paragraphs simply add miscellaneous comments — our expectations of order aren't always fulfilled). After some further hesitation, we decide that each of the follow-up paragraphs says something about who favors a particular purpose — and why. Tentatively, as we begin to find some of the phrasing we will use in our summary, we can map out our interpretation of how the piece is held together:

Purposes of Imprisonment
A. Punishment
    1. Justification: State is entitled to harm those who break its laws by harming others.
    2. Favored by parts of the general public who insist on retribution.
B. Deterrence
    1. Justification
        a. Imprisonment keeps offender from repeating if penalty is strong enough.
        b. Threat of imprisonment prevents "the great mass of citizens who totter on the edge" from falling into crime.
        c. Imprisonment at least keeps current inmates off the streets and so prevents the crimes they might commit if they were free.
    2. Favored by those "who are too humanitarian to claim vengeance" and "too cynical" to hope for real reform.
C. Reform
    1. Justification: Imprisonment provides the opportunity "to eradicate those causes of crime which lie within the individual."
    2. Favored by most people, but there is no agreement on how to reform criminals, except that most professionals believe prisoners will change only in a supportive atmosphere.
        a. Psychiatrists stress group therapy.
        b. Sociologists stress "self-government," meaningful work, education.

Such outlines aren't ends in themselves; the test of their value is how well they help you to summarize a text succinctly and accurately. Before attempting to write a summary from an outline, you'll probably want to check back to the text itself, reevaluating how well the outline represents the original. Notice that while conforming to general principles of balance, the outline we've constructed has also opened up subdivisions where points grow more complicated. Even so, at a last run-through we may discover important emphases that we've neglected. For example, we might feel that the outline doesn't reflect Sykes's objections about deterrence. Rather than finding some new slot in our outline for these objections, we can just jot ourselves a reminder in the margin: "Include something about the lack of evidence that deterrence works." Notice that we are preparing for the actual sentences we'll be using in the summary by paraphrasing and by quoting distinctive phrases.

One further consideration before trying to convert the outline to a summary: We need to ask ourselves how we want to begin. Remember that we passed over the opening paragraph in constructing the outline. It's possible that we pass over it again, moving right to the heart of the matter: "According to Gresham M. Sykes, three purposes are served by sending criminal offenders to prison." But do you see any difficulties in starting this way? In the first place, we've made Sykes sound enthusiastic about sending people to prison, but his own presentation sounds more neutral than that. Second, we're missing the opportunity to come closer to the way Sykes himself frames his material: How is imprisonment justified? So a better sentence might read, "In *The Society of Captives*, Gresham M. Sykes asks how we justify placing criminals in prison." Another alternative is to try framing our own version of the question before introducing Sykes at all: "We usually assume that people convicted of crimes should be imprisoned. But why? In *The Society of Captives*, Gresham M. Sykes reviews the traditional answers."

Here, after some collapsing and editing of the sort we practiced earlier, is one draft of a summary constructed from our outline:

> We usually assume that people convicted of crimes should be imprisoned. But why? In The Society of Captives (1958), Gresham M. Sykes reviews the three traditional answers to this question. First, we imprison people to punish them. We feel that those who hurt others should be hurt in return. Punishment is favored by most of the general public. Second, some feel that imprisonment deters further crime. It can do so in three ways: by discouraging released criminals from repeating crimes, by preventing citizens "who totter on

```
the edge" from falling into crime, and by keeping po-
tential repeaters off the streets.  Sykes says that
evidence is lacking to show a cause and effect relation
between punishment and deterrence, but he says that
people "too humanitarian to claim vengeance" and "too
cynical to hope for real reform" see deterrence as a
"comfortable compromise."  Third, we imprison people in
hopes of reforming them.  Imprisonment provides the op-
portunity "to eradicate those causes of crime which lie
within the individual."  Most people agree that this is
a good aim, but there is no general agreement about how
to accomplish it.  Psychiatrists stress group therapy,
while sociologists stress "self-government, meaningful
work, and education."
```

This is an effective summary. It preserves most of the main emphases of the original, and it holds together coherently in its own right, thanks partly to the clear signposts provided by "First . . . Second . . . Third." But if you still feel a little dissatisfied, as we do, try putting your finger on the difficulty.

So far we have been treating the excerpt as though our job were simply to report on the contents of the passage. In most academic situations, however, our summary would have some other purpose. Perhaps we've been asked to examine several writers' views on the functions of prisons; perhaps we've been asked to analyze and criticize Sykes's views; perhaps we're writing an essay on the role of psychologists and sociologists in prisons. In any case, our purpose will very much affect our summary. If, for example, we were writing about the function of prison psychiatry, we might be using our summary of Sykes's writing to show that psychiatrists' efforts to help inmates must compete with prison's other functions, and perhaps even with other professionals' strategies for helping prisoners. Summarizing Sykes's work might get us started on an essay about the resistance met by psychiatrists in prisons.

Let's assume, in following through just a little further with this example, that we are writing an essay on the topic "What Do We Want Our Prisons to Do and How Well Can They Do It?" In such a context, our use of Sykes's work might change significantly to fit our purposes without distorting his. Note some of the changes in this version:

```
In The Society of Captives, Gresham M. Sykes main-
tains that our prison system pursues three purposes:
punishment, reform, and deterrence.  Most of the gen-
eral public believes in imprisonment as punishment or
```

```
retribution; prisons are meant to hurt those who have
hurt others.  Many people also believe that prisons are
a place of reform; individuals get the opportunity to
"eradicate" the causes of crime in themselves.  Some
people also believe that the thought of prison deters
crime: by discouraging those convicted from repeating
their crimes, by frightening potential criminals, or by
keeping proven criminals out of circulation.

        Taken together, these three purposes may seem a
strong argument for our present prison system.  Yet
when we look more closely, we see that the first two
aims, punishment and reform, are conflicting; it's hard
to reform someone whom you're also punishing.  Perhaps
it's this contradiction that makes sensitive people
reach for the theory of deterrence, which Sykes sees as
a "comfortable compromise" for those who cannot believe
wholeheartedly in either punishment or reform.  But
Sykes, writing in 1958, could point to no solid evi-
dence that deterrence actually works.  Do we know any
more today?
```

What adjustments have been made in arrangement or emphasis? What purpose is the summary of Sykes now being asked to serve?

DECISIONS OF EMPHASIS: A CASE FROM FOLKLORE

Let's consider one last example of the problems and strategies of summary writing, this time working with a piece that does not lend itself to outlining. The following fairy tale, "The Singing Bone," taken from the collection of the Brothers Grimm, is the sort you might be asked to analyze in a folklore class.

> There was once in a country great trouble about a wild boar, who 1
> attacked the peasants in the fields, and had killed and torn to pieces
> several men with his tusks. The king of the country promised a large
> reward to anyone who would free the land from this plague. But the
> animal was so large and strong that no man would even venture near
> the forest where he lived.
>
> At last, the king made a proclamation that he would give his only 2
> daughter in marriage to any man who would bring the wild boar to him
> dead or alive.

.There lived two brothers in that country, the sons of a poor man, 3
who gave notice of their readiness to enter on this perilous undertaking.
The eldest, who was clever and crafty, was influenced by pride; the
youngest, who was innocent and simple, offered himself from kindness
of heart.

Thereupon the king advised that, as the best and safest way would 4
be to take opposite directions in the wood, the eldest was to go in the
evening, and the youngest in the morning.

The youngest had not gone far when a little fairy stepped up to him. 5
He held in his hand a black spear, and said, "I will give you this spear
because your heart is innocent and good. With this you can go out and
discover the wild boar, and he shall not be able to harm you."

He thanked the little man, took the spear, placed it on his shoulder, 6
and, without delay, went farther into the forest. It was not long before
he espied the animal coming towards him, and fiercely making ready to
spring. But the youth stood still, and held the spear firmly in front of
him. In wild rage the fierce beast ran violently towards him, and was
met by the spear, on the point of which he threw himself, and, as it
pierced him to the heart, he fell dead.

Then the youngster took the dead monster on his shoulder, and went 7
to find his brother. As he approached the other side of the wood, where
stood a large hall, he heard music, and found a number of people dancing,
drinking wine, and making merry. His eldest brother was amongst them,
for he thought the wild boar would not run far away, and he wished to
get up his courage for the evening by cheerful company and wine.

When he caught sight of his youngest brother coming out of the 8
forest laden with his booty, the most restless jealousy and malice rose
in his heart. But he disguised his bitter feelings and spoke kindly to his
brother, and said:

"Come in, and stay with us, dear brother, and rest awhile, and get 9
up your strength by a cup of wine."

So the youth, not suspecting anything wrong, carried the dead boar 10
into his brother's house, and told him of the little man he had met in the
wood, who had given him the spear, and how he had killed the wild
animal.

The elder brother persuaded him to stay and rest till the evening, 11
and then they went out together in the twilight, and walked by the river
till it became quite dark. A little bridge lay across the river, over which
they had to pass, and the eldest brother let the young one go before
him. When they arrived at the middle of the stream, the wicked man
gave his youngest brother a blow from behind, and he fell down dead
instantly.

But, fearing he might not be quite dead, he threw the body over 12
the bridge into the river, and through the clear waters saw it sink into
the sand. After this wicked deed he ran home quickly, took the dead
wild boar on his shoulders, and carried it to the king, with the pretense
that he had killed the animal, and that therefore he could claim the princess
as his wife, according to the king's promise.

But these dark deeds are not often concealed, for something happens 13 to bring them to light. Not many years after a herdsman, passing over the bridge with his flock, saw beneath him in the sand a little bone as white as snow, and thought that it would make a very nice mouthpiece for his horn.

As soon as they had passed over the bridge, he waded into the 14
middle of the stream, for the water was very shallow, took up the bone, and carried it home to make a mouthpiece for his horn.

But the first time he blew the horn after the bone was in, it filled 15
the herdsman with wonder and amazement; for it began to sing of itself, and these were the words it sang:

> Ah! dear shepherd, you are blowing your horn
> With one of my bones, which night and morn
> Lie still unburied, beneath the wave
> Where I was thrown in a sandy grave.
> I killed the wild boar, and my brother slew me,
> And gained the princess by pretending 'twas he.

"What a wonderful horn," said the shepherd, "that can sing of itself! 16
I must take it to my lord the king."

As soon as the horn was brought before the king and blown by the 17
shepherd, it at once began to sing the same song and the same words.

The king was at first surprised, but his suspicion being aroused, he 18
ordered that the sand under the bridge should be examined immediately, and then the entire skeleton of the murdered man was discovered, and the whole wicked deed came to light.

The wicked brother could not deny the deed; he was therefore 19
ordered to be tied in a sack and drowned, while the remains of his murdered brother were carefully carried to the churchyard, and laid to rest in a beautiful grave.

— "The Singing Bone" from *The Complete Brothers Grimm Fairy Tales*

As with other narratives, this one doesn't lend itself to outlining because there is no quick way to perceive a hierarchy of points: One event simply follows another. Our choices about which parts to emphasize are hard to make, and many of the choices we do make will seem arbitrary. But if outlining is not likely to help, some other form of note taking might. One possibility is to construct a "scratch" outline, simply listing in notation form (or even in sentences) the points that seem important enough to choose among later. Here's an example of a scratch outline made from "The Singing Bone":

```
                    "The Singing Bone"
Boar terrorizing a kingdom.

King's promise of reward.

King ups the ante by offering daughter.

Two brothers, oldest proud, younger kind, undertake the
    mission.
```

Young brother encounters fairy who gives him a spear.
He encounters the boar and kills it.
Goes to tell older brother the good news; older brother
    reacts as if pleased but feels malice.
At his first opportunity, older brother kills younger
    brother and tosses him into a stream.
He takes the boar and claims the princess.
Some years later a herdsman finds a bone in the stream.
He uses the bone to make a mouthpiece for his horn.
The horn plays itself and tells the story of the mur-
    dered young man.
The herdsman takes the horn to the king who makes the
    right deductions, discovers the body of the young
    brother.
The older brother is drowned, and the younger buried.

By combining some entries, passing over others, and retrieving a point or two that we decide we need after all, we might produce a summary like this one:

In the fairy story "The Singing Bone," a king offers his daughter to any man who can kill the wild boar
that has been ravaging his kingdom. Two brothers undertake the mission. While the older brother waits at
an inn, the younger brother enters the forest, where he
meets a fairy who gives him a magic spear. With the
spear, the young man soon kills the boar and returns to
tell his brother the good news. The older brother pre-
tends to be pleased, but at the first opportunity he
kills his brother, tosses the body into a river, and
takes the boar to the king. Some years later a herdsman finds a bone in the river and makes it into a
mouthpiece for his horn. The horn is capable of playing itself and tells the story of the murdered man.
The herdsman takes his horn to the king, who deduces
what has happened and orders his son-in-law drowned.

Note that even a straightforward summary like this is the product of dozens, if not hundreds, of very particular decisions about what to include, exclude, combine, and connect. For example, we decided not to characterize the two brothers as "innocent" and "proud," preferring to let those characteristics remain implied. We decided to ignore the slight upbeat of the ending emphasizing the younger brother's peaceful grave. We characterized the spear as "magic," even though there's no absolute evidence that it's anything more than a good spear. By omitting the king's stipulation that the two brothers hunt separately and at different times, we've made the older brother seem not only arrogant but slothful. Are these serious omissions and distortions of the original? It's hard to tell without knowing what purpose our summary is supposed to serve. Imagine how the retelling of this story might shift to accommodate the following perspectives: a student of folklore looking at a variety of tales that offer princesses as rewards, a child psychologist examining how fairy tales deal with sibling rivalries, or a literature student thinking about the conventional ways stories are opened and closed.

Let us risk a short summary of our comments on summarizing. In academic contexts, you'll be exposed to summaries as abstracts, as introductions and conclusions to textbook chapters, as reviews, as lectures, and as textbooks themselves. But the most common form of summary occurs when one writer summarizes the work of another, whether to understand it, to pass it on, to build on it, or to criticize it. Writing an effective summary calls on your ability to see relations between general points, to express those relations in a coherent way, to take advantage of parallels, to make use of apt quotations, and to edit for compression. Summaries can vary in length according to your purposes, gaining or losing detail at each level of abstraction. A summary will always attempt to represent the original fairly — in structure, in emphasis, in tone. But any summary involves numerous decisions and invariably becomes an interpretation of the original. Above all, you'll want any summary that you write to help express some purpose of your own.

Assignments: First Passes

1. Abstracting a Sequence of Events: Effects of a Nuclear Explosion

After reading the following passage, from Jonathan Schell's *The Fate of the Earth*, decide how it is organized and construct a summary that reflects that organization. Try writing your summary first as a paragraph and then as a single sentence.

> Whereas most conventional bombs produce only one destructive effect — the shock wave — nuclear weapons produce many destructive

effects. At the moment of the explosion, when the temperature of the weapon material, instantly gasified, is at the superstellar level, the pressure is millions of times the normal atmospheric pressure. Immediately, radiation, consisting mainly of gamma rays, which are a very high-energy form of electromagnetic radiation, begins to stream outward into the environment. This is called the "initial nuclear radiation," and is the first of the destructive effects of a nuclear explosion. In an air burst of a one-megaton bomb — a bomb with the explosive yield of a million tons of TNT, which is a medium-sized weapon in present-day nuclear arsenals — the initial nuclear radiation can kill unprotected human beings in an area of some six square miles. Virtually simultaneously with the initial nuclear radiation, in a second destructive effect of the explosion, an electromagnetic pulse is generated by the intense gamma radiation acting on the air. In a high-altitude detonation, the pulse can knock out electrical equipment over a wide area by inducing a powerful surge of voltage through various conductors, such as antennas, overhead power lines, pipes, and railroad tracks. The Defense Department's Civil Preparedness Agency reported in 1977 that a single multi-kiloton nuclear weapon detonated one hundred and twenty-five miles over Omaha, Nebraska, could generate an electromagnetic pulse strong enough to damage solid-state electrical circuits throughout the entire continental United States and in parts of Canada and Mexico, and thus threaten to bring the economies of these countries to a halt. When the fusion and fission reactions have blown themselves out, a fireball takes shape. As it expands, energy is absorbed in the form of X rays by the surrounding air, and then the air re-radiates a portion of that energy into the environment in the form of the thermal pulse — a wave of blinding light and intense heat — which is the third of the destructive effects of a nuclear explosion. (If the burst is low enough, the fireball touches the ground, vaporizing or incinerating almost everything within it.) The thermal pulse of a one-megaton bomb lasts for about ten seconds and can cause second-degree burns in exposed human beings at a distance of nine and a half miles, or in an area of more than two hundred and eighty square miles, and that of a twenty-megaton bomb (a large weapon by modern standards) lasts for about twenty seconds and can produce the same consequences at a distance of twenty-eight miles, or in an area of two thousand four hundred and sixty square miles. As the fireball expands, it also sends out a blast wave in all directions, and this is the fourth destructive effect of the explosion. The blast wave of an air-burst one-megaton bomb can flatten or severely damage all but the strongest buildings within a radius of four and a half miles, and that of a twenty-megaton bomb can do the same within a radius of twelve miles. As the fireball burns, it rises, condensing water from the surrounding atmosphere to form the characteristic mushroom cloud. If the bomb has been set off on the ground or close enough to it so that the fireball touches the surface, in a so-called ground burst, a crater will be formed, and tons of dust and debris will be fused with the intensely radioactive fission products and sucked up into the mushroom cloud. This mixture will return to earth as radioactive fallout, most of it in the form of fine ash, in the fifth destructive effect of the explosion.

Depending upon the composition of the surface, from forty to seventy percent of this fallout — often called the "early" or "local" fallout — descends to earth within about a day of the explosion, in the vicinity of the blast and downwind from it, exposing human beings to radiation disease, an illness that is fatal when exposure is intense. Air bursts may also produce local fallout, but in much smaller quantities. The lethal range of the local fallout depends on a number of circumstances, including the weather, but under average conditions a one-megaton ground burst would, according to the report by the Office of Technology Assessment, lethally contaminate over a thousand square miles. (A lethal dose, by convention, is considered to be the amount of radiation that, if delivered over a short period of time, would kill half the able-bodied young adult population.)

— Jonathan Schell, *The Fate of the Earth*

2. Summarizing a Table: Regional Distribution of World Trade

Table 1 is from *Africa and the International Economy, 1800–1960*, by J. Forbes Munro. Stressing the data that seem most significant, briefly summarize the information provided in the table in a way that takes the focus of Munro's book into consideration. You may encounter some difficulty in making generalizations about this table; discuss any frustrations you face in interpreting it in your essay. (For some suggestions on discussing the trends revealed in statistical tables, you might want to look back at pp. 52–54.)

TABLE 1. Regional Distribution of World Trade, 1876–1960

	TRADE AS % OF TOTAL WORLD TRADE		% CHANGE
	1876–80	1960	1876–1960
World	100	100	—
Europe	66.9	51.4	− 23.1
N. America	9.5	18.4	+ 93.6
C. & S. America	5.4	7.6	+ 40.7
Asia	12.9	14.3	+ 10.8
Africa	1.9	5.5	+ 189.4
Oceania	3.4	2.4	− 29.4

SOURCES: A. G. Kenwood and A. L. Lougheed, *The Growth of the International Economy, 1820–1960* (1971), p. 93; *U.N. Yearbook of International Trade Statistics* (1966).

3. Summarizing a Table: Trends in Higher Education

David A. Garvin includes the following table (Table 2) in his book *The Economics of University Behavior*. What conclusions can you draw about trends in American higher education from 1959 to 1975? Stressing the data that seem to you most significant, summarize, in one or two paragraphs, the general trends you see reflected in the table. (For some suggestions for discussing the trends revealed in statistical tables, you might want to look back at pp. 52–54.)

TABLE 2.   Institutions of Higher Education by Type of Control and Highest Degree Offered, 1959–1960 to 1975

	1959–1960		FALL 1965		FALL 1970		FALL 1975	
	NO.	%	NO.	%	NO.	%	NO.	%
TYPE OF CONTROL								
Public	703	35	790	36	1101	43	1454	48
Private	1325	65	1417	64	1472	57	1601	52
HIGHEST DEGREE OFFERED								
2 but less than 4 years	593	29	664	30	897	35	1141	37
B.A. or first professional	739	36	823	37	850	33	872	29
M.A. or more, but below Ph.D.	455	22	472	21	528	21	637	21
Ph.D. or equivalent	210	10	227	10	298	12	405	13
Other	31	2	21	1	0	0	0	0

PERCENTAGE INCREASE, 1959–1960 TO 1975

Public institutions	106.8
Private institutions	20.8
Institutions of 2 but less than 4 years	92.4
Institutions offering B.A. or first professional degrees	18.0
Institutions offering M.A. or more, but below the Ph.D.	40.0
Institutions offering Ph.D. or equivalent	92.9

SOURCE: Anderson (1976, pp. 76.141–76.143).

4. Rereading for Structure: Mycenaean Civilization

The following passage seems to read in a fairly straightforward way. But in an effort to summarize it paragraph by paragraph, you may run into difficulty keeping your summary coherent. After considering the source of this difficulty, write a summary paragraph expressing what you think is the author's main purpose.

In a separate paragraph, consider the following questions: What about the original made writing your summary easy or difficult? What did you have to omit, and how did you determine what to include or leave out?

About two thousand years before the Christian era, the first Greek-speaking peoples descended into the southern part of the Balkan Peninsula. There they found an indigenous population at whose origins and   1 antiquity it is impossible to guess. The initial contact resulted in the destruction of some sites, but succeeding centuries saw an integration of Greek and pre-Greek elements, rather than eradication of one by the other. By the beginning of the sixteenth century B.C. it is possible to speak of the first Greek civilization, called Achaean by Homer and Mycenaean by modern convention: a far-flung empire of princely citadels surrounded by the fields and villages of farmers and craftsmen.

About 1500 or so, the Mycenaean power expanded to include the island of Crete, where the non-Greek Minoans had created an elegant and wealthy civilization. The Mycenaeans evidently destroyed the Minoan capital of Knossos, occupied and rebuilt it, and remained as stewards of the whole island for the next four centuries. By 1300, the Mycenaean Empire had spread to the shores of Asia Minor and westward to Italy. But a major war against Troy, in about 1200, dangerously drained the power of Mycenae. A century later that civilization lay in ruins, while a ruder sort of Greek immigrant from northern lands willingly took over the fields and flocks, but not the palaces. There, only the wind moaned in the ruined battlements, lizards scampered in the great audience halls, and in the counting rooms spiders wove their webs. It would be another three centuries before an urban society of any complexity reappeared on the shores of the Aegean.

The evidence for Mycenaean society is threefold. The traditional tales were never forgotten and were preserved by Homer, the poets, and later mythographers. These legends describe the founding of the great Mycenaean states by sons and grandsons of the Gods, the great deeds of these heroes, and finally, the culmination of Mycenaean imperialism in the grand, tragic war of the Greeks against the Trojans. But legends preserved by oral tradition and folk memory can be confusing and contradictory. There is also an inevitable element of the supernatural and the miraculous in every legend which makes it easy for the skeptical to condemn the entire tradition. Therefore, as little as a hundred years ago, in an era when scientific method was beginning to be demanded of history, classical scholars treated the Greek myths only as a contribution to world folk literature; anyone who dared suggest that they contained a germ of historical truth was considered a fool or a charlatan.

One man held out against this attitude with stubborn courage. Heinrich Schliemann (1822–1890), a brilliant and wealthy German merchant, had been so captivated in his youth by Homer's account of the Trojan War that he resolved to find the actual site of Troy, long forgotten to the world. In 1870, despite the jeers of "professional" archaeologists, Schliemann started to dig at Hissarlik, in the northwestern corner of Turkey. Almost immediately he came upon massive fortifications, one level of which had been destroyed in a vast conflagration. Despite Schliemann's sometimes crude methods and overly romantic interpretation of the evidence uncovered, when he left Troy three years later he had laid the groundwork for classical archaeology. Few scholars would now deny that there was a Troy and that Schliemann had found it.

Crossing to the Greek mainland, Heinrich Schliemann began to excavate the great Mycenaean palaces, most of which were far better preserved than the city of the Trojans. His work, carried on by generation after generation of modern archaeologists, has demonstrated to the world that the Greek legends contain a considerable nucleus of accurate, historical data. The palaces of the Achaeans (as Homer had called them) are where Homer had said they were. Mycenaean cemeteries proved to contain a race of warrior nobles such as those described in the Greek epic tradition. And the uniformity of the pottery and other hardware found in graves and in the ruins of the citadels showed conclusively that Mycenaean society was the product of a civilization unified culturally and economically, as the tradition had suggested.

By the 1930s, archaeology had revealed a whole new world to historians of ancient Greece, who had once been content to scoff at myths and confine their research to libraries whole continents away from the shores of the Aegean. One thing only was lacking to provide better understanding of Mycenaean society and to confirm for once and for all that the Mycenaeans were the real ancestors of the Greeks: literary documents of some kind.

In 1939, the American archaeologist Carl Blegen located the ruined and forgotten palace of King Nestor of Pylos, known to all readers of the *Iliad* for his wise (and often lengthy) counsel. Almost the first day of work, the excavators came across thousands of clay tablets inscribed with a peculiar syllabic script and baked in the conflagration which had destroyed the palace. Similar tablets had been found many years previously in the great Minoan palace at Knossos, and it had been taken for granted that they were written in the unknown Minoan language. Now here was a far greater number, preserved in the archive rooms of a society that Blegen, for one, was convinced was Greek. The Second World War intervened to delay publication and study of the tablets, but in 1953, a brilliant young English architect named Michael Ventris deciphered the script and demonstrated to the world that the language was in fact an archaic form of Greek, written in a script borrowed from the Minoans (as the Greeks were later to borrow the Phoenician alphabet).

The tablets are records from the Mycenaean archives, and similar ones have subsequently been found at Mycenae and Thebes. Because of their nature they are often difficult to interpret, being no more than the accounts and receipts of a highly organized bureaucracy. But despite the difficulties and sometimes bitter controversy that surrounds the tablets and their use, they have provided a vitally important link in the network of evidence for the workings of Mycenaean society.

— Frank J. Frost, *Greek Society*

5. Rereading for Structure: Attitudes Toward Schooling

The following passage comes toward the end of Sara Lawrence Lightfoot's study of the effective American high school. You'll probably find some parts of it harder to read than others. After deciding what you think is Lightfoot's main purpose, write a summary paragraph. You may want to change the order of her observations or de-emphasize some parts in favor of others.

In a separate paragraph, evaluate your summary. What aspects of the original have you been able to capture, and what seemed elusive? Has your effort to summarize alerted you to anything in Lightfoot's text that you would like to question further?

The combined impact of the subtle negativisms of social science   1
investigations and the flagrant attacks of muckrakers over the last few decades has produced a cultural attitude towards schools which assumes their inadequacies and denies evidence of goodness. This pessimism and cynicism has had a peculiarly American cast. The persistent complaints seem to reflect a powerful combination of romanticism, nostalgia, and feelings of loss for a simpler time when values were clear; when children were well behaved; when family and schools agreed on educational values and priorities; when the themes of honor, respect, and loyalty directed human interaction. In comparison to this idealized retrospective view, the contemporary realities of school seem nothing short of catastrophic. David K. Cohen, in a powerful essay entitled "Loss as a Theme of Social Policy," talks about the ways in which our grief over a lost community frames our views of today's chaos. We envision an idealized past of homogeneous and firmly entrenched values, and the contemporary conflict over competing moral systems appears threatening. We envision a time long ago when communities and neighborhoods were glued together by mutual exchange, deeply felt gratitude, and common interests, making today's transient city blocks and urban anonymity appear profoundly troublesome.

However, the romanticism and idealization of the past is most vividly   2
felt when we look back at schooling. Rural and small town images flood our minds; pictures of earnest, healthy children sitting dutifully in a spare classroom; big students attending to the small ones. The teacher, a revered and dedicated figure, lovingly and firmly dispenses knowledge, and the conscientious children, hungry for learning, respond thoughtfully to the teacher's bidding. These romantic pictures, that many Americans continue to refer to when they look at today's schools, produce feelings of great disappointment and disenchantment.

Today's high schools, in particular, seem farthest away from this   3
idealized past. They appear grotesque in their permissiveness and impending chaos. The large, unruly adolescents appear threatening, and their swiftly changing, faddish preoccupations are baffling to their parents' conservative eyes. It is simply difficult for parents and the community to see them as "good." They are seen as scary and incomprehensible, or dull and boring. Rarely can adults look beyond their comparisons with idealized visions of a more simple and orderly world, beyond the mannerly high school scenes that they remember, beyond the often trivial swings of adolescent fashion and habit, to see the good inside the institutions adolescents inhabit.

After years of doing research in schools for very young children, I   4
recall these vague feelings of threat and disappointment when I began visiting high schools. I was struck by how physically large the students were, how I was sometimes confused about who was teacher and who was student. Boys with men's voices, bearded faces, and huge, bulky

frames filled the hallways with their large movements. Girls, with their painted faces, pseudo-sophisticated styles, lady's gossip, and casual swagger seemed to be so different from the pleated skirts, bobby socks, and ponytails that I remembered from my high school days. At first I was shocked by the children in adult frames, afraid of their groupiness, and saw the lingering dangers just below the surface of tenuous order. As I became increasingly accustomed to their presence, their habits, their rituals, I began to see the vulnerabilities and uncertainties of adolescents, rather than be preoccupied with the symbols of maturity and power. In a strange way, I began to be reminded of my own adolescence and saw great similarities between my high school days and the contemporary scene. But before I could explore and document "the good" in these high schools, I had to move inside them, grow accustomed to today's scene, and learn the difference between my own inhibitions and fears and the real warnings of danger. Perceptions of today's high schools, therefore, are plagued by romanticized remembrances of "the old days" and anxiety about the menacing stage of adolescence. Both of these responses tend to distort society's view of high schools and support the general tendency to view them as other than good.

— Sara Lawrence Lightfoot, *The Good High School:*
Portraits of Character and Culture

Assignments: Options

6. An Anthropology Option: Rites of Passage

This selection comes from an introductory anthropology text. Summarize it first. Then refocus your summary to help you write an essay about the rites of passage you find most typical of your culture. Come up with several examples, and discuss at least one of those examples in some detail.

From *Cultural Anthropology*
CONRAD PHILLIP KOTTAK

Early in this century Arnold van Gennep, a Belgian anthropologist, studied rites of passage in a variety of societies. Passage rites, found throughout the world, are exemplified by such phenomena as vision quests of certain Native American populations in North America. As boys moved from boyhood to socially recognized manhood, they temporarily separated themselves from their communities to journey alone to the wilderness. After a period of isolation, often accompanied by fasting and drug consumption, the young men would see a vision, which would become their personal guardian spirit. On return to their communities they would be reintegrated as adults. In contemporary societies, rites of passage include confirmations, baptisms, bar mitzvahs, and fraternity hazing. Passage rites do not refer only to such changes in social status as from boyhood to manhood, or from nonmember to fraternity brother, but apply more generally to any change in place, condition, social position, or age.

Examining data from a variety of societies, van Gennep generalized 2 that all rites of passage have three phases: separation, margin, and aggregation. Separation is exemplified by the initial detachment of individuals from the group or their initial movement from one place to another; aggregation, by their reentry into society after completion of the rite. More recently, anthropologist Victor Turner has focused on the marginal period or condition, the position between states, the limbo during which individuals have left one place or state but have not yet entered or joined the next. Van Gennep used the Latin term *limen* (threshold) to refer to this in-between period, and Turner's designation of it as the *liminal* phase of a passage rite will be used here.

On the basis of data from several societies, Turner identified generalized attributes of liminality. Liminal individuals occupy ambiguous social positions. They exist apart from ordinary status distinctions and expectations, living in a time out of time. They are cut off from normal social intercourse. Turner points out that liminal periods are ritually demarcated by a variety of contrasts with regular social life. For example, among the Ndembu of Zambia, whom Turner studied, a newly chosen chief had to undergo a passage rite before taking office. During the liminal period, his past and future positions in society were ignored, even reversed, and he was subjected to a variety of insults, harangues, instructions, and humiliations.

In contrast to the vision quest and the initiation of the Ndembu chief, 4 which are individualistic, passage rites are often collective. A group of people — boys undergoing circumcision, fraternity initiates, men attending military boot camps, football players at summer training camps, women becoming nuns — pass through the rites together. Turner lists contrasts or oppositions between liminality and normal social life. Most notable is a social aspect of collective liminality that he calls "communitas." People who experience liminality together characteristically form an egalitarian community; whatever social distinctions have existed before, or will exist afterwards, are temporarily forgotten. Liminal individuals experience the same treatment and conditions and are expected to act alike. Liminality may be marked ritually and symbolically by reversals of ordinary behavior. Sexual taboos may be intensified or, conversely, sexual excess may be encouraged.

Turner also points out that not only is liminality always a temporary 5 part of any passage rite, it may, in certain social contexts, become a permanent attribute of particular groups. This will occur, Turner suggests, in the most socially diverse societies, presumably state-organized societies and particularly modern nations. Religious sects often use liminal characteristics to set themselves off from the rest of the society. Such requirements as humility, poverty, equality, obedience, sexual abstinence, and silence may be conditions of sect membership. The ritual aspect of persons, settings, and events may also be communicated through liminal attributes that set them off as extraordinary — outside normal social space and regular time. Thus, like Radcliffe-Brown, Turner focuses on the social functions of rituals, in this case of passage rites. Their role in creating temporary or permanent social solidarity is his main interest.

7. A Sociology Option: The Barrio Economy

After reading the following excerpt, write a summary paragraph that reflects its organization. Then go back and rework your summary, using it in a short essay that responds to one of the following questions.

a. What are the economic obstacles faced by someone in the barrio?
b. What does Moore see as original about her approach to the subject of the barrio economy? What are the advantages of her approach?
c. If you grew up in a barrio — or a section of a city that resembled a barrio — discuss the accuracy of Moore's analysis. Does her analysis correspond to what you know about the economics of the community?

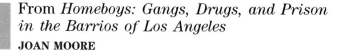

From *Homeboys: Gangs, Drugs, and Prison in the Barrios of Los Angeles*
JOAN MOORE

In the large cities of the Southwest (most notably, Los Angeles, San Diego, Phoenix, San Antonio, and El Paso), the Mexican ghetto appeared for the same reason as the ethnic and racial ghettos of the Eastern and Midwestern industrial cites — to meet the needs and opportunities of the local labor markets. But in the early decades of the twentieth century, when Mexicans first entered the U.S. in large numbers, Southwestern labor markets were different from those of New York and Chicago. Railroads, mines, and large-scale agriculture offered the major workplaces. In the East, new immigrants worked in such labor-intensive manufactures as the garment sweatshops of New York.   1

There was a much smaller range of labor-intensive industry in the Southwest; this difference dictated the pattern of settlement for Chicanos and for other racial minorities. Yet slowly, through the past few years, the market for workers at the bottom of the urban job structure has grown to resemble that of Eastern cities as the Western economy has diversified.   2

THE SEGMENTED LABOR MARKET OF THE BARRIOS

It is now common wisdom that the opportunity structure has changed substantially for the "new" urban minorities. In turn, the changing structure is greatly affecting community social structure — and therefore the ways in which people solve their problems of survival. . . . In general, this new structure is the segmented labor market. An understanding   3 of its structure and function is essential for understanding any of the social or cultural features of modern urban ethnic neighborhoods and communities.

We will begin with a sociological version of a rather controversial   4
theory in labor economics of labor market processes. In its assumption of a segmented labor market, this theory departs from both conventional economics and popular conceptions by arguing at the outset that the type of job always described in the American dream of normalcy (with security, good pay, and a career ladder) is relatively scarce. . . . The fact is that only a minority of American workers hold jobs with these features.

Yet it is more significant to our study that very few people on the   5
bottom of the labor market will ever have access to good jobs. This is because of the segmentation that is caused not only by differences between types of workers (varying levels of education, motivation, and skills, and more or less attractiveness because of age, race, and sex), but also by differences among the employing organizations. Urban minority workers are found disproportionately in the lowest-paying segments of the labor market. These are unstable jobs, often only part-time, with below-average wages and virtually no possibility of advancement. The only protections for such employees are those required by the government, such as compensation in case of injury and social security deductions in lieu of private pensions. These are *types* that we are talking about; peripheral firms (marginal employers) are as likely to demand workers with the job habits of the casual laborer as a large, well-established employer is to demand workers with the job habits of the middle-class Protestant ethic. These firms and employers constitute the "secondary labor market" to which many people in today's urban ghettos are largely confined. The employees are simply making do with the inadequate best that is available in the barrio or ghetto.

This view has important implications. Not the least of them is the   6
well-founded suspicion that, just as the inner-city schools produce workers for the secondary labor market, so do other schools in other areas produce workers for managerial positions. Rist has called the inner-city minority schools "factories for failure" after a careful study of interaction processes at the lower grade levels. This term accurately describes the chances of the individual failure to attain a good job. But, in another sense, the young school dropout is *well* prepared for jobs in the peripheral firms. He has been thoroughly socialized in the schools to expect very little: he learns to cope with, and finally abandons all hope of, pleasing the teacher, and he establishes patterns of "truancy, tardiness and evasion of school rules." Finally, the young dropout acquires habits and attitudes ("tastes for work" . . .) that can qualify him (or her) only for jobs in the secondary labor market. . . . It is essential for peripheral employers that their workers not expect much, as they must be hired and fired as finances permit and as the market demands. . . .

From the point of view of the employer, segmentation of the labor   7
market means that the ghetto worker rarely competes with the workers in the primary labor market for the scarce good jobs. . . .

Besides the normal wage-labor market, there are two important   8
economic structures in the poverty areas of American cities: the welfare
structure and the illegal structure. The welfare economy is the familiar
combination of income from food stamps, Aid to Families with Dependent
Children, programs for the aged and veterans, unemployment compensation, and other benefits. There are also occasional special programs,
such as the Cuban Refugee program. In the mid-1960s a careful survey
found that about a quarter of the residents of the barrios of Los Angeles
received income from welfare and related services. . . . One may also
add the numerous and elaborate manpower programs (such as the Neighborhood Youth Corps), which were intended to provide socialization experiences for youth in the secondary labor market but have become
straightforward programs to keep kids off the streets. . . . These employment and training programs tend to offer minimum wages for specified
periods of time for a limited number of jobs.

The second important economic structure in the barrios of Los An-   9
geles is the illegal economy. It is elaborate and well funded. It includes
casual labor (part-time drug dealers and, in some cities, numbers runners),
middle management, and top management. Of course, illegal structures
differ somewhat from legal businesses. Some economists consider them
the essence of the truly competitive enterprise in their response to market
conditions. Middle-management heroin dealers, for example, enter and
leave their business rapidly in response to supply factors and consumer
demand. In addition, they respond to warnings about law enforcement
activity. Bullock discusses the role of police corruption in the illegal
economy (what he calls the "sub-economy") of the black and Chicano
slums of Los Angeles. Providing information about impending "heat" that
leads to shutdowns of illegal businesses is a major aspect of police corruption and an additional element of barrio business operations in the
illegal economy. . . .

TRIPARTITE ECONOMIC STRUCTURE

This interpretation of three economic structures makes it difficult to   10
estimate the importance of the illegal economy in the total economic
structure of poor urban minority areas. . . .

It is common for a worker to migrate back and forth from positions   11
in one or another economic structure in the peripheral sector of the
economy. He may change, for example, from a minimum-wage job to
unemployment compensation to the illegal labor market. Many sources
of income in the welfare economy are conditional upon losing a position
in the work economy. . . . Multiple roles may also exist within one family,
with one member working part time, another receiving welfare or unemployment compensation, and yet another working some type of hustle.
In general, the welfare and illegal economies subsidize the marginal industries of the peripheral sector of the secondary labor market. Without
"fall-back" and supplementary sources of income, the minimum wage is
not enough to support a family. Even if an individual primarily identifies
himself with work — legitimate jobs, in the secondary labor market —

this person (or other members of his family) must often resort to alternative sources of income. . . .

IMPLICATIONS OF THE TRIPARTITE MODEL

The tripartite model offers a view of the American opportunity structure that differs from both common sense and many sociological writings. The model's primary assumption is rooted in the structure of the American economy; there are not enough jobs in the core or primary structure for all — or even most — Americans to attain the vision of normalcy. The model effectively illustrates the economic situation of the urban barrio resident. This is a world of limited opportunities, with legitimate jobs generally offering little prospect for lifetime satisfaction. In this respect, the segmented labor market becomes an essential concept for understanding the structure and context of the Chicano gang, the use and marketing of illegal drugs and stolen merchandise, and the prison involvements of the residents of the Los Angeles barrios. **12**

It is important to remember that the continuous shuttle from one economic structure to another consumes a great amount of time and energy. Each structure is differently organized. Hiring in the secondary labor market entails different and often informal job search patterns . . . , which take a great deal of time. Obtaining income from the welfare economy means establishing a status in at least one — and usually several — bureaucracies. Getting income from the illegal economy means establishing — and sustaining — yet another status with a very different set of income-givers. Economic survival, especially in times of inflation, is a more than full-time occupation for the barrio resident. While it is true that there are sometimes high levels of income, for most of the casual participants in the illegal economy the income generated is small. Ultimately, total income only maintains survival, even when an individual participates in several economic structures simultaneously. **13**

8. A History Option: China Versus Vietnam

The following is an account of China's invasion of Vietnam in 1979, written by *Newsweek* journalists in the midst of the invasion. After reading and re-reading the article, do one of the following assignments:

a. Summarize separately the observations of correspondent David Hatcher and correspondent Andrew Nagorski; then offer a general summary of the implications of the invasion for U.S. foreign policy as speculated by the *Newsweek* editors. Incorporate all three summaries in a single essay about the invasion.
b. See if you can locate a recent account of relations between China and Vietnam. Then write a short summary of the events described in the *Newsweek* article from a standpoint provided by the passage of time.
c. If you have recently immigrated from China or Vietnam and have knowledge about the relations between China and Vietnam, write a short

summary of the events described in the *Newsweek* article from your own point of view. (If someone in your family or circle of friends has recently immigrated, you could interview them and use that information to help you to do this assignment.)

Showdown in Asia

STEVEN STRASSER AND NEWSWEEK REPORTERS

As we drove in a Russian-made truck past the tiny settlement of Cam 1
Duong, we heard the unmistakable whistle of incoming artillery. A Chinese shell landed in the middle of the village, setting one of the thatch-roofed houses ablaze. Half a dozen survivors scurried to safety across a wooden footbridge suspended above the river. I didn't doubt that the entire village would be destroyed within hours. On another bridge nearby, a bright blue-and-gold sign bore Ho Chi Minh's favorite slogan: "Nothing is more precious than independence and freedom."

A potentially momentous Asian war was being fought in almost total 2 obscurity last week. *Newsweek*'s David Hatcher was one of the few Westerners to witness the shooting as Chinese attackers poured into Vietnam. Peking's forces overran four provincial capitals, including Lao Cai, 4 miles above Cam Duong on Vietnam's northwestern frontier. . . . To the east, a crucial battle seemed to be taking shape near the town of Lang Son, just down the road from the erstwhile "Friendship Pass" between the two Communist nations. The outcome of the Chinese invasion was even harder to discern than the details of the fighting. But as the two antagonists chewed methodically at each other's armies, it became clear that China's onslaught was more than just a short-lived punitive raid.

The longer the invasion lasted, China's gamble in Vietnam became 3 more perilous for all concerned. Before the attack, Deputy Prime Minister Teng Hsiao-ping said the object was to "punish" the Vietnamese for invading China's ally, Cambodia, and to "teach them a lesson" for incidents along the Chinese frontier. But Peking's troops continued to advance slowly along a front 12 to 20 miles deep, while the Vietnamese drew back, avoiding a set-piece battle. Western intelligence analysts monitoring the war through satellite photos and radio interceptions could not tell whether China was trying to expand its hold on Vietnamese territory or merely wanted to goad its enemy into a decisive fight. "Either way," said one expert in Bangkok, "they're escalating the risk of Soviet intervention. The Chinese must know that every day they stay in Vietnam, the risk gets bigger."

Vietnam's friend, the Soviet Union, warned China to "stop before it 4 is too late." Rhetoric aside, the initial Russian reaction was cautious. A flotilla of Soviet intelligence-gathering ships stationed off the Vietnamese coast was reinforced last week by a cruiser and a destroyer under Adm. Vladimir Maslov, commander of the Soviet Pacific Fleet. The Russians also continued a modest airlift of military supplies to Hanoi. As Hatcher left the Vietnamese capital, he saw two giant An-22 transports on the runway, along with six of Vietnam's Soviet-built MiG-21 fighters and nine American-made F-5s, captured nearly four years ago in South Vietnam. Beyond furnishing supplies and intelligence information, the Soviets could yet respond to China's invasion in a number of ways. . . . At worst, that response could plunge Russia and China into a nuclear war.

POISONING RELATIONS

To avert any such threat, Jimmy Carter sent a personal appeal for restraint to Soviet President Leonid Brezhnev on the Washington-Moscow hotline. Carter argued that the Chinese invasion was a direct result of Vietnam's actions in Cambodia. Brezhnev reportedly resisted that notion, but in general, a source said, his reply indicated that Russia would not "act precipitately or irrationally." But the Soviet Union could not resist blaming the U.S., in part, for China's attack, charging that the warm welcome given Teng last month [in Washington] led Peking to "draw the conclusion that the Americans would not object" to an invasion of Vietnam. Whatever the case, the dispute over China was poisoning relations between Washington and Moscow. Sources told *Newsweek* that senior officials in both capitals had begun to question whether the second-stage treaty on strategic arms limitation (SALT II) could ever be concluded. 5

Carter also sent Teng Hsiao-ping a personal appeal for restraint. The message was carried by Treasury Secretary Michael Blumenthal, who arrived in Peking late last week on a previously scheduled mission to discuss trade and finance. Some of Carter's critics argued that the trip should have been postponed to express U.S. disapproval of the Vietnamese invasion. But for the Administration, the watchword was business as usual. "This affair doesn't affect us," a top official said of the war in Vietnam, "so why should we punish ourselves?" In fact, the U.S. had decided that it would try to maintain its relations with both Russia and China, even if they got into a war with each other. 6

SENSATIONAL REPORTS

Despite some sensational reports in the press last week, China's invasion was no blitzkrieg. After his trip to the front, Hatcher reported: 7

> In Pho Lu, a command post 20 miles south of Lao Cai, a 40-second artillery barrage echoed at our backs — further evidence that the Chinese were continuing their slow but steady southward march. In the confusion, our convoy was held up at a Red River ferry crossing for more than an hour. A Russian correspondent, accompanied by a Polish interpreter and a Vietnamese television crew, took the opportunity to interview Georgia Congressman Billy Lee Evans, the ranking member of our expedition. The southern politician walked a verbal tightrope, describing the action he had witnessed at Cam Duong but declining the invitation to condemn the Chinese "aggressors" and praise the "heroic" Vietnamese defenders. 8

After a luncheon of East German blood sausage and yeasty Vietnamese beer, we were shown two Chinese prisoners captured near Lao Cai. They were infantryman Tung Fei-lin, 34, and "espionage agent" Wu Chien-tao, 22. Wu's hands were tied behind his back, his face was scraped and bruised and his eyes brimmed with contempt. After a photo session, the two prisoners were hauled off in a Soviet truck, and we continued our own journey back to Hanoi. We rested briefly at Yen Bai, where the local people's committee toasted us with peach liquor. On behalf of the dignitaries, our interpreter thanked us for coming to witness the "American invasion." When we burst into laughter, he quickly corrected his slip of the tongue. We all drank together to peace in Vietnam. 9

Peking had given ample warning that it intended to attack Vietnam, massing armor, attack planes, and 180,000 troops along the craggy, 800-mile border. Even so, the size and swiftness of China's predawn invasion on Feb. 17 stunned many Vietnamese. Sleepy border towns awoke to the thump of heavy artillery and the high-pitched whine of Chinese MiGs, and within hours villagers were dodging mortar shells. "The Chinese are coming," a Vietnamese border guard screamed into his radio transmitter. "We are surrounded. There are Chinese everywhere." 10

MOUNTED CAVALRYMEN

Waves of Chinese infantrymen poured into Vietnam's five northern provinces at 26 different points stretching from the Gulf of Tonkin to the jungled hills near Laos. Some of the assaults were spearheaded by tanks. Others, on narrow mountain trails, were led by mounted cavalrymen. The principal thrusts were directed at the classical invasion routes through the mountains from China: in the west, the Red River Valley and the provincial capital of Lao Cai; in the east, the "Friendship Pass" and the city of Lang Son. The sweeping nature of the attack left Hanoi's generals guessing about its ultimate objectives. 11

On the second day of the incursion, China's forces paused a modest 6 miles inside Vietnam's border, and some analysts predicted hopefully that Peking's invasion would be a mere hit-and-run attack. But the invaders, their war machine rusty from disuse, apparently had stopped only for reinforcements and supplies. By late last week, the Chinese force in the border area had swollen to 250,000 men or more, and the invasion had begun to press forward again. Soon the Chinese were launching a two-pronged attack on Lang Son. One Chinese column attacked from the captured rail center of Dong Dang; another closed in from the coastal plain as the Vietnamese sent reinforcements and heavy artillery up Highway 1 to the eastern front. 12

The commanders of China's forces were veterans of the civil war and the Korean conflict. . . . But they may have advanced cautiously because most of their soldiers were getting their first taste of battle. After a week of fighting, the Vietnamese claimed that they had killed 15,000 Chinese, and although that seemed to be a substantial exaggeration, there was no doubt that some clashes had been intense. 13

For its defense, Vietnam was relying primarily on 100,000 local mi-   **14**
litiamen, many of them veterans of Vietnam's long struggle against France
and the U.S. "Don't underestimate the Vietnamese militia," said an analyst
in Bangkok. "They're well-trained, battle-tested troops with modern
weapons, and they're fighting on their home turf. They defeated two
imperialist powers in the past 25 years and they're not awed by the
Chinese."

The militiamen were defending jagged mountain country, which is of   **15**
minimal value compared with the fertile bottom land and important industrial areas nearer Hanoi. "It's like Dante's inferno up there," said
French Gen. Marcel Bigeard, who spent six years in the border region
during France's colonial war. "There are hills, hidden ravines, rockpiles
and lots of jungle, and all the roads leading to the frontier are ideal for
ambush."

Except for one regiment near Lang Son, Vietnam had not committed   **16**
its regular-army divisions to battle by late last week. That seemed to be
a sound move; it preserved a force to defend Hanoi, it avoided a retreat
from Cambodia (where Vietnam has 150,000 troops), and it thwarted
China's efforts to lure main-force units into a meat grinder. "The Vietnamese saw through that trap," said an analyst in Bangkok. "Why get
your forces chewed up when the Chinese have already announced they're
not going to stay long?" Although Chinese warplanes flew about 500
sorties last week, there was no aerial threat to Hanoi. The Vietnamese
capital displayed a calm, business-as-usual atmosphere, and radio programs were only infrequently interrupted by war bulletins claiming sweeping Vietnamese victories.

All was strangely quiet as well on China's home front. Only late in   **17**
the week did the government publicly acknowledge that Chinese troops
were fighting on Vietnam's side of the border. *Newsweek*'s Andrew Nagorski, who visited Peking and other Chinese cities, filed this report:

> Most of the world learned fairly quickly about China's dawn attack on   **18**
> Vietnam — but not foreign diplomats in Peking. More than twelve hours
> after the war began, many diplomats gathered at the U.S. Liaison Office for
> a belated Valentine's Day party. Raising my voice over the disco beat of the
> Bee Gees, I asked one envoy about the prospects for a Chinese attack on
> Vietnam. "There was one radio report earlier that fighting had begun — but
> of course it turned out to be false," he replied. "My guess is that the Chinese
> won't invade." Only well past midnight did news of the crisis finally reach
> Peking's diplomatic community.
>
> Throughout China there was an almost detached attitude about the war.   **19**
> In a school outside Shanghai, I noticed a blackboard drawing of a Vietnamese
> peasant stooped under the weight of a Soviet missile on his back. But the
> prominent wall posters in major cities made no mention of the conflict until
> late in the week; then, surprisingly, one poster in Peking complained that
> "China has lost its international reputation" by invading Vietnam. More typ-
> ically, Chinese news media briefly mentioned the army's "counterattacks"
> along Vietnam's border. *People's Daily* reported: "We are still defeating the
> Vietnamese invaders." Foreign businessmen continued their stampede for
> the China market. "It has nothing to do with me," shrugged a Dutch busi-

nessman in Shanghai. "Production will keep going. That's what the Chinese are really interested in."

The same kind of optimism still seemed to characterize American   20
companies doing business with China. "This might become an all-out war, but so far it's just a border fracas," said a spokesman for Inter-Continental Hotels, whose corporate leaders were in Peking last week to nail down an agreement to build a chain of luxury hotels in China. "While we're not soothsayers, it's far too early to say this will affect our business with the Chinese."

A FLAT "NO"

The Carter Administration was also determined to keep on dealing   21
with China, even though some thought that the Blumenthal mission looked like an endorsement of China's invasion. Republican Sen. Charles Mathias of Maryland called the trip "part of the Administration's misplayed 'China card.'" Mathias complained that Washington had sent Moscow a series of unfriendly "signals" in recent months. "Now," he said, "while China is invading Vietnam, we are sending another signal — our Secretary of the Treasury." Administration officials saw no conflict. "The Blumenthal visit is the economic equivalent of Teng's trip to the U.S.," said one. "It was never in danger." En route to Peking, Blumenthal himself was asked whether the invasion of Vietnam would make his trade negotiations more difficult. He answered with a flat "No," adding that he was aiming for a "long-term relationship" unaffected by other factors.

To head off possible trouble between Russia and China, the U.S.   22
called late last week for an emergency meeting of the United Nations Security Council. The objective, said U.S. Ambassador Andrew Young, was "to get a cease-fire and to avoid a fight-to-the-death type of situation." As the debate began, the Soviet Union and its allies were seeking an arms embargo against China, while the U.S. was trying to show that China's invasion of Vietnam should be considered in tandem with Vietnam's invasion of Cambodia. But the Cambodian issue did not help Peking much, since there was little sympathy for the brutal regime of former Cambodian strongman Pol Pot.

Throughout the week, U.S. officials kept insisting, in the words of   23
one, "It's not our war." Administration officials soft-pedaled the fighting as much as they could, and they made a point of not placing U.S. forces in the Far East on combat alert. Fairly or not, however, Washington suffered from guilt by association in some quarters. "China would not have invaded if it had not first succeeded in building its links with the U.S. and Japan," maintained a spokesman for Taiwan's Foreign Ministry. Even a U.S. diplomat conceded: "It's interesting to ask to what extent Peking's designs on Indochina caused it to make concessions to the U.S. in return for normalization. Sure, the Chinese want our technology and our money for modernization. But they only started being really receptive when it looked as if the Vietnamese were going to take Cambodia."

AN UNCERTAIN COURSE

It was not known when or how Peking would change course. Unless 24
the Chinese can kill large numbers of Vietnamese troops or extract
significant concessions from Hanoi, they may decide to remain on Vietnamese soil for some time. "If they withdrew now, I don't think they'd
be satisfied with the public perception of what they've done," said a
Carter aide. "They may have to do more than they have already to get
credit in the world for 'punishing' Vietnam." Whatever China's intentions
were, there was little the U.S. could do about it — beyond begging both
Peking and Moscow to keep their heads.

9. A History Option: A Brief History of U.S. Immigration Laws

By selectively summarizing the following entries, describe the main historical trends in U.S. immigration policy through 1979. As a follow-up option,
briefly research the Simpson-Mazoli immigration bill passed in 1984; rework
your earlier summary to place this more recent legislation in historical context.

Chronology from *Coming to America: Immigrants from the Far East*
LINDA PERRIN

The authority to formulate immigration policy rests with Congress and 1
is contained in Article 1, Section 8, Clause 3 of the Constitution, which
provides that Congress shall have the power to "regulate commerce with
foreign nations, and among the several States, and with the Indian tribes."

Alien Act of 1798: authorized the deportation of aliens by the President. 2
Expired after two years.
    For the next seventy-five years there was no federal legislation
restricting admission to, or allowing deportation from, the United States.

Act of 1875: excluded criminals and prostitutes and entrusted inspection 3
of immigrants to collectors of the ports.

Act of 1882: excluded lunatics and idiots and persons liable to becoming 4
public charges.
    First Chinese Exclusion Act.

Acts of 1885 and 1887: contract labor laws, which made it unlawful to 5
import aliens under contract for labor or services of any kind. (Exceptions:
artists, lecturers, servants, skilled aliens in an industry not yet established
in the United States, etc.)

Act of 1888: amended previous acts to provide for expulsion of aliens 6
landing in violation of contract laws.

Act of 1891: first exclusion of persons with certain diseases; felons, also [7] persons having committed crimes involving moral turpitude; polygamists, etc.

Act of 1903: further exclusion of persons with certain mental diseases, [8] epilepsy, etc.; beggars; also "anarchists or persons who believe in, or advocate the overthrow by force or violence of the Government of the United States or of all government or of all forms of law or the assassination of public officials." Further refined deportation laws.

Acts of 1907, 1908: further exclusions for health reasons, such as [9] tuberculosis.
Exclusion of persons detrimental to labor conditions in the United States, specifically Japanese and Korean skilled or unskilled laborers.
Gentlemen's Agreement with Japan: in which Japan agreed to restrictions imposed by the United States.

Act of 1917: codified previous exclusion provisions, and added literacy [10] test. Further restricted entry of other Asians.

Act of 1921: First Quota Law, in which approximately 350,000 immigrants [11] were permitted entry, mostly from northern or western Europe.

Act of 1924: National Origins Quota System set annual limitations on the [12] number of aliens of any nationality immigrating to the U.S. The act also decreed, in a provision aimed primarily at the Japanese, that no alien ineligible for citizenship could be admitted to the U.S.

"Gigolo Act" of 1937: allowing deportation of aliens fraudulently marrying [13] in order to enter the United States either by having marriage annulled or by refusing to marry once having entered the country.

Act of 1940: Alien Registration Act provided for registration and finger- [14] printing of all aliens.

Act of 1943: Chinese Exclusion Acts repealed. [15]

Act of 1945: War Brides Act admitted during the three years of act's [16] existence approximately 118,000 brides, grooms, and children of servicemen who had married foreign nationals during World War II.

Act of 1949: Displaced Persons Act admitted more than four hundred [17] thousand people displaced as a result of World War II (to 1952).

Act of 1950: Internal Security Act excluded from immigrating any present [18] or foreign member of the Communist party, and made more easily deportable people of this class already in the U.S. Also provided for alien registration by January 10 of each year.

Act of 1952: Immigration and Nationality Act codified all existing legis- [19] lation; also eliminated race as a bar to immigration.

Acts of 1953–1956: Refugee Relief acts admitted orphans, Hungarians [20] after 1956 uprising, skilled sheepherders.

1957: special legislation to admit Hungarian refugees.   21

1960: special legislation paroled Cuban refugees into the U.S.   22

Act of 1965: legislation amending act of 1952 phased out national origins   23
quotas by 1968, with new numerical ceilings on a first come, first served
basis. Numerical ceilings (per annum): 120,000 for natives of the Western
Hemisphere; 170,000 for natives of the Eastern Hemisphere. New preference categories: relatives (74 percent), scientists, artists (10 percent),
skilled and unskilled labor (10 percent), refugees (6 percent).

Act of 1977: allowed Indo-Chinese who had been paroled into the U.S.   24
to adjust their status to permanent resident.

1979: Presidential directive allowed thousands of Vietnamese "boat peo-   25
ple" to enter the U.S.

10. A Composition Option: Revising Strategies

As is the case with many articles in academic journals, the following
article by composition researcher Nancy Sommers begins with a review of
the literature — that is, a review of other research that is related to hers
and an explanation of how her research will confirm or challenge the other
work. Then comes a discussion of the methods Sommers used in conducting
her research. Finally, Sommers presents her results and the implications of
those results for her discipline, in this case the teaching of writing.

Experiment with different kinds of summaries that could be used for
different purposes. You might try a single-sentence summary, of the kind you
would include in a literature review like Sommers's. You might also try writing
a brief paragraph, an abstract of Sommers's article for a paper you are writing
on research on the composing process of college writers. Or you might try
shifting your audience and writing an essay for other student writers your
age, reporting to them the results of Sommers's research and its implications
for them. Though Sommers's article lends itself to a neat review-methods-
results-implications summary, you also might want to consider the benefits
(and liabilities) of organizing your summary in other ways.

Revision Strategies of Student Writers and Experienced Adult Writers
NANCY SOMMERS

Although various aspects of the writing process have been studied ex-   1
tensively of late, research on revision has been notably absent. The reason
for this, I suspect, is that current models of the writing process have
directed attention away from revision. With few exceptions, these models
are linear; they separate the writing process into discrete stages. Two
representative models are Gordon Rohman's suggestion that the com-

posing process moves from prewriting to writing to rewriting and James Britton's model of the writing process as a series of stages described in metaphors of linear growth, conception–incubation–production.[1] What is striking about these theories of writing is that they model themselves on speech: Rohman defines the writer in a way that cannot distinguish him from a speaker ("A writer is a man who . . . puts [his] experience into words in his own mind" . . .); and Britton bases his theory of writing on what he calls (following Jakobson) the "expressiveness" of speech.[2] Moreover, Britton's study itself follows the "linear model" of the relation of thought and language in speech proposed by Vygotsky, a relationship embodied in the linear movement "from the motive which engenders a thought to the shaping of the thought, *first* in inner speech, *then* in meanings of words, and *finally* in words." . . . What this movement fails to take into account in its linear structure — "first . . . then . . . finally" — is the recursive shaping of thought by language; what it fails to take into account is *revision*. In these linear conceptions of the writing process revision is understood as a separate stage at the end of the process — a stage that comes after the completion of a first or second draft and one that is temporally distinct from the prewriting and writing stages of the process.[3]

The linear model bases itself on speech in two specific ways. First of all, it is based on traditional rhetorical models, models that were created to serve the spoken art of oratory. In whatever ways the parts of classical rhetoric are described, they offer "stages" of composition that are repeated in contemporary models of the writing process. Edward Corbett, for instance, describes the "five parts of a discourse" — *inventio, dispositio, elocutio, memoria, pronuntiatio* — and, disregarding the last two parts since "after rhetoric came to be concerned mainly with written discourse, there was no further need to deal with them,"[4] he produces a model very close to Britton's conception [*inventio*], incubation [*dispositio*], production [*elocutio*]. Other rhetorics also follow this procedure, and they do so not simply because of historical accident. Rather, the process represented in the linear model is based on the irreversibility of speech. Speech, Roland Barthes says, "is irreversible":

> A word cannot be retracted, except precisely by saying that one retracts it. To cross out here is to add: if I want to erase what I have just said, I cannot do it without showing the eraser itself (I must say *"or rather . . ."* *"I expressed myself badly . . ."*); paradoxically, it is ephemeral speech which

[1] D. Gordon Rohman and Albert O. Wlecke, "Pre-writing: The Construction and Application of Models for Concept Formation in Writing," Cooperative Research Project No. 2174, U.S. Office of Education, Department of Health, Education, and Welfare; James Britton, Anthony Burgess, Nancy Martin, Alex McLeod, Harold Rosen, *The Development of Writing Abilities (11–18)* (London: Macmillan Education, 1975).

[2] Britton is following Roman Jakobson, "Linguistics and Poetics," in T. A. Sebeok, *Style in Language* (Cambridge, Mass.: MIT Press, 1960).

[3] For an extended discussion of this issue see Nancy Sommers, "The Need for Theory in Composition Research," *College Composition and Communication*, 30 (February, 1979), 46–49.

[4] *Classical Rhetoric for the Modern Student* (New York: Oxford University Press, 1965), p. 27.

is indelible, not monumental writing. All that one can do in the case of a spoken utterance is to tack on another utterance.[5]

What is impossible in speech is *revision:* like the example Barthes gives, revision in speech is an afterthought. In the same way, each stage of the linear model must be exclusive (distinct from the other stages) or else it becomes trivial and counterproductive to refer to these junctures as "stages."

By staging revision after enunciation, the linear models reduce revision in writing, as in speech, to no more than an afterthought. In this way such models make the study of revision impossible. Revision, in Rohman's model, is simply the repetition of writing; or to pursue Britton's organic metaphor, revision is simply the further growth of what is already there, the "preconceived" product. The absence of research on revision, then, is a function of a theory of writing which makes revision both superfluous and redundant, a theory which does not distinguish between writing and speech.

What the linear models do produce is a parody of writing. Isolating revision and then disregarding it plays havoc with the experiences composition teachers have of the actual writing and rewriting of experienced writers. Why should the linear model be preferred? Why should revision be forgotten, superfluous? Why do teachers offer the linear model and students accept it? One reason, Barthes suggests, is that "there is a fundamental tie between teaching and speech," while "writing begins at the point where speech becomes *impossible.*"[6] The spoken word cannot be revised. The possibility of revision distinguishes the written text from speech. In fact, according to Barthes, this is the essential difference between writing and speaking. When we must revise, when the very idea is subject to recursive shaping by language, then speech becomes inadequate. This is a matter to which I will return, but first we should examine, theoretically, a detailed exploration of what student writers as distinguished from experienced adult writers *do* when they write and rewrite their work. Dissatisfied with both the linear model of writing and the lack of attention to the process of revision, I conducted a series of studies over the past three years which examined the revision processes of student writers and experienced writers to see what role revision played in their writing processes. In the course of my work the revision process was redefined as *a sequence of changes in a composition — changes which are initiated by cues and occur continually throughout the writing of a work.*

METHODOLOGY

I used a case study approach. The student writers were twenty freshmen at Boston University and the University of Oklahoma with SAT verbal scores ranging from 450–600 in their first semester of composition.

[5] Roland Barthes, "Writers, Intellectuals, Teachers," in *Image-Music-Text,* trans. Stephen Heath (New York: Hill and Wang, 1977), pp. 190–191.
[6] "Writers, Intellectuals, Teachers," p. 190.

The twenty experienced adult writers from Boston and Oklahoma City included journalists, editors, and academics. To refer to the two groups, I use the terms *student writers* and *experienced writers* because the principal difference between these two groups is the amount of experience they have had in writing.

Each writer wrote three essays, expressive, explanatory, and persuasive, and rewrote each essay twice, producing nine written products in draft and final form. Each writer was interviewed three times after the final revision of each essay. And each writer suggested revisions for a composition written by an anonymous author. Thus extensive written and spoken documents were obtained from each writer.   6

The essays were analyzed by counting and categorizing the changes made. Four revision operations were identified: deletion, substitution, addition, and reordering. And four levels of changes were identified: word, phrase, sentence, theme (the extended statement of one idea). A coding system was developed for identifying the frequency of revision by level and operation. In addition, transcripts of the interviews in which the writers interpreted their revisions were used to develop what was called a *scale of concerns* for each writer. This scale enabled me to codify what were the writer's primary concerns, secondary concerns, tertiary concerns, and whether the writers used the same scale of concerns when revising the second or third drafts as they used in revising the first draft.   7

REVISION STRATEGIES OF STUDENT WRITERS

Most of the students I studied did not use the terms *revision* or *rewriting*. In fact, they did not seem comfortable using the word *revision* and explained that revision was not a word they used, but the word their teachers used. Instead, most of the students had developed various functional terms to describe the type of changes they made. The following are samples of these definitions: 8

> *Scratch Out and Do Over Again:* "I say scratch out and do over, and that means what it says. Scratching out and cutting out. I read what I have written and I cross out a word and put another word in; a more decent word or a better word. Then if there is somewhere to use a sentence that I have crossed out, I will put it there."
>
> *Reviewing:* "Reviewing means just using better words and eliminating words that are not needed. I go over and change words around."
>
> *Reviewing:* "I just review every word and make sure that everything is worded right. I see if I am rambling; I see if I can put a better word in or leave one out. Usually when I read what I have written, I say to myself, 'that word is so bland or so trite,' and then I go and get my thesaurus."
>
> *Redoing:* "Redoing means cleaning up the paper and crossing out. It is looking at something and saying, no that has to go, or no, that is not right."
>
> *Marking Out:* "I don't use the word rewriting because I only write one draft and the changes that I make are made on top of the draft. The changes that I make are usually just marking out words and putting different ones in."
>
> *Slashing and Throwing Out:* "I throw things out and say they are not good. I like to write like Fitzgerald did by inspiration, and if I feel inspired then I don't need to slash and throw much out."

The predominant concern in these definitions is vocabulary. The 9 students understand the revision process as a rewording activity. They do so because they perceive words as the unit of written discourse. That is, they concentrate on particular words apart from their role in the text. Thus one student quoted above thinks in terms of dictionaries, and, following the eighteenth century theory of words parodied in *Gulliver's Travels*, he imagines a load of things carried about to be exchanged. Lexical changes are the major revision activities of the students because economy is their goal. They are governed, like the linear model itself, by the Law of Occam's razor that prohibits logically needless repetition: redundancy and superfluity. Nothing governs speech more than such superfluities; speech constantly repeats itself precisely because spoken words, as Barthes writes, are expendable in the cause of communication. The aim of revision according to the students' own description is therefore to clean up speech; the redundancy of speech is unnecessary in writing, their logic suggests, because writing, unlike speech, can be reread. Thus one student said, "Redoing means cleaning up the paper and crossing out." The remarkable contradiction of cleaning by marking might, indeed, stand for student revision as I have encountered it.

The students place a symbolic importance on their selection and 10 rejection of words as the determiners of success or failure for their compositions. When revising, they primarily ask themselves: can I find a better word or phrase? A more impressive, not so clichéd, or less hum-drum word? Am I repeating the same word or phrase too often? They approach the revision process with what could be labeled as a "thesaurus philosophy of writing"; the students consider the thesaurus a harvest of lexical substitutions and believe that most problems in their essays can be solved by rewording. What is revealed in the students' use of the thesaurus is a governing attitude toward their writing: that the meaning to be communicated is already there, already finished, already produced, ready to be communicated, and all that is necessary is a better word "rightly worded." One student defined revision as "redoing"; "redoing" meant "just using better words and eliminating words that are not needed." For the students, writing is translating: the thought to the page, the language of speech to the more formal language of prose, the word to its synonym. Whatever is translated, an original text already exists for students, one which need not be discovered or acted upon, but simply communicated.[7]

The students list repetition as one of the elements they most worry 11 about. This cue signals to them that they need to eliminate the repetition either by substituting or deleting words or phrases. Repetition occurs, in large part, because student writing imitates — transcribes — speech: attention to repetitious words is a manner of cleaning speech. Without a sense of the developmental possibilities of revision (and writing in general) students seek, on the authority of many textbooks, simply to clean up their language and prepare to type. What is curious, however, is that students are aware of lexical repetition, but not conceptual rep-

---

[7] Nancy Sommers and Ronald Schleifer, "Means and Ends: Some Assumptions of Student Writers," *Composition and Teaching*, II (in press).

etition. They only notice the repetition if they can "hear" it; they do not diagnose lexical repetition as symptomatic of problems on a deeper level. By rewording their sentences to avoid the lexical repetition, the students solve the immediate problem, but blind themselves to problems on a textual level; although they are using different words, they are sometimes merely restating the same idea with different words. Such blindness, as I discovered with student writers, is the inability to "see" revision as a process; the inability to "re-view" their work again, as it were, with different eyes, and to start over.

The revision strategies described above are consistent with the students' understanding of the revision process as requiring lexical changes but not semantic changes. For the students, the extent to which they revise is a function of their level of inspiration. In fact, they use the word *inspiration* to describe the ease or difficulty with which their essay is written, and the extent to which the essay needs to be revised. If students feel inspired, if the writing comes easily, and if they don't get stuck on individual words or phrases, then they say that they cannot see any reason to revise. Because students do not see revision as an activity in which they modify and develop perspectives and ideas, they feel that if they know what they want to say, then there is little reason for making revisions.   12

The only modification of ideas in the students' essays occurred when they tried out two or three introductory paragraphs. This results, in part, because the students have been taught in another version of the linear model of composing to use a thesis statement as a controlling device in their introductory paragraphs. Since they write their introductions and their thesis statements even before they have really discovered what they want to say, their early close attention to the thesis statement, and more generally the linear model, function to restrict and circumscribe not only the development of their ideas, but also their ability to change the direction of these ideas.   13

Too often as composition teachers we conclude that students do not willingly revise. The evidence from my research suggests that it is not that students are unwilling to revise, but rather that they do what they have been taught to do in a consistently narrow and predictable way. On every occasion when I asked students why they hadn't made any more changes, they essentially replied, "I knew something larger was wrong, but I didn't think it would help to move words around." The students have strategies for handling words and phrases and their strategies helped them on a word or sentence level. What they lack, however, is a set of strategies to help them identify the "something larger" that they sensed was wrong and work from there. The students do not have strategies for handling the whole essay. They lack procedures or heuristics to help them reorder lines of reasoning or ask questions about their purposes and readers. The students view their compositions in a linear way as a series of parts. Even such potentially useful concepts as "unity" or "form" are reduced to the rule that a composition, if it is to have form, must have an introduction, a body, and a conclusion, or the sum total of the necessary parts.   14

The students decide to stop revising when they decide that they   15
have not violated any of the rules for revising. These rules, such as
"Never begin a sentence with a conjunction" or "Never end a sentence
with a preposition," are lexically cued and rigidly applied. In general,
students will subordinate the demands of the specific problems of their
text to the demands of the rules. Changes are made in compliance with
abstract rules about the product, rules that quite often do not apply to
the specific problems in the text. These revision strategies are teacher-
based, directed towards a teacher-reader who expects compliance with
rules — with pre-existing "conceptions" — and who will only examine
parts of the composition (writing comments about those parts in the
margins of their essays) and will cite any violations of rules in those
parts. At best the students see their writing altogether passively through
the eyes of former teachers or their surrogates, the textbooks, and are
bound to the rules which they have been taught.

REVISION STRATEGIES OF EXPERIENCED WRITERS

One aim of my research has been to contrast how student writers   16
define revision with how a group of experienced writers define their
revision processes. Here is a sampling of the definitions from the experienced writers:

> *Rewriting:* "It is a matter of looking at the kernel of what I have written,
> the content, and then thinking about it, responding to it, making decisions,
> and actually restructuring it."
> *Rewriting:* "I rewrite as I write. It is hard to tell what is a first draft
> because it is not determined by time. In one draft, I might cross out three
> pages, write two, cross out a fourth, rewrite it, and call it a draft. I am
> constantly writing and rewriting. I can only conceptualize so much in my
> first draft — only so much information can be held in my head at one time;
> my rewriting efforts are a reflection of how much information I can encompass
> at one time. There are levels and agenda which I have to attend to in each
> draft."
> *Rewriting:* "Rewriting means on one level, finding the argument, and
> on another level, language changes to make the argument more effective.
> Most of the time I feel as if I can go on rewriting forever. There is always
> one part of a piece that I could keep working on. It is always difficult to
> know at what point to abandon a piece of writing. I like this idea that a piece
> of writing is never finished, just abandoned."
> *Rewriting:* "My first draft is usually very scattered. In rewriting, I find
> the line of argument. After the argument is resolved, I am much more
> interested in word choice and phrasing."
> *Revising:* "My cardinal rule in revising is never to fall in love with what
> I have written in a first or second draft. An idea, sentence, or even a phrase
> that looks catchy, I don't trust. Part of this idea is to wait a while. I am
> much more in love with something after I have written it than I am a day
> or two later. It is much easier to change anything with time."
> *Revising:* "It means taking apart what I have written and putting it back
> together again. I ask major theoretical questions of my ideas, respond to
> those questions, and think of proportion and structure, and try to find a

controlling metaphor. I find out which ideas can be developed and which should be dropped. I am constantly chiseling and changing as I revise."

The experienced writers describe their primary objective when re-   **17** vising as finding the form or shape of their argument. Although the metaphors vary, the experienced writers often use structural expressions such as "finding a framework," "a pattern," or "a design" for their argument. When questioned about this emphasis, the experienced writers responded that since their first drafts are usually scattered attempts to define their territory, their objective in the second draft is to begin observing general patterns of development and deciding what should be included and what excluded. One writer explained, "I have learned from experience that I need to keep writing a first draft until I figure out what I want to say. Then in a second draft, I begin to see the structure of an argument and how all the various sub-arguments which are buried beneath the surface of all those sentences are related." What is described here is a process in which the writer is both agent and vehicle. "Writing," says Barthes, unlike speech, "develops like a seed, not a line,"[8] and like a seed it confuses beginning and end, conception and production. Thus, the experienced writers say their drafts are "not determined by time," that rewriting is a "constant process," that they feel as if (they) "can go on forever." Revising confuses the beginning and end, the agent and vehicle; it confuses, *in order to find,* the line of argument.

After a concern for form, the experienced writers have a second   **18** objective: a concern for their readership. In this way, "production" precedes "conception." The experienced writers imagine a reader (reading their product) whose existence and whose expectations influence their revision process. They have abstracted the standards of a reader and this reader seems to be partially a reflection of themselves and functions as a critical and productive collaborator — a collaborator who has yet to love their work. The anticipation of a reader's judgment causes a feeling of dissonance when the writer recognizes incongruities between intention and execution, and requires these writers to make revisions on all levels. Such a reader gives them just what the students lacked: new eyes to "re-view" their work. The experienced writers believe that they have learned the causes and conditions, the product, which will influence their reader, and their revision strategies are geared towards creating these causes and conditions. They demonstrate a complex understanding of which examples, sentences, or phrases should be included or excluded. For example, one experienced writer decided to delete public examples and add private examples when writing about the energy crisis because "private examples would be less controversial and thus more persuasive." Another writer revised his transitional sentences because "some kinds of transitions are more easily recognized as transitions than others." These examples represent the type of strategic attempts these experienced writers use to manipulate the conventions of discourse in order to communicate to their reader.

[8] *Writing Degree Zero* in *Writing Degree Zero and Elements of Semiology,* trans. Annette Lavers and Colin Smith (New York: Hill and Wang, 1968), p. 20.

But these revision strategies are a process of more than commu- **19** nication; they are part of the process of *discovering meaning* altogether. Here we can see the importance of dissonance; at the heart of revision is the process by which writers recognize and resolve the dissonance they sense in their writing. Ferdinand de Saussure has argued that meaning is differential or "diacritical," based on differences between terms rather than "essential" or inherent qualities of terms. "Phonemes," he said, "are characterized not, as one might think, by their own positive quality but simply by the fact that they are distinct."[9] In fact, Saussure bases his entire *Course in General Linguistics* on these differences, and such differences are dissonant; like musical dissonances which gain their significance from their relationship to the "key" of the composition which itself is determined by the whole language, specific language (parole) gains its meaning from the system of language (langue) of which it is a manifestation and part. The musical composition — a "composition" of parts — creates its "key" as in an overall structure which determines the value (meaning) of its parts. The analogy with music is readily seen in the compositions of experienced writers: both sorts of composition are based precisely on those structures experienced writers seek in their writing. It is this complicated relationship between the parts and the whole in the work of experienced writers which destroys the linear model; writing cannot develop "like a line" because each addition or deletion is a reordering of the whole. Explicating Saussure, Jonathan Culler asserts that "meaning depends on difference of meaning."[10] But student writers constantly struggle to bring their essays into congruence with a predefined meaning. The experienced writers do the opposite: they seek to discover (to create) meaning in the engagement with their writing, in revision. They seek to emphasize and exploit the lack of clarity, the differences of meaning, the dissonance, that writing as opposed to speech allows in the possibility of revision. Writing has spatial and temporal features not apparent in speech — words are recorded in space and fixed in time — which is why writing is susceptible to reordering and later addition. Such features make possible the dissonance that both provokes revision and promises, from itself, new meaning.

For the experienced writers the heaviest concentration of changes **20** is on the sentence level, and the changes are predominantly by addition and deletion. But, unlike the students, experienced writers make changes on all levels and use all revision operations. Moreover, the operations the students fail to use — reordering and addition — seem to require a theory of the revision process as a totality — a theory which, in fact, encompasses the *whole* of the composition. Unlike the students, the experienced writers possess a nonlinear theory in which a sense of the whole writing both precedes and grows out of an examination of the parts. As we saw, one writer said he needed "a first draft to figure out what to say," and "a second draft to see the structure of an argument buried

[9] *Course in General Linguistics,* trans. Wade Baskin (New York, 1966), p. 119.
[10] Jonathan Culler, *Saussure* (Penguin Modern Masters Series; London: Penguin Books, 1976), p. 70.

beneath the surface." Such a "theory" is both theoretical and strategical; once again, strategy and theory are conflated in ways that are literally impossible for the linear model. Writing appears to be more like a seed than a line.

Two elements of the experienced writers' theory of the revision 21 process are the adoption of a holistic perspective and the perception that revision is a recursive process. The writers ask: what does my essay as a *whole* need for form, balance, rhythm, or communication. Details are added, dropped, substituted, or reordered according to their sense of what the essay needs for emphasis and proportion. This sense, however, is constantly in flux as ideas are developed and modified; it is constantly "re-viewed" in relation to the parts. As their ideas change, revision becomes an attempt to make their writing consonant with that changing vision.

The experienced writers see their revision process as a recursive 22 process — a process with significant recurring activities — with different levels of attention and different agenda for each cycle. During the first revision cycle their attention is primarily directed towards narrowing the topic and delimiting their ideas. At this point, they are not as concerned as they are later about vocabulary and style. The experienced writers explained that they get closer to their meaning by not limiting themselves too early to lexical concerns. As one writer commented to explain her revision process, a comment inspired by the summer 1977 New York power failure: "I feel like Con Edison cutting off certain states to keep the generators going. In first and second drafts, I try to cut off as much as I can of my editing generator, and in a third draft, I try to cut off some of my idea generators, so I can make sure that I will actually finish the essay." Although the experienced writers describe their revision process as a series of different levels or cycles, it is inaccurate to assume that they have only one objective for each cycle and that each cycle can be defined by a different objective. The same objectives and sub-processes are present in each cycle, but in different proportions. Even though these experienced writers place the predominant weight upon finding the form of their argument during the first cycle, other concerns exist as well. Conversely, during the later cycles, when the experienced writers' primary attention is focused upon stylistic concerns, they are still attuned, although in a reduced way, to the form of the argument. Since writers are limited in what they can attend to during each cycle (understandings are temporal), revision strategies help balance competing demands on attention. Thus, writers can concentrate on more than one objective at a time by developing strategies to sort out and organize their different concerns in successive cycles of revision.

It is a sense of writing as discovery — a repeated process of beginning 23 over again, starting out new — that the students failed to have. I have used the notion of dissonance because such dissonance, the incongruities between intention and execution, governs both writing and meaning. Students do not see the incongruities. They need to rely on their own internalized sense of good writing and to see their writing with their "own" eyes. Seeing in revision — seeing beyond hearing — is at the root of the word *revision* and the process itself; current dicta on revising blind our students to what is actually involved in revision. In fact, they blind them to what constitutes good writing altogether. Good writing disturbs: it creates dissonance. Students need to seek the dissonance of discovery, utilizing in their writing, as the experienced writers do, the very difference between writing and speech — the possibility of revision.

Acknowledgment: The author wishes to express her gratitude to Professor William Smith, University of Pittsburgh, for his vital assistance with the research reported in this article and to Patrick Hays, her husband, for extensive discussions and critical editorial help.

11. A Literature Option: A Poem

Read and reread the poem "Persimmons." Try summarizing what occurs in the poem. We suspect you'll find it hard at first to summarize the poem without doing violence to it. If so, think why. In a short essay, find a way to guide a reader gracefully and effectively through the poem.

Persimmons
LI-YOUNG LEE

In sixth grade Mrs. Walker
slapped the back of my head
and made me stand in the corner
for not knowing the difference   4
between *persimmon* and *precision.*
How to choose

persimmons. This is precision.
Ripe ones are soft and brown-spotted.   8
Sniff the bottoms. The sweet one
will be fragrant. How to eat:
put the knife away, lay down newspaper.
Peel the skin tenderly, not to tear the meat.   12
Chew the skin, suck it,
and swallow. Now, eat
the meat of the fruit,
so sweet,   16
all of it, to the heart.

Donna undresses, her stomach is white.
In the yard, dewy and shivering
with crickets, we lie naked,   20
face-up, face-down.
I teach her Chinese.
Crickets: *chiu chiu.* Dew: I've forgotten.
Naked: I've forgotten.   24

Ni, wo: you and me.
I part her legs,
remember to tell her
she is beautiful as the moon.   28

Other words
that got me into trouble were
fight and *fright, wren* and *yarn.*
Fight was what I did when I was frightened,   32
fright was what I felt when I was fighting.
Wrens are small, plain birds,
yarn is what one knits with.
Wrens are soft as yarn.   36
My mother made birds out of yarn.
I loved to watch her tie the stuff;
a bird, a rabbit, a wee man.

Mrs. Walker brought a persimmon to class   40
and cut it up
so everyone could taste
a *Chinese apple.* Knowing
it wasn't ripe or sweet, I didn't eat   44
but watched the other faces.

My mother said every persimmon has a sun
inside, something golden, glowing,
warm as my face.   48

Once, in the cellar, I found two wrapped in newspaper,
forgotten and not yet ripe.
I took them and set both on my bedroom windowsill,
where each morning a cardinal   52
sang, *The sun, the sun.*

Finally understanding
he was going blind,
my father sat up all one night   56
waiting for a song, a ghost.
I gave him the persimmons,
swelled, heavy as sadness,
and sweet as love.   60

This year, in the muddy lighting
of my parents' cellar, I rummage, looking
for something I lost.
My father sits on the tired, wooden stairs,   64
black cane between his knees,
hand over hand, gripping the handle.
He's so happy that I've come home.
I ask how his eyes are, a stupid question.   68
All gone, he answers.

Under some blankets, I find a box.
Inside the box I find three scrolls.
I sit beside him and untie   72
three paintings by my father:
Hibiscus leaf and a white flower.
Two cats preening.
Two persimmons, so full they want to drop from the cloth.   76

He raises both hands to touch the cloth,
asks, *Which is this?*

This is persimmons, Father.
Oh, the feel of the wolftail on the silk,   80
the strength, the tense
precision in the wrist.
I painted them hundreds of times
eyes closed. These I painted blind.   84
Some things never leave a person:
scent of the hair of one you love,
the texture of persimmons,
in your palm, the ripe weight.   88

CHAPTER 5

Comparing

General Considerations

Comparisons surround us. We naturally compare people, objects, experiences, and circumstances. We compare ourselves with others, compare present situations with past ones, compare our goals with our accomplishments. When confronted with something new, we try to see it in relation to what we already know. We are forever trying to get our bearings by comparing one thing with something else.

Comparisons are so fundamental to academic thinking that entire branches of study bear the word in their titles: comparative literature, comparative religion, comparative anatomy. Even where not so prominently announced, comparison can be a course's central method — the political science course that compares how governments work or the anthropology course that sets out a complex web of comparisons to study which behavior is fundamental to all humans and which varies from culture to culture.

Comparisons also serve as ways to present class material. A history lecture might subdivide the American colonies into three groups and then proceed to compare their social and economic characteristics. A philosophy course might begin by setting up Plato and Aristotle as the founders of two distinct philosophical traditions, with the teacher returning to fill in or modify the comparisons as later philosophers are introduced. You'll also notice that many of the chapters and articles you will read in college are organized as comparisons, pieces with titles like "Genetic Engineering: Two Schools of Thought" or "Sea Fiction: A Comparative Study of Jack London and Joseph Conrad."

College teachers use comparison not only to present information but also to elicit it. The comparison/contrast question is one of the standbys of essay examinations: "Compare and contrast the economic theories of Karl Marx and Adam Smith." "Compare the attitudes toward civil disobedience of Henry David Thoreau and George Wallace." "Contrast the function of pores in humans and stomata in plants." At their best, such questions do not elicit a simple recitation of a comparison already worked out by the instructor; rather, they call up two sets of material that you've learned, and they force you, through comparison, to restructure and reevaluate that material.

The comparison/contrast question is often extended to papers you are asked to write outside of class. In an art history course you might be asked to compare an Egyptian funerary figure with an early Greek statue. In a sociology class you might be asked to write an essay comparing the social impact of state and federal welfare programs. In a cultural geography class you might be asked to assess the comparative role played by climate in the national economies of Venezuela and Argentina. Topics like these usually contain some germ of comparison that has attracted a teacher toward the topic in the first place; once you've inferred or discovered that initial basis of comparison, you have taken your first strong step toward structuring an effective essay.

When asked to choose essay topics on your own, think of comparison as one of the options open to you. Even if the essay you eventually write turns out not to be structured as a comparison, the act of comparing may kick off your thinking in interesting and helpful ways. Faced with a discouragingly vague instruction like "Write an essay on the thought of Carl Jung," you could begin with the observation that Jung started as a disciple of Freud. Developing an essay on the similarities and differences of Jung and Freud is apt to get you somewhere (even though at first you may feel you've only doubled your difficulties).

Consider another example, from a political science class stressing constitutional law: "Write a short paper discussing the constitutional problems surrounding a contemporary issue such as gun control or abortion." The *a* in "a contemporary issue" explicitly prevents you from writing an essay comparing the constitutional aspects of gun control *and* abortion. But what's to prevent you from using a comparison to get your thinking started? Perhaps setting up such a comparison, even if you don't keep it as part of your essay, can help you discover a topic that can be managed effectively. You might decide, for instance, that some of the same points of conflict in the abortion issue can be found in the issue of euthanasia; then you start to see how the two issues part ways. Your chances are improving for writing a meaningful essay about a constitutional issue.

So far we've been speaking of extensive comparisons, comparisons used to structure whole disciplines, courses, books, lectures, articles, or essays. But this ignores their most frequent and flexible use. They are helpful along the way, in service of some larger purpose. Here is physicist Robert Jastrow turning to a startling comparison — a metaphor — to help us understand what we see when we look at the Milky Way.

> The Galaxy is flattened by its rotating motion into the shape of a disk, whose thickness is roughly one-fiftieth of its diameter. Most of the stars in the Galaxy are in this disk, although some are located outside it. A relatively small, spherical cluster of stars, called the nucleus of the Galaxy, bulges out of the disk at the center. The entire structure resembles a double sombrero with the galactic nucleus as the crown and the disk as the brim. The sun is located in the brim of the sombrero about three-fifths of the way out from the center to the edge. When we look into the sky in the direction of the disk we see so many stars that they are not visible as separate points of light, but blend together into a luminous band stretching across the sky.
>
> — Robert Jastrow, *Red Giants and White Dwarfs*

Comparisons like these provide momentary stopping points, fresh angles of vision, opportunities for clarification: we understand our position in our galaxy better when we can see the galaxy as a sombrero with ourselves on the brim. To work well, however, comparisons need not work so spectacularly. Often they will modestly occupy only a single sentence, or even flash past us in the midst of sentences. Here is a brief quotation from Helena Curtis's textbook *Biology*:

> A fruit is the mature, ripened ovary of an angiosperm and contains the seeds. Like the flower, the fruit has evolved as a payment to an animal visitor for transportation. (p. 477)

What is being compared to what in this passage? What new perspective does the comparison provide?

Writers often draw on comparisons in coordination with other writing strategies. Chapter 1 has already stressed how comparisons can help you define. In an economics course you get a surer sense of *fixed supply* when you compare it with *elastic supply*. Similarly, comparing often works in co-ordination with summarizing: In a political science essay you might find yourself summarizing two writers' views on the SALT treaty in order to compare them. For a biology essay on cell metabolism that is organized sequentially, you might find yourself shaping your account with the familiar comparison of a developing cell and a busy factory. And comparison will play a particularly important role in analysis, for when you analyze you are always asking yourself how well something particular corresponds to something general: Does the short story you've been assigned to write about go along with your English teacher's views about "Hemingway's rigid ideal of masculinity"?

Comparing is perhaps most intimately connected with classifying. In fact, we can say that comparison depends on classification. We're not always aware of the connection, however, because in many academic situations someone else has done the classifying in advance, leaving only the comparing for us. When you are presented with two illustrations, or case studies, or sets of statistics, the instructor presenting them has usually chosen them on the basis of some category they share. Sometimes that basis is obvious, and sometimes it needs to be coaxed out before you can proceed. You'll quickly recognize how to compare two articles on pneumonia or two experts' attitudes on diplomatic relations with China. But you'll have to do some harder searching if you're asked to compare a newspaper account of a press conference with a chapter from a sociology textbook.

It's important to recognize that some things cannot be compared effectively because they cannot be brought into categorical alignment. It's hard to compare two wildly different things — a mushroom, say, and a porcupine. And some comparisons seem logically impossible to make. For instance, an object like a cabinet cannot be compared with a process such as photosynthesis. Why is this so? Take a few moments and invent some pairings of terms that, you feel, cannot be compared. Be ready to explain why not. Are you sure?

Since most things in the universe do have *some* similarity, most things can be brought into some alignment for comparison. The question is always whether the act of comparing helps us understand something more clearly or look at it more freshly. The old saw "You can't compare apples and oranges" may hold for multiplication problems, but it doesn't hold up to inquisitive thinking: if you saw the need, you could compare apples and oranges for citric content, nutritional value, or agricultural yield; you could even compare them as aesthetic objects or as cultural symbols. What matters is the use to which the comparison is put.

Some potential comparisons are unlikely to be of interest if their basis is too broad. The porcupine and the mushroom could, after all, be compared as living things. But what would be the point of the comparison? Would we be likely to learn anything more about either porcupines or mushrooms? If we were to use something we knew about biological classification to help us refine the category further — they're both examples of organisms composed of eukaryotic cells (they are more like each other than they are like bacteria) — we wouldn't be much further along. However, if we refined our perception of the categories in a different way — recognizing, for example, that both organisms have evolved striking mechanisms for self-protection — we'd be on richer ground. We might be able to develop an effective comparison of porcupines and mushrooms as organisms capable of blending into their environmental backgrounds. Or, if we were to restrict the mushroom example to a poisonous type, we could look at the ways that the two organisms have developed adaptive strategies for warding off predators — namely, quills and toxins. Only by prodding a potential comparison inquisitively do we discover what it can yield.

The early assignments (First Passes) in this chapter ask you to think comparatively without giving you much to work with. They pressure you toward finding simple, basic lines of similarity and difference. The later assignments (Options), though more elaborate, put less emphasis on finding a basis of comparison. But they ask you to find more to say.

Cases

DISCOVERING GROUND FOR COMPARISON: TWO PROSE EXCERPTS

Let's work our way through a representative example of an early assignment, which asks you to take a first pass at comparing the following two passages. The first comes from psychiatrist Viktor Frankl's personal account of imprisonment in a Nazi concentration camp during World War II. The second is from Brett Easton Ellis's *Less than Zero*, a novel set in the wealthy youth culture of contemporary Los Angeles:

> One evening, when we were already resting on the floor of our hut, dead tired, soup bowls in hand, a fellow prisoner rushed in and asked us to run out to the assembly grounds and see the wonderful sunset. Standing outside we saw sinister clouds glowing in the west and the whole sky alive with clouds of ever-changing shapes and colors, from steel blue to blood red. The desolate gray mud huts provided a sharp contrast, while the puddles on the muddy ground reflected the glowing sky. Then, after minutes of moving silence, one prisoner said to another, "How beautiful the world *could* be!"
>
> — Viktor E. Frankl, *Man's Search for Meaning*

> There was a song I heard when I was in Los Angeles by a local group. The song was called "Los Angeles," and the words and images were so harsh and bitter that the song would reverberate in my mind for days. The images, I later found out, were personal and no one I knew shared them. The images I had were of people being driven mad by living in the city. Images of parents who were so hungry and unfulfilled that they eat their own children. Images of people, teenagers my own age, looking up from the asphalt and being blinded by the sun. These images stayed with me even after I left the city. Images so violent and malicious they seemed to be my only point of reference for a long time afterwards. After I left.
>
> — Brett Easton Ellis, *Less Than Zero*

When faced with the need for constructing a comparison from such passages, you may find it helpful to begin with a formula like the following as an aid to your thinking:

Both *A* and *B.* . . .
But *A.* . . .
Whereas *B.* . . .

In other words, you can try first to establish a similarity and then go on to find an important difference. (But if a difference between the passages seems easier to establish, then pursue it first.) In this example, you might decide to work with the vivid way both passages are written. The link between the two passages becomes their striking imagery:

> Both Frankl and Ellis rely on vivid images to add
> force to their writing. . . .

While considering the passages to find an important contrast, you may be fortunate enough to see an interesting one right away:

> Both Frankl and Ellis rely on vivid images to add
> force to their writing. . . .
> But Frankl's images are real descriptions of a
> prison camp and a striking sunset. . . .
> Ellis's images, however, are "personal" and occur
> only in his mind. . . .

These initial perceptions of the grounds for a comparison could, with development, become the basis of a full paragraph:

> Both Viktor Frankl and Brett Easton Ellis rely on
> vivid images to add force to their writing. Frankl
> presents prisoners in a "desolate" and "muddy" concen-
> tration camp looking upward to a "whole sky alive with
> clouds of ever-changing shapes and colors, from steel
> blue to blood red." Similarly, Ellis's narrator de-
> scribes a city of unhappy people with images of parents
> eating children and of teenagers "looking up from the
> asphalt and being blinded by the sun." But the sources
> of the images are very different. Frankl's images come
> from real life, from a concentration camp and prisoners

```
gathered together on the assembly grounds.  For Ellis's
character, the images are, in his own words, "personal."
They occur in his own head when he hears a certain
song, and "no one I knew shared them."
```

This paragraph focuses on the kinds of images each writer creates, on the writers' techniques. Now that the paragraph has been developed, does the basis of comparison seem satisfactory to you? What about the purpose of the images, the reasons the authors created them — in a sense, their messages? Is that aspect of the passages dealt with to your satisfaction? Let's try working on a different approach:

```
    Both Frankl and Ellis write about people who live
in conditions that cause great suffering....
    With Frankl, the conditions are created by politi-
cal and racial oppression: Jews imprisoned in a concen-
tration camp.
    But with Ellis, the conditions are more social and
psychological: people "hungry and unfulfilled" and
"driven mad by living in the city."
```

Developing these basic points with a few details from the two passages, you might arrive at a comparison like this one:

```
    Both Viktor Frankl and Brett Easton Ellis write
about people who live in conditions that cause great
suffering.  In Frankl's passage people imprisoned in a
concentration camp live in huts built on muddy ground,
and their terrible condition is made all the more
striking by its contrast with a beautiful sunset.  In
Ellis's passage, people are made unhappy by the city:
parents are "hungry and unfulfilled" and teenagers, a
little like the prisoners in the concentration camp,
look skyward for something else, though they're blinded
by the sun they see.  There is a big difference, how-
ever, between the two conditions described by the au-
thors.  In Frankl's passage, misery is caused by polit-
ical and racial oppression.  Huge numbers of people are
imprisoned because of their race, and many of them will
```

be killed. "The world <u>could</u> be" a beautiful place, but
it isn't because of Nazi atrocity. But in Ellis's passage, it's harder to determine exactly why people are
miserable. The causes seem personal and psychological.
"Harsh and bitter" images of "unfulfilled" people "re-
verberate" in the mind of the speaker. And, unlike the
prisoners in Frankl's work, this person can't even
imagine a better world. The "violent and malicious"
images stay "a long time" after he leaves the city.

As in the first attempt to establish a comparison, this paragraph contrasts
the images in the two passages: the particulars of the concentration camp
and the sky above it versus the tortured psychological cityscapes of upscale
Los Angeles. Here, however, the discussion of the images includes discussion
of the authors' reasons for creating them. Notice, too, that in this second
attempt at comparison, the contrast between the two sources of imagery
begins to establish a possible critique of Ellis. In the first attempt, there
doesn't seem to be much purpose for comparing the two passages — other
than accomplishing a comparison. In the second attempt, however, we are
trying to convince readers to consider the two passages in different ways,
thus making the comparison a kind of argument. In fact, most comparisons
are arguments for particular ways of seeing stories or theories or methods
or collections of data that writers have placed side by side.

WORKING OUT ANALOGIES: A CASE FROM THE HISTORY OF SCIENCE

Most comparisons move from similarities toward differences, but sometimes
they move in the opposite direction. When the things you are comparing
seem startlingly different, your main job often will be to uncover hidden
correspondences, basic similarities that don't at first meet the eye. Imagine
that your biology instructor has asked you to consider how a human blood
cell resembles an office building. At first you may be aware only of differences:
The building is vast, the cell microscopic; the building rectangular and vertical,
the cell spherical; the building composed of synthetic materials, the cell organic
molecules; the building has been built from architectural plans by construction
crews, the cell reproduces itself by passing on DNA, its genetic material.

Enumerating these differences may only strengthen the impression that
there is no comparison to be made. But consider the ingenious use made of
the comparison by Horace F. Judson, a historian of science. Judson describes
the state of biological knowledge before the discovery of the genetic importance of DNA. Most molecular biologists felt that a key role must be played

by proteins since proteins were present in tremendous variety, carrying on an extraordinary number of cellular functions. Proteins seem as omnipresent in the cell, Judson tells us, as metal in a high-rise under construction:

> Biologists looking into cells were like spectators at a building site, peering through a crack in the board fence at the hole in the ground where a new office tower is going up: so much to see, cranes, shovels, . . . scaffolding, pneumatic drills, electric cables, riveters, hoists raising rafts of pipe, a huge steel beam swinging precariously overhead — but yes, everything made of metal, even the folding table in the hut over there with a roll of blue paper spread out on it.
>
> — Horace F. Judson, *The Eighth Day of Creation*

In the same way that a building site appears to an outside observer to consist of metal beams and cables, most of what goes on inside a cell seems, at first glance, to involve proteins. But the key to all the activity is something that initially appears secondary, of minor interest: the strands of nucleic acid at the center of the cell and the roll of blue paper at the construction site. Both are blueprints, the sets of instructions without which none of the other construction could occur.

Comparisons like the one between the cell and the skyscraper are called metaphors when they occur in a single flash, like the comparison we quoted earlier likening the shape of our galaxy to that of a sombrero. When they can be developed in more detail, with several back-and-forth correspondences, they are called analogies. Analogies at their best make something difficult more understandable; metaphors at their best often make something familiar seem refreshingly strange. The emphasis in an analogy is on a set of structural similarities. It would be difficult to find other ways in which the Milky Way resembles a sombrero, but the comparison between a cell and a building, as we've seen, can be developed in some detail:

```
microbiologists ... spectators
proteins ... metals
DNA ... blueprints
microscope ... crack in the fence
```

Often, we discover that good analogies can be extended even further. If we wanted to extend Judson's analogy, for example, we could compare an office building's headquarters with the cell's nucleus, its air conditioning with the cell's homeostatic mechanisms, its position among other buildings on the street with the position of the cell in relation to other cells in the bloodstream. When you've tapped as rich an analogy as this one, extending it can be fun. But be careful. At some point such analogies may seem only to be showing off; don't lose sight of their clarifying purpose (unless your purpose *is* to show off, as sometimes it may be). Also remember that any comparison has limitations, and it's usually good to show that you're aware of these limitations:

Add all the high-rises in North America and you've got only a fraction of the cells in one person's bloodstream; blueprints, unlike DNA, do not reproduce more blueprints; and so on.

EXTENDED COMPARISON:
A CASE FROM AMERICAN HISTORY

The later assignments (Options) in this chapter invite some fairly detailed comparisons. As a way of getting your bearings with these potentially complex comparisons, you may want to try some preliminary device more flexible than the three-part formula we suggested on page 211. One such device is a two-column chart arranged like so:

```
                              A            B
Similarities  1.
              2.
              3.
              etc.
Differences   1.
              2.
              3.
              etc.
```

Or you might make it even simpler by using the two columns to line up your material without committing yourself to where similarities break off into differences or differences blur into similarities. Don't make filling in such a chart an end in itself. Just use it until you feel enough in control of the elements of the comparison that you can begin to write about them.

As an example of working up such a comparison, let's try a variation on an assignment traditionally given in American history classes: the comparison between Alexander Hamilton and Thomas Jefferson. Often this task is presented in a general form, such as "Compare the economic policies of Jefferson and Hamilton." As we noted earlier, such questions are sometimes thinly disguised requests for giving back an already well-organized lecture; but in other situations, the question forces you to synthesize or even rethink what you've learned.

To complicate the task, we ask you to consider two texts, one a set of selections from a biography of Hamilton and the other a set from a book about Jefferson. To keep the task from getting even more complicated, however, we've chosen books by the same scholar. John Chester Miller wrote his biography of Hamilton, *Alexander Hamilton: Portrait in Paradox*, in 1959.

In 1977 he wrote *The Wolf by the Ears: Thomas Jefferson and Slavery.* As you read the following excerpts, try taking notes in the rough two-column form we just suggested. As you jot down your notes for the first piece (Miller's more recent book, on Jefferson) which appears below, include not only points where you already sense a potential comparison but points that seem important in their own right. Leave yourself plenty of space for observations that may occur to you later.

1
Late in 1789, after witnessing the opening scenes of the French Revolution, Jefferson returned to Virginia, and in the spring of 1790 he went to New York to assume the post of secretary of state in the cabinet of President Washington. He brought with him to the temporary capital of the United States a retinue of household servants, footmen, and a coachman. Republican simplicity as practiced by Jefferson and other Southerners who came North to serve in Congress or the cabinet never required the renunciation of the services of slaves; and, in Jefferson's case, it did not require the sacrifice of fine furniture, French cooking, exquisite wines, horses, and carriages. On the strength of his appearance — he sported the latest fashions of the French *haut monde* — one would hardly have supposed that a great American democrat had arrived in town or, unless one had read the *Notes on Virginia*, that Jefferson felt the slightest repugnance to slavery. The truth is that he had grown up with slavery and his "people" were essential to his comfort and well being.

2
Amply as his physical comforts were ministered to, Jefferson found himself involved in some very unsettling diplomatic exchanges with George Hammond, the British minister to the United States who arrived in Philadelphia in 1791 as the first official representative sent by His Britannic Majesty to his former subjects in America. In his negotiations with Hammond, Jefferson distinguished himself as a champion of peculiarly Virginia interests and as a defender of the rights of property, especially that species of property represented by black slaves. In the first clearly defined postrevolutionary confrontation between the rights of black man and the rights of property, Jefferson aligned himself decisively on the side of property. His insistence that slaves be treated as property attributed significantly toward bringing Great Britain and the United States to an impasse from which war seemed the probable outcome.

3
The treaty of peace of 1783, which brought an end to the war between the United States and Great Britain and established the independence of the United States (a preliminary treaty had been agreed upon as early as November 1782) was ratified by the Continental Congress in January 1784. Among other provisions, the definitive treaty prohibited the British army, when it evacuated the United States, from carrying away "Negroes or other property" belonging to American citizens; it required the United States to desist from interposing any obstacles to the collection of debts owed by Americans to British citizens; and it committed the British to surrender the Northwest Posts (which had been ceded by the treaty of peace) "with all convenient speed" to the United States. In the negotiations conducted by Jefferson with George Hammond in 1791–1793, these three articles were of paramount importance. . . .

Had Jefferson's paramount objective been to gain possession of the   **4**
Northwest Posts and to make a commercial treaty with Great Britain
opening the British West Indies to American ships, he would hardly have
adopted the hectoring, abrasive, and unconciliatory tone he used with
Hammond. It served no constructive purpose to engage in recriminations,
and the question of which nation was guilty of the first infringement of
the treaty inevitably degenerated into a mere exercise in mutual vitu-
peration. Manifestly, Jefferson did not give the highest priority to effecting
a settlement with Great Britain; he was far more intent upon establishing
closer commercial relations with France than with Great Britain, and he
was more concerned with vindicating the reputation of the United States
than in promoting commercial intercourse with the former mother country
— intercourse that he feared might lead to military alliance between the
two countries. He still referred to Great Britain as "the enemy," and he
had by no means forgotten or forgiven the slights and humiliations he
had endured at the hands of high British officials in London in the spring
of 1786. Great Britain's governing principles, he had long since decided,
were "Conquest, Colonization, Commerce, and Monopoly of the Ocean."
Nor could he be persuaded that a nation pursuing such objectives seriously
intended to surrender the Northwest Posts or to make a commercial
treaty with the United States.

While these negotiations were in progress — if that is the right word   **5**
to describe this exchange of tirades and outcries of outraged virtue on
the part of both men — Alexander Hamilton, as secretary of the treasury,
was doing his utmost to undermine Jefferson's position. As early as 1783,
Hamilton had taken the position that the United States had no right to
demand the return of the slaves. Having been emancipated by British
military order, they became, he said, free men, and no compact, however
solemn, made between the United States and Great Britain, could alter
their status. Under these circumstances, for the United States to demand
the surrender of these slaves was, in Hamilton's opinion, "as *odius* and
immoral a thing as can be conceived." Moreover, Hamilton strongly
dissented from Jefferson's view that raising legal obstacles to the collection
of debts was a legitimate reprisal for prior British infractions of the treaty.
"The debts of private individuals are in no case a proper object of reprisals," he declared; in international law, debts were not subject to
confiscation, and public injuries could not discharge private obligations.

With convictions regarding the way American foreign policy ought to   **6**
be conducted quite as strong as but completely opposite to Jefferson's
governing principles, Hamilton took it upon himself to tell Hammond that
the American secretary of state was speaking for himself, not for the
government of the United States. Without consulting the president, he
tried to dissociate Washington and the cabinet from Jefferson's "intem-
perate violence" and Anglophobia. Jefferson and Madison, he told Hammond, were the victims of "a womanish attachment to France and a
womanish resentment against Great Britain." . . .

In his negotiations with George Hammond, Jefferson failed to achieve   **7**
any of his objectives: the British refused to admit that they were guilty
of the first breach of the treaty; they declined to compensate the slave-

owners whose "property" they had carried away; and they retained possession of the Northwest Posts. To his government, Hammond described Jefferson as a perfect Frenchman, imbued with all the Frenchman's hatred of "perfidious Albion." This report of Jefferson's Anglophobism had the untoward effect of stiffening the determination of the British government to retain possession of the Northwest Posts. In February 1794, Lord Grenville, the British foreign secretary, declared that because of the refusal of the United States to honor the peace treaty over a period of nine years, Great Britain no longer considered itself obliged to abide by it. Thus, after three years of desultory negotiations, Anglo-American relations were worse than when Jefferson had assumed the office of secretary of state. . . .

During his term of office as secretary of state, and, indeed, during 8 the entire decade of the 1790s, Jefferson was preoccupied with the struggle against Hamiltonian finance and the "monarchism" which seemed to him certain to follow in its train. By the summer of 1790, after a few months' residence in New York, he became convinced that a conspiracy against republicanism, no less formidable than the conspiracy against freedom that Americans had encountered and overcome in the British Empire, existed among highly placed officials in the new federal government and that President Washington was in danger of becoming an unsuspecting abettor of the plot.

In the course of his career, Jefferson was compelled to respond to 9 a succession of threats to freedom and republicanism which demanded his undivided attention. At no time did he permit slavery to take precedence over what he regarded as more immediate threats to the ideals and institutions he cherished. Jefferson viewed the American scene not merely as a philosopher-statesman but, more importantly, as a political activist fighting on many fronts against a legion of enemies hostile to republicanism. Conscious of being beset by dangers on every hand, he was never able to concentrate his attention upon slavery as the paramount, all-encompassing evil of the day.

For this reason, Jefferson appeared during the 1790s to be far more 10 eager to combat Hamiltonian finance and to liquidate the national debt than to eradicate slavery. Since he considered the assumption of state debts (to which he had been persuaded to assent) and the perpetuation of the national debt to be the prime engines of the system of corruption and centralization Hamilton was trying to foist upon the country, Jefferson naturally gave priority to his continuing struggle with the secretary of the treasury. If Hamiltonianism triumphed, the question of slavery would become academic: farmers and planters, Jefferson predicted, would then be reduced to a more cruel and certainly more exploitative form of slavery to Northern businessmen, bankers, and speculators than the relatively humane servitude experienced by Southern slaves. So fearful was he that these "conspirators against human happiness" would overthrow the republic that in the 1790s he demanded that all holders of government securities and bank stock be prohibited by federal law from sitting in Congress. Since he did not propose a similar morals test for slaveowners, many of whom were members of Congress, Jefferson put himself in the extraordinary position of holding that the ownership of human beings was less reprehensible than the ownership of stocks and bonds.

— John Chester Miller, *The Wolf by the Ears: Thomas Jefferson and Slavery*

Here now are some excerpts from Miller's earlier book on Hamilton. After you've read this second set of passages and taken some notes toward a comparison, try using those notes to develop a plan for an essay. Can you find several contrasts that seem particularly strong or worth noticing? Do you see some way of coordinating these points with one another? Can you think of a controlling idea to keep an essay unified? Take a crack at a plan as soon as you've read this second selection.

1   When Hamilton came to the Treasury, the foreign debt of the United States was about $10 million, plus $1,600,000 in arrears of interest. The domestic debt Hamilton estimated to be slightly over $27 million, not including $13 million in accrued interest. The total debt therefore stood at slightly over $50 million. But there was no certainty in these figures: how much debt in the form of certificates had been contracted by the various agencies of the government — the commissary and quartermaster accounts were especially confused — was known, as one congressman observed, only to the Supreme Being. Although commissioners had been appointed by the Continental Congress to settle the accounts of individuals holding claims against the government, their work had not been completed. Nor had the claims of the states against the general government been ascertained: here was a terra incognita, an impenetrable wasteland of unliquidated debt.

2   To a less sanguine and resolute man than Hamilton, the national debt might well have appeared more like an albatross hung about the neck of the federal government than a sword with which to vanquish the states. For this mass of paper seemed to lie like a dead weight upon the national economy, stifling governmental credit and diverting into speculation capital which might have been more profitably employed in business enterprise. And, despite all that the government could do, the debt was constantly increasing: revenue was inadequate to meet even the interest which the government had pledged itself to pay.

3   Under these circumstances, some Americans were of the opinion that the government ought to repudiate the national debt and start out with a clean financial slate. Why, they asked, should the federal government bankrupt itself in order to repay money that had served its purpose and from which everyone had profited in the form of independence of Great Britain? It seemed to them perfectly proper for the government to inform its creditors that, through no fault of its own, the debt was cancelled. . . .

4   Displaying an optimism to which nothing in the previous financial experience of the United States gave warrant, Hamilton took the position that the tariff could be made to furnish the government with sufficient revenue to liquidate the national debt and at the same time pay the operating expenses of the government. He admitted of no doubt that the

foreign debt must be paid in full, accrued interest and all, but at the same time he declared his determination to stretch every resource of the government in order to do justice to the domestic creditors. Everything he had said and done up to the time of his appointment as secretary of the treasury indicated that he held the satisfaction of these claims to be a prerequisite to the success of the Federal Constitution.

If the domestic creditors were to be paid, the question inevitably arose: Which creditors? For in 1789, the securities of the United States government were for the most part not in the possession of the original holders: they had been transferred — often at a fraction of their nominal value — to purchasers who bought them for speculative or investment purposes. As a result, the evidences of governmental debt had gravitated into the hands of a few, most of whom were residents of the northern states. A class and a section therefore stood to profit from the payment of the debt. . . . 5

Besides the mass of depreciated securities and paper money issued by the Continental Congress, the people of the United States labored under a heavy load of state debts. Like the national debt, the evidences of state indebtedness had followed the well-worn course from original holders to speculators and investors. Hamilton's constant objective was to bind these men to the national government by the durable ties of "*Ambition* and *Avarice*"; but as matters stood in 1789, ambition and avarice tended to attach the state creditors to the state governments. As long as the states possessed their debts, they were certain to compete with the federal government for the allegiance of the creditor class and for the citizens' tax dollar. The result, Hamilton feared, would be that the states would attempt to pre-empt (as the Constitution, by recognizing concurrent taxation, permitted them to do) the remaining objects of taxation and that the affluent citizens of the United States would be divided against themselves, the state creditors seeking to strengthen the states while the holders of federal securities endeavored to aggrandize the powers and the revenues of the national government.[1] 6

It can be said of Hamilton that whenever he saw a Gordian knot, he attempted to cut it forthwith. In this instance, he called in his Report on Public Credit for the assumption by the federal government of $25 million of state debts incurred in the prosecution of the War of Independence. Here he acted upon the principle that "if all the public creditors receive their dues from one source, distributed by an equal hand, their interest will be the same. And, having the same interests, they will unite in the support of the fiscal arrangements of the Government." Thus the most valuable members of the community — valuable because they were the most liberally endowed with the goods of this world — would bestow their affections and, Hamilton hoped, their money upon the federal gov- 7

---

[1] Hamilton regarded concurrent taxation as "the Gordion-knot [*sic*] of our political situation." In *The Federalist* he observed that the only way concurrent taxation could be made workable was for each government to exercise "reciprocal forbearance" by respecting the rights of the first occupant. As secretary of the treasury, Hamilton left no doubt that he intended the federal government to do the occupying, while forbearance was to be practiced by the states.

ernment. With all the creditors, state and national, gathered into the fold of the federal government, Hamilton's vision of a powerful national government, supreme over the states, would begin to assume concrete reality. . . .

Between Hamilton and Jefferson there was as much difference in **8** outward appearance as there was in the cast of their minds. Jefferson — tall, angular, loose-joined, awkward, ill at ease in company and reserved in his manners — was confronted by a small, well-shaped, meticulously dressed young man who exuded energy, youthfulness, and high spirits. Despite the fact that Jefferson had spent several years in the most polite circles in Europe, his ill-fitting clothes — they always seemed too small for him — his lounging, careless manner — he sprawled rather than sat in a chair — made him appear rather like a frontiersman playing the Virginia gentleman and who still had a long way to go before he mastered the part. Even some of Jefferson's friends felt that he abused a philosopher's privilege of negligence in dress. But Jefferson, the born aristocrat, was sure of himself and of his position in society, whereas Hamilton was a parvenu who could never afford to let down his guard; his family closet contained several skeletons over which he was compelled to mount guard.

Although Hamilton never made the mistake of taking Jefferson to be **9** a kindred spirit, he did not at this time regard him as an enemy. The Virginian's objections to the Constitution had been largely removed by the Bill of Rights; he held *The Federalist* in high esteem; he liked to think of commerce as the handmaiden of agriculture; he was a nationalist who favored making the federal judiciary supreme over the state judges; and he was no friend of an "elected despotism" such as had prevailed in some states during the period of the Articles of Confederation. Most important of all, he had not committed himself formally on the issues raised by Hamilton's report.

And so, when Hamilton encountered Jefferson one day near the **10** President's house, he seized the opportunity of sounding out the secretary of state. . . .

In this memorable conversation in front of the President's house, **11** Hamilton apparently offered Jefferson only the consolation of saving the union: although Hamilton undoubtedly had in mind some arrangements having to do with the site of the national capital, he did not broach the subject at this time. It was at dinner the next day, attended by Jefferson, Hamilton, and Madison, that the matter was brought up; and it was Madison and Jefferson who set the price for the passage of the funding-assumption bill — the permanent location of the national capital on the banks of the Potomac. And since assumption could not be carried without the support of the Pennsylvanians, it was agreed that Philadelphia should be made the temporary residence of the government for ten years.

That Hamilton should stoop to bargaining to achieve his objectives **12** struck some of his friends as beneath the dignity of a statesman. Rufus King, who as a United States senator ought to have known better, told Hamilton that "great & good schemes ought to succeed on their own merits and not by intrigue or the establishment of bad measures." But Hamilton was not such a babe in the political woods as to imagine that the purity of his intentions and the rectitude of his measures were a guarantee of success. Putting first things first, he told King, was a policy he had found to yield excellent results: "The funding System, including the assumption is the primary national object; all subordinate points which oppose it must be sacrificed; the project of Philadelphia & Potomack is bad, but it will ensure the funding System and the assumption." To carry that point, Hamilton probably would have been willing to put the national capital in an even hotter spot than the Potomac in mid-August. . . .

By means of the assumption of state debts and the funding of the   13
national debt, Hamilton had succeeded in attaining his first objective — the re-establishment of the credit of the national government. In the Bank of the United States, Hamilton had created an institution designed to concentrate the capital resources of the country in a central bank. Thus the United States was prepared for the capitalistic dispensation, but the answer to the question — to what ends were the new-found wealth of the country to be put? — had not yet been handed down from the Treasury. The answer was forthcoming in the Report on Manufactures Hamilton submitted to Congress in December, 1791.

In January, 1791, the House of Representatives requested the sec-   14
retary of the treasury to prepare a plan "for the encouragement and promotion of such manufactures as will tend to render the United States independent of other nations for essentials, particularly for military supplies." As was his settled habit, Hamilton gave the broadest possible interpretation to this directive. In consequence, what Congress received on December 5, 1791, when he submitted his report, was a comprehensive survey of the state of manufacturing in the United States — its extent, variety, the degree of success attained, the obstacles that needed to be overcome, its future prospects, and a disquisition upon the ways and means of promoting manufactures in the Republic. . . .

Other than serving as a guide, benefactor, and partner of business,   15
the government, in Hamilton's philosophy, left individual enterprise to itself. He would tolerate no price-fixing, for example, on the ground that competition was a better regulator of prices than governmental edict. Nor did he envisage governmental interference with business to secure social objectives. Hamilton's ideal was a free economy — free, that is, insofar as curbs upon individual initiative were concerned, but not free in that sense that government abstained from interference of any kind. He insisted only that the interference of government be benevolent and in the interests of the national welfare.

In his inventory of the resources of the United States, Hamilton did   16
not omit the distinctive talents and skills of the American people. He was especially impressed by the inventive genius and the "peculiar aptitude for mechanic improvements" displayed by his countrymen. To turn this aptitude to the account of the state was for Hamilton an essential part of his plan for the encouragement of manufactures; accordingly, he urged Congress "to induce the prosecution and introduction of useful discoveries" by a system of rewards and premiums. To those who introduced machinery into the United States from abroad, even in defiance of the laws of foreign countries prohibiting its exportation, he was prepared to

give cash rewards and the temporary grant of exclusive manufacturing privileges.

Nevertheless, no matter how elaborate the system of rewards, Ham-   17
ilton recognized that few businessmen would be inclined to risk their capital in the establishment of factories in the United States without the assurance of an adequate supply of labor. With western lands acting as a magnet that drew potential factory workers from the eastern states, the problem was not to keep Americans down on the farm but to per-suade them to live in cities and work in factories. Nevertheless, Hamilton did not despair of providing American factories with a labor force: there was a plentitude of women, children, and immigrants which might be used to work the machines. The men of the United States would learn their error when they saw the pay checks brought home by their wives and children; plow-jogging was not to be compared with a good steady job in a mill!

In England, little children were leading the factory owners to the   18
promised land of bigger factories and bigger profits. Blessed were these children, for they worked fourteen hours a day, six days a week, and were never known to engage in union activities. Hamilton carried his admiration of British industrialism even to the point of noting with approval that almost half the workers in British cotton factories were women and children, "of whom the greater proportion were children, and many of them of a tender age." That the United States should copy this example seemed to Hamilton highly beneficial not only for the national economy but even for the women and children involved: "In general," he asserted "women and children are rendered more useful, and the latter more early useful, by manufacturing establishments, than they would other wise be."
— John Chester Miller, *Alexander Hamilton:*
Portrait in Paradox

Once you've produced your own notes and a plan for an essay, read on. See if the following notes are like the ones you've taken, and evaluate our thinking as we describe the essay possibilities we see emerging.

JEFFERSON	HAMILTON
Secretary of state	Secretary of treasury
His time in France	
His ease with slavery as a way of life	
Slaves as property	
His negotiations with the British minister Hammond about enforcing the treaty of 1783	His efforts to interfere in J's handling of these negotiations
Defender of Virginian interests	Protector of interests of the North, particularly New York

JEFFERSON	HAMILTON
His hostile attitude toward Britain; his friendship with the French	His conciliatory attitude toward Britain; indifference to France?
Despised Hamilton's "monarchism"	Did Hamilton want a king?
Issue of Northwest Posts	
The issue of the return of slaves taken away to England	Slaves in England had become free.
	Tried to dissociate Washington's administration from Jefferson's "womanish" views
Slavery issue subordinate to threats against Republican form of government	
Opposed most of Hamilton's financial proposals:	
Assumption of state debts by national government (though at first he supported this)	Measures for centralizing national power over states and for creating capital with which to encourage industrialization
"Perpetuation of national debt"	
The formation of a national bank? A small group of financial people will have too much control.	National bank further centralized capital and decision making.
Saw interests of northern business opposed to southern agricultural interests	"Report on Manufactures"
Saw main "slavery" issue as exploitation of the South by the North	
His appearance: sloppy but aristocratically at ease	More proper, but nervous
	"Skeletons in the closet"
	Hamilton's anticipated areas of agreement with J: the Constitution, the importance of commerce, admiration for The Federalist, the advantages of more central authority than there had been during the revolution

JEFFERSON	HAMILTON
Accepted new location of nation's capital in return for letting H's financial plan pass	Made "the Potomac deal" as a way of getting his funding—assumption bill passed
	First to advocate large-scale weapons manufacture
	Valued factory work above farm labor; admired British system of children's and women's labor

How would we go about converting a set of notes like these to a plan for an essay? There's no single best way. We might try to construct the three-part formula demonstrated earlier (Both A and B. . . ./But A. . . ./ Whereas B. . . .), but judging from the material on our list, we wouldn't find much to develop for the "Both Hamilton and Jefferson . . ." part. Most of the general similarities will sound obvious and silly: "Both Hamilton and Jefferson were important politicians of their day," or "Both Hamilton and Jefferson served in George Washington's administration," or "Both Hamilton and Jefferson were men of strong political opinion." Which, if any, of these general points is worth developing in more detail as a major part of an essay? If we decide that none is, we'll turn away from this strategy.

A second strategy might be to leap to some central contrast, one we think capable of sustaining an entire essay. Often when comparing two passages, we might find, for example, that the perspectives of the authors differ in some fundamental way and that this difference in turn helps explain further differences. In this case, when we are dealing with two passages by the same author, that option will not seem so attractive. Still, after rereading the passages, we might decide that Miller does not approach his two subjects from the same point of view or that he does not maintain the same attitude toward them. In thinking about this possibility, we decided we couldn't detect meaningful differences in approach or tone — he seems equally cool to each. This time the quick leap didn't work.

A third strategy would be to proceed more deliberately, consolidating the list we made, passing over points that seem repetitious or unhelpful or points that simply don't lend themselves to comparison. We would want to be alert to general trends. We might think it odd, for instance, that so many of our notes about Jefferson pertain to the slavery issue; then, remembering the title of Miller's book — *The Wolf by the Ears: Thomas Jefferson and Slavery* — we would recognize that that emphasis is the book's central theme (maybe we've discovered a difference in point of view after all). Perhaps what we notice is important enough to become the controlling point of our essay. Or perhaps it's a point we want to hold on to, waiting to see how it will coordinate with others.

Whatever we do, we're looking for some way to simplify our material so that we can organize a coherent essay. It might help to arrive at some scheme of subtopics, something to suggest how our essay could move along. Here's one example of a plan that might work:

```
The contrasting personalities of Jefferson and Hamilton
The contrast in the regions and interests they
    represented
Their contrasting political philosophies
```

Here's another:

```
The treaty issue
The slavery issue
Financial issues
The manufacturing issue
```

And another:

```
The contrasting social values of Hamilton and Jefferson
Their contrasting political values
Their economic values
Their moral blind spots
```

We might create an effective essay out of a sequence of subtopics like these. It would depend of course on how well and in what detail we could develop clear comparisons for each subtopic. It would also depend on how well we could link our subtopics as we move from one part of our essay to another. For example, a sentence like this one could link the first and second subtopics in the last plan above: "Just as their social values depended on their upbringings, the political values of Hamilton and Jefferson had much to do with where and how they lived." Without such transitions, we'd risk giving readers the impression that they are reading several separate essays rather than a single sustained one. And even with such transitions readers may be left wondering what the whole has been about.

We're on the strongest ground when we discover a single idea, a thesis, capable of giving coherence to the rest of our points. Good theses can be quite general, and they also can get quite specific. A good thesis needs to be broad enough to cover the comparisons we think are important and focused enough to leave a reader persuaded about something in particular. Here's a short list of possible theses emerging from our notes about Jefferson and Hamilton.

```
    Jefferson and Hamilton illustrate a deep national
tension, one that would lead eventually to the Civil
War.
```

Politically Jefferson was more revolutionary than
Hamilton; but economically he was more conservative.

Although Jefferson is considered the foremost of
the "Founding Fathers" after Washington, Alexander Hamilton has had the more lasting influence on American
institutions.

John C. Miller treats Hamilton and Jefferson
equally; toward both he shows a healthy disrespect.

Jefferson and Hamilton each saw national interests
in terms most favorable to his own region of the
country.

The dispute between Hamilton and Jefferson was
really between two opposing images of aristocracy: one
of landed property, the other of monetary power.

Hamilton did not think the United States could be
self-sufficient; Jefferson felt that the nation had obtained true independence.

What do you see as some of the strengths and weaknesses of these statements as ideas for structuring an essay? Does any one of them look more promising than the others? You might select one and try planning an essay. Or go back and evaluate your own plan to determine if you would want to modify it in some way. Or wait until you've done some of the other assignments in this chapter and then return for a fresh look at these two important figures in American history. Finally, whether or not you decide to think further about Jefferson and Hamilton, we ask you to take a few moments to think about these two more general questions: What do we gain by acts of comparison? Do we take any risks in thinking comparatively?

Assignments: First Passes

1. Perceiving Comparisons: An Australian Creation Myth and an Account of the "Big Bang"

After finding a common basis for thinking about the following passages, write a brief comparative essay. The first excerpt is a creation myth collected from the Aranda tribe in Australia, and the second is a description of the "big bang" creation theory taken from an astronomy textbook.

In a separate paragraph — one that can be rough and experimental — consider what placing side by side these two very different accounts helped you to see. Consider as well the possibility that comparing the two accounts distorted one or both for you.

In the very beginning everything was resting in perpetual darkness: night oppressed all the earth like an impenetrable thicket. The gurra ancestor — his name was Karora — was lying asleep, in everlasting night, at the very bottom of the soak of Ilbalintja; as yet there was no water in it, but all was dry ground. Over him the soil was red with flowers and overgrown with many grasses; and a great tnatantja° was swaying above him. This tnatantja had sprung from the midst of the bed of purple flowers which grew over the soak of Ilbalintja. At its root rested the head of Karora himself: from thence it mounted up towards the sky as though it would strike the very vault of the heavens. It was a living creature, covered with a smooth skin like the skin of a man.   **1**

And Karora's head lay at the root of the great tnatantja: he had rested thus ever from the beginning.   **2**

And Karora was thinking, and wishes and desires flashed through his mind. Bandicoots began to come out from his navel and from his armpits. They burst through the sod above, and sprang into life.   **3**

And now dawn was beginning to break. From all quarters men saw a new light appearing: the sun itself began to rise at Ilbalintja, and flooded everything with its light. Then the gurra ancestor was minded to rise, now that the sun was mounting higher. He burst through the crust that had covered him: and the gaping hole that he left behind became the Ilbalintja Soak, filled with the sweet dark juice of the honeysuckle buds.   **4**

— T. G. H. Strenlow, ed., *Aranda Traditions*

Theoreticians have calculated a "standard" model of what the big bang may have been like. In the beginning we imagine a great primeval fireball of matter and radiation. We do not have to imagine any particular mass, or even a finite mass, for the fireball. Its density was very high and it was at a temperature of perhaps 10^{10} °K.   **1**

At first the matter consisted only of protons, neutrons, electrons, positrons, and neutrinos, all independent particles. After about 100 seconds, however, the temperature had dropped to 10^9 °K, and the particles began to combine to form some heavier nuclei. This nucleogenesis continued, according to the model, for a few hours until the temperature dropped to about 10^8 °K. During this time, about 20 percent of the mass of the material formed into helium. Some deuterium also formed (deuterium is an isotope of hydrogen with a nucleus containing one proton and one neutron) but only a small amount — probably less than one part in a thousand. The actual amount of deuterium formed depends critically on the density of the fireball; if it was fairly high, most of the deuterium would have been built up into helium. Scarcely any nuclei heavier than those of helium are expected to have survived. So the composition of the fireball when nuclear building ceased is thought to have been mostly hydrogen, about 20 percent helium, and a trace of deuterium.   **2**

For the next million years the fireball was like a stellar interior — hot and opaque, with radiation passing from atom to atom. During this   **3**

tnatantja: Decorated pole used in native ceremonies.

time, the temperature gradually dropped to about 3000 °K, and the density to about 1000 atoms/cm^3. At this point the fireball became transparent. The radiation was no longer absorbed and was able to pass freely throughout the universe. After about 1000 million years, the model predicts that the matter should have condensed into galaxies and stars.

We emphasize again that the fireball must *not* be thought of as a localized explosion — like an exploding superstar. There were no boundaries and no site of the explosion. It was everywhere. The fireball is still existing, in a sense. It has expanded greatly, but the original matter and radiation are still present and accounted for. The atoms of our bodies came from material in the fireball. We were and are still in the midst of it; it is all around us.

4

— George D. Abell, Exploration of the Universe

2. Comparing Two Quotations: Vincent van Gogh and Paul Gauguin on Art

Vincent van Gogh (1853–1890) and Paul Gauguin (1848–1903) were European painters, each contributing to the late nineteenth-century movement away from strictly realistic painting. In a paragraph, compare their attitudes toward art. Decide whether you prefer to stress how they agree or how they differ. If you are an artist yourself, you might want to consider which attitude most closely matches yours and work your personal perspective into the paragraph.

> But in the meantime I am getting well acquainted with nature. I exaggerate, sometimes I make changes in motif; but for all that, I do not invent the whole picture; on the contrary, I find it all ready in nature, only it must be disentangled.
>
> — Vincent van Gogh, letter quoted in Theories of Modern Art:
A Sourcebook by Artists and Critics

> Some advice: do not paint too much after nature. Art is an abstraction; derive this abstraction from nature while dreaming before it, and think more of the creation which will result than of nature. Creating like our Divine Master is the only way of rising toward God.
>
> — Paul Gauguin, letter quoted in Theories of Modern Art:
A Sourcebook by Artists and Critics

3. Comparing Three Quotations: Aimé Césaire, Karl Jaspers, and John Donne on the Human Condition

Write a short essay comparing the following brief quotations by African statesman Aimé Césaire (b. 1913), German psychiatrist and philosopher Karl Jaspers (1883–1969), and English poet John Donne (1572–1631). After establishing the message they share, discuss the differences in the ways these writers express that message: for example, the words chosen, the sound, the kind of audience you think each had in mind.

In the whole world no poor devil is lynched, no wretch is tortured, in whom I too am not degraded and murdered.

— Aimé Césaire

There exists among men, because they are men, a solidarity through which each shares responsibility for every injustice and every wrong committed in the world.

— Karl Jaspers

No man is an Island entire of it self; every man is a piece of the Continent, a part of the main. . . . Any man's death diminishes me, because I am involved in Mankind; and therefore never send to know for whom the bell tolls; It tolls for thee.

— John Donne

4. Comparing Three Quotations: H. G. Wells, Jacob Bronowski, and T. E. Hulme on Science

Compare the following three brief quotations by the science fiction novelist H. G. Wells (1866–1946), the mathematician and historian Jacob Bronowski (1908–1974), and the writer and philosopher T. E. Hulme (1883–1917). After deciding whether you want to emphasize their similarities or their differences, write a short essay comparing them.

As a postscript, reflect on any difficulties you had in reading or writing about these passages. Did they present similar difficulties? Did reading one help you to read another? Might reading one have caused you to misread another?

Science is a match that man has just got alight. He thought he was in a room — in moments of devotion, a temple — and that his light would be reflected from and display walls inscribed with wonderful secrets and pillars carved with philosophical systems wrought into harmony. It is a curious sensation, now that the preliminary splutter is over and the flame burns up clear, to see his hands lit and just a glimpse of himself and the patch he stands on visible, and around him, in place of all that human comfort and beauty he anticipated — darkness still.

— H. G. Wells, "The Rediscovery of the Unique"

Science is a very human form of knowledge. We are always at the brink of the known, we always feel forward for what is to be hoped. Every judgment in science stands on the edge of error, and is personal. Science is a tribute to what we can know although we are fallible. In the end the words were said by Oliver Cromwell: "I beseech you, in the bowels of Christ, think it possible you may be mistaken."

— Jacob Bronowski, *The Ascent of Man*

The aim of science and of all thought is to reduce the complex and inevitably disconnected world of grit and cinders to a few ideal counters,

which we can move about and so form an ungritlike picture of reality —
one flattering to our sense of power over the world.

— T. E. Hulme, *Speculations*

5. Comparing Arguments: Margaret O'Brien Steinfels and Lewis Thomas on *In Vitro* Fertilization

Journalist Margaret O'Brien Steinfels and science writer Lewis Thomas
both have written about *in vitro* fertilization (*in vitro* means "in glass" — in
a test tube as opposed to *in vivo,* inside a living organism). In a short essay,
compare their arguments and their styles of arguing.

In a separate paragraph, discuss what effect comparing these two essays
had on your opinion of each. That is, did you think differently about each
after closely comparing their arguments and style of arguing?

1　The once-simple connections between having sex and having babies,
between having babies and starting families, is fading. Medical science
and our social imagination are busy inventing novel ways to conceive, to
bear, and to raise children, alone or with others of the same or opposite
sex. The possibilities seem endless, and, if doctors become very adept,
perhaps the babies can even start conceiving themselves. A new maternal
smorgasbord is here and pregnant with possibilities.

2　Elizabeth Jordan Carr's birth in Norfolk, Virginia, on December 28
[1981] comes about nine months after her mother had the benefit of in
vitro fertilization (IVF). Conception outside the womb by fertilizing a
maternal egg with sperm and later inserting the fertilized egg into the
womb is almost, but not quite, old hat. Worldwide, Elizabeth is the 10th
reported birth following IVF. But she is the first American IVF conceived
and born on American soil.

3　Louise Brown, the first IVF baby, was born in England on July 25,
1978. Her birth rated front-page headlines around the globe and sparked
a heated debate on the morality of test-tube conceptions. Perhaps Elizabeth's birth will fan the dying embers of that discussion, which has
become increasingly academic as the number of IVF births has grown.
More likely, IVF's will become just another routine medical procedure
— although physicians caution that the failure rate will remain high for
some time — ultimately to join artificial insemination and hormone shots
for superovulation, as part of medicine's efforts to provide infertile women
and men the opportunity to have their own children. . . .

4　Variations of artificial insemination are not only possible, but probable.
Single women have become pregnant through this method, using an
anonymous donor. No doubt homosexual and lesbian couples, whether
through artificial insemination or surrogate motherhood, have been, or
will be, able to "have" children that are half-genetically their own. . . .

5　Many ethical questions and criticisms were raised about IVF when
Louise Brown was born. But in the three years since, none of the troubling
questions about IVF or surrogate motherhood or voluntary single motherhood have led to a cautionary pause in their use. If anything, their

incidence has increased. But, to be blunt, is it a good thing for a child
to grow up without a father? What rights or responsibilities should the
unwed father have? At what cost do we allow mothers to buy and sell
an infant like a commodity? What right does a couple have to arrange
for a woman to breed them a child? And is such an arrangement more
ethical if it is voluntary? Even if the surrogate just loves being pregnant?
Now that an egg can be fertilized in the laboratory, what is to prevent
an ambitious scientist from sustaining that life outside the womb for the
full nine months? The possibility is momentarily hindered by federal regulations and technological barriers, but both will surely be overcome by
a humanitarian impulse to give a baby to a woman who has no womb at
all. Having loosened the biological tie linking mother and infant, and the
psychological and social tie linking mother, infant, and father, are we so
far from the human hatchery described by Aldous Huxley in *Brave New
World?*

An alarmist question? Perhaps. . . .   6

Yet it is not so hard to imagine the day when human hatcheries,   7
having better quality control and greater efficiency, will become the home
of better babies. Or the day when family bonds, being no longer necessary, fade away and each of us, at last, can live and let live with a
minimum of human contact and human community. Or, perhaps, if human
hatcheries fail to take hold, the day when women are bought and sold
to breed children. It is not even hard to imagine the day when we produce
the child with good teeth, good bones, and just enough intelligence to
know that some questions shouldn't be raised.

It would be reassuring to think that these are delusions of pessimism. 8
But in the same year that technology brought about the birth of Elizabeth
Carr, technology also began to overwhelm us with its toxic wastes, failed
to build a safe nuclear power plant, and together with both nuclear and
conventional weapons, seemed to bring us closer to the brink of war. In
such a year, of course, Baby Elizabeth looks like a technological plus,
but then in the 1950s so did the peaceful use of nuclear power.

— Margaret O'Brien Steinfels, "Of Tubes and Motherhood:
Hatching Better Babies"

A short while ago, in mid-1978, the newest astonishment in medicine, 1
covering all the front pages, was the birth of an English baby nine months
after conception in a dish. The older surprise, which should still be fazing
us all, is that a solitary sperm and a single egg can fuse and become a
human being under any circumstance, and that, however implanted, a
mere cluster of the progeny of this fused cell affixed to the uterine wall
will grow and differentiate into eight pounds of baby; this has been going
on under our eyes for so long a time that we've gotten used to it; hence
the outcries of amazement at this really minor technical modification of
the general procedure — nothing much, really, beyond relocating the
beginning of the process from the fallopian tube to a plastic container
and, perhaps worth mentioning, the exclusion of the father from any role
likely to add, with any justification, to his vanity.

There is, of course, talk now about extending the technology beyond 2
the act of conception itself, and predictions are being made that the whole

process of embryonic development, all nine months of it, will ultimately be conducted in elaborate plastic flasks. When this happens, as perhaps it will someday, it will be another surprise, with more headlines. Everyone will say how marvelously terrifying is the new power of science, and arguments over whether science should be stopped in its tracks will preoccupy senatorial subcommittees, with more headlines. Meanwhile, the sheer incredibility of the process itself, whether it occurs in the uterus or *in* some sort of *vitro,* will probably be overlooked as much as it is today.

For the real amazement, if you want to be amazed, is the process.   3
You start out as a single cell derived from the coupling of a sperm and an egg, this divides into two, then four, then eight, and so on, and at a certain stage there emerges a single cell which will have as all its progeny the human brain. The mere existence of that cell should be one of the great astonishments of the earth. People ought to be walking around all day, all through their waking hours, calling to each other in endless wonderment, talking of nothing except that cell. It is an unbelievable thing, and yet there it is, popping neatly into its place amid the jumbled cells of every one of the several billion human embryos around the planet, just as if it were the easiest thing in the world to do.

— Lewis Thomas, "On Embryology"

6. Comparing Three Summaries: Theories of Language Acquisition

We have summarized the theories of language acquisition of three prominent social scientists: B. F. Skinner (b. 1904), Albert Bandura (b. 1925), and Noam Chomsky (b. 1928). Read the summaries and write a three-way comparison, indicating what you see as distinctive about each theory.

B. F. SKINNER: BEHAVIORAL THEORY

Children learn to speak the same way they learn other behaviors: by being rewarded for correct responses to their environment. Infants utter sounds spontaneously, either at random or in imitation of what they have heard. Parents and other adults then respond only to some of those sounds, those that approximate the sounds of words in the language. This response may only be a smile, a caress, or a brief hug, but for children it is a tangible reward that encourages them to do again what they did before getting the positive response. Thus children, through such rewards, or "reinforcement," more and more closely come to approximate adult speech.

ALBERT BANDURA: SOCIAL LEARNING THEORY

Much of what a child learns is a result of observation and imitation of a model, usually the mother. This imitation may or may not be accompanied by a reward of some kind. Research has indicated that such imitation is crucial to the child's development of language. Certainly, children cannot acquire vocabulary and grammatical structures *without* exposure to models. Even if they do not imitate speech at the moment it is uttered, through listening they acquire information that eventually appears in imitative behavior. Therefore, imitation of a model may be indispensable for language acquisition.

NOAM CHOMSKY: INNATE MECHANISM THEORY

To make sense of the language they hear around them, and to eventually produce correct elements of that language, infants must have some sort of built-in system that allows them to do this. This can be called, for lack of a more precise name, a "language acquisition device" (LAD). The LAD represents an innate capacity, a disposition to listen for speech sounds in the environment, make guesses about the grammatical rules that underlie those sounds, and in time produce appropriate, grammatical speech. Thus children who begin constructing their own sentences are not merely imitating what they have heard others say; they are acting on the basis of the grammatical rules that they have unconsciously formulated. They are then able to produce infinite varieties of utterances, not just to parrot fixed "chunks" that they have memorized.

Assignments: Options

7. A Literature Option: Two Poems About the Natural World

Following are a set of Papago Indian rain songs and a poem by Thom Gunn (b. 1929). Write an essay comparing the relationship between the speaker and the natural world established in the rain songs and in Gunn's poem. Your comparison should take into account the vantage point and attitude of the speaker as well as the way nature is described. Use passages from the songs and poem to support your comparison.

Papago Rain Songs

1

Clouds are standing in the east, they are approaching,
It rains in the distance;
Now it is raining here and the thunder rolls.

2

Green rock mountains are thundering with clouds.
With this thunder the Akim village is shaking.

4

The water will come down the arroyo
  and I will float on the water.
Afterward the corn will ripen in the fields.   8

    3

Close to the west the great ocean is singing.
The waves are rolling toward me, covered with many clouds.
Even here I catch the sound.
The earth is shaking beneath me and I hear deep rumbling.   12

    4

A cloud on top of Evergreen Mountain is singing,
A cloud on top of Evergreen Mountain is standing still.
It is raining and thundering up there,
It is raining here.   16
Under the mountain the corn tassels are shaking,
Under the mountain the slender spikes of child corn are glistening.

Flying Above California
THOM GUNN

Spread beneath me it lies — lean upland
sinewed and tawny in the sun, and

valley cool with mustard, or sweet with
loquat. I repeat under my breath   4

names of places I have not been to:
Crescent City, San Bernardino

— Mediterranean and Northern names.
Such richness can make you drunk. Sometimes   8

on fogless days by the Pacific,
there is a cold hard light without break

that reveals merely what is — no more
and no less. That limiting candor,   12

that accuracy of the beaches,
is part of the ultimate richness.

8. A Literature Option: Two Poems

Both of the following poems are by Gary Soto (b. 1952) and were published in a volume titled *Black Hairs* (1985). The speaker in each poem is entering adolescence and reacting to important first experiences. Write an essay comparing the speakers' reactions to these experiences: their attitudes

towards the events described, the words used, the tones of voice. Use
passages from the poems to support your comparison.

Oranges
GARY SOTO

The first time I walked
With a girl, I was twelve,
Cold, and weighted down
With two oranges in my jacket.   4
December. Frost cracking
Beneath my steps, my breath
Before me, then gone.
As I walked toward   8
Her house, the one whose
Porch light burned yellow
Night and day, in any weather.
A dog barked at me, until   12
She came out pulling
At her gloves, face bright
With rouge. I smiled,
Touched her shoulder, and led   16
Her down the street, across
A used car lot and a line
Of newly planted trees,
Until we were breathing   20
Before a drugstore. We
Entered, the tiny bell
Bringing a saleslady
Down a narrow aisle of goods.   24
I turned to the candies
Tiered like bleachers,
And asked what she wanted —
Light in her eyes, a smile   28
Starting at the corners
Of her mouth. I fingered
A nickel in my pocket,
And when she lifted a chocolate   32
That cost a dime,
I didn't say anything.
I took the nickel from
My pocket, then an orange,   36
And set them quietly on
The counter. When I looked up,
The lady's eyes met mine,
And held them, knowing   40

Very well what it was all
About.

> Outside,
A few cars hissing past,   44
Fog hanging like old
Coats between the trees.
I took my girl's hand
In mine for two blocks,   48
Then released it to let
Her unwrap the chocolate.
I peeled my orange
That was so bright against   52
The gray of December
That, from some distance,
Someone might have thought
I was making a fire in my hands.   56

Cruel Boys

GARY SOTO

First day. Jackie and I walking in leaves
On our way to becoming 8th graders,
Pencils behind our ears, pee-chee folders
Already scribbled with football players   4
In dresses, track star in a drooped bra.
We're tough. I'm Mexican
And he's an unkillable Okie with three
Teeth in his pocket, sludge under   8
His nails from scratching oily pants.
No one's going to break us, not the dean
Or principal, not the cops
Who could arrive in pairs, walkie-talkies   12
To their mouths, warning:
"Dangerous. They have footballs."
We could bounce them off their heads
And reporters might show up   16
With shirt sleeves rolled up to their ears,
Asking our age, if we're Catholic.
But this never happens. We go to first
Period, math, then second period, geography, 20
And in third period, English, the woman
Teacher reads us Frost, something
About a tree, and to set things straight,
How each day will fall like a tree.   24
Jackie raises his hand, stands up,
And shouts, "You ain't nothing but a hound dog,"
As the spitballs begin to fly.

9. A Music Option: Listening to Music

David Randolph (b. 1914) is a contemporary music critic, and Aaron Copland (b. 1900) is a modern composer. Compare their approaches to listening to music. Then incorporate this comparison in an essay about what you listen for in music.

From *This Is Music: A Guide to the Pleasures of Listening*

DAVID RANDOLPH

Let us see what it is that you respond to in music.   1

Do you find something appealing about the famous tune from Schubert's Unfinished Symphony? If so, then you are responding to one of the most important elements of music — *melody.*   2

Do you find that you feel like tapping your foot during the march movement of Tchaikovsky's Pathétique Symphony? If so, then you are responding to another extremely important element — *rhythm.* . . .   3

Now imagine how much less satisfying Schubert's melody would be if it were buzzed through a tissue-papered comb, instead of being played by the entire cello section of an orchestra. The melody and the rhythm would still be present as before; the difference would lie only in the quality of the sound that reached your ears. Therefore, when you enjoy the richness of the sound of the massed cellos playing the melody, you are responding to another of the basic elements — *tone color.* Your appreciation, then, really involves *three* elements.   4

Now, let us suppose that a pianist is playing one of your favorite songs — the melody in the right hand, the accompanying chords in the left. Suppose that his finger slips as he plays one of the chords, causing him to play a sour note. Your immediate awareness of that wrong note comes from your response to another of the basic elements — *harmony.* . . .   5

Do you have a sense of completeness at the conclusion of a performance of . . . Beethoven's Ninth Symphony? Are you left with a feeling of satisfaction as well as of elation? If so, part of that sense of satisfaction — of completion — comes from your feeling for *form,* which is the last of the . . . basic elements of music.   6

What to Listen For in Music

AARON COPLAND

We all listen to music according to our separate capacities. But, for the sake of analysis, the whole listening process may become clearer if we break it up into its component parts, so to speak. In a certain sense we all listen to music on three separate planes. For lack of a better terminology, one might name these: (1) the sensuous plane, (2) the expressive   1 plane, (3) the sheerly musical plane. The only advantage to be gained from mechanically splitting up the listening process into these hypothetical planes is the clearer view to be had of the way in which we listen.

The simplest way of listening to music is to listen for the sheer pleasure of the musical sound itself. That is the sensuous plane. It is the plane on which we hear music without thinking, without considering it in any way. One turns on the radio while doing something else and absent-mindedly bathes in the sound. A kind of brainless but attractive state of mind is engendered by the mere sound appeal of the music.

You may be sitting in a room reading this book. Imagine one note struck on the piano. Immediately that one note is enough to change the atmosphere of the room — proving that the sound element in music is a powerful and mysterious agent, which it would be foolish to deride or belittle.

The surprising thing is that many people who consider themselves qualified music lovers abuse that plane in listening. They go to concerts in order to lose themselves. They use music as a consolation or an escape. They enter an ideal world where one doesn't have to think of the realities of everyday life. Of course they aren't thinking about the music either. Music allows them to leave it, and they go off to a place to dream, dreaming because of and apropos of the music yet never quite listening to it. . . .

The second plane on which music exists is what I have called the expressive one. Here, immediately, we tread on controversial ground. Composers have a way of shying away from any discussion of music's expressive side. Did not Stravinsky himself proclaim that his music was an "object," a "thing," with a life of its own, and with no other meaning than its own purely musical existence? This intransigent attitude of Stravinsky's may be due to the fact that so many people have tried to read different meanings into so many pieces. Heaven knows it is difficult enough to say precisely what it is that a piece of music means, to say it definitely, to say it finally so that everyone is satisfied with your explanation. But that should not lead one to the other extreme of denying the music the right to be "expressive."

My own belief is that all music has an expressive power, some more and some less, but that all music has a certain meaning behind the notes and that that meaning behind the notes constitutes, after all, what the piece is saying, what the piece is about. This whole problem can be stated quite simply by asking, "Is there a meaning to music?" My answer to that would be, "Yes." And "Can you state in so many words what the meaning is?" My answer to that would be, "No." Therein lies the difficulty. . . .

Music expresses, at different moments, serenity or exuberance, regret or triumph, fury or delight. It expresses each of these moods, and many others, in a numberless variety of subtle shadings and differences. It may even express a state of meaning for which there exists no adequate word in any language. In that case, musicians often like to say that it has only a purely musical meaning. They sometimes go farther and say that *all* music has only a purely musical meaning. What they really mean is that no appropriate word can be found to express the music's meaning and that, even if it could, they do not feel the need of finding it. . . .

The third plane on which music exists is the sheerly musical plane. **8** Besides the pleasurable sound of music and the expressive feeling that it gives off, music does exist in terms of the notes themselves and of their manipulation. Most listeners are not sufficiently conscious of this third plane. . . .

The intelligent listener must be prepared to increase his awareness **9** of the musical material and what happens to it. He must hear the melodies, the rhythms, the harmonies, the tone colors in a more conscious fashion. But above all he must, in order to follow the line of the composer's thought, know something of the principles of musical form. Listening to all of these elements is listening on the sheerly musical plane.

Let me repeat that I have split up mechanically the three separate **10** planes on which we listen merely for the sake of greater clarity. Actually, we never listen on one or the other of these planes. What we do is to correlate them — listening in all three ways at the same time.

10. A Political Science Option: Colonialism in Africa

Kwame Nkrumah (1909–1972) was prime minister and president of Ghana in the years following its independence from Great Britain (1957); his government was overthrown in 1966. David K. Fieldhouse (b. 1925) is a British political scientist specializing in political economy. In a short essay, compare their political views on the relation between African nations and European ones.

If you have recently immigrated from an African country, or if you have studied African history and politics, you might want to add a section to your essay expressing your views on the issues raised by Nkrumah and Fieldhouse.

From *Neo-Colonialism: The Last Stage of Imperialism*
KWAME NKRUMAH

Africa is a paradox which illustrates and highlights neo-colonialism. Her **1** earth is rich, yet the products that come from above and below her soil continue to enrich, not Africans predominantly, but groups and individuals who operate to Africa's impoverishment. With a roughly estimated population of 280 million, about eight percent of the world's population, Africa accounts for only two percent of the world's total production. Yet even the present very inadequate surveys of Africa's natural resources show the continent to have immense, untapped wealth. We know that iron reserves are put at twice the size of America's, and two-thirds those of the Soviet Union's, on the basis of an estimated two billion metric tons. Africa's calculated coal reserves are considered to be enough to last for three hundred years. New petroleum fields are being discovered and brought into production all over the continent. Yet production of primary ores and minerals, considerable as it appears, has touched only the fringes.

Africa has more than 40 percent of the world's potential water power, a greater share than any other continent. Yet less than five percent of this volume has been utilized. Even taking into account the vast desert stretches of the Sahara, there is still in Africa more arable and pasture land than exists in either the United States of America or the Soviet Union. There is even more than in Asia. Our forest areas are twice as great as those of the United States. . . . 2

Africa is having to pay a huge price once more for the historical accident that this vast and compact continent brought fabulous profits to western capitalism, first out of the trade in its people and then out of imperialist exploitation. This enrichment of one side of the world out of the exploitation of the other has left the African economy without the means to industrialize. At the time when Europe passed into its industrial revolution, there was a considerably narrower gap in development between the continents. But with every step in the evolution of productive methods and the increased profits drawn from the more and more shrewd investment in manufacturing equipment and base metal production, the gap widened by leaps and bounds. . . . 3

When the countries of their origin are obliged to buy back their minerals and other raw products in the form of finished goods, they do so at grossly inflated prices. A General Electric advertisement carried in the March/April 1962 issue of *Modern Government* informs us that "from the heart of Africa to the hearths of the world's steel mills comes ore for stronger steel, better steel — steel for buildings, machinery, and more steel rails." With this steel from Africa, General Electric supplies transportation for bringing out another valuable mineral for its own use and that of other great imperialist exploiters. In lush verbiage the same advertisement describes how "deep in the tropical jungle of Central Africa lies one of the world's richest deposits of manganese ore." But is it for Africa's needs? Not at all. The site, which is "being developed by the French concern, Compagnie Minière de l'Ogooue, is located on the upper reach of the Ogooue River in the Gabon Republic. After the ore is mined it will first be carried 50 miles by cableway. Then it will be transferred to ore cars and hauled 300 miles by diesel-electric locomotives to the port of Point Noire for shipment to the world's steel mills." For "the world" read the United States first and France second. 4

From *The Economic Exploitation of Africa*
DAVID K. FIELDHOUSE

Exploitation, like imperialism, is no word for scholars because it has long been confused by ideological concepts. Semantics apart, two usages must be distinguished. The original French meaning can best be translated as "use" or "development." In English, however, "exploitation" is pejorative, 1 suggesting unfair or unrequited advantage obtained. In Marxist thought it implied extraction of surplus value from variable capital; and in contemporary neo-Marxist terminology it may indicate imperialist superprofit from a dependent economy. Since this chapter is concerned with the actual policies followed by Britain and France and their economic consequences rather than with theoretical questions, "exploitation" will be understood as "development," though some attempt will be made to assess the validity of Marxist assumptions.

Even so restricted, the economic development of British and French   2
Africa after about 1880 is too vast a subject to be comprehended in a single chapter. It must also be said that the materials now available are an insufficient basis for answering most questions with confidence. More work has been done and published on the British than on the French side, but even there the gaps remain large. For both it is possible to describe with some precision what may be called the imperial factor as it affected economic development — metropolitan policy on tariffs and currency, governmental intervention in Africa in such basic fields as law, land, and labor. But the actual working of the colonial economies, more particularly in the private sector, remains largely unknown. Public investment can be measured with some accuracy, but private direct investment and its profitability remain speculative at all periods. A leading economic role was taken by British and French trading, shipping, investment, and plantation companies, yet there are no detailed studies of any of these after about 1900. On the African side very little is known about the activities of merchants or entrepreneurs or about the response of producers to the stimulus of overseas markets. It need hardly be added that sophisticated data on production does not exist. . . .

The problem of exploitation in the pejorative sense is more difficult   3
to handle because it cannot be defined in measurable economic terms. The case against Britain and France, in a nutshell, is that through their political and economic power they took more out of Africa than they put in: that the *mise en valeur* was a cover for piracy. Evidence supporting this hypothesis is easy to produce but is often misleading. Least impressive is the accusation that, due to favorable conditions produced by colonialism, metropolitan investment in colonial Africa obtained "superprofit." There is insufficient data to prove or disprove this generally; but there is no reason to think that over a long period profits of capital in Africa were higher than those in Europe or elsewhere, though profits in extractive industries (such as wild rubber) might be very large for short periods. . . .

Fundamentally, however, it must be concluded that while the typical   4
patterns of colonial economy and the objectives of European entrepreneurs did not prevent "growth," equally they were not calculated to promote it, and did so largely by accident. . . . African colonies, like other parts of the world, were developed in order to produce raw materials while importing manufactures and capital. The result was inevitably a high degree of commercial metrocentrism, intense specialization in a few raw materials, and uneven development. By the 1950s much of French

Africa was so tied to France by high price levels and dependence on a protected market that independence brought little freedom to choose future economic policy. British Africa was far less tied to Britain by these factors, but in other respects the same problems had to be faced. . . .

A perspective view of British and French exploitation in Africa from the late nineteenth century onward is therefore dominated by half tints and qualifications. Development was neither as heroic as early enthusiasts for the *mise en valeur* wanted, nor as negative and disastrous for African interests as critics have commonly alleged. Under ideal conditions it might have been done better and with less pain to Africans without imperial control, though in the historical context it is difficult to see any practicable alternative. Tropical Africa was not like Japan. One thing at least is certain. Alien rule brought Africa forcibly into the world economy and ensured that future development would be in the direction of Western economic systems, whether capitalist, socialist, or mixed. This was the substantive product of exploitation. 5

11. An Education Option: Two Accounts of Reading

Write an essay comparing the following autobiographical accounts by the colonial patriot Benjamin Franklin (1706–1790), first published in 1791, and the Black Muslim leader Malcolm X (1925–1965), written in 1964.

You might want to reflect on your own involvement with reading and work your reflection into your essay or into a separate essay. In either case, situate your discussion in the context of Franklin and Malcolm X, using your own experience as a third element in the comparative discussion.

From *Autobiography*
BENJAMIN FRANKLIN

From a child I was fond of reading, and all the little money that came into my hands was ever laid out in books. Pleased with the *Pilgrim's Progress,* my first collection was of John Bunyan's works in separate little volumes. I afterward sold them to enable me to buy R. Burton's *Historical Collections*; they were small chapmen's books, and cheap, 40 or 50 in all. My father's little library consisted chiefly of books in polemic divinity, most of which I read, and have since often regretted that, at a time when I had such a thirst for knowledge, more proper books had not fallen in my way, since it was now resolved I should not be a clergyman. Plutarch's *Lives* there was in which I read abundantly, and I still think that time spent to great advantage. There was also a book of Defoe's, called an *Essay on Projects,* and another of Dr. Mather's called *Essays to Do Good,* which perhaps gave me a turn of thinking that had an influence on some of the principal future events of my life. 1

This bookish inclination at length determined my father to make me a printer, though he had already one son (James) of that profession. In 2

1717 my brother James returned from England with a press and letters to set up his business in Boston. I liked it much better than that of my father, but still had a hankering for the sea. To prevent the apprehended effect of such an inclination, my father was impatient to have me bound to my brother. I stood out some time, but at last was persuaded, and signed the indentures when I was yet but twelve years old. I was to serve as an apprentice till I was twenty-one years of age, only I was to be allowed journeyman's wages during the last year. In a little time I made great proficiency in the business, and became a useful hand to my brother. I now had access to better books. An acquaintance with the apprentices of booksellers enabled me sometimes to borrow a small one, which I was careful to return soon and clean. Often I sat up in my room reading the greatest part of the night, when the book was borrowed in the evening and to be returned early in the morning, lest it should be missed or wanted.

And after some time an ingenious tradesman, Mr. Matthew Adams, 3 who had a pretty collection of books, and who frequented our printing-house, took notice of me, invited me to his library, and very kindly lent me such books as I chose to read. I now took a fancy to poetry, and made some little pieces; my brother, thinking it might turn to account, encouraged me, and put me on composing occasional ballads. One was called *The Lighthouse Tragedy*, and contained an account of the drowning of Captain Worthilake, with his two daughters: the other was a sailor's song, on the taking of *Teach* (or Blackbeard) the pirate. They were wretched stuff, in the Grub-street-ballad style; and when they were printed he sent me about the town to sell them. The first sold wonderfully, the event being recent, having made a great noise. This flattered my vanity; but my father discouraged me by ridiculing my performances, and telling me verse-makers were generally beggars. So I escaped being a poet, most probably a very bad one; but as prose writing has been of great use to me in the course of my life, and was a principal means of my advancement, I shall tell you how, in such a situation, I acquired what little ability I have in that way.

There was another bookish lad in the town, John Collins by name, 4 with whom I was intimately acquainted. We sometimes disputed, and very fond we were of argument, and very desirous of confuting one another, which disputatious turn, by the way, is apt to become a very bad habit, making people often extremely disagreeable in company by the contradiction that is necessary to bring it into practice; and thence, besides souring and spoiling the conversation, is productive of disgusts and perhaps enmities where you may have occasion for friendship. I had caught it by reading my father's books of dispute about religion. Persons of good sense, I have since observed, seldom fall into it, except lawyers, university men, and men of all sorts that have been bred at Edinburgh.

A question was once, somehow or other, started between Collins 5 and me, of the propriety of educating the female sex in learning, and their abilities for study. He was of opinion that it was improper, and that they were naturally unequal to it. I took the contrary side, perhaps a little for dispute's sake. He was naturally more eloquent, had a ready plenty of words; and sometimes, as I thought, bore me down more by his fluency than by the strength of his reasons. As we parted without settling the point, and were not to see one another again for some time, I sat down to put my arguments in writing, which I copied fair and sent to him. He answered, and I replied. Three or four letters of a side had passed, when my father happened to find my papers and read them. Without entering into the discussion, he took occasion to talk to me about the manner of my writing; observed that, though I had the advantage of my antagonist in correct spelling and pointing (which I owed to the printing-house), I fell far short in elegance of expression, in method and in perspicuity, of which he convinced me by several instances. I saw the justice of his remarks, and thence grew more attentive to the manner in writing, and determined to endeavor at improvement.

About this time I met with an odd volume of the *Spectator*. It was the third. I had never before seen any of them. I bought it, read it over and over, and was much delighted with it. I thought the writing excellent, and wished, if possible to imitate it. With this view I took some of the papers, and, making short hints of the sentiment in each sentence, laid them by a few days, and then, without looking at the book, tried to complete the papers again, by expressing each hinted sentiment at length, and as fully as it had been expressed before, in any suitable words that should come to hand. Then I compared my *Spectator* with the original, discovered some of my faults, and corrected them. But I found I wanted a stock of words, or a readiness in recollecting and using them, which I thought I should have acquired before that time if I had gone on making verses; since the continual occasion for words of the same import, but of different length, to suit the measure, or of different sound for the rhyme, would have laid me under a constant necessity of searching for variety, and also have tended to fix that variety in my mind, and make me master of it. Therefore I took some of the tales and turned them into verse; and, after a time, when I had pretty well forgotten the prose, turned them back again. I also sometimes jumbled my collections of hints into confusion, and after some weeks endeavored to reduce them into the best order, before I began to form the full sentences and complete the paper. This was to teach me method in the arrangement of thoughts. By comparing my work afterwards with the original, I discovered many faults and amended them; but I sometimes had the pleasure of fancying that, in certain particulars of small import, I had been lucky enough to improve the method or the language, and this encouraged me to think I might possibly in time come to be a tolerable English writer, of which I was extremely ambitious. My time for these exercises and for reading was at night, after work or before it began in the morning, or on Sundays, when I contrived to be in the printing-house alone, evading as much as I could the common attendance on public worship which my father used to exact on me when I was under his care, and which indeed I still thought a duty, though I could not, as it seemed to me, afford time to practice it.

From *The Autobiography of Malcolm X*
MALCOLM X

It was because of my letters that I happened to stumble upon starting   1
to acquire some kind of a homemade education.

I became increasingly frustrated at not being able to express what   2
I wanted to convey in letters that I wrote, especially those to Mr. Elijah
Muhammad.[1] In the street, I had been the most articulate hustler out
there — I had commanded attention when I said something. But now,
trying to write simple English, I not only wasn't articulate, I wasn't even
functional. How would I sound writing in slang, the way I would *say* it,
something such as, "Look, daddy, let me pull your coat about a cat,
Elijah Muhammad —"

Many who today hear me somewhere in person, or on television,   3
or those who read something I've said, will think I went to school far
beyond the eighth grade. This impression is due entirely to my prison
studies.

It had really begun back in the Charlestown Prison, when Bimbi[2]   4
first made me feel envy of his stock of knowledge. Bimbi had always
taken charge of any conversations he was in, and I had tried to emulate
him. But every book I picked up had few sentences which didn't contain
anywhere from one to nearly all of the words that might as well have
been in Chinese. When I just skipped those words, of course, I really
ended up with little idea of what the book said. So I had come to the
Norfolk Prison Colony still going through only book-reading motions.
Pretty soon, I would have quit even these motions, unless I had received
the motivation that I did.

I saw that the best thing I could do was get hold of a dictionary —   5
to study, to learn some words. I was lucky enough to reason also that
I should try to improve my penmanship. It was sad. I couldn't even write
in a straight line. It was both ideas together that moved me to request
a dictionary along with some tablets and pencils from the Norfolk Prison
Colony school.

I spent two days just riffling uncertainly through the dictionary's   6
pages. I'd never realized so many words existed! I didn't know *which*
words I needed to learn. Finally, just to start some kind of action, I
began copying.

In my slow, painstaking, ragged handwriting, I copied into my tablet   7
everything printed on that first page, down to the punctuation marks.

I believe it took me a day. Then, aloud, I read back, to myself,   8
everything I'd written on the tablet. Over and over, aloud, to myself, I
read my own handwriting.

I woke up the next morning, thinking about those words — immensely   9
proud to realize that not only had I written so much at one time, but I'd

---

[1] *Elijah Muhammad:* U.S. clergyman (1897–1975); leader of the Black Muslims 1934–
1975.
[2] *Bimbi:* A fellow inmate.

written words that I never knew were in the world. Moreover, with a little effort, I also could remember what many of these words meant. I reviewed the words whose meanings I didn't remember. Funny thing, from the dictionary first page right now, that "aardvark" springs to my mind. The dictionary had a picture of it, a long-tailed, long-eared, burrowing African mammal, which lives off termites caught by sticking out its tongue as an anteater does for ants.

I was so fascinated that I went on — I copied the dictionary's next 10 page. And the same experience came when I studied that. With every succeeding page, I also learned of people and places and events from history. Actually the dictionary is like a miniature encyclopedia. Finally the dictionary's *A* section had filled a whole tablet — and I went on into the *B*'s. That was the way I started copying what eventually became the entire dictionary. It went a lot faster after so much practice helped me to pick up handwriting speed. Between what I wrote in my tablet, and writing letters, during the rest of my time in prison I would guess I wrote a million words.

I suppose it was inevitable that as my word-base broadened, I could 11 for the first time pick up a book and read and now begin to understand what the book was saying. Anyone who has read a great deal can imagine the new world that opened. Let me tell you something: From then until I left that prison, in every free moment I had, if I was not reading in the library, I was reading on my bunk. You couldn't have gotten me out of books with a wedge. Between Mr. Muhammad's teachings, my correspondence, my visitors — usually Ella and Reginald — and my reading of books, months passed without my even thinking about being imprisoned. In fact, up to then, I never had been so truly free in my life.

The Norfolk Prison Colony's library was in the school building. A 12 variety of classes was taught there by instructors who came from such places as Harvard and Boston universities. The weekly debates between inmate teams were also held in the school building. You would be astonished to know how worked up convict debaters and audiences would get over subjects like "Should Babies Be Fed Milk?"

Available on the prison library's shelves were books on just about 13 every general subject. Much of the big private collection that Parkhurst had willed to the prison was still in crates and boxes in the back of the library — thousands of old books. Some of them looked ancient: covers faded, old-time parchment-looking binding. Parkhurst . . . seemed to have been principally interested in history and religion. He had the money and the special interest to have a lot of books that you wouldn't have in general circulation. Any college library would have been lucky to get that collection.

As you can imagine, especially in a prison where there was heavy 14 emphasis on rehabilitation, an inmate was smiled upon if he demonstrated an unusually intense interest in books. There was a sizable number of well-read inmates, especially the popular debaters. Some were said by many to be practically walking encyclopedias. They were almost celebrities. No university would ask any student to devour literature as I did when this new world opened to me, of being able to read and *understand*.

I read more in my room than in the library itself. An inmate who   15
was known to read a lot could check out more than the permitted maximum number of books. I preferred reading in the total isolation of my
own room.

When I had progressed to really serious reading, every night at about   16
ten P.M. I would be outraged with the "lights out." It always seemed to
catch me right in the middle of something engrossing.

Fortunately, right outside my door was a corridor light that cast a   17
glow into my room. The glow was enough to read by, once my eyes
adjusted to it. So when "lights out" came, I would sit on the floor where
I could continue reading in that glow.

At one-hour intervals the night guards paced past every room. Each   18
time I heard the approaching footsteps, I jumped into bed and feigned
sleep. And as soon as the guard passed, I got back out of bed onto the
floor area of that light-glow, where I would read for another fifty-eight
minutes — until the guard approached again. That went on until three
or four every morning. Three or four hours of sleep a night was enough
for me. Often in the years in the streets I had slept less than that.

The teachings of Mr. Muhammad stressed how history had been   19
"whitened" — when white men had written history books, the black man
simply had been left out. Mr. Muhammad couldn't have said anything
that would have struck me much harder. I had never forgotten how when
my class, me and all of those whites, had studied seventh-grade United
States history back in Mason, the history of the Negro had been covered
in one paragraph, and the teacher had gotten a big laugh with his joke,
"Negroes' feet are so big that when they walk, they leave a hole in the
ground."

This is one reason why Mr. Muhammad's teachings spread so swiftly   20
all over the United States, among *all* Negroes, whether or not they
became followers of Mr. Muhammad. The teachings ring true — to every
Negro. You can hardly show me a black adult in America — or a white
one, for that matter — who knows from the history books anything like
the truth about the black man's role. In my own case, once I heard of
the "glorious history of the black man," I took special pains to hunt in
the library for books that would inform me on details about black history.

I can remember accurately the very first set of books that really   21
impressed me. I have since bought that set of books and I have it at
home for my children to read as they grow up. It's called *Wonders of the
World.* It's full of pictures of archeological finds, statues that depict,
usually, non-European people.

I found books like Will Durant's *Story of Civilization.* I read H. G.   22
Wells's *Outline of History. Souls of Black Folk* by W. E. B. Du Bois
gave me a glimpse into the black people's history before they came to
this country. Carter G. Woodson's *Negro History* opened my eyes about
black empires before the black slave was brought to the United States,
and the early Negro struggles for freedom.

J. A. Rogers's three volumes of *Sex and Race* told about race-mixing   23
before Christ's time; about Aesop being a black man who told fables;

about Egypt's Pharaohs; about the great Coptic Christian Empires; about Ethiopia, the earth's oldest continuous black civilization, as China is the oldest continuous civilization.

Mr. Muhammad's teaching about how the white man had been created 24 led me to *Findings in Genetics* by Gregor Mendel. (The dictionary's *G* section was where I had learned what "genetics" meant.) I really studied this book by the Austrian monk. Reading it over and over, especially certain sections, helped me to understand that if you started with a black man, a white man could be produced; but starting with a white man, you never could produce a black man — because the white chromosome is recessive. And since no one disputes that there was but one Original Man, the conclusion is clear.

During the last year or so, in the *New York Times*, Arnold Toynbee 25 used the word "bleached" in describing the white man. (His words were: "White (i.e., bleached) human beings of North European origin. . . ." Toynbee also referred to the European geographic area as only a peninsula of Asia. He said there is no such thing as Europe. And if you look at the globe, you will see for yourself that America is only an extension of Asia. (But at the same time Toynbee is among those who have helped to bleach history. He has written that Africa was the only continent that produced no history. He won't write that again. Every day now, the truth is coming to light.)

I never will forget how shocked I was when I began reading about 26 slavery's total horror. It made such an impact upon me that it later became one of my favorite subjects when I became a minister of Mr. Muhammad's. The world's most monstrous crime, the sin and the blood on the white man's hands, are almost impossible to believe. Books like the one by Frederick Olmstead opened my eyes to the horrors suffered when the slave was landed in the United States. The European woman, Fanny Kemble, who had married a Southern white slaveowner, described how human beings were degraded. Of course I read *Uncle Tom's Cabin*. In fact, I believe that's the only novel I have ever read since I started serious reading.

Parkhurst's collection also contained some bound pamphlets of the 27 Abolitionist Anti-Slavery Society of New England. I read descriptions of atrocities, saw those illustrations of black slave women tied up and flogged with whips; of black mothers watching their babies being dragged off, never to be seen by their mothers again; of dogs after slaves, and of the fugitive slave catchers, evil white men with whips and clubs and chains and guns. I read about the slave preacher Nat Turner, who put the fear of God into the white slavemaster. Nat Turner wasn't going around preaching pie-in-the-sky and "nonviolent" freedom for the black man. There in Virginia one night in 1831, Nat and seven other slaves started out at his master's home and through the night they went from one plantation "big house" to the next, killing, until by the next morning 57 white people were dead and Nat had about 70 slaves following him. White people, terrified for their lives, fled from their homes, locked themselves up in public buildings, hid in the woods, and some even left the state. A small army of soldiers took two months to catch and hang

Nat Turner. Somewhere I have read where Nat Turner's example is said to have inspired John Brown to invade Virginia and attack Harpers Ferry nearly thirty years later, with thirteen white men and five Negroes.

I read Herodotus, "the father of History," or, rather, I read about **28** him. And I read the histories of various nations, which opened my eyes gradually, then wider and wider, to how the whole world's white men had indeed acted like devils, pillaging and raping and bleeding and draining the whole world's non-white people. I remember, for instance, books such as Will Durant's *The Story of Oriental Civilization*, and Mahatma Gandhi's accounts of the struggle to drive the British out of India.

Book after book showed me how the white man had brought upon **29** the world's black, brown, red, and yellow peoples every variety of the sufferings of exploitation. I saw how since the sixteenth century, the so-called "Christian trader" white man began to ply the seas in his lust for Asian and African empires, and plunder, and power. I read, I saw, how the white man never has gone among the non-white peoples bearing the Cross in the true manner and spirit of Christ's teachings — meek, humble, and Christlike.

I perceived, as I read, how the collective white man had been actually **30** nothing but a piratical opportunist who used Faustian machinations to make his own Christianity his initial wedge in criminal conquests. First, always "religiously," he branded "heathen" and "pagan" labels upon ancient non-white cultures and civilizations. The stage thus set, he then turned upon his non-white victims his weapons of war.

I read how, entering India — half a *billion* deeply religious brown **31** people — the British white man, by 1759, through promises, trickery and manipulations, controlled much of India through Great Britain's East India Company. The parasitical British administration kept tentacling out to half of the subcontinent. In 1857, some of the desperate people of India finally mutinied — and, excepting the African slave trade, nowhere has history recorded any more unnecessary bestial and ruthless human carnage than the British suppression of the non-white Indian people.

Over 115 million African blacks — close to the 1930s population of **32** the United States — were murdered or enslaved during the slave trade. And I read how when the slave market was glutted, the cannibalistic white powers of Europe next carved up, as their colonies, the richest areas of the black continent. And Europe's chancelleries for the next century played a chess game of naked exploitation and power from Cape Horn to Cairo.

Ten guards and the warden couldn't have torn me out of those books. **33** Not even Elijah Muhammad could have been more eloquent than those books were in providing indisputable proof that the collective white man had acted like a devil in virtually every contact he had with the world's collective non-white man. I listen today to the radio, and watch television, and read the headlines about the collective white man's fear and tension concerning China. When the white man professes ignorance about why the Chinese hate him so, my mind can't help flashing back to what I read, there in prison, about how the blood forebears of this same white man raped China at a time when China was trusting and helpless. Those original white "Christian traders" sent into China millions of pounds of opium. By 1839, so many of the Chinese were addicts that China's desperate government destroyed twenty thousand chests of opium. The first Opium War was promptly declared by the white man. Imagine! Declaring *war* upon someone who objects to being narcotized! The Chinese were severely beaten, with Chinese-invented gunpowder.

34 The Treaty of Nanking made China pay the British white man for the destroyed opium: forced open China's major ports to British trade; forced China to abandon Hong Kong; fixed China's import tariffs so low that cheap British articles soon flooded in, maiming China's industrial development.

35 After a second Opium War, the Tientsin Treaties legalized the ravaging opium trade, legalized a British-French-American control of China's customs. China tried delaying that Treaty's ratification; Peking was looted and burned.

36 "Kill the foreign white devils!" was the 1901 Chinese war cry in the Boxer Rebellion. Losing again, this time the Chinese were driven from Peking's choicest areas. The vicious, arrogant white man put up the famous signs, "Chinese and dogs not allowed."

37 Red China after World War II closed its doors to the Western white world. Massive Chinese agricultural, scientific, and industrial efforts are described in a book that *Life* magazine recently published. Some observers inside Red China have reported that the world never has known such a hate-white campaign as is now going on in this non-white country where, present birth-rates continuing, in fifty more years Chinese will be half the earth's population. And it seems that some Chinese chickens will soon come home to roost, with China's recent successful nuclear tests.

38 Let us face reality. We can see in the United Nations a new world order being shaped, along color lines — an alliance among the non-white nations. America's U.N. Ambassador Adlai Stevenson complained not long ago that in the United Nations "a skin game" was being played. He was right. He was facing reality. A "skin game" *is* being played. But Ambassador Stevenson sounded like Jesse James accusing the marshal of carrying a gun. Because who in the world's history ever has played a worse "skin game" than the white man?

39 Mr. Muhammad, to whom I was writing daily, had no idea of what a new world had opened up to me through my efforts to document his teachings in books.

40 When I discovered philosophy, I tried to touch all the landmarks of philosophical development. Gradually, I read most of the old philosophers, Occidental and Oriental. The Oriental philosophers were the ones I came to prefer; finally, my impression was that most Occidental philosophy had largely been borrowed from the Oriental thinkers. Socrates, for instance, traveled in Egypt. Some sources even say that Socrates was initiated into some of the Egyptian mysteries. Obviously Socrates got some of his wisdom among the East's wise men.

41 I have often reflected upon the new vistas that reading opened to me. I knew right there in prison that reading had changed forever the course of my life. As I see it today, the ability to read awoke inside me

some long dormant craving to be mentally alive. I certainly wasn't seeking any degree, the way a college confers a status symbol upon its students. My homemade education gave me, with every additional book that I read, a little bit more sensitivity to the deafness, dumbness, and blindness that was afflicting the black race in America. Not long ago, an English writer telephoned me from London, asking questions. One was, "What's your alma mater?" I told him, "Books." You will never catch me with a free fifteen minutes in which I'm not studying something I feel might be able to help the black man.

Yesterday I spoke in London, and both ways on the plane across   42
the Atlantic I was studying a document about how the United Nations proposes to insure the human rights of the oppressed minorities of the world. The American black man is the world's most shameful case of minority oppression. What makes the black man think of himself as only an internal United States issue is just a catch-phrase, two words, "civil rights." How is the black man going to get "civil rights" before first he wins his *human* rights? If the American black man will start thinking about his *human* rights, and then start thinking of himself as part of one of the world's great peoples, he will see he has a case for the United Nations.

I can't think of a better case! Four hundred years of black blood and   43
sweat invested here in America, and the white man still has the black man begging for what every immigrant fresh off the ship can take for granted the minute he walks down the gangplank.

But I'm digressing. I told the Englishman that my alma mater was   44
books, a good library. Every time I catch a plane, I have with me a book that I want to read — and that's a lot of books these days. If I weren't out here every day battling the white man, I could spend the rest of my life reading, just satisfying my curiosity — because you can hardly mention anything I'm not curious about. I don't think anybody ever got more out of going to prison than I did. In fact, prison enabled me to study far more intensively than I would have if my life had gone differently and I had attended some college. I imagine that one of the biggest troubles with colleges is there are too many distractions, too much panty-raiding, fraternities, and boola-boola and all of that. Where else but in a prison could I have attacked my ignorance by being able to study intensely sometimes as much as fifteen hours a day?

12. A Literature Option: Two Short Stories

Find a basis for comparing the following short stories and then write a critical essay. You may find both stories tough going at first but easier to follow as you go along. H. G. Wells (1866–1946) is the British science fiction writer quoted in Assignment 4 of this chapter. Estela Portillo Trambley (b. 1936) is a Mexican-American writer from El Paso, Texas.

In a short postscript to your essay, offer some afterthoughts. Consider what placing these unusual stories next to each other did to your reading of each.

The Country of the Blind
H. G. WELLS

Three hundred miles and more from Chimborazo, one hundred from the snows of Cotopaxi, in the wildest wastes of Ecuador's Andes, there lies that mysterious mountain valley, cut off from the world of men, the Country of the Blind. Long years ago that valley lay so far open to the world that men might come at last through frightful gorges and over an icy pass into its equable meadows; and thither indeed men came, a family or so of Peruvian half-breeds fleeing from the lust and tyranny of an evil Spanish ruler. Then came the stupendous outbreak of Mindobamba, when it was night in Quito for seventeen days, and the water was boiling at Yaguachi and all the fish floating dying even as far as Guayaquil; everywhere along the Pacific slopes there were landslips and swift thawings and sudden floods, and one whole side of the old Arauca crest slipped and came down in thunder, and cut off the Country of the Blind for ever from the exploring feet of men. But one of these early settlers had chanced to be on the hither side of the gorges when the world had so terribly shaken itself, and he perforce had to forget his wife and his child and all the friends and possessions he had left up there, and start life over again in the lower world. He started it again but ill, blindness overtook him, and he died of punishment in the mines; but the story he told begot a legend that lingers along the length of the Cordilleras of the Andes to this day.

He told of his reason for venturing back from that fastness, into which he had first been carried lashed to a llama, beside a vast bale of gear, when he was a child. The valley, he said, had in it all that the heart of man could desire — sweet water, pasture, an even climate, slopes of rich brown soil with tangles of a shrub that bore an excellent fruit, and on one side great hanging forests of pine that held the avalanches high. Far overhead, on three sides, vast cliffs of gray-green rock were capped by cliffs of ice; but the glacier stream came not to them but flowed away by the farther slopes, and only now and then huge ice masses fell on the valley side. In this valley it neither rained nor snowed, but the abundant springs gave a rich green pasture, that irrigation would spread over all the valley space. The settlers did well indeed there. Their beasts did well and multiplied, and but one thing marred their happiness. Yet it was enough to mar it greatly. A strange disease had come upon them, and had made all the children born to them there — and indeed, several older children also — blind. It was to seek some charm or antidote against this plague of blindness that he had with fatigue and danger and difficulty returned down the gorge. In those days, in such cases, men did not think of germs and infections but of sins; and it seemed to him that the reason of this affliction must lie in the negligence of these priestless immigrants to set up a shrine so soon as they entered the valley. He wanted a shrine — a handsome, cheap, effectual shrine — to be erected in the valley; he wanted relics and such-like potent things of faith, blessed objects and mysterious medals and prayers. In his wallet he had a bar of native silver for which he would not account; he insisted there was none in the valley with something of the insistence of an inexpert liar. They had all clubbed their money and ornaments together, having little need for such treasure up there, he said, to buy them holy help against their ill. I figure this dim-eyed young mountaineer, sunburnt, gaunt, and anxious, hat-brim clutched feverishly, a man all unused to the ways of the lower world, telling this story to some keen-eyed, attentive priest before the great convulsion; I can picture him presently seeking to return with pious and infallible remedies against that trouble, and the infinite dismay with which he must have faced the tumbled vastness where the gorge had once come out. But the rest of his story of mischances is lost to me, save that I know of his evil death after several years. Poor stray from that remoteness! The stream that had once made the gorge now bursts from the mouth of a rocky cave, and the legend his poor, ill-told story set going developed into the legend of a race of blind men somewhere "over there" one may still hear to-day.

And amidst the little population of that now isolated and forgotten valley the disease ran its course. The old became groping and purblind, the young saw but dimly, and the children that were born to them saw never at all. But life was very easy in that snow-rimmed basin, lost to all the world, with neither thorns nor briars, with no evil insects nor any beasts save the gentle breed of llamas they had lugged and thrust and followed up the beds of the shrunken rivers in the gorges up which they had come. The seeing had become purblind so gradually that they scarcely noted their loss. They guided the sightless youngsters hither and thither until they knew the whole valley marvelously, and when at last sight died out among them the race lived on. They had even time to adapt themselves to the blind control of fire, which they made carefully in stoves of stone. They were a simple strain of people at the first, unlettered, only slightly touched with the Spanish civilization, but with something of a tradition of the arts of old Peru and of its lost philosophy. Generation followed generation. They forgot many things; they devised many things. Their tradition of the greater world they came from became mythical in color and uncertain. In all things save sight they were strong and able; and presently the chance of birth and heredity sent one who had an original mind and who could talk and persuade among them, and then afterwards another. These two passed, leaving their effects, and the little community grew in numbers and in understanding, and met and settled social and economic problems that arose. Generation followed generation. There came a time when a child was born who was fifteen generations from that ancestor who went out of the valley with a bar of silver to seek God's aid, and who never returned. Thereabouts it chanced that a man came into this community from the outer world. And this is the story of that man.

He was a mountaineer from the country near Quito, a man who had **4** been down to the sea and had seen the world, a reader of books in an original way, an acute and enterprising man, and he was taken on by a party of Englishmen who had come out to Ecuador to climb mountains, to replace one of their three Swiss guides who had fallen ill. He climbed here and he climbed there, and then came the attempt on Parascotopetl, the Matterhorn of the Andes, in which he was lost to the outer world. The story of the accident has been written a dozen times. Pointer's narrative is the best. He tells how the party worked their difficult and almost vertical way up to the very foot of the last and greatest precipice, and how they built a night shelter amidst the snow upon a little shelf of rock, and, with a touch of real dramatic power, how presently they found Núñez had gone from them. They shouted, and there was no reply; shouted and whistled, and for the rest of that night they slept no more.

As the morning broke they saw the traces of his fall. It seems impossible he could have uttered a sound. He had slipped eastward towards the unknown side of the mountain; far below he had struck a steep slope of snow, and ploughed his way down it in the midst of a snow avalanche. His track went straight to the edge of a frightful precipice, and beyond that everything was hidden. Far, far below, and hazy with distance, they could see trees rising out of a narrow, shut-in valley — the lost Country of the Blind. But they did not know it was the lost Country of the Blind, nor distinguish it in any way from any other narrow streak of upland valley. Unnerved by this disaster, they abandoned their attempt in the afternoon, and Pointer was called away to the war before he could make another attack. To this day Parascotopetl lifts an unconquered crest, and Pointer's shelter crumbles unvisited amidst the snows.

And the man who fell survived.

At the end of the slope he fell a thousand feet, and came down in the midst of a cloud of snow upon a snow slope even steeper than the one above. Down this he was whirled, stunned and insensible, but without a bone broken in his body; and then at last came to gentler slopes, and at last rolled out and lay still, buried amidst a softening heap of the white masses that had accompanied and saved him. He came to himself with a dim fancy that he was ill in bed; then realized his position with a mountaineer's intelligence, and worked himself loose, and after a rest or so, out until he saw the stars. He rested flat upon his chest for a space, wondering where he was and what had happened to him. He explored his limbs, and discovered that several of his buttons were gone and his coat turned over his head. His knife had gone from his pocket and his hat was lost, though he had tied it under his chin. He recalled that he had been looking for loose stones to raise his piece of the shelter wall. His ice-axe had disappeared.

He decided he must have fallen, and looked up to see, exaggerated **8** by the ghastly light of the rising moon, the tremendous flight he had taken. For a while he lay, gazing blankly at that vast pale cliff towering above, rising moment by moment out of a subsiding tide of darkness. Its phantasmal mysterious beauty held him for a space, and then he was seized with a paroxysm of sobbing laughter. . . .

After a great interval of time he became aware that he was near the lower edge of the snow. Below, down what was now a moonlit and practicable slope, he saw the dark and broken appearance of rock-strewn turf. He struggled to his feet, aching in every joint and limb, got down painfully from the heaped loose snow about him, went downward until he was on the turf, and there dropped rather than lay beside a boulder, drank deep from the flask in his inner pocket, and instantly fell asleep. . . .

He was awakened by the singing of birds in the trees far below.

He sat up and perceived he was on a little alp at the foot of a vast precipice, that was grooved by the gully down which he and his snow had come. Over against him another wall of rock reared itself against the sky. The gorge between these precipices ran east and west and was full of the morning sunlight, which lit to the westward the mass of fallen mountain that closed the descending gorge. Below him it seemed there was a precipice equally steep, but behind the snow in the gully he found a sort of chimney-cleft dripping with snow-water down which a desperate man might venture. He found it easier than it seemed, and came at last to another desolate alp, and then after a rock climb of no particular difficulty to a steep slope of trees. He took his bearings and turned his face up the gorge, for he saw it opened out above upon green meadows, among which he now glimpsed quite distinctly a cluster of stone huts of unfamiliar fashion. At times his progress was like clambering along the face of a wall, and after a time the rising sun ceased to strike along the gorge, the voices of the singing birds died away, and the air grew cold and dark about him. But the distant valley with its houses was all the brighter for that. He came presently to talus, and among 'the rocks he noted — for he was an observant man — an unfamiliar fern that seemed to clutch out of the crevices with intense green hands. He picked a frond or so and gnawed its stalk and found it helpful.

About midday he came at last out of the throat of the gorge into the plain and the sunlight. He was stiff and weary; he sat down in the shadow of a rock, filled up his flask with water from a spring and drank it down, and remained for a time resting before he went on to the houses.

They were very strange to his eyes, and indeed the whole aspect of that valley became, as he regarded it, queerer and more unfamiliar. The greater part of its surface was lush green meadow, starred with many beautiful flowers, irrigated with extraordinary care, and bearing evidence of systematic cropping piece by piece. High up and ringing the valley about was a wall, and what appeared to be a circumferential water-channel, from which the little trickles of water that fed the meadow plants came, and on the higher slopes above this flocks of llamas cropped the scanty herbage. Sheds, apparently shelters or feeding-places for the llamas, stood against the boundary wall here and there. The irrigation streams ran together into a main channel down the center of the valley, and this was enclosed on either side by a wall breast high. This gave a singularly urban quality to this secluded place, a quality that was greatly enhanced by the fact that a number of paths paved with black and white stones, and each with a curious little curb at the side, ran hither and thither in an orderly manner. The houses of the central village were quite

12

unlike the casual and higgledy-piggledy agglomeration of the mountain villages he knew; they stood in a continuous row on either side of a central street of astonishing cleanness; here and there their parti-colored facade was pierced by a door, and not a solitary window broke their even frontage. They were parti-colored with extraordinary irregularity; smeared with a sort of plaster that was sometimes gray, sometimes drab, sometimes slate-colored or dark brown; and it was the sight of this wild plastering first brought the word "blind" into the thoughts of the explorer. "The good man who did that," he thought, "must have been as blind as a bat."

He descended a steep place, and so came to the wall and channel that ran about the valley, near where the latter spouted out its surplus contents into the deeps of the gorge in a thin and wavering thread of cascade. He could now see a number of men and women resting on piled heaps of grass, as if taking a siesta, in the remoter part of the meadow, and nearer the village a number of recumbent children, and then nearer at hand three men carrying pails on yokes along a little path that ran from the encircling wall towards the houses. These latter were clad in garments of llama cloth and boots and belts of leather, and they wore caps of cloth with back and ear flaps. They followed one another in single file, walking slowly and yawning as they walked, like men who have been up all night. There was something so reassuringly prosperous and re-spectable in their bearing that after a moment's hesitation Núñez stood forward as conspicuously as possible upon his rock, and gave vent to a mighty shout that echoed round the valley.

The three men stopped, and moved their heads as though they were looking about them. They turned their faces this way and that, and Núñez gesticulated with freedom. But they did not appear to see him for all his gestures, and after a time, directing themselves towards the mountains far away to the right, they shouted as if in answer. Núñez bawled again, and then once more, and as he gestured ineffectually the word "blind" came up to the top of his thoughts. "The fools must be blind," he said.

When at last, after much shouting and wrath, Núñez crossed the **16** stream by a little bridge, came through a gate in the wall, and approached them, he was sure that they were blind. He was sure that this was the Country of the Blind of which the legends told. Conviction had sprung upon him, and a sense of great and rather enviable adventure. The three stood side by side, not looking at him, but with their ears directed towards him, judging him by his unfamiliar steps. They stood close together like men a little afraid, and he could see their eyelids closed and sunken, as though the very balls beneath had shrunk away. There was an expression near awe on their faces.

"A man," one said, in hardly recognizable Spanish — "a man it is — a man or a spirit — coming down from the rocks."

But Núñez advanced with the confident steps of a youth who enters upon life. All the old stories of the lost valley and the Country of the Blind had come back to his mind, and through his thoughts ran this old proverb, as if it were a refrain —

"In the Country of the Blind the One-eyed Man is King."

"In the Country of the Blind the One-eyed Man is King." 20

And very civilly he gave them greeting. He talked to them and used his eyes.

"Where does he come from, brother Pedro?" asked one.

"Down out of the rocks."

"Over the mountains I come," said Núñez, "out of the country beyond 24 there — where men can see. From near Bogotá, where there are a hundred thousands of people, and where the city passes out of sight."

"Sight?" muttered Pedro. "Sight?"

"He comes," said the second blind man, "out of the rocks."

The cloth of their coats Núñez saw was curiously fashioned, each with a different sort of stitching.

They startled him by a simultaneous movement towards him, each 28 with a hand outstretched. He stepped back from the advance of these spread fingers.

"Come hither," said the third blind man, following his motion and clutching him neatly.

And they held Núñez and felt him over, saying no word further until they had done so.

"Carefully," he cried, with a finger in his eye, and found they thought that organ, with its fluttering lids, a queer thing in him. They went over it again.

"A strange creature, Correa," said the one called Pedro. "Feel the 32 coarseness of his hair. Like a llama's hair."

"Rough he is as the rocks that begot him," said Correa, investigating Núñez's unshaven chin with a soft and slightly moist hand. "Perhaps he will grow finer." Núñez struggled a little under their examination, but they gripped him firm.

"Carefully," he said again.

"He speaks," said the third man. "Certainly he is a man."

"Ugh!" said Pedro, at the roughness of his coat. 36

"And you have come into the world?" asked Pedro.

"*Out* of the world. Over mountains and glaciers; right over above there, halfway to the sun. Out of the great big world that goes down, twelve days' journey to the sea."

They scarcely seemed to heed him. "Our fathers have told us men may be made by the forces of Nature," said Correa. "It is the warmth of things and moisture, and rottenness — rottenness."

"Let us lead him to the elders," said Pedro. 40

"Shout first," said Correa, "lest the children be afraid. This is a marvelous occasion."

So they shouted, and Pedro went first and took Núñez by the hand to lead him to the houses.

He drew his hand away. "I can see," he said.

"See?" said Correa. 44

"Yes, see," said Núñez, turning towards him, and stumbled against Pedro's pail.

"His senses are still imperfect," said the third blind man. "He stumbles, and talks unmeaning words. Lead him by the hand."

"As you will," said Núñez, and was led along, laughing.

It seemed they knew nothing of sight.   48

Well, all in good time he would teach them.

He heard people shouting, and saw a number of figures gathering together in the middle roadway of the village.

He found it tax his nerve and patience more than he had anticipated, that first encounter with the population of the Country of the Blind. The place seemed larger as he drew near to it, and the smeared plasterings queerer, and a crowd of children and men and women (the women and girls, he was pleased to note, had some of them quite sweet faces, for all that their eyes were shut and sunken) came about him, holding on to him, touching him with soft, sensitive hands, smelling at him, and listening at every word he spoke. Some of the maidens and children, however, kept aloof as if afraid, and indeed his voice seemed coarse and rude beside their softer notes. They mobbed him. His three guides kept close to him with an effect of proprietorship, and said again and again, "A wild man out of the rocks."

"Bogotá," he said. "Bogotá. Over the mountain crests."   52

"A wild man — using wild words," said Pedro. "Did you hear that — *Bogotá?* His mind is hardly formed yet. He has only the beginnings of speech."

A little boy nipped his hand. "Bogotá!" he said mockingly.

"Ay! A city to your village, I come from the great world — where men have eyes and see."

"His name's Bogotá," they said.   56

"He stumbled," said Correa, "stumbled twice as we came hither."

"Bring him to the elders."

And they thrust him suddenly through a doorway into a room as black as pitch, save at the end there faintly glowed a fire. The crowd closed in behind him and shut out all but the faintest glimmer of day, and before he could arrest himself he had fallen headlong over the feet of a seated man. His arm, out-flung, struck the face of someone else as he went down; he felt the soft impact of features and heard a cry of anger, and for a moment he struggled against a number of hands that clutched him. It was a one-sided fight. An inkling of the situation came to him, and he lay quiet.

"I fell down," he said; "I couldn't see in this pitchy darkness."   60

There was a pause as if the unseen persons about him tried to understand his words. Then the voice of Correa said: "He is but newly formed. He stumbles as he walks and mingles words that mean nothing with his speech."

Others also said things about him that he heard or understood imperfectly.

"May I sit up?" he asked, in a pause. "I will not struggle against you again."

They consulted and let him rise.   64

The voice of an older man began to question him, and Núñez found himself trying to explain the great world out of which he had fallen, and the sky and mountains and sight and such-like marvels, to these elders who sat in darkness in the Country of the Blind. And they would believe and understand nothing whatever he told them, a thing quite outside his expectation. They would not even understand many of his words. For fourteen generations these people had been blind and cut off from all the seeing world; the names for all the things of sight had faded and changed; the story of the outer world was faded and changed to a child's story; and they had ceased to concern themselves with anything beyond the rocky slopes above their circling wall. Blind men of genius had arisen among them and questioned the shreds of belief and tradition they had brought with them from their seeing days, and had dismissed all these things as idle fancies, and replaced them with new and saner explanations. Much of their imagination had shriveled with their eyes, and they had made for themselves new imaginations with their ever more sensitive ears and finger-tips. Slowly Núñez realized this; that his expectation of wonder and reverence at his origin and his gifts was not to be borne out; and after his poor attempt to explain sight to them had been set aside as the confused version of a new-made being describing the marvels of his incoherent sensations, he subsided, a little dashed, into listening to their instruction. And the eldest of the blind men explained to him life and philosophy and religion, how that the world (meaning their valley) had been first an empty hollow in the rocks, and then had come, first, inanimate things without the gift of touch, and llamas and a few other creatures that had little sense, and then men, and at last angels, whom one could hear singing and making fluttering sounds, but whom no one could touch at all, which puzzled Núñez greatly until he thought of the birds.

He went on to tell Núñez how this time had been divided into the warm and the cold, which are the blind equivalents of day and night, and how it was good to sleep in the warm and work during the cold, so that now, but for his advent, the whole town of the blind would have been asleep. He said Núñez must have been specially created to learn and serve the wisdom they had acquired, and for that all his mental incoherency and stumbling behavior he must have courage and do his best to learn, and at that all the people in the doorway murmured encouragingly. He said the night — for the blind call their day night — was now far gone, and it behooved everyone to go back to sleep. He asked Núñez if he knew how to sleep, and Núñez said he did, but that before sleep he wanted food.

They brought him food — llama's milk in a bowl, and rough salted bread — and led him into a lonely place to eat out of their hearing, and afterwards to slumber until the chill of the mountain evening roused them to begin their day again. But Núñez slumbered not at all.

Instead, he sat up in the place where they had left him, resting his limbs and turning the unanticipated circumstances of his arrival over and over in his mind.

Every now and then he laughed, sometimes with amusement, and sometimes with indignation.

"Unformed mind!" he said. "Got no senses yet! They little know they've been insulting their heaven-sent king and master. I see I must bring them to reason. Let me think — let me think."

He was still thinking when the sun set.

Núñez had an eye for all beautiful things, and it seemed to him that the glow upon the snowfields and glaciers that rose about the valley on every side was the most beautiful thing he had ever seen. His eyes went from that inaccessible glory to the village and irrigated fields, fast sinking into the twilight, and suddenly a wave of emotion took him, and he thanked God from the bottom of his heart that the power of sight had been given him. `72`

He heard a voice calling to him from out of the village.

"Ya ho there, Bogotá! Come hither!"

At that he stood up smiling. He would show these people once and for all what sight would do for a man. They would seek him, but not find him.

"You move not, Bogotá," said the voice. `76`

He laughed noiselessly, and made two stealthy steps aside from the path.

"Trample not on the grass, Bogotá; that is not allowed."

Núñez had scarcely heard the sound he made himself. He stopped, amazed.

The owner of the voice came running up the piebald path towards him. `80`

He stepped back into the pathway. "Here I am," he said.

"Why did you not come when I called you?" said the blind man. "Must you be led like a child? Cannot you hear the path as you walk?"

Núñez laughed. "I can see it," he said.

"There is no such word as *see*," said the blind man, after a pause. `84` "Cease this folly, and follow the sound of my feet."

Núñez followed, a little annoyed.

"My time will come," he said.

"You'll learn," the blind man answered. "There is much to learn in the world."

"Has no one told you, 'In the Country of the Blind the One-eyed `88` Man is King'?"

"What is blind?" asked the blind man carelessly over his shoulder.

Four days passed, and the fifth found the King of the Blind still incognito, as a clumsy and useless stranger among his subjects.

It was, he found, much more difficult to proclaim himself than he had supposed, and in the meantime, while he meditated his *coup d'état*, he did what he was told and learned the manners and customs of the Country of the Blind. He found working and going about at night a particularly irksome thing, and he decided that that should be the first thing he would change.

They led a simple, laborious life, these people, with all the elements `92` of virtue and happiness, as these things can be understood by men. They toiled, but not oppressively; they had food and clothing sufficient for their needs; they had days and seasons of rest; they made much of music and singing, and there was love among them, and little children.

It was marvelous with what confidence and precision they went about their ordered world. Everything, you see, had been made to fit their needs; each of the radiating paths of the valley area had a constant angle to the others, and was distinguished by a special notch upon its curbing; all obstacles and irregularities of path or meadow had long since been cleared away; all their methods and procedure arose naturally from their special needs. Their senses had become marvelously acute; they could hear and judge the slightest gesture of a man a dozen paces away — could hear the very beating of his heart. Intonation had long replaced expression with them, and touches gesture, and their work with hoe and spade and fork was as free and confident as garden work can be. Their sense of smell was extraordinarily fine; they could distinguish individual differences as readily as a dog can, and they went about the tending of the llamas, who lived among the rocks above and came to the wall for food and shelter, with ease and confidence. It was only when at last Núñez sought to assert himself that he found how easy and confident their movements could be.

He rebelled only after he had tried persuasion.

He tried at first on several occasions to tell them of sight. "Look you here, you people," he said. "There are things you do not understand in me."

Once or twice one or two of them attended to him; they sat with faces downcast and ears turned intelligently towards him, and he did his best to tell them what it was to see. Among his hearers was a girl, with eyelids less red and sunken than the others, so that one could almost fancy she was hiding eyes, whom especially he hoped to persuade. He spoke of the beauties of sight, of watching the mountains, of the sky and the sunrise, and they heard him with amused incredulity that presently became condemnatory. They told him there were indeed no mountains at all, but that the end of the rocks where the llamas grazed was indeed the end of the world; thence sprang a cavernous roof of the universe, from which the dew and the avalanches fell; and when he maintained stoutly the world had neither end nor roof such as they supposed, they said his thoughts were wicked. So far as he could describe sky and clouds and stars to them it seemed to them a hideous void, a terrible blankness in the place of the smooth roof to things in which they believed — it was an article of faith with them that the cavern roof was exquisitely smooth to the touch. He saw that in some manner he shocked them, and gave up that aspect of the matter altogether, and tried to show them the practical value of sight. One morning he saw Pedro in the path called Seventeen and coming towards the central houses, but still too far off for hearing or scent, and he told them as much. "In a little while," he prophesied, "Pedro will be here." An old man remarked that Pedro had no business on Path Seventeen, and then, as if in confirmation, that individual as he drew near turned and went transversely into Path Ten, and so back with nimble paces towards the outer wall. They mocked Núñez when Pedro did not arrive, and afterwards, when he asked Pedro questions to clear his character, Pedro denied and outfaced him, and was afterwards hostile to him.

Then he induced them to let him go a long way up the sloping meadows towards the wall with one complacent individual, and to him he promised to describe all that happened among the houses. He noted

96

certain goings and comings, but the things that really seemed to signify to these people happened inside of or behind the windowless houses — the only things they took note of to test him by — and of these he could see or tell nothing; and it was after the failure of this attempt, and the ridicule they could not repress, that he resorted to force. He thought of seizing a spade and suddenly smiting one or two of them to earth, and so in fair combat showing the advantage of eyes. He went so far with that resolution as to seize his spade, and then he discovered a new thing about himself, and that was that it was impossible for him to hit a blind man in cold blood.

He hesitated, and found them all aware that he snatched up the spade. They stood alert, with their heads on one side, and bent ears towards him for what he would do next.

"Put that spade down," said one, and he felt a sort of helpless horror. He came near obedience.

Then he thrust one backwards against a house wall, and fled past   **100** him and out of the village.

He went athwart one of their meadows, leaving a track of trampled grass behind his feet, and presently sat down by the side of one of their ways. He felt something of the buoyancy that comes to all men in the beginning of a fight, but more perplexity. He began to realize that you cannot even fight happily with creatures who stand upon a different mental basis to yourself. Far away he saw a number of men carrying spades and sticks come out of the street of houses, and advance in a spreading line along the several paths towards him. They advanced slowly, speaking frequently to one another, and ever and again the whole cordon would halt and sniff the air and listen.

The first time they did this Núñez laughed. But afterwards he did not laugh.

One struck his trail in the meadow grass, and came stooping and feeling his way along it.

For five minutes he watched the slow extension of the cordon, and   **104** then his vague disposition to do something forthwith became frantic. He stood up, went a pace or so towards the circumferential wall, turned, and went back a little way. There they all stood in a crescent, still and listening.

He also stood still, gripping his spade very tightly in both hands. Should he charge them?

The pulse in his ears ran into the rhythm of "In the Country of the Blind the One-eyed Man is King!"

Should he charge them?

He looked back at the high and unclimbable wall behind — unclimbable   **108** because of its smooth plastering, but withal pierced with many little doors, and at the approaching line of seekers. Behind these, others were now coming out of the street of houses.

Should he charge them?

"Bogotá!" called one. "Bogotá! where are you?"

He gripped his spade still tighter, and advanced down the meadows towards the place of habitations, and directly he moved they converged upon him. "I'll hit them if they touch me," he swore; "by Heaven, I will. I'll hit." He called aloud, "Look here, I'm going to do what I like in this valley. Do you hear? I'm going to do what I like and go where I like!"

They were moving in upon him quickly, groping, yet moving rapidly. It was like playing blind man's buff, with everyone blindfolded except one. "Get hold of him!" cried one. He found himself in the arc of a loose curve of pursuers. He felt suddenly he must be active and resolute. 112

"You don't understand," he cried in a voice that was meant to be great and resolute, and which broke. "You are blind, and I can see. Leave me alone!"

"Bogotá! Put down that spade, and come off the grass!"

The last order, grotesque in its urban familiarity, produced a gust of anger.

"I'll hurt you," he said, sobbing with emotion. "By Heaven, I'll hurt you. Leave me alone!" 116

He began to run, not knowing clearly where to run. He ran from the nearest blind man, because it was a horror to hit him. He stopped, and then made a dash to escape from their closing ranks. He made for where a gap was wide, and the men on either side, with a quick perception of the approach of his paces, rushed in on one another. He sprang forward, and then saw he must be caught, and *swish!* the spade had struck. He felt the soft thud of hand and arm, and the man was down with a yell of pain, and he was through.

Through! And then he was close to the street of houses again, and blind men, whirling spades and stakes, were running with a sort of reasoned swiftness hither and thither.

He heard steps behind him just in time, and found a tall man rushing forward and swiping at the sound of him. He lost his nerve, hurled his spade a yard wide at his antagonist, and whirled about and fled, fairly yelling as he dodged another.

He was panic-stricken. He ran furiously to and fro, dodging when there was no need to dodge, and in his anxiety to see on every side of him at once, stumbling. For a moment he was down and they heard his fall. Far away in the circumferential wall a little doorway looked like heaven, and he set off in a wild rush for it. He did not even look round at his pursuers until it was gained, and he had stumbled across the bridge, clambered a little way among the rocks, to the surprise and dismay of a young llama, who went leaping out of sight, and lay down sobbing for breath. 120

And so his *coup d'état* came to an end.

He stayed outside the wall of the valley of the Blind for two nights and days without food or shelter, and meditated upon the unexpected. During these meditations he repeated very frequently and always with a profounder note of derision the exploded proverb: "In the Country of the Blind the One-eyed Man is King." He thought chiefly of ways of fighting and conquering these people, and it grew clear that for him no practicable way was possible. He had no weapons, and now it would be hard to get one.

The canker of civilization had got to him even in Bogotá, and he could not find it in himself to go down and assassinate a blind man. Of course, if he did that, he might then dictate terms on the threat of assassinating them all. But — sooner or later he must sleep! . . .

He tried also to find food among the pine trees, to be comfortable 124 under pine boughs while the frost fell at night, and — with less confidence — to catch a llama by artifice in order to try to kill it — perhaps by hammering it with a stone — and so finally, perhaps, to eat some of it. But the llamas had a doubt of him and regarded him with distrustful brown eyes, and spat when he drew near. Fear came on him the second day and fits of shivering. Finally he crawled down to the wall of the Country of the Blind and tried to make terms. He crawled along by the stream, shouting, until two blind men came out to the gate and talked to him.

"I was mad," he said. "But I was only newly made."

They said that was better.

He told them he was wiser now, and repented of all he had done.

Then he wept without intention, for he was very weak and ill now, 128 and they took that as a favorable sign.

They asked him if he still thought he could *"see."*

"No," he said. "That was folly. The word means nothing — less than nothing!"

They asked him what was overhead.

"About ten times ten the height of a man there is a roof above the 132 world — of rock — and very, very smooth." . . . He burst again into hysterical tears. "Before you ask me any more, give me some food or I shall die."

He expected dire punishments, but these blind people were capable of toleration. They regarded his rebellion as but one more proof of his general idiocy and inferiority; and after they had whipped him they appointed him to do the simplest and heaviest work they had for anyone to do, and he, seeing no other way of living, did submissively what he was told.

He was ill for some days, and they nursed him kindly. That refined his submission. But they insisted on his lying in the dark, and that was a great misery. And blind philosophers came and talked to him of the wicked levity of his mind, and reproved him so impressively for his doubts about the lid of rock that covered their cosmic casserole that he almost doubted whether indeed he was not the victim of hallucination in not seeing it overhead.

So Núñez became a citizen of the Country of the Blind, and these people ceased to be a generalized people and became individualities and familiar to him, while the world beyond the mountains became more and more remote and unreal. There was Yacob, his master, a kindly man when not annoyed; there was Pedro, Yacob's nephew; and there was Medina-saroté, who was the youngest daughter of Yacob. She was little esteemed in the world of the Blind, because she had a clear-cut face, and lacked that satisfying, glossy smoothness that is the blind man's ideal of feminine beauty; but Núñez thought her beautiful at first, and presently the most beautiful thing in the whole creation. Her closed eyelids were not sunken and red after the common way of the valley, but lay as though they might open again at any moment; and she had long eyelashes, which were considered a grave disfigurement. And her voice was strong, and did not satisfy the acute hearing of the valley swains. So that she had no lover.

There came a time when Núñez thought that, could he win her, he would be resigned to live in the valley for all the rest of his days.   **136**

He watched her; he sought opportunities of doing her little services, and presently he found that she observed him. Once at a rest-day gathering they sat side by side in the dim starlight, and the music was sweet. His hand came upon hers and he dared to clasp it. Then very tenderly she returned his pressure. And one day, as they were at their meal in the darkness, he felt her hand very softly seeking him, and as it chanced the fire leaped then and he saw the tenderness of her face.

He sought to speak to her.

He went to her one day when she was sitting in the summer moonlight spinning. The light made her a thing of silver and mystery. He sat down at her feet and told her he loved her, and told her how beautiful she seemed to him. He had a lover's voice, he spoke with a tender reverence that came near to awe, and she had never before been touched by adoration. She made him no definite answer, but it was clear his words pleased her.

After that he talked to her whenever he could take an opportunity.   **140**
The valley became the world for him, and the world beyond the mountains where men lived in sunlight seemed no more than a fairy tale he would some day pour into her ears. Very tentatively and timidly he spoke to her of sight.

Sight seemed to her the most poetical of fancies, and she listened to his description of the stars and the mountains and her own sweet white-lit beauty as though it was a guilty indulgence. She did not believe, she could only half understand, but she was mysteriously delighted, and it seemed to him that she completely understood.

His love lost its awe and took courage. Presently he was for demanding her of Yacob and the elders in marriage, but she became fearful and delayed. And it was one of her elder sisters who first told Yacob that Medina-saroté and Núñez were in love.

There was from the first very great opposition to the marriage of Núñez and Medina-saroté; not so much because they valued her as because they held him as a being apart, an idiot, incompetent thing below the permissible level of a man. Her sisters opposed it bitterly as bringing discredit on them all; and old Yacob, though he had formed a sort of liking for his clumsy, obedient serf, shook his head and said the thing could not be. The young men were all angry at the idea of corrupting the race, and one went so far as to revile and strike Núñez. He struck back. Then for the first time he found an advantage in seeing, even by twilight, and after that fight was over no one was disposed to raise a hand against him. But they still found his marriage impossible.

Old Yacob had a tenderness for his last little daughter, and was   **144**
grieved to have her weep upon his shoulder.

"You see, my dear, he's an idiot. He has delusions; he can't do anything right."

"I know," wept Medina-saroté. "But he's better than he was. He's getting better. And he's strong, dear father, and kind — stronger and

kinder than any other man in the world. And he loves me — and, Father,
I love him."

Old Yacob was greatly distressed to find her inconsolable, and, besides — what made it more distressing — he liked Núñez for many
things. So he went and sat in the windowless council-chamber with the
other elders and watched the trend of the talk, and said, at the proper
time, "He's better than he was. Very likely, some day, we shall find him
as sane as ourselves."

Then afterwards one of the elders, who thought deeply, had an idea.   148
He was the great doctor among these people, their medicine-man, and
he had a very philosophical and inventive mind, and the idea of curing
Núñez of his peculiarities appealed to him. One day when Yacob was
present he returned to the topic of Núñez.

"I have examined Bogotá," he said, "and the case is clearer to me.
I think very probably he might be cured."

"That is what I have always hoped," said old Yacob.

"His brain is affected," said the blind doctor.

The elders murmured assent.   152

"Now, *what* affects it?"

"Ah!" said old Yacob.

"This," said the doctor, answering his own question. "Those queer
things that are called the eyes, and which exist to make an agreeable
soft depression in the face, are diseased, in the case of Bogotá, in such
a way as to affect his brain. They are greatly distended, he has eyelashes,
and his eyelids move, and consequently his brain is in a state of constant
irritation and distraction."

"Yes?" said old Yacob. "Yes?"   156

"And I think I may say with reasonable certainty that, in order to
cure him completely, all that we need do is a simple and easy surgical
operation — namely, to remove these irritant bodies."

"And then he will be sane?"

"Then he will be perfectly sane, and a quite admirable citizen."

"Thank Heaven for science!" said old Yacob, and went forth at once   160
to tell Núñez of his happy hopes.

But Núñez's manner of receiving the good news struck him as being
cold and disappointing.

"One might think," he said, "from the tone you take, that you did
not care for my daughter."

It was Medina-saroté who persuaded Núñez to face the blind
surgeons.

"You do not want me," he said, "to lose my gift of sight?"   164

She shook her head.

"My world is sight."

Her head drooped lower.

"There are the beautiful things, the beautiful little things — the   168
flowers, the lichens among the rocks, the lightness and softness on a
piece of fur, the far sky with its drifting down of clouds, the sunsets and
the stars. And there is *you.* For you alone it is good to have sight, to
see your sweet, serene face, your kindly lips, your dear, beautiful hands
folded together. . . . It is these eyes of mine you won, these eyes that

hold me to you, that these idiots seek. Instead, I must touch you, hear you, and never see you again. I must come under that roof of rock and stone and darkness, that horrible roof under which your imagination stoops. . . . No; you would not have me do that?"

A disagreeable doubt had arisen in him. He stopped, and left the thing a question.

"I wish," she said, "sometimes ——" She paused.

"Yes?" said he, a little apprehensively.

"I wish sometimes — you would not talk like that."   172

"Like what?"

"I know it's pretty — it's your imagination. I love it, but *now* ——"

He felt cold. *"Now?"* he said faintly.

She sat still.   176

"You mean — you think — I should be better, better perhaps ——"

He was realizing things very swiftly. He felt anger, indeed, anger at the dull course of fate, but also sympathy for her lack of understanding — a sympathy near akin to pity.

"Dear," he said, and he could see by her whiteness how intensely her spirit pressed against the things she could not say. He put his arms about her, he kissed her ear, and they sat for a time in silence.

"If I were to consent to this?" he said at last, in a voice that was   180
very gentle.

She flung her arms about him, weeping wildly. "Oh, if you would," she sobbed, "if only you would!"

For a week before the operation that was to raise him from his servitude and inferiority to the level of a blind citizen, Núñez knew nothing of sleep, and all through the warm sunlit hours, while the others slumbered happily, he sat brooding or wandered aimlessly, trying to bring his mind to bear on his dilemma. He had given his answer, he had given his consent, and still he was not sure. And at last work-time was over, the sun rose in splendor over the golden crests, and his last day of vision began for him. He had a few minutes with Medina-saroté before she went apart to sleep.

"Tomorrow," he said, "I shall see no more."

"Dear heart!" she answered, and pressed his hands with all her   184
strength.

"They will hurt you but little," she said; "and you are going through this pain — you are going through it, dear lover, for *me*. . . . Dear, if a woman's heart and life can do it, I will repay you. My dearest one, my dearest with the tender voice, I will repay."

He was drenched in pity for himself and her.

He held her in his arms, and pressed his lips to hers, and looked on her sweet face for the last time. "Good-bye!" he whispered at that dear sight, "good-bye!"

And then in silence he turned away from her.   188

She could hear his slow retreating footsteps, and something in the rhythm of them threw her into a passion of weeping.

He had fully meant to go to a lonely place where the meadows were beautiful with white narcissus, and there remain until the hour of his sacrifice should come, but as he went he lifted up his eyes and saw the morning, the morning like an angel in golden armor, marching down the steeps. . . .

It seemed to him that before this splendor he, and this blind world in the valley, and his love, and all, were no more than a pit of sin.

He did not turn aside as he had meant to do, but went on, and passed through the wall of the circumference and out upon the rocks, and his eyes were always upon the sunlit ice and snow.   192

He saw their infinite beauty, and his imagination soared over them to the things beyond he was now to resign for ever.

He thought of that great free world he was parted from, the world that was his own, and he had a vision of those further slopes, distance beyond distance, with Bogotá, a place of multitudinous stirring beauty, a glory by day, a luminous mystery by night, a place of palaces and fountains and statues and white houses, lying beautifully in the middle distance. He thought how for a day or so one might come down through passes, drawing ever nearer and nearer to its busy streets and ways. He thought of the river journey, day by day, from great Bogotá to the still vaster world beyond, through towns and villages, forest and desert places, the rushing river day by day, until its banks receded and the big steamers came splashing by, and one had reached the sea — the limitless sea, with its thousand islands, its thousands of islands, and its ships seen dimly far away in their incessant journeyings round and about that greater world. And there, unpent by mountains, one saw the sky — the sky, not such a disc as one saw it here, but an arch of immeasurable blue, a deep of deeps in which the circling stars were floating. . . .

His eyes scrutinized the great curtain of the mountains with a keener inquiry.

For example, if one went so, up that gully and to that chimney there, then one might come out high among those stunted pines that ran round in a sort of shelf and rose still higher and higher as it passed above the gorge. And then? That talus might be managed. Thence perhaps a climb might be found to take him up to the precipice that came below the snow; and if that chimney failed, then another farther to the east might serve his purpose better. And then? Then one would be out upon the amber-lit snow there, and halfway up to the crest of those beautiful desolations.   196

He glanced back at the village, then turned right round and regarded it steadfastly.

He thought of Medina-saroté, and she had become small and remote.

He turned again towards the mountain wall, down which the day had come to him.

Then very circumspectly he began to climb.   200

When sunset came he was no longer climbing, but he was far and high. He had been higher, but he was still very high. His clothes were torn, his limbs were blood-stained, he was bruised in many places, but he lay as if he were at his ease, and there was a smile on his face.

From where he rested the valley seemed as if it were in a pit and nearly a mile below. Already it was dim with haze and shadow, though the mountain summits around him were things of light and fire. The mountain summits around him were things of light and fire, and the little details of the rocks near at hand were drenched with subtle beauty — a vein of green mineral piercing the gray, the flash of crystal faces here and there, a minute, minutely beautiful orange lichen close beside his face. There were deep mysterious shadows in the gorge, blue deepening into purple, and purple into a luminous darkness, and overhead was the illimitable vastness of the sky. But he heeded these things no longer, but lay quite inactive there, smiling as if he were satisfied merely to have escaped from the valley of the Blind in which he had thought to be King.

The glow of the sunset passed, and the night came, and still he lay peacefully contented under the cold stars.

The Burning

ESTELA PORTILLO TRAMBLEY

The women of the barrio, the ones pock-marked by life, sat in council. Existence in dark cubicles of wounds had withered the spirit. Now, all as one, had found a heath. One tired soul stood up to speak. "Many times I see the light she makes of darkness, and that light is a greater blackness, still."

There was some skepticism from the timid. "Are you sure?"

"In those caves outside the town, she lives for days away from everybody. At night, when she is in the caves, small blinking lights appear, like fireflies. Where do they come from? I say, the blackness of her drowns the life in me."

Another woman with a strange wildness in her eyes nodded her head in affirmation. "Yes, she drinks the bitterness of good and swallows, like the devil-wolf, the red honey milk of evil." ⁴

A cadaverous one looked up into a darkened sky. "I hear thunder; lightning is not far." In unison they agreed, "We could use some rain."

The oldest one among them, one with dirty claws, stood up with arms outstretched and stood menacingly against the first lightning bolt that cleaved the darkness. Her voice was harsh and came from ages past. "She must burn!"

The finality was a cloud, black and tortured. Each looked into another's eyes to find assent or protest. There was only frenzy, tight and straining. The thunder was riding the lightning now, directly over their heads. It was a blazing canopy that urged them on to deeds of fear. There was still no rain. They found blistering words to justify the deed to come. One woman, heavy with anger, crouched to pour out further accusations. "She is the devil's pawn. On nights like this, when the air is heavy like thick blood, she sings among the dead, preferring them to the living. You know why she does it . . . eh? I'll tell you! She chases the dead back to their graves."

"Yes, yes. She stays and stays when death comes. Never a whimper, ⁸ nor a tear, but I sense she feels the death as life like one possessed. They say she catches the flitting souls of the dead and turns them into flies. That way the soul never finds heaven."

"Flies! Flies! She is a plague!"

A clap of thunder reaffirmed. The old one with nervous, clutching claws made the most grievous charge, the cause for this meeting of the judgment. She shaped with bony gestures the anger of the heart. "She is the enemy of God! She put obscenities on our doorsteps to make us her accomplices. Sacrilege against the holy church!"

There was a fervor now, rising like a tide. They were for her burning now. All the council howled that Lela must burn that night. The sentence belonged to night alone. The hurricane could feed in darkness. Fear could be disguised as outrage at night. There were currents now that wanted sacrifice. Sacrifice is the umbilical cord of superstition. It would devastate before finding a calm. Lela was the eye of the storm, the artery that must flow to make them whole when the earth turned to light. To catch an evil when it bounced as shadow in their lives, to find it trapped in human body, this was an effective stimulant to some; to others it was a natural depressant to cut the fear, the dam of frustration. This would be their method of revelation. The doubt of themselves would dissolve.

But women know mercy! Mercy? It was swallowed whole by chasms   12
of desire and fear of the unknown. Tempests grow in narrow margins that want a freedom they don't understand. Slaves always punish the free.

But who was Lela? She had come across the mountain to their pueblo many years before. She had crossed la Barranca del Cobre alone. She had walked into the pueblo one day, a bloody, ragged, half-starved young girl. In an apron she carried some shining sand. She stood there, like a frightened fawn, at the edge of the village. As the people of the pueblo gathered around her strangeness, she smiled, putting out her hand for touch. They drew back and she fell to the ground in exhaustion.

They took her in, but she remained a stranger the rest of her life in the pueblo upon which she had stumbled. At the beginning, she seemed but a harmless child. But, as time passed and she resisted their pattern of life, she was left alone. The people knew she was a Tarahumara from Batopilas. Part of her strangeness was the rooted depth of her own religion. She did not convert to Christianity. People grew hostile and suspicious of her.

But she had also brought with her the miracle sand. It had strange curative powers. In no time, she began to cure those in the pueblo who suffered from skin disease, from sores, or open wounds.

"Is it the magic of her devil gods?" the people asked themselves.   16
Still, they came for the miracle cure that was swift and clean. She became their *curandera*° outside their Christian faith.

The people in her new home needed her, and she loved them in silence and from a distance. She forgave them for not accepting her strangeness and learned to find adventure in the Oneness of herself.

Many times she wanted to go back to Batopilas, but too many people needed her here. She learned the use of medicinal herbs and learned to set broken bones. This was what she was meant to do in life. This

curandera: Folk healer.

purpose would not let her return to Batopilas. Still, she did not convert to Christianity. The people, begrudgingly, believed in her curative powers, but did not believe in her. Many years had passed and Lela was now an old woman, and the council of women this night of impending storm had decided her fate.

Lela lay dying in her one-room hut. There was a fire with teeth that consumed her body. She only knew that her time was near an end as she lay in her small cot. Above the bed was a long shelf she had built herself that held rows of clay figurines. These were painted in gay colors and the expression on the tiny faces measured the seasons of the heart. They were live little faces showing the full circle of human joy and pain, doubt and fear, humor and sobriety. In all expressions there was a fierceness for life.

Lela had molded them through the years, and now they stood over her head like guardians over their maker. . . . Clay figurines, an act of love learned early in her childhood of long ago. In Batopilas, each home had its own rural god. He was a friend and a comforter. The little rural gods were like any other people. They did not rule or demand allegiance. The little rural gods of river, sky, fire, seed, birds, all were chosen members of each family. Because they sanctified all human acts, they were the actions of the living, like an aura. They were a shrine to creation. 20

Lela's mother had taught the little girl to mold the clay figures that represented the rural gods. This was her work and that of Lela's in the village, to provide clay little gods for each home and for festive occasions. This is why Lela never gave them up in her new home. She had molded them with her hands, but they dwelled boundless in the center of her being. The little gods had always been very real, very important, in her reverence for life.

There had been in Batopilas a stone image of the greater god, Tecuat. He was an impressive god of power that commanded silence and obedience. People did not get close to Tecuat except in ritual. As a girl, Lela would tiptoe respectfully around the figure of Tecuat, then she would breathe a sigh of relief and run off to find the little gods.

This was her game, god-hunting. One day, she had walked too far towards the pines, too far towards a roar that spoke of rushing life. She followed a yellow butterfly that also heard a command of dreams. She followed the butterfly that flitted towards a lake. As she followed, she looked for little gods in the glint of the sun, and in the open branches that pierced the absoluteness of the sky. The soft breath of wind was the breath of little gods, and the crystal shine of rocks close to the lake was a winking language that spoke of peace and the wildness of all joy.

When she had reached the lake, she stepped into the water without hesitation. She felt the cool wet mud against her open toes. She walked into the water, touching the ripple of its broken surface with her finger tips. After a while, there was no more bottom. She began to cut the water with smooth, clean strokes, swimming out towards the pearl-green rocks that hid the roar. She floated for a while looking up at the light filtering through eternal trees. The silence spoke of something other than itself. It spoke in colors born of water and sun. She began to swim 24 more rapidly towards the turn that led to the cradle of the roar, the waterfall. . . .

This is what Lela, the old Lela dying on her bed, was remembering . . . the waterfall. It helped to ease the pain that came in waves that broke against her soul and blackened the world. Then, there was the calm, the calm into which the experience machine brought back the yesterdays that were now soft, kind memories. She opened her eyes and looked up at the row of clay figures. She was not alone. "The waterfall . . ." she whispered to herself. She remembered the grotto behind the waterfall. It had been her hermitage of dreams, of wonder. Here her Oneness had knitted all the little gods unto herself until she felt the whole of earth — things within her being. Suddenly, the pain cut her body in two. She gripped the edge of the cot. There were blurs of throbbing white that whirled into black, and all her body trembled until another interval of peace returned for a little while.

There was no thought; there was no dream in the quiet body. She was a simple calm that would not last. The calm was a gift from the little gods. She slept. It was a fitful, brief sleep that ended with the next crash of pain. The pain found gradual absorption. She could feel the bed sheet clinging to her body, wet with perspiration. She asked herself in a half-moan, "When will the body give way?" Give way . . . give way, for so long, Lela had given way and had found ways to open herself and the world she understood. It had been a vital force in her. She could have been content in Batopilas. The simple truths of Nature might have fulfilled her to the end of her days if she had remained in Batopilas. But there was always that reach in her for a larger self. Nature was a greatness, but she felt a different hunger and a different thirst.

There was a world beyond Batopilas; there were people beyond Batopilas. She was no longer a child. It was easy to find little gods in Nature, but as she grew older, it became a child's game. There was time to be a child, but there was now time for something more. That is why, one day, she had walked away from Batopilas.

Beyond the desert, she would find another pueblo. She knew there were many pueblos and many deserts. There was nothing to fear because her little gods were with her. On the first day of her journey, she walked all day. The piercing sun beat down on her and the world, as she scanned the horizon for signs of a way. Something at a distance would be a hope, would be a way to something new, a way to the larger self. At dusk, she felt great hunger and great thirst. Her body ached and her skin felt parched and dry. The night wind felt cold, so she looked for a shelter against the wind. She found a clump of mesquite behind some giant sahuaros. This was not the greenness she knew so well, but a garden of stars in the night sky comforted her until she fell asleep.

At first light she awakened refreshed and quickly resumed her journey. She knew she must make the best out of the early hours before the sun rose. By late morning, the desert yielded a mountain at a distance. She reached the mountain in time to rest from the sun and the physical effort of her journey. When the sun began to fall, she started up a path made narrow by a blanket of desert brush. It tore the flesh of her feet and legs as she made her way up the path. In a little while, it was hard to find sure footing. The path had lost itself in a cleavage of rocks. Night had fallen. She was not afraid, for the night sky, again, was full of blinking little gods.

Then it happened. She lost her footing and fell down, down over a crevice between two huge boulders. As she fell, her lungs filled with air. Her body hit soft sand, but the edge of her foot felt the sharpness of a stone. She lay there stunned for a few minutes until she felt a sharp pain at the side of her foot. Somewhat dizzy, she sat up and noticed that the side of her foot was bleeding profusely. She sat there and watched the blood-flow that found its way into the soft sand. She looked up at the boulders that silently rebuked her helplessness; then she began to cry softly. She had to stanch the blood. She wiped away her tears with the side of her sleeve and tore off a piece of skirt to use as a bandage. As she looked down at the wound again, she noticed that the sand where she had fallen was extremely crystalline and loose. It shone against a rising moon. She scooped up a handful and looked at it with fascination. "The sand of little gods," she whispered to herself. She took some sand and rubbed it on the wound before she applied the bandage. By now, she felt a burning fever. She wrapped the strip of skirt around the wound now covered with the fine, shining sand. Then she slept. But it was a fitful sleep, for her body burned with fever. Half awake and half in a dream, she saw the sands take the shapes of happy, little gods. Then, at other times, the pain told her she was going to die. After a long time, her exhausted body slept until the dawn passed over her head.

When she finally awakened, she felt extremely well. Her body was rested and her temperature, to her great surprise, was normal. She looked down at the wound. The blood was caked on the bandage. She took it off to look at the wound. She could hardly believe her eyes. There was no longer any open wound. There was a healthy scab, and the area around the wound had no infection. It was a healing that normally would have taken weeks. She stood on her foot and felt no pain. "My little gods!" she thought. She fell down on her knees and kissed the shining sand. After a while, she removed her apron and filled it with the shining sand. She secured it carefully before she set off on her climb. As she made her way out of the crevice, she marked the path leading to the shining sand to find her way to it again. It was hard making marks with a sharp stone, and it seemed to take forever. At last, she reached the top of the crevice and noticed, to her great joy, that it led down to a pueblo at a distance. She made her way to strangers that day. Now, at the end of a lifetime, Lela felt the pain roll, roll, roll, roll itself into a blindness. She struggled through the blackness until she gasped back the beginning of the calm. With the new calm came a ringing memory from her childhood. She saw the kindly face of the goddess, Ta Te. She who was born of the union of clean rock, she who was eternal. Yes, Ta Te understood all the verdant things . . . the verdant things.

And who were these women who sat in council? They were one full sweep of hate; they were one full wave of fear. Now these village women were outlined against a grayish sky where a storm refused to break.   32

Spiderlike, apelike, toadlike was the ferocity of their deadness. These were creatures of the earth who mingled with mankind. But they were minions to torture because the twist of littleness bound them to condemn all things unknown, all things untried. The infernal army could not be stopped now. The scurrying creatures began to gather firewood in the gloom. With antlike obedience they hurried back and forth carrying wood to Lela's hut. They piled it in a circle around her little house. The rhythm of their feet sang, "We'll do! We'll do!"

"The circle of fire will drain her powers!" claimed the old one with claws.

"Show me! Show me! Show me!" Voices lost as one.

As the old one with claws ordered more wood, the parish priest came running from his church. With raised arms he shouted as he ran, "Stop! Do you hear? Stop this madness!"

It can be argued that evil is not the reversal of good, but the vacuum of good. Thus, the emptiness is a standing still, a being dead, an infinite pain . . . like dead wood. No one listened to him. 36

"Burn! Burn! Burn!"

Life? The wood? The emptiness? The labor pains were that of something already lost, something left to the indefinite in life. The priest went from one woman to another begging, pleading, taking the wood from their hands.

"Burn! Burn! Burn!"

The old priest reasoned. "All is forgiven, my children. She only made some figurines of clay!" 40

There was a hush. The one woman with the claws approached the priest and spit out the condemnation, "She took our holy saints, Mary, Joseph, and many others and made them obscene. How can you defend the right hand of the devil? Drinking saints! Winking saints! Who can forgive the hideous suggestions of her clay devils? Who?"

The priest said simply, "You."

But if there is only darkness in a narrow belief, who can believe beyond the belief, or even understand the belief itself? The women could not forgive because they did not believe beyond a belief that did not go beyond symbol and law. Somehow, symbol and law, without love, leaves no opening. The clay figures in the church with sweet, painted faces lifted to heaven were much more than figures of clay to these women. Their still postures with praying hands were a security. Now, the priest who had blessed them with holy water said they were not a sanctuary of God. Why did he contradict himself?

The old one with the claws felt triumphant. "She has made our saints into pagan gods!" 44

The priest shook his head sadly. "It is not a sin, what she did!"

No one listened. The piling of wood continued until the match was lit. Happy . . . Happy fire . . . it would burn the sin and the sinner.

Something in Lela told her this was the last struggle now. She looked up at her clay figurines one last time. Her eyes had lost their focus. The little gods had melted into one another; all colors were mixed. They grew into silver strands of light that crossed and mingled and found new forms that pulled away from one center. In half consciousness, she whispered, "Yes, yes, pull away. Find other ways, other selves, grow. . . ."

She smiled; the last calm had taken her back to the caves outside   48
the pueblo. The caves were not like the grotto behind the waterfall, but they were a place for Oneness, where one could look for the larger self. Here the solitude of the heart was a bird in space. Here, in the silence of aloneness, she had looked for the little gods in the townspeople. In her mind, she had molded their smiles, their tears, their embraces, their seeking, their *just being*. Her larger self told her that the miracle of the living act was supreme, the giving, the receiving, the stumbling, and the getting up.

In the caves she had sadly thought of how she had failed to reach them as a friend. Her silences and her strangeness had kept them apart. But, she would find a way of communicating, a way of letting them know that she loved them. "If I give shape and form to their beauty," she thought. "If I cannot tell them I love them with words. . . ."

The light of the moving, mixing little gods was becoming a darkness. Her body would give in now. Yet, she still wished for Batopilas and the old ways with her last breath, "If only . . . if only I could be buried in the tradition of my fathers . . . a clean burning for new life . . . but here, here, there is a dark hole for the dead body. . . . Oh, little gods, take me back to my fathers. . . ."

The little gods were racing to the waterfall.

13. A History Option: Two Overviews of the American Revolution

Write an essay comparing the following two overviews of the American Revolution, written by British historian G. M. Trevelyan and American historian Edmund S. Morgan. Take into consideration how their perspectives help shape their historical accounts.

From *A Shortened History of England*
G. M. TREVELYAN

The disappearance of the French flag from the North American Continent   1
as a result of the Seven Years' War led to the disruption of the first British Empire. For it relieved the English colonists of the dangers which had made them look for protection to the mother country. At the same time the expenses of the late war and the heavy burden of debt and land-tax with which it had saddled Great Britain, suggested to her statesmen, in an evil hour, that the colonies might be made to contribute something towards the military expenses of the Imperial connection. An attempt to levy contributions towards the future upkeep of royal forces in America was first made through George Grenville's Stamp Duty on legal documents in the colonies. It was passed in 1765, but repealed next year by the

Rockingham Whigs on account of the violent opposition which it had aroused beyond the Atlantic. In 1767 indirect taxation on tea and certain other articles was imposed on America by Charles Townshend. Chatham, the strongest English opponent of the policy of taxing the colonies, was then Prime Minister in name, but in actuality he was far removed from the political scene by gout and melancholia. Of these unpopular taxes the tea duty alone was maintained in a much modified form by George III's henchman Lord North in 1773, for the sake of principle only, as the profits were utterly negligible. Unfortunately, eight years of controversy on the taxation question had so worked upon the average colonial mind, that the overthrow of that principle was regarded as worth almost any disturbance and sacrifice. "No taxation without representation" was the cry, and every farmer and backwoodsman regarded himself as a Hampden, and North as a Strafford.

It was natural that the Americans should object to being taxed, 2 however moderately and justly, by a Parliament where they were not even "virtually" represented. They had always acknowledged an indefinite allegiance to the Crown, though Massachusetts had made very light of it at certain times in the Stuart era, and had even gone to war with France without consulting the Crown in 1643. But Americans had never admitted the supremacy of Parliament, in the sense of conceding that the two Houses sitting at Westminster could vote laws and taxes binding on the Colonies, each of which had its own Assembly. On that issue, as on most issues of constitutional law that have divided the men of our race at great historical crises, there was a good legal case pleadable on either side. But as a matter of political expediency it was most desirable that the colonists should be taxed for imperial purposes by their own representatives rather than by the British Parliament.

Unfortunately they made no move to tax themselves, partly from 3 thrift and partly from indifference to the Imperial connection. When once the French danger had disappeared, the Empire seemed a far-off abstraction to the backwoodsman of the Alleghenies, like the League of Nations to the Middle West today. And even on the sea coast, where the Empire was better known, it was not always better loved: it was represented by Governors, Colonels, and Captains of the British upper class, often as little suited to mix with democratic society as oil with vinegar. Furthermore, the Empire was associated in the mind of the Americans with restrictions on their commerce and their industry, imposed for the benefit of jealous English merchants, or of West Indian sugar and tobacco planters who were then the favorite colonists of a mother country not yet disturbed about the ethics of slavery.

Chatham, or rather that more formidable person, William Pitt, had 4 made the imperial connection popular in America in time of war, and might have made it tolerable even in time of peace. But Chatham had ceased to influence the politics of the Empire, except as a Cassandra prophet warning George III in vain, and being called a "trumpet of sedition" for his pains.

In theory — or at least in the theory that was held in England — 5 the Empire was a single consolidated State. In practice it was a federation of self-governing communities, with the terms of federation undrawn and constantly in dispute. Such a situation was full of danger, the more so as the situation and the danger were alike unrecognized. The defunct Whig oligarchy can hardly be said to have had a colonial policy or any clear ideas about the future of the Empire. Pitt's great Ministry had come and gone. And now, to meet the pressing needs of Imperial finance, George III's Ministers had advanced partial and one-sided solutions that proved unacceptable, while the Americans refused to propose any solution at all. A way out could have been found by men of good will summoned to a round-table conference, at which Britain might have offered to give up the trade restrictions, and the Americans to make some contribution of their own to the military expenses incurred by the mother country on their behalf.

But such a conference was outside the range of ideas on either side [of] the Atlantic. England was still in the grip of "mercantile" and protectionist theories of the old type. She still regarded her colonies primarily as markets for her goods, and the trade of the colonials as permissible only so far as it seemed consistent with the economic interest of the mother country. As the historian of our British colonial policy has remarked, "That the measures of 1765 and 1767 precipitated the crisis is obvious enough; but that the crisis must sooner or later have come, unless Great Britain altered her whole way of looking at the colonies, seems equally certain." 6

As to the hope that America might voluntarily contribute to the Imperial expenses, "America" did not exist. The thirteen colonies were mutually jealous, provincial in thought, divided from one another by vast distances, great physical obstacles, and marked social and economic distinctions. They had failed in 1754 at Albany to combine even for the purpose of fighting the French at dire need, and they were little likely to unite in time of peace for the purpose of negotiating with England on an Imperial question which they denied to be urgent. 7

And so things drifted on to the catastrophe. On one side was the unbending stubbornness of George III, who dictated policy to Lord North, that easy, good-natured man, so fatally unwilling to disoblige his sovereign. On the other side was the uncompromising zeal of the Radical party among the Americans led by Samuel Adams, to whom separation gradually began to appear as a good in itself. 8

The general causes rendering it difficult for English and Americans to understand one another were then numerous and profound: many of them have been removed by the passage of time, while on the other hand the difference of race is much greater today. English society was then still aristocratic, while American society was already democratic. Six or seven weeks of disagreeable ocean tossing divided London from Boston, so that personal intercourse was slight, and the stream of emigration from the mother country had run very dry ever since 1640. In England politics and good society were closed to Puritans, while Puritanism dominated New England and pushed its way thence into all the other colonies; it was Anglicanism that was unfashionable in Massachusetts. English society was old, elaborate, and artificial, while American society was new, 9 simple, and raw. English society was based on great differences of wealth, while in America property was still divided with comparative equality, and every likely lad hoped some day to be as well-off as the leading man in the township. In England political opinion was mainly that of squires, while in America it was derived from farmers, water-side mobs, and frontiersmen of the forest.

In two societies so widely set apart in the circumstances and at-   10
mosphere of everyday life, it required people with imaginative faculties like Burke, Chatham, and Fox, to conceive what the issues looked like to ordinary men on the other side of the Atlantic. George III had strength of mind, diligence, and business ability, but he had not imagination.

After the famous outrage on the tea-chests in Boston harbor, the   11
English Government, naturally and deeply provoked, made its fatal mistake. It hurried through Parliament Penal Acts against Massachusetts, closing the port of Boston, canceling the charter of the colony, and ordering political trials of Americans to be conducted in England. These measures rallied the other colonies to Massachusetts and ranked up behind the Radicals doubtful and conservative forces for whose support the English Government might still have played with success. The Penal Acts meant in fact war with the colonies. They were defensible only as acts of war, and if adopted should have been accompanied by preparations to ensure armed victory. Yet in that very year the British Government reduced the number of seamen in the Navy, and took no serious steps to strengthen their forces in America. When the pot boiled over at last, and hostilities broke out of themselves at Lexington, Burgoyne wrote thus from Boston:

> After a fatal procrastination, not only of vigorous measures but of preparations for such, we took a step as decisive as the passage of the Rubicon, and now find ourselves plunged at once in a most serious war without a single requisition, gunpowder excepted, for carrying it on.

During the twelve months preceding Lexington, while the British   12
authorities, having defied New England to the arbitrament of force, contented themselves with the inactive occupation of Boston, the Radical party in the country outside had used the respite to organize revolutionary power and terrorize, or expel, its opponents. Indeed, ever since the original passage of the Stamp Act, the "Sons of Liberty" had employed tarring-and-feathering and other local methods of making opinion unanimous. Even so, the Loyalists in most of the thirteen colonies remained a formidable body. Few, if any, had approved the measures by which the British Government had provoked the war, but they were not prepared to acquiesce in the dismemberment of the Empire, and for social and political reasons of their own they disliked the prospect of Radical rule. Their strength lay among the mercantile and professional men and the large landowners of the coast, and they were stronger in the Middle and Southern Colonies than in New England. Against them were arrayed the humbler folk in most sections, the small farmers and the frontiersmen of the West, organized under leaders of amazing audacity and zeal. The Loyalists were slower to move, more anxious for compromise than war,

and they got little leadership either from their own ranks or from the British, who too often treated them very ill and drove them by ill-usage or neglect to join the rebel ranks.

Yet the Radicals would never have overcome the trained soldiers of   13
George III and their own Loyalist fellow-subjects, had they not been led by a statesman of genius who was also a first-class soldier, organizer, and disciplinarian. George Washington belonged by temper and anteced- ents rather to the Loyalist than the Radical classes. But, although he was first and foremost a gentleman of Virginia, he was also a frontiersman who had seen service against Indians and French beyond the Alleghenies, and who knew the soul of young America as it could only be known in the backwoods. Good Virginian as he was, he was no mere provincial, with feelings and experience limited to his own colony. He had a "con- tinental" mind, and foresaw the nation he created. Some well-informed vision of the astounding future of his country westwards, helped to decide George Washington to draw his sword for a cause which was bound, in the stress of war, to become the cause of American Independence. The American militiamen brought to the ranks qualities learnt in their hard struggle with nature — woodcraft and marksmanship, endurance, energy, and courage. But they grievously lacked discipline, save what the Puritan temper supplied to the individual, and what Washington imposed upon the army. His long struggle, as Commander-in-Chief in the field, with the exasperating ineptitude of the Continental Congress, was a war within the war. Fortunately for him, the British army, in spite of its fine qualities, made mistake after mistake not only in the military but in the political strategy of the contest.

It was a civil war, not a war between two nations, though when the   14
battle smoke at length subsided two nations were standing there erect. Because it was a civil war, and because its issue would decide among other things whether England should in future be ruled by the King acting through Parliament or by Parliament acting through the King, opinion was divided in England no less than in America. Once fighting began, the bulk of the British people supported their government, so long as there was any hope of reconquering the colonies. But they showed so little enthusiasm for the fratricidal contest that recruiting was very difficult, and the government largely employed German mercenaries whose con- duct further incensed the colonists. Moreover in England there was always a strong minority, speaking with powers as diversified as those of Chatham, Burke, and young Charles Fox, that denounced the whole policy of the war and called for concession to save the unity of the Empire before it was too late.

Military operations were as ill-conducted by the British as they had   15
been rashly provoked. The troops, as Bunker's Hill showed, were not inferior to the men of Blenheim and Minden. But the military mistakes of Generals Burgoyne and Howe were very serious, and they were rivaled by those of the government at home. Lord George Germain in England planned the Saratoga campaign as Pitt had planned the taking of Quebec, but with very different results. His plan gave the Americans the advantage of acting on the inner lines, for he sent Burgoyne to Canada to march

down the Hudson and isolate New England, but without making sure that Howe moved up to meet him from the South. The result was that, while Howe lingered in Philadelphia, Burgoyne and his 5000 regulars were cut off in the wilderness beside the great river, and surrendered at Saratoga to the American minutemen.

After Saratoga the French despotism felt encouraged to come to the aid of liberty in the New World. This remarkable decision dismembered the British Empire, but it did not thereby achieve its object of restoring the House of Bourbon to world power. For it turned out that the idea of revolution, if once successful in America, could traverse the Atlantic with unexpected ease. And no less unexpectedly, from the broken egg-shell of the old British Empire emerged two powers, each destined to rapid growth — a new British Empire that should still bestride the globe, still rule the seas, and still hold up its head against the Powers of the continent; and a united American State that should spread from Atlantic to Pacific and number its citizens by scores of millions, in the place of thirteen little, mutually jealous colonies upon the Atlantic coast. 16

It was well that America was made. It was tragic that the making could only be effected by a war with Britain. The parting was perhaps inevitable at some date and in some form, but the parting in anger, and still more the memory of that moment's anger fondly cherished by America as the starting-point of her history, have had consequences that we rue to this day. 17

From *The Birth of the Republic, 1763–89*
EDMUND S. MORGAN

The men who fixed their signatures to the Declaration of Independence would not have done so without some expectation of success. They knew that they and their countrymen would have to defeat the world's most formidable military and naval power, but in July, 1776, this did not look like an impossible task. They had had plenty of evidence in the preceding decade of the corruption and incompetence of British political leaders, and the events of the preceding year seemed to demonstrate that these men would be no better at running a war than they were at running an empire. On April 19, 1775, the uncoordinated militia of the towns of eastern Massachusetts had routed a considerable body of British regulars. Two months later, at Bunker Hill, the same militia met a frontal assault by British troops and punished them terribly. In March, 1776, after Washington took command and obtained some heavy guns, he was able to force British troops to evacuate Boston and withdraw to Halifax, Nova Scotia. 1

Against these facts had to be weighed one notable failure. In the autumn of 1775 the Americans sent an expedition to Canada, hoping to bring that area into the Revolution on their side. By the spring of 1776 it was clear that this expedition had failed. Though the failure was both military and political, Americans reassured one another that no such thing 2 could occur among themselves. If the Canadians lacked the noble urge to be free, if they would not help themselves, then they deserved slavery. Meanwhile American patriots would establish their rights on battlefields closer to home.

The assurance of the Americans was ultimately justified by events: they did win, and their greatest asset was, in fact, their desire to be free. Though this desire did not enable them to maintain in the field a force equal to that of the British, the American armies could always count on popular support. It is true that many Americans took the British side — the best current estimate is that they amounted to a fifth of the population. Many of them shared the view that England had violated colonial rights, but they did not think the violations insufferable, and they turned out in substantial numbers to help the British troops keep the colonies in the empire. Nowhere, however, were they strong enough to enable royal government to survive. At the beginning of the war all the royal governors fled, and only in Georgia, the least populous of the revolting colonies, was British civil government re-established during the remainder of the war.

A large portion of the population may have been indifferent at the outset, content to stay British if the British won or to go along with independence if the patriots could make it stick. But the war itself sooner or later obliged men to get off the fence on one side or the other. The independent state governments called on their people for military service again and again, for a tour of duty in either the militia or the Continental Army. When the call came, a man had to shoulder a musket in the cause or else abandon home and family and head for the British lines. Most preferred to go along with their countrymen; and once they had spent some months in camp, perhaps shooting at the British and being shot at by them, they were likely to return committed to the Revolution.

The Revolution, in other words, became a people's war, and it is doubtful that the British could ever have won more than a stalemate. They might defeat the American forces in the field, as they often did, but victory did not enable them to occupy the country without a much larger force than they ever had. Americans generally owned guns and knew how to use them. A century and a half of defending themselves against French and Indians, the reliance many placed on guns to protect their crops from animals and to provide themselves with meat — these had given them a familiarity with firearms that common people of the Old World lacked. It was this experience that told at Concord and at Bunker Hill. And it would tell again whenever a British army attempted to sweep through the country. Men would gather from the farms, snipe at the troops, ambush them, raid them, until the victory parade turned into a hasty retreat.

This great asset, which made a British victory most unlikely, unfortunately did not insure an American victory. The local militia were good at harassing the British, but they were the least reliable part of the American forces when it came to pitched battles, and they could never be kept in the field for more than a short time. As soon as a battle was over, sometimes before, they would be on their way home. It took something more than a militia to make the war end in American victory.

How much more it took began to be apparent very soon after Congress took the plunge to independence. On July 2, while the members were adopting their resolution, General William Howe was landing unopposed on Staten Island in New York with several thousand troops. Shortly afterward his brother, Admiral Lord Howe, arrived with a battle fleet, and during the rest of the summer men and supplies poured in until there were more than thirty thousand men in arms on the island. Along with this force the Howes bore a commission enabling them to offer pardon to all Americans, provided they submitted to the authority of King and Parliament. The offer was laughable at this stage, but the force accompanying it was not.

Washington was on hand to oppose the expected attack and had almost as many men available as Howe, but most of them were militia. Washington himself had had a good deal less experience in command than his opponent, and in the ensuing Battle of Long Island (August 26, 1776) he was badly beaten and only saved from losing most of his forces by good luck and by Howe's failure to take full advantage of opportunities. There followed a humiliating series of defeats in which Washington and his army were chased across New Jersey.

There now began to appear, however, two factors which were to weigh heavily in determining the outcome of the war. One was the mediocrity of the commanders England sent to subdue the colonists. It is always difficult to determine in advance whether a field commander will be up to his job — so much depends on chance and on making the right decision at precisely the right moment. There were doubtless men among the British officers in America who might have succeeded in crushing Washington and destroying his army in 1776; but General Howe was a cautious, methodical soldier, not given to taking chances. He pursued war by the rulebook, and though capable of brilliant planning he was not good at seizing unexpected opportunities. After pushing Washington across the Delaware River by December, he called a halt for the winter.

Washington and his subordinates meanwhile were learning about war the hard way. The fact that he and they had the talent to learn was a second factor working toward American success. In spite of numerous defeats and in spite of the vanishing militia, Washington still had the remnants of an army. When he found that the British were disposed to halt for the winter, he turned and hit them hard. On the famous night of December 25, 1776, he crossed the Delaware and with very little loss to his own men captured 1,000 Hessians under Colonel Rall at Trenton. It was not a battle of great importance in itself, but it showed which commander had the daring and the initiative to win a war, and it restored to the Americans some of the assurance they had begun to lose.

In the following year General Howe along with his subordinate, General Burgoyne, gave the Americans further reason for confidence. With Howe's approval Burgoyne conducted an expedition from Canada down the Hudson Valley to cut off New England from the other colonies. This was the old French strategy, and since the British already held New York, it would have been a simple matter to send a column up from New York to meet the other coming down from Canada. But instead of sending such a column from New York, Howe moved the main body of his troops to Philadelphia. Washington, baffled as he well might be by what Howe was doing, tried to bar the way, but the British troops swept triumphantly into the city. There was probably no city in America that Howe could not have taken with the force at his disposal. Neither did he gain much by his entry — most Americans did not live in Philadelphia.

And while Howe was receiving the encomiums of Pennsylvania loy-   **12** alists, the farmers of New England and New York were giving Burgoyne a bad time in the Hudson Valley. He had made his march from Canada to the accompaniment of manifestos calling upon the people to come in and be saved from the awful tyranny of the Revolution. They came in, but not to be saved, and Continental troops came in too. On October 17, 1777, at Saratoga, Burgoyne surrendered to them.

He surrendered not only the tattered remains of his forces but also   **13** much of the prestige which for Europeans still clung to British arms. Saratoga was a great turning point of the war, because it won for Americans the foreign assistance which was the last element needed for victory. The possibility of such assistance had played an important role in their calculations from the beginning. The Declaration of Independence itself was issued mainly for the purpose of assuring potential allies that Americans were playing for keeps and would not fly into the mother country's arms at the first sign of parental indulgence.

Among possible allies the most likely had always been France. Ever   **14** since the peace of 1763 she had been waiting for opportunities of revenge against Britain and observing the alienation of the colonies with growing satisfaction. On May 2, 1776, two months before the Americans declared themselves independent, before they had even asked for aid, Louis XVI, on the advice of his foreign minister Vergennes, made a million livres (about $185,000 or £41,666 sterling) available to them for the purchase of munitions. And Vergennes persuaded Spain to put up an equal amount. The money and supplies which reached America from Europe were of the utmost importance. The money, of which there was much more to come both in gifts and loans, bolstered the credit of the United States and made it possible to finance the war. The munitions were indispensable because America, not yet an industrial country, could scarcely produce what she needed in sufficient quantities.

But money and supplies furnished secretly were different from out-   **15** right military and naval assistance. France had been ready to give the one before she was asked; the other she was much slower to risk. Congress sent Benjamin Franklin to seek it, and if anyone could have got it by sheer persuasiveness, he could have. The French lionized him, pampered him, quoted him, but Vergennes retired behind his diplomatic fences and waited to see how much staying power the Americans would show. The Frenchman knew what a beating Washington had taken on Long Island, and he did not wish to expose France to a war with Great

Britain unless the Americans could carry a real share of the burden. Vergennes was still waiting — and so was Franklin — when news of Saratoga arrived.

It was now Vergennes' turn to move. Saratoga demonstrated that the Americans could force the surrender of a British army. It seemed likely now that with French help they could win. Even England seemed to have reached that conclusion, for a commission under the Earl of Carlisle was directed to offer them everything they had asked for short of independence. Reconciliation was the last thing Vergennes wished to see, and Franklin exploited his fear of it to win the greatest diplomatic victory the United States has ever achieved. In February, 1778, France signed two treaties, one of Amity and Commerce in which she recognized the United States and the two countries agreed to help each other commercially, the other of Alliance. This second treaty (on which Vergennes now insisted) gave the Americans all they could have hoped for and exacted almost nothing in return. It was to go into effect in case war should break out between England and France — as it did the following June (1778) — and it stated specifically that its essential purpose was to maintain the "liberty, sovereignty, and independence absolute and unlimited of the United States." France renounced all future possession of the Bermuda Islands and of any part of North America east of the Mississippi. If the United States conquered Canada or the Bermudas in the course of the war, France would recognize them as part of the United States. The two parties agreed to make no separate peace with Great Britain, and neither was to lay down arms until the independence of the United States was assured.

CHAPTER 6

Analyzing

If you've been doing assignments in the earlier chapters of this book, you already have been writing analytically. Analysis occurs whenever you look at something closely and selectively, interpreting what you see. So you have written analytically if you've defined a word by examining some of the ways in which it is used; you've analyzed a poem by moving through it serially; you've analyzed a group of images by sorting them into meaningful categories; you've analyzed two systems by comparing them; in the act of summarizing a reading, you've begun to analyze it. In this chapter, however, we take this general sense of analysis a little further, sharpening it to meet some of the biggest challenges of academic writing. For in most academic situations, analysis is seldom simply a matter of looking and selecting. What we see depends on how we look.

Imagine yourself standing on a local hill staring up at the night sky — cloudless and clear, dominated by clusters of stars, some brighter or denser than others. The view is exhilarating. Now imagine yourself having to write about that sky for an early assignment in your astronomy class, coming to some conclusions about the relationships of stars. Where would you begin?

Which of your first impressions would you put to use? What words would you choose? What else would you like to know? Without understanding something about the assumptions, methods, and terminology of astronomers, you would not get very far in your analysis — at least not far enough to please an astronomer. But if you approached the job equipped with some astronomical learning, you'd be on surer footing. Your analysis would still depend on what you could see and what you chose to look at carefully, but those choices would be better informed. If, after looking at the sky some more, you decided to let your analysis be guided by some single hypothesis or point of view — for example, the idea that the densest band of stars is likely to belong to the galaxy we ourselves inhabit — you'd be on your way to writing an effective analysis. To do more, you'd need to know more — about light, about telescopes, about atomic theory, about the movement of the earth, about the means of stellar measurement, about what you couldn't see as well as what you could.

Of course in a book like this we cannot hope to ground your analytical thinking in the sorts of experience you'll get within specific disciplines. But even without these fuller frameworks, we can offer assignments that ask you to look at particular texts from particular points of view. We think that such assignments help to demonstrate the power of such perspectives for shaping, or reshaping, what you see. We hope that this recognition, in turn, will encourage you to think critically about the perspectives sometimes imposed on you. Good analytical writing comes as frequently from resisting an offered point of view as from embracing it.

The early assignments (First Passes) in this chapter ask you to write about short texts from particular points of view. Gradually the texts get more substantial and the points of view more varied. The final two assignments put more pressure on your own inventiveness: one offers some perspectives but leaves the topic up to you; the other offers a text and asks you to establish your own perspective.

Cases

FRAMING AN ANALYSIS: A CASE FROM PSYCHOLOGY

Let us begin by imagining a classroom situation in which you are asked to perform analytically. For a class in the psychology of human relations, your instructor presents you with the following short reading passage and tells you that it is an excerpt from a novel called *The Collector* written by the British novelist John Fowles. You're asked to write a short analytical commentary on the interaction between the two characters. After reading the passage, try analyzing it.

I picked up my knitting and put it away. When I looked round he   1
was standing there with his mouth open, trying to say something. And
I knew I'd hurt him, I know he deserves to be hurt, but there it is. I've
hurt him. He looked *so* glum. And I remembered he'd let me go out in
the garden. I felt mean.

I went to him and said I was sorry and held out my hand, but he   2
wouldn't take it. It was queer, he really had a sort of dignity, he was
really hurt (perhaps that was it) and showing it. So I took his arm and
made him sit down again, and I said, I'm going to tell you a fairy story.

Once upon a time (I said, and he stared bitterly bitterly at the floor)   3
there was a very ugly monster who captured a princess and put her in
a dungeon in his castle. Every evening he made her sit with him and
ordered her to say to him, "You are very handsome, my lord," and every
evening she said, "You are very ugly, you monster." And then the
monster looked very hurt and sad and stared at the floor. So one evening
the princess said, "If you do this thing and that thing you might be
handsome," but the monster said, "I can't, I can't." The princess said,
"Try, try." But the monster said, "I can't, I can't." Every evening it was
the same. He asked her to lie, and she wouldn't. So the princess began
to think that he really enjoyed being a monster and very ugly. Then one
day she saw he was crying when she'd told him, for the fiftieth time,
that he was ugly. So she said, "You can become very handsome if you
do just one thing. Will you do it?" Yes, he said, at last, he would try to
do it. So she said, then set me free. And he set her free. And suddenly,
he wasn't ugly any more, he was a prince who had been bewitched. And
he followed the princess out of the castle. And they both lived happily
ever afterwards.

I knew it was silly as I was saying it. Fey. He didn't speak, he kept   4
staring down.

I said, now it's your turn to tell a fairy story.   5

He just said, I love you.   6

And yes, he had more dignity than I did then and I felt small, mean.   7
Always sneering at him, jabbing him, hating him and showing it. It was
funny, we sat in silence facing each other and I had a feeling I've had
once or twice before, of the most peculiar closeness to him — *not* love
or attraction or sympathy in any way. But linked destiny. Like being
shipwrecked on an island — a raft — together. In *every* way not wanting
to be together. But together.

I feel the sadness of his life, too, terribly. And of those of his miserable   8
aunt and his cousin and their relatives in Australia. The great dull hopeless
weight of it.

— John Fowles, *The Collector*

What did you decide was going on between the two people? If you
responded as most readers do, you may have said something like this:

```
It's a young woman and her boyfriend.  She's

throwing him over, and he seems to be pretty immature
```

```
about it.  She feels sympathy for him and wants to let
him down gently, but she's also determined to get out
of the relationship.
```

If pressed to provide evidence to support these conclusions, you could provide plenty:

```
        "I've hurt him.... I felt mean."
        "I went to him and said I was sorry....he was
really hurt...and showing it."
        "So I took his arm...."
        "He just said, I love you."
        "I feel the sadness of his life, too, terribly....
The great dull hopeless weight of it."
```

There's also the fairy story. Some readers have pointed out that the story the woman tells seems designed to equate her with the princess and him with the monster. The story thus pushes him away while also holding out a vague hope for a future together.

If you've analyzed the passage along these general lines, you may also feel some misgivings. Stop for a moment now. Can you think of any ways this general analysis falls short? On the one hand, it seems a plausible explanation. But do you find any moments that seem puzzling? Make a short list of such moments.

If you have read John Fowles's novel, you probably have been reading this discussion impatiently. The story, you know, is not about a typical romantic falling-out. It's about a hostage-taking. As one student has put it,

```
        He holds the woman captive because he's in love
with her.  He isn't violent, and he doesn't go after
her sexually, but he also doesn't want to let her
go.  She does her best to talk him out of keeping her
prisoner, hinting with the fairy tale that if he'll re-
lease her, they can be friends later.  She knows he
probably won't fall for this, but she's desperate.
```

Disappointed? Knowing what happens in the novel seems, in effect, to put an end to the analytical effort. If you were asked now to write about the passage, what would you find to say? There seems little to do but to summarize the story as the student we just quoted has done. In an odd way, what we know about the facts of the case seems to flatten out and deaden the analysis.

But consider what can happen when we approach the passage from a fresh perspective. Read the following paragraph about the Stockholm theory and then try writing about *The Collector* excerpt from the point of view suggested by the expert quoted here, Dr. Frank Ochberg.

> Most hostages suffer some degree of psychological damage, a mix of helplessness, fear, rage, and a sense of abandonment. . . . One sign of stress is known as the "Stockholm syndrome." . . . The syndrome is a kind of bonding between captors and captives, and is named for a Stockholm bank robbery in 1973 in which the hostages came to idolize their captors and ultimately refused to testify against them. In some cases, hostages have reportedly fallen in love with their jailers of the opposite sex, and the captors have become protective of their hostages. "When someone captures you, he places you in an infantile position," says Dr. Frank Ochberg, director of the Michigan Department of Mental Health. "It sets the stage for love as a response to infantile terror — he could kill you but he doesn't, and you are grateful."
>
> — *Time*, December 24, 1979

The Stockholm theory suddenly provides a powerful lens through which to view what happens between the two characters in Fowles's story. Or, to put it another way, the idea can become a kind of analytical searchlight: as we reread the passage, it throws some features into sudden prominence, illuminating details we hadn't noticed or didn't know how to interpret. For instance, some of the same phrases that at first kept us from recognizing the situation as a hostage-taking now take on a new meaning: "I've hurt him. . . . I felt mean"; "I had a feeling . . . of the most peculiar closeness to him"; "I felt the sadness of his life." Here is how one student analyzed the passage in light of the Stockholm theory:

> In this passage from The Collector, we see a clas-
> sic example of someone caught up in the "Stockholm syn-
> drome." As Dr. Frank Ochberg has described it, the
> Stockholm syndrome occurs when victims of a hostage-
> taking form attachments to their captors. Captives,
> Ochberg says, usually feel "a mix of helplessness,
> fear, rage, and a sense of abandonment." In such situ-
> ations captives may be impressed by the seriousness of
> their captors, while they themselves begin to feel
> small and dependent. Captives become grateful for
> small favors. "He could kill you," says Ochberg, "but
> he doesn't, and you are grateful." In this way a
> strong bond can develop between captor and captive--
> they are living through a stressful situation together.

This helps to explain why the captive in The Collector can feel guilty about hurting the feelings of the person she should hate.   She displays the mixture of feelings that Ochberg describes when she says, "I know he deserves to be hurt, but there it is.   I've hurt him.... I felt mean." She feels petty and "small" when she tries to trick him with the fairy story, and she sees him, by contrast, as a person of "dignity." She feels great sympathy for him: "I felt the sadness of his life, too, terribly." Above all, she feels the power of the bond that has developed between them. Even though this is a situation that he has created, it now feels as though they both are captive to it:

> It was funny, we sat in silence facing each other and I had a feeling I've had once or twice before, of the most peculiar closeness to him—not love or attraction or sympathy in any way.   But linked destiny.   Like being shipwrecked on an island—a raft—together.

In her own confusion and stress, she's formed an enormous attachment to the person who has made her vulnerable.

This is a persuasive piece of analysis, isn't it? Notice how the writer has made skillful use of the theoretical material about the Stockholm syndrome, using it as a preliminary set-up for discussing the passage itself in the second paragraph. Also notice the skillful blend of short quotations and paraphrasings throughout both paragraphs. The energy of the analysis seems to build with the gathering evidence. Where once there seemed only "the facts" of the kidnapping, there now seems a strong point of view to be applied, a case to be made.

Yet it's also possible to feel dissatisfied with the above analysis. Did you? Sometimes a powerful point of view can block out other ways of looking; and clear, coherent explanations can smother potential disagreements and objections. For that reason, it's a good intellectual habit to practice a little resistance. With some skeptical prodding — what if it isn't so? — you'll sometimes find yourself with opportunities to show your independence. Here, for example, is how another student resisted the Stockholm explanation, organizing her objections into an effective essay:

The relationship we see in <u>The Collector</u> does not conform to the Stockholm syndrome. According to the theory described by Dr. Frank Ochberg, victims of hostage-takings develop strong feelings of affection for their captors, coming to idolize them, sometimes even falling in love with them. Fearing for their lives, they become infantilized, and they feel love "as a response to infantile terror."

The young woman in <u>The Collector</u> doesn't seem to fit this description at all. In the first place, she feels no terror. She begins by leisurely putting down her knitting, and she proceeds calmly to tell her captor a belittling story. Second, she isn't infantilized. In fact, it's the other way around--the captor is infantilized, becoming in effect a big baby. She sits him down to tell her fairy tale, and he sulks in response. Third, there's clearly no idolization involved. She admits he has some dignity, but basically she regards him with pity: "I feel the sadness of his life." Pity involves looking down--and that's the opposite of idolization. Finally, she does not love him. She explicitly says this twice. She admits she was "always sneering at him, jabbing him, hating him and showing it." And even when she admits to feeling as if she has been shipwrecked with him, she is careful to say that the feeling is "<u>not</u> love or attraction" but simply a feeling of "linked destiny."

The Stockholm syndrome may occur in some captor/captive relationships, but this isn't one of them. Perhaps the theory applies only to true hostage-takings, when the captor has some ulterior ambition. Here the kidnapper has what he wants and seems helpless about what to do next. We should be reluctant to slap an abstract theory onto a case as strange as this one.

Do you find this analysis persuasive too? More or less so than the first essay? What are some of the decisions that this writer has made in developing her counteranalysis? Notice that in this essay the theoretical passage about the Stockholm syndrome has become as much the subject of attention as the passage from *The Collector.* Notice also that in helping the writer think about the relation between the two characters, the theory proves useful even in rejection.

Of course it isn't always necessary to either accept or reject the application of a theory in its entirety. Thus, one legitimate approach to the question of whether the passage from *The Collector* conforms to the Stockholm theory is to argue both sides. But here you need to be careful. Few readers respond favorably to an analysis that seems to say, "Maybe it is, but then again maybe it isn't." If well handled, however, a two-sided approach allows you to balance one set of evidence against another, while coming to a complex but emphatic judgment. Here is the opening paragraph of one such essay:

> At first sight, the passage from The Collector
> seems to lend itself well to the Stockholm theory. The
> Stockholm syndrome offers a way of understanding the
> mixture of anger and tenderness we see in the victim.
> But on more careful reading, the narrator's feelings
> toward her abductor cannot be explained so neatly.

Notice how this paragraph forecasts an analytical structure: First we'll see how the theory *might* be applied, and then we'll see the ways in which it doesn't work. By contrast, here's another opening that reverses these emphases, promising first to show what makes the theory and the case an ill fit and then to show an underlying similarity more important than the differences:

> The relationship in The Collector is far from a
> classic illustration of the Stockholm syndrome. There
> are half a dozen ways in which the relationship between
> the young woman and her captor does not resemble that
> of the Stockholm bank robbers and their hostages. Yet
> the Stockholm theory does apply in one fundamental and
> crucial way--the formation of a strong emotional bond.

Both of these opening paragraphs promise interesting analyses. Both writers will use the perspective offered by the Stockholm theory to arrive at their own interpretations of the passage from *The Collector.*

Most of the assignments in this chapter take the form we have been demonstrating: one text serves as an object of analysis and another offers a perspective from which to analyze it. Sometimes we offer the objects first, sometimes the perspectives. As you approach the assignments, we urge you to try out strategies like those we've just described. Don't simply clamp one text on the other. See what you can say about the two texts independently; then see what you can say about one from the perspective offered by the other; then see what you can say in resistance to that view. When you've thought about your choices and tried out a few sentences, decide how you want to approach your analysis and proceed with a general plan. The key is to stay flexible in your thinking — observe, respond, question, evaluate, reconsider. Write when you're ready, but keep in mind that the act of writing will itself lead to more thinking, perhaps even to a new plan.

PATTERN AND VARIATION: A SAMPLING OF ANALYTICAL ASSIGNMENTS

To pair texts as we do in this chapter is to risk oversimplifying academic analysis. Seldom in your courses will you simply be given two compact texts and asked to analyze one in terms of the other. But this basic relation between object and perspective can be found in any analytic assignment. To see what we mean, consider the following assortment, a mixture of exam questions and paper topics from various disciplines. What do they have in common?

1. Explain Paley's design argument for the existence of God. Examine his reasoning in relation to Hume's criticisms of it. What is your opinion? (Philosophy)
2. Define the concept of the "American Adam." Discuss *Huckleberry Finn* in light of that concept. (American Literature)
3. In *The Mirage of Health*, René Dubos makes the point that men and women will have a good chance of escaping disease if they live reasonably harmoniously with the external environment. Explain why this may or may not be true. Consider two or more of the following disorders in your answer: mental illness, depression, stress-related diseases, drug abuse, unwanted pregnancy, divorce. Use material from all your readings and from class lectures. (Public Health)
4. "Superstitions" is a category of beliefs that we recognize within our own cultural tradition. Interview ten people and ask them if they are aware of beliefs or actions that they would include within this category. Collect as many examples as you can from each individual. Then analyze the results of your survey. (Anthropology)
5. Explain the results of the "conformity experiment" using the following theories: (1) symbolic interaction, (2) reinforcement theory, (3) social exchange theory. Explain which theory provides the most comprehensive understanding of the experiment's results. (Sociology)
6. In the centrist view, the American system does a satisfactory job of providing a range of alternative policies. Present a careful assessment of

this view with particular reference to the roles of political parties, election campaigns, the media, and interest groups. (Political Science)

7. We have talked about a number of areas (sleep cycles, motor development, language) where the nature and course of early development seem to have a lasting impact on adult functioning. Using material from these or other areas, draw your own conclusions about the relationship between early development and adult behavior. (Psychology)

Notice that each assignment specifies not only what is to be analyzed but the perspective to be used. Look at the first four questions. You are asked to consider Paley's argument from the point of view of Hume, *Huckleberry Finn* from the point of view of the scholar who coined the phrase "American Adam," a modern public health problem from the point of view of Dubos, and survey data from the point of view provided by an anthropological definition of "superstition." Questions 5 and 6 complicate the pattern by asking you to consider more than a single point of view. Question 5 does this explicitly by asking you to look at a classic sociology experiment from the perspectives of three sociological theories. Question 6 is not so overt, but the expectation of multiple perspectives can be inferred from the way the question is worded: the term "centrist" (meaning politically central, neither liberal nor conservative) together with the instruction "Present a careful assessment" suggests that there are other points of view to be considered from the left and the right. What about question 7? How do you interpret what is being asked there?

Each analysis question identifies what is to be analyzed and suggests one or more perspectives from which to analyze it. Of course, as these questions illustrate, not all analysis questions make equal demands. Having to work from more than one perspective can account for one sort of extra difficulty, but what are some of the other sources of variation?

One difference lies in the difficulty of establishing perspectives. Any analysis requires you to establish a point of view, but some are much more easily established than others. With question 3, for example, you could establish Dubos's point of view simply by rewording the phrasing of the question: "According to René Dubos, health is a matter of living harmoniously with the environment." The main work of the essay would involve applying this generalization to the examples you choose. In question 2, by contrast, establishing what is meant by the phrase "American Adam" will take more doing — you may have to summarize a fairly complicated theory before you can begin writing about *Huckleberry Finn*. With any such questions, you will have to rely on your abilities to quote, paraphrase, or summarize, but with some questions these activities will take up a major portion of your analysis. In question 5, for example, you will have to establish each of the three sociological theories (symbolic interaction, reinforcement, social exchange) distinctly enough to make effective comparisons. Doing that will probably become the main effort of the essay — and will be at least as important as what you say about the experiment being analyzed. To establish points of view in some cases requires only an alert eye for a key quotation, while in others it requires much digestion, synthesis, and judgment.

Analytical assignments also vary in the difficulty of establishing the objects of analysis — *Huckleberry Finn* in question 2, the conformity experiment in question 5, and so on. Some assignments give you little responsibility for choosing or setting up what you are to analyze; others give you much responsibility. Look at how the first four questions differ in this respect. For question 1 you merely need to paraphrase Paley's argument. Question 2, by contrast, forces you to think selectively about an entire novel, choosing incidents and details relevant to the question. Question 3 forces you to choose a problem for analysis and to construct a description using more than one source. For question 4 you need to compile your evidence from scratch, in the form of a survey you must design and carry out. What about questions 5, 6, and 7? Which give you more choices and impose more responsibilities in setting up the objects of analysis?

Another important variable among analysis assignments is harder to judge: To what extent are you invited to resist the suggested points of view? Are you being asked only to apply theory X to text Y? To simply apply the theory of the Stockholm syndrome to the situation in *The Collector*? Or are you encouraged to make your analysis more problematic, seeking out limitations and expressing reservations? "The Stockholm theory applies only so far. . . ." Deciding how strenuously to struggle with the suggested points of view is partly a matter of judging the tone of a class and the attitudes of a teacher — it's possible that you're being asked to apply theory to case without raising distracting objections. But it's also a matter of consulting yourself — are you convinced? Do you have something to say in disagreement? The wording of a question is not always the best guide to whether you should offer resistance. For example, question 1 says to "Give your opinion," but after analyzing Paley's argument from the point of view of Hume, you may find yourself with little to add to his critique. If so, you probably wouldn't be expected to include an "In my opinion . . ." section in your essay. Rather, you would simply make your basic agreement with Hume apparent from how you approach the question: "Hume offers a persuasive demolition of Paley's argument. . . ."

In contrast, the absence of a request for an opinion shouldn't prevent you from seizing the opportunity to give one. Look again at question 2:

2. Define the concept of the "American Adam." Discuss *Huckleberry Finn* in light of that concept.

Taken literally, the question asks you to do no more than analyze the novel from the perspective offered by the "American Adam" idea. According to that theory, as developed by the literary critic R. W. B. Lewis, works of American literature in the early nineteenth century frequently depicted a hero who, like Adam before the Fall, found himself in a new world, as "an individual standing alone, self-reliant and self-propelling, ready to confront whatever awaited him with the aid of his own unique and inherent resources." This hero was "fundamentally innocent" and uncorrupted by the inheritances of history. Now imagine that having tried to apply this theory to *Huckleberry Finn*, you find yourself unconvinced that it fits. Rather than being content to go through the analytical motions, you should try to articulate your dissatisfactions. A well-presented set of objections may undermine the analysis, but it will strengthen the impression of intellectual independence. Here's how such an essay might be structured:

> The critic R. W. B. Lewis, with his powerful conception of the "American Adam" as a theme in American literature, gives us a promising way of reading Huckleberry Finn. Huck can be seen as a new Adam in several respects....
>
> Viewed in this way, then, Huckleberry Finn is about the shedding of innocence. Although, as I've shown, there is much in the book to support this interpretation, I think there are limitations to this view. Does Huck Finn really have much innocence to shed? The character that we meet at the outset of the book is already cunning and sophisticated in the ways of the world....

An essay carried out in this way has the advantage of going beyond the assignment while fulfilling it. In suggesting that the one way of looking at the novel is not fully adequate and can be complicated, the writer introduces a problem worth exploring. In general, the more often you can make your analyses problematic, the more successful you will be.

Sometimes assignments are slanted so as to help you discover such problems. Look back at question 3:

3. In *The Mirage of Health*, René Dubos makes the point that men and women will have a good chance of escaping disease if they live reasonably harmoniously with the external environment. Explain why this may or may not be true. Consider two or more of the following disorders in your answer: mental illness, depression, stress-related diseases, drug abuse, unwanted pregnancy, divorce. Use material from all your readings and from class lectures.

We've said that you could establish Dubos's point of view simply by paraphrasing the question. But if this is true, what do you make of the health care problems you are asked to work with? Do you see anything odd about the list of "disorders" from which you are asked to choose? What is the effect of including depression and divorce? Do such objects of analysis make it easier or more difficult to support the view that health is simply a matter of living harmoniously with the environment? How might you be able to reject a simplistic way of approaching this question in favor of a more complex discussion?

Let us put our advice more boldly: Wherever you can reasonably complicate your analysis, do it. Take as another example question 4, the one asking for a survey of superstitions. Much of the work in fulfilling this assignment will come in conducting the survey. So to set up what you mean by "superstition," it may be convenient to take a definition from class notes or perhaps from the glossary of your anthropology textbook. But you can make your analysis problematic, thus strengthening the essay, if you recognize that there are several possible definitions of "superstition" and that the definition you use will strongly influence how you conduct and interpret your survey.

Consider one last example. We asked earlier how you would interpret question 7, the one on early childhood development. What are you being asked to do? It's possible, perhaps even likely, that you are being asked something very straightforward. Certainly you can choose to answer the question with information compiled from your notes and reading, information in support of the announced point of view that childhood patterns shape adult behavior. The evidence in support of this view is probably vast, and your psychology instructor may be expecting little more than a rehashing of some of it. Yet there is that nagging wording of the last sentence: "Draw your own conclusions." How can you draw your own conclusions if nothing seems to be at issue? Even if the information that you have is overwhelmingly in support of the offered point of view, you'd do well to show at least the flash of a counterperspective, if only to then override it with the analysis that follows:

```
    Not all forms of adult behavior are shaped by the
developmental patterns of childhood.  Some childhood
patterns--reticence, for example--have been found to
have little correlation with adult behavior.  But on
the whole, the child is father of the man, or mother of
the woman.
    Studies of sleep cycles have shown....
```

IS ANALYTICAL INDEPENDENCE POSSIBLE? CASES FROM BIOLOGY AND LITERATURE

Up to now we have been looking at assignments that specify, or at least imply, perspectives to be used analytically. Sometimes, however, you will be asked to analyze without being offered a perspective. Apparently in such cases you are free to write from whatever point of view you choose.

This apparent freedom is sometimes deceiving. Analytical assignments never come entirely free of context, and usually they are meant to draw on something specific that a class has provided. Consider the following analytical assignment from a biology exam. You are given Table 1 along with the terse instruction "Analyze the following data."

How do we find a perspective for interpreting these data, and how free are we to choose? We can tell that the experiment concerns fertilization in a species of sea urchin at various times and temperatures, but what about it? We could begin by consulting what we've learned in the course about marine animals in general or about sea urchins in particular. For example, we might know that sea urchins range widely along both coasts of North America, that they consume kelp, and that they have relatively few predators. We would also have learned that, like other marine animals, they fertilize externally (eggs are fertilized outside the female's body). Information like this seems to go partway toward establishing a perspective, at least by orienting us to the animal under investigation. But when we look back at the table, we may see that generalizations about sea urchin behavior won't really be of much help in establishing a perspective for interpreting these particular data.

More useful will be what we've learned about how to read tables and about how experiments are designed. We would have learned, for instance, that the data presented in this table must be the results of a specific experiment designed to ask and tentatively answer a single question — a hypothesis. In looking closely at the table we will not be so much choosing *our* perspective as trying to deduce the hypothesis expressing the perspective of the experimenter. What question guided this experiment? We may not be able to tell for certain, but as we look at how the data are presented, we can close in on a few possibilities: a question about fertilization success over time, a question about fertilization success across a range of temperatures, a question about the interaction of time and temperature on fertilization success.

If we look a little more closely at how the table is set up, we can gather something more about the experiment's assumptions and expectations. Look at the row corresponding to each sperm temperature. What do you notice about 17°C? At 17°C sea urchin fertilization was more successful than at the

TABLE 1. Fertilization of Sea Urchin Eggs (*Strongylocentrotus purpuratus*) at 17°C by Sperm at Various Temperatures

SPERM TEMPERATURE (°C)	PERCENT FERTILIZATION AT ELAPSED TIME				
	0–2 MIN.	2–5 MIN.	30 MIN.	60 MIN.	24 HR
3	2	22	10	4	0
10	95	85	65	25	0
17	100	98	64	31	9
24	61	70	50	28	0
31	0	2	0	0	0

other temperatures. Do you notice anything else? We can see that the 17°C readings occupy the central position in the rows, with two equally spaced readings above and below. Notice also from the title on the table that 17°C was the temperature at which the eggs were maintained. What do these two details imply about what the experimenter expected? Take a moment and write out what you think. What can you conclude about how we should approach the data?

Here's how one student decided to go about answering the question:

> The hypothesis here seems to be that sea urchin sperm are most successful in fertilizing at 17°C; and the results seem to confirm that hypothesis. The results also suggest that as the temperature moves away from 17°C, fertilization percents decline, but not equally. Sperm colder than 17°C do better than sperm warmer than 17°C. At 10°C the youngest sperm attained 95% fertilization, whereas at 24°C the freshest sperm achieved only 61% fertilization.
>
> Another interesting result was that the sperm in the experiment seemed to rapidly lose their fertilizing ability. Even at 17°C, only 31% of the eggs were fertilized by sperm after 60 minutes. But some fertilizing ability was retained even after 24 hours, suggesting that at the optimal temperature, fertilization is at least possible one day after sea urchins have released their sperm and eggs.
>
> There are also some oddities in the results. One would expect the maximum fertilization to occur, across all temperatures, with the freshest sperm. But for two of the temperatures, 3°C and 24°C, the percent of fertilization is actually greater in the 2–5 minute range than in the 0–2 minute range. And at 3°C the sperm at 30 minutes were more successful (10%) than those at 0–2 minutes (2%). Does this suggest that sperm at more extreme temperatures go through some sort of "adjustment period" that lasts at least a few minutes? Even at the extremely warm 31°C, some fertilization occurred, but not instantaneously.

> Overall the results confirm that sea urchin fer-
> tilization is most successful at 17°C. But the results
> also indicate that there isn't a narrow band of temper-
> ature within which sea urchins must fertilize. Even at
> extremes of temperature, some fertilization occurs—at
> least if sperm get to eggs fairly quickly.

This analysis succeeds not by establishing an independent perspective but by deducing the perspective from which the experiment itself was conducted. The expectation about 17°C becomes a kind of interpretive backbone for the rest of the discussion. In relation to that central observation, other trends become observable. There is plenty of freedom for the inventive observation of details once the main experimental point of view has been established. But this freedom becomes meaningful only after recognizing the basic perspective built into the table.

The success of the preceding analysis does not mean, however, that more critical approaches aren't available. One student did find a way to show some further independence. After analyzing the experiment's main results in a fashion similar to the first student, this writer moves on to look at what the data *don't* tell us. Notice how she maintains a productive skepticism by thinking about gaps in the data, odd bits of evidence, and features that might have biased the results.

> These results leave me unconvinced about several
> points. First, there is the presumption that 17°C is
> the optimal temperature for sea urchin fertilization.
> Yet the table can't establish whether 17°C is really
> any better than 14°C, or even 19°C. We would have to
> test other temperatures between 10°C and 24°C to be
> confident that we were testing the optimal temperature.
>
> Another problem is that maintaining the eggs at
> 17°C may have biased the results. It's possible that
> sperm kept at 17°C are simply more efficient in fertil-
> izing eggs at the same temperature, without having to
> adjust to a temperature change. Sperm in the ocean
> might have to function at various temperatures, but how
> often would they have to adjust to a 7°C or more shift
> in temperature between the time they leave the male and
> the time they reach the eggs? This is further evidence

that 17°C may not necessarily be the optimal temperature for fertilization. I suspect that sperm might be
able to do equally well, or better, at lower temperatures. In fact, if we look at the data, we can see
that, for several time spans, there aren't great differences between the percent fertilization at 10°C and
at 17°C. In fact, at 30 minutes, the fertilization
success at 10°C is even slightly higher.

        Finally, what does this experiment reveal about
sea urchin fertilization in nature? It's impossible to
tell from this table alone how the sperm and egg were
brought together, but probably the fertilization took
place in laboratory glassware, not in the more chaotic
ocean environment. But even under such controlled conditions, if sperm quickly lose their ability to fertilize eggs, what does that imply about the efficiency of
fertilization of sea urchins in their natural habitat?
Wouldn't successful fertilization be much less likely
than these readings suggest? How would sea urchins
even arrive at the fertilized stage in significant
enough numbers to survive all the rest that will happen to them before getting the chance to mature? On the
other hand, these long odds against success may explain
why there is not more of a population explosion among
sea urchins.

These additional paragraphs add something rare and welcome. The writer
thoughtfully examines both the evidence and its limitations and also looks for
ways to place the experimental results in a larger context — the sea urchins'
natural environment. The writing is inventively skeptical, but also speculative
and curious.

Let's look at another example in which a student is granted analytical
independence, this time in a literature class. The assignment: "Analyze the
poem 'Diving into the Wreck' by Adrienne Rich."

First having read the book of myths,
and loaded the camera,
and checked the edge of the knife-blade,

I put on   4
the body-armor of black rubber
the absurd flippers
the grave and awkward mask.
I am having to do this   8
not like Cousteau with his
assiduous team
aboard the sun-flooded schooner
but here alone.   12

There is a ladder.
The ladder is always there
hanging innocently
close to the side of the schooner.   16
We know what it is for,
we who have used it.
Otherwise
it is a piece of maritime floss   20
some sundry equipment.

I go down.
Rung after rung and still
the oxygen immerses me   24
the blue light
the clear atoms
of our human air.
I go down.   28
My flippers cripple me,
I crawl like an insect down the ladder
and there is no one
to tell me when the ocean   32
will begin.

First the air is blue and then
it is bluer and then green and then
black I am blacking out and yet   36
my mask is powerful
it pumps my blood with power
the sea is another story
the sea is not a question of power   40
I have to learn alone
to turn my body without force
in the deep element.

And now: it is easy to forget   44
what I came for
among so many who have always
lived here
swaying their crenellated fans   48
between the reefs

and besides
you breathe differently down here.

I came to explore the wreck.   52
The words are purposes.
The words are maps.
I came to see the damage that was done
and the treasures that prevail.   56
I stroke the beam of my lamp
slowly along the flank
of something more permanent
than fish or weed   60

the thing I came for:
the wreck and not the story of the wreck
the thing itself and not the myth
the drowned face always staring   64
toward the sun
the evidence of damage
worn by salt and sway into this threadbare beauty
the ribs of the disaster   68
curving their assertion
among the tentative haunters.

This is the place.
And I am here, the mermaid whose dark hair   72
streams black, the merman in his armored body.
We circle silently
about the wreck
we dive into the hold.   76
I am she: I am he

whose drowned face sleeps with open eyes
whose breasts still bear the stress
whose silver, copper, vermeil cargo lies   80
obscurely inside barrels
half-wedged and left to rot

we are the half-destroyed instruments
that once held to a course   84
the water-eaten log
the fouled compass

We are, I am, you are
by cowardice or courage   88
the one who find our way
back to this scene
carrying a knife, a camera
a book of myths   92
in which
our names do not appear.

Of course we expect literature classes to encourage a variety of points of view, and many literature teachers make an assignment such as this an open invitation, even challenging you to develop your own interpretation. Students sometimes misinterpret this challenge, however, translating it to mean that any interpretation is as good as another. But like the biology teacher behind the exam question we just discussed, the literature teacher who assigned this poem for analysis would expect you to be influenced by what had gone on in the course. Your interpretation would be oriented by lectures, other readings, and class discussions.

Let us invent a context for this particular analysis by sketching in some emphases that might have occurred in an introductory literature course. Imagine that in the first few classes your teacher spent time talking about the variety of verse forms employed by modern poets, putting a special emphasis on the conversational qualities of free verse — poetry unconstrained by the regularity of line lengths or by the necessity of rhymes. Another early class or two introduced some poems called "imagist" — short, fragmentary glimpses of everyday life, captured in just a few well-chosen phrases. A bit later, you covered "narrative poems," which you discussed as straightforward, powerfully told stories. More recently, your teacher has turned toward a different sort of poetry, poems that seem to be about some particular event or experience but seem also to be going after something else. The subjects of such poems — a field, a damaged airplane, a path in the woods — have been treated as "psychological metaphors," ways of expressing complex states of mind in a few evocative images.

Throughout the entire class, your teacher has been stressing the reading of poems for coherence; that is, with attention to how their parts connect with one another. You've been asked to puzzle over the moments in a poem that don't seem connected, usually discovering that these baffling moments become keys to interpreting the poem as a whole. It's in this context, then, that you're given the poem by Adrienne Rich to analyze. You haven't been told much about the poet, but you've read in a brief biographical heading that "her poetry in recent years has become more and more strongly feminist." "Diving into the Wreck" was published in 1973.

How do you start? After having carefully read through the poem, don't be reluctant to jump in anywhere, trying out any line of thought that occurs to you. Yet at the same time you want to be hard on yourself, tossing aside those perspectives that don't seem to take you very far in working with the poem as a whole. For instance, if you recognize the reference to marine scientist Jacques Cousteau, you might think for a moment of analyzing the poem from an environmentalist point of view; but you quickly reject the idea when you see that very little in the poem has anything to do with the environment. Similarly, in thinking about the wreck in the poem, you suddenly recall out of nowhere the phrase "the ship of state" and wonder for a moment if this poem could have political overtones. Once again, there seem to be few, if any, details in the poem to support such an interpretation. Ideas like these, as lively as they might be, are quickly rejected when they don't link up with any emphasis in the course or with more than a few parts of the poem.

Let's follow the thinking of a student who has gotten a little further. Without yet committing himself to a single direction of analysis, he jots out some notes, trying to find a promising perspective from which to write:

```
1.  I could write about this poem as an example of free
    verse.  It's not a poem without form, but its form
    is very free-floating and relaxed.  It seems to
    suit the experience it's describing.
2.  I could write about the poem as a story, an attempt
    to describe the narrator's experience of losing
    herself underwater.  It's about how strange it
    feels to leave our world for underwater, an effort
    to imagine what underwater explorers like Cousteau
    must feel.
3.  I could try writing about this poem in psychologi-
    cal terms, the way we've been doing in class.  The
    dive or the wreck might represent something about
    the state of mind of the speaker, especially during
    the second half.
4.  The headnote says Rich is a feminist.  I bet I
    could find a way of discussing this poem as one
    about female experience.  A lot seems to be going
    on in the second half, the mermaid and merman cir-
    cling each other...maybe something about man and
    woman here.
```

Each of these perspectives seems at least briefly attractive, because each corresponds to some emphasis in the course and responds to something in the poem. But almost immediately the writer begins to evaluate these perspectives critically. Here, as he tries some free writing to get his thoughts on paper, we see him rejecting the first two possibilities.

```
    I know I've got a good point about the free verse,
but it's not much more than a point.  I could probably
say the same thing about lots of poems.  I'm not going
to be comfortable basing my whole analysis on the form
--or formlessness--of the poem.  It's not going to help
me get at the rest of what is going on, whatever that
is.  I can probably incorporate some points about free
verse within the paper anyway--I'll subordinate those
points to whatever turns out to be my main one.
    I'd like to write about this poem as a story about
the experience of going underwater.  It doesn't have to
```

be one of those poems that's about more than it says
it's about. I'm having trouble with some of the lines,
though. These, for instance, make me uneasy:

> There is a ladder.
> The ladder is always there
> hanging innocently
> close to the side of the schooner.
> We know what it is for,
> we who have used it.

Why "innocently"? Why apply that word to a ladder?
Why the odd emphasis on "we who have used it," as if
there's a special club. Doesn't anyone know what the
ladder on a boat is for? Maybe she's just saying that
only those who have dived can know how powerful the experience is. But now that I'm looking for things that
don't fit, what about the "book of myths" back in line
1? Is that realistic gear on a diving expedition?

There's an even greater problem at line 73. Here's
where this way of reading the poem as about an actual
experience falls apart:

> This is the place.
> And I am here, the mermaid whose dark hair
> streams black, the merman in his armored body.
> We circle silently
> about the wreck

I can understand how she might feel herself like a mermaid, but where does the merman come from? How come
suddenly there's a "We" in the poem? Was there another
diver there at the beginning of the poem? No, she said
she was having to do this, not like Cousteau, "but here
alone."

By discovering parts of the poem that don't lend themselves to a straight
reading of a deep-sea diving experience, this student finds himself moving,
almost reluctantly, away. He hasn't gotten very far toward an analysis, but
he is beginning to read the poem alertly and he is casting about for a perspective that will bring more of the poem to light.

Where do you think he is headed? Where would you go? If you would like to try your hand at an analysis, here is your chance. Look for a perspective you find promising and work out a rough draft. Don't try for a complete essay; just see what you can find to say.

A LAST ANALYTICAL PROBLEM: A CASE FROM A HISTORY EXAM

One other type of analytical assignment leaves you almost too free. Here is a question from a take-home exam in a U.S. history course:

Analyze the trends in U.S. foreign policy since 1945.

Not only does this assignment suggest no particular perspective, it provides only the vaguest of analytical objects. Sometimes, despite the word *analyze* in the question, such assignments are calling only for summary: "Tell me what I've told you about U.S. foreign policy." But when calling for genuine analysis, such questions are worded so broadly as to leave the crucial decisions to the students. And the choices can be bewildering. Which of the myriad events and relations are you to choose, and from which perspectives should you consider them? How do you define the term "foreign policy" anyway? Does it include only what has happened or also what has not? What do you write about, and how?

Of course, in practice, the question is not so frightening. In fact, if forced, most of us could write a response in a few minutes (as an experiment you might want to try doing this; then compare your response to someone else's). Besides, the question does imply some framework. The phrasing "since 1945" suggests that that year should be treated as pivotal, a time when something important began or shifted (you could start your essay "When World War II ended . . ." or "Foreign policy in the nuclear age . . ."). More important, in the context of the history course you would not really face a limitless number of possibilities — you'd have read or heard about particular events and issues that, by consensus, have been treated as crucial in U.S. foreign policy, and you'd have been exposed to several perspectives, including your teacher's, for interpreting them. In fact, these perspectives will have done much to determine which issues and events you see as important.

The difference between this question in theory and in practice helps us to reiterate a closing point about analysis. Objects of analysis seldom come to us neutrally, as something dispassionately to be examined from whatever perspectives we choose. They invariably come to us already shaped by those who have found them worth our attention. Knowing that should keep us restless. The best informed and most thoughtful analyses will recognize and negotiate this limitation, using a perspective both to help us see and to provoke us to see more.

Assignments: First Passes

1. Applying a Perspective: Children's Views of Death

In a study published in the late 1940s, psychologist Maria Nagy investigated children's attitudes toward death. The children she interviewed lived in or near Budapest, Hungary, and ranged in age from three to ten. We include excerpts from two of her discussions.

After reading the excerpts, apply as perspective the quotation that follows by the Swiss psychiatrist Carl Jung (1875–1961).

INTERVIEWS

H. G. [eight years old]: "I don't know if it is alive, if it is a person. If it is a man it is like the woodcutter. It has a white cloak on, a scythe in its hand, as one imagines it in a picture. It's not something you can see. I'm not sure if there is really any such thing."

"If there is, where is it?"

"Spirit forms haven't any country."

"Haven't angels either?"   4

"Yes, but they are good spirits. I only mean the bad ones. Bad men haven't any home. They come and go, wander about, loiter around, doing damage."

"Is death a bad spirit?"

"Yes."

"Why?"   8

"Because somehow it's cold. I imagine it would be terrible if you saw it. You would kneel down, pray to it, and still death would make you die. I've often imagined I ran away from death."

"Ran away?"

"In my room, by myself, I imagine it. I don't dare to go out. I shut the door after myself so he can't catch me. It's as if he were there. I play like that, often."

"Is it a game?"   12

"I don't know. I often pretend about him."

"Are you afraid when you are alone?"

"No, I just pretend to myself."

"The whole thing isn't true?"   16

"No."

"Why are you afraid if it isn't true?"

"Somehow I'm afraid. Death is the most powerful ruler in the world, except the good God. Death is a companion of the devil. Death is like a ghost. If death has servants, then the ghosts are its servants. If death dances, then a lot of ghosts come in white cloaks and dance the ghost dance. It could be so beautiful."

"What would be beautiful about it?"   20

"I don't know, but there's something so beautiful about it. Death and ghosts go together, like fairies and angels. Spirits and the devil go together with death. But the most terrible of all is death."

"Do you often think of death?"

"I often do. But such things as when I fight with death and hit him on the head, and death doesn't die. Death hasn't got wings."

"Why?"   24

"I imagine somehow that he hasn't. The angels have, and the fairies in the stories, but death hasn't. But he can fly for all of that. He can fly without wings, too. Death has got some kind of invisible wings. In reality they can't be seen."

G. P. [six years old]: "He stretched out his arms and lay down. You couldn't push down his arms. He can't speak. He can't move. Can't see. Can't open his eyes. He lies for four days."

"Why for four days?"

"Because the angels don't know yet where he is. The angels dig him   28
out, take him with them. They give him wings and fly away."

"What stays in the cemetery?"

"Only the coffin stays down there. Then people go there and dig it up. They take out the coffin for it to be there if somebody dies. If they couldn't make one quickly it would be there. They clean it up, good and bright."

"What happens to him?"

"If it's a woman, she does the cleaning. If it's a man, then he'll be   32
an angel. He brings the Christmas trees. Who doesn't, bakes cakes in the sky, and brings toys. It's bad to go to heaven because you have to fly. It's a good thing to be in heaven. You can't get wet, don't get soaked if it rains. It only rains on the earth."

"Well, what are you going to do if you ever get there?"

"I'm going to bake cakes the whole year. Each angel has got his own stove."

"Won't there be an awful lot of cakes if you bake the whole year round?"

"Lots of houses. Lots of children. If the cakes are done we can play   36
hide-and-seek. Then the children hide in the clouds. You can hide very well up there. One flies up, the other flies down."

— Interviews by Maria Nagy in *The Meaning of Death*

PERSPECTIVE

Unfortunately, the mythic side of man is given short shrift nowadays.   1
He can no longer create fables. As a result, a great deal escapes him; for it is important and salutary to speak also of incomprehensible things. Such talk is like the telling of a good ghost story, as we sit by the fireside and smoke a pipe. . . .

We cannot visualize another world ruled by quite other laws, the   2
reason being that we live in a specific world which has helped to shape our minds and establish our basic psychic conditions. We are strictly limited by our innate structure and therefore bound by our whole being and thinking to this world of ours. Mythic man, to be sure, demands a "going beyond all that," but scientific man cannot permit this. To the intellect, all my mythologizing is futile speculation. To the emotions,

however, it is a healing and valid activity; it gives existence a glamour which we would not like to do without. Nor is there any good reason why we should.

— Carl Jung, *Memories, Dreams, Reflections*

2. Applying a Perspective: A Passage from Camus' *The Stranger* and a Quotation by Alfred North Whitehead

The Stranger (1942) is an early novel of the French existentialist Albert Camus (1913–1960). In the excerpt presented here, the speaker, Meursault, who is awaiting execution for murder, comes to a series of philosophical understandings about his own life. Following this excerpt is an observation by British mathematician and philosopher Alfred North Whitehead (1861–1947) about the limitations of certain kinds of knowledge. In a paragraph, apply Whitehead's observation to the passage by Camus.

It was at one of these moments that I refused once again to see the   1
chaplain. I was lying down and could mark the summer evening coming on by a soft golden glow spreading across the sky. . . . Then . . . the chaplain walked in, unannounced. . . . He remained quite still at first, his arms resting on his knees, his eyes fixed on his hands. . . .

All of a sudden he jerked his head up and looked me in the eyes.   2
"Why," he asked, "don't you let me come to see you?"   3
I explained that I didn't believe in God. . . .   4
Then, I don't know how it was, but something seemed to break   5
inside me, and I started yelling at the top of my voice. I hurled insults at him, I told him not to waste his rotten prayers on me. . . . I'd taken him by the neckband of his cassock, and, in a sort of ecstasy of joy and rage, I poured out on him all the thoughts that had been simmering in my brain. He seemed so cocksure, you see. And yet none of his certainties was worth one strand of a woman's hair. Living as he did, like a corpse, he couldn't even be sure of being alive.

— Albert Camus, *The Stranger*

When you understand all about the sun, and all about the atmosphere, and all about the rotation of the earth, you may still miss the radiance of the sunset.

— Alfred North Whitehead

3. Applying a Perspective: Harvey Graff and Excerpts from Nineteenth-Century Schoolbooks

The following passage comes from a historical study by Harvey J. Graff. The penmanship (p. 312) and vocabulary (p. 313) lessons — taken from nineteenth-century schoolbooks used in Toronto, Canada — also appear in his book. In a short essay, analyze one or both of the lessons from Graff's point of view.

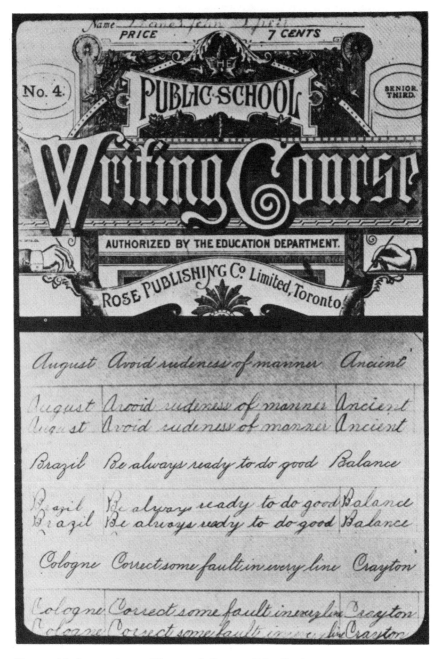

Penmanship Lesson from a Nineteenth-Century Schoolbook

Literacy's benefits were primarily social and integrating, and only 1 rarely connected with job pursuits. Nonetheless, literacy could be essential, for the promise of the school had to be conveyed: "Every man, unless he wishes to starve outright, must read and write, and cast accounts, and speak his native tongue well enough to attend to his own particular business." These were ominous tones, but the implications of these needs were nowhere elaborated: Did the individual benefits from the everyday uses of literacy make the worker more skilled, more knowledgeable about his work? Yes, but only partly so; educated labor, it was claimed, was more productive than uneducated labor. The educated mechanic was not disruptive; he was superior because he was orderly, punctual, and content.

These moral functions of schooling intersected with work in another 2 way, too. Schooling had the additional important task of assuring that manual workers did not aspire to rise above their station in life. Farmers or agricultural workers, for example, must be educated *not* to view their activities as narrow or regard them with contempt and disgust; they were not to be schooled so that they would want to leave their work, "in order to attain to a position of importance and influence." Education meant the cultivation of the workers (that is, if properly conducted) not the alienation of them from their positions.

— Harvey J. Graff, *The Literacy Myth: Literacy and Social Structure in the Nineteenth-Century City*

VOCABULARY LESSON XXI

cause	fraud	pause
clause	gauze	sauce
daub	laud	vault

James daubs his clothes with clay. Pause at the stops or points. It is fraud to take what is not yours. To laud is to praise. Read this clause. Jane has torn her gauze frock; that is the cause of her tears. Let me have sauce to my fish, if you please. It is not my fault, if you do not learn to read. Paul is a man's name. Wine is kept in vaults. *You must not vaunt or boast of your skill.*

4. Evaluating a Perspective: Thomas Rohlen and Behavior in Four College Classrooms

People who study schooling sometimes claim it teaches us much more than bodies of knowledge like science, geography, and history. Here is one perspective, that of Thomas P. Rohlen, on the extracurricular effects of schooling.

Following Rohlen's excerpt are four descriptions of instructor and student behaviors in community college classrooms. Analyze these four descriptions from the perspective of Rohlen's ideas in a short essay that supports, disagrees with, or modifies his generalizations.

In a separate short essay, you might want to describe — as accurately and precisely as you can — scenes from one or more classes you are currently taking, then apply Rohlen's framework to your descriptions.

PERSPECTIVE

1 Schools in a very real sense teach us modern time. Only when we start school do we begin to experience an extraordinary need for regularity that centers on the clock. Schools begin and end at set hours, meals can be taken only when the clock allows, and activities are all fixed by the daily schedule. A decade or more of going to school and we are all perfectly prepared to abide by the sense of time that runs through the organizational life of industrial society.

2 In school, furthermore, we learn that time is serious. It is productive and it is social. That is, being late or being confused about time is a social disturbance that affects others and causes the group to be inconvenienced and less productive. We learn in school the rhythms of the days, weeks, and years. Balances are fixed between work and rest, between different forms of work, between sitting and exercise. Difficult subjects are mixed with "fun" ones. Balances are sought between passive and active learning. In American education we make sure to build in "free" time.

3 Schools thus set a pace that prepares the young for adult society. They establish the crucial categories of time, and they shape the meaning these categories have as they contrast and interrelate, as they affect different social groups, and as they become fundamental assumptions of a modern cultural system.

— Thomas P. Rohlen, *Japan's High Schools*

CLASSROOM 1

1 He always starts off his lecture by reviewing what we just discussed the class before. You know, he'll say something like "Well, last time we were talking about the Keynesian theory, and today we'll want to compare this with the classical theory." Sometimes this is a little confusing if you're trying to take notes on what he says, but that doesn't usually really matter so much, because, like me, most students just put into their notes what the instructor writes on the board anyhow. He uses the board a lot to put all his main points on and to go over diagrams, so if you just write down what he puts on the board and maybe add a few remarks he makes in the margins, you have good notes.

2 Once he starts lecturing, he mostly goes right on through the class period. He knows a lot, a lot more than us, about economics, and he always tries to give us good information on the topic. Usually, a few students will ask him some questions. Mostly they ask him about something on the board or from the text. The instructor answers all questions, but he usually doesn't spend much time. I mean, he's got a lot of material to get us through in just a semester.

3 So, anyway, that's what usually happens in a class — the instructor

lectures, we listen and take notes, and some of us answer questions or ask them. One or two students in the back of the room I've noticed sleep through most of the class, but the instructor never says anything.

CLASSROOM 2

When I arrived, most of the students were already seated at their machines and had started working. . . . Ms. Krono was demonstrating to students working on the editing typewriter. She said, "If you've read the book, and I hope you did, you'll recognize this." Before she started demonstrating to the editing typewriter section, she collected materials for the duplicating section and got them started. As Ms. Krono was explaining to the editing typewriter group, Lois noticed something on her Executive typewriter and called all the other women around her, plus Fay. . . . Meanwhile, Laura had jumped up to help Lucy three times. She tried verbally to explain, first, but this didn't work; she had to get up and explain it to her. . . . 1

In the transcription area, Sue Ellen told Veronica, "No, it's *i* before *e* except after *c*." All three of them compared their letters for style. Sue Ellen said, "I know. Doesn't it look like it should be down a little farther?" The folder that accompanied the tape that they type from explains whom the letter was from, the letter style, suggested margins, the date on which it was to be typed, and so on. 2

Three of the duplicating girls looked for materials. They were illustrating and typing poems to duplicate on ditto. At 8:25, the instructor became aware that the transcription girls were having problems. Sue Ellen's tape was erased halfway through. Ms. Krono said, "Okay, girls, what's your problem?" She investigated. 3

Meanwhile, Faye and Ruth were quizzing each other on the parts of the ditto machine with a diagram, since the ditto was broken. 4

CLASSROOM 3

The instructor turned her back on the class and wrote the first entry of today's lecture outline on the board. Then she returned to the lectern on her desk and looked at us. Everyone got quiet and we were all ready to take notes. We wrote down what was on the board, and then the instructor began to lecture in her soft, soothing voice about diseases caused by certain microbes. She used the board often to write down more outline entries and to draw the structure of various microbes. She wrote the genus and species name of the microbes as she described them and what their functions were. Whatever she wrote or drew on the board the students put in their notes. This was all important information for the test coming up. 1

The instructor always stayed on the topic and very seldom even brought in personal references to illustrate a point. The few times she mentioned her family or a personal experience, it was a surprise but always relevant to the topic. The instructor very seldom asked students 2 questions during the lecture. If she did, it was usually informal, and whoever knew the answer would blurt it out.

. . . She told them outright that the textbook was of "high reading level and difficult." She told them not to spend lots of time reading before they came to class, but afterwards. She said to skim the chapter, come to class, take notes, and then read the chapter. She also told students they didn't have to know so much chemistry. "Your textbook really gets into chemistry." Although she never directly told the students not to use the textbook, she did tell them, "I will never ask a question on a test that I haven't covered in class." She also said, "Your textbook is an aid." 3

The instructor also used a study guide, and when she handed it out, she said, "I can guarantee you that if you can answer these questions, you're going to pass the course, but your grade depends on how well you answer the questions." Throughout the semester, before a test, the instructor freely answered student questions on the study guide. She gave examples of test questions and what names to know and not know. She also explained various techniques for answering different types of questions. 4

The instructor's strategy for allowing students to succeed in her class included giving organized class lectures, writing notes on the board, telling explicitly her requirements and what she wanted them to know, giving a study guide over each unit, and going over each exam after it was graded. When the instructor saw that students were writing only what she did on the board, she adapted her own notes and made them much more complete. She also said it slowed her down so students could keep up. 5

CLASSROOM 4

I arrived at the classroom at about 1:00 P.M. The students were working in three groups, and at times the noise level got very loud. This was especially true when several groups were working on oral exercises. One section of seven students was writing sentences from the cards. The cards were pictures of different things that are found around the home. On one side of the card, which was about $8\frac{1}{2} \times 11$, was the picture, and on the other side was the same picture, but the name of the thing was also printed — for example, *cabinet*. The aide held up the card, then asked the student what the thing was. The student was then asked to say what the thing was used for. These cards consisted of items such as television, stairs, telephone, teapot, desk, or lamp. 1

Another section was working from their workbooks. These six students were writing the exercises that deal with where people get services, such as the bank, general store, post office. In these exercises, the students copied an example from the workbook, and then they filled in the sentences like the examples. During these exercises, the aide circulated among the students and corrected them as the student finished the exercises. 2

The third section was working on verbal communication. They were practicing speaking the "I ams." The conversation would involve a student 3 doing something and saying what he was doing. Don got up and walked around his desk. He then stated, "I am walking around the desk." The students in the group then responded, "You are walking around the desk." Some of the other examples used were "I am talking"; "I am sitting at the desk."

The three groups continued working on the above exercises until 4 1:45 P.M. They were then given a break. At 2:00, a counselor came, and he was going to work with the students who needed to fill out their financial aid packets.

— Richard C. Richardson, Jr., Elizabeth C. Fisk, and Morris A. Okun,
Literacy in the Open-Access Classroom

5. Evaluating a Perspective: A Hostage Drama and Martin E. P. Seligman's Theory of Helplessness

Read the following newspaper story and then the passage by psychologist Martin Seligman. Then write a short essay in which you consider to what extent the incident reported in the newspaper can be understood in terms of Seligman's theory of helplessness.

GUNMAN KILLS HIMSELF AFTER HOSTAGE DRAMA

A night-long siege and hostage drama in a Hollywood hotel room 1 ended early Saturday when a 26-year-old gunman killed himself. He apparently was depressed over having multiple sclerosis.

No one else was injured by the gunman, whose 17-year-old hostage 2 was grabbed by police officers and pulled to safety minutes before he committed suicide.

The tense drama was played out in a 22nd floor room of Holiday Inn 3 in the heart of Hollywood, forcing the evacuation of guests from three floors and from a busy nightclub in the building.

The gunman, armed with a rifle, was identified by police as Robert 4 B. Rose of Leucadia, a town about 30 miles north of San Diego. The hostage was not identified.

Rose's mother, Mary, said after the incident that her son had been 5 under intensive psychiatric care for a number of years. She said he learned in January that he had multiple sclerosis, a disease of the central nervous system.

"I think this was sort of the last straw as far as he was concerned," 6 she said.

Police said Rose checked into the hotel late Saturday night, went 7 out, returned with the 17-year-old girl and went to his room.

There, a police department statement said, he pointed the rifle at 8 the girl, threatened her life, warned that he would commit suicide and ordered her to take off her clothes. When she did, he threw the clothing out the window.

Shots were fired from the window at about 11:15 p.m. By coinci- 9 dence, amateur radio operators from a group known as EARS were on the roof of the building at the time as part of a new program to help the police keep watch in high-crime areas of Hollywood.

They reported the shooting to the police, who closed off the top of the hotel, evacuated the other guests and summoned the Special Weapons and Tactics team.   10

Guests waited out the confrontations in the lobby, many wearing pajamas and wrapped in blankets.   11

Most appeared to be foreign tourists. They were startled by the sudden arrival of scores of police officers, some carrying automatic rifles, and house detectives from the hotel.   12

"It's just like that television program, SWAT," said John Edwards, a tourist from Perth, Australia.   13

During telephone negotiations between the police and the girl, Rose reportedly asked to see a Roman Catholic priest and have food brought to the room.   14

A pizza was left outside the barricaded room. Rose, according to police, forced the girl, then wearing only a towel, to pick it up. When the girl stepped outside, she was grabbed by officer Donnelley D. Mowry and pulled to safety.   15

Police said Rose pointed his rifle at other officers in the corridor. The police fired one shot and Rose retreated, closed the door and fired four times. The police returned fire and one shot apparently grazed Rose's chest.   16

At 2 a.m., police heard a gunshot in the room. Three hours later, after using tear gas, police stormed the room and found Rose dead. They said he had shot himself in the mouth.   17

Rose's mother said she last talked to her son on Monday. He told her that he was living with a friend in Los Angeles and driving a taxi.   18

Rose, the youngest of five children, was a "very brilliant young man and a very depressed man," she said.   19

His mother, who learned of the incident when a friend told her husband about hearing a news account on the radio, said she is thankful that no one else was injured.   20

— Charles P. Wallace and Tim Waters, *Los Angeles Times*, May 10, 1981

PERSPECTIVE

When a traumatic event first occurs, it causes a heightened state of emotionality that can loosely be called fear. This state continues until one of two things happens: if the subject learns that he can control the trauma, fear is reduced and may disappear altogether; or if the subject finally learns he cannot control the trauma, fear will decrease and be replaced with depression.   1

For example, when a rat, a dog, or a man experiences inescapable trauma he first struggles frantically. Fear, I believe, is the dominant emotion accompanying this state. If he learns to control the trauma, frenetic activity gives way to an efficient and nonchalant response. If the trauma is uncontrollable, however, struggling eventually gives way to the helpless state I have described. The emotion that accompanies this state   2 is, I believe, depression. Similarly, when an infant monkey is separated from its mother, great distress is produced by the traumatic experience. The monkey runs around frantically, making distress calls. Two things can happen: if the mother returns, the infant can now control her again, and distress will cease; or if the mother does not return, the infant eventually learns that it cannot bring mother back, and depression ensues, displacing the fear. The infant curls up in a ball and whines. Such a sequence is in fact what happens in all primate species that have been observed. . . .

3   Many theorists have talked about the need or drive to master events in the environment. In a classic exposition, R. W. White proposed the concept of *competence*. He argued that the basic drive for control had been overlooked by learning theorists and psychoanalytic thinkers alike. The need to master could be more pervasive than sex, hunger, and thirst in the lives of animals and men. Play in young children, for example, is motivated not by "biological" drives, but by a competence drive. . . .

4   A drive for competence . . . is, from my point of view, a drive to avoid helplessness. The existence of such a drive follows directly from the emotional premise of our theory. Since being helpless arouses fear and depression, activity that avoids helplessness thereby avoids these aversive emotional states. Competence may be a drive to avoid the fear and depression induced by helplessness.

— Martin E. P. Seligman, *Helplessness:*
On Depression, Development, and Death

6. Evaluating a Perspective: Immigration Statistics and a Passage by Karl Marx

First look at the statistics in Table 2 on page 320 and think about the story they tell. Then read the fragment from *Capital* by Karl Marx (1818–1883), which follows. How would Marx tell the story of the immigration statistics? Write a short essay about U.S. immigration patterns, either taking Marx's point of view or resisting it. (The Marx is not easy, so it will take several readings and some discussion.)

If a surplus laboring population is a necessary product of accumulation or of the development of wealth on a capitalist basis, this surplus population becomes, conversely, the lever of capitalistic accumulation, nay, a condition of existence of the capitalist mode of production. It forms a disposable industrial reserve army, that belongs to capital quite as absolutely as if the latter had bred it at its own cost. Independently of the limits of the actual increase of population, it creates, for the changing needs of the self-expansion of capital, a mass of human material always ready for exploitation. . . . The mass of social wealth, overflowing with the advance of accumulation, and transformable into additional capital, thrusts itself frantically into old branches of production, whose market suddenly expands, or into newly formed branches, such as railways, etc., the need for which grows out of the development of the old ones. In all such cases, there must be the possibility of throwing great masses of men suddenly on the decisive points without injury to the scale of production in other spheres. Over-population supplies these masses. The course characteristic of modern industry, viz., a decennial cycle (interrupted by smaller oscillations), of periods of average activity, production at high pressure, crisis and stagnation, depends on the constant formation, the greater or less absorption, and the re-formation of the industrial reserve army of surplus population. In their turn, the varying phases of the industrial cycle recruit the surplus population, and become one of the most energetic agents of its reproduction.

— Karl Marx, *Capital*

TABLE 2.   Immigration: 1820 to 1986

[In thousands, except rate. For fiscal years ending in year shown, except as noted; see text, section 9. For definition of immigrants, see text, section 1. For 1820–1867, alien passengers arriving; 1868–1891 and 1895–1897, immigrants arriving; 1892–1894 and 1898 to the present, immigrants admitted. Rates based on Bureau of the Census estimates as of July 1 for resident population through 1929, and for total population thereafter (excluding Alaska and Hawaii prior to 1959). See also *Historical Statistics, Colonial Times to 1970*, series C 89]

PERIOD OR YEAR	TOTAL		YEAR	TOTAL	
	NUMBER	RATE[1]		NUMBER	RATE[1]
1820–1986	53,122	3.4			
1820–1830[2]	152	1.2	1968	454	2.3
1831–1840[3]	599	3.9	1969	359	1.8
1841–1850[4]	1,713	8.4	1970	373	1.8
1851–1860[4]	2,598	9.3	1971	370	1.8
1861–1870[5]	2,315	6.4	1972	385	1.8
1871–1880	2,812	6.2	1973	400	1.9
1881–1890	5,247	9.2	1974	395	1.9
1891–1900	3,688	5.3	1975	386	1.8
1901–1910	8,795	10.4	1976	399	1.9
1911–1920	5,736	5.7	1977	462	2.1
1921–1930	4,107	3.5	1978	601	2.8
1931–1940	528	.4	1979	460	2.1
1941–1950	1,035	.7	1980	531	2.3
1951–1960	2,515	1.5	1981	597	2.6
1961–1970	3,322	1.7	1982	594	2.6
1971–1980[6]	4,493	2.1	1983	560	2.4
1981–1986	3,466	2.4	1984	544	2.3
1965	297	1.5	1985	570	2.4
1966	323	1.6	1986	602	2.5
1967	362	1.8			

[1] Annual rate per 1,000 U.S. population. Rate computed by dividing sum of annual immigration totals by sum of annual U.S. population totals for same number of years.   [2] Oct. 1, 1819–Sept. 30, 1830.   [3] Oct. 1, 1830–Dec. 31, 1840.   [4] Calendar years.   [5] Jan. 1, 1861–June 30, 1870.   [6] Includes transition quarter, July 1 to Sept. 30, 1976.
SOURCE: U.S. Immigration and Naturalization Service, *Statistical Yearbook*, annual; and releases.

Assignments: Options

7. A Psychology Option: An Example of Alienation

The first reading is a case study modeled on the type that psychologists use and that is assigned in courses in human relations. Following that is a reading from the philosopher Karl Jaspers (1883–1969) on the effect certain kinds of modern work has on men and women. In an essay, analyze the case history of Angelo Cacci from the perspective offered by Jaspers, either accepting or rejecting Jaspers's ideas as a way of understanding Cacci.

The Case History of Angelo Cacci
MIKE ROSE

A young man visited a local counseling center because he was feeling "very down in the dumps." Angelo Cacci was thirty-two years old, lived alone, and was employed as a clerk in a large insurance company. The counselor noted that Angelo was fairly good-looking, clean-shaven, and dressed nicely, though not expensively. He spoke articulately, though not with any particular flair; however, the lack of emphasis in his speech could have been related to his depression. He seemed to be willing to discuss his history and his feelings. 1

Angelo stated that he had had passing periods of the "blues" before but that his present feelings of depression were more severe. Several months earlier, Angelo had broken up with his girlfriend. "It just wasn't working out," he explained. "We used to go out — go to the park, a ball game, the movies — but after a while it fizzled. I just didn't feel that much for her anymore." He added that a similar event had occurred with a different woman five years earlier. 2

Angelo talked a great deal about his past. He comes from an Italian working-class family. He has a brother and sister but doesn't see either one any longer. His brother was transferred to another large city because the automotive industry was booming there. His sister moved out west after she got married. When Angelo was younger, the Cacci family lived in a predominantly Italian neighborhood. Both of his paternal grandparents died when Angelo was quite young. Still, some of Angelo's fondest memories are of his grandfather. The old man used to take him fishing outside the city. Angelo's father, on the other hand, didn't have much time for his children. Mr. Cacci supported the family as a dockworker, but he left when Angelo was eleven. After the separation, Mrs. Cacci got a job in a clock factory, and she has worked there ever since. 3

Angelo explained that his childhood was a very unhappy period. His father was seldom home, and when he was present, he was constantly fighting with Mrs. Cacci. Mrs. Cacci usually became sullen and withdrawn after an argument, refused to speak to her husband, and became uncommunicative with her children. Angelo remembered that many times 4 as a child he was puzzled because it seemed that his mother was angry with him too. Sometimes after an argument, Mrs. Cacci told her children that she ruined her life by marrying a "truck driver." Angelo went on, explaining that his mother rarely smiled or laughed and did not converse very much with the children. When she came home from work she would usually put on her robe, cook dinner, and spend the evening watching television. This pattern continued well into Angelo's young adulthood.

After high school, Angelo went into the army, where he developed good typing, clerical, and basic accounting skills. He describes the army as being uneventful. He put in his time and was honorably discharged.   5

Angelo characterized his job as being "OK." "It pays the bills and leaves me a decent amount for entertainment." His particular task is to certify damage claims by checking customer estimates against insurance investigator reports. This provides the company with the information it needs to challenge possibly exaggerated or even fraudulent claims. On an average day, Angelo said he examines and registers twenty to twenty-five estimates and reports. The counselor noted that Angelo's work record must be a good one. He has been with the company for ten years and regularly gets the raises afforded employees in good standing.   6

The reason for Angelo's visit to the counseling center was that his depression puzzled him. He recounted a dream he has had several times in the last month, wondering if it is connected to his depression. The counselor described the dream in Angelo's case history, but, though he might have offered an interpretation, he didn't write it down. In the dream Angelo and a man from another department in the insurance firm are walking in an open field. Horses are roaming the area as are several large dogs. One of the dogs seems to be injured and limps by Angelo and his friend. A third man appears and begins attending to the dog. Here either the dream fades or Angelo wakes up. Angelo then turned to other aspects of his life, but didn't see any immediate connection between them and his situation. "Sure I broke up with my girl," he speculated, "but I wasn't in love with her. Besides, I've been through this before." As for his job, "like I explained, it's all right. I've got a good record and the pay is satisfactory." As for his mother, "I go to see her now and then. She's still gloomy as always, but I realize there's little I can do about it. She's been that way for a long time."   7

From *Man in the Modern Age*
KARL JASPERS

It has been said that in modern times men have been shuffled together like grains of sand. They are elements of an apparatus in which they occupy now one location, now another. . . . What a man can do nowadays can only be done by one who takes short views. He has occupation, indeed, but his life has no continuity. What he does is done to good purpose, but is then finished once for all. The task may be repeated after the same fashion many times, but it cannot be repeated in such an intimate way as to become, one might say, part of the personality of the doer; it does not lead to an expansion of the selfhood. What has been done, no longer counts, but only that which is actually being done. Oblivion is the basis of such a life, whose outlooks upon past and present shrink so much that scarcely anything remains in the mind but the bald present. Thus life flows on its course devoid of memories and foresights, lacking the energy derivable from a purposive and abstract outlook upon the part played in the apparatus. Love for things and human beings wanes and disappears. The machine-made products vanish from sight as soon as made and consumed, all that remains in view being the machinery by which new commodities are being made. The worker at the machine, concentrating upon immediate aims, has no time or inclination left for the contemplation of life as a whole.

8. A Composition Option: The Writing Process of a College Student

The first reading is a discussion of the composing process. Read and discuss it before moving on to the case study that follows it. Consider it in light of your own writing. Does it make sense when you think about the way you learned to write and what you do now when you write?

Writing Around Rules
MIKE ROSE

Writing is a phenomenally complex learned activity. To write in a way that others can understand we must employ a large and complicated body of conventions. We learn from our parents or earliest teachers that script, in English, goes left to right straight across the page. We learn about letter formation, spelling, sentence structure, and so on. Some of this information we absorb more or less unconsciously through reading, and some of it we learn formally as guidelines, as directives . . . as rules.   1

And there are all kinds of rules. Some tell us how to format our writing (for example, when to capitalize, how to paragraph, how to footnote). There are grammar rules (for example, "Make a pronoun agree in number with its antecedent"). There are preferences concerning style that are often stated as rules ("Avoid passive voice"). There are usage rules ("*That* always introduces restrictive clauses; *which* can introduce both restrictive and nonrestrictive clauses"). There are rules that tell us how to compose ("Before you begin writing, decide on your thesis and write it down in a single declarative sentence"). The list goes on and on. Some of these rules make sense; others are confusing, questionable, or contradictory. Fortunately, we assimilate a good deal of the information they contain gradually by reading other writers, by writing ourselves, or   2 by simply being around print. Therefore, we can confirm or alter or reject them from experience.

But all too often the rules are turned into absolutes. And that's where the trouble begins. Most rules about writing should not be expressed (in textbooks), stored (in our minds), or enacted (on the page) as absolutes, as mathematical, unvarying directives. True, a few rules apply in virtually all situations (for example, certain formatting rules or capitalization rules). But most rules do not. Writing rules, like any rules about language, have a history and have a time and place. They are highly context-bound. 3

Should you always, as some textbooks suggest, place your thesis sentence at the beginning of your first paragraph or, as others suggest, work up to it and place it at the end of the paragraph? Well, the answer is that both injunctions are right . . . and wrong. Students writing essay exams would be well-advised to demonstrate their knowledge and direct the reader's attention as soon as possible. But the writer who wants to evoke a mood might offer a series of facts and events that gradually lead up to a thesis sentence. The writing situation, the rhetorical purpose, and the nature of the material one is working with will provide the answer. A single-edged rule cannot. 4

How about our use of language, usage rules? Certainly there's a right and a wrong here? Again, not quite. First of all, there's a time in one's writing to worry about such things. Concern yourself with questions of usage too early in your composing and you'll end up . . . worrying about the minutiae of language while your thought fades to a wisp. Second, the social consequences of following or ignoring such rules vary widely depending on whether you're writing formal or informal prose. Third, usage rules themselves have an evolutionary history: we aren't obliged to follow some of the rules that turn-of-the-century writers had to deal with, and our rules will alter and even disappear as the English language moves on in time. No, there are no absolutes here either. 5

Well, how about some of the general, commonsense rules about the very act of writing itself? Certainly, rules like "Think before you write" ought to be followed? Again, a qualification is in order. While it certainly is good advice to think through ideas before we record them for others to see, many people, in fact, use writing as a way of thinking. They make major decisions *as* they write. There are times when it's best to put a piece of writing aside and ponder, but there are also times when one ought to keep pen in hand and attempt to resolve a conceptual tangle by sketching out what comes to mind. Both approaches are legitimate. 6

I'll stop here. I hope I've shown that it's difficult to make hard and fast statements about the structure, the language, or the composing of an essay. Unfortunately, there's a strong push in our culture to make absolute statements about writing, especially where issues of style and usage are concerned. But I hope by now the reader of this essay believes that most rules about writing — about how to do it, about how it should be structured, about what words to use — are not absolute, and should be taught and enacted in a flexible, context-dependent way. Given certain conditions, you follow them; given other conditions you modify or suspend 7 them. A teacher may insist that a young writer follow a particular dictum in order to learn a pattern, but there must come a time when the teacher extends the lesson and explains when the dictum is and isn't appropriate.

The second reading is a case study of a student writing on the materials from assignment 7 (see pp. 321–323; you might want to take a moment to read, or reread, those materials). A few words about Liz, the focus of the case study: Although she is a senior English major in good standing, she says she has a great deal of trouble completing her papers. She was given the materials from Assignment 7 and asked to interpret Angelo Cacci's situation in light of Jaspers's discussion. She was told to compose as she normally would for sixty minutes, and that if she couldn't finish a draft in that length of time, that would be okay. We present first the writing she completed in sixty minutes and follow that with a summary of what she did as she wrote.

Write an essay in which you consider Liz's case from the perspective provided in "Writing Around Rules."

Case Study of Liz
MIKE ROSE

LIZ'S ESSAY

The depression Angelo experiences and the dis-continuity Jaspers 1 describes can both be accounted for, at least in some sense by the quality of city life; by the modern experience. Angelo's "blues" for example may result directly from breakup with his girlfriend but even if they do

LIZ'S SESSION

At the 60-minute deadline, Liz turned in a draft of 45 words — a 2 topic sentence and part of a second, apparently qualifying, sentence. This extremely brief product, however, belied the amount of writing she actually produced. After rereading the assignment materials for 2½ minutes, Liz began underlining the Jaspers passage and the case history, glossing the former and jotting down fragments and sentences on scratch paper. Liz did not pause a great number of times while writing (62), but her pauses were relatively long (28.9 seconds on the average). During most of these pauses, Liz was weighing ideas and rehearsing sentences. She often spoke aloud and gestured with her hand while rehearsing, apparently testing the rhythm of her sentences, measuring rhythm with the waves of her hand in the air.

From the beginning, Liz "was trying to make a connection . . . 3 between" the passages. (A sentence from the first page of her scratch paper revealed this attempt at fusion: "Jaspers attributes the personal unhappiness of people like Cacci to the noncreative nature of their jobs.")

But, at the same time, Liz was wrestling with the legitimacy of the Jaspers passage itself. . . . Simultaneous with her attempts to effect a connection between Angelo's life and Jaspers's vision (mentally arguing with Jaspers's vision all the while), Liz was also making a number of word to phrase-level changes in her glossing and rough draft. Within the first 10 minutes of writing, Liz made the following alterations: passive constructions were changed to active ones; "to be" forms were changed to more striking verbs; certain words (e.g., "says") were rejected as being "too colloquial"; other words (e.g., "like") were rejected for being "too simple . . . too easy"; clauses were rejected or accepted by the way they sounded; clauses were also rejected for containing a preposition; and, finally, spelling was corrected. These changes were supported with rules like "You're not supposed to have passive verbs"; "You can't start a sentence with 'says' "; "If you can singsong it, it's not good stylistically." Sometimes Liz's decisions were based on rules and concepts she did not fully understand: "When he's [a textbook author] talking about 'to be' verbs, I don't really even understand what he's saying." Other times, her rules and resulting word choices would conflict. When she changed "is saying" to "says," she noted that the new verb "would . . . be too colloquial" and thus would not be acceptable. Further on she wrote "to the noncreative nature of their jobs" and said it "is good [because it sounds good], and it's bad because of the 'of.' " Finally, there were times when Liz's preoccupation with editing resulted in her forgetting her thought. Very early in the hour she wrote an interpretive note under the Jaspers passage: "is saying that not having creative (generative) work is the"; she stopped and changed "is saying" to "says" and "is the" to "causes." Then came a long pause. She couldn't remember the rest of her insight. "That happens a lot," she later observed.

Through the second third of her hour, Liz continued to pause, rehearse, and jot down ideas on scratch paper. The ideas of this period were expressed in strings of sentences as Liz's disagreement with Jaspers (and her attempt to work that disagreement into the assignment) was becoming more evident (e.g., "The breakup between Angelo and his girlfriend is probably the reason for his depression. Jaspers, if you accept the little that is given in this selection, might attribute the breakup to the kind of job that he is talking about"). As Liz continued to attempt new sentences and rephrase old ones, it became obvious that she was trying to form an approach to the assignment that would allow her to work with Jaspers's vision while taking issue with it. This approach would become the stuff of a topic sentence as well as a conclusion, and, for Liz, thinking of some sort of a conclusion fairly early is important: "A place to end up. I always have that." But mid-way through the hour, she had not yet found her approach. When asked if, at this point, she could have told what her paper was going to be about, she replied, "No. No way." She was experiencing "real confusion" as she continued to think of and set down one and two sentence "blocks of information," wrestling with Jaspers all the while. Then, at this mid-point, she suddenly put her scratch paper aside and began the draft she would turn in, framing a beginning sentence and part of another that gave some structure to her complex stance toward Jaspers and the case of Angelo Cacci.

After working on her introductory sentences for 5½ minutes, Liz went back to the case study and began to gloss it. (She had originally only underlined it.) "It's from this sort of stuff that I get my best ideas." She was asked why, then, she did not begin her 60 minutes by performing this interpretive glossing. "I don't know," she answered.

As Liz moved through the last third of the hour, she continued reading the case study closely, following line by line with her finger, glossing every tenth line or so. At one point she commented, "Well, maybe he [Jaspers] is right," only to return to her original skepticism several minutes later: "All he [Jaspers] is really saying is that you don't get to see the end of your work. That means all these terrible things?" Liz was asked again if she was any closer to a thesis: "I don't know. Can't tell. Because it [is] actually only an hour. You know, you can't exactly judge. . . . [You can] never really tell what it is until you're halfway done." Queried about the continual conflict between her quarrel with Jaspers and the requirements of the assignment as she understood them, she replied, "I just really didn't think it out well enough."

9. A Sociology Option: The Phases of Culture Shock

Culture shock is a general term for describing the problems that people experience in making the transition from a familiar to an unfamiliar setting. The first reading is an excerpt from a book written for nursing professionals by medical anthropologists. The authors define four distinct phases of culture shock.

That reading is followed by descriptions of the experiences of three people adjusting to life in the United States. Mary Antin (1881–1949) arrived in the United States as a young girl from Russia at the turn of the century. Maxine Hong Kingston (b. 1940) grew up in Stockton, California, where she experienced tension between the Chinese and American cultures. Wood Chuen Kwong came to San Francisco from Canton, China, as an adult in 1979.

From the perspective offered by Brink and Saunders, write an essay analyzing the culture shock experienced by the three people. Does the theoretical model of culture shock help you understand all three cases? In a separate brief paper — one that can be rough and experimental — reflect on this experience of trying to apply a theoretical model to cases: the ways it helped you understand people's experience and the ways it narrowed or misrepresented that experience.

For those of you who have immigrated to the United States or have spent a significant amount of time in another culture, we offer a further option: Write an essay analyzing your own experience of crossing cultures using Brink and Saunders's theoretical model, specifically considering the ways the model fits and illuminates your experience and the ways it doesn't.

From *Transcultural Nursing: A Book of Readings*

PAMELA BRINK AND JUDITH SAUNDERS

[The researcher] Oberg's original paper isolated and described four phases   1
of culture shock and named the first phase the "Honeymoon Phase." . . .
The other three phases were described but not named. The following
discussion is an attempt to name and extend Oberg's discussion.

Phase One. "The Honeymoon Phase" is marked by excitement.   2
The desire to learn about the people and their customs is great; sight-
seeing is anticipated with pleasure; and getting to work and accomplishing
all the goals envisioned at home provide the basis for this phase. Travelers, visiting dignitaries, and other temporary functionaries may never
experience any other phase but this one.

Phase Two. "The Disenchantment Phase" generally does not be-   3
gin until the individual has established residence, i.e., when he begins to
become aware of the setting as his area of residence. This sense of
awareness often is associated with the realization that one is "stuck here"
and cannot get out of the situation. What was "quaint" may become
aggravating. Simple tasks of living are time consuming because they must
be done in a different way. This beginning awareness often results in
frustration — either frustration because the indigenous population is too
stubborn to see things your way or frustration because you can't see
things their way and are constantly making social errors. Embarrassment
coupled with feelings of ineptness attack self-image or self-concept.

Particular, individual styles of behavior are developed over the years   4
through the principles of inertia and economy. Usually the individual is
unaware of the operation of these principles and their effect to him. They
form part of ethnocentrism: "The way I do things is the right way (and
perhaps for some the only way) to do things." The disenchantment phase
directly threatens ethnocentrism because the host country believes exactly the same way about its customs and sees no reason to change its
ways. Phase two includes a reexamination of one's self from the vantage
point of another set of values. In this phase failure often outweighs
success.

To this, add loneliness. No one knows you well enough to reaffirm   5
your sense of self-worth. The distance from home is magnified. Home
itself assumes the aura of Mecca — distant, unattainable, beautiful. This
form of nostalgia for the past and the familiar seems to have two effects.
Mail and visitors from home assume immense importance as a contact
with people who believe in you and think you are important. To protect
yourself from these feelings of loneliness and lack of self-esteem, you
attack the presumed cause of these feelings — the host country. Feelings
of anxiety and inadequacy are often expressed through depression, withdrawal, or eruptions of anger at frustration; or by seeking out fellow

countrymen to the exclusion of the indigenous population. This period in the culture shock syndrome is the most difficult to live through and this is the period where people "give up and go home."

Phase Three. "The Beginning Resolution Phase." Oberg de- 6 scribed this phase . . . as the individual seeking to learn new patterns of behavior appropriate to the setting, attempting to make friends in the indigenous population, and becoming as much of a participant-observer as possible in the ceremonies, festivals, and daily activities of the new setting.

This phase seems to be characterized by the reestablishment of a 7 sense of humor. Social errors no longer are devastating to the ego. The host culture no longer is considered all bad and home all wonderful. This phase seems to be facilitated greatly by the arrival of fellow countrymen who are "worse off" and need help. You can show off what you have learned, you are important because you are sought for advice, you feel needed by the newcomer.

At this point also, the individual becomes aware that things seem 8 easier; friendships are being developed; home is still distant, but less relevant. Letters from home somehow seem peripheral to current interests and concerns. Letters to home become more superficial; explanation of what is becoming familiar would take up too much time. Current friendships have the same frame of reference for conversation, a frame of reference that is unknown at home.

Without really becoming aware of the process one slowly adapts to 9 the new situation. Each small discovery, each small victory in learning the new rules is satisfying, and helps to restore one's sore and damaged ego.

Phase Four. "The Effective Function Phase." This means being 10 just as comfortable in the new setting as in the old. Having achieved this phase, the individual will probably experience reverse culture shock when he returns home. Or, the individual may decide only to go home for visits, but make the new culture his own.

From *The Promised Land*
MARY ANTIN

Anybody who knows Boston knows that the West and North Ends are 1 the wrong ends of that city. They form the tenement district, or, in the newer phrase, the slums of Boston. Anybody who is acquainted with the slums of any American metropolis knows that that is the quarter where poor immigrants foregather, to live, for the most part, as unkempt, half-washed, toiling, unaspiring foreigners; pitiful in the eyes of social missionaries, the despair of boards of health, the hope of ward politicians, the touchstone of American democracy. The well-versed metropolitan knows the slums as a sort of house of detention for poor aliens, where they live on probation till they can show a certificate of good citizenship.

He may know all this and yet not guess how Wall Street, in the West End, appears in the eyes of a little immigrant from Polotzk. What would the sophisticated sight-seer say about Union Place, off Wall Street, where my new home waited for me? He would say that it is no place at all, but a short box of an alley. Two rows of three-story tenements are its sides, a stingy strip of sky is its lid, a littered pavement is the floor, and a narrow mouth its exit.   2

But I saw a very different picture on my introduction to Union Place. I saw two imposing rows of brick buildings, loftier than any dwelling I had ever lived in. Brick was even on the ground for me to tread on, instead of common earth or boards. Many friendly windows stood open, filled with uncovered heads of women and children. I thought the people were interested in us, which was very neighborly. I looked up to the topmost row of windows, and my eyes were filled with the May blue of an American sky!   3

In our days of affluence in Russia we had been accustomed to up-holstered parlors, embroidered linen, silver spoons and candlesticks, gob-lets of gold, kitchen shelves shining with copper and brass. We had feather-beds heaped halfway to the ceiling; we had clothes presses dusky with velvet and silk and fine woollen. The three small rooms into which my father now ushered us, up one flight of stairs, contained only the necessary beds, with lean mattresses; a few wooden chairs; a table or two; a mysterious iron structure, which later turned out to be a stove; a couple of unornamental kerosene lamps; and a scanty array of cooking-utensils and crockery. And yet we were all impressed with our new home and its furniture. It was not only because we had just passed through our seven lean years, cooking in earthen vessels, eating black bread on holidays and wearing cotton; it was chiefly because these wooden chairs and tin pans were American chairs and pans that they shone glorious in our eyes. And if there was anything lacking for comfort or decoration we expected it to be presently supplied — at least, we children did. Perhaps my mother alone, of us newcomers, appreciated the shabbiness of the little apartment, and realized that for her there was as yet no laying down of the burden of poverty.   4

Our initiation into American ways began with the first step on the new soil. My father found occasion to instruct or correct us even on the way from the pier to Wall Street, which journey we made crowded together in a rickety cab. He told us not to lean out of the windows, not to point, and explained the word "greenhorn." We did not want to be "greenhorns," and gave the strictest attention to my father's instructions. I do not know when my parents found opportunity to review together the history of Polotzk in the three years past, for we children had no patience with the subject; my mother's narrative was constantly inter-rupted by irrelevant questions, interjections, and explanations.   5

The first meal was an object lesson of much variety. My father produced several kinds of food, ready to eat, without any cooking, from little tin cans that had printing all over them. He attempted to introduce   6 us to a queer, slippery kind of fruit, which he called "banana," but had to give it up for the time being. After the meal, he had better luck with a curious piece of furniture on runners, which he called "rocking-chair." There were five of us newcomers, and we found five different ways of getting into the American machine of perpetual motion, and as many ways of getting out of it. One born and bred to the use of a rocking-chair cannot imagine how ludicrous people can make themselves when attempting to use it for the first time. We laughed immoderately over our various experiments with the novelty, which was a wholesome way of letting off steam after the unusual excitement of the day.

In our flat we did not think of such a thing as storing the coal in the bathtub. There was no bathtub. So in the evening of the first day my father conducted us to the public baths. As we moved along in a little procession, I was delighted with the illumination of the streets. So many lamps, and they burned until morning, my father said, and so people did not need to carry lanterns. In America, then, everything was free, as we had heard in Russia. Light was free; the streets were as bright as a synagogue on a holy day. Music was free; we had been serenaded, to our gaping delight, by a brass band of many pieces, soon after our installation on Union Place. 7

Education was free. That subject my father had written about repeatedly, as comprising his chief hope for us children, the essence of American opportunity, the treasure that no thief could touch, not even misfortune or poverty. It was the one thing that he was able to promise us when he sent for us; surer, safer than bread or shelter. On our second day I was thrilled with the realization of what this freedom of education meant. A little girl from across the alley came and offered to conduct us to school. My father was out, but we five between us had a few words of English by this time. We knew the word school. We understood. This child, who had never seen us till yesterday, who could not pronounce our names, who was not much better dressed than we, was able to offer us the freedom of the schools of Boston! No application made, no questions asked, no examinations, rulings, exclusions; no machinations, no fees. The doors stood open for every one of us. The smallest child could show us the way. 8

This incident impressed me more than anything I had heard in advance of the freedom of education in America. It was a concrete proof — almost the thing itself. One had to experience it to understand it. 9

It was a great disappointment to be told by my father that we were not to enter upon our school career at once. It was too near the end of the term, he said, and we were going to move to Crescent Beach in a week or so. We had to wait until the opening of the schools in September. What a loss of precious time — from May till September! 10

Not that the time was really lost. Even the interval on Union Place was crowded with lessons and experiences. We had to visit the stores and be dressed from head to foot in American clothing; we had to learn the mysteries of the iron stove, the washboard, and the speaking-tube; we had to learn to trade with the fruit peddler through the window, and not to be afraid of the policeman; and, above all, we had to learn English. 11

The kind people who assisted us in these important matters form a 12 group by themselves in the gallery of my friends. If I had never seen them from those early days till now, I should still have remembered them with gratitude. When I enumerate the long list of my American teachers, I must begin with those who came to us on Wall Street and taught us our first steps. To my mother, in her perplexity over the cookstove, the woman who showed her how to make the fire was an angel of deliverance. A fairy godmother to us children was she who led us to a wonderful country called "uptown," where, in a dazzlingly beautiful palace called a "department store," we exchanged our hateful homemade European costumes, which pointed us out as "greenhorns" to the children on the street, for real American machine-made garments, and issued forth glorified in each other's eyes.

With our despised immigrant clothing we shed also our impossible 13 Hebrew names. A committee of our friends, several years ahead of us in American experience, put their heads together and concocted American names for us all. Those of our real names that had no pleasing American equivalents they ruthlessly discarded, content if they retained the initials. My mother, possessing a name that was not easily translatable, was punished with the undignified nickname of Annie. Fetchke, Joseph, and Deborah issued as Frieda, Joseph, and Dora, respectively. As for poor me, I was simply cheated. The name they gave me was hardly new. My Hebrew name being Maryashe in full, Mashke for short, Russianized into Marya (*Mar-ya*), my friends said that it would hold good in English as *Mary;* which was very disappointing, as I longed to possess a strange-sounding American name like the others.

I am forgetting the consolation I had, in this matter of names, from 14 the use of my surname, which I have had no occasion to mention until now. I found on my arrival that my father was "Mr. Antin" on the slightest provocation, and not, as in Polotzk, on state occasions alone. And so I was "Mary Antin," and I felt very important to answer to such a dignified title. It was just like America that even plain people should wear their surnames on week days.

As a family we were so diligent under instruction, so adaptable, and 15 so clever in hiding our deficiencies, that when we made the journey to Crescent Beach, in the wake of our small wagon-load of household goods, my father had very little occasion to admonish us on the way, and I am sure he was not ashamed of us. So much we had achieved toward our Americanization during the two weeks since our landing.

From *The Woman Warrior*
MAXINE HONG KINGSTON

Long ago in China, knot-makers tied string into buttons and frogs, and rope into bell pulls. There was one knot so complicated that it blinded the knot-maker. Finally an emperor outlawed this cruel knot, and the nobles could not order it anymore. If I had lived in China, I would have been an outlaw knot-maker.

Maybe that's why my mother cut my tongue. She pushed my tongue up and sliced the frenum. Or maybe she snipped it with a pair of nail scissors. I don't remember her doing it, only her telling me about it, but all during childhood I felt sorry for the baby whose mother waited with scissors or knife in hand for it to cry — and then, when its mouth was wide open like a baby bird's, cut. The Chinese say "a ready tongue is an evil."

I used to curl up my tongue in front of the mirror and tauten my frenum into a white line, itself as thin as a razor blade. I saw no scars in my mouth. I thought perhaps I had had two frena, and she had cut one. I made other children open their mouths so I could compare theirs to mine. I saw perfect pink membranes stretching into precise edges that looked easy enough to cut. Sometimes I felt very proud that my mother committed such a powerful act upon me. At other times I was terrified — the first thing my mother did when she saw me was to cut my tongue.

"Why did you do that to me, Mother?"   4

"I told you."

"Tell me again."

"I cut it so that you would not be tongue-tied. Your tongue would be able to move in any language. You'll be able to speak languages that are completely different from one another. You'll be able to pronounce anything. Your frenum looked too tight to do those things, so I cut it."

"But isn't 'a ready tongue an evil'?"   8

"Things are different in this ghost country."

"Did it hurt me? Did I cry and bleed?"

"I don't remember. Probably."

She didn't cut the other children's. When I asked cousins and other   12
Chinese children whether their mothers had cut their tongues loose, they said, "What?"

"Why didn't you cut my brothers' and sisters' tongues?"

"They didn't need it."

"Why not? Were theirs longer than mine?"

"Why don't you quit blabbering and get to work?"   16

If my mother was not lying she should have cut more, scraped away the rest of the frenum skin, because I have a terrible time talking. Or she should not have cut at all, tampering with my speech. When I went to kindergarten and had to speak English for the first time, I became silent. A dumbness — a shame — still cracks my voice in two, even when I want to say "hello" casually, or ask an easy question in front of the check-out counter, or ask directions of a bus driver. I stand frozen, or I hold up the line with the complete, grammatical sentence that comes squeaking out at impossible length. "What did you say?" says the cab driver, or "Speak up," so I have to perform again, only weaker the second time. A telephone call makes my throat bleed and takes up that day's courage. It spoils my day with self-disgust when I hear my broken voice come skittering out into the open. It makes people wince to hear it. I'm getting better, though. Recently I asked the postman for special-issue stamps; I've waited since childhood for postmen to give me some of their own accord. I am making progress, a little every day.

My silence was thickest — total — during the three years that I covered my school paintings with black paint. I painted layers of black over houses and flowers and suns, and when I drew on the blackboard, I put a layer of chalk on top. I was making a stage curtain, and it was the moment before the curtain parted or rose. The teachers called my parents to school, and I saw they had been saving my pictures, curling and cracking, all alike and black. The teachers pointed to the pictures and looked serious, talked seriously too, but my parents did not understand English. ("The parents and teachers of criminals were executed," said my father.) My parents took the pictures home. I spread them out (so black and full of possibilities) and pretended the curtains were swinging open, flying up, one after another, sunlight underneath, mighty operas.

During the first silent year I spoke to no one at school, did not ask before going to the lavatory, and flunked kindergarten. My sister also said nothing for three years, silent in the playground and silent at lunch. There were other quiet Chinese girls not of our family, but most of them got over it sooner than we did. I enjoyed the silence. At first it did not occur to me I was supposed to talk or to pass kindergarten. I talked at home and to one or two of the Chinese kids in class. I made motions and even made some jokes. I drank out of a toy saucer when the water spilled out of the cup, and everybody laughed, pointing at me, so I did it some more. I didn't know that Americans don't drink out of saucers.

I liked the Negro students (Black Ghosts) best because they laughed 20 the loudest and talked to me as if I were a daring talker too. One of the Negro girls had her mother coil braids over her ears Shanghai-style like mine; we were Shanghai twins except that she was covered with black like my paintings. Two Negro kids enrolled in Chinese school, and the teachers gave them Chinese names. Some Negro kids walked me to school and home, protecting me from the Japanese kids, who hit me and chased me and stuck gum in my ears. The Japanese kids were noisy and tough. They appeared one day in kindergarten, released from concentration camp, which was a tic-tac-toe mark, like barbed wire, on the map.

It was when I found out I had to talk that school became a misery, that the silence came a misery. I did not speak and felt bad each time that I did not speak. I read aloud in first grade, though, and heard the barest whisper with little squeaks come out of my throat. "Louder," said the teacher, who scared the voice away again. The other Chinese girls did not talk either, so I knew the silence had to do with being a Chinese girl.

Reading out loud was easier than speaking because we did not have to make up what to say, but I stopped often, and the teacher would think I'd gone quiet again. I could not understand "I." The Chinese "I" has seven strokes, intricacies. How could the American "I," assuredly wearing a hat like the Chinese, have only three strokes, the middle so straight? Was it out of politeness that this writer left off strokes the way a Chinese has to write her own name small and crooked? No, it was not politeness; "I" is a capital and "you" is lowercase. I stared at that middle line and waited so long for its black center to resolve into tight strokes and dots that I forgot to pronounce it. The other troublesome word was "here," no strong consonant to hang on to, and so flat, when "here" is two mountainous ideographs. The teacher, who had already told me every day how to read "I" and "here," put me in the low corner under the stairs again, where the noisy boys usually sat.

When my second-grade class did a play, the whole class went to the auditorium except the Chinese girls. The teacher, lovely and Hawaiian, should have understood about us, but instead left us behind in the class-room. Our voices were too soft or nonexistent, and our parents never signed the permission slips anyway. They never signed anything unnec-essary. We opened the door a crack and peeked out, but closed it again quickly. One of us (not me) won every spelling bee, though.

I remember telling the Hawaiian teacher, "We Chinese can't sing   24 'land where our fathers died.' " She argued with me about politics, while I meant because of curses. But how can I have that memory when I couldn't talk? My mother says that we, like the ghosts, have no memories.

After American school, we picked up our cigar boxes, in which we had arranged books, brushes, and an inkbox neatly, and went to Chinese school, from 5:00 to 7:30 P.M. There we chanted together, voices rising and falling, loud and soft, some boys shouting, everybody reading to-gether, reciting together and not alone with one voice. When we had a memorization test, the teacher let each of us come to his desk and say the lesson to him privately, while the rest of the class practiced copying or tracing. Most of the teachers were men. The boys who were so well behaved in the American school played tricks on them and talked back to them. The girls were not mute. They screamed and yelled during recess, when there were no rules; they had fistfights. Nobody was afraid of children hurting themselves or of children hurting school property. The glass doors to the red and green balconies with the gold joy symbols were left wide open so that we could run out and climb the fire escapes. We played capture-the-flag in the auditorium, where Sun Yat-sen and Chiang Kai-shek's pictures hung at the back of the stage, the Chinese flag on their left and the American flag on their right. We climbed the teak ceremonial chairs and made flying leaps off the stage. One flag headquarters was behind the glass door and the other on stage right. Our feet drummed on the hollow stage. During recess the teachers locked themselves up in their office with the shelves of books, copybooks, inks from China. They drank tea and warmed their hands at a stove. There was no play supervision. At recess we had the school to ourselves, and also we could roam as far as we could go — downtown, Chinatown stores, home — as long as we returned before the bell rang.

At exactly 7:30 the teacher again picked up the brass bell that sat on his desk and swung it over our heads, while we charged down the stairs, our cheering magnified in the stairwell. Nobody had to line up.

Not all of the children who were silent at American school found voice at Chinese school. One new teacher said each of us had to get up and recite in front of the class, who was to listen. My sister and I had memorized the lesson perfectly. We said it to each other at home, one chanting, one listening. The teacher called on my sister to recite first. It was the first time a teacher had called on the second-born to go first.

My sister was scared. She glanced at me and looked away; I looked down at my desk. I hoped that she could do it because if she could, then I would have to. She opened her mouth and a voice came out that wasn't a whisper, but it wasn't a proper voice either. I hoped that she would not cry, fear breaking up her voice like twigs underfoot. She sounded as if she were trying to sing though weeping and strangling. She did not pause or stop to end the embarrassment. She kept going until she said the last word, and then she sat down. When it was my turn, the same voice came out, a crippled animal running on broken legs. You could hear splinters in my voice, bones rubbing jagged against one another. I was loud, though. I was glad I didn't whisper. There was one little girl who whispered.

From *New Immigrants: Portraits in Passage*
THOMAS BENTZ

WOOD CHUEN KWONG

"I wouldn't leave Chinatown, even if I were offered a job somewhere else," said Wood Chuen Kwong from his apartment in the heart of the world's largest Chinese community outside of Asia. This city is wonderfully textured with the Chinese sensibility. Graceful calligraphy blinks brilliantly from neon signs on banks, fish markets, and boutiques. The Chinese language is spoken at every turn and other aspects of Chinese culture are seen everywhere. Chinatown is like a haven between hemispheres, an oasis of the Orient firmly planted on our western shore. 1

"I wanted to stay in San Francisco for a year or two, to get acquainted, to get to know the people here. It is such a beautiful city and the weather is wonderful. But it is very difficult to find a job." For now, Wood and his son, Ching Yu, work as dishwashers and busboys, but they hope this is only temporary. Wood is a mechanical engineer and has an extensive background in electronics. 2

"In Canton, I was a radio repairman for thirty-two years in my spare time. The locally made radios and parts were easy to come by in China, and we always saved any extra parts. In America I see people who are so wasteful. They will throw out a radio if a single part breaks down. All these electric gadgets you have here are luxuries you don't need. We had to cook in China on a messy coal stove. It would be very helpful to have what you have here, the Japanese-made electric frying pans, rice cookers, and toasters. But there the people couldn't afford them even if they were available. Here you have useless electric razors and toothbrushes too. 3

"In Canton our whole family was allowed only 10 kilowatts of electricity each month. One 40-watt lightbulb and one 60-watt fan were all we could afford. All our work and reading had to be done by that one bulb. We also had one three-watt fluorescent lamp we could put in the socket for dim and minimal lighting. There was, of course, no air-con- 4 ditioning in our apartment, or anywhere else in Canton, even though the heat hit 90 degrees in the autumn and 100 degrees in the summer.

"Living in China, you have to learn how to fix almost anything and everything in your household. For others to fix what you have would take too long and cost too much. So I learned carpentry and began to make tables and chairs. If a leg on something broke, or our bed broke down, I had to fix it. Soon I had repaired a whole house. So did all the other workers that I knew who got about $40 a month for their normal labors.   5

"All the people were willing to help. If you needed to move something or paint a wall, you could just call on your friends and they would all come and give you a hand to do anything or go anywhere. And they didn't need to be paid." It is just this sort of cooperation between people that Wood finds to be lacking in the United States. Even though he and his wife, Foong Ying Dang, and their son, Ching Yu, and daughter, Ming Yu, feel relatively secure within the cultural haven of Chinatown, they know that they are now living in more threatening surroundings. Rival Chinese street gangs have been trying to assert their dominance, and their presence breeds fear in the new and old residents alike.   6

"I would not come home late at night, or go out of Chinatown," admitted Wood. "I have never had any trouble, but I don't feel safe. In China I knew everybody who lived on our block, but here, even people in the same building don't say hello. There may not be enough freedom in China but there is too much here. They have far less crime, very little theft or murder, because the offender in China is handled much more thoroughly and properly. Picking someone's pocket there would get you twenty days to three months in jail. Burglary draws at least two years, armed robbery is ten to twenty years. Murder is for life, with no probation. When the rule and punishment are straight and strong, then you can have restraint. There is no gambling in China because the people don't have the greed that makes them want to take what doesn't belong to them instead of earning it themselves."   7

Wood takes pride in being able to earn what his family needs though he has known disappointment along these lines and understands that fairness and justice are not always available to everyone. "For about eight years in the 1950s I took part in a Chinese government-promoted plan to provide housing, employment, and services. We put our money in the bank, and with the interest the government built homes and left the principal in the bank for future investment. No one person in China could build or afford to buy a house. So the money made some housing available. And each new year we drew lots and several people won the houses. The Cultural Revolution wiped this out before I could win my house. But you know, if the savings and loans in San Francisco would follow that scheme, there would be lots of investors and we could both build houses and provide employment for people in the process."   8

Wood can see that there is good and bad in both countries. He knows that China could certainly use some American technology and suspects that the U.S. would do well to have more of the will and spirit that the   9

Chinese worker has. "Opening trade has been and will continue to be beneficial to both the U.S. and China. If China doesn't look to the U.S. for technical progress it will never catch up to the new and better ways that the world can work. And if the U.S. doesn't meet the real spirit of the Chinese people, it will never get out of its old red-devil fear. We are different, but each of us has good points and weaknesses. If we come together we can learn to complement each other."

"I just finished a manpower training program in the Chinatown Re- 10
sources Development Center and I have already had several interviews for jobs. I've just applied and taken a written examination in English for a government position that I have high hopes for. It is a civil service mechanical technician at $800 a month."

In Canton he made much less money, $113 a month, but his expenses 11
were much less too. His food cost about $10 a month and his rent, for a three-bedroom apartment, was $13.49 a month. He was not dissatisfied with his life there and though he applied for a visa to come here for six years, he only wanted to visit and to see his parents. However the Chinese government refused his requests. Finally his father's influence made the difference.

"My father had studied at Ohio State University before spending his 12
life teaching, first in Canton and then from 1946 to 1968 in Hong Kong. In 1952 one of my sisters and her husband came to the United States. In 1968, my parents followed after my sister's petition for reunification was accepted. None of the rest of us seven children could come out of China with them then.

"In 1979 my father petitioned for me to come out because of the 13
special case of his illness. He was also a commissioner on the housing authority in San Francisco, so through his connections, my case was expedited. I was able to come and be with him before he died. It had been so difficult to get out of China just for a visit that I decided that once I came here I would want to stay. I am now a permanent resident alien. I think I'll decide after five years whether I want to become a U.S. citizen."

Meanwhile one of his sisters has no such choice. She is now a 14
permanent resident alien in a country she doesn't want to be in. She came out of China to Hong Kong at the same time that Wood flew to San Francisco to be with his father. "Father also petitioned for Kin. But when she came out of China in June of 1979, a lot of other people were going to Hong Kong to be processed for America. So the U.S. consulate just listed people in the order of the requests for immigration. She was put way back on the list. When our father died, so did his petition for Kin. The case was closed. Now she cannot come to America nor can she go back to China.

"Kin was a doctor in China, but she can't get recognized in Hong 15
Kong, so she works as an aide in a school for the blind. Her husband was an X-ray specialist in China, but he can't find a job in Hong Kong. They have a very difficult life now. I don't know who is to blame. I often write to her and send money to help. I don't know what else to do."

10. An Art Option: Surrealism

In the following excerpts, written in 1924, the Frenchman André Breton defines and elaborates what he means by *surrealism*. Breton first used the term to describe a kind of automatic poetry writing by which a poet abandons rational control of his writing and opens up to images provided unconsciously. By extension, the term has been applied to other art forms in which the artist uses this method to bring together startling juxtapositions of images.

The first surrealists, who were heavily influenced by Freud's beliefs about the unconscious, tried to exploit the material of dreams, hallucinations, and semiwaking states. They saw themselves very much in revolt against the social and artistic standards of their time, particularly against the idea that the best art was created by "reasonable" means. For example, Breton quotes the line "Day unfolded like a white tablecloth" and declares that it cannot have been premeditated. Such an image is created out of two terms too dissimilar to have been intentionally composed. The artist's role is simply to be receptive to the surprising combinations brought together unconsciously.

Accompanying the excerpts from Breton's work are copies of works of art by two surrealist artists. The first is a painting by the Spanish artist Salvador Dali (1904–1989), the second a collage composed by the French-German artist Max Ernst (1891–1976). This collage is one of a series of such images that make up Ernst's "novel" *Une Semaine de Bonté* ("A Week of Kindness"), published in 1934.

From the perspective offered by Breton, write an analytical essay about one or both of the works of art.

From *Manifesto of Surrealism*
ANDRÉ BRETON

I believe in the future resolution of these two states, dream and reality, which are seemingly so contradictory, into a kind of absolute reality, a *surreality*, if one may so speak. . . .   1

Let us not mince words: the marvelous is always beautiful, anything marvelous is beautiful, in fact only the marvelous is beautiful. . . .   2

Surrealism is based on the belief in the superior reality of certain forms of previously neglected associations, in the omnipotence of dream, in the disinterested play of thought. . . .   3

It is true of Surrealist images as it is of opium images that man does not evoke them; rather [as Baudelaire said] they "come to him spontaneously, despotically. He cannot chase them away; for the will is   4

Above: Salvador Dali.
Illumined Pleasures.
1929. Oil and collage
on composition board,
9⅜ × 13¾″.
Collection, The
Museum of Modern
Art, New York. The
Sidney and Harriet
Janis Collection.
Right: Max Ernst.
Une Semaine de Bonté
from *Dimanche.*
Editions Jeanne
Bucher, Paris, 1934.

powerless now and no longer controls the faculties." It remains to be seen whether images have ever been "evoked." . . .

In my opinion, it is erroneous to claim that "the mind has grasped   5 the relationship" of two realities in the presence of each other. First of all, it has seized nothing consciously. It is, as it were, from the fortuitous juxtaposition of the two terms that a particular light has sprung, *the light of the image,* to which we are infinitely sensitive. . . . Now, it is not within man's power, so far as I can tell, to effect the juxtaposition of two realities so far apart. . . . We are therefore obliged to admit that the two terms of the image are not deduced one from the other . . . for the specific purpose of producing the spark, that they are the simultaneous products of the activity I call Surrealist, reason's role being limited to taking note of, and appreciating, the luminous phenomenon. . . .

The mind which plunges into Surrealism relives with glowing excite-   6 ment the best part of its childhood. . . . From childhood memories, and from a few others, there emanates a sentiment of being unintegrated, and then later of *having gone astray,* which I hold to be the most fertile that exists. It is perhaps childhood that comes closest to one's "real life." . . . Thanks to Surrealism, it seems that opportunity knocks a second time. It is as though we were still running toward our salvation, or our perdition. In the shadow we again see a precious terror. Thank God, it's still only Purgatory. With a shudder, we cross what the occultists call *dangerous territory.* In my wake I raise up monsters that are lying in wait; they are not yet too ill-disposed toward me, and I am not lost, since I fear them. Here are "the elephants with the heads of women and the flying lions" which used to make Soupault [another surrealist] and me tremble in our boots to meet, here is the "soluble fish" which still frightens me slightly.

11. A Social Science Option: The Early Days of Punk Rock in the United States

The first account here describes the punk rock scene during the early 1980s. Following that reading are excerpts from the works of several social theorists. Sigmund Freud (1856–1939) was the founder of psychoanalysis. *Frustration and Aggression* by John Dollard (1900–1980) has been a standard in the field of social psychology. Sociologist David Riesman (b. 1909) wrote the influential book *The Lonely Crowd* (1950), which established "other-directedness" as a popular term for describing contemporary behavior. Socio-biologist Konrad Lorenz (1903–1989) did research with animals that he later extended to a theory about human aggression (*On Aggression,* 1963). R. D. Laing (1927–1989), a controversial Scottish psychiatrist, wrote about the relation of madness to social life. One of his best-known works is *The Politics of Experience* (1967), which was popular and influential in the late 1960s and early 1970s.

After considering the perspectives of these theorists, write an essay analyzing the punk rock movement.

Violence Sneaks into Punk Scene
PATRICK GOLDSTEIN

Holding one of his front teeth in his hands, Eric, 10, stands on the sidewalk in front of the Roxy, surveying the throngs of clubgoers along the Sunset Strip. He's from Sherman Oaks and it's only his second pilgrimage to the late-night rock mecca. 1

Eric grins, wiping a smudge of blood from his chin. "We were all jumping on top of this guy when someone hit me from behind," he says, gingerly tugging at his other front tooth. "I got flipped upside down and hit my chin on the floor." 2

He wipes some more blood off his lip. "It didn't really hurt much after a while." 3

Most 10-year-olds lose their front teeth playing ball. Eric got his knocked out at the Roxy, dancing to the music of 999, a raucous British punk band whose most popular song is called "Homicide." 4

The followers of punk acts like 999 — most of whom are a little older than Eric — don't just dance anymore. They mug each other. 5

It's part of a new "dance" craze called the Slam, whose popularity, especially with organized gangs of punk youths, has led to numerous incidents of violence at many area clubs. 6

The accounts of senseless violence, vandalism and even mutilation at some area rock clubs read like reports from a war zone. 7

— Lynda Nichols, a 23-year-old Hollywood receptionist, was knifed in the back at a recent show by the group called X at the Whisky. "I was standing up close to the stage to watch the band when I felt this weird pressure in my back," she said. "I put my hand back there and it was covered with blood." She was treated by paramedics for a five-inch knife wound and has been out of work for almost a month. 8

— The lead singer of the Diodes, a new-wave band from Canada, was attacked by a member of the audience at the Hong Kong Cafe recently after a spitting contest between the audience and the group got out of hand. "Our bouncers had to pull the guy off him," said club booker Kim Turner, who said there were several other fights in the audience that night. Later that evening, punk fans broke several windows and littered the square in front of the club with broken beer bottles. 9

— A bouncer for one area rock club stopped one young fan at the door who was carrying a buckskin-sheathed hunting knife. "I asked him to leave it at the door and pick it up on his way out." 10

— Several eyewitnesses reported recently that a group of young punks got into a shouting match with motorists driving by a Sunset Strip rock club. After exchanging obscenities, the punks began lobbing beer bottles into an open convertible, showering the occupants with broken glass. 11

— Two girls in an Orange County punk band called Sexual Frustration   12
pleaded with the manager of the Hong Kong Cafe one night to book their
band into the club. "While one was talking to me, the other went into
the girls' room and broke a bunch of beer bottles in the sink and ran her
hands through the glass. Then she came out to talk to me, blood streaming
down her arms."

— Several girls reported a similar occurrence in the bathroom at an   13
X date at the Whisky where a couple of girls carved X's into their arms
with broken glass.

While most club-owners agree that only a small minority of punk fans   14
actively incite violence, several area clubs have banned bands like the
Germs, the Circle Jerks and Black Flag, whose followers provoke the
most trouble. Hong Kong Cafe manager Turner now has blacklisted more
than half a dozen groups, mostly Orange County–based punkers like
AgentOrange, Middle Class and Eddie and the Sub-titles.

"No one's saying these groups encourage violence," he conceded,   15
"but they do attract it and they do tolerate it. We're just not going to
put up with vandals who have no respect for people or property."

Other club managers and regular clubgoers blamed the violence on   16
organized Huntington Beach–area punk gangs who make a practice of
pummeling each other and Slam dancing at area clubs.

"What happens is they end up knocking down someone's girlfriend   17
and he gets upset and starts a fight," explained Rod Firestone, singer
for the Rubber City Rebels. "They don't care about the bands at all.
They just hog all the attention and distract people who want to see the
group."

According to Firestone, it's the novice punks, not veterans of the   18
scene, who provoke the most trouble. "It's these beach kids who missed
out on the punk era and don't know it's passé now," he said. "They just
want to come out and throw beer bottles and get their licks in. I wish
they'd go start their own teen club where they could beat each other
up."

Other local bands were not so critical. "I don't want to see somebody   19
stabbed out there," said Lee Ving of Fear, "but I want to make sure
there's lots of action. That's our aim — to get people riled up. It's much
better than them just sitting on their hands."

The Germs, an area band that has been periodically banned from   20
many local clubs for attracting rowdy followers, also sympathized with
the young punk dancers. "It doesn't bother me. It's always been like that
at our shows," Pat Smear admitted, saying that Germs singer Darby
Crash has been hospitalized "lots of times" after savage audience
skirmishes.

Claiming that he's been beaten up by bouncers at his own show,   21
Smear said he didn't care if his fans beat each other up. "If they're doing
that, then I know they're having fun."

However, even Rodney Bingenheimer, an indefatigable supporter of   22
the punk scene who hosts a twice-weekly disco at the Starwood, admits
the antics of many punk fans have gotten out of hand. "It's getting worse
now that kids are out of school," he said. "Kids complain to me that they

can't even see the bands anymore. It's just too rough sometimes — a lot of young girls get hurt at these shows."

Lynda Nichols, who was stabbed at the X show, wholeheartedly agrees, complaining about lax security at area clubs. "They hassle me about wearing a belt with spikes," she said, "but kids can obviously get in with knives. I used to think the worst that could happen at these shows was a gigantic bruise or something. I never figured on getting stabbed." 23

"It's not much fun going to see a band if you have to fear for your life." 24

Visitors to local clubs featuring punk bands like the Germs, Fear, the Weirdos and Black Flag often are treated to the sight of dozens of fans hurtling across the dance floor like kamikaze pilots taking aim on an aircraft carrier. Other audience members dance in a loose circle around the action, either taking a spill themselves or throwing the most avid celebrants back into the fray. 25

Unlike previous dances, the Slam is neither elegant nor erotic. You don't twirl, twist or bump your partner. The object is to knock each other down. 26

"It's no wonder there's so many fights," said Kara, a young punk fan from Hollywood. "We were at a Weirdos show a few weeks ago and these idiots kept punching us in the back. Finally I got fed up and started hitting these guys, even though they were bigger than me." 27

The mindless ferocity of this Slam dancing bothers longtime L.A. punk enthusiasts who view the younger, beach-area punks as outside agitators bent on destroying the local punk community. 28

"Sure there was violence in the Masque days," said one longtime scene maker, referring to the city's first punk stronghold, "but it was more like play-acting violence, like guerrilla theater. The older punk audience was a family of writers, artists and college kids — people who cared about the music. Now we get these crazy, pathetic jerks who just want some cheap new thrill." 29

Though L.A. area club owners sympathize with these complaints, they offered few solutions to the recent wave of random violence. "There's nothing much we can really do," admitted Gaylord, who books the Whisky. "It's not the same person every time. Even the most normal-looking kid can cause trouble. 30

"We really haven't hired any extra security. We just eyeball the kids when they come in and now we serve paper cups so no one gets a bottle thrown at them." 31

According to David Forest, manager of the Starwood, the club frequently shakes down patrons for crowbars and weapons, as well as refusing admittance to any kids wearing "Gestapo-style" spikes, heavy gloves and boots. The club also now refuses to allow bands to invite kids up on stage, where they often dive back into the audience. 32

"We have security guys keeping a close eye on what goes on," Forest said. "If some prankster gets out of hand and starts clobbering people, trying to injure somebody, then we eject them immediately. But most of this wild stuff is just good fun. It's not violence, because we don't allow violence." 33

Most observers agree that eventually the bands themselves will have to initiate any serious crackdowns on this rising tide of violence and vandalism. "After all, it's their fans," said one club manager. "If the bands don't speak out or make some show of contempt, the kids can only assume they fully approve of all this crap." 34

Unfortunately, all too many disgruntled punk fans want to take matters in their own hands. "It's gotten to the point where you can't even watch the stage anymore because of these idiots," one fan said after a recent Fear show. "All they want to do is fight. And next time I'm gonna be ready to give 'em one." 35

PERSPECTIVES

The bit of truth behind all this — one so eagerly denied — is that men are not gentle, friendly creatures wishing for love, who simply defend themselves if they are attacked, but that a powerful measure of desire for aggression has to be reckoned as part of their instinctual endowment. The result is that their neighbor is to them not only a possible helper or sexual object, but also a temptation to them to gratify their aggressiveness on him, to exploit his capacity for work without recompense, to use him sexually without his consent, to seize his possessions, to humiliate him, to cause him pain, to torture and to kill him. *Homo homini lupus;*° who has the courage to dispute it in the face of all the evidence in his own life and in history? This aggressive cruelty usually lies in wait for some provocation, or else it steps into the service of some other purpose, the aim of which might as well have been achieved by milder measures. In circumstances that favor it, when those forces in the mind which ordinarily inhibit it cease to operate, it also manifests itself spontaneously and reveals men as savage beasts to whom the thought of sparing their own kind is alien.

— Sigmund Freud, *Civilization and Its Discontents*

In American society the process of becoming mature involves the inhibition and redirection of behavior resulting from several sources of instigation, and the predominant behavior symptoms of adolescence are aggression against the frustrating forces and substitute responses for those goal-responses which suffer interference.

— John Dollard et al., *Frustration and Aggression*

In the smaller families of urban life, and with the spread of "permissive" child care to ever wider strata of the population, there is a relaxation of older patterns of discipline. Under these newer patterns the peer-group (the age- and class-graded group in a child's school and neighborhood) becomes much more important to the child, while the parents make him feel guilty not so much about violation of inner standards as 1

Homo homini lupus: From the Latin, "man's inhumanity to man"; literally, "man is a wolf to man."

about failure to be popular or otherwise to manage his relations with these other children. Moreover, the pressures of the school and the peer-group are reinforced and continued . . . by the mass media: movies, radio, comics, and popular culture media generally. Under these conditions types of character emerge that we shall here term other-directed. To them much of the discussion in the ensuing chapters is devoted. *What is common to all other-directed is that their contemporaries are the source of direction for the individual — either those known to him or those with whom he is indirectly acquainted, through friends and through the mass media. This source is of course "internalized" in the sense that dependence on it for guidance in life is implanted early. The goals toward which the other-directed person strives shift with that guidance; it is only the process of striving itself and the process of paying close attention to the signals from others that remain unaltered throughout life.* This mode of keeping in touch with others permits a close behavioral conformity, not through drill in behavior itself, as in the tradition-directed character, but rather through an exceptional sensitivity to the actions and wishes of others.

Of course, it matters very much who these "others" are: whether   2
they are the individual's immediate circle or a "higher" circle or the anonymous voices of the mass media; whether the individual fears the hostility of chance acquaintances or only of those who "count." But his need for approval and direction from others — and contemporary others rather than ancestors — goes beyond the reasons that lead most people in any era to care very much what others think of them. While all people want and need to be liked by some of the people some of the time, it is only the modern other-directed types who make this their chief source of direction and chief area of sensitivity.

— David Riesman, *The Lonely Crowd*

The increase in number of individuals belonging to the same com-   1
munity is in itself sufficient to upset the balance between the personal bonds and the aggressive drive. It is definitely detrimental to the bond of friendship if a person has too many friends. It is proverbial that one can have only a few really close friends. To have a large number of "acquaintances," many of whom may be faithful allies with a legitimate claim to be regarded as real friends, overtaxes a man's capacity for personal love and dilutes the intensity of his emotional attachment. The close crowding of many individuals in a small space brings about a fatigue of all social reactions. Every inhabitant of a modern city is familiar with the surfeit of social relationships and responsibilities and knows the disturbing feeling of not being as pleased as he ought to be at the visit of a friend, even if he is genuinely fond of him and has not seen him for a long time. A tendency to bad temper is experienced when the telephone rings after dinner. That crowding increases the propensity to aggressive behavior has long been known and demonstrated experimentally by sociological research.

On the other hand, there is, in the modern community, no legitimate   2
outlet for aggressive behavior. To keep the peace is the first of civic duties, and the hostile neighboring tribe, once the target at which to

discharge phylogenetically programmed aggression, has now withdrawn to an ideal distance, hidden behind a curtain, if possible of iron. Among the many phylogenetically adapted norms of human social behavior, there is hardly one that does not need to be controlled and kept on a leash by responsible morality.

— Konrad Lorenz, *On Aggression*

The condition of alienation, of being asleep, of being unconscious, of being out of one's mind, is the condition of the normal man.   1

Society highly values its normal man. It educates children to lose themselves and to become absurd, and thus to be normal.   2

Normal men have killed perhaps 100,000,000 of their fellow normal men in the last fifty years.   3

Our behavior is a function of our experience. We act according to the way we see things.   4

If our experience is destroyed, our behavior will be destructive. . . .   5

Personal action can either open out possibilities of enriched experience or it can shut off possibilities. Personal action is either predominantly validating, confirming, encouraging, supportive, enhancing, or it is invalidating, denying, discouraging, undermining and constricting. It can be creative or destructive.   6

In a world where the normal condition is one of alienation, most personal action must be destructive both of one's own experience and of that of the other.   7

— R. D. Laing, *The Politics of Experience*

12. A Health Science Option: Nutrition Statistics

Table 3 (p. 348), Table 4 (p. 349), and Figure 1 (p. 350) present worldwide and national statistics bearing on diet and nutrition. Consider some of the implications of these statistics — social, economic, and political. Then consider the perspectives of the health and nutrition commentators. Write an essay analyzing U.S. diets in a worldwide context.

In a postscript or perhaps an alternative essay, you might write about any problems or frustrations you encounter with this assignment. What limitations did you find in the data or the commentary? What else would you like to know? What further questions can you raise?

PERSPECTIVE 1

At this Bicentennial Conference, which observes the beginning of American political independence, we would like to draw your attention to the bicentennial of another event which significantly influenced the way in which the food industry has been able to affect American nutrition during these past 200 years. We refer, of course, to the publication of *The Wealth of Nations*, in which Adam Smith defined the basic laissez-faire capitalist economic system. This is essentially the same system under which the American food industry operates today. His classic analysis of the processes of the marketplace, and his observations concerning   1

TABLE 3.   World Daily Dietary Energy Supply in Relation to Requirements

REGION	DIETARY ENERGY[1]				SUPPLY AS PERCENT OF REQUIREMENT[2]			
	1966–68	1969–71	1972–74	1975–77	1966–68	1969–71	1972–74	1975–77
Developing market economies	2,122	2,206	2,193	2,219	81	85	84	85
Africa	2,136	2,194	2,174	2,206	82	84	84	85
Latin America	2,511	2,531	2,518	2,552	97	97	97	96
Near East	2,413	2,431	2,498	2,657	93	94	96	102
Far East	1,959	2,079	2,053	2,053	75	80	80	80
Others	2,268	2,326	2,371	2,345	87	89	91	90
Asian centrally planned economies	2,087	2,224	2,317	2,420	80	86	89	93
Total developing countries	2,110	2,211	2,233	2,282	81	85	86	88
Developed market economies	3,200	3,275	3,323	3,329	123	126	128	128
North America	3,384	3,467	3,493	3,519	130	133	134	135
Western Europe	3,256	3,333	3,389	3,378	125	128	130	130
Oceania	3,288	3,360	3,365	3,418	126	129	129	131
Others	2,701	2,769	2,852	2,872	104	107	110	110
Eastern Europe and the U.S.S.R.	3,300	3,379	3,413	3,465	127	130	131	133
Total developed countries	3,232	3,308	3,353	3,373	124	127	129	130
World	2,457	2,541	2,500	2,580	95	96	98	90

[1] Calories per capita per day.
[2] Daily calorie requirement is 3,000 for men, 2,200 for women.
SOURCE: UN Food and Agriculture Organization. From *The World Almanac & Book of Facts*, 1984 edition. Copyright © Newspaper Enterprise Association, Inc. 1983, New York, NY 10166.

TABLE 4.   What's in Fast Foods?

ITEM	CALORIES	PROTEIN (g)	CARBO-HYDRATES (g)	FATS (g)	SODIUM (mg)
McDonald's Big Mac	541	26	39	31	962
Burger King Whopper	606	29	51	32	909
Burger Chef Hamburger	258	11	24	13	393
Dairy Queen Cheese Dog	330	15	24	19	N.A.[1]
Taco Bell Taco	186	15	14	8	79
Pizza Hut Thin 'N Crispy Cheese Pizza (½ of 10-inch pie)	450	25	54	15	N.A.[1]
Pizza Hut Thick 'N Chewy Pepperoni Pizza (½ of 10-inch pie)	560	31	68	18	N.A.[1]
Arthur Treacher's Fish Sandwich	440	16	39	24	836
Burger King Whaler	486	18	64	46	735
McDonald's Filet-O-Fish	402	15	34	23	709
Long John Silver's Fish (2 pieces)	318	19	19	19	N.A.[1]
Kentucky Fried Chicken Original Recipe Dinner	830	52	56	46	2,285
Kentucky Fried Chicken Extra Crispy Dinner (3 pieces chicken)	950	52	63	54	1,915
McDonald's Egg McMuffin	352	18	26	20	914
Burger King French Fries	214	3	28	10	5
Arthur Treacher's Coleslaw	123	1	11	8	266
Dairy Queen Onion Rings	300	6	33	17	N.A.[1]
McDonald's Apple Pie	300	2	31	19	414
Burger King Vanilla Shake	332	11	50	11	159
McDonald's Chocolate Shake	364	11	60	9	329
Dairy Queen Banana Split	540	10	91	15	N.A.[1]

[1] N.A. = not available.
SOURCE: Data supplied by the companies to the Senate Select Committee on Nutrition and Human Needs.

the conditions under which companies produce and sell goods and services are, in many respects, as valid today as they were in 1776. . . .

In effect, the relationship works as follows: On one hand is the scientific and academic community telling consumers what they *should* eat; on the other are the consumers telling one and all what they *want* to eat. In between is the food industry, trying to satisfy both groups and itself as well. . . .

The very system by which food is gathered, prepared, and distributed to consumers throughout the United States and other developed nations, by any standard a major achievement, is fueled by profit. Thus, profit is an integral aspect of the food industry's ability to improve public nutrition.

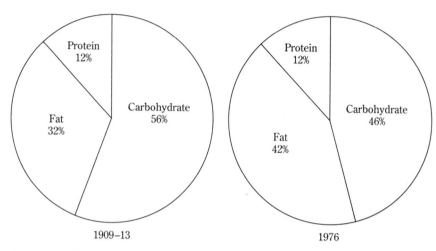

FIGURE 1.   Where Our Calories Come From
SOURCE: *1978 Handbook of Agriculture Charts*, USDA, Agriculture Handbook No. 551, p. 56.

I believe that the providing of a wide range of products within the   4
framework of free competitive enterprise is an essential feature of efforts
to improve nutrition. This process is further enhanced by the feedback
which consumers continually provide to industry through their purchases.
— William O. Beers and John F. White, Kraft Inc.,"Contributions of
American Industry to the Improvement of American Nutrition"

PERSPECTIVE 2

In the course of this century, an imbalance has crept into the American   1
diet. Since the early 1900s, the percentage of our diet derived from
carbohydrates has dropped, and the proportion of fat has risen dramatically. . . .

Another unhealthful change relates to the *kinds* of carbohydrates in   2
the American diet. . . . At the turn of the century, most of our carbohydrates were the *complex starches* in nutrient-rich grains and beans and
the *natural simple sugars* in fruits and vegetables. Today a major portion
of carbohydrates in the American diet comes from *refined and processed
sugars* often found in relatively nutrient-deficient and high-calorie foods.
. . . This emphasis on "sweets" has been linked to a number of health
problems, especially tooth decay and obesity.

Part of the problem is that there's no powerful, profit-making industry   3
selling Americans on natural forms of complex carbohydrates at every
commercial break on radio and TV. The growers of fruits, vegetables,
grains, and potatoes are hard put to compete with the meat, dairy, and
processed-foods industries for the consumer's attention.

The fall-off in consumption has been particularly dramatic for flour   4
and cereal products. Today Americans typically consume half the amount
of these foods their counterparts ate in 1910. . . . At that time, flour

(used in bread and pasta) and cereals were America's *chief* sources of protein, supplying 36 percent of the day's protein. Today they account for only 17 percent of protein consumed, having been replaced by fattier sources of protein, primarily meats.

— Jane E. Brody, *Jane Brody's Nutrition Book*

PERSPECTIVE 3

Coronary atherosclerosis is the number-one health problem in the United States, with one million Americans killed or permanently disabled every year. In many ways it must be considered a "disease of civilization" brought about in part by our mode of life: a diet overabundant in calories derived from saturated fat (and sucrose) and too high in cholesterol, an almost total lack of physical activity, and heavy cigarette smoking. These have created conditions new to the human race. The United States is particularly hard hit by this new pandemic. . . .   1

We need to modify our national diet to cut drastically our intake of saturated fat and cholesterol, particularly for middle-aged men; [and we need] to cut down the unnecessary calories in our diet. . . .   2

Following the recommendation of the Inter-Society Commission, the food industry should be encouraged by the health professions and the government . . . to make available leaner meats and processed meats, . . . dairy products, and baked goods reduced in saturated fats, cholesterol, and calories. . . .   3

Meat products should be manufactured so as to be as high in protein and as low in fat and cholesterol as possible.   4

— Jean Mayer, *U.S. Nutrition Policies in the Seventies*

13. A History of Science Option: Scientific Fraud and the Case of Cyril Burt

Cyril Burt (1883–1971) was a highly influential British psychologist whose IQ studies, based on research with twins, were once thought authoritative but have now come under severe criticism. The first reading is an account of the controversy written for *Science* in 1976.

Following that reading are three critical commentaries on Burt.

Suspicion Beclouds Classic Experiment
NICHOLAS WADE

Charges of scientific fraud, as yet unproved, have been made against an eminent English psychologist, the late Cyril Burt, whose work has featured prominently in the debate about racial differences and intelligence.   1

Burt is accused by his critics of having doctored or even invented his extensive and partly unique collection of IQ test data in order to support his theory that intelligence is determined primarily by heredity.   2

Should the accusation prove true, the forgery may rank with that of   3 the Piltdown Man in that for years it remained undetected while occupying a pivotal place in a fierce scientific controversy. . . .

As a government adviser in the 1930s and 1940s, [Burt] was influential in setting up the three-tier system of British education. In accordance with Burt's views that intelligence is largely innate, children were irredeemably assigned to one of the three educational levels on the basis of a test given at the age of 11.

Burt's conclusions have been under suspicion for several years because of internal inconsistencies in his data. What has sparked off accusations of outright fraud is an article in the London *Sunday Times* of 24 October. The newspaper's medical correspondent, Oliver Gillie, reported his failure to find any evidence that Burt's two chief coauthors on his later papers, Miss Margaret Howard and Miss J. Conway, had ever existed.

Gillie could find no sign of Howard or Conway in the records of London University, the address given on their scientific papers, and none of 18 acquaintances of Burt could remember having ever met or heard of them. "It must be considered a possibility," Gillie concluded, "that Margaret Howard and J. Conway never existed, but were the fantasy of an aging professor who became increasingly lonely and deaf." Burt died in 1971 at the age of 88, having retired from the chair of psychology at University College, London, some 20 years earlier.

For those who were in any case skeptical of the notable fit between Burt's data and his theories, the failure to trace his collaborators has come as clinching evidence of fraud. Leon Kamin of Princeton University says of Burt's work, "It was a fraud linked to policy from the word go. The data were cooked in order for him to arrive at the conclusions he wanted." On the other side of the Atlantic Liam Hudson, professor of psychology at Edinburgh University, considers that the inconsistencies in Burt's data and the difficulty in tracking down his coauthors put the question of Burt's fraudulence "beyond argument." . . .

Burt's continuing importance has been due to the still unrivaled collection of data on heredity and IQ which he gathered as research psychologist to the London school system from 1913 to 1932, and later as professor of psychology at University College, London. Burt's data were cited by Jensen in his furiously debated *Harvard Educational Review* article of 1969. The article suggested that the large genetic component of intelligence might underlie racial differences in IQ scores and hence the failure of compensatory education programs addressed to minorities. . . .

[One of Burt's first critics] was Kamin, a psychologist who specializes in the conditioned reflex and who had never ventured into the IQ field until 1972 when a student urged him to read one of Burt's papers. "The immediate conclusion I came to after 10 minutes of reading was that Burt was a fraud," he says. Being an outsider to the field, Kamin spotted what no one inside had seen, that Burt's results are riddled with internal implausibilities and basic methodological oversights.

For example, the pearl of Burt's data collection is a survey of separated identical twins. Since the twins have the same genes, any difference in their intelligence should be due to environment alone, so that the correlation of their IQ scores in theory gives a pure measure of the influence of heredity on intelligence. This is a classical experiment in psychology, but one that is not often done because of the rarity of separated identical twins.

Burt published the first full report of his twins in 1955, when he had located 21 pairs, a second report in 1958 when the collection amounted to "over 30" pairs, and a final report in 1966 with 53 pairs. What Kamin noticed was that the correlation between the IQ scores of the separated twins was given as 0.771 for all three studies. For the correlation to remain unchanged through different sample sizes is improbable even at one occurrence, but the IQ correlation between identical twins reared together sticks at 0.944 through three different sample sizes, and there are many other such examples. For whatever reason, there is a strange imperturbability in the results Burt obtains from a changing data base.

Kamin also noticed that Burt often failed to record facts quite basic to the methodology of his surveys, such as the sexes of the children, the age at which they were tested, or even what particular test was applied. "The numbers left behind by Professor Burt," Kamin concluded in a lecture given in 1973, "are simply not worthy of serious scientific attention." . . .

Are the errors in Burt's papers the results of a deliberate attempt to deceive, or simply the inattention to detail of an elderly and ailing man? Burt is not around to defend himself, but [some] believe that there are innocent explanations of what happened. Kamin, on the other hand, has come to suspect that Burt consistently invented data from his very first work published in 1909. . . .

Most of Burt's data on IQ and kinship correlations were published after his retirement in 1950. According to Leslie Hearnshaw of Liverpool University, who is preparing a biography, Burt was hard up during this time and had to do a lot of hack work to make ends meet. He was suffering from a form of deafness known as Ménière's disease which made it hard for him to communicate. He wrote several papers on psychical research, in which he had long been interested. Philip Vernon, a collaborator of Burt's who is now at the University of Calgary, Alberta, says of Burt's state of mind that he was always a bit paranoiac. "He would train students brilliantly but once they turned against him he would turn on them with a vengeance. He was very helpful if one was with him, as long as one did not criticize the theories he built up in the 1910s and 1920s. Unfortunately, he never changed his theories."

Old, ailing, embattled in numerous controversies, it is quite possible that Burt was simply careless with his data and neglectful of accuracy. [Heredity researcher Arthur] Jensen, for example, says that though he can't offer any explanation for the errors, "they seem to be too haphazard and not planned. If Burt was trying to fake the data a person with his statistical skills would have done a better job."

[Hans] Eysenck's suggestion, somewhat more damaging to Burt, is that to avoid the chore of recalculating the correlations with the new data, Burt simply carried over the correlation figures from his earlier papers. Though quite inadmissible as a scientific procedure, a shortcut of this nature would fall a long way short of fraud since not done with intent to deceive.

A similar explanation is proposed by G. C. Drew, present occupant   17
of Burt's chair of psychology. "As he got old he was remembering old figures that stuck in his mind from earlier papers." But Drew still sees the affair as purely a matter of carelessness. "Burt was totally convinced of the rightness of his views and he became exceedingly careless with the data," he says.

Such evidence as suggests that Burt might have been inventing data   18
revolves chiefly around Burt's two collaborators, Miss Margaret Howard and Miss J. Conway. The failure of the London *Sunday Times* to find them or anyone who knew them is provocative but not conclusive. Indeed the paper has since reported the account of a Manchester University professor who knew Howard at least in the late 1930s: "She used to wear tinted glasses and a dark blouse with a ribbon. She had a lovely smile," the professor remembers.

Even if Howard and Conway existed once, there is another reason   19
for doubting their reported collaboration with Burt in his crucial papers of the late 1950s. Howard and Conway appear frequently during this period as the authors of book reviews in the journal that Burt edited, the *British Journal of Statistical Psychology*. The style of the reviews is similar to Burt's own highly distinctive style. It is of course possible that the similarity reflects Burt's hand as editor, not as author. But the reviews struck people even at the time as being Burt's work. Vernon, for example, says he had long suspected that Burt used pseudonyms for the book reviews, an act that he describes as "silly but not particularly heinous." . . .

Reading Burt's final paper on the twin survey in the light of such   20
suspicions, it is hard not to be struck by the patness with which crucial, yet hitherto unpublished, data are adduced to demolish each of his critics' arguments. The paper appeared in the *British Journal of Psychology* in 1966, when Burt was 83. The number of separated identical twin pairs had grown from "over 30" in 1958 to 53, making the study by far the largest of its kind. But the study was now revealed to possess a feature that made it even more unique and authoritative. The anti-hereditarians had been claiming that the high IQ correlations found between separated twins might have a lot to do with a correlation between their environments. This was a plausible argument — and one that is true of all the other twin studies — because adopted children are indeed usually placed in homes similar to their own. Though it was not mentioned in the earlier reports of 1955 and 1958, the 1966 paper now reveals the remarkable fact that the homes of Burt's twin pairs, as judged by the occupational categories of the parents and foster parents, are entirely uncorrelated. (The correlation, though Burt gives only the raw figures, is -0.4.) "These figures," Burt then proceeds to observe, "should dispose of one of the commonest explanations advanced by thoroughgoing environmentalists — namely, that the high correlations for the separated twins is due to the way the foster-parents were chosen."

Burt's figures were unlikely enough to have prompted an inquiry from   21 at least one psychologist. Sandra Scarr-Salapatek of the University of California wrote in 1970 asking Burt for more information because the data "looked funny" to her. And Vernon says he thought at the time that the result was highly unlikely. "I could not stomach that, I could not believe that. I didn't know what he had done." Asked why no one had disputed Burt's result, Vernon says that "there were certainly grave doubts although nobody dared to put them into print, because Burt was enormously powerful." Burt's power seemed to have stemmed not so much from patronage — he was by then retired — as from the way he would use his formidable prose style and mastery of statistics to take out after this critics. "He would write a 50-page paper denouncing any criticisms," says Vernon. . . .

The flaws in Burt's work, whatever the reason for them, are obvious 22 enough now that Kamin and Jensen have pointed them out. Yet Burt's work was never challenged during his lifetime. He was preeminent among his colleagues in England, being the first psychologist to receive a knighthood, and the American Psychological Association awarded him its Thorndike prize in 1971. At least from 1969 onward, his data occupied a central position in controversy, in a subject which is presumably no less rigorous than other disciplines. Why were the flaws not detected earlier? Why did journal editors and journal boards not require that he report his results in a more complete or accurate form?

"The sober fact is that scholarly penetration of the literature, and 23 endless delving into primary sources, occurs only very rarely," suggests Hudson. "It reflects on us all that these figures should have been in the literature of a highly contentious and important area for more than a decade before anyone went back to examine them as Kamin did. It strikes me as very damaging to us as a profession that articles were coming from someone called Conway whom no one had ever heard of. That is not the way that a community of scholars should be working."

Kamin's interpretation is that Burt's data remained unchallenged be- 24 cause they confirmed what everyone wanted to believe. "Every professor knew that his child was brighter than the ditch-digger's child, so what was there to challenge?" The moral of the tale, according to Kamin, is "Caveat emptor! The people who buy social science should remember that those who have collected the data may have axes to grind."

Others see the episode as less far-reaching. Scarr-Salapatek, one of 25 the early doubters of Burt's data, says that "people trusted Burt to be reporting accurately what he did, so I don't think it is surprising they accepted his data even if they were implausible." In fact, apart from the strange lack of environmental correlation in the twin study, Burt's results for the IQ correlations of his twins are well in line with those of other studies. This, and the fact that the data are published in such scattered form that the discrepancies are not readily apparent, are reasons why the flaws remained undetected, suggests Jensen.

Consider the case of Cyril Burt from the next three perspectives. The first point of view is that of Burt's biographer, L. S. Hearnshaw; the second is that of William Broad and Nicholas Wade, whose *Betrayers of the Truth* (1983) is an investigation of the phenomenon of scientific fraud; and the last is that of the authors of *Not in Our Genes* (1984), an argument against the overdeterministic applications of research in genetics. R. C. Lewontin and Steven Rose are biologists, and Leon J. Kamin is a psychologist. (Note that Kamin played a role in the Burt controversy.)

With these perspectives in mind, write an analytical essay about the life and work of Cyril Burt.

PERSPECTIVE 1

Burt was an extremely introverted, extremely private person, who rarely expressed his feelings to others, and, perhaps, did not always admit them to himself. He hardly ever displayed anger, or lost his temper, and he maintained a devastating politeness even when engaged in controversy. He showed what one colleague described as "benign equanimity." And this external composure revealed itself not only in social situations, but when confronted with physical danger. When, after his return to London in the autumn of 1944, a rocket fell on Primrose Hill breaking the windows of his flat, Burt displayed no panic, but calmly analyzed his feelings introspectively. There was an inwardness about Burt which detached him from close social contacts. He confided in nobody; there was no sharing of his intimate thoughts and feelings. He appreciated an audience to whom he could display his accomplishments — though even this was not perhaps essential to him — but sociability for its own sake meant nothing to him. He disliked and shunned social gatherings. It is said that he had never even entered a public house. The rowdyism of the sporting undergraduates at Oxford had been deeply repellent to him, and he never showed the slightest interest in any form of sport. His wife, who was both sport-loving and social, completely failed to modify his aversions, and they soon found they had almost nothing in common. . . .

He was utterly disinterested in wealth or place. He never showed any signs of using his many contacts with those in positions of power to enhance his own interests, and he never exploited his own abilities for personal gain. He responded when called on to sit on committees and advisory bodies, but he never sought office, and never pushed himself forward. He was always glad to retreat into the background and get on with his own work. In most of the mundane affairs of life he was dependent on others, his secretaries, housekeepers, and for a time his wife. Even in his professional work he did not mobilize his forces to the last effect. Particularly after his retirement he failed to utilize his time advantageously, showed no interest in obtaining financial support, and made no effort to recruit assistants. He neither expounded his ideas systematically for the benefit of psychologists, nor, apart from occasional broadcasts, popularly for the benefit of the general public; and thereby lost a considerable potential income. In all such matters he seemed totally disinterested, while to make ends meet he slogged away at menial tasks more suited to a struggling junior.

Yet Burt was unquestionably ambitious, and the impulse to dominate   3
was perhaps the driving force of his life — but it was domination on his
terms. He sought neither wealth nor power, but intellectual supremacy.
There was something egotistical, exalted, and grandiose about the resolutions he solemnly wrote down while still an Oxford undergraduate:

> My purpose in life concerns primarily myself. It is to produce one perfect
> being for the universe. The question then for each moment is this: is my
> present attitude a manifestation of, or conducive to, my perfection. . . .

His whole world was insecure. His home had broken up; his research   4
data had perished; his health was precarious; his old department had
defected; he had been robbed of his journal; new modes of thinking and
younger rivals were ousting him from the center of the stage; the doc-
trines he believed in were being rejected. The changes in his personality
from the late 1930s onwards were responses to these threats, and as
the threats grew, so the changes became more marked. Burt could no
longer respond creatively by going out and doing more research. He had
neither the physical fitness, nor the assistants, nor the resources to make
this possible. Instead he had recourse to the well-established mechanisms
of defense, compensation, and regression; on the one hand, inflated claims
as to his own achievements, and on the other a regression to earlier
ways of coping with threats — ways he had learned we must suppose
in the tough Board School playground of his early boyhood, where survival
involved outsmarting his opponents. There was in Burt's reactions, beneath the bland exterior, a compulsive, almost phrenetic, quality, which
suggests such a deep motivational origin. He was a lonely man, who had
few close friends, and who did not communicate his anxieties to others.
He attempted to fight his battles single-handed, and in doing so became
distinctly paranoic.

Paranoia in its fully developed form is generally classed as a delusional   5
psychosis. The delusional system is commonly a circumscribed one, leaving the personality otherwise intact, and in many respects capable of
perfectly normal functioning. Moreover it often occurs in the milder form
of a marginal psychical abnormality, in which the delusional element is
fairly inconspicuous. Characteristic features of such marginal forms are
self-aggrandizement and inflated egocentricity, oversensitiveness and sus-
piciousness, querulousness, secretiveness, compulsive drive ("a temperament which never allows itself to flag"), and hypochondria.

— L. S. Hearnshaw, *Cyril Burt: Psychologist*

PERSPECTIVE 2

Where the conventional ideology [of science] goes most seriously   1
astray is in its focusing on the process of science instead of on the motives
and needs of scientists. Scientists are not different from other people.
In donning the white coat at the laboratory door, they do not step aside
from the passions, ambitions, and failings that animate those in other
walks of life. Modern science is a career. Its stepping-stones are published
articles in the scientific literature. To be successful, a researcher must

get as many articles published as possible, secure government grants, build up a laboratory and the resources to hire graduate students, increase the production of published papers, strive to be awarded a tenured post at a university, write articles that may come to the notice of committees that award scientific prizes, gain election to the National Academy of Sciences, and hope one day to win an invitation to Stockholm.

Not only do careerist pressures exist in contemporary science, but the system rewards the appearance of success as well as genuine achievement. Universities may award tenure simply on the quantity of a researcher's publications, without considering their quality. A laboratory chief who has skillful younger scientists working for him will be rewarded for their efforts as if they were his own. Such misallocations of credit may not be common, but they are common enough to encourage a certain evident cynicism.

— William Broad and Nicholas Wade, *Betrayers of the Truth*

PERSPECTIVE 3

Biological determinism . . . is . . . an attempt at a total system of explanation of human social existence, based on the two principles that human social phenomena are the direct consequences of the behaviors of individuals, and that individual behaviors are the direct consequences of inborn physical characteristics. Biological determinism is, then, a reductionist explanation of human life in which the arrows of causality run from genes to humans and from humans to humanity. But it is more than mere explanation: It is politics. For if human social organization, including the inequalities of status, wealth, and power, are a direct consequence of our biologies, then, except for some gigantic program of genetic engineering, no practice can make a significant alteration of social structure or of the position of individuals or groups within it. What we are is natural and therefore fixed. We may struggle, pass laws, even make revolutions, but we do so in vain. The natural differences between individuals and among groups played out against the background of biological universals of human behavior will, in the end, defeat our uninformed efforts to reconstitute society.

— R. C. Lewontin, Steven Rose, and Leon J. Kamin, *Not in Our Genes*

14. A Political Science Option: Analyzing Political Decision Making

The Cuban missile crisis in October 1962 is considered to be the closest the United States has come to a nuclear confrontation with the Soviet Union. The decisions made by the Kennedy administration at the time of the crisis have been the subject of much attention by historians and political scientists. One historian, Graham T. Allison, has offered an overview of how the Cuban missile crisis can be used to illustrate and test three distinct but overlapping theories about the ways in which important political decisions are made.

After reading the excerpts from an article Allison wrote in 1969, try paraphrasing the three models he describes.

Then, for an essay, choose one of the following assignments.

a. Research the Cuban missile crisis. Based on what you can discover, which of Allison's theoretical models seems best to account for events?
b. Choose another international crisis that called for decision making at a high level. Which of Allison's models is most persuasive in accounting for how decisions were reached? In thinking about this question, take into account limitations in your sources of information and try to imagine how a particular decision might be explained under each model.
c. If you or your friends or your parents have any first-hand knowledge of decision making in a government agency or a corporation, test each of Allison's models against that knowledge. Which model, if any, is most persuasive?

From *Conceptual Models and the Cuban Missile Crisis*
GRAHAM T. ALLISON

RATIONAL POLICY MODEL

Most analysts explain (and predict) the behavior of national govern-　1
ments in terms of various forms of one basic conceptual model, here entitled the Rational Policy Model (Model I).

In terms of this conceptual model, analysts attempt to understand　2
happenings as the more or less purposive acts of unified national governments. For these analysts, the point of an explanation is to show how the nation or government could have chosen the action in question, given the strategic problem that it faced. For example, in confronting the problem posed by the Soviet installation of missiles in Cuba, rational policy model analysts attempt to show how this was a reasonable act from the point of view of the Soviet Union, given Soviet strategic objectives. . . .

What is striking about . . . the literature of foreign policy and inter-　3
national relations are the similarities among analysts of various styles when they are called upon to produce explanations. Each assumes that what must be explained is an action, i.e., the realization of some purpose or intention. Each assumes that the actor is the national government. Each assumes that the action is chosen as a calculated response to a strategic problem. For each, explanation consists of showing what goal the government was pursuing in committing the act and how this action was a reasonable choice, given the nation's objectives. This set of assumptions characterizes the rational policy model. . . .

ORGANIZATIONAL PROCESS MODEL

A "government" consists of a conglomerate of semifeudal, loosely　4
allied organizations, each with a substantial life of its own. Government leaders do sit formally, and to some extent in fact, on top of this con-

glomerate. But governments perceive problems through organizational sensors. Governments define alternatives and estimate consequences as organizations process information. Governments act as these organizations enact routines. Government behavior can therefore be understood according to a second conceptual model, less as deliberate choices of leaders and more as *outputs* of large organizations functioning according to standard patterns of behavior.

To be responsive to a broad spectrum of problems, governments   5
consist of large organizations among which primary responsibility for particular areas is divided. Each organization attends to a special set of problems and acts in quasi-independence on these problems. But few important problems fall exclusively within the domain of a single organization. Thus government behavior relevant to any important problem reflects the independent output of several organizations, partially coordinated by government leaders. Government leaders can substantially disturb, but not substantially control, the behavior of these organizations.

To perform complex routines, the behavior of large numbers of in-   6
dividuals must be coordinated. Coordination requires standard operating procedures: rules according to which things are done. Assured capability for reliable performance of action that depends upon the behavior of hundreds of persons requires established "programs." Indeed, if the eleven members of a football team are to perform adequately on any particular down, each player must not "do what he thinks needs to be done" or "do what the quarterback tells him to do." Rather, each player must perform the maneuvers specified by a previously established play which the quarterback has simply called in this situation.

At any given time, a government consists of *existing* organizations,   7
each with a *fixed* set of standard operating procedures and programs. The behavior of these organizations — and consequently of the government — relevant to an issue in any particular instance is, therefore, determined primarily by routines established in these organizations prior to that instance. But organizations do change. Learning occurs gradually, over time. Dramatic organizational change occurs in response to major crises. Both learning and change are influenced by existing organizational capabilities. . . .

BUREAUCRATIC POLITICS MODEL

The leaders who sit on top of organizations are not a monolithic   8
group. Rather, each is, in his own right, a player in a central, competitive game. The name of the game is bureaucratic politics: bargaining along regularized channels among players positioned hierarchically within the government. Government behavior can thus be understood according to a third conceptual model not as organizational outputs, but as outcomes of bargaining games. In contrast with Model I, the bureaucratic politics model sees no unitary actor but rather many actors as players, who focus not on a single strategic issue but on many diverse intranational problems as well, in terms of no consistent set of strategic objectives, but rather according to various conceptions of national, organizational, and personal

goals, making government decisions not by rational choice but by the pulling and hauling that is politics.

The apparatus of each national government constitutes a complex arena for the intranational game. Political leaders at the top of this apparatus plus the men who occupy positions on top of the critical organizations form the circle of central players. Ascendancy to this circle assures some independent standing. The necessary decentralization of decisions required for action on the broad range of foreign policy problems guarantees that each player has considerable discretion. Thus power is shared. 9

The nature of problems of foreign policy permits fundamental disagreement among reasonable men concerning what ought to be done. Analyses yield conflicting recommendations. Separate responsibilities laid on the shoulders of individual personalities encourage differences in perceptions and priorities. But the issues are of first order importance. What the nation does really matters. A wrong choice could mean irreparable damage. Thus responsible men are obliged to fight for what they are convinced is right. 10

Men share power. Men differ concerning what must be done. The differences matter. This milieu necessitates that policy be resolved by politics. What the nation does is sometimes the result of the triumph of one group over others. More often, however, different groups pulling in different directions yield a resultant distinct from what anyone intended. What moves the chess pieces is not simply the reasons which support a course of action, nor the routines of organizations which enact an alternative, but the power and skill of proponents and opponents of the action in question. 11

15. A Literature Option: A Short Story for Analysis

Find your own perspective for writing an analytical essay about the following story. Paule Marshall (b. 1929) is of Caribbean descent but has spent most of her life in the United States. Her books include *Brown Girl, Brownstones*; *Praisesong for the Widow*; and *Reena*, the collection from which this story is taken.

To Da-duh, in Memoriam
PAULE MARSHALL

> ". . . Oh Nana! all of you is not involved in this evil business Death,
> Nor all of us in life."
> — From "At My Grandmother's Grave," by Lebert Bethune

I did not see her at first I remember. For not only was it dark inside the crowded disembarkation shed in spite of the daylight flooding in from outside, but standing there waiting for her with my mother and sister I was still somewhat blinded from the sheen of tropical sunlight on the water of the bay which we had just crossed in the landing boat, leaving behind us the ship that had brought us from New York lying in the offing. Besides, being only nine years of age at the time and knowing nothing of islands I was busy attending to the alien sights and sounds of Barbados, the unfamiliar smells.

I did not see her, but I was alerted to her approach by my mother's hand which suddenly tightened around mine, and looking up I traced her gaze through the gloom in the shed until I finally made out the small, purposeful, painfully erect figure of the old woman headed our way.

Her face was drowned in the shadow of an ugly rolled-brim brown felt hat, but the details of her slight body and of the struggle taking place within it were clear enough — an intense, unrelenting struggle between her back which was beginning to bend ever so slightly under the weight of her eighty-odd years and the rest of her which sought to deny those years and hold that back straight, keep it in line. Moving swiftly toward us (so swiftly it seemed she did not intend stopping when she reached us but would sweep past us out the doorway which opened onto the sea and like Christ walk upon the water!), she was caught between the sunlight at her end of the building and the darkness inside — and for a moment she appeared to contain them both: the light in the long severe old-fashioned white dress she wore which brought the sense of a past that was still alive into our bustling present and in the snatch of white at her eye; the darkness in her black high-top shoes and in her face which was visible now that she was closer.

It was as stark and fleshless as a death mask, that face. The maggots   4 might have already done their work, leaving only the framework of bone beneath the ruined skin and deep wells at the temple and jaw. But her eyes were alive, unnervingly so for one so old, with a sharp light that flicked out of the dim clouded depths like a lizard's tongue to snap up all in her view. Those eyes betrayed a child's curiosity about the world, and I wondered vaguely seeing them, and seeing the way the bodice of her ancient dress had collapsed in on her flat chest (what had happened to her breasts?), whether she might not be some kind of child at the same time that she was a woman, with fourteen children, my mother included, to prove it. Perhaps she was both, both child and woman, darkness and light, past and present, life and death — all the opposites contained and reconciled in her.

"My Da-duh," my mother said formally and stepped forward. The name sounded like thunder fading softly in the distance.

"Child," Da-duh said, and her tone, her quick scrutiny of my mother, the brief embrace in which they appeared to shy from each other rather than touch, wiped out the fifteen years my mother had been away and restored the old relationship. My mother, who was such a formidable figure in my eyes, had suddenly with a word been reduced to my status.

"Yes, God is good," Da-duh said with a nod that was like a tic. "He has spared me to see my child again."

We were led forward then, apologetically because not only did Da-   8 duh prefer boys but she also liked her grandchildren to be "white," that is, fair-skinned; and we had, I was to discover, a number of cousins, the outside children of white estate managers and the like, who qualified. We, though, were as black as she.

My sister being the oldest was presented first. "This one takes after the father," my mother said and waited to be reproved.

Frowning, Da-duh tilted my sister's face toward the light. But her frown soon gave way to a grudging smile, for my sister with her large mild eyes and little broad winged nose, with our father's high-cheeked Barbadian cast to her face, was pretty.

"She's goin' be lucky," Da-duh said and patted her once on the cheek. "Any girl child that takes after the father does be lucky."

She turned then to me. But oddly enough she did not touch me. Instead leaning close, she peered hard at me, and then quickly drew back. I thought I saw her hand start up as though to shield her eyes. It was almost as if she saw not only me, a thin truculent child who it was said took after no one but myself, but something in me which for some reason she found disturbing, even threatening. We looked silently at each other for a long time there in the noisy shed, our gaze locked. She was the first to look away. 12

"But Adry," she said to my mother and her laugh was cracked, thin, apprehensive. "Where did you get this one here with this fierce look?"

"We don't know where she came out of, my Da-duh," my mother said, laughing also. Even I smiled to myself. After all I had won the encounter. Da-duh had recognized my small strength — and this was all I ever asked of the adults in my life then.

"Come, soul," Da-duh said and took my hand. "You must be one of those New York terrors you hear so much about."

She led us, me at her side and my sister and mother behind, out of 16 the shed into the sunlight that was like a bright driving summer rain and over to a group of people clustered beside a decrepit lorry. They were our relatives, most of them from St. Andrews although Da-duh herself lived in St. Thomas, the women wearing bright print dresses, the colors vivid against their darkness, the men rusty black suits that encased them like straitjackets. Da-duh, holding fast to my hand, became my anchor as they circled round us like a nervous sea, exclaiming, touching us with their calloused hands, embracing us shyly. They laughed in awed bursts: "But look Adry got big-big children!" / "And see the nice things they wearing, wrist watch and all!" / "I tell you, Adry has done all right for sheself in New York. . . ."

Da-duh, ashamed at their wonder, embarrassed for them, admonished them the while. "But oh Christ," she said, "why you all got to get on like you never saw people from 'Away' before? You would think New York is the only place in the world to hear wunna. That's why I don't like to go anyplace with you St. Andrews people, you know. You all ain't been colonized."

We were in the back of the lorry finally, packed in among the barrels of ham, flour, cornmeal and rice and the trunks of clothes that my mother had brought as gifts. We made our way slowly through Bridgetown's clogged streets, part of a funereal procession of cars and open-sided buses, bicycles and donkey carts. The dim little limestone shops and offices along the way marched with us, at the same mournful pace, toward the same grave ceremony — as did the people, the women balancing huge baskets on top their heads as if they were no more than hats they wore to shade them from the sun. Looking over the edge of the lorry I watched as their feet slurred the dust. I listened, and their voices, raw and loud and dissonant in the heat, seemed to be grappling with each other high overhead.

Da-duh sat on a trunk in our midst, a monarch amid her court. She still held my hand, but it was different now. I had suddenly become her anchor, for I felt her fear of the lorry with its asthmatic motor (a fear and distrust, I later learned, she held of all machines) beating like a pulse in her rough palm.

As soon as we left Bridgetown behind though, she relaxed, and while the others around us talked she gazed at the canes standing tall on either side of the winding marl road. "C'dear," she said softly to herself after a time. "The canes this side are pretty enough." 20

They were too much for me. I thought of them as giant weeds that had overrun the island, leaving scarcely any room for the small tottering houses of sunbleached pine we passed or the people, dark streaks as our lorry hurtled by. I suddenly feared that we were journeying, unaware that we were, toward some dangerous place where the canes, grown as high and thick as a forest, would close in on us and run us through with their stiletto blades. I longed then for the familiar: for the street in Brooklyn where I lived, for my father who had refused to accompany us ("Blowing out good money on foolishness," he had said of the trip), for a game of tag with my friends under the chestnut tree outside our aging brownstone house.

"Yes, but wait till you see St. Thomas canes," Da-duh was saying to me. "They's canes father, bo," she gave a proud arrogant nod. "To-morrow, God willing, I goin' take you out in the ground and show them to you."

True to her word Da-duh took me with her the following day out into the ground. It was a fairly large plot adjoining her weathered board and shingle house and consisting of a small orchard, a good-sized canepiece and behind the canes, where the land sloped abruptly down, a gully. She had purchased it with Panama money sent her by her eldest son, my uncle Joseph, who had died working on the canal. We entered the ground along a trail no wider than her body and as devious and complex as her reasons for showing me her land. Da-duh strode briskly ahead, her slight form filled out this morning by the layers of sacking petticoats she wore under her working dress to protect her against the damp. A fresh white cloth, elaborately arranged around her head, added to her height, and lent her a vain, almost roguish air.

Her pace slowed once we reached the orchard, and glancing back at me occasionally over her shoulder, she pointed out the various trees. 24

"This here is a breadfruit," she said. "That one yonder is a papaw. Here's a guava. This is a mango. I know you don't have anything like these in New York. Here's a sugar apple." (The fruit looked more like artichokes than apples to me.) "This one bears limes. . . ." She went on for some time, intoning the names of the trees as though they were those of her gods. Finally, turning to me, she said, "I know you don't have anything this nice where you come from." Then, as I hesitated: "I said I know you don't have anything this nice where you come from. . . ."

"No," I said and my world did seem suddenly lacking.

Da-duh nodded and passed on. The orchard ended and we were on the narrow cart road that led through the canepiece, the canes clashing like swords above my cowering head. Again she turned and her thin muscular arms spread wide, her dim gaze embracing the small field of canes, she said — and her voice almost broke under the weight of her pride, "Tell me, have you got anything like these in that place where you were born?"

"No." **28**

"I din' think so. I bet you don't even know that these canes here and the sugar you eat is one and the same thing. That they does throw the canes into some damn machine at the factory and squeeze out all the little life in them to make sugar for you all so in New York to eat. I bet you don't know that."

"I've got two cavities and I'm not allowed to eat a lot of sugar."

But Da-duh didn't hear me. She had turned with an inexplicably angry motion and was making her way rapidly out of the canes and down the slope at the edge of the field which led to the gully below. Following her apprehensively down the incline amid a stand of banana plants whose leaves flapped like elephants' ears in the wind, I found myself in the middle of a small tropical wood — a place dense and damp and gloomy and tremulous with the fitful play of light and shadow as the leaves high above moved against the sun that was almost hidden from view. It was a violent place, the tangled foliage fighting each other for a chance at the sunlight, the branches of the trees locked in what seemed an immemorial struggle, one both necessary and inevitable. But despite the violence, it was pleasant, almost peaceful in the gully, and beneath the thick undergrowth the earth smelled like spring.

This time Da-duh didn't even bother to ask her usual question, but **32** simply turned and waited for me to speak.

"No," I said, my head bowed. "We don't have anything like this in New York."

"Ah," she cried, her triumph complete. "I din' think so. Why, I've heard that's a place where you can walk till you near drop and never see a tree."

"We've got a chestnut tree in front of our house," I said.

"Does it bear?" She waited. "I ask you, does it bear?" **36**

"Not anymore," I muttered. "It used to, but not anymore."

She gave the nod that was like a nervous twitch. "You see," she said. "Nothing can bear there." Then, secure behind her scorn, she added, "But tell me, what's this snow like that you hear so much about?"

Looking up, I studied her closely, sensing my chance, and then I told her, describing at length and with as much drama as I could summon not only what snow in the city was like, but what it would be like here, in her perennial summer kingdom.

". . . And you see all these trees you got here," I said. "Well, they'd   **40**
be bare. No leaves, no fruit, nothing. They'd be covered in snow. You
see your canes. They'd be buried under tons of snow. The snow would
be higher than your head, higher than your house, and you wouldn't be
able to come down into this here gully because it would be snowed
under. . . ."

She searched my face for the lie, still scornful but intrigued. "What
a thing, huh?" she said finally, whispering it softly to herself.

"And when it snows you couldn't dress like you are now," I said.
"Oh no, you'd freeze to death. You'd have to wear a hat and gloves and
galoshes and ear muffs so your ears wouldn't freeze and drop off, and a
heavy coat. I've got a Shirley Temple coat with fur on the collar. I can
dance. You wanna see?"

Before she could answer I began, with a dance called the Truck
which was popular back then in the 1930s. My right forefinger waving,
I trucked around the nearby trees and around Da-duh's awed and rigid
form. After the Truck I did the Suzy-Q, my lean hips swishing, my
sneakers sidling zigzag over the ground. "I can sing," I said and did so,
starting with "I'm Gonna Sit Right Down and Write Myself a Letter,"
then without pausing, "Tea For Two," and ending with "I Found a Million
Dollar Baby in a Five and Ten Cent Store."

For long moments afterwards Da-duh stared at me as if I were a   **44**
creature from Mars, an emissary from some world she did not know but
which intrigued her and whose power she both felt and feared. Yet
something about my performance must have pleased her, because bending
down she slowly lifted her long skirt and then, one by one, the layers
of petticoats until she came to a drawstring purse dangling at the end of
a long strip of cloth tied round her waist. Opening the purse she handed
me a penny. "Here," she said half-smiling against her will. "Take this to
buy yourself a sweet at the shop up the road. There's nothing to be done
with you, soul."

From then on, whenever I wasn't taken to visit relatives, I accompanied Da-duh out into the ground, and alone with her amid the canes
or down in the gully I told her about New York. It always began with
some slighting remark on her part: "I know they don't have anything this
nice where you come from," or "Tell me, I hear those foolish people in
New York does do such and such. . . ." But as I answered, recreating
my towering world of steel and concrete and machines for her, building
the city out of words, I would feel her give way. I came to know the
signs of her surrender: the total stillness that would come over her little
hard dry form, the probing gaze that like a surgeon's knife sought to cut
through my skull to get at the images there, to see if I were lying; above
all, her fear, a fear nameless and profound, the same one I had felt beating
in the palm of her hand that day in the lorry.

Over the weeks I told her about refrigerators, radios, gas stoves,
elevators, trolley cars, wringer washing machines, movies, airplanes, the
cyclone at Coney Island, subways, toasters, electric lights: "At night,
see, all you have to do is flip this little switch on the wall and all the

lights in the house go on. Just like that. Like magic. It's like turning on the sun at night."

"But tell me," she said to me once with a faint mocking smile, "do the white people have all these things too or it's only the people looking like us?"

I laughed. "What d'ya mean," I said. "The white people have even better." Then: "I beat up a white girl in my class last term."

"Beating up white people!" Her tone was incredulous.

"How you mean!" I said, using an expression of hers. "She called me a name."

For some reason Da-duh could not quite get over this and repeated in the same hushed, shocked voice, "Beating up white people now! Oh, the lord, the world's changing up so I can scarce recognize it anymore."

One morning toward the end of our stay, Da-duh led me into a part of the gully that we had never visited before, an area darker and more thickly overgrown than the rest, almost impenetrable. There in a small clearing amid the dense bush, she stopped before an incredibly tall royal palm which rose cleanly out of the ground, and drawing the eye up with it, soared high above the trees around it into the sky. It appeared to be touching the blue dome of sky, to be flaunting its dark crown of fronds right in the blinding white face of the late morning sun.

Da-duh watched me a long time before she spoke, and then she said very quietly, "All right, now, tell me if you've got anything this tall in that place you're from."

I almost wished, seeing her face, that I could have said no. "Yes," I said. "We've got buildings hundreds of times this tall in New York. There's one called the Empire State Building that's the tallest in the world. My class visited it last year and I went all the way to the top. It's got over a hundred floors. I can't describe how tall it is. Wait a minute. What's the name of that hill I went to visit the other day, where they have the police station?"

"You mean Bissex?"

"Yes, Bissex. Well, the Empire State Building is way taller than that."

"You're lying now!" she shouted, trembling with rage. Her hand lifted to strike me.

"No, I'm not," I said. "It really is, if you don't believe me I'll send you a picture postcard of it soon as I get back home so you can see for yourself. But it's way taller than Bissex."

All the fight went out of her at that. The hand poised to strike me fell limp to her side, and as she stared at me, seeing not me but the building that was taller than the highest hill she knew, the small stubborn light in her eyes (it was the same amber as the flame in the kerosene lamp she lit at dusk) began to fail. Finally, with a vague gesture that even in the midst of her defeat still tried to dismiss me and my world, she turned and started back through the gully, walking slowly, her steps groping and uncertain, as if she were suddenly no longer sure of the way, while I followed triumphant yet strangely saddened behind.

The next morning I found her dressed for our morning walk but   60
stretched out on the Berbice chair in the tiny drawing room where she
sometimes napped during the afternoon heat, her face turned to the
window beside her. She appeared thinner and suddenly indescribably old.

"My Da-duh," I said.

"Yes, nuh," she said. Her voice was listless and the face she slowly
turned my way was, now that I think back on it, like a Benin mask, the
features drawn and almost distorted by an ancient abstract sorrow.

"Don't you feel well?" I asked.

"Girl, I don't know."   64

"My Da-duh, I goin' boil you some bush tea," my aunt, Da-duh's
youngest child, who lived with her, called from the shed roof kitchen.

"Who tell you I need bush tea?" she cried, her voice assuming for
a moment its old authority. "You can't even rest nowadays without some
malicious person looking for you to be dead. Come girl," she motioned
me to a place beside her on the old-fashioned lounge chair, "give us a
tune."

I sang for her until breakfast at eleven, all my brash irreverent Tin
Pan Alley songs, and then just before noon we went out into the ground.
But it was a short, dispirited walk. Da-duh didn't even notice that the
mangoes were beginning to ripen and would have to be picked before
the village boys got to them. And when she paused occasionally and
looked out across the canes or up at her trees it wasn't as if she were
seeing them but something else. Some huge, monolithic shape had imposed itself, it seemed, between her and the land, obstructing her vision.
Returning to the house she slept the entire afternoon on the Berbice
chair.

She remained like this until we left, languishing away the mornings   68
on the chair at the window gazing out at the land as if it were already
doomed; then, at noon, taking the brief stroll with me through the ground
during which she seldom spoke, and afterwards returning home to sleep
till almost dusk sometimes.

On the day of our departure she put on the austere, ankle length
white dress, the black shoes and brown felt hat (her town clothes she
called them), but she did not go with us to town. She saw us off on the
road outside her house and in the midst of my mother's tearful protracted
farewell, she leaned down and whispered in my ear, "Girl, you're not to
forget now to send me the picture of that building, you hear."

By the time I mailed her the large colored picture postcard of the
Empire State Building she was dead. She died during the famous '37
strike which began shortly after we left. On the day of her death England
sent planes flying low over the island in a show of force — so low,
according to my aunt's letter, that the downdraft from them shook the
ripened mangoes from the trees in Da-duh's orchard. Frightened, everyone in the village fled into the canes. Except Da-duh. She remained in
the house at the window so my aunt said, watching as the planes came
swooping and screaming like monstrous birds down over the village, over
her house, rattling her trees and flattening the young canes in her field.

It must have seemed to her lying there that they did not intend pulling out of their dive, but like the hardback beetles which hurled themselves with suicidal force against the walls of the house at night, those menacing silver shapes would hurl themselves in an ecstasy of self-immolation onto the land, destroying it utterly.

When the planes finally left and the villagers returned they found her dead on the Berbice chair at the window.

She died and I lived, but always, to this day even, within the shadow   72 of her death. For a brief period after I was grown I went to live alone, like one doing penance, in a loft above a noisy factory in downtown New York and there painted seas of sugar-cane and huge swirling Van Gogh suns and palm trees striding like brightly plumed Tutsi warriors across a tropical landscape, while the thunderous tread of the machines down-stairs jarred the floor beneath my easel, mocking my efforts.

Readings for
Academic Argument:
A Sourcebook

CHAPTER 7

Sustaining Academic Argument: General Considerations

To argue is to attempt to persuade with evidence and reasoning. In this general sense, most academic writing argues. Certainly you've done plenty of arguing if you've attempted some of the earlier exercises in this book. Defining, serializing, classifying, summarizing, comparing, and analyzing all can be seen as strategies of argument. When a writer defines "health" not merely as the absence of disease but as "a positive moral outlook on one's life," that definition, particularly when elaborated and defended against possible objections, is an argument. Similarly, if you were to write an essay comparing the features of Buddhism and Christianity, that comparison would become an argument if you organized your points to support a single controlling idea. Analysis is particularly close to argument. If you analyzed the immigration statistics on page 320 using the framework provided by the Karl Marx quotation, your argument was, in effect, "Here's how I think Marx would explain these statistics." If you decided to analyze punk rock violence not from the perspective of Sigmund Freud but from that of David Riesman, you were arguing for one interpretation over another.

No one feature of an argument distinguishes it absolutely from other writing strategies. But several generalizations hold for most academic arguments. Usually an argument draws on a breadth of material and knowledge, seldom relying solely on a single text. Usually an argument treats a topic about which there are differences of opinion; some real persuading needs to be done. A good argument usually takes into consideration a variety of points of view — not necessarily balancing them, but acknowledging that they exist. Most arguments emphasize their own logic: A writer questions other people's assumptions and clarifies his or her own. A writer calls attention to the relations among starting points, evidence, and conclusions: "If X is true, then it follows. . . ." Good arguments make effective use of specific details; a writer either provides a lot of supportive detail or gives the impression that such detail *could* be provided. Finally, most good arguments are versatile, taking advantage of diverse materials: personal anecdotes, statistics, analogies, descriptions, clever phrasings, quotations, and the various strategies you've been practicing in this book — whatever helps to get the job done.

Here are some examples of representative academic assignments calling for argument:

From a philosophy class. Are there circumstances under which euthanasia is morally justifiable?

From an American history class. Assess the lasting influence of the Roosevelt administration on U.S. institutions.

From a biology class. Do species adapt to changing environments, or is this a misleading way to think of evolution?

From a literature class. The critic Randall Jarrell characterized Robert Frost as a "terrifying" poet. Considering what you've read of Frost, and in the context of other poetry you've read for this course, do you agree with this characterization?

From a political science class. What has been the influence of the Western powers on modern African politics? Is the legacy of colonialism a disruptive or a stabilizing factor?

Some assignments get quite specific in defining a question to argue pro or con. Others do not frame a specific question but only provide a general topic within which you must choose from a wide range of possibilities. Consider the difference between the following assignments:

From a speech class. You will be asked in class to defend or refute the following proposition. "Resolved: Because crime in the United States is steadily increasing, sentencing policies must be made more stringent."

From a sociology class. Drawing on pertinent readings in the course and any further research that you choose to do on your own, write a term paper on some sociological aspect of crime in the United States.

These two assignments represent extremes. Seldom will you be so restricted in topic and language as in the first example, and seldom will you be left so entirely on your own as in the second.

AN EXAMPLE OF A DEVELOPING ARGUMENT: CRIMINAL PUNISHMENT

To illustrate the process of searching for and developing an argument, let's imagine ourselves setting out to write a paper on crime and punishment for an introductory course in criminology (the study of crime). The course began by looking at several theories of criminal behavior, then went on to examine the varieties of crime in the United States, and has recently turned to look at the American system of criminal justice. Here is the wording of our assignment, neither so narrow as the assignment from the speech class nor so broad as the sociology assignment:

> For your term paper, consider whether the problem of crime in the United States has reached epidemic proportions and whether the administration of criminal justice should be changed to deal with the problem more effectively. You may use any of the assigned or suggested readings of the course, as well as any further research you do on your own.

Before jumping headfirst into an argument, we had better begin by asking ourselves a few preliminary questions. In the first place, what are we being asked to do? This assignment seems to consist of two separate questions — Is there an epidemic? and What should we do about it? — but is the first question merely a way of getting at the second? That is, should we take the question to really mean "Since there is a great crime problem in the United States, what can you propose to do about it?"

Second, we can ask ourselves how free we are to find our own topic within the general one. For example, if we decided to make our paper entirely about issues of the U.S. parole system, would we be fulfilling the expectations of the assignment? Many instructors advise their students to find a tight focus for their research papers, since it's impossible to treat a broad subject in much detail. But some instructors, particularly in introductory courses, are looking to see how well students have acquired an overview of their disciplines. Overfocusing a paper might risk sacrificing that overview.

Third, we can ask whether the wording of the assignment or the conduct of the course itself inclines us toward some particular perspective or interpretation. Is the word *epidemic,* for example, consistent with the language of the instructor's lectures, or does it seem out of keeping? Is the question a genuinely open one, or does the entire experience of the course point us in one direction rather than another?

Finally, and most important, we can ask ourselves what we already feel about the topic. Do we have strong feelings about whether there is an epidemic of crime? Do we have a gut feeling about what should be done? Such a question helps keep us aware of our own inclinations and biases; it also makes us more likely to produce a paper that engages us and is intellectually honest. Having examined our own initial feelings and checking them as we go along, we'll be less likely to construct a paper shaped simply by what we think an instructor wants to hear. Moreover, we'll be more alert as we gather material — it's not just a matter of what that material tells us; it's also what we can make of it. This does not mean we should be closed off to opinions that run counter to our own initial ones. On the contrary, it means we can be more open to discovering how new material complicates or clashes with our preliminary thinking.

Let's say that we've come to the following judgments on our preliminary questions. We're disposed to think that there is a tremendous crime problem in the United States, perhaps an epidemic, and we tentatively favor enacting tougher measures of law enforcement and criminal punishment. We feel the course has not pointed us toward this conclusion — in fact, the instructor has seldom seemed to take a stand on issues of government policy. We're undecided about whether to narrow the topic. On the one hand, the course has stressed the amount of recidivism in American prisons (convicted criminals tend to wind up back in prison after release), and we feel that we can construct an entire paper about inadequacies of the parole system. On the other hand, it may be hard to write about parole issues without considering the whole context of crime in America. Since we're free to explore the topic, we decide to hold off choosing prematurely. As for whether we are being asked one question or two, we decide that the question does have two real parts. If we can establish that there *is* an epidemic, we'll be better situated to choose what to do next.

So we begin the search to document the severity of the crime problem. In looking over our criminology textbook, we notice that in one section, the authors have dramatically represented the national state of crime through the use of a mosaic of short, graphic capsules.

> *Burglary in the Country.* Vivian and Al Weber lived in Battle   1
> Creek, Mich., working 6:30 a.m.-to-3 p.m. shifts in two different factories
> — and hating city life. In 1976 they realized what Mrs. Weber calls "our
> dream, our lifelong dream," moving to a 50-acre site near the tiny village
> of Burlington and commuting 35 minutes to work. "Everything we had,
> we put into this home," she recalls. One afternoon the Webers came
> home to find "glass all over. They'd smashed the window into the kitchen.
> Everything was gone through — every drawer, every room."
>
> Mrs. Weber felt that their house had been sullied. "I scrubbed the   2
> walls. I took the curtains down and washed them. I would open a drawer
> to put on clean clothes and think about my personal things, 'Oh, God,
> I've got to wash them.'" She and her husband took different shifts so
> one of them would always be home. They started locking their doors,
> even if one of them was merely going out to the garden.
>
> Eventually they decided to work the same hours again. Al got home   3
> first one day and met Vivian outside the door. He was white as a sheet.
> "Honey," he said, "we've been ripped off again." This time the burglars
> took some of the items the Webers had bought as replacements — and
> keepsakes as well. "They've got us timed," thought Mrs. Weber. "They

know when we go and when we come home." She quit work and would not even go shopping unless Al was home. He gave up his annual hunting trips. They put dead-bolt locks on all the outside doors, wired a back-room window with a siren, and even bought a third car to park as a decoy in the driveway if they could not avoid being gone at the same time.

The Webers placed their dream house up for sale, then reconsidered.   4
"I have friends here who are more like family than friends," she explains. But their lives have changed. "I try to be normal, but I'm afraid. I have turned around and driven 15 miles back home because I had a funny feeling in my stomach. I feel watched constantly. I never feel safe."

Brutality in Phoenix.   Suzanne Marie Rossetti, 26, a technician   5
at a burn treatment center in Phoenix, had attended a performance of *Dancin'* at Arizona State University. On her way home, she drove into a grocery-store parking lot, and mistakenly locked her car with the keys inside. Two young white men helpfully unlocked the door, asked for a short lift — then forced her to drive to her apartment, where they beat and raped her for several hours.

According to Phoenix Police Detective Richard Fuqua, the men then   6
drove 50 miles to an isolated desert area and hurled Suzanne off a cliff. They heard her moaning and climbed down to her side. She pleaded with them to leave her alone because, she said, "I'm dying anyway." The response was swift. "Damn right you are," one of the men said, and picked up a large rock and crushed her head to still her sounds. . . .

Gang Shooting in Chicago.   Steven Watts had everything to live   7
for. A 6-ft. 3-in., 212-lb. lineman, he had been named the outstanding defensive football player in Chicago public high schools and had been given an athletic scholarship by Iowa State University. He was walking home from a Friday-night dance at Julian High with several friends when a car carrying three youths passed. The trio, who were members of a black street gang, apparently thought Watts and his friends, also black, belonged to a rival gang, and began shooting. Running for cover, Watts was hit in the back by one bullet and died before he reached a hospital. Said his coach, Gregory Brooks: "He was a kid who had worked hard all his life for something and was about to get it. Then it's all taken away by some fool with a gun."

> — *Time*, March 23, 1981, quoted in Martin R. Haskell and
> Lewis Yablonsky, *Criminology: Crime and Criminality*

Stories like this make a strong, visceral impact. We read them, and we want people punished. If we decide to use such stories to help make our case, we know we can get similar material by following the newspapers for a week or so. Such stories, particularly fresh, local ones, will lend emotional power to our argument. But do you see any limitations in this kind of evidence?

We could also start to compile crime statistics. Table 1 appeared in the same criminology textbook. What do these statistics seem to tell us?

TABLE 1. FBI Crime Rates, 1980

POPULATION[1]	CRIME INDEX TOTAL[2]	VIOLENT CRIME	PROPERTY CRIME	MURDER AND NONNEGLIGENT MANSLAUGHTER
NUMBER OF OFFENSES				
1971 — 206,212,000	8,588,200	816,500	7,771,700	17,780
1972 — 208,230,000	8,248,800	834,900	7,413,900	18,670
1973 — 209,851,000	8,718,100	875,910	7,842,200	19,640
1974 — 211,392,000	10,253,400	974,720	9,278,700	20,710
1975 — 213,124,000	11,256,600	1,026,280	10,230,300	20,510
1976 — 214,659,000	11,304,800	986,580	10,318,200	18,780
1977 — 216,332,000	10,935,800	1,009,500	9,926,300	19,120
1978 — 218,059,000	11,141,300	1,061,830	10,079,500	19,560
1979 — 220,099,000	12,152,700	1,178,540	10,974,200	21,460
1980 — 225,349,264	13,295,400	1,308,900	11,986,500	23,040
RATE PER 100,000 INHABITANTS				
1971	4,164.7	396.0	3,768.8	8.6
1972	3,961.4	401.0	3,560.4	9.0
1973	4,154.4	417.4	3,737.0	9.4
1974	4,850.4	461.1	4,389.3	9.8
1975	5,281.7	481.5	4,800.2	9.6
1976	5,266.4	459.6	4,806.8	8.8
1977	5,055.1	466.6	4,588.4	8.8
1978	5,109.3	486.9	4,622.4	9.0
1979	5,521.5	535.5	4,986.0	9.7
1980	5,899.9	580.8	5,319.1	10.2

[1] Populations are Bureau of Census provisional estimates as of July 1, except April 1, 1980 preliminary census counts, and are subject to change.
[2] Due to rounding, the offenses may not add to totals.

If we try serializing these data to tell a year-by-year story or to seek out a general trend, what conclusions can we draw? Will the data help us to argue for stiffer punishments? What other sorts of questions do these statistics raise? What *don't* they tell us? What other sorts of information will we need to look for?

Another way to argue the severity of the crime problem is to look for readings that also make a claim about its severity. If we can find some authority who asserts that the United States has been undergoing a prolonged crime wave, we can summarize or quote from his or her argument in addition to using our other evidence. Looking through the list of suggested readings that our criminology instructor has provided, we run across a likely title, "The Alarming Increase of Crime," by former FBI Director J. Edgar Hoover. At one point in the course, the instructor mentioned Hoover as a powerful political figure, but otherwise he has received no special mention. We surmise that

TABLE 1.   (Continued)

FORCIBLE RAPE	ROBBERY	AGGRAVATED ASSAULT	BURGLARY	LARCENY-THEFT	MOTOR VEHICLE THEFT
42,260	387,700	368,700	2,399,300	4,424,200	948,200
46,850	376,290	393,090	2,375,500	4,151,200	887,200
51,400	384,220	420,650	2,565,500	4,347,900	928,800
55,400	442,400	456,210	3,039,200	5,262,500	977,100
56,090	464,970	484,710	3,252,100	5,977,700	1,000,500
56,730	420,210	490,850	3,089,800	6,270,800	957,600
63,020	404,850	522,510	3,052,200	5,905,700	968,400
67,130	417,040	558,100	3,104,500	5,983,400	991,600
75,990	466,880	614,210	3,299,500	6,577,500	1,097,200
82,090	548,810	654,960	3,759,200	7,112,700	1,114,700
20.5	188.0	178.8	1,163.5	2,145.5	459.8
22.5	180.7	188.8	1,140.8	1,993.6	426.1
24.5	183.1	200.5	1,222.5	2,071.9	442.6
26.2	209.3	215.8	1,437.7	2,489.5	462.2
26.3	218.2	227.4	1,525.9	2,804.8	469.4
26.4	195.8	228.7	1,439.4	2,921.3	446.1
29.1	187.1	241.5	1,410.9	2,729.9	447.6
30.8	191.3	255.9	1,423.7	2,743.9	454.7
34.5	212.1	279.1	1,499.1	2,988.4	498.5
36.4	243.5	290.6	1,668.2	3,156.3	494.6

SOURCE: FBI Crime Index, 1980. Table as appeared in Martin R. Haskell and Lewis Yablonsky, *Criminology: Crime and Criminality.*

as FBI director, he would probably have taken a strong stand on law-and-order issues. So we decide to see what he has to say. When we locate Hoover's piece, it turns out to be a speech he delivered in the early 1960s; it is anthologized in a collection called *Readings in Criminology and Penology.* Our first thought is that the speech will be too dated for our purposes, but as we read it, sparks start to fly.

> Is America as a nation being swept by an epidemic of spiritual mal- [1]
> nutrition? I fervently hope not; but the danger signs are all too clear. I
> fear that the public may be coming to accept widespread lawlessness as
> an unavoidable adjunct to our way of life. . . .
> Despite the continuing efforts of some self-professed experts to min- [2]
> imize the crime problem, the undeniable fact remains that crime is in-
> creasing — in both numbers and intensity — at an alarming rate. It is
> growing six times as fast as our expanding population.

Last year, more than 2,600,000 serious offenses were reported to law enforcement agencies throughout the United States. This is the largest total on record. It means that more Americans felt the ravages of crime last year than ever before.   3

Today, the onslaught continues — with five serious offenses being recorded every minute. There is a vicious crime of violence — a murder, forcible rape or assault to kill — every 2½ minutes; a robbery, each 5 minutes, a burglary, every 28 seconds; and 52 automobiles are stolen every hour.   4

These figures are based on facts — unlike the illogical and inane criticism which has been voiced by the peculiar clique of sociologists and criminologists who are apparently suffering armchair fatigue. These impractical theorists who attempt to define away our crime problem should step from their paper castles into the world of reality. . . .   5

There is an urgent need today for realistic thought and realistic action in meeting the challenge of crime and immorality. This is especially true in the critical area of youthful criminality — where society has too long been asked to endure gross abuses of public and private trust by shallow-minded juvenile authorities. . . .   6

In complaining last year of what it termed "turnstile justice," a major newspaper in New York demanded, "it's time that the public was told just why so many young criminals and terrorists are passed through this turnstile and sent back to the streets to kill, rape, rob, and assault the innocent."   7

Exaggerated charges? Not in the least. From 1960 through 1964, no less than 225 police officers were killed in line of duty. Nearly one-third of the hoodlums arrested in connection with these murders were on parole or probation when the killings occurred.   8

The lives of six of these officers were claimed by criminals who had been paroled for a prior murder. Eleven lives were taken by offenders who had been paroled after confinement for felonious assault; and 32 of these officers were killed by paroled robbers.   9

We recently completed an examination of the records of nearly 93,000 criminals who were arrested in 1963 and 1964. This disclosed that 76 percent — more than three-quarters — had been arrested on at least one previous occasion. Over one-half of them had received lenient treatment, including parole, probation, and suspended sentences, at some point in their criminal careers — and these criminals recorded an average of more than three additional arrests after their first encounter with the school of soft justice and official leniency.   10

Forty-one years ago, an experienced attorney and jurist in New York issued a strong warning: "It is not the criminals, actual or potential, that need a neuropathic hospital. It is the people who slobber over them in an effort to find excuses for their crimes. The demand of the hour in America, above all other countries, is for jurors with conscience, judges with courage, and prisons which are neither country clubs nor health resorts."   11

The same "demands of the hour" continue to exist today. Tragically, the atmosphere of many courtrooms is still polluted by some jurors who   12 deliberately close their minds to the evidence before them. Too many of our judges seek out technicalities rather than guilt or innocence. A trial should truly represent an enlightened search for truth so that deception, surprise, technicalities, and delay will be obliterated. The jousting in legal mumbo-jumbo resorted to by too many of our judges makes a farce of our judicial system.

But even if he should be convicted, the criminal knows that regardless **13** of his past record there is steadily increasing hope for a suspended or a probationary sentence or an early release on parole. . . .

Those who seek equal rights under the law should be taught to **14** assume equal responsibility before the law. Certainly, civil rights and individual dignity have their vital place in life, but what about the common good and the law and order that preserve us all from lapsing back into the jungle?

We must have a world ruled by law. I am not one of those who **15** believe in adding a great many more laws. The crux of the problem is that we do not observe the laws we already have; nor is the spirit of these laws interpreted by our courts to give equal justice to the criminal and to law-abiding citizens who are the victims of the savagery perpetrated on our streets and highways.

— J. Edgar Hoover, "The Faith of Free Men"

Pretty strong stuff, we think, and kind of fanatical. But we're pleased to see that Hoover uses the very term — *epidemic* — that plays such a prominent role in the assignment. We're also struck by how similar Hoover's criticisms sound to complaints made by political candidates today. Has crime been rising steadily all this time? If so, has nothing been done about it? If not, why not? We also notice that Hoover touches on the parole issue we've been thinking about, though he sees liberal parole policies as only one of the areas in need of remedy.

Though it's odd, we are starting to feel that Hoover's speech can be of great use to us, so we pause to try summarizing it. We may be able to use the summary when we write our paper, but in the meantime it will also be useful to tie down, with a summary, what Hoover is saying:

FBI Director J. Edgar Hoover argued in a speech delivered in the early 1960s that America was undergoing an epidemic of crime. Over 2,600,000 serious crimes had been committed in one year alone. In opposition to "armchair sociologists" who would define away crime, Hoover argues for realistic action. We should tighten the "turnstile justice" given to juveniles. We should decrease the number of convicted criminals receiving parole, probation, and suspended sentences. We should also eliminate the "country club" atmosphere of

```
prisons, and we should pressure judges to disregard le-
gal technicalities and "mumbo-jumbo." Our laws, says
Hoover, were never intended to provide equal justice to
criminals and the people they victimize.
```

Partly as a result of having summarized Hoover's argument, a strategy for organizing our own argument occurs to us. We can borrow Hoover's structure. Since his speech was composed more than a generation ago, it would be powerful to claim that since Hoover made this speech things have only gotten worse. We might even draft an opening paragraph that uses the summary we've just written:

```
FBI Director J. Edgar Hoover warned in a speech
delivered in the early 1960s that America was undergo-
ing an epidemic of crime....
```

Then in separate phases of our paper we might examine one by one the institutions Hoover criticized: juvenile sentencing; parole, probation, and suspended sentences; living conditions in prisons; and legal maneuverings. Our argument would be that the situations of which Hoover complained have only deteriorated, and remedies are needed now more than ever.

One problem with this plan is that we don't yet have much evidence. And if we do follow through, we'll have to research each of the four subtopics we just listed. That won't be easy. And what if we discover that some of those topics do not significantly contribute to the crime rate? Or that the policies for some have grown stricter yet have had no effect? After reflecting for a moment, it occurs to us that such complications might not turn out to be disadvantages. In fact, they might help us to develop an argument that, while using the framework provided by Hoover's points, is more our own. For instance, if we learned that the number of convictions averted by legal technicalities is insignificant and that few of today's prisons — or yesterday's prisons either — could really be accused of maintaining country club atmospheres, we might be able to construct an argument along the following lines:

```
In the early 1960s FBI Director J. Edgar Hoover
argued that....
    Hoover's criticisms of "legal mumbo-jumbo" no
longer hold....
    His attack on the ease of prison life never did
ring true....
    But Hoover's criticisms of this country's sentenc-
ing policies, both for juveniles and adults, do still
```

```
hold.  If anything, our courts have grown more lax
lately in the administration of probation, suspended
sentences, and parole.  In this paper I would like to
look at one of these major shortcomings in our criminal
system, the institution of parole....
```

So we needn't find that each of Hoover's points still applies. In fact we needn't accept any of these points themselves. But if we find his speech helpful as a jumping-off platform, we can adapt its structure to accommodate what we learn. Excited by the possibilities of this new and more flexible strategy for developing our argument, we're eager to get on with investigating which features of the criminal justice system have continued to be abused.

But before pushing on, we might take a critical pause. Are we losing sight of anything important? Are we too heavily invested in finding that an epidemic, in some form, exists? Before considering the supposed abuses of the system, don't we still need to establish the gravity of the general problem? Should we be looking for opposing views? It turns out that one good place to look for such views is in front of us. The anthology in which we found Hoover's speech is designed to bring together conflicting viewpoints. As we browse through the section of the book in which Hoover's speech appears, we come across another piece that seems sharply in contrast. It's an excerpt from a book called *Rules of Sociological Method* by the French sociologist Émile Durkheim. Unlike Hoover, Durkheim is someone who has been mentioned in class; he has been credited with having a great influence on other sociologists. Here are some excerpts from the passage that appears in the criminology anthology.

> There is no society that is not confronted with the problem of crim-   1
> inality. Its form changes; the acts thus characterized are not always the
> same everywhere; but everywhere and always, there have been men
> who have behaved in such a way as to draw upon themselves penal
> repression. If, in proportion as societies pass from the lower to the higher
> types, the rate of criminality, i.e., the relation between the yearly number
> of crimes and the population, tended to decline, it might be believed that
> crime, while still normal, is tending to lose this character of normality.
> But we have no reason to believe that such a regression is substantiated.
> Many facts would seem rather to indicate a movement in the opposite
> direction. . . . There is, then, no phenomenon that presents more in-
> disputably all the symptoms of normality, since it appears closely con-
> nected with the conditions of all collective life. . . . No doubt it is possible
> that crime itself will have abnormal forms, as, for example, when its rate
> is unusually high. This excess is, indeed, undoubtedly morbid in nature.
> What is normal, simply, is the existence of criminality, provided that it
> attains and does not exceed, for each social type, a certain level, which
> it is perhaps not impossible to fix in conformity with the preceding rules.
> . . . To classify crime among the phenomena of normal sociology is not

to say merely that it is an inevitable, although regrettable phenomenon, due to the incorrigible wickedness of men; it is to affirm that it is a factor in public health, an integral part of all healthy societies. This result is, at first glance, surprising enough to have puzzled even ourselves for a long time. Once this first surprise has been overcome, however, it is not difficult to find reasons explaining this normality and at the same time confirming it.

In the first place crime is normal because a society exempt from it   2
is utterly impossible. Crime . . . consists of an act that offends certain very strong collective sentiments. In a society in which criminal acts are no longer committed, the sentiments they offend would have to be found without exception in all individual consciousnesses, and they must be found to exist with the same degree as sentiments contrary to them. Assuming that this condition could actually be realized, crime would not thereby disappear; it would only change its form, for the very cause which would thus dry up the sources of criminality would immediately open up new ones. . . .

From this point of view the fundamental facts of criminality present   3
themselves to us in an entirely new light. Contrary to current ideas, the criminal no longer seems a totally unsociable being, a sort of parasitic element, a strange and unassimilable body, introduced into the midst of society. On the contrary, he plays a definite role in social life. Crime, for its part, must no longer be conceived as an evil that cannot be too much suppressed. There is no occasion for self-congratulation when the crime rate drops noticeably below the average level, for we may be certain that this apparent progress is associated with some social disorder. Thus, the number of assault cases never falls so low as in times of want. With the drop in the crime rate, and as a reaction to it, comes a revision, or the need of a revision in the theory of punishment. If, indeed, crime is a disease, its punishment is its remedy and cannot be otherwise conceived; thus, all the discussions it arouses bear on the point of determining what the punishment must be in order to fulfill this role of remedy. If crime is not pathological at all, the object of punishment cannot be to cure it, and its true function must be sought elsewhere.

— Émile Durkheim, *Rules of Sociological Method*

Are we persuaded? Before reading Durkheim, most of us would not have regarded crime as part of a healthy society, nor would we have viewed dropping crime rates with alarm, as evidence of some social disorder. What a strange idea. Do you think there is anything to be said for this point of view? Other people take Durkheim's views seriously, so perhaps we can use him in some way, even if he doesn't persuade us. For instance, we might be able to generate part of our argument by setting up a Durkheim quotation with which we can disagree.

Without yet deciding whether we intend to put the Durkheim piece to some direct use, we might as well try to get a grip on it by writing about it, as we did with the Hoover passage. But this time instead of a summary, let's try a few notes. And let's try comparing Durkheim's views to Hoover's.

> Hoover sees crime as an epidemic. Durkheim sees it as part of a healthy society.
>
> For Hoover, the remedy for crime seems to be punishment. For Durkheim, punishment is no remedy. His last sentence is puzzling, though: "its true function [punishment's?] must be sought elsewhere." Where? What does he mean by this?
>
> Hoover accuses "armchair sociologists" of defining away crime. Is that what Durkheim is doing? Not exactly, but he is concerned with definition. Any society, he says, will define <u>something</u> as crime. If burglary is successfully suppressed, he might say, failing to mow your lawn might become a crime. But we might be willing to make lawn negligence a crime if that got rid of homicides....
>
> Can Durkheim be right that the number of assaults goes <u>down</u> in "times of want"? Hoover would scoff at that one, I bet. When was Durkheim writing? And in what society? What were the punishments?
>
> Durkheim and Hoover might not be in total opposition. Durkheim allows that crime, though healthy, will sometimes have "abnormal forms, as for example when its rate is unusually high." And he uses a disease word—— <u>morbid</u>——to describe such states. I wonder if he'd agree that our crime rate is morbidly high.

Pitting Durkheim and Hoover against each other in this way may not shake our intent to use Hoover to shape our argument, but it makes us a little wary. It also makes us more certain than ever that we should find some further statistics that help us to say whether or not the contemporary crime rate is especially high. The statistics we've already found (pp. 378–379) will be helpful, but they point to a rising crime rate only through 1980. We know from our class that there is quite a lag in the compilation of national crime statistics, but at the library, with the help of a reference librarian, we do manage to locate a table (Table 2, pp. 386–387) that takes us further into the 1980s. What do you make of it? Does it suit our purposes?

In trying to draw on the data in this table for our argument, what problems emerge? At first, the categories may not seem to match those of our earlier statistics. And the numbers aren't in a single frame of reference — the rate

TABLE 2. Number and Rate (per 1,000 units of each respective category) of Personal and Household Victimizations

TYPE OF VICTIMIZATION	BY TYPE OF VICTIMIZATION, UNITED STATES, 1973–85 (NUMBER OF VICTIMIZATIONS IN THOUSANDS)												
	1973	1974	1975	1976	1977	1978	1979	1980	1981	1982	1983	1984	1985
PERSONAL VICTIMIZATION (RATE PER 1,000 PERSONS 12 YEARS OF AGE AND OLDER)													
CRIMES OF VIOLENCE													
Number	5,351	5,510	5,573	5,599	5,902	5,941	6,159	6,130	6,582	6,459	5,903	6,021	5,823
Rate	32.6	33.0	32.8	32.6	33.9	33.7	34.5	33.3	35.3	34.3	31.0	31.4	30.0
RAPE													
Number	156	163	154	145	154	171	192	174	178	153	154	180	138
Rate	1.0	1.0	0.9	0.8	0.9	1.0	1.1	0.9	1.0	0.8	0.8	0.9	0.7
ROBBERY													
Number	1,108	1,199	1,147	1,111	1,083	1,038	1,116	1,209	1,381	1,334	1,149	1,097	985
Rate	6.7	7.2	6.8	6.5	6.2	5.9	6.3	6.6	7.4	7.1	6.0	5.7	5.1
ASSAULT													
Number	4,087	4,148	4,272	4,344	4,664	4,732	4,851	4,747	5,024	4,973	4,600	4,744	4,699
Rate	24.9	24.8	25.2	25.3	26.8	26.9	27.2	25.8	27.0	26.4	24.1	24.7	24.2
AGGRAVATED ASSAULT													
Number	1,655	1,735	1,631	1,695	1,738	1,708	1,769	1,707	1,796	1,754	1,517	1,727	1,605
Rate	10.1	10.4	9.6	9.9	10.0	9.7	9.9	9.3	9.6	9.3	8.0	9.0	8.3
SIMPLE ASSAULT													
Number	2,432	2,413	2,641	2,648	2,926	3,024	3,082	3,041	3,228	3,219	3,083	3,017	3,094
Rate	14.8	14.4	15.6	15.4	16.8	17.2	17.3	16.5	17.3	17.1	16.2	15.7	15.9
CRIMES OF THEFT													
Number	14,971	15,889	16,294	16,519	16,933	17,050	16,382	15,300	15,863	15,553	14,657	13,789	13,474
Rate	91.1	95.1	96.0	96.1	97.3	96.8	91.9	83.0	85.1	82.5	76.9	71.8	69.4
PERSONAL LARCENY WITH CONTACT													
Number	504	520	524	497	461	549	511	558	605	577	563	530	523
Rate	3.1	3.1	3.1	2.9	2.7	3.1	2.9	3.0	3.3	3.1	3.0	2.8	2.7
PERSONAL LARCENY WITHOUT CONTACT													
Number	14,466	15,369	15,770	16,022	16,472	16,501	15,871	14,742	15,258	14,976	14,095	13,259	12,951
Rate	88.0	92.0	92.9	93.2	94.6	93.6	89.0	80.0	81.9	79.5	74.0	69.1	66.7
TOTAL POPULATION AGE 12 AND OLDER	164,363	167,058	169,671	171,901	174,093	176,215	178,284	184,324	186,336	188,497	190,504	191,962	194,097

RATE PER 1,000 HOUSEHOLDS

HOUSEHOLD VICTIMIZATION													
HOUSEHOLD BURGLARY													
Number	6,459	6,721	6,744	6,663	6,765	6,704	6,685	6,973	7,394	6,663	6,063	5,643	5,594
Rate	91.7	93.1	91.7	88.9	88.5	86.0	84.1	84.3	87.9	78.2	70.0	64.1	62.7
HOUSEHOLD LARCENY													
Number	7,537	8,933	9,223	9,301	9,418	9,352	10,630	10,468	10,176	9,705	9,114	8,750	8,703
Rate	107.0	123.8	125.4	124.1	123.3	119.9	133.7	126.5	121.0	113.9	105.2	99.4	97.5
MOTOR VEHICLE THEFT													
Number	1,344	1,358	1,433	1,235	1,297	1,365	1,393	1,381	1,439	1,377	1,264	1,340	1,270
Rate	19.1	18.8	19.5	16.5	17.0	17.5	17.5	16.7	17.1	16.2	14.6	15.2	14.2
TOTAL NUMBER OF HOUSEHOLDS	70,442	72,163	73,560	74,956	76,412	77,980	79,499	82,753	84,095	85,211	86,635	88,039	89,263

SOURCE: U.S. Department of Justice, Bureau of Justice Statistics, *Criminal Victimization in the U.S.: Summary Findings of 1978–79 Changes in Crime and of Trends Since 1973,* National Crime Survey Report SD-NCS-N-18 (Washington, DC: U.S. Department of Justice, 1980), Table 1; U.S. Department of Justice, Bureau of Justice Statistics, *Criminal Victimization in the U.S.,* Technical Report NCJ-87577 (Washington, DC: U.S. Department of Justice, March 1983), p. 2, Table 1; U.S. Department of Justice Statistics, *Criminal Victimization in the United States,* Special Report NCJ-90541 (Washington, DC: U.S. Department of Justice, September 1983), p. 2, Table 1; and U.S. Department of Justice, Bureau of Justice Statistics, *Criminal Victimization 1984,* Bulletin NCJ-98904, p. 2; *Criminal Victimization 1985,* Bulletin NCJ-102534, p. 2 (Washington, DC: U.S. Department of Justice). Table adapted by Katherine M. Jamieson and Timothy J. Flanagan, *Sourcebook of Criminal Justice Statistics, 1987.*

of the earlier table was per 100,000 people; these figures are per 1,000. Once we learn to read past these difficulties, however, a more disconcerting problem awaits us. This new table is evidently not going to support our claim of a rising crime rate. The rate of "crimes of violence," for example, though it did rise from 32.6 in 1973 to 34.5 in 1979, declined by 1985 to 30.0. Overall from the year 1973 to 1985 the rate of violent crimes went *down*. Similar, in some cases sharper, declines can be seen for burglaries and motor vehicle thefts. In fact, on the entire table, only the category "simple assaults" supports the claim of a rising crime rate through 1985.

It's starting to look as though our argument will not flow along as we had envisioned it. Before turning away in disappointment from the table, however, we ought to see if there's anything more it can tell us. Play around with the numbers a little. Can you notice anything else? Are there any further inferences to be made? One guess might be that something happened in the 1980s to bring down the crime rate. But we don't know of any major changes in criminal policies. Researching the possible causes for this crop might turn into a dismal enterprise: We feel tired before we start.

But something else has caught our eye. When we think comparatively about this table in relation to the earlier one, we realize that the two overlap in the years 1973 through 1980. That doesn't seem particularly interesting at first; it only means that some of the information must be repetitive. Yet when we actually compare the numbers for any given year, we notice something very puzzling. The statistics from the two tables — both the totals and the rates — seem weirdly out of touch with each other. We can illustrate these strange discrepancies by creating a new table of our own. (To compare the rates from the two tables we translate the second from a rate per 1,000 to a rate per 100,000.)

	FBI INDEX		DEPT. OF JUSTICE FIGURES	
	Violent Crimes Total	Rate per 100,000 people	Violent Crimes Total	Rate per 100,000 people
1973	875,910	417.4	5,351,000	3,260
1974	974,720	461.1	5,510,000	3,300
1975	1,026,280	481.3	5,573,000	3,280
1976	986,580	459.6	5,599,000	3,260
1977	1,009,500	466.6	5,902,000	3,390
1978	1,061,830	486.9	5,941,000	3,370
1979	1,178,540	535.5	6,159,000	3,450
1980	1,308,900	580.8	6,130,000	3,300

When we look at the two sets of figures now, they are bewildering. First, in total number of violent crimes, the figures in the right columns dwarf the figures at the left. In any given year, the Department of Justice lists five times as many violent crimes as the FBI Index. Stranger still, though, is a comparison between the two rate columns. According to the FBI statistics, there were 417.4 victims per 100,000 people in 1973 and 580.8 victims per 100,000 in 1980. Those were the figures that enabled us to decide, when we first looked at them, that these years show a steady increase in crime. If we calculate the overall change as a percent ($580.8 - 417.4 = 163.4$; $163.4 \div 580.8 = 0.28$), this eight-year period shows a genuinely alarming 28 percent increase in violent crime. If we perform the same calculations with the numbers on the right, we arrive at a 2.1 percent increase for the same years, a negligible increase. If we wanted to play with the numbers still further, we could also say that while the FBI figures show an increase from 1974 to 1980 of more than 20 percent, the Department of Justice figures show no rate increase at all.

Clearly the two sets of statistics tell very different stories. Where does that leave us in relation to our argument? Maybe there's some way to turn this problem with statistics to our advantage, making *them* a part of our topic. After all, this problem was our discovery. But are we again losing touch with our topic? Is it time to consult with our criminology teacher?

If we look to our criminology textbook for some further help, we find these illuminating paragraphs about how the FBI statistics are compiled.

> In general we have a limited idea of the percentage of crime that is [1] committed by any category of individuals or groups in our society. The actual amount of crime in the United States today is, according to reliable surveys, several times that reported in the *Uniform Crime Reports*. We have no idea of the age, sex, or race of persons who committed crimes that were not reported to the police. Only about 20 percent of the crimes known to the police are cleared by arrest. We have no idea who committed the remaining 80 percent, and therefore we cannot attribute these crimes to any age, sex, or racial group. Moreover, people arrested by the police are not necessarily guilty. Many are released without being charged, and many more are acquitted. The statistics reveal that *almost half the people arrested were not found guilty of a crime.*
>
> The general and complex statistical issue is that FBI statistics re- [2] garding the age, sex, and race of criminals are mainly based on data obtained from those arrested. These are the *suspects* and the *failures* in crime. We know little or nothing about people who successfully commit crimes and are not apprehended.
>
> — Martin R. Haskell and Lewis Yablonsky, *Criminology: Crime and Criminality*

If we pursue this question further, we can learn from another book on the suggested reading list that the second table must have been compiled from a more recently developed method of data gathering called "victimization studies." Victimization studies are compiled by asking samplings of individuals whether members of their households have been the recent victims of crimes.

Are the figures in the second table more reliable than the first? Perhaps, perhaps not. Has the U.S. crime rate been rising throughout the 1970s and well into the 1980s? Only according to the statistics of the FBI.

If we try to step back a little further from this problem with the evidence, we encounter an even more fundamental problem. If statisticians have such difficulty assembling authoritative data about the *facts* of crime, what will statistics be able to tell us about relationships of cause and effect? We must face a problem that we haven't been facing until now. If increasing punishment *did* decrease crime, how would we ever be able to tell? What would the evidence look like? Where would we find it? We've been assuming that at some later point we can look into questions such as whether stiffer sentences for juveniles or fewer grants of parole lead to a decrease in crime. Now we are starting to doubt whether any such evidence has ever been compiled. What if a sudden change in judicial policy had been instituted in some particular year, and a change in the crime rate could be detected in that same year? Would that prove that the two factors were causally connected, or might some other factor be responsible?

We have now reached a very frustrating point in our search for an argument. We know that the argument we had originally intended — even in its more flexible form — will be hard to manage. But we don't have an alternative to turn to — unless we make our argument about the limitations of the evidence itself. Is crime getting worse? We don't know. What will work to bring the crime rate down? We can't say for sure.

Not every effort to develop an argument will lead you into this kind of argumentative swamp. But if you find yourself getting bogged down, look for something else to keep you afloat.

What we're running up against, we now are starting to realize, is a classic problem in criminology — the question of deterrence. What actions, short of killing all potential criminals (ourselves included), will effectively deter crime? We cannot tell with certainty, for a crime not committed — deterred crime — cannot be directly measured. We know, though, that there are some criminologists who have written *theoretically* about deterrence, and back again we go to the list of suggested readings. There we find listed an article, written by an economist, the title of which asks the blunt question "Does Punishment Deter Crime?" Here are some key passages.

> Traditionally there have been three arguments for the punishment of criminals. The first of these is that punishment is morally required or, another way of putting the same thing, that it is necessary for the community to feel morally satisfied. I will not discuss this further. The two remaining explanations are that punishment deters crime and that it may rehabilitate the criminal. The rehabilitation argument was little used before about 1800, presumably because the punishments in vogue up to that time had little prospect of producing any positive effect upon the moral character of the criminal. 1
>
> But with the turn to imprisonment as the principal form of punishment — a movement which occurred in the latter part of the 18th and early part of the 19th century — the idea that the prison might "rehabilitate" 2

the prisoner became more common. The word "penitentiary" was coined with the intent of describing a place where the prisoner has the time and the opportunity to repent of his sins and resolve to follow a more socially approved course of action after his release. The idea that prisons would rehabilitate the criminal and that this was their primary purpose gradually replaced the concept of deterrence as the principal publicly announced justification for the punishment system. . . . I should like to point out that, whatever the motive or the reason for this change, it certainly was not the result of careful scientific investigation.

So far as I have been able to discover, there were no efforts to test   3 the deterrent effect of punishment scientifically until about 1950. At that time, several studies were made investigating the question whether the death penalty deterred murder more effectively than life imprisonment. These studies showed that it did not, but they were extremely primitive statistically. This is not to criticize the scholars who made them. Computers were not then readily available, the modern statistical techniques based on the computer had not yet been fully developed, and, last but by no means least, the scholars who undertook the work were not very good statisticians. Under the circumstances, we cannot blame them for the inadequacies of their work, but neither should we give much weight to their findings. . . .

Most economists who give serious thought to the problem of crime   4 immediately come to the conclusion that punishment will indeed deter crime. The reason is perfectly simple: Demand curves slope downward. If you increase the cost of something, less will be consumed. Thus, if you increase the cost of committing a crime, there will be fewer crimes. The elasticity of the demand curve, of course, might be low, in which case the effect might be small; but there should be at least some effect.

Economists, of course, would not deny that there are other factors   5 that affect the total number of crimes. Unemployment, for example, quite regularly raises the amount of crime and, at least under modern conditions, changes in the age composition of the population seem to be closely tied to changes in the crime rate. The punishment variable, however, has the unique characteristic of being fairly easy to change by government action. Thus, if it does have an effect, we should take advantage of that fact. . . .

It should be emphasized that the question of whether the death   6 penalty deters murder is a different one from the question of whether we wish to have the death penalty. One widespread minor crime is failing to return to the parking meter and put in a coin when the time expires. I take it that we could reduce the frequency with which this crime is committed by boiling all offenders in oil. I take it, also, that no one would favor this method of deterrence. Thus, the fact that we can deter a crime by a particular punishment is not a sufficient argument for use of that punishment.

In discussing the concept of deterrence, I find that a great many   7 people seem to feel that, although it would no doubt work with respect to burglary and other property crimes, it is unlikely to have much effect on crimes of impulse, such as rape and many murders. They reason that people who are about to kill their wives in a rage are totally incapable of making any calculations at all. But this is far from obvious. The prisoners in Nazi concentration camps must frequently have been in a state of well-justified rage against some of their guards; yet this almost never led to their using violence against the guards, because punishment — which, if they were lucky, would be instant death, but was more likely to be death by torture — was so obvious and so certain. Even in highly emotional situations, we retain some ability to reason, albeit presumably not so well as normally.

It would take much greater provocation to lead a man to kill his wife   8
if he knew that, as in England in the 1930s, committing murder meant a two-out-of-three chance of meeting the public executioner within about two months than if — as is currently true in South Africa — there were only a one-in-100 chance of being executed after about a year's delay. . . .

It should be noted that thus far I have said nothing whatsoever about   9
how well-informed criminals or potential criminals are as to the punishments for each crime in each state. For punishment to have a deterrent effect, potential criminals must have at least some information about its likely severity and frequency. Presumably, the effect of variations in punishment would be greater if criminals were well-informed than if they were not. In practice, of course, potential criminals are not very well-informed about these things, but they do have some information.

Reports of crimes and punishments are a major part of most news-   10
papers. It is true that most intellectuals tend to skip over this part of the newspaper, but the average person is more likely to read it than some things that appeal to intellectuals. And an individual who is on the verge of committing a crime or has already taken up a career of crime is apt to be much more interested in crime stories than is the average man. He should have, therefore, a rough idea of the severity of punishments and of the probability that they will be imposed. This information should affect the likelihood that he will choose to commit a given crime.

Nevertheless, the information that he will have is likely to be quite   11
rough. Undoubtedly, if we could somehow arrange for people to have accurate information on these matters, we would get much better coefficients on our multiple regression equations for the deterrence effect of punishment. But since governments have a motive to lie — i.e., to pretend that punishment is more likely and more severe than it actually is — it is unlikely that we can do much about improving this information. Still, the empirical evidence is clear. Even granting the fact that most potential criminals have only a rough idea as to the frequency and severity of punishment, multiple regression studies show that increasing the frequency or severity of the punishment does reduce the likelihood that a given crime will be committed.

Finally, I should like to turn to the issue of why "rehabilitation"   12
became the dominant rationale of our punishment system in the latter part of the 19th century and has remained so up to the present, in spite of the absence of any scientific support. The reasons, in my opinion,

have to do with the fallacy, so common in the social sciences, that "all good things go together." If we have the choice between preventing crime by training the criminal to be good — i.e., rehabilitating him — or deterring crime by imposing unpleasantness on criminals, the former is the one we would like to choose. . . .

If, . . . we can think of the prison as a kind of educational institution 13 that rehabilitates criminals, we do not have to consciously think of ourselves as injuring people. It is clearly more appealing to think of solving the criminal problem by means that are themselves not particularly unpleasant than to think of solving it by methods that are unpleasant. But in this case we do not have the choice between a pleasant and an unpleasant method of dealing with crime. We have an unpleasant method — deterrence — that works, and a pleasant method — rehabilitation — that (at least so far) never has worked. Under the circumstances, we have to opt either for the deterrence method or for a higher crime rate.
— Gordon Tullock, "Does Punishment Deter Crime?"

After rereading Tullock's article and once again taking stock of where we are, we find ourselves with some new possibilities and some revived ones:

1. We could use Tullock's article to support the idea that increased punishment must deter crime. Thus we could use Tullock in support of the plan to follow Hoover's structure.
2. Tullock confirms what we've discovered for ourselves about FBI statistics. And he makes us aware that governments may have their own interests in how crime statistics are presented. Our argument could be entirely about the problems with crime statistics.
3. We notice that Tullock classifies the motives for punishment into three types: social morality, rehabilitation, and deterrence. He goes on to say why he finds the deterrence argument more persuasive than the rehabilitation argument. Maybe we could use Tullock's classification system to sort out the motives of those who write about imprisonment. Tullock writes from the motive of deterrence, Hoover seems to mix the motives of deterrence and morality, and Durkheim — well, we're not sure about Durkheim. He seems to say that society punishes criminals for moral reasons, but we'd need to read more Durkheim to be sure. And can we find someone who argues for prison sentences as rehabilitation?
4. Now that we're thinking in terms of classification, perhaps we ought to think about classifying crimes themselves. Doesn't it make a difference which *types* of crime we're talking about? We might want to distinguish between violent and nonviolent crimes and then subdivide the categories. Or we might want to classify crimes into those directed against people and those directed against property. Or maybe, with some more research, we could divide crimes into those that may be decreased by deterrence and those that will remain unaffected.
5. Could we argue that it's naive to think that we punish criminals *only*

to deter crime? There's something socially satisfying about such punishment: It says to those doing the punishing, "We, not they, are in control." Here's where Durkheim might be very helpful.

6. Tullock warns against letting his general points become the basis for public policies. He points out that we can't assume that criminals will be well informed about increases in punishments, but the whole idea of deterrence is based on information. He also cautions that "the fact that we can deter a crime by a particular punishment is not a sufficient argument for use of that punishment." We might make the argument that while increasing punishments should in theory reduce crimes, there are all sorts of practical hindrances working against it.

7. The "economics of crime" approach is a new perspective. The idea that crimes can be seen as rational acts based on cost-benefit analyses seems strange but interesting. Perhaps our argument could be for or against this approach to understanding crime. Or perhaps our argument could simply be that this is a perspective worth considering. We'd have to look at other economists' writing about crime.

Spurred on by this last possibility, let's imagine one last rush to the supplementary reading list, where we find some helpful pieces. First is an article "The Economics of Crime and Punishment," which seems to support some of Tullock's points while also raising new ones. Here are some excerpts.

> Is there a relationship between punishment and the number and types of crimes committed? If so, what are the available alternatives to punishing guilty offenders? Should we impose large fines instead of incarceration? Should we have public whippings? Should capital punishment be allowed? To establish a system of crime deterrence, we would need to assess carefully the value of different supposed deterrents.   1
>
> One thing we can be sure of. Uniformly heavy punishments for all crimes will lead to a larger number of major crimes being committed. Let's look at the reasoning. All decisions are made on the margin. If an act of theft will be punished by hanging and an act of murder will be punished by the same fate, there is no marginal deterrence to murder. If a theft of $5 is met with a punishment of ten years in jail and a theft of $50,000 incurs the same sentence, why not steal $50,000? Why not go for broke? There is no marginal deterrence to prevent one from doing so.   2
>
> A serious question is how our system of justice can establish penalties that are appropriate from a social point of view. To establish the correct (marginal) deterrents, we must observe empirically how criminals respond to changes in punishments. This leads us to the question of how people decide whether to commit a "crime." A theory needs to be established as to what determines the supply of criminal offenses.   3
>
> Adam Smith once said: 4
>
>> The affluence of the rich excites the indignation of the poor, who are often both driven by want, and prompted by envy, to invade his possessions. It

is only under the shelter of the civil magistrate that the owner of that valuable property, which is acquired by the labor of many years, or perhaps by many successive generations, can sleep a single night in security. He is at all times surrounded by unknown enemies, whom, though he never provokes, he can never appease, and from whose injustice he can be protected only by the powerful arm of the civil magistrate continually held up to chastise it. The acquisition of valuable and extensive property, therefore, necessarily requires the establishment of civil government. Where there is no property, or at least none that exceeds the value of two or three days' labor, civil government is not so necessary.[1]

Smith is pointing out that robberies involve the taking of valuable   5
property. Thus, we can surmise that individuals who engage in robberies are seeking income. Therefore, before acting, a professional criminal might be expected to look at the anticipated returns and the anticipated costs of criminal activity. These could then be compared with the net returns from legitimate activities. We note that the civil government which Smith refers to above would be imposing the cost on the criminal, if apprehended. That cost would include, but not be limited to, apprehension, conviction, and jail. (The criminal's calculations are analogous to those made by a professional athlete when weighing the cost of possible serious injury.)

Viewing the supply of offenses thusly, we can come up with methods   6
by which society can lower the net expected rate of return for committing any illegal activity. That is, we can figure out how to reduce crime most effectively. We have talked about one particular aspect — the size of penalties. We also briefly mentioned another — the probability of detection for each offense. When either of these costs of crime goes up, the supply of offenses goes down; that is, less crime is committed. . . .

One can analyze criminal acts as economic activities. The potential   7
criminal makes an economic decision in which he or she does a cost-benefit analysis of criminal activities versus legal consequences. A key set of variables in such an analysis involves the costs of criminal activity, which include the costs of getting caught, being sentenced, and suffering punishment. In most major cities, the probabilities of being caught, sentenced, going to trial, and serving time are very low. Hence, when they are multiplied together and the product is multiplied times the potential punishment, the expected cost is extremely small. The potential criminal's cost-benefit analysis therefore often implicitly shows that crime does indeed pay. In order to reduce criminal activities, including murder, an economist would argue that the price paid by the criminal must be increased.

— Douglass C. North and Roger L. Miller, *The Economics
of Public Issues*

This piece increases our interest in using economists' points of view to help construct our argument. But we also notice that although this article

---

[1] Adam Smith, *The Wealth of Nations*, 1776.

makes a general case for deterrence, North and Miller add further reservations. Increasing punishments for some crimes, they say, can make other crimes more severe. Like Tullock, they disqualify themselves from recommending specific policies, and they admit that there is no adequate theory for judging which penalties will decrease which crimes without counterproductive side effects. Finally, they admit that there are also moral problems: "A serious question is how our system of justice can establish penalties that are appropriate from a social point of view." *Whose* social point of view? we might add.

Nagged by such reservations, we're very interested when we come upon a third article that, while sharing much with the first two, is written from a more outright political point of view. David Gordon, writing from the political left, is concerned not so much with the problem of reducing crime as with analyzing its place within our larger economic system. His article also looks frankly at another part of the problem we've been avoiding: More violent crime is committed by poor people, particularly those living in ghettos. Gordon asks why this is and what should or shouldn't be done about it. Here are some excerpts.

> Capitalist societies depend, as radicals often argue, on basically competitive forms of social and economic interaction and upon substantial inequalities in the allocation of social resources. Without inequalities, it would be much more difficult to induce workers to work in alienating environments. Without competition and a competitive ideology, workers might not be inclined to struggle to improve their relative income and status in society by working harder. Finally, although rights of property are protected, capitalist societies do not guarantee economic security to most of their individual members. Individuals must fend for themselves, finding the best available opportunities to provide for themselves and their families. At the same time, history bequeaths a corpus of laws and statutes to any social epoch which may or may not correspond to the social morality of that epoch. Inevitably, at any point in time, many of the "best" opportunities of economic survival open to different citizens will violate some of those historically determined laws. Driven by the fear of economic insecurity and by a competitive desire to gain some of the goods unequally distributed throughout the society, many individuals will eventually become "criminals." As Adam Smith himself admitted, "Where there is no property, . . . civil government is not so necessary." 1

> In that respect, therefore, radicals argue that nearly all crimes in capitalist societies represent perfectly *rational* responses to the structure of institutions upon which capitalist societies are based. Crimes of many different varieties constitute functionally similar responses to the organization of capitalist institutions, for those crimes help provide a means of survival in a society within which survival is never assured. . . . 2

> It seems especially clear, first of all, that ghetto crime is committed by people responding quite reasonably to the structure of economic op- 3

portunities available to them. Only rarely, it appears, can ghetto criminals be regarded as raving, irrational, antisocial lunatics. The "legitimate" jobs open to many ghetto residents, especially to young black males, typically pay low wages, offer relatively demeaning assignments, and carry the constant risk of layoff. In contrast, many kinds of crime "available" in the ghetto often bring higher monetary return, offer even higher social status, and — at least in some cases like numbers running — sometimes carry relatively low risk of arrest and punishment. Given those alternative opportunities, the choice between "legitimate" and "illegitimate" activities is often quite simple. . . . The fact that these activities are often "illegal" sometimes doesn't really matter; since life out of jail often seems as bad as life inside prison, the deterrent effect of punishment is negligible. . . .

4   If most crime in the United States in one way or another reflects the same kind of rational response to the insecurity and inequality of capitalist institutions, what explains the manifold differences among different kinds of crimes? Some crimes are much more violent than others, some are much more heavily prosecuted, and some are much more profitable. Why? . . .

5   First, I would argue that many of the important differences among crimes in this society derive quite directly from the different socioeconomic classes to which individuals belong. Relatively affluent citizens have access to jobs in large corporations, to institutions involved in complicated paper transactions involving lots of money, and to avenues of relatively unobtrusive communication. Members of those classes who decide to break the law have, as Clark puts it, "an easier, less offensive, less visible way of doing wrong." Those raised in poverty, on the other hand, do not have such easy access to money. If they are to obtain it criminally, they must impinge on those who already have it or direct its flow. As Robert Morgenthau, a former federal attorney, has written, those growing up in the ghetto "will probably never have the opportunity to embezzle funds from a bank or to promote a multimillion dollar stock fraud scheme. The criminal ways which we encourage [them] to choose will be those closest at hand — from vandalism to mugging to armed robbery."

— David M. Gordon, "Class and the Economics of Crime"

By forcing us to think about criminals not just as individuals making choices but as members of a class with limited choices to make, Gordon further sharpens the issues. By this point in our search we have grown aware of the different analytical perspectives that various writers bring to matters of crime and punishment. Not only is Durkheim's point of view opposed to Hoover's, but the economists bring to the issues a different set of emphases altogether. Further, *within* the community of economists the detached analysis of Tullock differs sharply from the more impassioned analysis of Gordon. And while we see that all the economists are writing analytically, they differ sharply in what they assume, select, and emphasize. As we imagine their different ways of looking at the facts, as well as the different facts they choose to look at and connect, the analytical possibilities for our own argument expand. We may even feel the impulse to do more research. We still haven't researched the workings of the parole system, for example.

We can't always pursue the questions that we raise, though it's good to raise as many as we can. At some point in our search, however, we'll need to cut ourselves off. Although there's more we could do, let's try a draft now. We have plenty of material to work with, and there are a number of possible arguments from which to choose. Let's choose an approach that reflects our latest understanding of the issues, making sure that it's one we can pursue in sufficient detail. We might try sketching an outline or jump right in with a looser plan. Let's say that we've decided to start off with Hoover, connect his recommendations with deterrence theory and then go on to show how economists look at deterrence. Maybe we can try to add up the hidden factors that make deterrence strategies less attractive than they first appear. Here is what we produce. In brackets we've indicated parts of the argument we intend to fill in later. The citations in parentheses conform to the documentation guidelines of the American Psychological Association (APA), the format most often used in the social sciences. In its final form, an essay like this one would include at the end a reference list consisting of all the sources used in the essay.

A DRAFT OF AN ESSAY ON CRIMINAL PUNISHMENT

                            Title?

        "Is America as a nation being swept by an epidemic
of spiritual malnutrition?" asked FBI Director J. Edgar
Hoover in a speech delivered in the early 1960s (1972).
He then went on to say that the signs of disease were
all too clear: 2,600,000 serious crimes in one year
alone, five offenses per minute. He claimed that crime
was "increasing--in both numbers and intensity--at an
alarming rate" (p. 29). His remedy? Enforce existing
laws more strictly: get tougher in sentencing juveniles, cut back on suspended sentences and paroles,
make prisons less comfortable places to be, and reduce
the number of convictions lost to legal technicalities.
Is the epidemic that Hoover saw then still with us today? Was there ever an epidemic at all? Could the
treatments urged by Hoover help reduce crime today?

        At first glance, the problem of crime in the U.S.

has only gotten worse since Hoover's warning. In 1980,
for example, the FBI reported a total of 13,295,400 serious crimes, six times the number that alarmed Hoover.
Even if we take into account that the U.S. population
has also been growing, there has apparently been a continual increase in crime. In the 1970s the rate of
crime per 100,000 inhabitants increased from 4,164.7 in
1971 to 5,899.9 in 1980, an increase of over 40 percent
in that ten-year span (Haskell & Yablonsky, 1983, pp.
68-69). The problem with such statistics is that they
are notoriously unreliable. [We can then go on to demonstrate the difference between the FBI statistics and
those compiled in the victimization studies, coming to
the conclusion that the crime rate may not be increasing at all.]

Is our current crime rate an epidemic then? Not
if by an epidemic we mean a sudden outbreak of something disease-like. In the first place, there's nothing sudden about the large amount of crime in the U.S.
Even Hoover admitted as much in the speech quoted above.
In calling for stiffer penalties, he quotes a distinguished jurist who made the same complaints and gave
the same recommendations forty-one years earlier. Crime
has always been a presence in our society, and although
the amount of crime is disturbing—even a single crime
is disturbing if we or someone we know is a victim—
there's little to suggest it is spreading contagiously.

Disease may also be an inappropriate image for understanding crime. Sociologist Emile Durkheim, for example, maintained that crime goes along with a healthy
society. "There is," he says, "no phenomenon that presents more indisputably all the symptoms of normality,
since it appears closely connected with the conditions
of all collective life" (1983, p. 4). He goes on to
declare that crime "is a factor in public health, an
integral part of all healthy societies." We needn't go

so far as Durkheim in claiming that our crime rate is a
sign of a healthy, relatively free society. But it's
hard to see ourselves in the midst of an epidemic.
That's not to say we should be complacent about the
level of crime in the U.S. Why shouldn't we want to
reduce it if we can? The real question is: What actions can we take? And what will they cost, not just
financially but in human terms?

Traditionally, there are three reasons offered for
imprisoning people or extending their imprisonment
(Tullock, 1974). [Using Tullock's framework, we can
then go on to classify Hoover's four recommendations as
strategies of deterrence.]

But how effectively does deterrence work? Until
fairly recently, most sociologists felt that prison had
little if any deterring effects on crime. The main explanations for criminal acts were to be sought in their
social environments or in the personalities of the
criminals themselves. These social and personal factors determined whether an individual was likely to
commit criminal acts. The few studies that were undertaken seemed to show that criminals' expectations of
punishment played little role in their decisions to
commit crimes (Tullock, 1974). Thus, strategies like
Hoover's would have little influence on crime rates—
only to the extent that criminals could not commit
crimes while in prison. But their imprisonment wouldn't
deter others from committing crimes, nor lessen their
own criminal inclinations when released.

With the entry of economists into the study of
crime, the case for the effectiveness of deterrence has
grown stronger. Economists perform more sophisticated
statistical tests—multiple regression studies, they
are called—and these have suggested that a greater
threat of punishment does tend to decrease the number
of crimes committed. Although these tests are hard to

comprehend, it's not hard to understand economists' explanations of <u>why</u> deterrence does work. Here's how
Gordon Tullock puts it:

> Most economists who give serious thought to
> the problem of crime immediately come to the con-
> clusion that punishment will indeed deter crime.
> The reason is perfectly simple: Demand curves
> slope downward. If you increase the cost of some-
> thing, less will be consumed. Thus, if you in-
> crease the cost of committing a crime, there will
> be fewer crimes. (p. 129)

Similarly the economists Douglass North and Roger
Miller (1983) explain how the principle of cost-benefit
analysis applies to crime:

> One can analyze criminal acts as economic
> activities. The potential criminal makes an
> economic decision in which he or she does a cost-
> benefit analysis of criminal activities versus le-
> gal consequences. A key set of variables in such
> an analysis involves the costs of criminal activ-
> ity, which include the costs of getting caught,
> being sentenced, and suffering punishment. In
> most major cities, the probabilities of being
> caught, sentenced, going to trial, and serving
> time are very low. Hence, when they are multi-
> plied together and the product is multiplied times
> the potential punishment, the expected cost is ex-
> tremely small. The potential criminal's cost-
> benefit analysis therefore often implicitly shows
> that crime does indeed pay. In order to reduce
> criminal activities, including murder, an econo-
> mist would argue that the price paid by the crimi-
> nal must be increased. (p. 181)

Such an explanation may at first seem unconvincing.
It's hard to picture a criminal doing "a cost-benefit
analysis of criminal activities versus legal conse-

quences." Imagine an addict about to mug someone. It seems ludicrous to say of such a situation, "The potential criminal makes an economic decision." But is it really so ludicrous? Don't most criminals, at least in the back of their minds, weigh the possibility of getting caught and the severity of their possible punishment? More important, for the theory to apply, it isn't necessary that <u>every</u> criminal think this way, only that <u>some</u> number will. To put such decisions in terms of deterrence, imagine 100 potential armed robbers contemplating 100 acts of armed robbery. The sentence for armed robbery has recently been raised from one to ten years. [We can go on to further develop this invented example.] Increasing the price (punishment) will make <u>some</u> consumers (criminals) turn away from the crime market.

If this view of crime and punishment is persuasive—and I admit that it is—then it follows, doesn't it, that if we want to reduce the crime rate, all we have to do is increase the penalties for all crimes? Well, yes and no. There are several reasons why we should not expect such changes to have much effect and why, from a social point of view, we should be hesitant to make them.

First, listen to this hesitation from North and Miller. "One thing we can be sure of," they say. "Uniformly heavy punishments for all crimes will lead to a larger number of major crimes being committed." Their reasoning? Let's go back to the addict on the street. He has decided to rob you. What are the chances he may kill you too? If the cost of getting caught robbing you is almost the same as the cost of killing you, he may decide, without much further calculation, to kill you—after all, you're the main witness to the robbery. The more I think about this example, the more I realize that I'd rather have a mugger know there is a great

difference in possible punishment costs between taking
my money and killing me. Viewed in this way, questions of deterrence become more problematic--which
crimes do we want to deter, and what are we willing to
pay to deter them? Are we willing to increase the
homicide rate in order to cut down the robbery rate?

We also need to keep in mind that increased punishment is only one of the factors contributing to a
criminal's judgment of costs. [We then go on to develop, in separate paragraphs, other practical and
moral hesitations that our reading has helped us to
raise, culminating with the following final objection.]

There is one further reservation that, in my opinion, is even stronger than the rest. Imposing stiffer
prison sentences punishes one social class more than
others. Upper classes benefit, lower classes pay. I
say this partly on the expectation that any likely
changes in criminal sentencing will be directed at violent crime, that is, street crime, rather than white-
collar crimes. And street crimes are committed by poor
people, often ghetto residents. Why should people living in ghettos be disproportionately involved in crime?
Here is the explanation offered by the radical economist David Gordon:

> It seems especially clear, first of all, that
> ghetto crime is committed by people responding
> quite reasonably to the structure of economic op-
> portunities available to them. Only rarely, it
> appears, can ghetto criminals be regarded as rav-
> ing, irrational, antisocial lunatics. The "legiti-
> mate" jobs open to many ghetto residents, espe-
> cially to young black males, typically pay low
> wages, offer relatively demeaning assignments, and
> carry the constant risk of layoff. In contrast,
> many kinds of crime "available" in the ghetto
> often bring higher monetary return, offer even

>higher social status, and—at least in some cases
>like numbers running—sometimes carry relatively
>low risk of arrest and punishment. Given those
>alternative opportunities, the choice between "le-
>gitimate" and "illegitimate" activities is often
>quite simple. (pp. 379–380)

What effect will the increased possibility of punishment have on someone for whom there are relatively few
alternatives? The perception of cost would have to become quite large before influencing someone's behavior.

Gordon points out that a ghetto criminal is actually, in a strange way, conforming to social norms.
"Capitalist societies depend," he argues, "on basically
competitive forms of social and economic interaction
and upon substantial inequalities in the allocation of
social resources" (p. 378). He goes on to conclude
that "Driven by the fear of economic insecurity and
by a competitive desire to gain some of the goods un-
equally distributed throughout the society, many individuals will eventually become 'criminals'" (p. 379).
Hoover would call this "armchair sociology," but it's
a point of view that takes into consideration not just
the criminal act but its social context.

The penal system, as Hoover and Gordon would agree
(though they wouldn't agree on much else), amounts to a
kind of conveyer belt (Hoover, 1972, p. 32). It picks
up criminals over here, holds them awhile, then drops
them off back over here, where they are soon picked
up again. Increasing the time they spend inside the
prison system only increases the likelihood that they
will remain on the belt. The reason is that regardless
of how severely the penalties are increased, there will
be a large portion of criminals for whom life presents
few favorable alternatives to criminal activity—risks
and all. It's no coincidence, as Gordon points out,
that the rate of crime usually drops when the rate of
unemployment also drops.

It may seem that I've come around to the view of crime argued by the liberal sociologists before the economists arrived on the crime scene. Not entirely. It's clear that to some extent increased prison sentences will deter crime. And in some cases we certainly should increase the cost to criminals of their criminal acts. It seems to me that the system of juvenile justice and the system of paroles could both benefit from stiffer penalties. By increasing the costs, we may be able to discourage some crimes. Gang killings, for example, might go down if murderers under eighteen knew they faced a long prison sentence without the possibility of parole. Parole has become a particularly disturbing institution in this country because it influences the general perception that a sentence is never to be taken literally. Fifteen years is always something less—or so it seems. Particularly in need of reform are the paroles granted in cases of homicide. Perhaps severely cutting back the paroles granted in homicide cases could make a dent in the obscene number of homicides our society seems to tolerate.

But we need to keep in mind which crimes we really want to deter. All crimes? Violent crimes? Homicides? Simply increasing punishments across the board is no cure-all. In fact, such measures will at best disguise, and at worst inflame, what really needs treatment. If our generally healthy society is sick in some way, it's in the living conditions that perpetuate poverty and extreme class differences. An unemployment rate of 30 percent among young black males is as alarming a statistic as any crime rate—and of course the two kinds of statistics must be related. Economic analysis teaches us that we can bring down some crime rates by increasing criminal costs. But what can we do to raise the benefits of not committing crimes?

This paper may not be complete or fully polished, but it's a very solid draft. And now that we've written it, we can look back at what we've done and see our argument itself more clearly — as something to reevaluate, adjust, or even turn away from. In this case, we hadn't realized when we started how central the economic analyses would become. But we decide that that's all right. And now that we know, we can paraphrase our argument more precisely: We're arguing that the strategies of deterrence, despite the support from economic theory, offer only limited possibilities for dealing with the crime problems in the United States. At this point, we might even try to give our paper a title. Any suggestions?

The argument in this draft is only one among many that we might have made. It may not seem a very exciting one — "Here's why we need to be cautious about applying theories of deterrence." But look at all the paper has accomplished. It has responded fully and coherently to both parts of the original assignment (and found a bridge between the parts). It has grown in power, moving through the series of reservations about deterrence until climaxing with its fifth and most important point about social inequalities. It draws on an assortment of evidence — not only statistics and quotations, but vivid invented examples. It employs strategies like definition, summary, and comparison both in thinking through and in presenting the argument. And by bringing into one arena perspectives as varied as those of Hoover, Durkheim, Tullock, and Gordon, it conveys a sense of controversy and shows someone coming to careful, informed judgments.

The four chapters that follow — "Women and Power: Perspectives from Anthropology"; "Nathaniel Hawthorne's 'Young Goodman Brown': Historical Imaginings"; "Schizophrenia: Causes and Treatments"; and "What's Funny: Investigating the Comic" — lend themselves to argument. We hope, in fact, that they lend themselves to the discovery and development of numerous arguments. They present you not with positions to defend or questions to argue pro or con, but with topics worth thoughtfully exploring.

Our method is to offer a mix of primary and secondary materials — texts to bring into conversation with one another. The primary materials consist of stories, case studies, descriptions, statistics, histories, and jokes. The secondary materials consist mainly of critical opinions written from a variety of points of view. Because of restricted space, we have deleted many of the footnotes and citations that usually accompany scholarly articles. We've only kept them where they are necessary for you to understand the text and where they might be necessary for your response to the questions we pose. We also realize that we cannot offer you the fuller backgrounds you would have acquired if you were writing for a particular course or discipline. Nor can we open up quite so freewheeling a search as we've illustrated in the example about criminal punishment. But the mix of materials should provide you with plenty to search and think about.

Besides these materials, each chapter contains two sets of questions, both of which call on the strategies developed in the first half of this book. After an initial cluster of readings meant to orient you to issues emerging from the general topic, we've included "Preliminary Questions" calling for reflection and critical thinking. These questions can serve as stimuli for classroom discussion, for individual study or group work, or for relatively brief in-class writing assignments. In some cases, where they spark your interest, the questions can become the basis for more fully developed essays. The second set of questions, "Questions for Argument," comes at the end of each chapter, after you have had a chance to extend, refine, and challenge your original perceptions by reading a fuller selection of pertinent materials. These final questions, while also meant to lead to reflection and stimulate discussion, are offered as writing assignments. They encourage you to draw on and make connections among a wide range of materials. They ask you to operate from a strong point of view, framing arguments of some sophistication.

CHAPTER 8

Women and Power: Perspectives from Anthropology

Framing the Issues

Do the biological differences between women and men translate in all cultures to differences in status, roles, and power? Are there cultures in which women and men are equals? Have such cultures existed in the past? Are differences not necessarily inequalities? Where inequalities seem strongest, what is responsible? Where powers are more balanced, what is responsible? What are the possibilities?

These are cross-cultural questions asked by modern feminists, and they are asked primarily of anthropologists. Anthropology, the study of cultures, is itself a field once dominated by men. But from the early years of this century onward, women have played an increasingly large part both in the fieldwork that provides anthropological evidence and in the writing that interprets that evidence. By enabling us to look insightfully at cultures other than our own, anthropology enables us to better understand what is common to all people and what varies from one group to another. Anthropological perspectives also encourage us, after looking at how others live, to look at our own culture with fresh eyes. Patterns that we accept as natural because they are familiar begin to look more strange.

We begin with some overviews — generalizations that may suggest some lines of thought and argument. The first passage is from *Male and Female* (1949) by Margaret Mead, America's most prominent anthropologist and one of the earliest women in the field. The next is by Simone de Beauvoir, who is not an anthropologist but a philosopher and whose book *The Second Sex* (1953) has had a strong influence on the contemporary women's movement. E. E. Evans-Pritchard is one of the founding fathers of modern anthropology. His often quoted comments, originally part of a public lecture, appeared in his article "The Position of Women in Primitive Societies and in Our Own" (1955). The passage by Sherwood Washburn and C. S. Lancaster is from an article first presented at a symposium called "Man the Hunter" (1968). Eleanor Leacock, Sherry Ortner, and Karen Sacks are all contemporary anthropologists writing from feminist perspectives; their selections were published in 1972, 1974, and 1975, respectively. The "Preliminary Questions" that follow these selections are meant to help you sharpen your sense of the issues and to prepare you for reading the more detailed cultural descriptions that form the core of this section. The cultural descriptions range widely — from southwest African bushwomen to Sicilian peasants to cocktail waitresses in an American bar — but you'll find, along with the obvious dissimilarities, some interesting parallels. The chapter closes with suggestions for writing arguments about women and power.

From *Male and Female*
MARGARET MEAD

In every known human society, the male's need for achievement can be   1
recognized. Men may cook, or weave or dress dolls or hunt humming-birds, but if such activities are appropriate occupations of men, then the whole society, men and women alike, votes them as important. When the same occupations are performed by women, they are regarded as less important. In a great number of human societies men's sureness of their sex role is tied up with their right, or ability, to practice some activity that women are not alllowed to practice. Their maleness, in fact, has to be underwritten by preventing women from entering some field or performing some feat. Here may be found the relationship between maleness and pride; that is, a need for prestige that will outstrip the prestige which is accorded to any woman. There seems no evidence that it is necessary for men to surpass women in any specific way, but rather that men do need to find reassurance in achievement, and because of this connection, cultures frequently phrase achievement as something that women do not or cannot do, rather than directly as something which men do well.

The recurrent problem of civilization is to define the male role sat-   2
isfactorily enough — whether it be to build gardens or raise cattle, kill game or kill enemies, build bridges or handle bank-shares — so that the male may in the course of his life reach a solid sense of irreversible

achievement, of which his childhood knowledge of the satisfactions of child-bearing have given him a glimpse. In the case of women, it is only necessary that they be permitted by the given social arrangements to fulfill their biological role, to attain this sense of irreversible achievement. If women are to be restless and questing, even in the face of child-bearing, they must be made so through education. If men are ever to be at peace, ever certain that their lives have been lived as they were meant to be, they must have, in addition to paternity, culturally elaborated forms of expression that are lasting and sure. Each culture — in its own way — has developed forms that will make men satisfied in their constructive activities without distorting their sure sense of their masculinity. Fewer cultures have yet found ways in which to give women a divine discontent that will demand other satisfactions than those of child-bearing.

From *The Second Sex*
SIMONE DE BEAUVOIR

But is it enough to change laws, institutions, customs, public opinion, and the whole social context, for men and women to become truly equal? "Women will always be women," say the skeptics. Other seers prophesy that in casting off their femininity they will not succeed in changing themselves into men and they will become monsters. This would be to admit that the woman of today is a creation of nature; it must be repeated once more that in human society nothing is natural and that woman, like much else, is a product elaborated by civilization. The intervention of others in her destiny is fundamental: if this action took a different direction, it would produce a quite different result. Woman is determined not by her hormones or by mysterious instincts, but by the manner in which her body and her relation to the world are modified through the action of others than herself. The abyss that separates the adolescent boy and girl has been deliberately opened out between them since earliest childhood; later on, woman could not be other than what she *was made,* and that past was bound to shadow her for life. If we appreciate its influence, we see clearly that her destiny is not predetermined for all eternity.

From *The Position of Women in Primitive Societies and in Our Own*
E. E. EVANS-PRITCHARD

If we bear in mind that every disability primitive women may be said to suffer has compensations our own women may no longer enjoy, we may come to the conclusion that, taking everything into consideration and on balance, it cannot be said, certainly not without many qualifications, that women are much more favorably situated in our own society than in primitive societies. Lest this should seem to you an extravagant, even absurd, statement I hasten to emphasize again that I am speaking of women's position relative to men. Certainly, and obviously, English women enjoy comforts and leisure and luxuries and the advantages of Christianity, education, medicine, mechanization — everything, in fact, which we speak of as civilization; and all this primitive women lack; but then the men lack them too. Indeed it might reasonably be held that where our womenfolk are most conspicuously better off than primitive women, this is due not so much to alteration of women's status in society, which means vis-à-vis men, as to innovations which have affected everybody equally, both men and women, woman's status remaining in essentials, and in spite of all formal and conventional appearances, relatively constant. If this is true, it suggests that some of the changes which have come about with regard to her situation in our own society which present a contrast with primitive conditions may prove to be transitory, especially where we find that they are recent developments which have taken place in very peculiar historical circumstances.

I would take the risk of going even further, and say that I find it difficult to believe that the relative positions of the sexes are likely to undergo any considerable or lasting alteration in the foreseeable future. Primitive societies and barbarous societies and the historical societies of Europe and the East exhibit almost every conceivable variety of institutions, but in all of them, regardless of the form of social structure, men are always in the ascendancy, and this is perhaps the more evident the higher the civilization. I am not wishing to be provocative — it might be better were it not so — but, so far as I can see, it is a plain matter of fact that it is so. Feminists have indeed said that this is because women have always been denied the opportunity of taking the lead; but we would still have to ask how it is that they have allowed the opportunity to be denied them, since it can hardly have been just a matter of brute force. The facts seem rather to suggest that there are deep biological and psychological factors, as well as sociological factors, involved, and that the relation between the sexes can only be modified by social changes, and not radically altered by them.

2

From *The Evolution of Hunting*
SHERWOOD L. WASHBURN AND C. S. LANCASTER

Human hunting, if done by males, is based on a division of labor and is a social and technical adaptation quite different from that of other mammals. Human hunting is made possible by tools, but it is far more than a technique or even a variety of techniques. It is a way of life, and the success of this adaptation (in its total social, technical, and psychological dimensions) has dominated the course of human evolution for hundreds of thousands of years. In a very real sense our intellect, interests, emotions, and basic social life — all are evolutionary products of the success of the hunting adaptation. When anthropologists speak of the unity of mankind, they are stating that the selection pressures of the hunting and gathering way of life were so similar and the result so successful that populations of *Homo sapiens* are still fundamentally the same everywhere.

From The Introduction to *The Origin of the Family, Private Property, and the State* by Friedrich Engels
ELEANOR BURKE LEACOCK

An interesting subject for reassessment is the mystique that surrounds the hunt and, in comparison, that surrounding childbirth. A common formulation of status among hunter-gatherers overlooks the latter and stresses the importance and excitement of the hunt. Albeit the primary staple foods may be the vegetable products supplied by the women, they afford no prestige, it is pointed out, so that while not precisely subservient women are still of lower status than men. However, women's power of child-bearing has been a focus for awe and even fear as long ago as the Upper Paleolithic, judging from the fertility figurines that date from that period. This point is easy to overlook, for the ability to bear children has led in our society not to respect but to women's oppressed status. Similarly, the mystique surrounding menstruation is underestimated. Attitudes of mystery and danger for men are interpreted in terms of our cultural judgment as "uncleanliness." Indeed, the semantic twists on this subject would be amusing to analyze. Women are spoken of as "isolated" in "menstrual huts" so that the men will not be contaminated. Where men's houses exist, however, they are written about respectfully; here the exclusion of women betokens men's high status. Doubtless this congeries of attitudes was first held by missionaries and traders, and from them subject peoples learned appropriate attitudes to express to whites.

From *Is Female to Male as Nature Is to Culture?*
SHERRY B. ORTNER

Woman is not "in reality" any closer to (or further from) nature than man — both have consciousness, both are mortal. But there are certainly reasons why she appears that way. . . . The result is a (sadly) efficient feedback system: various aspects of woman's situation (physical, social, psychological) contribute to her being seen as closer to nature, while the view of her as closer to nature is in turn embodied in institutional forms that reproduce her situation. The implications for social change are similarly circular: a different cultural view can only grow out of a different social actuality; a different social actuality can only grow out of a different cultural view.

It is clear, then, that the situation must be attacked from both sides. Efforts directed solely at changing the social institutions — through setting quotas on hiring, for example, or through passing equal-pay-for-equal-work laws — cannot have far-reaching effects if cultural language and imagery continue to purvey a relatively devalued view of women. But at the same time efforts directed solely at changing cultural assumptions — through male and female consciousness-raising groups, for example, or through revision of educational materials and mass-media imagery — cannot be successful unless the institutional base of the society is changed to support and reinforce the changed cultural view. Ultimately, both men and women can and must be equally involved in projects of creativity and transcendence. Only then will women be seen as aligned with culture, in culture's ongoing dialectic with nature.

From *Engels Revisited*
KAREN SACKS

Men are more directly exploited and more often collectively so — a situation which gives them the possibility of doing something about it. Women's field of activity and major responsibility is restricted to the household, which neither produces nor owns the means of production for more than domestic subsistence, a level of organization at which little can be done to institute social change in a class society. This situation has several consequences. First, women are relegated to the bottom of a social pecking order (a *man's* home is his castle). Second, because of their isolation and exclusion from the public sector, women can be used as a conservative force, unconsciously upholding the status quo in their commitment to the values surrounding maintenance of home, family, and children. Finally, the family is the sole institution with responsibility for consumption and for the maintenance of its members and rearing of its children, the future generation of exchange workers. It is necessary labor for the rulers, but women are forced to perform it without compensation.

Modern capitalism has maintained this pattern of exploiting the private *domestic* labor of women, but since industrialization women have also been involved heavily in public or wage labor. Meeting the labor burden that capitalism places on the family remains socially women's responsibility. Responsibility for domestic work is one of the material bases for present barriers to women working for money and for placing them in a more exploitable position than men in the public labor force. As Margaret Benston shows, this domestic work is not considered "real" work because it has only private use value and no exchange value — it is not public labor. . . .

The distinction between production for use and production for exchange places a heavy responsibility on women to maintain themselves as well as exchange workers and to rear future exchange and maintenance workers. In this context, wage work (or social labor) becomes an additional burden and in no way changes women's responsibility for domestic work. For full social equality, men's and women's work must be of the same kind: the production of social use values. For this to happen, family and society cannot remain separate *economic* spheres of life. Production, consumption, child-rearing, and economic decision-making all need to take place in a single social sphere — something analogous to the Iroquois *gens* as described by Engels, or to the production brigades of China during the Great Leap Forward. What is now private family work must become public work for women to become fully social adults.

Preliminary Questions

1. Write a short report classifying and then briefly comparing the preceding overviews. Make sure your report adequately represents the range of opinions.
2. From your reading of these passages, what do you take to be some of the key anthropological questions in thinking about women's issues?
3. What is "natural" and what is "cultural"? What are the fundamental differences of opinion on this question? Show how defining these terms can make a difference.
4. Do the authors express any disagreement about relations between the sexes in contemporary Western societies? If so, illustrate the differences. If not, describe the basic point of view they seem to share.
5. Some of the authors offer or imply views of how modern societies have evolved from primitive ones. Do they agree on an interpretation?
6. Define *primitive* and *civilized* as complementary terms. How does one definition depend on the other? How do we draw the line between them? Do these terms contain hidden assumptions?
7. What does Simone de Beauvoir mean by "the abyss" that separates male and female adolescents? Does your own experience substantiate this view?
8. From Margaret Mead's perspective, what is the relationship between civilization and discontent?
9. What are "hunter-gatherers"; how would you define this term? In what ways does the organization of a hunter-gatherer society seem to be different from our own?
10. Karen Sacks's view of women's situations seems attached to an interpretation of their economic situations. Summarize her view.
11. In what ways might earlier anthropologists have distorted the roles of women in the cultures they analyzed? Speculate, as well, on attitudes and assumptions found in America today that could distort our perceptions of women's roles in other cultures and in our own.

Complicating the Issues

One culture in which women apparently had great power was that of the Iroquois in the American Northeast during the time of early contact between whites and Native Americans. In this article, originally published in 1970, anthropologist Judith K. Brown reviews the evidence and offers her own analysis of the social position of Iroquois women.

From *Iroquois Women: An Ethnohistoric Note*
JUDITH K. BROWN

In the political sphere, Iroquois matrons had the power to raise and depose the ruling elders, the ability to influence the decisions of the Council, and occasional power over the conduct of war and the establishment of treaties. Although women could not serve on the Council of Elders, the highest ruling body of the League, the hereditary eligibility for office passed through them, and the elective eligibility for office was also largely controlled by them. Alexander Goldenweiser gives a retrospective account of the power of the matrons to raise and depose the ruling elders (whom he called chiefs): 1

> When a chief died, the women of his tribe and clan held a meeting at which a candidate for the vacant place was decided upon. A woman delegate carried the news to the chiefs of the clans which belonged to the "side" of the deceased chief's clan. They had the power to veto the selection, in which case another women's meeting was called and another candidate selected.

The actions of the new elder were closely watched, and if his behavior deviated from the accepted norms, he was warned by the woman delegate. If after several warnings he still did not conform, she would initiate impeachment proceedings.

It is surprising that Lewis Morgan, whose *League of the Ho-De'-No-Sau-Nee, Iroquois* stands as a classic to this day, should have taken no particular note of the political power of the Iroquois matrons. His account of the raising of the elders in *Ancient Society* differs in some details from the account given by Goldenweiser. Speaking of the election, he states, "Each person of adult age was called upon to express his *or her* preference" (italics mine). The right to depose "was reserved by members of the gens." Thus Morgan's observations do not contradict the fact that the matrons had a voice in these important matters. But for some reason, he did not find this remarkable or did not choose to comment upon it. However, in a later work, Morgan quotes from a letter written by the Reverend Ashur Wright (who had been a missionary among the Iroquois for forty years) as follows: 2

> The women were the great power among the clans, as everywhere else. They did not hesitate, when occasion required, to "knock off the horns," as it was technically called, from the head of a chief and send him back to the

ranks of the warriors. The original nomination of the chiefs also always rested with them.

Morgan's next paragraph begins, "The mother-right and gyneocracy among the Iroquois here plainly indicated is not overdrawn." He ends his paragraph with a footnote to Bachofen. It is therefore surprising when sixty-odd pages later he states:

> But this influence of the woman did not reach outward to the affairs of the gens, phratry, or tribe, but seems to have commenced and ended with the household. This view is quite consistent with the life of patient drudgery and of general subordination to the husband which the Iroquois wife cheerfully accepted as the portion of her sex.

In his earlier work, however, Morgan noted that women had the power of life or death over prisoners of war, which must certainly be regarded as an influence reaching beyond the household. Furthermore, the women could participate in the deliberations of the Council through their male speakers, such as the Council of 1791, the Council of 1804, and the Council of 1839, and had a voice concerning warfare and treaties. Schoolcraft sums up these powers as follows:

> They are the only tribes in America, north and south, so far as we have any accounts, who gave to woman a conservative power in their political deliberations. The Iroquois matrons had their representative in the public councils; and they exercised a negative, or what we call a veto power, in the important question of the declaration of war. They had the right also to interpose in bringing about a peace.

It appears from the evidence (some of it Morgan's) that the political influence of the Iroquois matron was considerable. The nation was not a matriarchy, as claimed by some, but the matrons were an *éminence grise.* In this respect the Iroquois were probably not unique. What is unusual is the fact that this power was socially recognized and institutionalized.

In addition, Iroquois matrons helped to select the religious practitioners of the tribe. Half of these "keepers of the faith" were women and, according to Morgan, "They had an equal voice in the general management of the festivals and of all their religious concernments." As Randle and Quain have pointed out, women's activities were celebrated in the ceremonial cycle, and female virtues of food-providing, cooperativeness, and natural fertility were respected and revered. Women might become clairvoyants or could join medicine societies; for several of the latter, women were managing officers.

Kin-group membership was transmitted through the mother, and since there were rules of exogamy, the father belonged to a kinship group other than that of his wife and children. Morgan describes the rules of inheritance and succession as follows:

> Not least remarkable among their institutions, was that which confined transmission of all titles, rights and property in the female line to the exclusion of the male. . . .
> If the wife, either before or after marriage, inherited orchards, or

planting lots, or reduced land to cultivation, she could dispose of them at her pleasure, and in case of her death, they were inherited, together with her other effects, by her children.

Marriages were arranged by the mothers of the prospective couple, and they also took responsibility for the success of the union thus created. Both marriage and divorce involved little ceremony. The latter could be instigated by either the wife or the husband. In the case of a separation, the children usually remained with the mother. Arthur Parker mentions that spacing the births of children was in the hands of the mother and there was greater delight at the birth of a daughter than at that of a son. The mother often had the power to confer a name on her child. Furthermore, Quain notes that "the women of the maternal line chose the child successors to a series of names which might culminate in high administrative titles of community or nation." . . .

THE ECONOMIC ORGANIZATION OF SUBSISTENCE ACTIVITIES

Agricultural Activities. The Iroquois supplemented cultivated foods with food gathered by the women, with meat hunted by the men (although women occasionally joined hunting expeditions), and with fish obtained by both men and women. However, the tribe depended upon shifting cultivation for the major portion of its food supply. Agricultural activity consisted of four stages: clearing the ground, planting, cultivating, and harvesting.   6

Men were in charge of preparing the fields, although Waugh and Quain claim that the women helped. Trees were girdled and allowed to die. The following spring, the underbrush was burned off. Planting and cultivating were conducted by the women in organized work groups. Elderly men occasionally helped, but for other men to do this work was considered demeaning. As Sara Stites has pointed out, the warrior in the field was always an assistant, never an owner or director. Men did join in the harvest, although this was occasionally done by women alone. Husking of the corn was a festive occasion, usually joined by the men. The work would be followed by a special meal and by singing and dancing. . . .   7

The economic organization of the Iroquois was remarkable (and far from unique), for the great separateness of the sexes which it fostered. Men were often away on war parties for years at a time. Although wives or temporary wives, appointed especially for the purpose, occasionally accompanied men on the hunt, it was more usual for this to be a male pursuit. Even at the daily meal the sexes ate separately. It is no wonder that Morgan wrote: 8

> Indian habits and modes of life divided the people socially into two great classes, male and female. The male sought the conversation and society of the male, and they went forth together for amusement, or for the severer duties of life. In the same manner the female sought the companionship of her own sex. Between the sexes there was but little sociality, as this term is understood in polished society.

Factors of Production. In agricultural production, land constitutes   9
the natural resource, seeds constitute the raw materials, and agricultural
implements constitute the tools. The ownership of these factors of production — the land, the seeds, and the implements — among the Iroquois
is difficult to establish from existing evidence. Goldenweiser offers the
following information: "The husband, in ancient times, could regard as
his own only his weapons, tools, and wearing apparel, his wife owned
the objects of the household, the house itself, and the land."

It is also not entirely clear who owned the land. . . .   10

Morgan stressed that land was communally owned and that its in-   11
dividual ownership was unknown. Snyderman mentions the belief that
land belonged to future generations as well as to the present generation.
However, according to Randle, land was often registered in female names.
Hewitt states that women owned the lands, the village sites, and the
burial grounds. Nominal female ownership is indicated in the following
statement by Red Jacket, speaker for the women at the Council of 1791:
"You ought to hear and listen to what we women shall speak . . . for
we are the owners of the land and it is ours." In short, the lands of the
Iroquois appear to have been communally owned, but held by the women.

The Food Produced. A great variety of corn was raised. Frank   12
Speck estimates from fifteen to seventeen varieties, and it was prepared
in numerous ways. Murdock suggests as many as fifty. Even the husks,
silk, cobs, and leaves were used to make a number of useful articles.
Beans were also a popular food — Speck estimates that there were sixty
varieties — as were squashes, of which there were eight varieties,
according to Speck. All three of these foods were provided by the women
and held in high esteem by the Iroquois. The foods were represented in
their pantheon as "The Three Sisters," "Our Life," and "Our Supporters."

These staples were supplemented by foods gathered by the women   13
— maple sugar, berries, wild fruit, nuts, roots, mushrooms, leaf foods
— and by other cultivated foods, such as melons. Schoolcraft referred
to the apple as "the Iroquois banana." The fruit was one of several
introduced by the Dutch and the French. According to Parker, during
the Revolutionary War "General Sullivan in his famous raid against the
hostile Iroquois cut down a single orchard of 1500 trees." Thus an impressive commissariat was supplied by the women of the tribe. The diet
of the Iroquois was ample, varied, and nutritious. One is forced to agree
with Morgan, who considered the indigenous diet of the Iroquois far
superior to that typical of the Europeans of pre-contact times.

Distributing and Dispensing Food. The generous hospitality that   14
was customary among the Iroquois was probably the most salient feature
of their food distribution. The rule of hospitality was perpetuated and its
protocol codified by Handsome Lake, the early nineteenth-century
prophet. Hospitality was extended to all strangers, and the stranger was
to be fed before he was questioned about his mission. Hospitality was
also extended to other members of the village, to the extent that no one

went hungry. It is of interest to note Morgan's comment: "It [hospitality] rested chiefly upon the industry, and therefore upon the natural kindness of the Indian women." This statement demonstrates that the hospitality of the household reflected favorably on its women, not on its men. Furthermore, hospitality was motivated by generosity, which was valued in and of itself.

There is conflicting evidence concerning the distribution of the fruit   15
of the chase. Beauchamp says that the meat was given to the hunter's wife. Carr claims it was given to the hunter's mother-in-law. Lafitau mentions that the legitimate wife had a prior claim to that of the temporary hunting wife. (The Iroquois were not rigidly monogamous.) Hunting expeditions often lasted as long as a year, and if the hunter's wife refused to go, a special temporary wife might accompany him instead.

Stites cites one *Jesuit Relation* to the effect that one of the women's   16
chief winter tasks was to go into the forest to bring home the deer their husbands had slain. Citing a different *Jesuit Relation*, however, she states that women were sometimes not given a share of the meat at all. Wright, quoted by Morgan, seems to suggest that the meat was contributed by the hunter to his wife's household. Morgan makes a similar statement himself, and this is probably the most correct description.

Thus the distribution of the food of the tribe, even the food procured   17
by the men, appears to have been at the discretion of the matrons. By observing the rules of hospitality, the matrons made it possible for every member of the tribe and for visitors to obtain a share of the food supply. . . .

It was not only in the domestic realm that the matrons controlled   18
the dispensing of food. By supplying the essential provisions for male activities — the hunt, the warpath, and the Council — they were able to control these to some degree. Thus Randle writes, "Indirectly, too, it is stated that the women could hinder or actually prevent a war party which lacked their approval by not giving the supplies of dried corn and the moccasins which the warriors required."

Stites makes a similar assertion: "They also had control of the cul-   19
tivated land and its produce, and gave support to the warriors only in return for their military services." This control was effected by the monopoly that the matrons exercised on the staple food used on both the hunt and the warpath. According to Morgan, this food was prepared while the warriors performed their dance. He gives the recipe for the dried corn-maple syrup provision, and concludes, "The warrior could carry without inconvenience in his bear-skin pocket a sufficient supply for a long and perilous expedition." Further on he states, "This [the same recipe] was carried in the bear-skin pocket of the hunter, and upon it alone he subsisted for days together."

The importance of these provisions was also mentioned by Loskiel,   20
who observed that hunting was not possible on the warpath for fear of giving warning to the enemy. He also describes the importance of the food provided by the matrons for the Council: "Provisions must always be in plenty in the council-house; for eating and deliberating take their turns."

Iroquois women were in charge of the ingenious methods of pre-   21
serving and storing the abundant food supplies. Corn, meat, fish, berries,
squashes, and even fats were preserved. Some of these foods were
buried in specially constructed pits, and some were kept in the longhouse.
Stored food constituted one of the major forms of wealth of the tribe.
Stites claims, "It was the women's organization which controlled the
surplus and represented the owning class." Hewitt describes a tribal public
treasury which contained wampum belts, quill and feather work, furs,
and assorted stored foods. Its contents were scrupulously guarded by
the matrons.

In sum, among the Iroquois, the distribution of food within the tribe   22
was the responsibility of the matrons. They also controlled the provisions
within the household, as well as those that made the major male activities
possible. Some authors claim that the matrons also controlled the wealth
of the tribe (much of it in stored food).

SUMMARY

Iroquois women controlled the factors of agricultural production, for   23
they had a right in the land which they cultivated, and in the implements
and the seeds. Iroquois agricultural activities, which yielded bountiful
harvests, were highly organized under elected female leadership. Most
important, Iroquois women maintained the right to distribute and dispense
all food, even that procured by men. This was especially significant, as
stored food constituted one of the major forms of wealth for the tribe.
Through their control of the economic organization of the tribe, Iroquois
matrons were able to make available or withhold food for meetings of
the Council and for war parties, for the observance of religious festivals
and for the daily meals of the household. These economic realities were
institutionalized in the matrons' power to nominate Council Elders and
to influence Council decisions. They had a voice in the conduct of war
and the establishment of treaties. They elected "keepers of the faith"
and served in that capacity. They controlled life in the longhouse.

The unusual role of Iroquois women in politics, religion, and domestic   24
life cannot be dismissed simply as a historical curiosity. It cannot be
explained by Iroquois kinship structure, nor can it be attributed to the
size of the women's contribution to Iroquois subsistence. The powerful
position of Iroquois women was the result of their control of the economic
organization of their tribe.

*The !Kung are a much-studied people living in southwestern Africa (the ! before
their name signals a clicking sound unrepresentable in our standard alphabet).
The !Kung attract much anthropological interest because they are one of the few
remaining groups who maintain their existence by hunting and gathering rather
than by some form of agriculture. Theories about the lives of the ancient hunter-
gatherers are sometimes tested against observations of the !Kung. In the following*

article, published in 1975, Patricia Draper considers why the !Kung lifestyle makes for relatively equal relations between the sexes.

!Kung Women: Contrasts in Sexual Egalitarianism in Foraging and Sedentary Contexts
PATRICIA DRAPER

Most members of the Harvard !Kung Bushman Study Project who have thought about the subject of !Kung women's status agree that !Kung society may be the least sexist of any we have experienced. This impression contradicts some popularly held stereotypes about relations between the sexes in hunting and gathering societies. Because sex is one of the few bases for the differentiation of social and economic roles in societies of this type, it has probably been attributed more weight than it deserves. The men are commonly depicted in rather romantic terms, striving with their brothers to bring home the precious meat while their women humbly provide the dull, tasteless vegetable food in the course of routine, tedious foraging. Contrary evidence is now emerging from several researchers that men and women of band-level societies have many overlapping activities and spheres of influence. The distinction between male and female roles is substantially less rigid than previously supposed, though there is variation among band-level peoples in the degree of autonomy and influence that women enjoy.   1

This paper describes relations between the sexes for two groups of !Kung: those living a traditional hunting and gathering life at /Du/da and those who have recently adopted a settled way of life in the !Kangwa Valley and who are now living by agriculture, animal husbandry, and a small amount of gathering.   2

The point to be developed at some length is that in the hunting and gathering context, women have a great deal of autonomy and influence. Some of the contexts in which this egalitarianism is expressed will be described in detail, and certain features of the foraging life which promote egalitarianism will be isolated. They are women's subsistence contribution and the control women retain over the food they have gathered; the requisites of foraging in the Kalahari which entail a similar degree of mobility for both sexes; the lack of rigidity in sex-typing of many adult activities, including domestic chores and aspects of child socialization; the cultural sanction against physical expression of aggression; the small group size; and the nature of the settlement pattern.   3

Features of sedentary life that appear to be related to a decrease in women's autonomy and influence are increasing rigidity in sex-typing of adult work; more permanent attachment of the individual to a particular place and group of people; dissimilar childhood socialization for boys and girls; decrease in the mobility of women as contrasted with men; changing nature of women's subsistence contribution; richer material inventory   4 with implications for women's work; tendency for men to have greater access to and control over such important resources as domestic animals, knowledge of Bantu language and culture, wage work; male entrance into extra-village politics; settlement pattern; and increasing household privacy. . . .

ETHNOGRAPHIC BACKGROUND TO THE !KUNG:
TRADITIONAL POPULATION

The !Kung are a hunting and gathering people living today mostly   5
on the western edge of the Kalahari sand system in what is now southern Angola, Botswana, and South-West Africa. The great majority of !Kung-speaking people have abandoned their traditional hunting and gathering way of life and are now living in sedentary and semi-squatter status in or near the villages of Bantu pastoralists and European ranchers. A minority of !Kung, amounting to a few thousand, are still living by traditional hunting and gathering techniques. It is to these bush-living peoples and a few groups of very recently settled !Kung that this paper refers.

The bush-living peoples subsist primarily on wild vegetable foods and   6
game meat. They are semi-nomadic, moving their camps at irregular intervals of from several days to several weeks. The average size of individual groups (also referred to as bands or camps) is about thirty-five people, though the numbers range from seventeen to sixty-five people. Season and the availability of water are the chief factors affecting group size. During the rainy season (October to March), group censuses are lower due to the fact that water and bush foods are widely available in most regions of the !Kung range. Smaller numbers of people in the form of two- and three-family groups spread out over the bush. As the dry season approaches, the small, temporary water pans dry up and the people begin to regroup and fall back on the remaining water sources that continue throughout the dry season. As there are relatively few water sources in the heart of the drought, as many as two or three different camps may be found within one to three miles of the same water hole.

The rules governing the composition of these bands are extremely   7
flexible. It appears there is no such thing as "band membership." Close relatives move together over much of the year, though individuals and segments of large kin groups frequently make temporary and amicable separations to go live some miles distant with other relatives and affines.

Material technology is extremely simple. Men hunt with small bows   8
and arrows (tipped with poison) and metal-pointed spears. Women's tools include a simple digging stick, wooden mortar and pestle, and leather kaross which doubles as clothing and carrying bag. Both sexes use leather carrying bags, hafted adzes, and net slings made from handwoven vegetable fiber. Clothing, particularly among the bush people, consists of leather garments; in addition, various cloth garments are worn, especially by the settled !Kung, but also by the peoples of the bush.

SETTLED POPULATION

. . . [T]he great majority of !Kung-speaking peoples are settled 9
around the villages of technologically more advanced peoples and have
been there for as many as three generations. Among other !Kung, se-
dentarization is much more recent. In the case of the Mahopa people,
in the !Kangwa area of Botswana, !Kung commitment to settled life is
perhaps fifteen to twenty years old. I observed these people and the
people of /Du/da for two years in 1968 and 1969. . . .

The subsistence practices of the recently settled !Kung are mixed. 10
The women continue to gather bush food, but not with the effort or
regularity of the women of the traditional groups. Hunting by Mahopa
men has virtually ceased. The people keep small herds of goats and plant
small gardens of sorghum, squash, melons, and corn. For the most part,
the Mahopa !Kung do not own their own cattle (at least, they did not
during my fieldwork). Some !Kung women receive milk in payment for
regular chores they do for nearby Herero women.

In the first discussion of !Kung women my remarks will pertain to 11
women of the bush-living groups, unless otherwise specified. Description
of the women's life in the settled Mahopa villages of the !Kangwa area
will be handled second. The traditional, or bush-living !Kung lived in the
/Du/da area, which straddles the border of Botswana and South-West
Africa and stretches over a north-south distance of about seventy miles.

SELF-ESTEEM DERIVED FROM
SUBSISTENCE CONTRIBUTION

Women are the primary providers of vegetable food, and they con- 12
tribute something on the order of 60 to 80 percent of the daily food
intake by weight (Lee, 1965). All !Kung agree that meat is the most
desirable, most prestigious food, but the hunters cannot always provide
it. Without question, women derive self-esteem from the regular daily
contribution they make to the family's food.

A common sight in the late afternoon is clusters of children standing 13
on the edge of camp, scanning the bush with shaded eyes to see if the
returning women are visible. When the slow-moving file of women is
finally discerned in the distance, the children leap and exclaim. As the
women draw closer, the children speculate as to which figure is whose
mother and what the women are carrying in their karosses.

Often when women return in the evening they bring information as 14
well as bush food. Women are skilled in reading the signs of the bush,
and they take careful note of animal tracks, their age, and the direction
of movement. On several occasions I have accompanied gathering expeditions in which, when the group was about thirty to forty minutes out
of camp, one of the women discovered the fresh tracks of several large
antelope. This find caused a stir of excitement in the group. Quickly the
women dispatched one of the older children to deliver the report to the
men in camp. In general, the men take advantage of women's recon-

naissance and query them routinely on the evidence of game movements, the location of water, and the like.

A stereotype of the female foraging role in hunting and gathering societies (in contrast with men's work, which is social in character) is that the work is individualized, repetitious, and boring. Descriptions of the work of gathering leave the reader with the impression that the job is uninteresting and unchallenging — that anyone who can walk and bend over can collect wild bush food. This stereotype is distinctly inappropriate to !Kung female work, and it promotes a condescending attitude toward what women's work is all about. Successful gathering over the years requires the ability to discriminate among hundreds of edible and inedible species of plants at various stages in their life cycle. This ability requires more than mere brute strength. The stereotype further ignores the role women play in gathering information about the "state of the bush" — presence of temporary water, evidence of recent game movements, etc. On a given day, !Kung hunters consciously avoid working the same area in which women are foraging, knowing that movements of the women may disturb the game, but also knowing that the women can be questioned at the end of the day.

!Kung women impress one as self-contained people with a high sense of self-esteem. There are exceptions — women who seem forlorn and weary — but for the most part, !Kung women are vivacious and self-confident. Small groups of women forage in the Kalahari at distances of eight to ten miles from home with no thought that they need the protection of the men or of the men's weapons should they encounter any of the several large predators that also inhabit the Kalahari (for instance, hyena, wild dog, leopard, lion, and cheetah). . . .

CONTROL BY WOMEN OVER GATHERED FOOD

Not only do women contribute equally, if not more than men, to the food supply, they also retain control over the food they have gathered after they return to the village. This is even more true of the vegetable food of women than of the meat brought in by the men. Lorna Marshall and Richard B. Lee have described how the distribution of meat is circumscribed by social rules as well as by the spontaneous demands of fellow camp members. With the exception of small game kills, a hunter has little effective control over the meat he brings into the camp. In contrast, the gatherer determines the distribution of vegetable food, at least when it concerns anyone outside her immediate family. An example may help to illustrate this point. One late afternoon I watched N!uhka return from an unusually long gathering trip. Her kaross was bulging with food, and her face showed fatigue from the weight and from dust, heat, and thirst. She walked stolidly through camp to her own hut. When she reached her hearthside, still stooping with the load, she reached to her shoulder, where the kaross was knotted. Wearily she gave the knot one practiced yank. The bush food spilled out of kaross, clattering and thumping onto the sand behind her. She had not even squatted before releasing the burden. At the sound, several people looked up, but only briefly. No

15

16

17

one greeted her or came over to look at the day's collection. N!uhka sat down at her hut, reached inside for an ostrich-egg shell, and slowly drank water from it for several minutes, sitting with her elbows on her knees and staring blankly ahead. Fifteen minutes later her grown daughter and a younger son joined her. The daughter, without talking, blew the coals back to life and started a fire. By then N!uhka had regained her strength, the listlessness had gone, and she picked up a wooden poke and began raking some of the freshly picked ≠nd≠dwa bean pods into the hot ashes for roasting. This done, she began gathering up the bush food she had dropped earlier. Most of it she heaped into the rear of her own hut, but she also made two additional small piles. Calling next door to her twelve-year-old grandnephew, she said, "Take this to your grandmother" (her brother's wife), and she motioned for him to take one of the heaps of bean pods. Later, when her daughter rose to return to her own fire, N!uhka had her take away the second pile for her own use. It is common for women to make these individual gifts, but it is not mandatory. Food that is brought in by women may also be redistributed during a family meal when other people visit at the fire and are served along with family members.

The fact that !Kung women retain control over their own production   18
is, of course, related to the simplicity of !Kung economy, technology, rules of ownership, and social organization. In more complex societies, there are kin groups, lineages, or other corporate units that control essential resources. Even in the relatively rare cases (matrilineages) where women nominally own the land and household property, it is usually men who control the production and distribution of resources. The gathering work of !Kung women can be done by women alone. They do not need to ask permission to use certain lands; they do not need the assistance of men in order to carry out their work, as in the case of many agricultural societies where men must do the initial heavy work of clearing fields, building fences, and the like, before the less strenuous work of women can begin.

SIMILAR ABSENTEEISM FOR MEN AND WOMEN

A similarity in the gathering work of women and the hunting work   19
of men is that both activities take adults out of the camp, sometimes all day for several days each week. The pattern of both sexes being about equally absent from the dwelling place is not typical of most middle-range, agriculturally based tribal societies. In these latter groups one finds an arrangement whereby women, much more than men, stay at home during child tending, domestic chores, food preparation and the like, while the men are occupied with activities that take them outside the household and keep them away for many hours during the day. Frequent (daily) male absence may result in viewing men as a scarce commodity with higher value than women, who are constantly present in the household. If men in this sense are a scarce commodity, their homecoming must have greater significance to those who stay at home, and their influence even in routine domestic affairs may be heightened simply because others

are less habituated to their presence. Among the !Kung a case could be argued for the equal, or nearly equal, scarcity value of men and women. Both leave the village regularly, and the return of both is eagerly anticipated — as illustrated earlier in this paper with reference to women. . . .

SEXUAL DIVISION OF LABOR

When asked, !Kung will state that there is men's work and women's [20] work, and that they conceive of most individual jobs as sex-typed, at least in principle. In practice, adults of both sexes seem surprisingly willing to do the work of the opposite sex. It often appeared to me that men, more than women, were willing to cross sex lines.

One afternoon while visiting in one of the /Du/da camps, I came [21] across Kxau, a rather sober middle-aged man, industriously at work building his own hut. Building huts is predominantly women's work, and I had never seen such a thing. It happened that Kxau's wife was away visiting at another settlement many miles distant, or she would have made the hut. However, Kxau's daughter, an unmarried girl about seventeen years old, was in camp, and even she did not offer to make the hut or help him once he had started. Kxau proceeded to build the structure methodically and without embarrassment. I deliberately stayed in the vicinity to observe the reaction of other people. No one commented or joked with him about how his women were lazy.

Gathering is women's work, but there are times when men also [22] gather. Some married couples collected mongongo nuts together, but in my observation, the couples most likely to do this were elderly couples and a young couple who had been married for several years but had no children. Water collection is normally considered to be women's work, particularly when the water source is close to camp, perhaps fifteen to twenty minutes' walk. However, when the people are camped several miles from water, men participate regularly in carrying water back to camp. In the months of August, September, and October of 1969, I observed two of the /Du/da camps where water was three miles distant. In this situation men and women both worked at bringing in water. Only on the occasions when several of the men were absent from camp for several nights on hunting trips did their wives collect water daily for the remaining members of the family. . . .

CHILD-REARING PRACTICES AND
SEXUAL EQUALITY

As children grow up there are few experiences which set one sex [23] apart from the other. Living in such small groups, !Kung children have relatively few playmates to choose from. Play groups, when they do form, include children of both sexes and of widely differing ages. This habit of playing in heterogeneous play groups probably minimizes any underlying, biologically based sex differences in style — differences which in other societies may be magnified and intensified by the opportunity of playing in same-sex, same-age play groups.

The child nurse is a regular feature of many African agricultural   24
societies. The custom of assigning child-tending responsibility to an older
child (usually a girl) in a family is one example of sex-role typing which
can begin at an early age. This responsibility shapes and limits the behavior
of girls in ways not true for boys, who are usually passed over for this
chore. The training a girl receives as an infant caretaker doubtless has
benefits for her eventual role performance and more immediately for the
family economy, since she frees the mother from routine child care and
allows her to resume subsistence production. However, the typical nine-
year-old who is saddled with carrying and supervising a toddler cannot
range as widely or explore as freely and independently as her brothers.
She must stay closer to home, be more careful, more nurturant, more
obedient, and more sensitive to the wishes of others. Habits formed in
this way have social value, but my point is that such girls receive more
training in these behaviors and that they form part of the complex of
passivity and nurturance which characterizes adult female behavior in
many cultures.

!Kung do not use child nurses of either sex on a routine basis; this   25
fact follows from the long birth intervals and the pattern of adult subsistence work. The average birth interval is approximately four years.
!Kung mothers can and do give lengthy, intensive care to each child
because no new infant arrives to absorb her attention. Such mothers are
comparatively unpressured and do not need to delegate the bulk of child-
tending responsibility to another caretaker. Naturally, older children interact with younger children and in the process give help, protection,
and attention to them. But one or more older children are rarely, if ever,
the sole caretakers of younger charges for an appreciable length of time.

The rhythm of adult work also makes the role of child nurse unnec-   26
essary. !Kung adults work about three days per week, and they vary
their time of being in and out of the camp, with the result that on any
given day one-third to one-half of the adults are in camp. They can easily
supervise their own children and those whose parents are absent. Older
children are helpful in amusing and monitoring younger children, but they
do so spontaneously (and erratically), and not because they are indoc-
trinated with a sense of responsibility for the welfare of a particular child
or children.

A reflection of !Kung women's effectiveness in family life is the fact   27
that a mother deals directly with her children when they are in need of
correction. . . . !Kung women do not resort to the threat "I'll tell your
father . . . !"

Among the !Kung, both parents correct the children, but women   28
tend to do this more often because they are usually physically closer to
the children at any given time than the men. When such situations arise,
a mother does not seek to intimidate the children with the father's wrath.
In this milieu children are not trained to respect and fear male authority.
In fact, for reasons which will be elaborated later, authoritarian behavior
is avoided by adults of *both* sexes. The typical strategy used by !Kung
parents is to interrupt the misbehavior, carry the child away, and try to
interest him or her in some inoffensive activity.

This way of disciplining children has important consequences in terms   29
of behaviors that carry over into adulthood. Since parents do not use
physical punishment, and aggressive postures are avoided by adults and
devalued by the society at large, children have relatively little opportunity
to observe or imitate overtly aggressive behavior. This carries over into
relations between adult men and women in the society. Evidence from
various sources is mounting in support of the notion that human males
(and males of nonhuman species) are innately more aggressive than their
female counterparts. But among the !Kung there is an extremely low
cultural tolerance for aggressive behavior by anyone, male or female. In
societies where aggressiveness and dominance are valued, these behaviors accrue disproportionately to males, and the females are common
targets, resulting in a lowering of their status. !Kung women are not
caught by this dimension of sex-role complementarity. They customarily
maintain a mild manner, but so do their men.

RELATIONS OF MEN WITH CHILDREN

A further example of the equality between the sexes and the amount   30
of overlap in their activities is the relationship between men and their
children. In cultures where men have markedly superordinant status,
women and children are expected to show deference to the male head
of the family by staying away from him, observing routine formalities.
!Kung fathers, in contrast, are intimately involved with their children and
have a great deal of social interaction with them. The relation between
fathers and young children is relaxed and without stylized respect or
deference from the children. In fact, the lack of tact with which some
children treated their parents was at first quite shocking to me.

As an example, I can relate an incident in which Kxau was trying to   31
get his youngest son, Kashe, to bring him something from the other side
of camp. Kxau was sitting at one edge of the village clearing with another
man older than himself. Kxau repeatedly shouted to his son to bring him
his tobacco from inside the family hut. The boy ignored his father's shouts,
though !Kung camps are small, and the boy clearly could hear his father.
Finally Kxau bellowed out his command, glaring across at his son and
the other youngsters sitting there. Kashe looked up briefly and yelled
back, "Do it yourself, old man." A few minutes later Kxau did do it
himself, and Kashe received no reprimand.

Most fathers appear ill-at-ease when they hold very young infants,   32
although by the time a child is nine or ten months old it is common to
see the father playing with the child and holding it close to his face,
blowing on its neck, and laughing. In the late afternoon and evening in
a !Kung camp one often sees a father walking among the huts with a
two- or three-year-old boy perched on his shoulder. The father ambles
along, accepting an offer of a smoke at one hut, then moving on to squat
elsewhere while watching a kinsman scraping a hide or mending a tool.
At such times the father is mindful of the boy at his shoulder but pays
him no special attention, aside from now and then steadying the child's
balance. . . .

EFFECT OF GROUP SIZE AND SETTLEMENT PATTERN
ON RELATIONS BETWEEN THE SEXES

!Kung camps are typically quite small; the average camp size at 33 /Du/da was thirty-four with a range of seventeen to sixty-five. The small group size is related to the low order of specialization of sex roles. Given the rather small numbers of able-bodied adults who manage group life and subsistence in these camps, the lack of opposition (or specialization) of the sexes is highly practical. Especially in the rainy seasons when local group size falls to about fifteen people, it is useful and necessary for adults to be relatively interchangeable in function.

Observing the way people group themselves during leisure hours in 34 a !Kung camp gives one a feeling for the tone of informal heterosexual interaction. Men and women (children, too) sit together in small clusters — talking, joking, cracking and eating nuts, passing around tobacco. Individuals pass among these groups without causing a rift in the ambiance, without attracting attention. In general, the sexes mix freely and un-selfconsciously without the diffidence one might expect to see if they thought they were in some way intruding.

If there were a prominent opposition between the sexes, one would 35 expect some expression of this in the organization and use of space within the !Kung camps. However, there are no rules and definitions that limit a person's access to various parts of the village space on the basis of sex. The overall small size of the settled area almost removes this type of symbolism from the realm of possibility.

To an outsider, particularly a Westerner, the small size of !Kung 36 camps and the intimate, close living characteristic of them can seem stifling. Essentially, thirty to forty people share what amounts to (by our standards) a large room. The individual grass scherms, one to each married couple, ring an elliptical village space. The huts are often placed only a few feet apart and look a mere forty to fifty feet across the cleared, central space into the hearth and doorway of the hut on the opposite side of the circle. Daily life goes on in this small, open space. Everything is visible with a glance; in many camps conversations can be carried on in normal tones of voice by people sitting at opposite ends of the village. In this setting it is easy to see why the sexes rub elbows without embarrassment. In other societies, where sex roles and the prerogatives which attach to them are more exclusively defined, one generally finds architectural features used to help people manage their interaction and/or avoidance: walls, fences, separate sleeping and/or eating arrangements, designated spaces allocated to only one sex, etc.

In summary, many of the basic organizing features of this hunting 37 and gathering group contribute to a relaxed and egalitarian relationship between men and women. The female subsistence role is essential to group survival and satisfying to the women. The foregoing remarks have illustrated a framework within which egalitarian relations are a natural or logical outcome. There are other issues bearing on the question of women's influence and control which are not answered here. Decision-making is one such issue. Leadership and authority are difficult problems to research in band-level societies generally, and in this one in particular.

Still, the question of whether women or men more often influence group or family decisions is an empirical one, albeit one on which I have no data. Other areas that bear on the topic of women's influence and power are marital relations, access to extramarital relations, the influence of young women in determining the selection of their first husbands, changes in women's influence over their life cycles, etc. So far as I know, these issues have yet to be researched in a systematic way among the !Kung.

THE SEDENTARY !KUNG OF MAHOPA

As stated earlier, my fieldwork was conducted in two areas of north-   38
western Botswana: the /Du/da area and the !Kangwa area. The second area was the locus of research similar to that conducted on the social life of the bush-living !Kung at /Du/da. Within the !Kangwa area (about seventy miles from the /Du/da water hole) I worked at Mahopa, one of several permanent water sources in the !Kangwa Valley. Around Mahopa are various settlements, of which three were the focus of my study. The three settlements were composed almost exclusively of !Kung. . . .

THE EFFECT OF SEDENTISM ON
SEX EGALITARIANISM

Stated most simply, my strong impression is that the sexual egali-   39
tarianism of the bush setting is being undermined in the sedentary !Kung villages. One obvious manifestation of status inequality is that at Mahopa sex roles are more rigidly defined, and at the same time women's work is seen as "unworthy" of men. In the bush setting, although adult roles are sex-typed to some extent — particularly with respect to the exclusive male hunting, and the fact that gathering is primarily done by women — men do not lose face when they do work typically done by women, such as gathering. But in the sedentary villages of Mahopa there is definitely a feeling that it is unmanly for a man to do the jobs that should be done by women. The following example is offered as an illustration of this and of how the community brings social pressure on women (not, in this case, men) to conform.

At the largest of the three Mahopa villages lived a wife, !Uku, about   40
sixteen years of age, and her husband /Gau, about thirty. Like many first marriages of !Kung women, this union was not happy and had not been for some time. The primary source of discontent was the wife's refusal to do the normal domestic chores expected of her. Her husband ranted publicly, claiming that she refused to collect water for their household. !Uku in those days was looking sullen; she avoided her husband and refused to sleep with him. This kind of marital standoff was not unusual among any of the !Kung I knew. !Kung brides are notorious for being labile, uncooperative, and petulant. Young husbands, though usually five to ten years older than their wives, can also be fractious and emotionally ill-equipped to make a first marriage last. !Kung have an expression which invariably crops up when one or both partners to a young

marriage sabotage domestic life. They say *"Debi !oa kxwia //wa,"* which translates literally: *"Children spoil marriage."*

The atypical feature of the Mahopa couple's difficulty was that the husband made a continuing issue of it. He berated his wife's behavior loudly in public and enlisted her relatives to "shame" her into good behavior, etc. Though I never observed a precisely parallel episode in the bush, my prediction is that such a husband would have grumbled quietly, shrugged his shoulders, and either collected the water himself or tried to drink the water of friends and relatives. He also might have waited until his wife complained that he never provided her with meat and then reminded her that he could not spend all day hunting and still have to supply his own water.

By the time I was living at Mahopa and knew of this marital problem, it appeared to me that the elders of the village were working harder at trying to keep the couple together than would be usual in the bush. In the bush concerned relatives will work to keep a young couple together up to a certain point, but if the individuals themselves feel mismatched, there are few, if any, arguments that will persuade them to stay together. When (as often happens) the young couple divorces, no one loses a great deal — no property of any economic weight has changed hands, etc. If both the ex-spouses (together with some of their respective kin) go their separate ways, their departure causes no special disruption in the context of routinely shifting residence patterns.

At Mahopa there were larger political factors at work in the village that may have accounted for the pressure on the couple to get along. Both spouses were related in different ways to the most influential couple of the largest of the three villages. The wife, !Uku, was indirectly related as "niece" to the man who was spoken of as the "owner" of the village. !Uku's husband, /Gau, was the actual brother of the village "owner's" wife. This older, influential couple needed to attract stable, permanent residents to their village. They were extremely "progressive" in comparison with other !Kung of the !Kangwa area. Both had had many years of experience living in various Bantu cattle camps but were now striving to maintain a separate community of sedentary !Kung who could live by agriculture and animal husbandry. Their village needed personnel; /Gau and !Uku were, in theory, ideal recruits to the village on account of their age and kin connections.

What is important for us here is that certain influential persons had vested interests in the success of the marriage, and that the bulk of social criticism was directed at the wife, not the husband. In this sedentary situation, various persons stood to lose a good deal in the event of a divorce. From the point of view of the village "owner" and his wife, a divorce might result in both young people leaving the village. This would be undesirable for reasons already stated. From the point of view of !Uku's parents, who also lived in this village — if their daughter divorced the brother of the "landlady," then their own welcome in the village might become jeopardized.

Although social pressure was being brought to bear on !Uku, it appeared that these pressures were not having the desired effect. !Uku's mother told me privately that she was disgusted with her daughter, that she had tried to get her to change her ways, but that !Uku was obdurate and had even used insulting language to her. !Uku at this time seemed to go out of her way to irritate her husband, had seriously offended her mother, and appeared quite regressive in her behavior. For example, although she was then sixteen years old, she spent hours each day playing dolls with three other girls, ten, nine, and seven years of age. From the bush-living groups I was well acquainted with five adolescent females (both married and unmarried, and approximately the age of !Uku), but I never observed any of them playing so continuously and with such absorption with children five or six years younger.

In the sedentary situation individuals have a different kind of commitment to the place and the persons with whom they are living. People have invested time and energy in building substantial housing, collecting a few goats, clearing and planting fields, and processing and storing the harvested food. It is not easy for an individual to leave these resources behind merely because he or she is at odds with someone else in the village. The couple just described were aware of what they had to lose; the head couple needed neighbors and village mates, not only for the purposes of economic cooperation but because they wanted the human company that would come of a stable settlement around them. 46

The unhappy marriage remained with no solution or even the hint of one during the time I observed it. Neither party to the marriage appeared ready to leave, so their plight festered and spread into the lives of other people in the village. It was not clear to me why the greatest criticism was leveled at the wife. At sixteen, she was at least fifteen years younger than her husband (a greater age difference than is usual for !Kung couples), and as a juvenile she may have been an easier target than her mature husband. /Gau was known for his hot temper and general unpredictability. The concerned parties may have felt uneasy about urging him to a compromise. Such a marriage in the bush setting would have had a different history. !Uku would have left her husband long before, in all likelihood to spend another year or two in casual flirtations before marrying again. 47

CHILDHOOD PRACTICES AND THE GREATER SEPARATION OF ADULT SEX ROLES

Previously I have stated that in the bush children of both sexes lead very similar lives. Girls and boys do equally little work within the village. For similar reasons both girls and boys are not encouraged to routinely accompany adults of the same sex on their respective food-getting rounds. Children sometimes accompany the women on gathering trips (particularly in the rainy season when the women do not have to carry drinking water for them), but up to about twelve years of age the children make little or no contribution to the collected food which their mothers carry home. Children do, however, pick their own food and eat it during the trek. 48

In the settled life children continue to have a great deal of leisure, but there is a shift in the adult attitude toward a child as a potential or 49 real worker. Boys, for example, are expected to help with the animal tending. They do not herd the animals during the day, but at sundown they are expected to scout the outskirts of the village and to hasten the returning animals into their pens. In each of the three Mahopa villages there was one boy who was primarily responsible for herding chores. In the largest village there were other boys also available, and these youths were frequently asked to help with the herding. Girls were not expected to help in the animal tending, and they in fact made no regular contribution.

An important feature of the herding work of the boys was that it   50
regularly took them out of the village, away from adults and out on their own. There was no comparable experience for girls. They tended to stay in or near the village, unless they were accompanying older women to the water hole to collect water. On such occasions they quickly walked the mile or more to the well, where they filled their buckets and then returned more or less promptly to the village. In contrast, the boys drove their animals to the water and then, their work done, they lingered at the water hole. Herero men also came to the well, driving animals to water. Herero and Tswana women frequently came to the well to wash clothing. !Kung boys hung around the fringes of this scene, listening and observing. Experiences like these are no doubt related to the superior knowledge of Bantu languages which !Kung men exhibit in comparison to !Kung women. Such experiences must foster for boys a better and earlier knowledge of the greater !Kangwa area and a more confident spirit when moving within it — or outside of it, for that matter.

Women and girls appear to inhabit more restricted space — that   51
space being largely their own village or neighboring villages. The Mahopa women gather wild plant foods, but they do this infrequently and forage in an area much closer to the village and for shorter intervals as compared with the bush women.

Overall, the Mahopa women seem homebound, their hands are bus-   52
ier, and their time is taken up with domestic chores. A number of factors enter into this change. Under settled conditions food preparation is more complicated, although the actual diet is probably less varied in comparison with that of the foragers. Grains and squash must be brought in from the fields and set up on racks to dry. Sorghum and corn are pounded into meal; squash and melons are peeled and then boiled before eating. Women do the greatest part of the cooking, and they also do most of the drying and storing.

The material inventory of the settled villagers is richer than that of   53
the bush-living !Kung. People have more possessions and better facilities, and all of these things require more time and energy for maintenance. Housing, for example, is more substantial than in the bush. Round, mud-walled houses with thatched roofs are replacing the traditional grass scherms at Mahopa. More durable structures are a response to at least two changes. Once committed to settled life, it makes sense to build better and more permanent shelters. Also, the presence of domestic animals in and near the villages means that grass houses are either protected by barricades or they are literally eaten up. Most people believe it is easier to build the mud-dung earth houses and to close them with

inedible doors, rather than being continually on the lookout against stock. These structures provide better shelter, but they also require more upkeep. The women periodically resurface the interior walls and lay new floors. The men do some domestic maintenance work, but it is more likely to be fencing, roof-thatching, and other nonroutine work. It appears that the Mahopa men are becoming peripheral to their households in ways that are completely uncharacteristic of the easy integration of bush-living men into their own households. More will be said about this later.

At Mahopa the work of adult women is becoming more specialized, 54 time-consuming, and homebound, and these women are quite willing to integrate their daughters into this work. Girls have no regular chores to compare with the herding work of some of the boys, but their mothers give them frequent small tasks such as pounding grain, carrying away a troublesome toddler, fetching earth from termite hills to be used in making mud, etc. The little girls are usually on the premises and easy targets for their mothers' commands; little boys seem to be either gone from the village (on errands already described) or else visible but distant enough from the women so that their help cannot be enlisted conveniently.

Earlier in this paper I suggested that bush-living men and women 55 are about equally absent from their respective households, due to the similarities in the location and frequency of their work. This is less true at Mahopa. Women are in the village a great deal. The greatest part of their work takes place there, and foraging occupies only a small part of their weekly work. Mahopa men are increasingly absent from the households as their women become more consistently present. There are tasks and activities for men in the village which have already been described, though they are not routine. What work the men do often takes them away from the village. They water animals, and when the goats are giving birth to kids the men who own pregnant goats check on the grazing herd during the day to make sure the newborn are not lost or rejected by the mothers. During planting season the men clear the fields and erect brush fences around the gardens to keep out the animals. Some men leave home for several days at a time to do wage work for Bantu employers living at other settlements in the !Kangwa Valley.

It is difficult to specify precisely what effect this increasing male 56 absenteeism had on family life or relations between the sexes. The activities of the sedentary men are different not only in form but in content from those of the women. They leave home more frequently, travel more widely, and have more frequent interaction with members of other (dominant) cultural groups. In their own villages the men carry an aura of authority and sophistication that sets them apart from the women and children. For example, occasionally some incident, such as a legal case pending before the Tswana headman at !Xabi, would attract attention in the !Kangwa area. In the afternoons I often saw a group of men composed of several !Kung and one or two Hereros sitting in a shady area of one of the !Kung villages. The men would be discussing the case, carrying on the talks in a Bantu language. Women never joined these groups, and even children seemed to give these sessions a wide berth.

What these episodes conveyed to me is that at Mahopa political affairs 57
are the concern of men, not women. Why or how women have been
"eased out" (at least in comparison with the influence they had in the
bush) is not clear. The /Du/da people, so long as they remained in the
bush, had only rare and fleeting contacts with members of different cultural
groups. If one postulates that men are the natural political agents in
intergroup contacts, then the /Du/da milieu would not elicit that potential
of the male role. At Mahopa three cultural groups mixed. !Kung men,
as already described, were more sophisticated than the women, and on
those occasions when !Kung became involved in extragroup events, the
!Kung men came prominently to the fore.

ORGANIZATION OF SPACE AND PRIVACY
IN THE BUSH SETTING

To recapitulate, in the bush, village space is small, circular, open, 58
and highly intimate. Everyone in the camp can see (and often hear)
everyone else virtually all of the time, since there are no private places
to which people can retire. Even at nightfall people remain in the visually
open space, sleeping singly or with other family members around the
fires located outside the family huts. Elsewhere, I have suggested that
!Kung egalitarianism and commitment to sharing are more than coinci-
dentally associated. The intensity of social pressure, in combination with
the absence of privacy, makes hoarding virtually impossible, at least for
individuals who wish to remain within the group. I am suggesting that
the nature of village space in the bush acts as a "lock" on other aspects
of culture that are congruent but capable of sliding apart. While it is true
that !Kung values oppose physical fighting and anger, ranking of individuals
in terms of status, material wealth, and competition, the context in which
social action occurs is such that the earliest and subtlest moves in these
directions can be perceived immediately by the group. Various forms of
negative reinforcement can be employed by anyone and everyone, and
the effect is to discourage anti-social behavior, whatever form it may
take.

Obviously a continuous socialization process is not unique to the 59
!Kung. All of us experience our fellows shaping our behavior throughout
our lives. What I would like to stress about the !Kung is that in this
small, face-to-face society it is much more difficult to compartmentalize
one's motives, feeling states, and (most of all) actions. In ways not true
of our life, !Kung remain in continuous communication, though they may
not be directly conscious of the exchanges of information that are
occurring. . . .

Another argument can be made for why an egalitarian, mutual in- 60
terdependence prevails among these people. The nature and distribution
of the resources used by the hunting and gathering !Kung probably have
indirect consequences for potential competition between and within !Kung
groups. Both vegetable and animal foods are thinly and unevenly distributed over the bush. This is particularly true of the large antelope, which

move erratically and seldom in the large herds that are more typical in East Africa and Arctic North America. Under conditions as these, hunting success for a particular individual depends as much on luck as it does on skill. Among the !Kung, even the best hunters readily admit that there are times when game is unavailable or when conditions do not permit the stalk-and-close approach to game required by bow-and-arrow hunting. As a result, any individual man cannot count on success, and in this context sharing of meat is an essentil form of social insurance — a way of distributing food to the have-nots against the time when their fortunes change. Not surprisingly, the rules about sharing meat constitute one of the most important values in !Kung culture. My guess is that in such a system where males are continually leveled and divested of their ownership of the single most valued item (meat), the potential for male competition is largely removed. The strict sharing ethic, together with the values against interpersonal aggression described earlier, are checks on male agonistic behavior that leave the field open for female autonomy and influence.

ORGANIZATION OF SPACE AND PRIVACY IN THE SETTLED VILLAGES

In the settled villages the organization of space and the notion of privacy have undergone some interesting changes. Instead of the circular, closed settlement pattern of the bush, the settled villages typically are arranged in an open crescent; individual households have moved farther apart; and household privacy is substantially increased, particularly for those people who have acquired more material wealth. With individual houses farther apart, the pattern of social usage of the village space is different. The average distance between interactive clusters of people also increases. In the settled village different activities are more typically separated in space, as contrasted with the bush setting where it is typical to find people carrying on a conversation and/or activity while sitting back-to-back with other people who are engaged in a wholly different enterprise. **61**

At the time I was living at Mahopa a few families already lived in permanent mud-walled houses and some other families were in the process of building Bantu-style rondavels to replace their smaller grass scherms. Occupants of the completed rondavels build log fences around their houses; slender logs or poles are placed upright in the ground, reaching to a height of five to six feet, and spaced one to two inches apart. These fences encircle individual households and create an inner courtyard. Obviously, privacy is increased substantially by the changed house type, settlement pattern, and fencing. **62**

When I asked settled villagers why people erected the fences, the typical response was that it is a means of keeping domestic animals away from people's living quarters. Goats, in particular, can be a nuisance. They steal food, knock over pots, even come into houses in search of food. Their fresh dung attracts flies which are also bothersome. If domestic animals entail a new style of building, the solid, roomy houses, **63** fences, and more linear placement of separate households also change the quality of social interaction in the villages. There are internal boundaries within the village space, which people recognize and manipulate in ways completely foreign to the bush setting. In the bush people can see each other and determine, on a variety of grounds, whether it is appropriate or timely to initiate social interaction. In the Mahopa villages one heard such exchanges as "So-and-so, are you at home?" and "Shall I enter [your space]?"

There are differences in material wealth among the people of the 64 settled villages that would not be tolerated in the bush. These differences are manifest in terms of household size and elaborateness of construction, unequal ownership of domestic animals, clothing, jewelry, and food reserves. The differences are not large in an absolute sense, but in comparison with the similar material wealth of individuals in the bush, the differences are impressive. Some !Kung live simply, still using grass scherms and owning few possessions; others are better off, though the men in particular seem to avoid some kinds of ostentation. For example, the two men who were the most influential males in their villages often dressed very simply and did not have the outward appearance of "big men."[1] Yet, if invited into their houses, one would see a remarkable collection of *things:* clothing, dishes, blankets, bottles, trunks with locks, etc. As a guest in such a house one could sit on the floor, lean back against the cool, sound-deadening wall, and enjoy being *alone* with one's host while he or she made tea and murmured small talk.

Ranking of individuals in terms of prestige and differential wealth has 65 begun in the settled villages. Men, more than women, are defined as the managers or owners of this property. One would hear, for example, such expressions as "Kxau's [a man's name] house" or "Kxau's village." Children are most often identified as being the child of the father rather than the child of the mother. Goats are also referred to as belonging to one or another adult male, though in fact a given man's herd generally includes several animals which in fact belong to his wife or other female relatives. These expressions can be heard in the bush setting, for individual ownership exists among the foragers as well, but the "owners" referred to are as likely to be women as men. At Mahopa this linguistic custom is being replaced by one in which the adult male stands as the symbol of his domestic group. It is a linguistic shorthand, but I believe it signifies changes in the relative importance attached to each sex.

Earlier I referred to the increasing peripheralization of males in the 66 settled villages and the opposite centripetal moving of women to the local domestic sphere. As households and possessions become private, I believe women are becoming private as well. (Perhaps this is one reason the women can afford to be ostentatious of their wealth.) In contrast bush men and women are equally "public," mobile, and visible. I believe this exposure of women is a form of protection in the bush setting. For instance, residence choices of bush-living couples are such that over time

---

[1] Yet the middle-aged wives of these men often wore jewelry and clothing beyond the means of other women living in the settled villages.

the couples live about equally (often simultaneously) with the kin of both husband and wife. (At present there is not even an ideal of patrilocal residence, so far as my own interviews could establish.) This means that the wife typically has several of her own close kin nearby. These people are already on the premises and can support her interests should they conflict with the interests of her husband or his close kin. When husbands and wives argue, people are at hand to intervene if either spouse loses self-control. Wife-beating in these settings is extremely difficult to effect. . . .

In this paper I have pointed out differences in sexual egalitarianism   67
in the hunting and gathering groups versus the settled groups of !Kung. I have discussed factors in the bush setting which favor high autonomy for females and freedom from subordination by males. Once the !Kung shift their subsistence to animal husbandry and crop planting, a number of changes occur in the area of sex roles. A major aspect of this change is the decrease in women's autonomy and influence relative to that of the men.

In "Illusion and Reality in Sicily" (1977), anthropologist Constance Cronin examines the social structure of a small Sicilian town, finding the public display of male power at odds with social realities.

Illusion and Reality in Sicily
CONSTANCE CRONIN

A Sicilian town is almost totally devoid of greenery. The center of every   1
town is a piazza where men gather to talk, surrounded by stores, coffee bars, and the main church. Off the piazza runs the main street, the Corso. The wealthy and higher-status families live on or near the Corso. The rest of the streets are narrow and roughly cobbled with small one- and two-room houses directly adjacent to each other. Most towns are divided into named quarters that have no administrative recognition; but aside from vague beliefs that the people in each quarter share some characteristics, these are not viable entities.

Towns are heterogeneous for occupation and class. They contain not   2
only persons with typical urban occupations such as doctors, lawyers, and white-collar employees, but also farmers and agricultural day laborers. Sicilians prefer to live in urban environments that have entertainment, action, life, and a never-ending flow of people and activities. Most of the farmers are poor and along with shepherds rank at the bottom of the social stratification scale; professionals and shop and office workers are middle-class; some towns have a resident upperclass, usually aristocratic, but most do not. Therefore, while the variation in the class system is limited, the gulf between the majority of farmers and all the rest is vast.

There is no positive view of peasantry. On the contrary, a number   3
of proverbs completely devalue farming as a way of life: it is said that

"a man who farms the land is his own slave." Until World War II there were few opportunities for upward social mobility; today, however, while mobility between classes is still difficult, it is possible to move upward within a class. Young men are rapidly abandoning their fathers' farms to become coffee-bar attendants, construction helpers, and auto mechanics, and always with their parents' approval. Girls and their parents prefer marriage with a nonfarmer because of the possibilities for more money and greater prestige.

Since agricultural plots lie outside the town, farmers must travel to   4
their land. However, this is not a simple round trip. Italian law, which in this case mirrors customary law, stipulates equal inheritance for all children, so that shares of the family patrimony must be given at the marriage of each child or divided equally at the death of the father. Since this system has been in effect for over 100 years, limited land resources plus large families have today resulted in extremely small fields. Each person or nuclear family, if fortunate, will own several of these plots, but they are usually widely dispersed. Therefore, the farmer spends inordinate amounts of time traveling first to the countryside and then to the various sections he must work. Many spend up to half their time slowly moving on mules or carts. To complicate matters, most of the land is rocky and impoverished, water must be brought in by cart, and modern fertilization techniques are generally unknown. Many families are even worse off since they have no land at all. The father must hire out as a day laborer and work an average of fewer than 100 days a year, or he may sharecrop under conditions disadvantageous to him. Women may not and do not work; in most areas of Sicily they may not even help out in the fields during busy periods. . . .

Even though there are national, regional, communal, and subcom-   5
munal institutions, these do not serve as a focus for groups. Sicilians have no sense of belonging in reference to the country or the town and do not share with others any beliefs or actions based on shared membership. The town is there, it picks up the garbage and supplies water erratically, but it is not an entity to which one owes anything. People do not perform services voluntarily, and community-action programs have proven to be totally unworkable. People from other towns are foreigners and therefore highly suspect, but there is not a reciprocal respect or concern for those of one's own town. The only grouping in the society that has any real validity is the nuclear family. [Other researchers] have all noted this phenomenon for southern Italy, which is often called "amoral familism," a term coined by Banfield.

Sicilian kinship is bilateral. "The relatives" (*i parenti*) is a category   6
comprising all affinal and consanguineal kin outside one's nuclear family. Relatives are supposed to be good to each other, to render aid when necessary, and always to show *rispetto* (respect) for one another. But relatives are not a corporate group; they do not hold property together, they do not live together, and they do not meet as a group to make decisions, work, or socialize. The nuclear family does all these things.

This family unit is the hub of the society to which each individual   7
owes his complete loyalty and from which he derives his greatest rewards. The members of the nuclear family should live together, love each other,

obey those in positions of authority, contribute all earnings to the family coffers, make decisions together, and demonstrate total undivided loyalty. The demands of this family group militate against the development of strong friendships outside it, for these would tend to weaken family loyalty and are therefore discouraged for both children and adults. In the same fashion and for the same reasons, closeness to other relatives, strangers, priests, the city, the country, and even oneself is a potential threat to the unity and integrity of the nuclear family. A well-known proverb states that "the real relatives are those inside the house" (*lu veru parenti sunnu chiddi dintra la casa*). This exclusivity extends to all others who are not "real relatives."

Within this family there is a complex but clear set of rules for re-   8
lationships. The husband-father should command his wife and children and oversee the activities of the family both inside and outside the house. The wife should obey her husband and direct activities inside the house, while the mother should guide the children in carrying out the commands of the father. Sons should obey their father, help their mother, and oversee their sisters, while daughters should obey father, mother, and brothers. Brothers should respect one another and sisters should care for and help each other.

As males and females, always within a family setting, the rules are   9
even more vivid. The *onore* (honor) of the family and the relatives depends ultimately upon the purity of the women. Women are weak and easily led astray; therefore, it is the responsibility of men and of other women to maintain the virginity of unmarried women and the constancy of married women. The best way to maintain *onore* is to ensure the protection of all women, and seclusion from others is believed to be the most effective method. Thus women must obey men who are stronger and remain in the house guarded by the men and other women in the family. On the rare occasions when women leave the house they should always be accompanied by others.

The culture does recognize the fallibility of men also, for God and   10
His mother alone are perfect. Therefore, men too must be controlled. This control comes somewhat from other men, but the most important agent of control is the family — not the individual members, who are controlled themselves, but rather the family as a collective and single unit. Members of the community help in this regard and so do the rules and beliefs of the Church. Thus we now have stated the ideal by which Sicilian society functions. But ideals or norms are only rules for behavior and in practice are often not observed. To get a complete picture of the life of a society, it is necessary to observe both norms and behaviors, noting the congruencies and the inconsistencies.

PROBLEMS AND SOLUTIONS

The major problem, from which all others derive, stems from the   11
culture's demand that men do everything — make all decisions, carry out most of them themselves, and delegate the rest of the tasks to others while still remaining responsible for them. To do all this requires not only

a considerable amount of time, but, more important, skill — intelligence, farsightedness, craftiness, and the ability to manipulate situations and people. Unfortunately, very few men have all the requisite skills. They desperately desire them and they feel unworthy and inferior because they are not as capable as the culture demands. One hears constant references by men to themselves as "poor things" or as having "hard heads": they do not understand everything they hear about and grow angry and hostile; they apologize for their stupidity and lack of sophistication. This does not mean that they can do nothing but rather that they cannot do everything. The cultural demands are so great and the societal opportunities so meager that failure is almost preordained. Men never really have a chance to be successful in their own world. However, so long as they appear to be in control, they and they alone receive public rewards.

One of the key words in understanding the complexity that is Sicily   12
is the local meaning of the Italian word *rispetto*. The English definition of respect is "to feel or show honor or esteem for," and the Italian is almost identical. But when used in Sicily the word means "to keep up the appearances." One hears constant references to "having respect for the relatives," "I respect my brother," and "that is a man of respect." All this means is that the cultural front is kept in place; it does not necessarily imply love, loyalty, help, or admiration. The man who maintains the proper public stance has *rispetto* and his family has *onore*. In this he is aided by members of his family.

In contrast to a man, the only obligation for a woman is to maintain   13
her honor, which she does by keeping shame intact. The concept "honor and shame" has for years been a key concept in Mediterranean studies, but for Sicily at least the meaning is at variance with other societies. One of the reasons we have not understood this critical difference is that little work has been done in Sicily, and another reason is that the Italian terms translate so easily into exact English equivalents. Thus *shame* in English means "a painful emotion arising from a consciousness of something dishonoring, ridiculous, or indecorous in one's own conduct or circumstances." We use the term with the verbs *to be* or *to feel*. It is a transitory state that induces slight or serious reactions in the individual, reactions that must be resolved. However, in Sicily the term *vergogna* is used with the verb *to have* (*avere*) and indicates a quality with which persons, especially women, are born. A good woman, a proper woman of *rispetto*, has *vergogna*. One is born with it and keeps it by decorous actions such as using a low voice or sitting correctly in a chair, behaving submissively to authority figures, and cherishing one's own purity. The more proper translation from the Italian would appear to be "an enduring sense of modesty and decorum." A woman loses her *vergogna* by violations of these cultural codes and is then called a *svergognata* (indicating the opposite of the original word).

The almost total emphasis in the literature on the fact that honor   14
and shame equal virginity is highly exaggerated. For while the easiest and surest way for a woman to lose her *vergogna* is to have sexual relations with a man not her spouse, there are other ways as well. But all that the culture demands of women is that they maintain *vergogna* by

remaining pure and modest and obeying figures of authority such as father and husband. Very few women violate these rules, for punishment is swift and awful. The majority have *vergogna* and with it do not need intelligence, wit, ability, or any of the other impressive qualities that men must exhibit. This very insistence upon one factor, or cluster of factors, leaves the woman free to choose what else she will be. She can sit back and spin out her life in total physical and mental laziness, relying on father, husband, son, and daughter to carry the demands of culture and society. But she can also choose to operate in the system of adjustment and use the many skills and talents she feels are hers. (This, of course, leaves out the important question of whether she really has any ability; but since even women who are incapable attempt to work through the system, we will not be concerned here with actual ability.)

Thus the prison of culture restricts a man from being and doing what   15
he wants, whereas the fetters placed on the woman, although seemingly more rigid, actually allow her much greater personal freedom if she will but publicly maintain her *vergogna*.

Problems and solutions for both women and men come from the   16
operation of the social system. There are a number of critical problem areas. One of these is the relation between the systems of education and social stratification. While schooling is available to all, it is, with very few exceptions, only the middle class who can take advantage of it. The two main reasons for this are home environment and finances. Working-class parents in their one- or two-room houses cannot provide quiet study areas for their children, nor do they see the need for such a luxury. It is assumed by most that learning is done in school and that homework is an exercise in obedience rather than in learning. Therefore children are told they should study in school and help out at home or in the fields after school. As a result, peasant children begin leaving school either voluntarily or by failing repeatedly — usually after two or three years. There are other families who for financial gain must take children, especially boys, out of school and put them to work as early as possible. Almost none of these parents think that education is a waste of time, again especially for boys, but they simply do not understand what is necessary for success in a modern school system.

Children from middle-class families do continue in school with varying   17
rates of success, although their social-class standing ensures that no teacher will fail even the dullest pupil. Teachers, middle class themselves, frequently draw public comparisons between middle-class and working-class children to the children. So a growing feeling of inadequacy in a seven-year-old peasant is reinforced by teachers, middle-class success, and his parents' characterization of him as a *cretino* or a *testa dura* (hardhead). In a very short time this results in his first real failure when he drops out of school at nine or ten. This process is directed specifically at boys.

Girls are not expected to do well in school nor is it necessary for   18
them to do so. The skills they will need to manage a house and family are learned at home; education beyond the ability to read, write, and

work simple arithmetic is not only superfluous but damaging, because it will eventually make girls dissatisfied with their homebound role. Exceptionally bright little boys are praised, but little girls who display high intelligence are a constant source of worry to their parents, whose most frequent comment is *che peccato* (what a pity).

By the age of ten, boys have already experienced their first major 19 setback, and whatever native intelligence and capacity they have has been effectively covered over by feelings of ignorance and inability. With girls it is different. They too may fail in school, but there is little if any public censure. They can reassure themselves that they are intelligent but left school, as many do, because they didn't like it. It is their decision, and they emerge with ego and self-esteem intact.

The boys then go to work with their fathers or in the town while 20 girls remain at home helping mothers, learning housekeeping tasks, and beginning the embroidery of linens which will form part of their dowry at marriage. Engagements are early; marriages are late. During this rather long period, boys work and are, for the most part, isolated from social contact. If they go to the fields then the isolation is all but complete. If they work in town there is more contact with others, but employers expect a lot from their workers and there is very little time or opportunity for socializing or discussion. Workdays, six or seven days a week, are long, and there is only time for an hour or so after work to stand in the piazza with other men.

Girls remain home and the limits of their physical world are narrow 21 — the house and the street extending for the block on which the house is located. But this street, the living room of all working-class families, is filled with people. Most are women of all ages, but usually there are a few men as well: artisans who repair shoes, carts, and implements or make barrels or bridles at home. Here, among the women, age differences have a tendency to blur and girls learn early to take an equal place in these women's groups. They take on the gestures, postures, speech patterns, and ideas of the older women and have an opportunity to learn not only the necessary housewifely skills but also the techniques of influencing decisions and controlling others without seeming to. Not just gossip but, more importantly, strategies are communicated. For example, in chatting about a husband and wife who have recently fought, an older woman will digress and enlarge to make a more general case: "Now see, a type like this Signor Tizio who is so brutal is not common but you might just marry one. The problem here is his wife who doesn't know how to handle him. She does so-and-so but what she should do is this. . . ." The girls listening learn a valuable lesson.

By the time marriage takes place personalities are developing and 22 the scene is set. The prime task of the couple is to establish and even increase the prestige of this new nuclear family. This is accomplished in a variety of ways, such as eating and dressing well, keeping a neat house, bringing up properly behaved children, owning a house, later owning more houses as rental property, and generally maintaining everything and everyone in order. When a person marries he and she say they are going to *sistemarsi* (to settle, arrange oneself). This, properly and consistently done, will bring praise and prestige to the family itself and to the husband in particular, since he is in total command.

The culture dictates that the husband-father must direct all activities, make all decisions, ensure they are carried out, and represent the family and its members to the public. In addition, men should perform all the tasks outside the house, such as paying bills, visiting experts and professionals, buying groceries, and conferring with relatives and outsiders if advice is needed. This plus a full-time job proves impossible. The man is at work six to seven days a week from at least sunup to sundown (and farmers normally work much longer hours than this), and thus he is not available to perform all his obligations in the public arena. There are no other adult males in the house, and only the members of the nuclear family would even be considered for these tasks. Boys work also, unmarried girls never leave the block, and so most of these activities fall to the wife. It is she who visits the doctor and lawyer and goes from one government office to another paying bills, arranging accounts, and keeping up with identity papers. It is also she who makes rounds of visits to relatives, friends, advisers, and others for counsel on legal problems or financial affairs, and to determine whether a son in another family is a likely spouse for their daughter. 23

It is rare that the casual visitor will see her doing all this, because she leaves the house early in the morning with the long mourning veil pulled low across her face, tracing a path around and about the back streets where she will be seen only by other women. Quite a bit of impromptu visiting and chatting occurs on these travels and much information is exchanged. She will never admit that she was across town. If you visit her house when she is out, family members tell you that she is next door or across the street, and if you ask a neighbor she gives the same reply. Women do feel that their *vergogna* is liable to harm in these forays because these trips are potentially dangerous, but they also derive a great deal of satisfaction from them. 24

When the husband at last returns home, they confer together on their day's activities. Women are said to be much more verbal in these exchanges and in general, but information received is weighed and judged by both and decisions are reached together. Even though the woman gathers most of the information, the man can still make the decisions by himself. Very few do because they realize that their wives are intelligent, concerned, and often more skillful than they themselves. Women are frequently said to be *furbe* (crafty, cunning, sly), which is generally considered to be a female attribute. Note that no claim is being made for Sicilian women taking over male roles; it is simply that the social system places the woman, in practice, on the same level with the man. Each has his or her own skills and specialties and these together help the couple to maintain an orderly family that enjoys the respect and prestige of the entire community. While women are skilled at conversation, manipulation, and intrigue, men have greater seriousness, farsightedness, and sophistication in other aspects of the public sector of life. Together they are a good pair. 25

All of this is carried out in secret, but everyone else knows that it   26
happens and works to keep it in the private sector — the house. It is
extremely important that the cultural rules concerning male and female
roles be maintained; if it appears that they have been broken, disaster
will result. The man who does not command is not a man, while the
woman who does command has lost her *vergogna;* and the family will
become the laughing-stock of the community, the public butt of jokes,
ridicule, and scorn. Therefore, the fewer who know the better.

It is impossible to hide the truth from children in the house, but they   27
will not talk. Neighbors also know what really happens, but so long as
appearances are maintained the neighbors will aid in the public deception,
partly to protect an honest situation and partly because they are doing
precisely the same thing. Others may guess and gossip but they need
never know. It is not a fiction that is being maintained because there is
an earnest and sincere desire to conform as closely as possible to the
cultural ideal. It is interesting to note that Mafia families are constantly
being held up as examples of how things should be. They, with their
special resources and ultrarigid code, are said to be the only families who
can maintain themselves in the proper way. The term *mafioso* can be
used for one who is involved in underworld activities, but it can also be
applied as a compliment, a term of respect, to any man who is scrupulous
in carrying out the cultural dictates to command, to be proud, to keep
silent. While most families cannot measure up, they do try. It is said that
a poor wife is one who lets everyone know she is important; a good wife
is one who lets only her husband know; and a perfect wife is one who
lets no one know.

Another serious chink in the cultural armor is caused by the child   28
socialization practices. Children are taught from the earliest age possible
that the world outside the house is dangerous and that the streets are
peopled with individuals who will "do bad things to you." The only safety
and protection lie with family members inside the house. It is also emphasized that all people are weak and imperfect and not capable either
of making decisions by themselves or of assuming responsibility for decisions once made. Therefore, all decisions are made by the group of
capable adults in the family: father, mother, and adult children. Decisions
are considered in the light of what is best for the family prestige, not
for the wishes of the individual involved. If a child wishes to continue in
school but the interests of the family will be better served by putting
him to work and using his earnings to buy a house, then his desire and
possibilities for the future are sacrificed. Parents are assumed to know
more than even adult children and to have their best interests at heart;
therefore, they will not put the child on the wrong road. There is little
rebellion against the strongly stated decisions of the group, because one
person alone does not feel capable of making decisions and probably is
not. Decision making is a learned skill, and if one learns it in a group it
will be extremely difficult later to stand alone, particularly against group
pressure.

But this is another area in which both adult men and women feel   29
inadequate, and it is reassuring for the man who is not, or at least does

not feel, up to culturally imposed standards to have an intelligent spouse who can help shoulder these responsibilities. Men say and probably feel that most women are not as whole in their humanness as men, with the exception of one's own wife who has been tested in the trials that marriage brings.

This cooperation between husband and wife and among family mem-   30
bers does not imply emotional closeness and intimacy. The entire social system of interpersonal relations fosters at best affective distance and at worst outright hostility. Here is another of the discrepancies between culture and the social system. The total effect of the socialization practices is to isolate individuals each from all others. Women feel the brunt of this more than men, but women also have ways of using the system to lessen the felt isolation.

Young adults do not date; they have no contact whatsoever with   31
members of the opposite sex who are not close relatives or neighbors. Engagements are long but the contact pattern is one of seeing each other every few days in a living room with others in the family always present. Not only is conversation difficult and strained, but isolation from all boys tends to make girls very shy and embarrassed in front of their fiancés. After marriage, affection and love do develop in a few cases. For most couples a working relationship of mutual dependence develops; intimacy, companionship, and frank disclosure of feelings is impossible. . . .

If a man is able to follow the cultural dictates to appear strong,   32
independent, self-reliant, commanding, serious, and silent the society will heap its greatest rewards and acclaim upon him. He is said by all to be a true Sicilian and is constantly praised for his demeanor, his family, his house, his daughter's marriage, and everything else commendable that he and his family members do. He is a man of honor and prestige, and if he also has money and social position better still, although these are not prime ingredients. He is deserving of deference and respect even from those who avoid him socially. If he is poor and of the working class they will not live with him or marry into his family, but they will admire him and hold him up as an example of what a Sicilian of his class should be. There are actually very few men who do not perform this part well.

Privately, he may know that he is not all that he projects in public.   33
He is not very capable, he can't figure things out easily or well, he must have help, which he receives primarily from his wife. Deep feelings of inferiority, insecurity, and fear result; he worries that his public face may be lifted to expose the poor fallible man underneath. He has the satisfaction of knowing that he is trying as hard as he knows how to meet cultural demands that are too great. Still, the public reinforcement seems enough to enable most men to cope with their self-professed incapacity.

The pattern for women is very different because there is very little   34
public reward and the costs to the individual are enormous. A woman is culturally rewarded only for maintaining her *vergogna,* which she can do very simply by remaining pure, modest, and circumspect with outsiders. This is not a difficult task and almost no women fail. Therefore, no one individual can feel that she has accomplished something unusual or difficult.

Women can be rewarded and praised by a small circle of people for   35
other more specialized skills. Women of at least middle age can appear

in a variety of contexts that call for an expert. There are four major roles of this sort, all of which demand a person with highly developed social sensitivity and an ability to talk well — two attributes women are felt to possess.

The first of these roles is the marriage matchmaker (*ruffiana*). These   36 individuals serve as representatives of families when engagements are in the beginning stages. They may or may not be the friend or neighbor who first suggested the match, but they know all the intricacies of bargaining and dowry settlement, and the histories of the two families. This is considered an extremely difficult job and calls for a person who is not only skilled but trusted implicitly. The *ruffiana* is usually not paid for this work but may be given a present later.

The second job for which women are suited is the peacemaker. When   37 arguments develop between branches of a family or between two families and there is a possibility that control may be lost and outright fighting or a *vendetta* may develop, then one or several people are called in as arbitrators in a collective-bargaining session in which the litigants have agreed to abide by the decision of the judges.

Both of these roles may be carried out by men and women, but a   38 third is almost exclusively the province of women — the social expert. These are generally older women who know everything about everyone going very far back into the past. If, for instance, an engagement is contemplated by a family who want to know everything about the other family, they will send someone, usually a woman, informally to a social expert known to them and ask for a rundown on the family and all its members. These experts can usually go back long before their own lifetimes because they have, as younger women, learned from social experts now dead.

The fourth area of expertise, ribaldry, is one known only among   39 women. There are women who function in the role of comedians or social satirists, always in an explicitly sexual context. They can make any subject and any person a figure of such hilarity, ridicule, and grotesqueness that the person will never again appear to be the same. The joking can be teasing and affectionate when applied to a person who is present, but it usually concerns someone who is not there and is strong, biting, and, underneath all the laughter, bitter. The women's groups that sit outside in good weather and indoors in the winter sewing and embroidering usually contain one woman who is such an expert. Her quips, jokes, and impersonations are circulated among other groups of women and her fame spreads. Men know who these women are but to my knowledge are never permitted to participate. The young girls and women who have such *vergogna* that no one can mention giving birth in their presence are privy to these shows, which often appear intended for their edification and education. This is not always rough humor, for most such women are also virtuosas at puns, word plays, and bits of drama. Humor at this level is usually sophisticated and smooth and would be the envy of any professional comedian.

Although some of this is humor for humor's sake, much is an effective   40 form of social control. For instance, three teen-age girls were sewing with a group of women inside the house one afternoon. The satirist mentioned the marriage soon to take place between an aged widower and a forty-year-old spinster. She assembled her props and began to act out what it would be like to be married to an old man, to a spinster, and then to a young man. The skit was screamingly funny and quite explicit, but when this woman left the young girls began to talk seriously about the problems portrayed. The point of the older woman's acts was that girls who are too romantic and wait for the knight in shining armor end up with nothing but an old man; it was a point these three girls understood and believed. This entire complex of sexual joking and satire is a powerful covert strategy used only by women to give notice publicly that they are not always the innocent, ignorant, and put-upon creatures demanded by the culture. For while men do not participate in these sessions, they know of them, acknowledge the experts, and fear the day when they will be the subjects of these female dramas.

But the price to be paid for being a woman in Sicily is high. Women, who do develop excessively romantic notions about love and marriage, are doomed to spend their lives without love and companionship with their husbands. In addition, they must never admit their skill at decision making and manipulation, and neither must anyone else, because to do so would ruin the husband and thereby the family. Thus no one ever alludes to these abilities nor do they ever praise or commend a woman for a job well done. She knows how good she is and so do her children, but for the rest she must remain the little submissive wife sitting quietly in the corner.   41

Anthropologists Jane Margold and Donna Bellorado interviewed women on the Micronesian island of Palau; the section of their study presented here, which was published in 1985, reveals the strains and changes Palauan culture has undergone since coming into contact with the U.S. government.

From *Matrilinear Heritage: A Look at the Power of Contemporary Micronesian Women*
JANE MARGOLD AND DONNA BELLORADO

The Republic of Palau (or Belau) is an archipelago of 350 lushly vegetated islands, coral atolls, and mushroom-shaped, rocky outcroppings, about 500 miles east of the Philippines. Hot, humid, and rainy throughout most of the year, the islands support a population of some 12,000 people, of whom about 7,000 are adults. There are only 3,200 jobs in the wage sector and almost half of these are in government work (including education); the rest are in light industry, tourism, and private retail trade. Fishing and subsistence agriculture supplement cash incomes and are the sole livelihood for many people.   1

Despite a succession of four foreign administrations (Spanish, German, Japanese, and American), the traditional culture in Palau has not   2 been overtaken by the transitional culture (an amalgam of American, Japanese, and European bureaucratic structures, styles of political protest, etc.). The two cultures coexist side by side. At department of education meetings, many of the Palauans chew betel nuts, as they discuss problem-solving models and goal-setting procedures. And the electronic ping of Pac-Man is heard in the distance, as the women inform a male administrator that he should have provided coffee for a long work session.

PALAUAN WOMEN: "A MAN WHO HAS
NO SISTERS IS UNLUCKY"

When I began interviewing the Palauan women, several informants   3
stressed that Palauan women traditionally choose the male chief of their own clan — an important social and political responsibility that is mentioned only once in the literature even though much of the material on Palau is specifically about political leadership and factionalism. Because the chief is looked up to as the person who defends his people's rights and customs, his is not an empty role in Palauan society, and the women's right to choose him means that they partake in his power. Whoever aspires to be chief must pay close attention to the thoughts, needs, and feelings of the women who appoint him. The men of the village can veto this appointment, but as one informant explained, their veto is merely an expression of disapproval that the women can override:

> The chiefs in the village can object to the women's choice. If the females of the clan have another alternative, they might reconsider their decision. But if they choose the same one again, that guy is going to be it. Already, there has been a court case where the chiefs of one village got together and signed a petition to get rid of a chief who is now deceased. They didn't like him. So they took it to the court and the chiefs lost because they have no right whatsoever to decide who will be chief. Now they each have to pay $500, plus seven percent interest, and they have a certain time left to do it. If they do not pay, they will probably be in jail, those ten chiefs.

It's the women's prerogative to decide who the chief will be, she   4
added, because it's the women who will provide the chief with the money he needs to carry out the many traditional obligations he has as the clan's leader. The women will also prepare and contribute any feast food that the chief needs for the rest of his life, which is likely to mean that the women are committing themselves to an enormous financial responsibility.

It is this type of financial obligation, which is far more binding upon   5
both single and married women than it is upon men, that is a major source of women's power and prestige. For many, it's also a burden. Women are expected to provide money and food for every Palauan "custom." The customs are observed not only to mark births, deaths, and marriages, but to celebrate and assist with house-building, boat-buying, and other expensive endeavors. Women have been known to come up with as much as $5,000 to contribute to a brother's new house — a demand that would strain the budget of all but an upper middle-class American and is especially difficult on Palauan salaries. It's no wonder that people in Palau

say, "A man who has no sisters is unlucky" and "A Palauan woman is a Palauan man's money." . . .

The system of mutual obligation was explained in detail by another woman who stressed that Palauan women are in many ways more powerful than the men, not only because of their financial role but because they make all the major decisions about the food that is exchanged at the customary feasts. In Micronesia (and other Pacific Island areas), it should be noted that food and feasting have profound social, emotional, political, and economic significance that has no counterpart in Western culture. The securing of food is a major preoccupation that until recently consumed most of an islander's time and work life. Food thus symbolizes work and is at the same time a reward for working. The amount of food provided at a feast not only indicates the feast-giver's economic, social, and sometimes political importance, but the sharing of food also serves to cement the bonds of kinship and community, reminding everyone that generosity, sharing, and concern for the group are the basis of island culture. Guests not only consume food during the festivities, but take home baskets of food in an amount proportionate to their social and political position, marital status, and willingness to contribute money to that particular custom. The money doesn't pay for the food. It is a more abstract exchange that ties the giver and receiver together in the knowledge that eventually there will be reciprocation, more exchange, and again more reciprocation. Women are at the epicenter of this intricate network, determining the nature and extent of the exchanges and who the givers and receivers will be. . . .

Although men, too, contribute money to the customs, a single man from a clan that is high in the Palauan hierarchy might be expected to give $5 or $10, whereas a married woman from the same high clan would be expected to give a vastly greater amount. "If my brother has a house party, my brother who is younger may give $5 or $10 just to help," one woman said, "but I might be expected to give up to $10,000. It's the sisters who will buy the house." . . .

Most often, the hard-working women will not only collect the money, but will also be the ones to earn it. "When I think about words to describe Palauan women, I think of beautiful but oppressed," one outspoken woman teacher said. This informant, who has run for political office and lost, feels that "it is like shoveling a pile of sand with your eyelashes" for a woman to try to progress to an administrative job within the educational bureaucracy. Highly conscious of her own and other women's positions within the traditional and transitional cultures, she offered this assessment of her own and others' status:

> . . . As far as being a woman in this society, I think a woman is more oppressed than a man, because the responsibility for customs falls on her. She contributes money, almost to the point where she doesn't have enough to provide for the people she lives with. It's unfortunate because then she cannot begin to bloom in her own environment or grow. . . . The women are so giving. They contribute when it's called for, and when they return to the family, they still have to perform, to take care of the children, the

household responsibilities. . . . The men contribute their little share, they give it to the wife, and then they float. But the females feel the burden. They keep it in their hearts, day in and day out. Women cannot grow if they're overburdened with these kinds of cultural responsibilities and family expectations.

In her clan, this woman said, her female relatives had innovated a type of Christmas club, in which the 14 women who participated set aside $10 every pay period, and took turns being the recipients of that sum. They were also beginning to insist that the men contribute more money to customs: 9

We're beginning to have more male participation because everything is costing more money and the pressure is building up. Before, someone would announce that something was needed and a single man would say, "Well, should I [contribute] or not?" But as a woman, single or not, I have to do it. It's a duty. So now, in my family, the men are made to give. We go collect contributions from them.

Although the women's role in carrying out the customs pervaded all the interviews, some of the women pointed to several other social mechanisms that buttress female influence and prestige. If being able to tap into formal and informal lines of communication/information is one characteristic of powerful people within organizations, Palauan women could step into the top ranks of company management with aplomb. Aside from the formal women's networks that all but one of the women belonged to, an informal system ensured that women could be called together on the strength of the convoker's social status. The purpose of the meeting was unimportant, my informant explained, since attendance depended on the social and political credibility of the other participants. "We women have our messengers," she said, adding: 10

If I send the word that there will be a meeting, the women will say, "Oh, who will be there?" And if the right women are there, everyone will make sure to come. But if you [as a non-Palauan] call a meeting and you have no introduction, it doesn't matter what you have to offer. The women won't make it.

Finally, as one woman pointed out, there is the sense of power inherent in the matrilineal tradition, in knowing that, no matter what happens, you have the land you inherited from your mother's lineage: 11

The women here are so sure of themselves . . . maybe it's that we know for sure that we have land. . . . Even if I don't get land from my husband, I still have it from my mother and nothing can change that. . . . Also, some women today convince the man to build a house on their family's land, so if anything happens (to the marriage), they have the house. . . .

The women, I think, work harder than the men. But speaking for myself, I would say we have equal power. Right now, my husband cannot stop me from going to work. Sometimes he tries, I cannot picture myself staying home all the time, doing the housework. I'd rather be out working. . . . The women here have equality with the men.

The Basque people, while citizens of Spain, have a separate language and a long history of cultural independence. Sally L. Hacker, with the help of Clara Elcorobairutia, a Basque, has provided an account of women's roles (published in 1987) and opportunities in Basque industrial cooperatives. These cooperatives first sprang up in the city of Mondragon and have since expanded to other parts of the country. Unlike privately owned factories, the industrial cooperatives are collectively owned by the workers employed in them. We should note that Hacker is a sociologist rather than an anthropologist.

Women Workers in the Mondragon System of Industrial Cooperatives
SALLY L. HACKER AND CLARA ELCOROBAIRUTIA

The Mondragon system of large worker-owned and worker-managed industrial cooperatives in Euskadi, the semiautonomous Basque Country in northern Spain, has the reputation of the most successful organizational model. Economists comparing Mondragon to firms in Yugoslavia, Japan, and Great Britain generally are favorable to Mondragon. This article asks how women fare in comparison to men when working in such cooperatives and concludes that — as in private firms — women workers in cooperatives cluster at the bottom of pay and occupational hierarchies, but they are more likely to get jobs and to earn more money in cooperatives than in private firms. Lower-level workers earn more in cooperatives than in private firms, and when they are predominantly women, the economic differential between men and women is lessened. Cooperatives also offer more job security to all workers than do private firms. [1]

Three major problems obstruct the goal of workplace equality for women in cooperatives: the gendered domestic sphere for women and public sphere for men, where distribution of goods and services is based on the work one does or one's wage, rather than on need, where housework and child care are still the parents' and primarily the mother's unpaid responsibility, and where the family is the basic economic unit; the capitalist market, which reinforces occupational gender stratification; and the concentration of craft skills and professional and technical knowledge among men. [2]

Cooperatives are workplaces owned and managed in varying degrees by the workers themselves, where labor hires capital, instead of the reverse. . . . [3]

The Mondragon system comprises over 100 firms in Basque Country and Spain, and employs 19,000 worker-owners. There are about 20 percent non-Basque members, roughly their proportion in the Basque Country. The firms produce machine tools, stoves, refrigerators, electronic equipment, kitchen furniture, bicycles, and agricultural products and do high-technology research and development. The cooperatives provide supportive education, health, and social services. The system also partly supports Basque nursery schools, but with places for only 125 children over one year old. The highest paid cooperative director earns [4] no more than three times the lowest paid worker (the average Basque ratio is 15:1, in large U.S. corporations, it is over 100:1). Individual workers' private, interest-bearing accounts receive 70 percent of the profit surplus; the other 30 percent is allocated to community needs and cooperative investment. Workers receive 100 percent of their accounts upon retirement; or 80 percent if they leave earlier. Redundant workers return to school or are given jobs in other cooperatives. . . .

WOMEN IN BASQUE SOCIETY

In 1985–1986 I lived and worked in the Basque Country in the city 5 of Donostia (San Sebastian), 30 miles from Mondragon. (The Basque name for this town of 30,000 is Arrasate, but the system uses the Spanish name, Mondragon.) I chose Mondragon to study the condition of women workers in cooperatives because of the system's reputation for democratic structure and process and successful economic performance. I interviewed about 50 cooperative and private employees in management, education, research, and service work and some unemployed members of the community, and gathered data on jobs and pay from two cooperatives and from two comparable Basque private firms. As a guest and as a participant in the social activities of cooperative production workers in the city of Mondragon, I was able to observe the elements of Basque society that affect expectations and opportunities for working women.

Basque culture seemed to me solidaristic and egalitarian, holding in 6 tension elements of individualism and collectivity barely felt in the United States. Antihierarchical values pervaded every daily interaction — on buses, in offices, in bars, and on the streets. Dress or demeanor offered little evidence of class background or social status. People dressed casually, spoke up and out freely. No one sought advantage over another without hearing about it. Mental and manual work were equally valued; status came from being Basque.

Basque social life centers in groups. Children grow up in single- or 7 mixed-gender *cuadrillas,* which are play groups in residential areas where playmates come from all walks of life and do not learn to defer to those of higher status. Autonomy is highly valued; it is important that Basque children be allowed their "no." Relationships are strong, life-long, and often more significant than family.

Familiar U.S. patterns of solitariness at play or work are virtually 8 absent in Basque culture. Asked what kinds of leisure activity she liked, one woman said it was going to the mountains with friends (a favorite weekend activity), biking with friends, talking in the bars with friends. What about going to a park, I asked. "I would go with my friends who wanted to go." And what if she wanted to be alone, perhaps think, or read a book under a tree? Her answer was puzzled: "Oh, well, people would *look,* you know, give you the *look.*" Not in hostility, but from curiosity or worry over what might be wrong. Did she have to go away for her college education? "Yes! Thirty miles!" I also asked her, a management-level worker in one of the major cooperatives, about her plans for the future. In the United States, a person with her education and experience might be looking for the next rung up the ladder or a better position somewhere else. Her response: "Me? Move to Barcelona?! To Madrid?! Pah!" she spit. "With whom would I drink?"

Basques socialize in streets and bars, not homes. . . . In the bars — many with the atmosphere of a well-lit, old-fashioned American kitchen — business is transacted and news and messages are exchanged. The main purpose is social and political, not sexual or alcoholic. . . . 9

Basque social equality and solidarity, however, are set in a culture of gender-differentiated and stratified spheres. Waged work is central for men, who dominate the crafts, engineering, and heavy industry. The unwaged private sphere of hearth and home is married women's responsibility. Technological knowledge and skill form an important aspect of the definition of Basque masculinity, while skills of culture, intimacy, and child rearing are central for women. *Indarra* — inner strength — for men occurs in their public activities, with women only in childbirth and the family. *Adur,* or mystic and mysterious power, both good and evil, is associated with women. Women's power, however, translates into responsibility toward husband and family. Even in radical politics, women are expected to support their men in the revolution. 10

Although 39 percent of Basque college graduates are women, they concentrate in traditional women's fields of education and health. Single women's labor force participation equals that of men, but less than 10 percent of married women work, figures similar to Spain's. Data from one school show only 3 percent of engineering graduates are women. Although the traditional family remains strong in this Catholic country, younger women search for alternatives to economic dependence on a husband's wages. 11

The subordinate status of women is under attack by a vigorous feminist movement. The movement is, as in most colonized countries, characterized by a political dimension. The Basques seek autonomy within the Spanish state, or independence within a federation of European cultures, and this issue is important to women's organizations. . . . 12

However egalitarian the roots of Basque culture and society, and despite the vitality of feminists, men's power in the public sphere has not diminished. A democratic workplace ideology in cooperatives is offset by occupational stratification based on access to technological knowledge and skills and by a traditional gendered division of labor. 13

WOMEN WORKERS IN THE MONDRAGON SYSTEM

In principle, cooperatives offer a model of more humane and productive alternatives to bureaucratic organization. [One] analysis of 80 experiments in more than a dozen countries of East and West defines three dimensions along which one can evaluate aspects of worker participation: the *degree* of control employees enjoy over any particular decision, the *issues* over which control is exercised, and the organizational *level* at which workers have control. Minimally, all employees should have access to the same information as management, protection from reprisal for voicing criticisms, an independent board of appeals, a share in profits, and attitudes and values of cooperativeness. 14

Bernstein says the Mondragon system more than meets these re- 15 quirements. We shall see that they are not sufficient to guarantee workplace democracy for women. I shall first compare the status of women and men in two of the largest cooperatives, Ulgor and Fagorelectronica, and describe the women-only cleaning and cooking cooperative, Auzo Lagun, and then I will compare the status of women workers in similar cooperative and private firms.

Ulgor, the oldest cooperative, manufactures kitchen appliances for a 16 national and international market. One-fifth of the 2,000 workers are women, clustered toward the lowest pay and skill levels. Workers jointly assign jobs a grade, from 3 (highest) to 1 (lowest), based on skill. Of the women, 86 percent were employed in jobs graded below level 1.50, compared to 37 percent of the men. Ten percent of the men, but less than 1 percent of women held upper-level jobs, above 2.00. Only one woman has ever directed one of these larger, older manufacturing cooperatives.

Fagorelectronica manufactures electronic components for TV channel 17 selectors, automobiles, and kitchen appliances. Of 580 workers, 70 percent are women. Of these, 96 percent are employed in jobs graded below level 1.50, compared to 56 percent of the men; 20 percent of the men, but only 1 percent of women, work at jobs above level 2.00. There has been some increase in women in management, and two women have joined the nine-member Social Council since 1980.

Men at the upper levels are more likely to be married than men at 18 the lower levels. For women, the reverse is true. Care for children over one year old is provided by nurseries, community women, or in some instances, husbands on different shifts. Parental leave for childbirth preserves one's position; available to both sexes, it is taken only by women.

Auzo Lagun, the married women's cooperative, was formed in 1969, 19 contrary to Spanish law, which barred married women from working at most occupations in private firms until 1970 and in cooperatives until 1973. It has 317 women, average age 47, who provide hot meals, cleaning, and other services for cooperatives in or near Mondragon. Twenty-four craftswomen construct the heavy industrial equipment needed for this work. The director is a man, the only man in Auzo Lagun. Since home and family remain women's responsibility, women work four-hour shifts. Absenteeism nonetheless is a problem. When a child or husband is ill, the woman misses work. The women say they enjoy cooperative work more than staying at home or working for a private firm, citing the greater degree of freedom and autonomy on the job, and the sociability and feeling of community.

WOMEN WORKERS IN PRIVATE VERSUS COOPERATIVE EMPLOYMENT

No private Basque firms matched the largest cooperatives. To assess 20 opportunities for women in the cooperative and private sectors, I compared two smaller cooperatives with two Basque capitalist firms that manufactured the same products and were similar in size and location.

The cooperatives were Danona, a printing and publishing firm, and Leniz, which manufactured kitchen furniture. Danona's counterpart was Valverde; Leniz's counterpart was Vega. I collected data on work and pay hierarchies at all four firms.

Leniz and Danona shared the structure and governance procedure   21
common to all the cooperatives, large and small. The few experiments with work teams and job rotation are more likely to be found in smaller cooperatives, but Leniz and Danona were not among them. The physical layout of plants is similar for large and small cooperatives, which are less capital intensive than private firms. The ambience at both small and large cooperatives is much less formal than in private firms. In Leniz and Danona, for example, workers moved about and chatted freely. At the private printing plant, the women binders stood working quietly, only glancing up sideways as we passed by. At the private furniture plant, despite several requests, I was unable to observe women production workers.

Employment.   Compared with Basque private firms, one might expect   22
Mondragon firms to have a much smaller proportion of women workers, since most cooperative employment is devoted to heavy industry and manufacturing, traditionally men's work. Yet 28 percent of Basque cooperative workers are women, compared with 25 percent in the country as a whole. Danona and Leniz had 20 percent and 22 percent women workers, respectively; at Valverde, 25 percent of the workers were women, and at Vega, 9 percent. Thus there is somewhat better job opportunity for Basque women workers in manufacturing cooperatives than in similar private firms.

Location in the Occupational Structure.   In both the private and the   23
cooperative printing firms, the lowest-level workers were helpers or handymen and all-women crews who worked in the bindery, inserting material by hand (see Table 1). In the cooperative, these women earned more than the men helpers. The women employed in administrative services, as clerical workers or assistants, made less than men in sales and clerical jobs in both types of firms. Except for a few women in photoreproduction or composition, all pressmen, other craft workers, and management in both the cooperative and private firms were men.

In kitchen-furniture manufacture, the women worked in gender-seg-   24
regated assembly work at the lowest level, and clerical or administrative assistant positions, with, again, the private firm using women more for clerical positions than for production work. Except for two women in the private firm, skilled craft and upper-level office and managerial jobs were held by men.

Women's and Men's Pay Scales.   In the Basque cooperatives, average   25
salaries are set to match those of private firms in the area. Within each cooperative, the 3:1 pay ratio means that managers and professional people earn less than their counterparts in private industry, but lower-level workers earn more. Since women are more often found at the lower

TABLE 1. Distribution of Men and Women in Basque Cooperatives and Private Firms (in percentages)[1]

TYPE OF FIRM	COOPERATIVE		PRIVATE FIRM	
	M	F	M	F
PRINTING				
Unskilled, semiskilled	35	70	18	53
Skilled	48	10	65	10
Sales and clerical	7	20	8	37
Management	10	0	8	0
Totals	100	100	99	100
	(42)	(10)	(72)	(19)
FURNITURE MANUFACTURING				
Unskilled, semiskilled	0	79	0	14
Skilled	65	0	78	8
Clerical	0	21	10	77
Highly skilled			4	0
Management[2]	35	0	8	0
Totals	100	100	100	99
	(88)	(29)	(184)	(22)

[1] Data from personnel directors, interviews, and observation.
[2] In the data I received from the cooperatives, highly skilled and management were grouped.

levels, their earning capacity should be greater in cooperatives than in private industry. Women workers in the private printing firm who worked in clerical and unskilled production jobs were paid less than men in similar jobs. In the cooperative, women worked in the bindery and unskilled production work, which was better paid than men's similar work. In general, women receive higher wages in the Basque cooperatives than in comparable private firms, except for some clerical workers (see Table 2, p. 458).

THE STRUCTURE OF WOMEN'S OPPORTUNITIES
IN BASQUE COOPERATIVES AND PRIVATE FIRMS

In terms of type of work, the two Basque private firms provided women with more clerical jobs than did comparable cooperatives, where most women worked in unskilled or semiskilled production jobs. These job structures reflected the private firms' greater automation. There was little incentive to automate lower-level work in the cooperatives, since other work would have to be found for those displaced. In private firms, many production jobs had been automated, or the work passed on to the consumer. The private furniture manufacturer did no final assembly, for example, and employed four women who filled plastic bags with screws.

26

TABLE 2.   Wages for Selected Occupations in Basque Cooperatives and Private Firms[1]

	PRINTING		FURNITURE MANUFACTURING	
	COOPERATIVE	PRIVATE FIRM	COOPERATIVE	PRIVATE FIRM
Unskilled (binder, assembly)	$ 3.05	$1.99	$3.18	$2.51
Skilled (e.g., photo reproduction, carpentry)	3.39	2.79	3.90	3.97
(e.g., make-up, mechanicals)	3.62	2.98	4.64	4.79
Clerical/administrative assistant	3.62	2.98	3.66	4.29
Management	11.30[2]	5.98	7.32	8.73

[1] All data from personnel directors.
[2] This salary is one of the "temporary exceptions"; the manager was at 5:1 rather than 3:1 because the difficulty of recruiting a manager at the cooperative's standard wage.

27   Although cooperative workers are never laid off, some women production workers did complain about being sent home during slack time more readily than men craft workers, who sometimes were given makework. For married women, the economic effects of this downtime are not considered so serious, since the family is the basic economic unit. For women who are single, the economic implications are severe.

28   Pay scales are set by the market, and the market is not gender blind. Each cooperative has its own 3:1 pay ratio, and traditional men's industries, such as heavy manufacturing, pay better than traditional women's work, such as cooking and cleaning. In 1986, the starting income for the lowest-level job at the Caja, the cooperative bank, and at Ikerlan, the high-technology research and development cooperative, was $3.42. For the combined group of heavy industry cooperatives it was $3.34; for Leniz, the furniture manufacturing cooperative, $3.18; for Danona, the printing cooperative, $3.05, and for Auzo Lagun, the all-woman cooking and cleaning cooperative, $2.74.

29   Contracting lower-level work to nonmembers (Russell 1982) is another practice that disadvantages women. In the Mondragon system, if a cooperative is not served by Auzo Lagun, women nonmembers are hired from the private sector for janitorial services. These workers are not included in the published 3:1 pay ratio, nor do they receive cooperative benefits. Women contract laborers for the Fagor cooperative plant in Madrid visited houses, cleaning and inspecting components of kitchen appliances produced by Fagor. This work had traditionally been performed by wives of male cooperative members who obtained benefits through their husbands. When single women contract workers asked for membership and its benefits, they lost their jobs, because the cooperatives

did not find it competitive to take on new members in these temporary positions.

Feminists at the cooperatives reported that most women had no complaints about low wages or job segregation. It was therefore difficult for single women to argue that each community member, rather than family, be taken as the basic economic unit. Said one: 30

> The biggest problem is the women's attitudes. All they want to talk about is what they saw on television, kids, clothes, houses. Many of them come by bus from small villages around Mondragon and go home immediately after work.

There is little chance to discuss these issues on the job, because many women take only half-hour lunch breaks so that they can go home early to do household chores. More information on gendered inequality in income and opportunity would make no difference, I was told, because "they already know," and "they don't care."

A major contributor to gender inequality is growing reliance on professional expertise as the Basque cooperative system modernizes its technological core. Professionalism entails control over specialized knowledge and is a major obstacle to democratic participation in cooperatives whose production is based on complex technology. While the autonomy and participation of most workers is diminished, women, who have less technical and professional training than men, are especially at a disadvantage. 31

In *The Cooperative Workplace*, Rothschild and Whitt praise Mondragon for diffusing technical knowledge to worker-members through technical education. I found, however, that few women cooperative workers participated in technological research, development, or maintenance. Mostly they operate machinery as production workers, rather than as craft, technical, or scientific workers, or as managers. When I interviewed managers at Mondragon about decisions on choosing new work systems and technologies, selecting machine tools for import, or research and development priorities, I found that, in contrast to the philosophy of worker participation, all agreed that most lower-level workers did not know enough to participate meaningfully in such decisions. Most of the lower-level workers excluded from this process are women. 32

On the crucial issue of expertise, most workers with whom I spoke also agreed that it takes a university education or its equivalent to equip people for managing, and a technical education to make decisions on technology. An informal criterion for election to management has now become a university technical, economic, or engineering degree, not a likely achievement for many workers, and especially unlikely for Basque women. 33

However, women have made some gains in technical education. The Mondragon Polytecnica, a cooperative of faculty, students, staff, and supporting institutions, offers technical and engineering education at lower, middle, and university levels. Women's participation has steadily increased from 3 percent in 1978 to 14 percent in 1986, and among the higher-level students, from zero to 4 percent. Of the 105 workers at 34

Ikerlan, the high-technology research and development cooperative, 14 are women, half of whom are scientists and half clericals.

WOMEN COOPERATIVE WORKERS' VIEWS

Women officers and members of boards adhered to the belief that cooperativism is more humane and productive than either monopoly capitalism or authoritarian socialism. They recognized problems of equality for women within the system, but placed priority on the continued capability of the cooperatives to create new jobs, in a country now suffering 30 percent unemployment in private industry. Managers, did, however, perceive diminishing enthusiasm for the cooperative project among all lower-level workers. 35

Most of the 20 women production workers and technicians from several industrial sectors that I spoke with saw no difference — other than job security, an important exception — between working for a private firm or a cooperative. "No different from capitalism," according to one. "How can that be?" I asked. "The workers own the means of production." "Well, maybe, but you're not treated any differently." In a similar conversation with more politically active women, I said it must be very different from capitalism, where owners take most of the profits rather than using them for the needs of the community. "What needs?" one asked. I replied, "Well, education." "But what are we taught? Not to question the system." 36

These workers, representing about 10 percent of the total, spoke of a "professional" mentality on the part of management, which excludes most people's participation in practice. Management agreed this is a problem. Feminists and other activists did not feel excluded from, but lacked interest in, management as currently structured. As one said: 37

> If I went in and said, "Oh, cooperativism is good" and so on, I could be put up [for a higher position]. But I don't want to do that. We want the system to change. [To what?] To be more responsive, to lead to a better life. Yes, people have money and security and live very well. But they are not happy. Work is not all. But then, what is happiness? We must all think about it.

Women who would not identify themselves as activists, such as one who worked in a high-technology cooperative, chaffed under what she saw as a distant and disinterested management. I asked if she could speak out on these concerns at the general assembly meeting:

> No, I don't feel comfortable doing that. [Why?] The bosses speak a different language. They stand up there and read these things I don't understand — "economy, productivity" — and so on. [What would you like to say if you could?] I have no say.

TECHNOLOGY, PROFESSIONALISM, AND GENDER STRATIFICATION

As Mondragon struggles to remain on the cutting edge of industry and high-technology research and development in Spain, and to survive in the world market, it faces tough decisions about the microelectronic 38 revolution and automation. Some men among the professional and technical elite, not necessarily management, now argue for layoffs, less democratic structure and participation, and more hierarchy in income levels. That course would affect low-level women production workers disproportionately.

These ideas reveal elements of patriarchal ideology and interest. They **39** are, in part, imported through European and U.S. models of technical and professional education, and return with Mondragon Polytecnica graduates who study abroad. Such technical professionalism is rooted historically in patriarchal military institutions, which define technical knowledge and skill as core elements in the concept of masculinity. These institutions stabilize patriarchal relations during times of rapid social and technological change. Here I have sketched one of the ways in which patriarchal modernization, today cast in the new technical professionalism in the cooperatives, can maintain gender stratification during times of change.

Mondragon workers increasingly elect a professional, university- **40** trained elite to make important decisions about the technological core of the system, which weakens workplace democracy. For women, the gendered and hierarchical organization of technology and professions is likely to continue to exclude them from management positions and cooperative government.

CONCLUSIONS AND SUGGESTIONS

Cooperatives are intended to provide social and economic advantages **41** for their members and the surrounding community. Successful cooperatives such as Mondragon do provide jobs, security, reduced labor-management strife, and flexibility in hours and work location. All profits return to workers or to community welfare. Cooperatives face disadvantages as well, but Mondragon's innovative patterns of ownership and investment seem to have overcome the most frequent, such as a preference for higher pay over long-term investment and new hires. There are structural disadvantages, however, for cooperatives operating within a capitalist market. They must produce goods and services and use methods of production of that market, and these are particularly disadvantageous to women workers. Also, since Mondragon workers are management, they sometimes decline to join noncooperative workers in their general strikes.

Our question here, however, was not the value of cooperative, dem- **42** ocratic workplaces in general but whether or not women, absolutely and compared to men, fare better in the Mondragon cooperatives than in comparable Basque capitalist firms.

I found that women in general, and low-income and unemployed **43** women in particular, benefit from the surplus returned to the community for health, education, and welfare. Further, the upper limit on worker income means that the wage differential between women workers, clustered at the bottom, and men workers, is much narrower than in private firms whose top layer of wealthy owners and managers tend to be men. Finally, cooperatives are less likely than private firms to automate routine work, since they are responsible for the displaced worker; thus employment opportunity for women remains somewhat greater within the co-operatives than the private firms. Overall, however, this study concludes, as others have, that women's position in noncapitalist workplaces is as disadvantaged as in capitalist workplaces.

Elizabeth Croll's data from a production brigade of a people's com-   **44**
mune in China showed that 68 percent of the women compared to 40 percent of the men clustered at jobs given low-wage grades, while at the highest grades, 2 percent were women and 23 percent were men. Kotlyar and Turchaninova's data for a typical industrial city in the Soviet Union are comparable; 66 percent of unskilled workers were women and 19 percent were men; in the most skilled work, 4 percent were women, 31 percent were men. Swafford's data for the Soviet Union displays as much gender segregation and income inequality as in capitalist countries. Blumberg and Nazzari also reveal considerable segregation of women to work assigned less prestige and pay on the Israeli kibbutz and in Cuba, respectively. . . .

MODIFYING GENDER HIERARCHIES IN COOPERATIVES

The greatest distance at Mondragon exists between unemployed   **45**
mothers in the community and the men who make top-level decisions about technological development and the organization of work within the cooperatives. An intermediate group between these two might be formed by a feminist coalition, already partly in place, of unemployed women, workers at Auzo Lagun, and the small but growing number of women "technicos" and managers in the cooperatives.

That there are feminists at all these levels, and that many do work   **46**
and socialize together, should not lead us to underestimate the divisions faced by the women's movement here as elsewhere. Basque culture, however, supports diversity within groups. What, then, are the truly nongendered criteria for workplace democracy toward which such a co-alition might move?

Women and men should be encouraged at every level of work and   **47**
in the community to gain access to information on technological devel-opment and the organization of work. Then they can question the way such knowledge and skill is organized and introduce their own concerns into the decision-making process.

Feminists might meet and work independently and with Mondragon's   **48**
League for Education and Culture, which warned 10 years ago of creating a "female class of industrial drudges: if steps were not taken to improve girls' and women's participation in technical education at all levels." Fem-inist critique is nowhere systemized in the cooperatives at present, and the general assembly, which meets only once a year, with a falling rate of attendance, surely does not suffice.

The Caja could gather systematic information, suggested by those   **49**
most concerned, on women, unpaid labor in home and family, as well as on economic differentials between men and women at work. They, with

feminist boards of organizations, could begin to analyze the implications of the family as the economic foundation on which the cooperatives are based.

I have examined women in cooperatives in light of the traditional literature on industrial democracy and find reason to encourage women to experiment with cooperative structure in the context of economic and of societal transformation. Without counteractive measures, women will fall behind men in ability to participate in cooperative structures so long as the traditional family remains the basic economic unit; distribution is based on position in the work force, not need; and modernization follows patriarchal modes, wherein control of craft and technical knowledge and skill is concentrated among men and is a core element in the definition of masculinity.

The following is an excerpt from a book by Patricia Zavella about the canning industry in northern California. In other sections of the book, Zavella, an anthropologist, discusses the history of the industry, the nature and culture of cannery work, the dynamics of the Chicano family, and the impact of women's employment on the Chicano family. This excerpt deals with the effects of various affirmative action programs on working conditions in the canneries and on the attitudes of both employers and employees. The women Zavella quotes are, for the most part, in their forties and have worked seasonally in the canning industry for at least fifteen years. Zavella's book was published in 1987.

From *Women's Work and Chicano Families: Cannery Workers of the Santa Clara Valley*
PATRICIA ZAVELLA

Women had contrasting views about the Affirmative Action Program, but generally they supported the principle of equal opportunity for women. Cristina noted, "It was about time. We should be equal with men in everything." Lupe believed that "it's really good. Women are going into mechanics, forklift driver, regardless of their race. Everybody in the U.S. should have that right." Vicki agreed with the notion but had questions about whether women could handle men's work: "I'm all for it if you're capable of doing it." Vicki's job injury, incurred while she trained for a man's job, no doubt led to her caution. A woman entering a man's job created a stir. Lupe recalled the first time a woman went to work on the seamer machine: "Everybody was flabbergasted. They said, 'What's the world coming to?' 'This is terrible, a woman doing a man's job!' I was shocked." Workers referred to the program derisively as "women's lib."

There were many reasons why the changes ordered by the Affirmative Action Program would be slow in coming. Most women indicated that they were not adequately informed of the proposed changes and had to rely on rumors. As a floorlady, Luz had not had much direct experience with the program. She shrugged: "Things haven't changed that much. I don't think there's too much to it." Gloria, who worked in the lab, also saw few changes. Connie was dissatisfied with the training program because it focused on job bidding: "The affirmative-action training program is a farce." She explained her dissatisfaction:

> The first day we toured canneries. I had them come to my plant and took them all over, even in the basement where the women work and there are all the rats. The head of the training program told me, "You'll do anything to make a point." I told her, "You're right." Then they showed us slides of different jobs, which were right out of the Appendix A book [of the union contract]. [She rolled her eyes.] Next they were going to show us a videotape of how we look when we put in a bid for a job to management. I told them to forget it. I didn't give a shit how I looked when I put in a bid. What really mattered was if I was qualified, if I had the seniority for the job. I refused to participate.

By contrast, Lupe had a positive experience in her plant: "She [the personnel officer] explained it real good, with everything in Spanish and English. She told us about the different positions that would be opened, how you were hired, what wages and health benefits, everything. I was pleased; they had never done it before." Lupe hoped that she would qualify for a promotion in the near future and believed that the Affirmative Action Program was "the greatest thing that ever happened to the cannery." Luz had problems with the training program also: "They don't allow a person to learn the job unless they want that particular person."

Some women did not support the notion of women taking men's jobs. **3** Estela, for example, said: "I don't go for that. Those jobs should be for men; they have a family. I don't like to work hard anyway. I wouldn't take a man's job because they're harder. It's good for widows and divorcees, but if we have our husbands, why bother?" Lupe concurred, believing women are physically weaker: "I myself wouldn't want to work that hard. We can't handle it; our bodies can't handle it." Yet she observed women successfully performing men's jobs: "Women drive semis, work on axles." She had a look of amazement. "Some of them are pretty and are not built that big." Celia felt guilty because she had taken a man's greaser job. "Sometimes I feel bad because I've taken a man's job for the last five years. And I figure we women with hard hats, we took men's jobs." Celia also did not like to see men in women's jobs: "It's unusual for men to work on the line. But when they do, they have to wear a hair net, the women's aprons, gloves, like a woman. It makes me feel kind of funny. To me, they must feel kind of, you know. . . ." She couldn't bring herself to conclude her statement, that men in aprons are emasculated. She stammered a bit longer and then pronounced that at least she would not take a warehouse job, "because those are men's jobs."

Vicki believed that conflict among workers was precipitated by the **4** Affirmative Action Program: "Yes, there is competition because of women's lib." Celia did not like the program: "There should be something different." She hoped that "women's lib" would remain confined to the job: "Women should get paid if they work a man's job, but I don't believe in all the other stuff. I like to have my door opened and other things."

Connie, on the other hand, did not support the view that women and   5
men should be confined to certain jobs: "We have families, too, that have to live. And I don't feel like I'm hurting any man by supporting my own family."

The men also apparently believed that women should remain in wom-   6
en's jobs. This can be seen in the harassment women received when they got promoted. Women clearly had difficulties in using plant seniority as a vehicle for moving up the job ladder.

Men were sometimes temporarily assigned to women's jobs, but   7
women had to fight through a series of steps to gain men's jobs. First they had to put in bids, since a man's job almost always meant a promotion. Workers did not wear badges with their seniority numbers on them; the only way women could ascertain another worker's seniority was through gossip networks or a visit to the personnel office. Thus to bump someone took initiative and nerve. Women were discouraged not only by supervisors but through fear of the possible repercussions by their coworkers.

Once they succeeded in getting new jobs, women were often subject   8
to devastating harassment. Supervisors insured that women received inadequate training. Vicki, for example, almost burned her face with acid while working with a cleanup crew because she was not advised of the dangers: "They don't teach you; they're in a hurry, and they don't go for women up there." Women would fail their job trials or receive job-related injuries and get discouraged. Familiar with this scenario, the bold Connie anticipated her treatment when she was promoted to shipping clerk. She told her supervisor and union representative alike: "I want it to go on the record that I have been told already that I'm going to be disqualified. But the only way you are going to disqualify me is to run me over with that boxcar. I am going to make it." She described her training period:

> I learned to stack cases, which weigh up to a hundred pounds, and put up bars to the box cars, which weigh about twenty-five to thirty pounds, and you must lift them over your head. I wasn't taught to drive a forklift until I'd been there about six months. It would have made my job a lot easier, since I have to go up and down the dock, which is about two-and-a-half blocks long. But the boys there weren't allowed to teach me. They were told "definitely not; teach her to hand stack and put up bars." I used to come home so tired I'd just flop out on that bed, and I was out until the next day. I was *completely* exhausted!

Supervisors would add tasks to jobs and even assigned one woman   9
work that formerly had been split between two men's jobs. For example, four-foot-nine-inch Maricela Hernández had to climb a ten-foot ladder to check temperature gauges, a task never assigned to the prior male worker. Lisa observed about her mother's experiences: "They used to

hassle her! They turned her meter back; she knew because she wrote the numbers down before she left. It was like a ritual: Every year they'd try and take her job away; she'd call in the union." Lupe observed: "The foremen were really upset because they had to train this one girl. They felt men should have the job because of the prestige; that's mostly what it was."

Patronizing comments by supervisors were commonplace. During   10
her interview for an oiler-greaser job, one woman was told, "We don't want you using your sex appeal to get the men to do your work." Connie observed: "Most company people are male Anglos, and for some asinine reason they don't like working with women. They just don't want to give you the chance to advance."

Women's new male coworkers were also a source of irritation or   11
outright harassment. On a new job, women were alternately ignored and taunted. They were admonished for depriving a man's family of its support, accused of being "man chasers," or called "uppity" or "loud-mouthed bitches." Men made fun of women's awkwardness in a new job with comments such as "leave it to a woman to do that" or teased them with statements such as "you wanted a man's job, now do it." Connie's coworkers were explicit: "They said, 'You're going to learn the hard way. Then it's up to you to learn the easy way.' " Luz, who worked temporarily in a higher-bracket job, said, "I know I sound paranoid, but those men who are fair are moved; they were very biased as to who you are. Men assume women can't do it with no testing." Cristina was upset: "They tell us vulgar things; all of this is very bad. It's discrimination, and sometimes even your own race is the worst." Celia had what seems to be a unique experience. She found her coworkers to be "real nice, very helpful. If I needed anything they helped and didn't make me feel like I took a man's job; they made me feel at ease." The fact that her husband, a Portuguese-American, was a foreman in another department in the same plant may have contributed to the cooperation she found from male coworkers.

Even subordinates discouraged the entry of women into better-paying   12
jobs by refusing to respect their authority as supervisors. Connie supervised three crews of workers as part of her job. One of the new male workers refused to follow her directions on how to load the boxcars properly. This was during a rush period and created a lot of tension until she finally confronted him, demanding to know why he refused to work for her. According to Connie, he had responded: " 'It's just that I'm not used to a woman telling me what to do, much less yell at me. That made me mad.' " Connie observed: "I get my biggest problems from Chicano men. Any time I get a new worker out there, if he's Mexican or if he's Chicano, he's the one that gives me a hassle." I asked, "Why is that?" "Because Chicano men, Mexican men, have always dominated their women, and they don't want a woman to tell them what to do," she replied. She found it easiest to work with black men: "They have more respect for women." The fact that Chicanas were often placed in men's jobs in which they competed with Chicanos probably made these women more sensitive to slurs from them.

Furthermore, Chicanas may have responded differently to Chicano   13
men because of their prior experiences with them. Connie described her
own response to being in a man's role:

> It's just like in your home. Women are much more liberated now; we dare
> to answer back, but still a lot of times you feel guilty. There's times when
> I feel guilty, when I have to tell a man "you must do this because I'm telling
> you to do it." I revert back to when I was a child, and you didn't dare tell
> Daddy that. And you grew up, and you didn't tell your husband that either.
> It's just another male you're talking to, but it's the whole mystique of being
> a man: "You're so big, and you're so strong." Women are supposed to be
> intimidated by men.

Apparently, male intimidation carried more force when the men were
Chicano, because Chicano men conjured up images in Chicanas' minds
that were more personal.

Women's complaints did not change things. Vicki noted, "Personnel   14
could care less." Hence besides experiencing the difficulties of learning
new jobs, women often felt humiliated and frustrated. Liz said: "I'm
surprised I didn't get an ulcer. It was too much: I felt discriminated
against as a Chicana and as a woman." Lisa observed, "My mom was a
nervous wreck." Connie stated: "Every time a woman goes into a 'man's'
job, she's harassed to the point that some women say 'you can have it.' "

The frequency of such harassment is subject to debate. A U.S.   15
Department of Labor study claims that only one-quarter of the women
they interviewed received such treatment. But every one of the women
I interviewed who was working at a "man's" job had received patronizing
treatment in one form or another and knew of other women who had
also. Almost all of the women I interviewed had heard of such incidents.
The consequent "spillover" effect of such intimidation went far beyond
the individuals who faced it directly.

Women witnessed management practices that flouted the new system   16
of promotions. Job openings were not posted; a foreman would inform
friends of coming job openings so that they could apply first and so on.
Connie worried because the incumbency rule was being used again. Luz
believed that she could get promoted faster if "they ran the whole place
fair; if jobs were openly and honestly available." Most women who were
Spanish speakers believed that they needed more education and a command of English to move up. Lisa instead recalled the significance of
work-based networks: "I'd have to be related to somebody important,
to have the right friends and more contacts." Women clearly understood
the stakes involved if they tried to move out of the "women's"
departments.

*This second-to-last cultural description introduces a particular subculture within
mainstream American culture. Anthropologists James P. Spradley and Brenda
J. Mann investigated the social structure of the owners, employees, and customers
in a college bar. To compile the evidence for this book-length ethnographic study,*

Mann worked for a year as a waitress in "Brady's" — a college bar in a large midwestern city. The following is a chapter from their study, published in 1975.

From *The Cocktail Waitress*
JAMES P. SPRADLEY AND BRENDA J. MANN

Denise moves efficiently through her section, stopping at a few of her tables. "Another round here?" she asks at the first table. They nod their assent and she moves on. "Would you like to order now?" "Two more of the usual here?" She takes orders from four of the tables and heads back to the bar to give them to the bartender. The work is not difficult for her now, but when she first started at Brady's, every night on the job was confusing, frustrating, embarrassing, and exhausting. Now it is just exhausting.

Her first night was chaos. When introduced to the bartender, Mark Brady, he responded with: "Haven't I seen you somewhere before?" Flustered, she shook her head. "He's not going to be one of those kind, is he?" she thought. Then later, following previous instruction, she asked two obviously underaged girls for identification, which they didn't have. As she was asking them to leave, Mark called Denise over and told her not to card those two particular girls. Embarrassed, Denise returned to their table, explained they could stay, and took their order. A customer at the bar kept grabbing her every time she came to her station, and tried to engage her in conversation. Not knowing what to do, she just smiled and tried to look busy. She asked one customer what he wanted to drink and he said, "the usual" and she had to ask him what that was. An older man seated at the bar smiled and said, "Hello, Denise," as he put a dollar bill on her tray. Again, she didn't know what to say or do so she just smiled and walked away, wondering what she had done or was supposed to do to make her worth the dollar. Another customer at a table grabbed her by the waist each time she walked past his table and persistently questioned her: "Are you new here?" "What nights do you work?" "What are you doing after work?" And so went the rest of the evening. It wasn't until several nights later and following similar encounters that she began to sort out and make sense of all this. She began to learn who these people were, what special identities they had in the bar culture, and where each one was located in the social structure of Brady's Bar.

The bartender's initial question, albeit a rather standard come-on, had been a sincere and friendly inquiry. The two girls she carded were *friends of the Brady family* and often drank there despite their young age. The grabby and talkative customer at the bar was Jerry, a *regular customer* and harmless drinker. The dollar tip came from *Mr. Brady,* the patriarch of the business. The man with the hands and persistent questions was a *regular* from the University who had a reputation with the other waitresses as a *hustler* to be avoided. These people were more than just

customers, as Denise had initially categorized them. Nor could she per-
sonalize them and treat each one as a unique individual. They were
different *kinds* of people who came into Brady's, and all required different
kinds of services and responses from her.

SOCIAL STRUCTURE

Social structure is a universal feature of culture. It consists of an   4
organized set of social identities and the expected behavior associated
with them. Given the infinite possibilities for organizing people, anthropologists have found it crucial to discover the particular social structure
in each society they study. It is often necessary to begin by asking
informants for the social identity of specific individuals. "He is a *big man*."
"That's my *mother*." "She is my *co-wife*." "He is my *uncle*." "She is my
sister." Then one can go on to examine these categories being used to
classify people. A fundamental feature of every social structure is a set
of such categories, usually named, for dividing up the social world. In
the area of kinship, for example, some societies utilize nearly 100 categories, organizing them in systematic ways for social interaction.

When we began our research at Brady's Bar, the various categories   5
of the social structure were not easy to discern. Of course the different
activities of waitresses, bartenders, and customers suggested these three
groupings, but finer distinctions were often impossible to make without
the assistance of informants. At first we thought it would be possible to
arrange all the terms for different kinds of people into a single folk
taxonomy, much like an anthropologist might do for a set of kinship terms.
With this in mind, we began listening, for example, to the way informants
talked about customers and asked them specifically, "What are all the
different kinds of customers?" This procedure led to a long list of terms,
including the following:

girl	regular	cougar
jock	real regular	sweetie
animal	person off street	waitress
bartender	policeman	loner
greaser	party	female
businessman	zoo	drunk
redneck	bore	Johnny
bitch	pig	hands
creep	slob	couple
bastard	hustler	king and his court
obnoxo	Annie	

This list was even more confusing as we checked out the various   6
terms. For example, we asked, "Would a waitress say that a bartender
is a kind of customer?" Much to our surprise, the answer was affirmative.

Then we discovered that a *regular* could be an *obnoxo* or a *bore,* a *party* could be a *zoo,* a *cougar* was always a *jock,* but a *jock* could also be a *regular* or *person off the street.* Even though it seemed confusing, we knew it was important to the waitresses to make such fine distinctions among types of customers and that they organized all these categories in some way. As our research progressed it became clear that waitresses operated with several different sets of categories. One appeared to be the basis for the formal social structure of the bar, the others could only be understood in terms of the specific social networks of the waitresses. Let us examine each briefly.

The formal social structure included three major categories of people: *customers, employees,* and *managers.* When someone first enters the bar and the waitresses look to see who it is, they quickly identify an individual in terms of one or another category in this formal social structure. The terms used form a folk taxonomy shown in Figure 1. Waitresses use these categories to identify who people are, anticipate their behavior, and plan strategies for performing their role.   7

Although waitresses often learn names and individual identities, it is not necessary. What every girl must know is the category to which people belong. It is essential, for example, to distinguish between a real regular and a person off the street. Both are customers, but both do not receive identical services from her. For example, a waitress should not have to ask a real regular what he's drinking, she should expect some friendly bantering as she waits on him, and she won't be offended if he puts his arm around her waist. A person off the street, however, receives only minimal attention from the waitress. Denise will have to inquire what he or she wants to drink, she won't be interested in spending her time talking with him, and she will be offended if he makes physical advances. It is important that Denise recognize these differences and not confuse the two kinds of customers. Being a good waitress means she can make such important distinctions. Although a knowledge of this formal social structure is essential to waitresses, it is not sufficient for the complexities of social interaction in Brady's Bar. In order to understand the other categories for identifying people and also to see how waitresses use the social structure, we need to examine the nature of *social networks.*   8

SOCIAL NETWORK

Social network analysis shifts our attention from the social structure as a formal system to the way it is seen through the eyes of individual members, in this case, the cocktail waitresses. Each waitress is at the center of several social networks. [See Figure 2, p. 472.] Some link her to specific individuals in the bar; other networks have strands that run outside the bar to college professors, roommates, friends, and parents. In addition to the formal social structure, we discovered at least three different sets of identities that make up distinct social networks. Only through an awareness of these networks is it possible to understand the way waitresses view their social world.   9

KINDS OF PEOPLE AT BRADY'S BAR	MANAGERS		
	EMPLOYEES	Bartenders	Night bartenders
			Day bartenders
		Bouncers	
		Waitresses	Day waitresses
			Night waitresses
	CUSTOMERS	Regulars	Real regulars
			Regulars
		People off the street	Loners
			Couples
			Businessmen
			People off the Street
			Drunks
		Female customers	

FIGURE 1.   Formal Social Structure of Brady's Bar

The first is a social network determined by the behavioral attributes 10
of people. As the girls make their way between the bar and tables each
night, identities such as *customer, waitress,* and *bartender* become less
significant than ones like *bitch,* and *obnoxo* based on specific actions of
individuals. Sue returns to a table of four men as she balances a tray of
drinks. No sooner has she started placing them on the table than she
feels a hand on her leg. In the semidarkness no one knows of this
encounter but the customer and the waitress. Should she ignore it or call
attention to this violation of her personal space? She quietly steps back
and the hand disappears, yet every time she serves the table this regular
makes a similar advance. By the middle of the evening Sue is saying
repeatedly, "Watch the hands." When Sandy takes over for her break,
Sue will point out *hands,* a man who has taken on a special social identity
in the waitresses' network. The real regular, businessman, loner, person

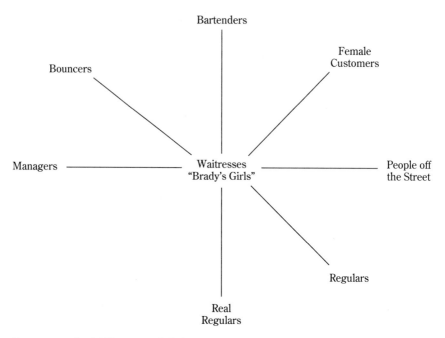

FIGURE 2.   Social Network of Waitresses

off the street, or almost any kind of male customer can fall into the same network category if his behavior warrants it. A customer who peels paper off the beer bottles and spills wax from the candle becomes a *pig*. The person who slows down the waitress by always engaging her in conversation, perhaps insisting that she sit at his table and talk, becomes a *bore*. As drinking continues during an evening, the behavior of some individuals moves so far outside the bounds of propriety that they become *obnoxos*. *Hustlers* gain their reputation by seeking to engage the waitress in some after-work rendezvous. The bartender who is impatient or rude becomes someone for the waitress to avoid, a real *bastard*. Even another waitress can be a *bitch* by her lack of consideration for the other girls. When a new waitress begins work, she doesn't know what kind of actions to expect nor how to evaluate them. Part of her socialization involves learning the categories and rules for operating within this network.

A second social network is based on social identities from outside the bar itself. Holly's roommate from college often visits the bar and one or another waitress serves her. Although she is a *customer,* they treat her as one of the other girl's *roommates* who has a special place in this social network. Each waitress will reciprocate when the close friends of other waitresses come to the bar, offering special attention to these customers. The colleges attended by customers and employees provide another basis for identifying people. "That's a table of Annie's," Joyce will say about the girls from St. Anne's College. *Cougars* are customers who also play on the University football team. Even *bartenders* and *wait-* 11 *resses* can be terms for kinds of customers when they have these identities from other bars where they work.

Finally, there is a special network of insiders that crosscuts the formal social structure. This is *the Brady Family,* made up of managers, employees, and customers — especially real regulars. The new waitress does not know about this select group of people when she first starts work. Sooner or later she will end up hanging around after work to have a drink on the house and talk. In this inner circle she will no longer think of the others as waitresses, bartenders, or customers, but now they are part of the Brady family. This network overarches all the specific categories of people in a dualistic kind of organization, a system not uncommon in non-Western societies. For example, a Nuer tribesman in Africa organizes people primarily on the basis of kinship. He has dozens of kinship terms to sort people into various identities and to anticipate their behavior. But every fellow tribesman, in a general sense, is either *both* or *mar,* distinctions that are important for social interaction. For the waitress, everyone in the bar is either in the Brady family or outside of it.

The social life of Brady's Bar derives its substance and form from the formal social structure as well as the various networks that waitresses and others activate for special purposes. Each waitress finds herself linked in some way to others in the bar with varying degrees of involvement. In order to gain a clearer picture of the social interaction that occurs within these frameworks, let us examine some of the major social relationships in the bar, examining them from the viewpoint of Brady's Girls.

THE BRADY PATRIARCHY: MANAGERS

The Brady family owns and runs the bar. Originally, three brothers owned the bar, but two died and now Mr. Brady and his brother's sons are managers. He no longer bartends and rarely comes into the bar in the evenings. He leaves all the hiring of the night employees to his two nephews, Mark and John, who manage the bar and take care of things around the place. Most of the waitresses, then, rarely meet Mr. Brady until they have been working at the bar for some time. "You hear a lot about him before you ever meet him," Sandy says. "Sharon told me all sorts of things like, 'Don't ever let Mr. Brady catch you sitting down. He fired one girl on the spot when he caught her sitting. And don't ever let him see you drinking while you're working either!'" The first time he came into the bar while Sandy was working, however, Sharon went running over to tell her to watch herself: "Mr. Brady's here." Sandy, somewhat apprehensive that evening, was careful to do everything exactly right while he was there. He sits at the bar, usually right next to the lower waitress station so he can talk to the bartenders and watch the waitresses. From that vantage point he observes the bartenders, giving them advice on how to mix drinks and handle customers, and he also checks on bar supplies. Most of this supervision is unnecessary, however, since his nephews handle those details. His presence is a symbolic affirmation of his authority as patriarch of the family and also of the bar.

"He's one of those men," says Sandy, "who seem really nice and jovial, but if you do anything the least bit wrong, he doesn't hesitate to tell you about it." All of the girls respect Mr. Brady's authority and pay special attention to any instructions or requests he makes. In addition, anything Mr. Brady asks one of the girls to do comes before looking after anyone else, be they customers or bartenders.

Sue was drinking while she worked one night when Mr. Brady came   15
in the bar so she shoved her drink behind the straws where it couldn't be seen. She kept especially busy to show him how industrious she was. She emptied clean ash trays and double checked her tables. John interrupted her display of industriousness to put a dollar in her hand: " 'My uncle wants you to have that,' " he said. "I didn't know exactly why he gave it to me. I hadn't even been introduced to him, but he knew who I was. I told John to say thank you and I smiled down to him." Sue told Sharon about it, wondering why she had been singled out for this extra tip. Sharon responded, "Mr. Brady knows the tips aren't good in here so once in a while he gives one of his girls a dollar." . . .

The personality of the Brady family permeates the bar. In fact, the   16
employees as well as many customers believe it is their individual personalities which account for the business in the bar. The saga is often told of the three brothers' long years of tending bar in other people's establishments, their efforts to make a name for themselves around town, how their successes finally made it possible for them to purchase a liquor license, and then the tragic deaths of two of the brothers, leaving Mr. Brady and his nephews. Like a "big man" in some tribe in the Highlands of New Guinea who gives feasts, has many wives, controls large herds of pigs, and attracts many loyal followers, Mr. Brady now stands at the top of the informal status hierarchy of people who frequent the bar. . . .

BARTENDERS AND BOUNCERS

Aside from the management, and especially Mr. Brady, most casual   17
observers in the bar would not suspect that the bar is a highly stratified society. The status hierarchy is played down and it seems to many that the employees at Brady's constitute one big happy family. . . .

One reason it appears that little hierarchy exists, even between   18
employees and customers, is the fluidity among roles. People change from customer to employee rapidly: an off-duty employee enters the bar as a customer, former customers become employees. In addition, both customers and employees are a homogeneous age group. Furthermore, a large proportion of them go or have gone to the same colleges. On campus, most of the men were called "jocks" or at least known as sports enthusiasts. The social atmosphere at Brady's seems designed to make everyone feel equal. Here is a world devoid of the pecking orders that exist in the rest of society; a place to get away from the competition of status striving. But waitresses are very much aware of the hidden hierarchy and they learn to act in terms of it. They see themselves near the bottom of a stratified social structure (see Figure 3), with managers and bartenders and most customers enjoying a higher status than the waitress.

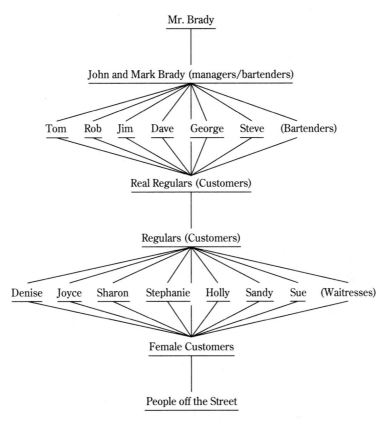

FIGURE 3.   Informal Status Hierarchy

The bartenders, who also double as bouncers, are about the same   19
age and share similar attitudes about life. To the waitress, they represent
a stronghold of masculinity and authority. There are eight bartenders,
including John and Mark: Jim, Dave, George, Steve, Rob, and Tom. All
of them are college students or recent graduates, with the exception of
Steve, whom the waitresses refer to as a "professional bartender."
Nevertheless, he easily assimilates into the group and is not normally
distinguished by the fact that he has not been to college.

Again and again, our informants emphasized the importance of bar-   20
tenders. One of the first things they learn upon starting the job was that
"bartenders are very important people." A good waitress is not so much
one who serves customers well but one who knows how to please the
bartenders. When Sandy started work a more experienced waitress told
her:

> Forget the customers, worry about the bartender. You have to keep him
> on your side. You've got to make him happy. Let the customers sit and
> wait.

This kind of advice is commonplace. Usually a new girl hears even more
specific admonitions that make her sensitive to the needs of bartenders.

"Look," says Stephanie to a girl who started one Tuesday night, "the bartender comes first. If he decides at some particular moment that he is going to stop and make a joke, you have to cater to his particular personality. That's what makes for good relationships in the bar." Because nearly everyone at Brady's accepts the myth of complete equality and informality, waitresses do not come to their job with expectations that they will have to show the proper deference to bartenders. After all, these guys seem almost like other college students. But slowly, through trial and error, and from advice given one another, all the girls learn to act in terms of the rigid hierarchy.

This learning process increases the anxiety of every girl, and these   21
feelings continue long after they have been through the rites of passage that make them one of Brady's girls. The girls often reflected with amusement on their first encounters with bartenders and the numerous mistakes they made. On one of her first nights, Joyce was assigned to work with Tom. It was busy and she tried valiantly to keep up with the rush of customers. At one table of guys she took an order for three Grain Belt beers, a Screwdriver, a Budweiser, and a vodka tonic. She gave Tom the order just as she had received it from the table, without grouping the drinks, and Tom gave her an exasperated look as he filled the order and set it on her tray. He then leaned over the bar and told Joyce: "Next time, put all the beer together and the drinks with the same kind of alcohol together, okay?" Joyce nodded and apologized. Tom said, "It's okay this time," but as Joyce walked back to the table she knew it wouldn't be the last time she would have to apologize to a bartender. . . .

The girls learn a multitude of other rules for dealing with the bar-   22
tenders: you don't yell for the bartender when you need him to mix drinks but instead wait to get his attention when he isn't busy; you cheerfully run errands for him before you wait on your own customers at tables; you don't correct the bartender when he makes a mistake with change; you don't bitch when he confuses drinks in an order; you don't demand when he forgets to hand you beer glasses; you don't show impatience when he makes you wait to give him your order; you don't scowl when he messes up your tray with foaming beer bottles. For bartenders in general, the waitresses have one fundamental principle: *don't assert yourself but let the bartender's wants determine the course of each encounter.*

But waitresses discover that each individual bartender has his own   23
special requirements. For example, when giving an order to Rob, the waitress knows she must name the beers *last* instead of first as with the others. Steve *always* leaves the "extras" such as fruit and straws for the waitresses to take care of while some of the other bartenders will occasionally help with those items. John likes waitresses to indicate the size of the bill they are handing him for a drink and to hold out both hands for change so that he can drop the bills in one hand, the coins in the other. When giving an order to Mark, the girls know they must speak quite loudly for him or he doesn't hear the order. Tom, a new bartender, needs the girls to give him their orders one or two drinks at a time since he hasn't yet developed the speed and memory of the other bartenders.

Waitresses gradually master these rules for interacting with individual bartenders, and they acquire a reputation for being a "good waitress," a label girls work diligently toward.

WAITRESSES

All of the waitresses at Brady's are friends, although some are closer to one another than are others. Denise and Sue, for example, are especially close since they have been roommates at St. Anne's for a couple of years, and both date bartenders. The four of them are often inseparable, going to college football games together, and when not working, drinking together. Sharon is held at arm's length by most of the girls because of her domineering tendencies. Because of her engagement, Stephanie is somewhat more marginal, preferring to spend her spare time with her fiancé. And Sandy has a kind of free-wheeling social attitude, finding and making friends with almost everyone in the bar. Despite these individual differences and the different degrees of friendship and participation in social life at the bar, the girls are closely united in most instances by their shared, common status as waitress. 24

Being a waitress at Brady's has brought girls together who might otherwise never have known one another. Sandy went to St. Anne's for four years and never met Stephanie, Denise, or Sue until she started at Brady's. Now they often spend Friday afternoons in other local bars, eating lunch and drinking together. Holly probably would never have met any of these girls and neither would Sharon had it not been for the job. 25

The girls share with one another their experiences in the bar with customers and bartenders, and are important sources of information when a new girl is learning the job. They pick up especially on one another's bad experiences and are thus able to help reduce the number of unknown and unprepared for, encounters. Denise had an unusually weird customer one evening who sat in her section and observed her every move. He was young and looked like a college student except for his clothing, a corduroy suit with vest and tie — too formal for Brady's. She did her best to ignore him most of the evening but right after last call, when she was standing by the bar smoking a cigarette and sipping a drink, waiting for her section to clear, he approached her and handed her a card with a dollar bill clipped to it. "You're really beautiful, you know. I've been watching you all evening. I'm a photographer and I would like to take your picture sometime. Why don't you call me?" Denise just nodded and stared at him. She was used to being propositioned around closing time, but this man's approach was rather unique and less direct than most, and she wasn't sure what he was implying with the card and the money. She showed the card with the money attached to it to Mark after the guy had left. He tore up the card and handed back the dollar with a grin. Denise told the other girls about this particular encounter and when it happened to Holly two nights later, she wasn't too surprised by the incident. Swapping stories like this after work informs waitresses about individuals in the bar and their behavior, without subjecting each girl to a totally unexpected type of encounter. 26

More experienced waitresses, especially Sharon, take upon them-   27
selves the task of relating important gossip and folklore of the bar to the
new waitress. It is Sharon, for example, who takes the initiative to explain
the Brady family and the historical events leading up to the opening of
Brady's Bar. This is because she has been working for Brady's since it
opened, longer than any of the other girls. And whenever a waitress has
a question about a customer, such as "Who is he?" "What's his name?"
"What does he do?" or any other personal information, they only have
to ask Sharon and she will share her vast knowledge of individuals or
else get the information for you.

Waitresses are especially supportive of one another when it comes   28
to dealings with the bartenders, and usually unite against direct "attack"
concerning their collective ability or intelligence. One night after closing,
around 2 A.M., all the bartenders and waitresses sat around the bar
drinking and having a few friendly arguments. Holly brought up the subject
of empty beer bottles — a subject that the girls had been discussing off
and on for the past week. "I *know*," said Holly emphatically, "that all the
beer bottles don't weigh the same when empty!"

"That's right," agreed Sandy.   29

"You broads are crazy," answers Tom. "No matter what label those   30
bottles have on them, all those bottles weigh the *same*." This remark
was met with a chorus of protests as the girls began to disagree. Mark
held up his hands and said, "Quiet. Quiet! We'll just see." He took two
empty bottles from a cardboard case, closed his eyes and weighed one
in each hand. "Nope. You're wrong. They weigh the same. Anyway, how
would you broads know?"

"But we lift more than you do, checking to see if they're empty or   31
full," replies Holly. "And, they don't all weigh the same because we can't
tell without looking if they are empty or not!" The argument continued
with all the bartenders united against the waitresses, each sticking to
their original claims. The issue was never settled, but each group remained united against the other: bartenders versus waitresses.

Not only do the girls stick together in such arguments, but they   32
provide mutual assistance when working. Because of the girls' pride in
the ability to handle the job, however, it is an unwritten rule that one
waitress never enters another's section without being asked to do so.
For example, Sharon looks down to the lower section and can immediately
see that Joyce is swamped with customers, messy tables, and is behind
in her job because of a sudden rush of people into her section. She knows
that Joyce will not ask for help, but it is Sharon's obligation to inquire
whether she would like extra help for a few minutes. When she asks,
Joyce may accept the offer but will probably say, "No." It is an important
rule of etiquette among the girls that such an offer is extended.

The importance of this rule can be seen in the fact that if one of the   33
waitresses is angry with another girl, one of the best ways to retaliate
or to express this anger is by invading the other waitress's territory,
thus insulting the girl whose territory is being invaded. It is as if the
offending waitress is saying: "You aren't a good waitress. You can't handle
your section." Sharon was working the lower section one night, and she

was mad because Denise had a particularly attractive group of males in her section while Sharon was stuck with groups of female customers. This was a reversal of the normal arrangement. In fact, Sharon had chosen to work the lower section to have primarily male customers for the night. To express her anger, she came up into Denise's section and cleaned off a couple of tables. This was a particularly direct insult to Denise because the upper section is much smaller and less work and while girls who work the upper section often offer to assist those in the lower, it is rarely the other way around.

While waitresses often stick together as a group, the strongest bonds 34 within the bar link men together, and these associations contrast with the bonding of females. Like a number of brothers the bartenders form a cohesive, loyal group of men. Together with the most regular customers they present a united front to the world, provide each other with mutual support and recognition, and they enjoy a sense of unity and closeness. We could discover hardly any cultural processes that divided this inner group of men. They did compete for the attention of women, but almost never did such competition occur at the expense of another male. While these men did consider all the girls in the bar as fair game for all the men, once any male indicated more serious intentions toward a waitress or female customer, competition quickly ended. The other men immediately redefined this particular female as "John's girl" or "Tom's girl," and the rule of loyalty to the male group resulted in looking out for Tom's or John's interests.

In contrast, the girls in the bar *depend* on male approval for their 35 sense of well-being. Because of the status hierarchy the waitresses need the approval and praise of bartenders and regular customers, but the reverse is not true. This feature of bar social structure has important consequences for female bonds — often weakening them and creating divisions among the waitresses. For example, the girls compete for the attention, affection, and recognition of bartenders by doing good work. But when one of the girls receives recognition of bartenders it is often at the expense of another. Holly was working the lower section one night, running from table to table because it was very busy. Joyce, however, who was stuck in the smaller, upper section had little work to do. The waitresses' code of ethics prevented her from stepping into Holly's section and helping her out, especially because Holly had already turned down one offer for assistance. But Mark looked out over the bar and what he saw were two waitresses: one "working her ass off," and the other "just standing around." So he told Joyce loudly, "Look at that, Holly's running her ass off taking care of customers and you're just standing there. Get to work." It would have been useless for Joyce to try to explain to Mark why she was just standing there, but she had lost favor in Mark's eyes while Holly had gained a compliment and recognition from Mark for her "industriousness." These kinds of incidents are usually remembered for only a night, but they occur often enough to remind the girls that male recognition is important, even if it means turning waitress loyalty away from each other.

Beyond the work relationship, waitresses seek attention from par- 36 ticular males but in doing so they are restricted to more passive strategies than are the men. A bartender or regular customer can purchase a drink for a girl, approach her table and ask direct questions, or in other ways actively "hustle" a member of the opposite sex. Waitresses generally employ a more passive strategy spoken of as "having your eye on someone."

It often happens, however, that a particular customer takes a fancy **37** to another waitress, other than the one who has her eye on him, and this also sets off a complex reaction of gossip, hurt feelings, and misunderstandings — all of which divide waitresses, weakening the bonds of this female group. . . .

The girls' relationships with one another is characterized by a thin **38** veneer of solidarity. Underneath runs a potentially strong current of hostility, competitiveness, and divisiveness. The solidarity functions in a few instances to maximize the girls' power against the males; but it is weakened or useless in most situations when the girls resort to individual strategies.

REAL REGULARS

No customer enters the social life at Brady's Bar as a *real regular*. **39** It is a position that develops over time, usually through friendship with the bartenders, occasionally as the regular boyfriend of a waitress. Whatever the link, only men have access to this high status position. Real regulars arrive early and stay late; they seldom miss more than one or two nights each week. Seated around the horseshoe end of the bar, they will swap stories, tell jokes, laugh with the bartender, and inquire about other real regulars who are absent. They all know the waitresses by name and in many respects act toward them like the bartenders do. Of all the customers, real regulars are the most important to waitresses.

Larry, Bobby, Skeeter, and Ron are charter members of the group. **40** All went to high school and college with Mark Brady, and the bar is the meeting place where they continue their long association with one another. On a typical evening they will rendezvous at Brady's around seven to drink and plan for the night's activities: barhopping, playing games, or eating a late dinner. They will hang around and drink, leave the bar on one or another venture, but always make it back to Brady's by last call. "It's practically an obsession with them," says Holly. She dated Dave and each time they went out, he either had to make certain that he had her home early enough to make it back to Brady's before last call or else he returned to the bar with her. Holly recalled that she usually went home because "Dave felt I would get in the way of his visiting with his buddies." . . .

Real regulars are probably the first individuals, other than employees, **41** that the girls learn to know by name. The process of getting acquainted with these customers is quite easy for the girls because real regulars take upon themselves the task of approaching each new Brady girl. The waitresses enjoy exchanging stories among themselves about the routine they each encountered when meeting one or another of the real regulars.

Holly started work at Brady's on a Saturday and by the end of her **42** first night on the job every real regular had introduced himself; by the end of her second week of work every real regular had tried to hustle her. Later Holly recalled those first weeks of work: "I didn't know what was going on. I would walk up to the bar and this guy would say 'Hi, Holly. How do you like working here?' I couldn't figure out how he knew my name or that I had just started working there and it really had me shook. Later, the other girls told me it's standard procedure for most guys, and especially guys like Skeeter, Ron, and Larry who are real regulars, to just ask Mark or whoever's tending bar, what the new girl's name is. It's a good thing I didn't know then how they all evaluate and talk about new waitresses or I would have been very embarrassed. I couldn't have handled it then at all. I would guess that they even had bets on me, as to who could take me out first. They're all so eager to find out what kind of girl you are, you know. At first I was really flattered. I mean, when you get asked out three or four times in one night by some pretty good looking guys, that is a compliment. That's what I thought then, but now I wouldn't think so. Now I know all about these guys and their little games and you couldn't get me to go out with any of them. Most of the other girls won't go either. They never really give up though. Each time Bobby asks me out for breakfast, for example, after work, I have to make sure he understands it's only for breakfast."

New girls rapidly learn how to deal with the twelve or fifteen real **43** regulars, and though they seldom accept dates, they are still considered special customers and every waitress gives them special service. If a waitress has free time during an evening she will often spend it with these customers, talking and joking. With the employees, real regulars share many "in" jokes about one another and never tire of endlessly repeating them, each time with some new twists.

When Sue saw Skeeter sitting at the bar one night she started to **44** banter with him. "Why, hello, Skeeter, I didn't see *you* come in!"

"You were probably working so hard you didn't see me. How are **45** you tonight, anyway?"

"I'm *cold.* Markie won't turn up the heat because *he's hot!*" **46**

"Hey, Mark!" Skeeter calls down the bar, eager to pick up on Sue's **47** comment. "Get over here and warm this girl up, we've got a frigid dame on our hands."

But Sue quickly intervenes, "That's okay, I'm warm now." **48**

"C'mon, Mark, get over here and take care of her," Skeeter says, **49** loud enough for other customers at the bar to hear. Before Sue turns to walk to her section she retorts, "Look, Skeeter, don't you know that two cold people don't make any heat?" In addition to the humor both enjoy in these encounters, they provide an opportunity for real regulars to tell other customers of their preferred position as members of the inner circle of the bar. . . .

REGULARS

The relative prestige of customers can be measured by their famil- **50** iarity with bartenders and waitresses. It is a symbol of status to walk in to the bar on some crowded night and have the bartender recognize you, call out your name, and refer obliquely to some past experiences shared by the inner circle. Regulars, while not members of the innermost clique, find personal recognition at Brady's. They drink there frequently and often speak to waitresses and bartenders by name, and, in turn, are addressed personally, if not by name at least by what they drink. "He's scotch and water," or "Here's whiskey sour," a waitress will say. But while regulars have strong ties to Brady's Bar as a *place,* they do not have close ties to the "Brady Family." Rather than strong affective bonds to waitresses or bartenders, their links to these people are based on a friendly, commercial relationship. Regulars include policemen, members of the Cougar football team, many Johnnies, and a few Hampton jocks, and the Shell station crowd (two mechanics and their girlfriends). Waitresses learn to identify these various individuals through frequent interaction, from information gleaned from the other girls, and sometimes by listening to the bartenders. Although the girls are generally careful to be courteous to all the regulars, they are almost in unanimous agreement as to who[m] they like and dislike.

By their actions regulars often announce to the audience of other customers how "well known" they are in the bar. Two regulars known to Sandy as "whiskey sour" and "bourbon sour" come in about every other night, and usually take a seat in the lower section. "When I see them," says Sandy, "I just cringe and want to run and hide." Instead, Sandy runs over immediately to take their order, trying to prevent them from starting their routine. If she is unable to get to their table right away, they will yell across the bar: "Nurse. Oh, nurse. We need some medicine over here." They refer to themselves as "Sandy's patients" and order loudly by saying, "Bring us our usual medicine." Sandy finds it embarrassing to serve them, but their approach is like a public announcement to their status in the bar hierarchy.   51

Waitresses gain familiarity with the drinking habits of regulars, and this leads to making games out of ordering and serving. When a regular comes in with some of his friends who are strangers to Brady's, these games can be an important demonstration to them of his status and ability with women. Sue sees a Cougar regular come into the bar one night with three friends she knows are strangers to Brady's.   52

She walks up to their table but they are engaged in intense conversation. She puts her hand on the regular's shoulders in order to get his attention. He immediately turns and looks at her as if to say, "Don't you touch me!" Sue knows he is kidding but she quickly removes her hand: "I'm sorry!" She asks if he would like to order anything now, but he says "No." In a few minutes she walks by him again and this time *he* reaches out and grabs her by the waist. "Hey, now, watch the hands," scolds Sue. Even though her tone of voice indicates she is kidding, he profusely apologizes and then says, "I guess I will have a beer now." She takes the other orders and when she returns the game continues: "That was fast!" says the Cougar regular while his friends look on.   53

"That's because I'm a fast girl."   54

"Oh, you mean with beer?"   55

"What did you think I meant?" laughs Sue as she leaves the table to wait on her other customers.   56

When a waitress waits on a table of regulars, it is seldom the case   57
that her interaction with them is "strictly business." Such encounters
often include verbal games, brief inquiries into the well-being of the
customer, and the rehashing of private jokes or shared confidences. For
example, if Stephanie were to walk up to a table where Jeff and Fred
were sitting, they might tell her how much they missed their favorite
lucky charm when they were chugging the other night when she wasn't
working. Or, she might inquire as to who the most frequent loser has
been recently in these contests. In any case, the waitress seldom escapes
without some brief and friendly conversation. . . .

FEMALE CUSTOMERS

The constant friction between waitresses and female customers   58
makes this the most antagonistic relationship in the bar. Most of the girls
had first come to Brady's as female customers and so the unexpected
difficulties in this relationship surprised them. After a few months at
work, Stephanie admitted, "When I first started out I tried to treat
everyone equally, give good service to everyone, but now I find myself
being nicer to the guys because I know it won't get me anywhere with
the girls." Female customers become the topic of conversation almost
every evening. Sue runs into Stephanie in the kitchen for a brief moment
and says, "I wish those bitches in my section would leave." Stephanie's
response is no less harsh, "Did you see that blonde girl at the corner
table in my section? She is such a bitch! I can't believe it." When we
asked Joyce how she felt toward female customers, her words came
quickly, "I'm getting so I hate every one of them. Hate is a little strong,
let's say they make me angry. No matter how good your service is to
them, they are never pleased or grateful. Nothing you do seems acceptable. They're so obnoxious when they start drinking. They get drunk,
or *appear* to, very quickly and they become giggly, loud, and silly. They
hang all over the guys and brandish their cigarettes in my face. The sillier
they get, the worse they treat me."

The waitresses clearly feel that their own dislike for female customers   59
is a response to treatment received. Unlike men, they feel women who
come to Brady's behave in ways that make their work more difficult.
Holly approaches a table of men and without hesitation they order a round
of Hamm's. One guy pays for the round and tells her to keep the change;
it doesn't amount to much money but it is a relief not to search for
change while balancing her tray. Throughout the evening they will order
the same thing, each time in rounds for the entire table. A few minutes
later a table in her section fills up with four girls. She approaches their
table and the first girl says, "What kind of beer do you have?" "Bud.
Grain Belt. Heineken. Schlitz. Pabst. Hamm's. Special Export. Michelob.
Schmidt." No response. Holly waits for their order and finally says,
"Would you like a beer?" "I don't know," the female customer says slowly,
and then, "I guess, umm, I'll have a Harvey Wallbanger. No. Wait, I'll
have a Tom Collins." By the time the other girls have gone through
similar hesitations and questions, Holly has not only wasted time but will
have difficulty remembering what they all ordered.

It has now been five minutes since she served these girls and the   60
one who ordered the Tom Collins calls her over to the table again. "This
tastes orangey." Holly looks at her drink and asks, "You ordered a Tom
Collins, didn't you?" "Yes, but it tastes orangey." Before she leaves the
table Holly picks up the drink and holds it to the light to examine it and
says, "Are you sure you didn't get your friend's Harvey instead?" The
evening wears on and Holly makes her way in a continuous circle, cleaning
ash trays, taking orders, and checking on tables. She brings a second
round of beers to one table, and a third round of bar booze to another
before stopping to ask the girls if they would like another drink. "Yes,
I'll have a banana daiquiri," one of the girls says. Holly looks to the others
who are sitting in silence before empty glasses and asks, "Does anyone
else want anything?" No one does so she goes to the bar and returns,
after the usual complaints of the bartender at fixing this fancy drink, with
the banana daiquiri. Before she can leave, one of the other female customers says, "Oh, I decided I want another blackberry brandy and seven."
No one else wants anything, so back at the bar she places a single order,
returns to her table of girls and then cleans off an empty table nearby.
By this time the third girl wants to try a scotch and soda, the last one
still has no order. But sure enough, when she returns, the last female
customer asks for a frozen daiquiri and when Holly gets to her station
to place the order she is muttering about the "dumb bitches" in her
section.

The waitresses can hardly discuss female customers without referring   61
to them at least once as "bitches." Inside the bar, this term does not
carry the strong connotations it would in other social settings. A girl at
a cocktail party who used the term "bitch" to describe a female she knows
would probably be considered quite coarse and crude. But in the bar,
the term is used freely by waitresses, bartenders, and male customers
to refer to any woman who is considered a nuisance, including waitresses.
It becomes almost a synonym for woman.

Furthermore, waitresses accuse females of an assortment of bad   62
manners and obnoxious behavior. Girls don't tip. Girls complain about
every little thing. Girls order exotic drinks like banana daiquiris, Gold
Cadillacs, and Pink Ladies, upsetting the bartenders who don't like to
make them. Girls pay separately, handing the waitress five, ten, and
twenty dollar bills for drinks that seldom cost more than $1.25. Girls
hold out their hands for even a nickel of change for their dollar drink.
Girls repeatedly pester the waitress to clean their tables. Girls don't
know how to order or what to order. Girls change their orders. The list
goes on and on and can be heard any night when waitresses can talk to
each other or to the bartenders. . . .

Antagonism between waitresses and female customers is also in-   63
creased due to the mobility of waitresses and their knowledge of the
men in the bar. Sandy is working the upper section. Seated at one table
is Dick, a familiar regular and his girlfriend, whom Sandy has never seen
before. When she stops at the table to take the order, Dick puts his arm
around her waist. His date's response is immediate: "Don't you touch
her!" Dick quickly removes his arm and Sandy turns to Dick to ask what

they would like to drink. Most waitresses usually wait for the male to give both orders, and so Sandy uses this strategy to act as if she doesn't see the other woman at the table. Sandy smiles and leaves for the bar with the order, secure in the knowledge that Dick will probably leave her a substantial tip out of embarrassment for the scene his date has created. . . .

Strategies for dealing with girls include automatically cashing in dollar bills in order to have change ready for a table of female customers; not checking female tables as often to avoid extra requests for service; double checking when taking an order to make sure they don't want to order anything else. The waitresses are aware that many problems created by female customers are due to ignorance; most women do not know the rules for behaving in a bar. They lack even a basic understanding of bar etiquette: buying drinks in rounds, knowing how to tip the waitress. But knowledge of these facts does not make the waitresses more understanding. They must still operate in a male-dominated institution and play by the set of rules and rewards available to them in this setting. And since female customers have nothing to offer the waitress, and because they endlessly hassle her, the waitresses continue to see most of them as "real bitches." 64

PEOPLE OFF THE STREET

Within weeks after they start work, most waitresses become experts at identifying customers. When they see girls enter the bar, whether newcomers or oldtimers, they immediately become *female customers,* perhaps to become *bitches* before the evening ends. Familiar male faces become regulars, real regulars, or employees. But almost every night at Brady's newcomers walk in and take their places along the bar or at a table. Some of these people off the street come with regulars or female customers who frequent Brady's; they may be guys from St. John's, the University, Hampton College, or one of the other schools in the area. Other newcomers find their way to the bar as friends of the waitresses or bartenders. While they are still "people off the street," the girls eagerly seek information to link them with some member of the inner circle. Sue is working the lower section on a Friday night and three guys she has never seen before take the last table against the wall. Her first task is to find some social network tie to them. She looks at Sandy in the upper section who has also noticed them arrive, but the questioning look tells her that Sandy doesn't know them either. Sue takes their order and when she gets the bartender's attention asks him, "Have you seen those guys before? The ones over by the wall?" "No," he says. "They've never been in here before." When Sue takes the order back to their table, everything is formal and polite, no joking or friendly banter as with regulars. Later in the evening Sue is talking to Andy, a regular from St. John's who is sitting next to her station; she asks him about the three guys. "Oh, they're jocks from school. I think one of them plays basketball." Two nights later, a regular comes in with a date, a guy who plays basketball at St. John's, and so Sue describes the three guys she 65 had seen earlier in the week and finds out they are close friends of this regular customer. If she sees them again she will probably surprise them by saying, "You're friends of Fred Morris, aren't you? How's the Johnnies' basketball team this fall?" The search to identify people off the street is not always successful; customers come and go, some never to be seen again, others to enter the small society of Brady's at the bottom of the hierarchy as people off the street. Eventually, they may even work their way up to become real regulars and finally be adopted into the Brady Family inner circle. . . .

The personal networks of each waitress at Brady's is constructed   66
out of different kinds of people — managers, bartenders, waitresses, real regulars, regulars, female customers, and people off the street. When a new girl begins work she has no concept of the many different kinds of people with whom she will interact. She may hope to treat them all as individuals, but like people in every culture, she soon begins to act on the basis of categories of people with certain characteristics. Like a social map, these cultural categories enable the girls to sort people into groups, anticipate their behavior, and plan for dealing with them. If you work as a waitress at Brady's Bar, it is necessary to know your way up and down the hierarchy. A sense of security and satisfaction on the job comes, in part, from knowing your place in this pecking order.

We close this chapter with a section from Studs Terkel's Working *(1974), an exceptionally popular collection of first-person accounts of "people talk[ing] about what they do all day and how they feel about what they do." Terkel is not an anthropologist — he is a journalist — but his accounts are engaging and revealing, and those he interviews give the reader a strong sense of the attractions and limitations of particular occupations. Read Barbara Herrick's story, then, for the firsthand information it provides about one woman's successful journey through a high-status, traditionally male-dominated occupational culture.*

Barbara Herrick
STUDS TERKEL

She is thirty; single. Her title is script supervisor/producer at a large   1
advertising agency; working out of its Los Angeles office. She is also a vice president. Her accounts are primarily in food and cosmetics. "There's a myth: a woman is expected to be a food writer because she is assumed to know those things and a man doesn't. However, some of the best copy on razors and Volkswagens has been written by women."

She has won several awards and considerable recognition for her com-   2
mercials. "You have to be absolutely on target, dramatic and fast. You have to be aware of legal restrictions. The FTC gets tougher and tougher. You must understand budgetary matters: will it cost a million or can it be shot in a studio in one day?"

She came off a Kansas farm, one of four daughters. "During high   3
school, I worked as a typist and was an extremely good one. I was compulsive
about doing every tiny job very well." She graduated from the University
of Missouri. According to Department of Labor statistics, she is in the upper
one percent bracket of working women.

In her Beverly Hills apartment are paintings, sculpted works, recordings   4
(classic, folk, jazz, and rock), and many books, most of them obviously
well thumbed.

Men in my office doing similar work were being promoted, given   5
raises and titles. Since I had done the bulk of the work, I made a stand
and was promoted too. I needed the title, because clients figured that
I'm just a face-man.

A face-man is a person who looks good, speaks well, and presents   6
the work. I look well, I speak well, and I'm pleasant to have around after
the business is over with — if they acknowledge me in business. We go
to the lounge and have drinks. I can drink with the men but remain a
lady. (Laughs.)

That's sort of my tacit business responsibility, although this has never   7
been said to me directly. I know this is why I travel alone for the company
a great deal. They don't anticipate any problems with my behavior. I
equate it with being the good nigger.

On first meeting, I'm frequently taken for the secretary, you know,   8
traveling with the boss. I'm here to keep somebody happy. Then I'm
introduced as the writer. One said to me after the meeting was over and
the drinking had started, "When I first saw you, I figured you were a
— you know. I never knew you were the person *writing* this all the
time." (Laughs.) Is it a married woman working for extra money? Is it
a lesbian? Is it some higher-up's mistress?

I'm probably one of the ten highest paid people in the agency. It   9
would cause tremendous hard feelings if, say, I work with a man who's
paid less. If a remark is made at a bar — "You make so much money,
you could buy and sell me" — I toss it off, right? He's trying to find out.
He can't equate me as a rival. They wonder where to put me, they
wonder what my salary is.

Buy and sell me — yeah, there are a lot of phrases that show the   10
reversal of roles. What comes to mind is swearing at a meeting. New
clients are often very uptight. They feel they can't make any innuendoes
that might be suggestive. They don't know how to treat me. They don't
know whether to acknowledge me as a woman or as another neuter
person who's doing a job for them.

The first time, they don't look at me. At the first three meetings of   11
this one client, if I would ask a direction question, they would answer
and look at my boss or another man in the room. Even around the
conference table. I don't attempt to be — the glasses, the bun, and
totally asexual. That isn't the way I am. It's obvious that I'm a woman
and enjoy being a woman. I'm not overly provocative either. It's the thin,
good nigger line that I have to toe.

I've developed a sixth sense about this. If a client will say, "Are you   12 married?" I will often say yes, because that's the easiest way to deal with him if he needs that category for me. If it's more acceptable to him to have a young, attractive married woman in a business position comparable to his, terrific. It doesn't bother me. It makes me safer. He'll never be challenged. He can say, "She'd be sensational. I'd love to get her. I could show her what a real man is, but she's married." It's a way out for him.

Or there's the mistress thing: well, she's sleeping with the boss. 13 That's acceptable to them. Or she's a frustrated, compulsive castrator. That's a category. Or lesbian. If I had short hair, wore suits, and talked in a gruff voice, that would be more acceptable than I am. It's when I transcend their labels, they don't quite know what to do. If someone wants a quick label and says, "I'll bet you're a big women's libber, aren't you?" I say, "Yeah, yeah." They have to place me.

I travel a lot. That's what gets very funny. We had a meeting in 14 Montreal. It was one of those bride's magazines, honeymoon-type resorts, with heart-shaped beds and the heated pool. I was there for three days with nine men. All day long we were enclosed in this conference room. The agency account man went with me. I was to talk about the new products, using slides and movies. There were about sixty men in the conference room. I had to leave in such a hurry, I still had my gaucho pants and boots on.

The presentation went on for an hour and a half. There was tittering 15 and giggling for about forty minutes. Then you'd hear the shift in the audience. They got interested in what I was saying. Afterwards they had lunch sent up. Some of them never did talk to me. Others were interested in my life. They would say things like, "Have you read *The Sensuous Woman*?" (Laughs.) They didn't really want to know. If they were even more obvious, they probably would have said, "Say, did you hear the one about the farmer's daughter?" I'd have replied, "Of course, I'm one myself."

The night before, there was a rehearsal. Afterwards the account 16 man suggested we go back to the hotel, have a nightcap, and get to bed early. It was a 9:00 A.M. meeting. We were sitting at the bar and he said, "Of course, you'll be staying in my room." I said, "What? I have a room." He said, "I just assumed. You're here and I'm here and we're both grown up." I said, "You assumed? You never even asked me whether I wanted to." My feelings obviously meant nothing to him. Apparently it was what you *did* if you're out of town and the woman is anything but a harelip and you're ready to go. His assumption was incredible.

We used to joke about him in the office. We'd call him Mr. Straight, 17 because he was Mr. Straight. Very short hair, never grew sideburns, never wore wide ties, never, never swore, never would pick up an innuendo, super-super-conservative. No one would know, you see?

Mr. Straight is a man who'd never invite me to have a drink after 18 work. He would never invite me to lunch alone. Would never, never make an overture to me. It was simply the fact that we were out of town and who would know? That poor son of a bitch had no notion what he was doing to my ego. I didn't want to destroy his. We had to work together the next day and continue to work together.

The excuse I gave is one I use many times. "Once when I was much   19
younger and innocent, I slept with an account man. The guy turned out
to be a bastard. I got a big reputation and he made my life miserable
because he had a loose mouth. And even though you're a terrifically nice
guy and I'd like to sleep with you, I feel I can't. It's my policy. I'm older
and wiser now. I don't do it. You have to understand that." It worked.
I could never say to him, "You don't even understand how you insulted
me."

It's the always-having-to-please conditioning. I don't want to make   20
any enemies. Only of late, because I'm getting more secure and I'm
valued by the agency, am I able to get mad at men and say, "Fuck off!"
But still I have to keep egos unruffled, smooth things over . . . I still
work with him and he never mentioned it again.

He'll occasionally touch my arm or catch my eye: We're really sym-   21
patico, aren't we baby? There may be twelve men and me sitting at a
meeting and they can't call on one of the girls or the receptionist, he'd
say, "Let's have some coffee, Barbara. Make mine black." I'm the waitress. I go do it because it's easier than to protest. If he'd known my
salary is more than his I doubt that he'd have acted that way in Denver
— or here.

Part of the resentment toward me and my salary is that I don't have   22
a mortgage on a home in the Valley and three kids who have to go to
private schools and a wife who spends at Saks, and you never know
when you're going to lose your job in this business. Say, we're having
a convivial drink among peers and we start grousing. I'm not allowed to
grouse with the best of them. They say, "Oh, you? What do you need
money for? You're a single woman. You've got the world by the balls."
I hear that all the time. . . .

"I've had a secretary for the last three years. I hesitate to use her . . .   23
I won't ask her to do typing. It's hard for me to use her as I was used.
She's bright and could be much more than a secretary. So I give her research
assignments, things to look up, which might be fun for her. Rather than
just say, 'Here, type this.'

"I'm an interesting figure to her. She says, 'When I think of Women's   24
Lib I don't think of Germaine Greer or Kate Millett. I think of you.' She
sees my life as a lot more glamorous than it really is. She admires the
externals. She admires the apartment, the traveling. We shot two commer-
cials just recently, one in Mexico, one in Nassau. Then I was in New
York to edit them. That's three weeks. She takes care of all my travel details.
She knows the company gave me an advance of well over a thousand dollars.
I'm put up in fine hotels, travel first class. I can spend ninety dollars at
a dinner for two or three. I suppose it is something — little Barbara from
a Kansas farm, and Christ! look where I am. But I don't think of it,
which is a funny thing."

It used to be the token black at a big agency was very safe because   25
he always had to be there. Now I'm definitely the token woman. In the
current economic climate, I'm one of the few writers at my salary level
getting job offers. Unemployment is high right now among people who

do what I do. Yet I get calls: "Will you come and write on feminine hygiene products?" Another, involving a food account: "We need you, we'll pay you thirty grand and a contract. Be the answer for Such-an-such Foods." I'm ideal because I'm young enough to have four or five solid years of experience behind me. I know how to handle myself or I wouldn't be where I am.

I'm very secure right now. But when someone says to me, "You don't have to worry," he's wrong. In a profession where I absolutely cannot age, I cannot be doing this at thirty-eight. For the next years, until I get too old, my future's secure in a very insecure business. It's like a race horse or a show horse. Although I'm holding the job on talent and responsibility, I got here partly because I'm attractive and it's a big kick for a client to know that for three days in Montreal there's going to be this young brunette, who's very good, mind you. I don't know how they talk about me, but I'd guess: "She's very good, but to look at her you'd never know it. She's a knockout." 26

I have a fear of hanging on past my usefulness. I've seen desperate women out of jobs, who come around with their samples, which is the way all of us get jobs. A lot of women have been cut. Women who had soft jobs in an agency for years and are making maybe fifteen thousand. In the current slump, this person is cut and some bright young kid from a college, who'll work for seven grand a year, comes in and works late every night. 27

Talk about gaps. In a room with a twenty-two-year-old, there are areas in which I'm altogether lost. But not being a status-quo-type person, I've always thought ahead enough to keep pace with what's new. I certainly don't feel my usefulness as a writer is coming to an end. I'm talking strictly in terms of physical aging. (Laughs.) It's such a young business, not just the consumer part. It's young in terms of appearances. The client expects agency people, especially on the creative end, to dress a certain way, to be very fashionable. I haven't seen many women in any executive capacity age gracefully. . . . 28

The part I hate — it's funny. (Pause.) Most people in the business are delighted to present their work and get praise for it — and the credit and the laughter and everything in the commercial. I always hate that part. Deep down, I feel demeaned. Don't question the adjectives, don't argue, if it's a cologne or a shampoo. I know, 'cause I buy 'em myself. I'm the biggest sucker for buying an expensively packaged hoax thing. Face cream at eight dollars. And I sell and convince. . . . 29

Do I ever question what I'm selling? (A soft laugh.) All the time. I know a writer who quit a job equivalent to mine. She was making a lot of money, well thought of. She was working on a consumer finance account. It's blue collar and black. She made this big stand. I said to her, in private, "I agree with you, but why is this your test case? You've been selling a cosmetic for years that is nothing but mineral oil and women are paying eight dollars for it. You've been selling a cake mix that you know is so full of preservatives that it would kill every rat in the lab. Why all of a sudden . . . ?" 30

If you're in the business, you're in the business, the fucking business! You're a hustler. But because you're witty and glib . . . I've never pre- 31 tended this is the best writing I can do. Every advertising writer has a novel in his drawer. Few of them ever do it.

I don't think what I do is necessary or that it performs a service. If 32
it's a very fine product — and I've worked on some of those — I love it. It's when you get into that awful area of hope, cosmetics — you're just selling image and a hope. It's like the arthritis cure or cancer — quackery. You're saying to a lady, "Because this oil comes from the algae at the bottom of the sea, you're going to have a timeless face." It's a crock of shit! I know it's part of my job, I do it. If I made the big stand my friend made, I'd lose my job. Can't do it. I'm expected to write whatever assignment I'm given. It's whorish. I haven't written enough to know what kind of writer I am. I suspect, rather than a writer, I'm a good reader. I think I'd make a good editor. I have read so many short stories that I bet you I could turn out a better anthology than anybody's done yet, in certain categories. I remember, I appreciate, I have a feeling I could . . .

POSTSCRIPT: *Shortly afterward she was battling an ulcer.* 33

_____ *Questions for Argument* _____

1. Does women's power ever equal men's? Develop your argument based on the cultures described in this section and any others with which you are familiar. Note that much of your essay will depend on how you define power and whether you choose to treat that definition as something problematic.
2. Are all cultures fundamentally alike, as Sherwood L. Washburn and C. S. Lancaster suggested in "The Evolution of Hunting," or are there crucial differences? Develop an argument that supports your point of view.
3. Anthropological evidence, critics sometimes say, is not really scientific. What do you think they mean by that? Evaluate the use of evidence by some of the writers in this chapter. After deciding which evidence you find most compelling, explain your reasons by developing an argument that supports your opinion.
4. Anthropologist Nancy Rogers has seen three motives operating behind the work of her colleagues who write about the roles of women:

   > While some anthropologists explicitly state that their work is motivated by a desire to mobilize direct action to change the contemporary power structure, others are more modestly attracted to the problem of rethinking the roles of women in society. Still others are simply interested in understanding the female experience in various societies, and in opening up a formerly neglected area of study. ("Woman's Place: A Critical Review of Anthropological Theory," *Comparative Studies in Society and History* 20 [1978])

Based on what you have read so far or on any supplementary reading you choose to do, try to use Rogers's framework for distinguishing among the women anthropologists represented in this chapter. In other words, develop the argument that some anthropologists are more politically motivated than others.

5. What distinguishes "women's work" from "men's work"? Argue on the basis of cross-cultural evidence.

6. Develop the argument that women's status relative to men depends on their economic power.

7. Support or argue against the idea that modern industrial societies have widened the differences between men and women.

8. Unlike the other writers in this chapter, Sally L. Hacker is identified as a sociologist. Reread her article "Women Workers in the Mondragon System of Industrial Cooperatives" and describe the difference you see between her sociological perspective and one or more of the anthropological perspectives in this chapter. Are the similarities between Hacker's perspective and the others more important than the differences? Develop an argument about which you consider more illuminating: Hacker's particular sociological perspective, or that of the anthropologist(s) of your choice.

9. How is James P. Spradley and Brenda J. Mann's piece different from the other readings? Compare it with several others, and argue whether you find it more or less effective for what it tells about cultural relationships.

10. Which of the introductory overviews (pp. 409–414) has the most to tell us about Brady's Bar? Argue for the applicability of the perspective you choose by analyzing the bar culture described by Spradley and Mann.

11. Think of a subculture that you personally know well enough to describe in structural detail. Argue whether or not that structure subjugates women.

12. When people are subjugated, they often develop alternative ways — sometimes covert, often shrewd — to maintain some measure of control over their lives. Develop the argument that there are many forms of women's power and that these are influenced by cultural circumstances. You might also want to consider the advantages and disadvantages of these forms of power. In addition to the cases presented in this chapter, you can also include cases you're familiar with — ones you've read about or know first-hand.

13. *Research Project.* Psychologist Helen Astin has developed a theoretical model to help explain women's occupational behavior. For her full presentation of that model, see her article "The Meaning of Work in Women's Lives: A Sociopsychological Model of Career Choice and Work Behavior" (*The Counseling Psychologist* 12:4 [1984]). Astin argues that all people's motives for working are the same (we work for survival, for pleasure, and for a sense of contribution) but that men and women do not have similar working outcomes because of their socialization as children, be-

cause of their expectations about possible options they'll have in the world of work, and because of the structure of actual opportunities available to them.

From an early age children in our society are socialized along gender lines through the games they play, the chores they do, and the first jobs they hold. They form different images of the choices open to them and of how they can satisfy their needs for survival, pleasure, and social contribution. And the world of work conforms in large part to their expectations of it. Astin claims that the socialization process and the opportunity structure are interactive: "The socialization process probably sets limits to changes in the structure of opportunity, whereas the structure of opportunity ultimately influences the values that are transmitted through the socialization process."

Astin sees in our recent cultural history several trends that may be influencing this relationship between expectations and opportunities. Specifically, she lists increased longevity, declining birth rates, increased divorce rates, changes in lifestyles, medical advances, the "codification of women's rights," and changes in the national economy. Such developments help to explain recent changes in the working lives of women.

Using Astin's model as a framework and using her list of trends as suggestions, develop a series of interview questions. Then conduct a set of interviews. Devise a scheme that will allow you to draw some conclusions. For example, you might interview six of your classmates and their mothers: What were the work expectations and experiences of the mothers? What are the expectations of the sons or daughters? Be creative in thinking about how to conduct interviews that will support meaningful conclusions. Think, as well, about how to best classify your data and what perspectives and opinions presented in this chapter (other than Astin's) might help you make sense of your data. Develop an argument based on the results of your survey.

CHAPTER 9

Nathaniel Hawthorne's "Young Goodman Brown": Historical Imagining

Framing the Issues

Developing an argument about a work of literature usually means offering an interpretation of that work — a set of observations held together by some strong central perception or point of view. In offering such an argument, think of yourself as a guide: Your job is to take others through the work in a way that enlightens their reading of it. The primary support for your argument will usually come from the text of the work itself — as you write analytically, you will selectively use summary and direct quotations to help you make your points. The first section of this chapter presents the text of a classic American short story, Nathaniel Hawthorne's "Young Goodman Brown," published in 1835. The preliminary questions following the story invite you to begin trying out some interpretive arguments.

In developing an interesting argument about "Young Goodman Brown," you will probably not want to rely on the story alone. It's a story that provokes curiosity about Hawthorne's life and times and about the historical setting Hawthorne chose. Like Hawthorne's well-known novel *The Scarlet Letter* (1850), the short story is set in Salem, Massachusetts, Hawthorne's birthplace and the site of the notorious witch trials conducted by Puritan authorities in the 1690s. Why did the Puritans so interest Hawthorne? What did he gain by setting his story in colonial Salem — at a time so distant from his own? Do the circumstances of his own life help you to understand his fictional choices? As you learn more about Hawthorne's life and thought, including his imaginative grasp of Salem's history, you may develop and sharpen your sense of what you want to argue about "Young Goodman Brown."

Our emphasis in this chapter on biographical and historical influences on the writer coincides with a recent trend in literary analysis called "the new historicism." New historicists react against "new criticism," the style of textual analysis that has dominated literary studies since World War II. New criticism typically trains readers to pay little attention to factors outside of the literary work itself but to concentrate exclusively on how its formal characteristics (imagery, tone, diction, structure) reveal its meaning. In contrast, the new historicists view literary works not as self-contained artifacts but as "social acts." They believe that one must analyze literature within its full historical context, or much of its meaning will be lost. A work of literature, as new historicist Jerome J. McGann puts it, "does not hold a mirror up to an immobilized 'Human Nature'; it reflects — and reflects upon — human nature in its social and historical reality."

In "Complicating the Issues," excerpts from several Hawthorne biographies are followed by a bit of autobiography, part of the preface Hawthorne wrote for *The Scarlet Letter*. The next selection describes what is known about the composing and publishing of "Young Goodman Brown" and will acquaint you with Hawthorne's own reading and possible literary influences. Then we offer a sequence of readings about Salem history: first a modern account of Puritan culture and of the Salem witch trials and then two accounts of those events that Hawthorne himself must have read. Finally, before suggesting some argument topics, we offer a short anthology of critical commentaries, published from 1879 to 1985.

Young Goodman Brown
NATHANIEL HAWTHORNE

Young Goodman Brown came forth at sunset into the street at Salem village; but put his head back, after crossing the threshold, to exchange a parting kiss with his young wife. And Faith, as the wife was aptly named, thrust her own pretty head into the street, letting the wind play with the pink ribbons of her cap while she called to Goodman Brown.

"Dearest heart," whispered she, softly and rather sadly, when her lips were close to his ear, "prithee put off your journey until sunrise and sleep in your own bed to-night. A lone woman is troubled with such dreams and such thoughts that she's afeared of herself sometimes. Pray tarry with me this night, dear husband, of all nights in the year."

"My love and my Faith," replied young Goodman Brown, "of all nights in the year, this one night must I tarry away from thee. My journey, as thou callest it, forth and back again, must needs be done 'twixt now and sunrise. What, my sweet, pretty wife, dost thou doubt me already, and we but three months married?"

"Then God bless you!" said Faith, with the pink ribbons; "and may   4
you find all well when you come back."

"Amen!" cried Goodman Brown. "Say thy prayers, dear Faith, and go to bed at dusk, and no harm will come to thee."

So they parted; and the young man pursued his way until, being about to turn the corner by the meeting-house, he looked back and saw the head of Faith still peeping after him with a melancholy air, in spite of her pink ribbons.

"Poor little Faith!" thought he, for his heart smote him. "What a wretch am I to leave her on such an errand! She talks of dreams, too. Methought as she spoke there was trouble in her face, as if a dream had warned her what work is to be done to-night. But no, no; 't would kill her to think it. Well, she's a blessed angel on earth; and after this one night I'll cling to her skirts and follow her to heaven."

With this excellent resolve for the future, Goodman Brown felt himself   8
justified in making more haste on his present evil purpose. He had taken a dreary road, darkened by all the gloomiest trees of the forest, which barely stood aside to let the narrow path creep through, and closed immediately behind. It was all as lonely as could be; and there is this peculiarity in such a solitude, that the traveller knows not who may be concealed by the innumerable trunks and the thick boughs overhead; so that with lonely footsteps he may yet be passing through an unseen multitude.

"There may be a devilish Indian behind every tree," said Goodman Brown to himself; and he glanced fearfully behind him as he added, "What if the devil himself should be at my very elbow!"

His head being turned back, he passed a crook of the road, and, looking forward again, beheld the figure of a man, in grave and decent attire, seated at the foot of an old tree. He arose at Goodman Brown's approach and walked onward side by side with him.

"You are late, Goodman Brown," said he. "The clock of the Old South was striking as I came through Boston, and that is full fifteen minutes agone."

"Faith kept me back a while," replied the young man, with a tremor   12
in his voice, caused by the sudden appearance of his companion, though not wholly unexpected.

It was now deep dusk in the forest, and deepest in that part of it where these two were journeying. As nearly as could be discerned, the second traveller was about fifty years old, apparently in the same rank of life as Goodman Brown, and bearing a considerable resemblance to him, though perhaps more in expression than features. Still they might have been taken for father and son. And yet, though the elder person was as simply clad as the younger, and as simple in manner too, he had an indescribable air of one who knew the world, and who would not have felt abashed at the governor's dinner table or in King William's court, were it possible that his affairs should call him thither. But the only thing about him that could be fixed upon as remarkable was his staff, which bore the likeness of a great black snake, so curiously wrought that it might almost be seen to twist and wriggle itself like a living serpent. This, of course, must have been an ocular deception, assisted by the uncertain light.

"Come, Goodman Brown," cried his fellow-traveller, "this is a dull pace for the beginning of a journey. Take my staff, if you are so soon weary."

"Friend," said the other, exchanging his slow pace for a full stop, "having kept covenant by meeting thee here, it is my purpose now to return whence I came. I have scruples touching the matter thou wot'st of."

"Sayest thou so?" replied he of the serpent, smiling apart. "Let us walk on, nevertheless, reasoning as we go; and if I convince thee not thou shalt turn back. We are but a little way in the forest yet."   16

"Too far! too far!" exclaimed the goodman, unconsciously resuming his walk. "My father never went into the woods on such an errand, nor his father before him. We have been a race of honest men and good Christians since the days of the martyrs; and shall I be the first of the name of Brown that ever took this path and kept" —

"Such company, thou wouldst say," observed the elder person, interpreting his pause. "Well said, Goodman Brown! I have been as well acquainted with your family as with ever a one among the Puritans; and that's no trifle to say. I helped your grandfather, the constable, when he lashed the Quaker woman so smartly through the streets of Salem; and it was I that brought your father a pitch-pine knot, kindled at my own hearth, to set fire to an Indian village, in King Philip's war. They were my good friends, both; and many a pleasant walk have we had along this path, and returned merrily after midnight. I would fain be friends with you for their sake."

"If it be as thou sayest," replied Goodman Brown, "I marvel they never spoke of these matters; or, verily, I marvel not, seeing that the least rumor of the sort would have driven them from New England. We are a people of prayer, and good works to boot, and abide no such wickedness."

"Wickedness or not," said the traveller with the twisted staff, "I   20 have a very general acquaintance here in New England. The deacons of many a church have drunk the communion wine with me; the selectmen of divers towns make me their chairman; and a majority of the Great and General Court are firm supporters of my interest. The governor and I, too — But these are state secrets."

"Can this be so?" cried Goodman Brown, with a stare of amazement at his undisturbed companion. "Howbeit, I have nothing to do with the governor and council; they have their own ways, and are no rule for a simple husbandman like me. But, were I to go on with thee, how should I meet the eye of that good old man, our minister, at Salem village? Oh, his voice would make me tremble both Sabbath day and lecture day."

Thus far the elder traveller had listened with due gravity; but now burst into a fit of irrepressible mirth, shaking himself so violently that his snake-like staff actually seemed to wriggle in sympathy.

"Ha! ha! ha!" shouted he again and again; then composing himself, "Well, go on, Goodman Brown, go on; but, prithee, don't kill me with laughing."

"Well, then, to end the matter at once," said Goodman Brown, 24 considerably nettled, "there is my wife, Faith. It would break her dear little heart; and I'd rather break my own."

"Nay, if that be the case," answered the other, "e'en go thy ways, Goodman Brown. I would not for twenty old women like the one hobbling before us that Faith should come to any harm."

As he spoke he pointed his staff at a female figure on the path, in whom Goodman Brown recognized a very pious and exemplary dame, who had taught him his catechism in youth, and was still his moral and spiritual adviser, jointly with the minister and Deacon Gookin.

"A marvel, truly that Goody Cloyse should be so far in the wilderness at nightfall," said he. "But with your leave, friend, I shall take a cut through the woods until we have left this Christian woman behind. Being a stranger to you, she might ask whom I was consorting with and whither I was going."

"Be it so," said his fellow-traveller. "Betake you to the woods, and 28 let me keep the path."

Accordingly the young man turned aside, but took care to watch his companion, who advanced softly along the road until he had come within a staff's length of the old dame. She, meanwhile, was making the best of her way, with singular speed for so aged a woman, and mumbling some indistinct words — a prayer, doubtless — as she went. The traveller put forth his staff and touched her withered neck with what seemed the serpent's tail.

"The devil!" screamed the pious old lady.

"Then Goody Cloyse knows her old friend?" observed the traveller, confronting her and leaning on his writhing stick.

"Ah, forsooth, and is it your worship indeed?" cried the good dame. 32 "Yea, truly is it, and in the very image of my old gossip, Goodman Brown, the grandfather of the silly fellow that now is. But — would your worship believe it? — my broomstick hath strangely disappeared, stolen, as I suspect, by that unhanged witch, Goody Cory, and that, too, when I was all anointed with the juice of smallage, and cinquefoil, and wolf's bane" —

"Mingled with fine wheat and the fat of a new-born babe," said the shape of old Goodman Brown.

"Ah, your worship knows the recipe," cried the old lady, cackling aloud. "So, as I was saying, being all ready for the meeting, and no horse to ride on, I made up my mind to foot it; for they tell me there is a nice young man to be taken into communion to-night. But now your good worship will lend me your arm, and we shall be there in a twinkling."

"That can hardly be," answered her friend. "I may not spare you my arm, Goody Cloyse; but here is my staff, if you will."

So saying, he threw it down at her feet, where, perhaps, it assumed   36
life, being one of the rods which its owner had formerly lent to the
Egyptian magi. Of this fact, however, Goodman Brown could not take
cognizance. He had cast up his eyes in astonishment, and, looking down
again, beheld neither Goody Cloyse nor the serpentine staff, but his
fellow-traveller alone, who waited for him as calmly as if nothing had
happened.

"That old woman taught me my catechism," said the young man;
and there was a world of meaning in this simple comment.

They continued to walk onward, while the elder traveller exhorted
his companion to make good speed and persevere in the path, discoursing
so aptly that his arguments seemed rather to spring up in the bosom of
his auditor than to be suggested by himself. As they went, he plucked
a branch of maple to serve for a walking stick, and began to strip it of
the twigs and little boughs, which were wet with evening dew. The
moment his fingers touched them they became strangely withered and
dried up as with a week's sunshine. Thus the pair proceeded, at a good
free pace, until suddenly, in a gloomy hollow of the road, Goodman Brown
sat himself down on the stump of a tree and refused to go any farther.

"Friend," he said, stubbornly, "my mind is made up. Not another
step will I budge on this errand. What if a wretched old woman do choose
to go to the devil when I thought she was going to heaven: is that any
reason why I should quit my dear Faith and go after her?"

"You will think better of this by and by," said his acquaintance,   40
composedly. "Sit here and rest yourself a while; and when you feel like
moving again, there is my staff to help you along."

Without more words, he threw his companion the maple stick, and
was as speedily out of sight as if he had vanished into the deepening
gloom. The young man sat a few moments by the roadside, applauding
himself greatly, and thinking with how clear a conscience he should meet
the minister in his morning walk, nor shrink from the eye of good old
Deacon Gookin. And what calm sleep would be his that very night, which
was to have been spent so wickedly, but so purely and sweetly now, in
the arms of Faith! Amidst these pleasant and praiseworthy meditations,
Goodman Brown heard the tramp of horses along the road, and deemed
it advisable to conceal himself within the verge of the forest, conscious
of the guilty purpose that had brought him thither, though now so happily
turned from it.

On came the hoof tramps and the voices of the riders, two grave
old voices, conversing soberly as they drew near. These mingled sounds
appeared to pass along the road, within a few yards of the young man's
hiding-place; but, owing doubtless to the depth of the gloom at that
particular spot, neither the travellers nor their steeds were visible.
Though their figures brushed the small boughs by the wayside, it could
not be seen that they intercepted, even for a moment, the faint gleam
from the strip of bright sky athwart which they must have passed. Goodman Brown alternately crouched and stood on tiptoe, pulling aside the
branches and thrusting forth his head as far as he durst without discerning
so much as a shadow. It vexed him the more, because he could have

sworn, were such a thing possible, that he recognized the voices of the minister and Deacon Gookin, jogging along quietly, as they were wont to do, when bound to some ordination or ecclesiastical council. While yet within hearing, one of the riders stopped to pluck a switch.

"Of the two, reverend sir," said the voice like the deacon's, "I had rather miss an ordination dinner than to-night's meeting. They tell me that some of our community are to be here from Falmouth and beyond, and others from Connecticut and Rhode Island, besides several of the Indian powwows, who, after their fashion, know almost as much deviltry as the best of us. Moreover, there is a goodly young woman to be taken into communion."

"Mighty well, Deacon Gookin!" replied the solemn old tones of the minister. "Spur up, or we shall be late. Nothing can be done, you know, until I get on the ground." **44**

The hoofs clattered again; and the voices, talking so strangely in the empty air, passed on through the forest, where no church had ever been gathered or solitary Christian prayed. Whither, then, could these holy men be journeying so deep into the heathen wilderness? Young Goodman Brown caught hold of a tree for support, being ready to sink down on the ground, faint and overburdened with the heavy sickness of his heart. He looked up to the sky, doubting whether there really was a heaven above him. Yet there was the blue arch, and the stars brightening in it.

"With heaven above and Faith below, I will yet stand firm against the devil!" cried Goodman Brown.

While he still gazed upward into the deep arch of the firmament and had lifted his hands to pray, a cloud, though no wind was stirring, hurried across the zenith and hid the brightening stars. The blue sky was still visible, except directly overhead, where this black mass of cloud was sweeping swiftly northward. Aloft in the air, as if from the depths of the cloud, came a confused and doubtful sound of voices. Once the listener fancied that he could distinguish the accents of towns-people of his own, men and women, both pious and ungodly, many of whom he had met at the communion table, and had seen others rioting at the tavern. The next moment, so indistinct were the sounds, he doubted whether he had heard aught but the murmur of the old forest, whispering without a wind. Then came a stronger swell of those familiar tones, heard daily in the sunshine at Salem village, but never until now from a cloud of night. There was one voice, of a young woman, uttering lamentations, yet with an uncertain sorrow, and entreating for some favor, which, perhaps, it would grieve her to obtain; and all the unseen multitude, both saints and sinners, seemed to encourage her onward.

"Faith!" shouted Goodman Brown, in a voice of agony and desperation; and the echoes of the forest mocked him, crying, "Faith! Faith!" as if bewildered wretches were seeking her all through the wilderness. **48**

The cry of grief, rage, and terror was yet piercing the night, when the unhappy husband held his breath for a response. There was a scream, drowned immediately in a louder murmur of voices, fading into far-off laughter, as the dark cloud swept away, leaving the clear and silent sky above Goodman Brown. But something fluttered lightly down through the air and caught on the branch of a tree. The young man seized it, and beheld a pink ribbon.

"My Faith is gone!" cried he after one stupefied moment. "There is no good on earth; and sin is but a name. Come, devil; for to thee is this world given."

And, maddened with despair, so that he laughed loud and long, did Goodman Brown grasp his staff and set forth again, at such a rate that he seemed to fly along the forest path rather than to walk or run. The road grew wilder and drearier and more faintly traced, and vanished at length, leaving him in the heart of the dark wilderness, still rushing onward with the instinct that guides mortal man to evil. The whole forest was peopled with frightful sounds — the creaking of the trees, the howling of wild beasts, and the yell of Indians; while sometimes the wind tolled like a distant church bell, and sometimes gave a broad roar around the traveller, as if all Nature were laughing him to scorn. But he was himself the chief horror of the scene, and shrank not from its other horrors.

"Ha! ha! ha!" roared Goodman Brown when the wind laughed at him. 52 "Let us hear which will laugh loudest. Think not to frighten me with your deviltry. Come witch, come wizard, come Indian powwow, come devil himself, and here comes Goodman Brown. You may as well fear him as he fear you."

In truth, all through the haunted forest there could be nothing more frightful than the figure of Goodman Brown. On he flew among the black pines, brandishing his staff with frenzied gestures, now giving vent to an inspiration of horrid blasphemy, and now shouting forth such laughter as set all the echoes of the forest laughing like demons around him. The fiend in his own shape is less hideous than when he rages in the breast of man. Thus sped the demoniac on his course, until, quivering among the trees, he saw a red light before him, as when the felled trunks and branches of a clearing have been set on fire, and throw up their lurid blaze against the sky, at the hour of midnight. He paused, in a lull of the tempest that had driven him onward, and heard the swell of what seemed a hymn, rolling solemnly from a distance with the weight of many voices. He knew the tune; it was a familiar one in the choir of the village meeting-house. The verse died heavily away, and was lengthened by a chorus, not of human voices, but of all the sounds of the benighted wilderness pealing in awful harmony together. Goodman Brown cried out, and his cry was lost to his own ear by its unison with the cry of the desert.

In the interval of silence he stole forward until the light glared full upon his eyes. At one extremity of an open space, hemmed in by the dark wall of the forest, arose a rock, bearing some rude, natural resemblance either to an altar or a pulpit, and surrounded by four blazing pines, their tops aflame, their stems untouched, like candles at an evening meeting. The mass of foliage that had overgrown the summit of the rock was all on fire, blazing high into the night and fitfully illuminating the whole field. Each pendent twig and leafy festoon was in a blaze. As the red light arose and fell, a numerous congregation alternately shone forth, then disappeared in shadow, and again grew, as it were, out of the darkness, peopling the heart of the solitary woods at once.

"A grave and dark-clad company," quoth Goodman Brown.

In truth they were such. Among them, quivering to and fro between   56
gloom and splendor, appeared faces that would be seen next day at the
council board of the province, and others which, Sabbath after Sabbath,
looked devoutly heavenward, and benignantly over the crowded pews,
from the holiest pulpits in the land. Some affirm that the lady of the
governor was there. At least there were high dames well known to her,
and wives of honored husbands, and widows, a great multitude, and
ancient maidens, all of excellent repute, and fair young girls, who trembled
lest their mothers should espy them. Either the sudden gleams of light
flashing over the obscure field bedazzled Goodman Brown, or he recognized a score of the church members of Salem village famous for their
especial sanctity. Good old Deacon Gookin had arrived, and waited at
the skirts of that venerable saint, his revered pastor. But, irreverently
consorting with these grave, reputable, and pious people, these elders
of the church, these chaste dames and dewy virgins, there were men of
dissolute lives and women of spotted fame, wretches given over to all
mean and filthy vice, and suspected even of horrid crimes. It was strange
to see that the good shrank not from the wicked, nor were the sinners
abashed by the saints. Scattered also among their pale-faced enemies
were the Indian priests, or powwows, who had often scared their native
forest with more hideous incantations than any known to English
witchcraft.

"But where is Faith?" thought Goodman Brown; and, as hope came
into his heart, he trembled.

Another verse of the hymn arose, a slow and mournful strain, such
as the pious love, but joined to words which expressed all that our nature
can conceive of sin, and darkly hinted at far more. Unfathomable to mere
mortals is the lore of fiends. Verse after verse was sung; and still the
chorus of the desert swelled between like the deepest tone of a mighty
organ; and with the final peal of that dreadful anthem there came a sound,
as if the roaring wind, the rushing streams, the howling beasts, and every
other voice of the unconcerted wilderness were mingling and according
with the voice of guilty man in homage to the prince of all. The four
blazing pines threw up a loftier flame, and obscurely discovered shapes
and visages of horror on the smoke wreaths above the impious assembly.
At the same moment the fire on the rock shot redly forth and formed a
glowing arch above its base, where now appeared a figure. With reverence
be it spoken, the figure bore no slight similitude, both in garb and manner,
to some grave divine of the New England churches.

"Bring forth the converts!" cried a voice that echoed through the
field and rolled into the forest.

At the word, Goodman Brown stepped forth from the shadow of the   60
trees and approached the congregation, with whom he felt a loathful
brotherhood by the sympathy of all that was wicked in his heart. He
could have well-nigh sworn that the shape of his own dead father beckoned
him to advance, looking downward from a smoke wreath, while a woman,
with dim features of despair, threw out her hand to warn him back. Was
it his mother? But he had no power to retreat one step, nor to resist,

even in thought, when the minister and good old Deacon Gookin seized his arms and led him to the blazing rock. Thither came also the slender form of a veiled female, led between Goody Cloyse, that pious teacher of the catechism, and Martha Carrier, who had received the devil's promise to be queen of hell. A rampant hag was she. And there stood the proselytes beneath the canopy of fire.

"Welcome, my children," said the dark figure, "to the communion of your race. Ye have found thus young your nature and your destiny. My children, look behind you!"

They turned; and flashing forth, as it were, in a sheet of flame, the fiend worshippers were seen; the smile of welcome gleamed darkly on every visage.

"There," resumed the sable form, "are all whom ye have reverenced from youth. Ye deemed them holier than yourselves and shrank from your own sin, contrasting it with their lives of righteousness and prayerful aspirations heavenward. Yet here are they all in my worshipping assembly. This night it shall be granted you to know their secret deeds: how hoary-bearded elders of the church have whispered wanton words to the young maids of their households; how many a woman, eager for widows' weeds, has given her husband a drink at bedtime and let him sleep his last sleep in her bosom; how beardless youths have made haste to inherit their fathers' wealth; and how fair damsels — blush not, sweet ones — have dug little graves in the garden, and bidden me, the sole guest, to an infant's funeral. By the sympathy of your human hearts for sin ye shall scent out all the places — whether in church, bedchamber, street, field, or forest — where crime has been committed, and shall exult to behold the whole earth one stain of guilt, one mighty blood spot. Far more than this. It shall be yours to penetrate, in every bosom, the deep mystery of sin, the fountain of all wicked arts, and which inexhaustibly supplies more evil impulses than human power — than my power at its utmost — can make manifest in deeds. And now, my children, look upon each other."

They did so; and, by the blaze of the hell-kindled torches, the wretched man beheld his Faith, and the wife her husband, trembling before that unhallowed altar.

"Lo, there ye stand, my children," said the figure, in a deep and solemn tone, almost sad with its despairing awfulness, as if his once angelic nature could yet mourn for our miserable race. "Depending upon one another's hearts, ye had still hoped that virtue were not all a dream. Now are ye undeceived. Evil is the nature of mankind. Evil must be your only happiness. Welcome again, my children, to the communion of your race."

"Welcome," repeated the fiend worshippers, in one cry of despair and triumph.

And there they stood, the only pair, as it seemed, who were yet hesitating on the verge of wickedness in this dark world. A basin was hollowed, naturally, in the rock. Did it contain water, reddened by the lurid light? or was it blood? or, perchance, a liquid flame? Herein did the shape of evil dip his hand and prepare to lay the mark of baptism upon their foreheads, that they might be partakers of the mystery of sin, more conscious of the secret guilt of others, both in deed and thought, than they could now be of their own. The husband cast one look at his pale wife, and Faith at him. What polluted wretches would the next glance show them to each other, shuddering alike at what they disclosed and what they saw!

"Faith! Faith!" cried the husband, "look up to heaven, and resist the wicked one."   **68**

Whether Faith obeyed he knew not. Hardly had he spoken when he found himself amid calm night and solitude, listening to a roar of the wind which died heavily away through the forest. He staggered against the rock, and felt it chill and damp; while a hanging twig, that had been all on fire, besprinkled his cheek with the coldest dew.

The next morning young Goodman Brown came slowly into the street of Salem village, staring around him like a bewildered man. The good old minister was taking a walk along the graveyard to get an appetite for breakfast and meditate his sermon, and bestowed a blessing, as he passed, on Goodman Brown. He shrank from the venerable saint as if to avoid an anathema. Old Deacon Gookin was at domestic worship, and the holy words of his prayer were heard through the open window. "What God doth the wizard pray to?" quoth Goodman Brown. Goody Cloyse, that excellent old Christian, stood in the early sunshine at her own lattice, catechizing a little girl who had brought her a pint of morning's milk. Goodman Brown snatched away the child as from the grasp of the fiend himself. Turning the corner by the meeting-house, he spied the head of Faith, with the pink ribbons, gazing anxiously forth, and bursting into such joy at sight of him that she skipped along the street and almost kissed her husband before the whole village. But Goodman Brown looked sternly and sadly into her face, and passed on without a greeting.

Had Goodman Brown fallen asleep in the forest and only dreamed a wild dream of a witch-meeting?

Be it so if you will; but, alas! it was a dream of evil omen for young   **72** Goodman Brown. A stern, a sad, a darkly meditative, a distrustful, if not a desperate man did he become from the night of that fearful dream. On the Sabbath day, when the congregation were singing a holy psalm, he could not listen because an anthem of sin rushed loudly upon his ear and drowned all the blessed strain. When the minister spoke from the pulpit with power and fervid eloquence, and, with his hand on the open Bible, of the sacred truths of our religion, and of saint-like lives and triumphant deaths, and of future bliss of misery unutterable, then did Goodman Brown turn pale, dreading lest the roof should thunder down upon the gray blasphemer and his hearers. Often, awaking suddenly at midnight, he shrank from the bosom of Faith; and at morning or eventide, when the family knelt down at prayer, he scowled and muttered to himself, and gazed sternly at his wife, and turned away. And when he had lived long, and was borne to his grave a hoary corpse, followed by Faith, an aged woman, and children and grandchildren, a goodly procession, besides neighbors not a few, they carved no hopeful verse upon his tombstone, for his dying hour was gloom.

Preliminary Questions

1. Experiment with a variety of ways to summarize the events of "Young Goodman Brown."

    a. Summarize Goodman Brown's experiences from his own point of view.
    b. Summarize Goodman Brown's experiences from the point of view of Hawthorne's narrator.
    c. Inventively summarize what happens to Goodman Brown from the point of view of a Salem townsperson (you can use a character in the story or make one up). Compare your invented point of view with those of your classmates.
    d. Treat "Young Goodman Brown" as though it were a parable or a sermon, something that can be summed up in a tidy moral, a lesson you can extract from the story. Summarize the story using your moral as your final sentence.
    e. Summarize the events of "Young Goodman Brown" in a way that raises doubts about what has happened or about the meaning of what has happened.

2. If you've done some part of question 1, write an extended paragraph about the way in which summary helps shape interpretation. How is the meaning of the story affected by the decisions you make on what to include and leave out, what to stress and ignore? Use specific examples from "Young Goodman Brown" to support your response.

3. "Young Goodman Brown" appeared in 1835, but it obviously is set much earlier. Gather clues from the text that suggest an approximate date imagined by Hawthorne (you may have to do a little research, but a good dictionary should be a sufficient source). Try dividing your evidence into "general" and "specific," and then write a short report verifying the date of the story's setting, moving from the general evidence toward your most clinching points.

4. Before looking at the rest of the materials in this chapter, try guessing which features of this story have most interested literary critics. List or perhaps classify those features and write a short paragraph explaining your choices. Save this paragraph to compare with what you think later.

5. "Had Goodman Brown fallen asleep in the forest and only dreamed a wild dream of a witch-meeting?" This question, which Hawthorne made prominent as the next-to-last paragraph of his story, has stirred some lively debate among readers. Before deciding whether you think Goodman Brown has dreamed, try assembling all the evidence you can on the side of the dream interpretation. List that evidence, indicating where his dream might begin and end and highlighting key dreamlike moments along the way. As a conclusion, say whether you find your evidence persuasive or doubtful.

6. "Be it so if you will." Why does Hawthorne's narrator call attention to

the possibility that Goodman Brown has dreamed and then turn away from his own question? Write a two-part essay exploring this problem. First show how a portion of the story might be read as a dream (see question 5). Then show why a full interpretation of the story cannot depend entirely on whether or not Goodman Brown has dreamed.

7. Judging from this story, define sin. Which sins are worst? Do some sins seem more prevalent than others among the Puritans? Does Hawthorne's view of sin seem to coincide with theirs?

8. Define "faith." Does the story seem to offer a definition or elude one?

9. In many places "Young Goodman Brown" seems to have been written from the point of view of Brown, in that we frequently move into his consciousness to learn what he is thinking — a perspective we are offered with no other character. But the story isn't told entirely from the perspective of Goodman Brown — the voice telling the story provides more. What are some of these extra elements, features that do not seem to be part of Brown's consciousness? Can you classify them? Think further about this gap between the narrator and Brown, and assess its importance to the way you read the story.

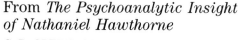

Complicating the Issues

What attracted Hawthorne to the Puritan past? Some biographical explanations are suggested by psychoanalyst C. P. Oberndorf, whose article "The Psychoanalytic Insight of Nathaniel Hawthorne" was published in The Psychoanalytic Review *in 1942. An excerpt from that article follows.*

From *The Psychoanalytic Insight of Nathaniel Hawthorne*
C. P. OBERNDORF

Hawthorne's father died on a trip to the Indies when his son was only four years old. After that his mother never left her room during the day, even had her meals served in solitude. Hawthorne's wife has recorded that when she, Hawthorne (now aged forty), and their first child went to spend Thanksgiving at his mother's home in Salem, which he nicknamed "Castle Dismal," this was the "first time since my husband can remember, he dined with his mother!" Only on rare occasions would his mother wander through the dark Salem streets while the village slept. Such seclusion and night excursions are habits attributed to the colonial witches of her native Salem.

The childhood environment of Hawthorne resembled more closely a psychopathological picture of group derangement than of a healthy home setting. Each member of the Hawthorne household in Salem was a recluse. Hawthorne's two sisters were also subject to the pathological mother's regime of strict isolation. In this atmosphere of feminine authority Hawthorne grew up — a seclusive, sensitive child. He seemed to be constantly stimulated by an urge to fulfill his mother's ambitions and hopes. At the same time he suffered from a feeling of thwarted pride, a heritage of the home environment, which made him resentful of the crippling elements in his own character and of the morbid nature of his daily life. From these unhappy influences he fled to a refuge of books, of fantasy and of unreality.

The mental attitude which tortured Hawthorne steeped his thought   3
in the fantasies of the past, and deterred him from bringing his writings to print for many years. Even then he used frequently changing noms de plume and recalled from circulation and destroyed his first novel, "Fanshawe." In early manhood, always despairing and despondent, the chances are that Hawthorne, with his feminine diffidence, would never have had sufficient faith to expose his work to a critical world had it not been for the unwavering encouragement of his only intimate friend, Horatio Bridge.

Hawthorne's first recorded depression occurred at the age of fifteen   4
when he returned from his uncle's farm on the free frontier of Lake Sebago, Maine, to his maternal uncle's gloomy home in Salem. There he stayed to prepare for entrance to Bowdoin, then a small, young country college, rigidly Calvinistic in spirit. After graduation at twenty-one, he returned to the maternal family home in Salem and, says Morris, "The addition of a man to this eccentric nunnery effected few changes in a routine of which the only common habit was to have no habits in common." Here Hawthorne passed the next ten years, shunning real experiences, brooding over the austere world of his family's past, and allowing fantasy to become more real than actuality. He was thrown into deep despair by each new failure to receive recognition from his meager literary productions.

There is something pitiable in his helpless despondency as shown in   5
a letter to Longfellow in 1837 — Hawthorne is now thirty-three years old — indicating the extent to which his duality, already apparent at college, had progressed. He writes that "by some witchcraft or other — for I really cannot assign any reasonable why and wherefore" (perhaps in modern terms, because of some unconscious force) "I have been carried apart from the main current of life and find it impossible to get back again. I have secluded myself from society and yet I never meant any such thing, nor dreamed what sort of life I was going to lead. I have made a captive of myself, and put me in a dungeon, and now I cannot find the key to let myself out — and if the door were open, I should be almost afraid to come out. For the last ten years, I have not lived, but only dreamed of living. Sometimes through a peephole, I have caught a glimpse of the real world and the two or three articles in which I have portrayed these glimpses, please me better than the others."

The above letter was written during the most desolate period of   6
Hawthorne's life, when he was frequently threatening suicide. He was sustained at this time only by the vigor and loyalty of Bridge with whom he stayed for a while. At Hawthorne's request later in life, Bridge de-

stroyed all of Hawthorne's letters written during these miserable years. Here is the picture of a patient well known to psychiatrists and especially analysts — a man struggling with mysterious forces which he cannot comprehend, and urgently pleading with his friends for help but unwilling to seek medical aid for fear that it might lead to the revelation of facts which he could not bear.

During his early manhood Hawthorne had been "technically chaste;   7
his code of sexual morality was exceedingly strict; his desires had been aggravated by prolonged asceticism. The frustration of his sexual life must have played a large part in giving his mood of despondency a morbid, almost hysterical, turn" (Morris).[1] During this time he was preoccupied with the idea of marriage — possibly accounted for by long sexual frustration.

Hawthorne was literally dragged out of his retirement by Elizabeth   8
Peabody, the older and bolder daughter of Dr. Nathaniel Peabody. His courtship of Elizabeth's sister, Sophia, a delicate, child-like woman, had the effect of bringing him partially out of his solitude. At least falling in love turned the tide from the habit of seclusion to an urge in the direction of contact with the exigencies of life. Falling in love, the fruition of marriage, and his insight into mechanisms were not sufficient to cure Hawthorne's periods of psychic depression, apathy, and inertia, which recurred and persisted up to the time of his death in 1864.

[1] Lloyd Morris, *The Rebellious Puritan* (1927), p. 354.

In his biography of Hawthorne, Randall Stewart offers a picture of Hawthorne quite different from Oberndorf's. Stewart's biography Nathaniel Hawthorne *was published in 1948.*

From *Nathaniel Hawthorne: A Biography*
RANDALL STEWART

ANCESTRY AND BOYHOOD

Nathaniel Hawthorne's earliest American ancestor, William Hathorne,   1
came from England to Massachusetts in 1630, the year of John Winthrop's migration, and settled first at Dorchester and later at Salem. He became an important man in the young colony, rising to the office of speaker in the House of Delegates and to the rank of major in the Salem militia. Hawthorne wrote of him in "The Custom House":

> The figure of that first ancestor, invested by family tradition with a dim and dusky grandeur, was present to my boyish imagination as far back as I can remember. It still haunts me, and induces a sort of home feeling with the past. . . . I seem to have a stronger claim to residence here [in Salem] on account of this grave, bearded, sable-cloaked and steeple-crowned progenitor — who came so early, with his Bible and his sword, and trode the unworn street with such a stately port, and made so large a figure, as a man of war

and peace — a stronger claim than for myself. . . . He was a soldier, legislator, judge; he was a ruler in the Church; he had all the Puritanic traits, both good and evil. He was likewise a bitter persecutor, as witness the Quakers, who have remembered him in their histories, and relate an incident of his hard severity towards a woman of their sect, which will last longer, it is to be feared, than any record of his better deeds, although these were many.

Hawthorne liked to remember particularly his ancestor's bold defiance of an edict of Charles II ordering Hathorne and the governor of Massachusetts to come to England and explain, if they could, the colony's persistent insubordination to royal authority. One of his most prized possessions was a document which he endorsed as follows: "Copy of a letter supposed to have been written by Major William Hathorne of Massachusetts defending that Colony against the accusations of the Commissioners of Charles II, and excusing the General Court for declining to send over Governor Bellingham and himself in compliance with the King's order." An ancestor who had defied a king was obviously one to be proud of, whatever his faults may have been.

William's son, John, is famous and infamous in history as one of the [2] three judges in the Salem witchcraft trials of 1692 — the other two being William Stoughton and Samuel Sewall — though, unlike Sewall, he is not known to have repented of his error. "He made himself so conspicuous in the martyrdom of the witches," Hawthorne wrote in "The Custom House," "that their blood may fairly be said to have left a stain upon him." There was a tradition in the family that one of the witches had pronounced a curse upon Judge Hathorne and all his posterity. Hawthorne seems to have had a superstitious respect for this curse, for — more than half seriously, perhaps — he attributed the subsequent decline of the Hathornes to its influence.

The intervening Hathorne ancestors were relatively obscure. The [3] judge's son, Joseph, was a farmer in the Salem township. Joseph's son, Daniel, went to sea and commanded a privateer during the Revolutionary War. Daniel's son, Nathaniel, born in 1775, also followed the sea. In 1801 he married Elizabeth Clarke Manning and their children were Elizabeth Manning, born in 1802, Nathaniel, the subject of this biography, born July 4, 1804, and Maria Louisa, born in 1808. While on a long voyage in 1808, Captain Nathaniel Hathorne died in Dutch Guiana.

Hawthorne could have seen but little of his father, who was much [4] absent on voyages to distant parts of the earth. The Salem *Gazette* on October 19, 1804, for example, announced the arrival of the "ship Mary and Eliza, Capt. Nathaniel Hathorne, in 118 days from Batavia." After greeting his family and saluting his three months' old son, the captain gave a brief account to the press of the commerce of the Dutch East Indies, reporting that all the crop of coffee had been exhausted and no more was to be had for the season, and that no less than forty-five neutral ships, principally American, had loaded there from September to June. The captain's son was later to cherish a logbook kept by his father during one of his voyages to the Far East; Hawthorne inscribed his name in it several times and copied in the margins and between the lines many nautical phrases taken from the text of the log — "moderate breeze, hazy weather and variable," "heavy head swell" and the like. Though he was never to spend much time on the sea, the sea was congenial to him and stimulated his imagination. He preferred a seaside residence to any other, and he relished accounts of sea adventures.

Less is known of Hawthorne's ancestry on his mother's side. The   5
Mannings migrated from England in 1679 and for a century and a half in Massachusetts they showed a talent for business. Hawthorne's uncle, Robert Manning, for many years operated a stagecoach line. The Salem *Gazette* advertised in 1818, for example, "Manning's Daily Stages" to Marblehead, Newburyport, and Boston. Between Salem and Boston there were four stagecoaches daily each way. The stage line was an important and profitable business. Robert Manning also cultivated and experimented with fruit trees; by the time of his death in 1842 he had acquired considerable fame as a pomologist. It was Uncle Robert who looked after the business affairs of the widow Hathorne and made financially possible the education of her son. . . .

After the death of Captain Hathorne the widow returned with her   6
three children to the Manning house. It was a large and hospitable household, including four uncles and four aunts, all unmarried. Nathaniel was "particularly petted," his sister Elizabeth recalled many years later, "the more because his health was then delicate and he had frequent illnesses." He was said to have been a very handsome boy and a great favorite not only with the members of his family but with the drivers of the Manning stages. At the age of nine he injured his foot while playing ball at school, and suffered a lameness which persisted for a long while. The prescribed therapy consisted of pouring showers of cold water from a window in the second story upon the lame foot, extended from the window below. At the time of his injury Hawthorne was attending the school taught by J. E. Worcester, and throughout the period of his lameness the great lexicographer came to the house to hear the boy's lessons. His earliest extant letter dated December 9, 1813, reports that he had been absent from school for four weeks, had been carried to the doorstep and to the stage office, and once had "hopped out into the street." Later he was able to walk with the aid of crutches. Not until after some three years, when he was twelve, was the lameness completely overcome.

A natural love of books, encouraged by the leisure thus enforced,   7
led to his acquiring early the habit of reading. Spenser's *Fairie Queene*, Thomson's *Castle of Indolence*, Bunyan's *Pilgrim's Progress*, and Shakespeare were boyhood favorites. Elizabeth remembered that he used to lie upon the carpet while reading, or that he would sit in a large chair in the corner of the room, near a window, and read half the afternoon without speaking. He liked to quote with mock heroic effect a line from *Richard III*, "My Lord, stand back, and let the coffin pass." Cats also amused him, and the Manning household was well supplied with felines bearing such Bunyanesque names as "Apollyon" and "Beelzebub." . . .

All told, Hawthorne's boyhood was not as abnormal as has sometimes   8
been supposed. Although it is true that, except while at Raymond, he may not have played with other boys as much as would have been good

for him, and that his activities were too much centered in his immediate family, his life was by no means physically inactive or socially impoverished. After his recovery from the lameness which handicapped him between the ages of nine and twelve, he became healthy and strong. Especially in Maine, where he spent a good deal of time between the ages of twelve and seventeen, he enjoyed a variety of outdoor sports — swimming, skating, fishing, hunting. A large family of uncles and aunts, sisters and cousins, stimulated his inclination to study the varieties of human nature. His relations with his mother and sisters were affectionate; his sister Louisa was especially congenial to him because of her fun-loving disposition. He did considerable reading — though not an excessive amount for a person who likes books — and began, in a juvenile way, to write. His was not a precocious development, but slow rather, and substantial. . . .

THE "SOLITARY YEARS," 1825–1837

. . . The period from 1825 until 1837, when he published the *Twice-Told Tales*, has often been called the "solitary years." Doubtless they were solitary to an unusual degree, but not in the sense of a hermit's deliberate withdrawal from the world. Hawthorne was actively interested in the world about him and maintained a reasonable amount of contact with it. But his chief object was to master the writer's difficult art — something which cannot be done in the hubbub of social activity. Probably his life at Bowdoin had been more social than was compatible with a severe literary discipline. The degree of compositional skill which Hawthorne achieved during the post-college years can be appreciated in some measure if it is recalled that the almost flawless writing of his notebooks was done rapidly, with scarcely an erasure or emendation. **9**

After graduation Hawthorne settled down to a serious literary career. He did a great deal of reading and writing. Although he destroyed much that he wrote, he had published by 1838 a novel of indifferent merit and at least forty-four tales and sketches, many of which were of high excellence. . . . **10**

[Hawthorne's] "solitary" years have often been described somewhat sentimentally. In a famous letter addressed to his fiancée, Miss Sophia Peabody, October 4, 1840, Hawthorne himself gave encouragement to a sentimental view of his apprentice years: **11**

> Here sits thy husband in his old accustomed chamber [he wrote], where he used to sit in years gone by, before his soul became acquainted with thine. Here I have written many tales — many that have been burned to ashes — many that doubtless deserved the same fate. This deserves to be called a haunted chamber; for thousands upon thousands of visions have appeared to me in it; and some few of them have become visible to the world. If ever I should have a biographer, he ought to make great mention of this chamber in my memoirs, because so much of my lonely youth was wasted here, and here my mind and character were formed; and here I have been glad and hopeful, and here I have been despondent; and here I sat a long, long time, waiting patiently for the world to know me, and sometimes wondering why

it did not know me sooner, or whether it would ever know me at all — at least, till I were in my grave. And sometimes (for I had no wife then to keep my heart warm) it seemed as if I were already in the grave, with only life enough to be chilled and benumbed. But oftener I was happy — at least, as happy as I then knew how to be, or was aware of the possibility of being. By and bye, the world found me out in my lonely chamber, and called me forth — not, indeed, with a loud roar of acclamation, but rather with a still, small voice; and forth I went, but found nothing in the world that I thought preferable to my old solitude, till at length a certain Dove was revealed to me, in the shadow of a seclusion as deep as my own had been. And I drew nearer and nearer to the Dove, and opened my bosom to her, and she flitted into it, and closed her wings there — and there she nestles now and forever, keeping my heart warm, and renewing my life with her own. So now I begin to understand why I was imprisoned so many years in this lonely chamber, and why I could never break through the viewless bolts and bars; for if I had sooner made my escape into the world, I should have grown hard and rough, and been covered with earthly dust, and my heart would have become callous by rude encounters with the multitude; so that I should have been all unfit to shelter a heavenly Dove in my arms. But living in solitude till the fulness of time was come, I still kept the dew of my youth and the freshness of my heart, and had these to offer to my Dove.

The phrases "lonely youth" and "lonely chamber" recur with affecting iteration; his life was one of "solitude" and "seclusion"; he was "chilled and benumbed." It is not necessary to question the writer's sincerity or the core of truth in the description. For a young man of Hawthorne's sensibilities and literary aspirations, the Muse was an exacting mistress. He spent many lonely and despondent hours in the chamber where fame was won. The life of a serious writer is likely to be in large part lonely. But the pathos which pervades the letter just quoted must be discounted somewhat in the light of the circumstances of composition. When writing a love letter, a man may be tempted to darken his former years so as to brighten by contrast his present felicity. In a more sober and responsible mood, Hawthorne later described these same years as "tranquil and not unhappy." . . .

In his journeys about New England, which he knew in its entirety   12 better than any other of the great New England authors, his attention was not confined to the beauties of nature and the humors of Shakers and villagers. Hawthorne always had an appreciative eye for female beauty, and there is reason to believe that he was interested in several girls. The evidence, though fire may not be clearly visible, provides a good deal of smoke. Elizabeth Hawthorne recalled her brother's captivation by a girl in Swampscott, the daughter of a fisherman and the keeper of a little shop. This village maiden had, Hawthorne said, a great deal of what the French call *espièglerie*. Their affair was apparently only a summer flirtation. The young man brought home as a memento a pink sugar heart, which he kept a long while before eating it. "I should have feared that he was really in love with her," Elizabeth remarked, "if he had not talked so much about her." Elizabeth doubted if her brother was quite serious, furthermore, because there had been others — for example, "a girl in the interior of Massachusetts as captivating in a different style."

A more serious romance apparently occurred in Edgartown on Martha's Vineyard. An unpublished reminiscence by a resident of Edgartown tells of Hawthorne's proposal of marriage to Miss Eliza Gibbs, "a tall, darkeyed queenly maiden." The date is unknown, but Bridge's letters in the spring of 1837 suggest that Hawthorne was contemplating marriage: "Are you seriously thinking of getting married," he asked; and again, "What has become of your matrimonial ideas? Are you in a good way to bring this about?" In a letter to Longfellow in June, 1837, Hawthorne spoke of soon having a "sharp spur to exertion" which he had previously lacked. But whether Miss Gibbs or another was the lady in question, it is impossible to say.   13

Hawthorne appears, at any rate, to have enjoyed friendly relations with women during the "solitary" years. On several occasions he was actively interested, and his experiences seem to have ranged from ephemeral flirtations to more serious entanglements. But he had not yet, apparently, been deeply in love.   14

The years from 1825 to 1837 were active, busy, productive ones. Hawthorne was doing just what a young author ambitious of enduring fame should and must do. He was reading much and writing much. Severely critical of his own work, he was mastering the writer's craft. By his travels over New England, he was recreating his mind, enlarging his knowledge of human nature, and gathering impressions which could be used in his writings (was making himself indeed the chief literary authority in New England life and manners). Recognition was slow, but the appearance of the *Twice-Told Tales* in 1837 was the beginning of an enduring reputation, for the volume contained some of the finest productions of his pen.   15

James R. Mellow published his biography of Nathaniel Hawthorne in 1980. In reading over the following excerpts, you might consider whether Mellow's emphases differ in significant ways from Stewart's. Also consider whether the two biographers' accounts support Oberndorf's interpretation of Hawthorne's personality.

From *Nathaniel Hawthorne in His Times*
JAMES R. MELLOW

The Hathorne family — it was Nathaniel Hawthorne who added the *w* to the ancient spelling some time after he left college — provided the future writer with an ambiguous heritage, stretching back to the days of colonial settlement. For Hawthorne, the history and fortunes of his family became a kind of literary property, all the more dramatic since the family, in its brush with Salem history, had suffered a decline.   1

William Hathorne, the first of the American settlers in the family, had been a member of John Winthrop's historic Massachusetts Bay Colony, arriving between 1630 and 1633 and settling in Dorchester. By 1636,   2 he had moved to Salem, where he distinguished himself as a major in the Salem militia. Eventually, he became speaker and, subsequently, deputy of the House of Delegates. In religion, William was a man of pious but uncompromising principles, remembered by his descendant for having ordered, in orthodox Puritan fashion, that a heretic Quaker woman, Anne Coleman, be whipped out of town. Hawthorne admired a family tradition that held that the stalwart William had once defied an order from King Charles II to return to London with the aged Governor Bellingham to explain the unruly conduct of His Majesty's fractious colony. Hawthorne treasured the transcript of a letter, purportedly written by his ancestor two centuries before, the copy of which he had obtained himself, in 1856, from the State Paper Office in London. The letter, written in 1666, signed Samuel Nadhorth — a possible pseudonym — is addressed to Sir William Morice, one of the king's secretaries of state. With an unusual combination of political tact and abrasive integrity, the writer exonerates himself and his fellow colonists by citing the hardships of life in a "waste and howling wilderness," the continuing loyalty of the colonists to the crown, and, more pointedly, their undeniable services to His Majesty's treasury. He goes on to condemn the abuses of the royal commissioners who are attempting to deprive the colonists of their liberties — "sacred and civil" liberties, that had been granted them by a royal charter. To offset the colonists' refusal to comply with the king's wishes, the writer notes that a present of two great masts and a shipload of twenty-eight large masts is being sent to the king. The colonists had been "forced to take up money at interest" in order to make this "small present"; nonetheless, they are "not without hope of a favorable acceptance, which will be to their souls as a cloud of latter rain." Hawthorne could scarcely have overlooked — or failed to admire — that the exquisite courtesy of the letter-writer's style concealed a number of sharp barbs.

William Hathorne's son John reached an even greater eminence — 3 and notoriety — as one of the judges in the Salem witchcraft trials, that outbreak of hysteria and harsh justice in which the testimony of eight "afflicted girls" brought about the hanging of nineteen unoffending victims and the death by torture of another. It was a family legend that one of the victims, before her execution on Gallow's Hill, had placed a curse on Judge Hathorne and his descendants.

Hawthorne was to remain fascinated by those darker regions of the 4 human mind that had been exposed in the courtroom presided over by his seventeenth-century ancestor. Witches and witches' Sabbaths, diabolical persuasions, the guilt of unmentioned crimes, whether real or circumstantial, were to become the themes of many of Hawthorne's stories and romances. Long after Judge Hathorne, in 1717, in his seventy-sixth year, was laid to rest in Salem burying ground, Nathaniel Hawthorne, in the preface to *The Scarlet Letter*, offered to take on himself the family curse that "the dreary and unprosperous condition of the race, for many a long year back, would argue to exist."

The Hathorne family had, indeed, fallen on poorer days. In his will, 5 John Hathorne had requested the repayment of certain sums he had borrowed from his surviving sons, Ebenezer and Joseph — an indication, perhaps, of financial embarrassment in his old age. Joseph inherited the family farm in Salem township, Ebenezer having died, probably of small-pox, in 1717, before his father's will was probated. Joseph remained a simple farmer. His son Daniel, born in 1731, achieved fame as a privateer during the Revolutionary War. But "Bold Daniel," as he was known both in a popular ballad and in the family annals, did little to increase the Hathorne wealth. In 1772, after selling the family homestead, he bought a small house and property on Union Street from the Pickmans, relatives of his wife, Rachel. It was there that Nathaniel Hawthorne's father — named Nathaniel before him — was born, on May 19, 1775. . . .

On August 2, 1801, Nathaniel Hathorne married Elizabeth Clarke   6
Manning, the daughter of a neighbor, Richard Manning, who lived on nearby Herbert Street. The Mannings were a prospering family of four sons and four daughters that could trace its lineage back to the colonial period, having arrived in America in 1679. Through industry and acumen, Richard Manning, a blacksmith by trade, had established himself as the proprietor and manager of the Boston and Salem Stage Company. He had also invested considerable sums in land grants in Maine, then a territory of Massachusetts. His daughter Betsey, an attractive but shy young woman with "remarkable eyes, full of sensibility and expression," was five years her husband's junior. Nathaniel Hathorne was remembered as "a warm-hearted and kindly man, very fond of children," but "somewhat inclined to melancholy, and of a reticent disposition." It was said that he was "a great reader, employing all his leisure time at sea over books." The couple's first child, a daughter whom they named Elizabeth, was born on March 2, 1802, seven months after their marriage, a circumstance that may have accounted, in part, for Elizabeth Hawthorne's later reclusive tendencies. In family circles Elizabeth was known as Ebe or Abby, names acquired from her brother, Nathaniel, who found it impossible to pronounce Elizabeth. A second daughter, Maria Louisa, was born on January 9, 1808. . . .

Hawthorne spent much of his childhood in a household of active   7
women. He lived with his grandmother, Miriam Manning, two aunts, his mother and sisters, and Hannah Lord, a Manning niece who worked as a servant. Among the Herbert Street women, he sometimes felt isolated — particularly when his mother and sisters were away in Maine. On one such occasion, writing to his Uncle Robert, who was visiting in Raymond, he expressed his hope that his sister Ebe would return to Salem, since he had "nobody to talk to but Grandmother, Aunt Mary and Hannah and it seems very lonesome here." . . .

Hawthorne considered his childhood years in Maine one of the hap-   8
piest periods of his life, though he had few companions his age except for his sisters. In the summers, he was free to roam the woods at his own will, hunting for partridges and hen hawks with his father's ancient fowling gun. The brooks were full of trout. In the winter, he skated, often in complete solitude, on the frozen lake, the dark pines looming on the horizon as the sun set. When he was cold, he installed himself in one of the many vacant cabins along the lake and settled on the broad hearth in front of a crackling log fire. The slow progress of the days and the seasons, the sense of isolation, seemed to agree with him. . . .

Hawthorne nonetheless read a good deal during this period and was   9 to form some opinions about his own education. He could recall reading, on rainy days in Maine, "in Shakespeare and 'The Pilgrim's Progress,' and any poetry or light books within my reach." Interestingly, in view of his later development as a writer of allegories, his two favorite books of these earlier years were Spenser's *Faerie Queene* and Bunyan's *Pilgrim's Progress*, which he read and reread (and frequently alluded to) throughout his life. He could recall his pleasure as a small boy, standing on tiptoe to pull down books from his Grandfather Manning's shelf, shutting himself off in the pages of some barely comprehensible work, but understanding it more through sensibility than intellect. Only a solitary child, "left much to such wild modes of culture as he chooses for himself while yet ignorant what culture means," Hawthorne maintained, could develop the special intimacy with an author that he thought was worth having.

In later life, Hawthorne idealized his Maine childhood, stressing the   10
natural setting: "Those were delightful days, for that part of the country was wild then, with only scattered clearings, and nine tenths of it primeval woods." He once told a friend, "I lived in Maine like a bird of the air, so perfect was the freedom I enjoyed." But he had, by then, acquired that doubleness of mind that marked him as a writer: the ability to recognize the rare, glowing occasions that life offered — and the price that it exacted. For he added, "It was there I first got my cursed habits of solitude." . . .

THE LONG SECLUSION

It was my fortune or misfortune . . ." Hawthorne later wrote, "to   11
have some slender means of supporting myself; and so, on leaving college, in 1825, instead of immediately studying a profession, I sat myself down to consider what pursuit in life I was best fit for. My mother had now returned, and taken up her abode in her deceased father's house . . . in which I had a room. And year after year I kept on considering what I was fit for, and time and my destiny decided that I was to be the writer that I am."

Behind that laconic statement lies one of the more curious chapters   12
in the career of a great American writer. On leaving Bowdoin, Hawthorne entered upon what he termed his "long seclusion," a decade in which he served his apprenticeship as a writer immured behind the family walls. Much of his boyhood and youth had been spent away from his native Salem; as a consequence, he had few acquaintances and friends there. "I doubt whether so much as twenty people in the town were aware of my existence," he remembered.

In later years, he was to be of two minds about his Salem life,   13
uncertain whether it should be construed as "fortune or misfortune." At times, he viewed it simply as a very tolerable period, one in which he "seemed cheerful and enjoyed the very best bodily health." His lengthy seclusion had neither made him "melancholy or misanthropic," nor had it unfitted him for "the bustle of life." At such moments, he was inclined to trust the instinct that had taught him the disciplines of solitude.

On other occasions, however, he viewed those Salem years as a   14 form of limbo, a long and weary imprisonment. In his youth, Hawthorne displayed none of the irascible temperament of the genius and little of that pose of the artist-as-romantic-hero. He remained remarkably level-headed about his profession. Still, there were to be moments in his career — solemn moments — when the matter-of-fact surfaces of life seemed to open up, revealing chasms below. Revisiting his upstairs room in the Herbert Street house as a mature writer, he was to have some gloomy reflections. "If ever I should have a biographer," he mused, "he ought to make great mention of this chamber in my memoirs, because so much of my lonely youth was wasted here, and here my mind and character were formed." In his small chamber under the eaves, he had "sat a long, long time, waiting patiently for the world to know me, and sometimes wondering why it did not know me sooner, or whether it would ever know me at all — at least, till I were in my grave. And sometimes . . . it seemed as if I were already in my grave . . ." Ebe Hawthorne, recalling those years, maintained, "It was only after his return to Salem and when he felt as if he could not get away from there and was conscious of being utterly unlike every one else in the place that he began to withdraw into himself." . . .

In the summer of 1832, Hawthorne planned an extensive trip to 15 northern New York and on into Canada. An outbreak of cholera in Canada, though, made him defer his plans. In June, he wrote to his friend Franklin Pierce, in New Hampshire, expressing his disappointment. "I was making preparations for a northern tour," he wrote, "when this accursed Cholera broke out in Canada. It was my intention to go by way of New York and Albany to Niagara, from thence to Montreal and Quebec . . ." With a touch of irony, he added, "I am very desirous of making this journey, on account of a book by which I intend to acquire an (undoubtedly) immense literary reputation."

The chief purpose of his letter, however, was to congratulate his 16 friend Pierce on his recent election as speaker in the New Hampshire legislature. Far from being uninterested in politics, Hawthorne went on to sketch — prophetically — a complete career for his college friend. "I sincerely congratulate you on all your public honors, in possession or in prospect," he wrote. "If they continue to accumulate so rapidly, you will be at the summit of political eminence, by that time of life when men are usually just beginning to make a figure. . . . If I were in your place, I should like to proceed by the following steps; after a few years in Congress, to be chosen Governor, say, at thirty years old — next a Senator in Congress — then minister to England — then to be put at the head of one of the Departments (that of War would suit you, I should think) — and lastly — but it will be time enough to think of the next step, some years hence." It says something about Hawthorne's grasp of American politics that he should have sketched out so accurately Pierce's route to political success. Pierce served in the House and Senate for nine years; he was offered the cabinet post of attorney general by the Polk administration (but declined it); he was a brigadier general in the Mexican War; and, finally, in 1852, he was elected President — that last step Hawthorne had stopped short of predicting.

Somehow, the consideration Hawthorne gave to his friend's bright 17 prospects served only to reflect on his own obscure future. "You cannot imagine how proud I feel," Hawthorne wrote Pierce, "when I recollect that I myself was once in office with you on the standing committee of the Athenaean Society. That," he concluded somewhat regretfully, "was my first and last appearance in public life."

In September, Hawthorne began his journey, probably the most ex-   18
tensive he made during this period of his life. His travels can be reconstructed on only scanty documentary evidence: a letter written to his mother from Burlington, Vermont, in mid-September; a printed certification that Nathaniel Hawthorne had "passed behind the Great Falling Sheet of Water to Termination Rock" at Niagara Falls, on September 28, 1832. Circumstantial details of at least one lengthy northern excursion are related in a series of fragmentary travel pieces, "Sketches from Memory, By a Pedestrian," published three years later in the November and December 1835 issues of the *New-England Magazine*. . . .

In his sketches, it is the pedestrian Hawthorne who appears — the   19
sometime traveler, the occasional man of the world, the observer of the American scene. This Hawthorne affects an air of diffidence and casual interest, is somewhat debonair. At times, he poses as the dandy, fussy about his appearance, a bit disdainful of his compatriots. Yet Hawthorne is never the outsider, the stranger. He is another character in the scene, the amused and amusing commentator on what he once described as "a text of deep and varied meaning" — the circumstance of being American.

But there is another Hawthorne: the solitary writer and journalizer,   20
spending the long hours in the upstairs bedroom in the Herbert Street house; the student of his own vague dreams and emotions; the man of a sometimes morbid turn of mind. He is the captive of time, the sensitive man who, in a moment of weariness, scribbles in an undated entry in his journal: "A recluse, like myself, or a prisoner, to measure time by the progress of sunshine through his chamber." In such moments, the record of his solitary life seemed reduced to the barest essentials, the slow passage of the sunlight across the bedroom carpet, along the furniture of his mind.

The darker side of Hawthorne's mind seemed reserved for his early   21
tales. The presiding themes there — the secret springs of shame, the hidden nature of guilt, the communion of sinners — speak of the tormented mind. But the style is always fastidious and elegant; it scarcely ever verges on prurience of despair. His researches into the interior self bring him to a shadowy world of "shapeless half-ideas which throng the dim region beyond the daylight of our perfect consciousness." Morality — the codes of a particular society at a particular time — does not become his real province as a writer, as it did for Dickens or Trollope, whose grasp of society and the real world he so much admired. Hawthorne was seldom to be a judgmental writer. Often enough, with Hawthorne's sinners, the deed is only hinted at. The crime may occur in some penumbral past, but the conscience will be explored with the skill of a surgeon probing diseased flesh. The mystery of sin is what absorbs him.

In this excerpt from a feminist analysis of Nathaniel Hawthorne, published in 1987, Louise DeSalvo focuses on Hawthorne's marriage and the language he used in speaking with his wife, Sophia.

From *Nathaniel Hawthorne and Feminists*
LOUISE DeSALVO

According to Julian Hawthorne, "the most fortunate event of [Hawthorne's] life was, probably, his marriage with Sophia Peabody." After her marriage to Nathaniel, Sophia found a new source for strength, and she was, for the first time since her infancy, in perfect health; nor did she ever afterwards relapse into her previous condition of invalidism, in all likelihood caused by the medications she had been given as a child. After their marriage, Hawthorne encouraged her talent as an artist, and, at one point, wrote to Margaret Fuller about his wishes for Sophia: 1

> I wish to remove everything that might impede her full growth and development, — which in her case, it seems to me, is not to be brought about by care and toil, but by perfect repose and happiness. . . . Besides, she has many visions of great deeds to be wrought on canvas and in marble during the coming autumn and winter; and none of these can be accomplished unless she can retain quite as much freedom from household drudgery as she enjoys at present.

Hawthorne and Sophia colluded in creating a mythology of their marriage in which they were the new Adam and Eve, which, according to T. Walter Herbert, was an example of a widespread nineteenth-century phenomenon, "the sacralization of domestic intimacy." This myth seriously distorted the truth of the reality of their lives, and presented grave and almost insurmountable problems for Sophia after Hawthorne's death. Although his love letters to her describe what has been called "a passionate, physical relationship," none the less, in letters to her during their courtship — he destroyed almost all of hers to him — she is his Dove, embodying "the Holy Spirit," or "naughty Sophie Hawthorne":   2

> Belovedest, I love thee. But then that naughty Sophie Hawthorne — it would be out of the question to treat her with tenderness. Nothing shall she get from me . . . save a kiss upon her nose; and I should not wonder if she were to return the favor with a buffet upon my ear. Mine own Dove, how unhappy art thou to be linked with such a mate! . . . — and me unhappy, too, to be forced to keep such a turbulent little rebel in my inmost heart.

Repeatedly, throughout his love letters, Hawthorne describes his feelings of unworthiness in the face of her divine goodness: "I suppose I should have pretty much the same feeling if an angel were to come from Heaven and be my dearest friend." And he describes his terror of losing her, should she decide to follow the dictates of her nature and desert him by becoming mere spirit. (Hawthorne had written a poem at sixteen about "a young man dying for love of a ghost.")   3

Because she is an angel, she is expected to forgive him, and she is   4
expected, as well, not to suffer if he wrongs her: "Oh, let me feel that
I may even do you a little wrong without your avenging it (oh how cruelly)
by being wounded." After their marriage, he was the husband to whom
she would willingly submit: "my Dove is to follow my guidance and do
my bidding. . . . My love gives me the right, and your love consents
to it."

*In his biography of Hawthorne, Randall Stewart quotes the passages about
Hawthorne's ancestors from the autobiographical preface, called "The Custom
House," that Hawthorne provided for* The Scarlet Letter *(see paragraphs 1–3
of the Stewart reading on pp. 508–509). Here are those passages again, but in
a somewhat fuller context. Does this context make Hawthorne's attitude toward
his ancestry easier or more difficult to judge?*

From *The Custom House*
NATHANIEL HAWTHORNE

This old town of Salem — my native place, though I have dwelt much   1
away from it, both in boyhood and maturer years — possesses, or did
possess, a hold on my affections, the force of which I have never realized
during my seasons of actual residence here. Indeed, so far as its physical
aspect is concerned, with its flat, unvaried surface, covered chiefly with
wooden houses, few or none of which pretend to architectural beauty,
— its irregularity, which is neither picturesque nor quaint, but only tame,
— its long and lazy street, lounging wearisomely through the whole extent
of the peninsula, with Gallows Hill and New Guinea at one end, and a
view of the alms-house at the other, — such being the features of my
native town, it would be quite as reasonable to form a sentimental attachment to a disarranged checkerboard. And yet, though invariably happiest elsewhere, there is within me a feeling for old Salem, which, in
lack of a better phrase, I must be content to call affection. The sentiment
is probably assignable to the deep and aged roots which my family has
struck into the soil. It is now nearly two centuries and a quarter since
the original Briton, the earliest emigrant of my name, made his appearance
in the wild and forest-bordered settlement, which has since become a
city. And here his descendants have been born and died, and have mingled
their earthy substance with the soil; until no small portion of it must
necessarily be akin to the mortal frame wherewith, for a little while, I
walk the streets. In part, therefore, the attachment which I speak of is
the mere sensuous sympathy of dust for dust. Few of my countrymen
can know what it is; nor, as frequent transplantation is perhaps better
for the stock, need they consider it desirable to know.

But the sentiment has likewise its moral quality. The figure of that   2 first ancestor, invested by family tradition with a dim and dusky grandeur, was present to my boyish imagination, as far back as I can remember. It still haunts me, and induces a sort of home-feeling with the past, which I scarcely claim in reference to the present phase of the town. I seem to have a stronger claim to a residence here on account of this grave, bearded, sable-cloaked, and steeple-crowned progenitor, — who came so early, with his Bible and his sword, and trode the unworn street with such a stately port, and made so large a figure, as a man of war and peace, — a stronger claim than for myself, whose name is seldom heard and my face hardly known. He was a soldier, legislator, judge; he was a ruler in the Church; he had all the Puritanic traits, both good and evil. He was likewise a bitter persecutor; as witness the Quakers, who have remembered him in their histories, and relate an incident of his hard severity towards a woman of their sect, which will last longer, it is to be feared, than any record of his better deeds, although these were many. His son, too, inherited the persecuting spirit, and made himself so conspicuous in the martyrdom of the witches, that their blood may fairly be said to have left a stain upon him. So deep a stain, indeed, that his old dry bones, in the Charter Street burial-ground, must still retain it, if they have not crumbled utterly to dust! I know not whether these ancestors of mine bethought themselves to repent, and ask pardon of Heaven for their cruelties; or whether they are now groaning under the heavy consequences of them, in another state of being. At all events, I, the present writer, as their representative, hereby take shame upon myself for their sakes, and pray that any curse incurred by them — as I have heard, and as the dreary and unprosperous condition of the race, for many a long year back, would argue to exist — may be now and henceforth removed.

Doubtless, however, either of these stern and black-browed Puritans **3** would have thought it quite a sufficient retribution for his sins, that, after so long a lapse of years, the old trunk of the family tree, with so much venerable moss upon it, should have borne, as its topmost bough, an idler like myself. No aim, that I have ever cherished, would they recognize as laudable; no success of mine — if my life, beyond its domestic scope, had ever been brightened by success — would they deem otherwise than worthless, if not positively disgraceful. "What is he?" murmurs one gray shadow of my forefathers to the other. "A writer of story-books! What kind of a business in life, — what mode of glorifying God, or being serviceable to mankind in his day and generation, — may that be? Why, the degenerate fellow might as well have been a fiddler!" Such are the compliments bandied between my great-grandsires and myself, across the gulf of time! And yet, let them scorn me as they will, strong traits of their nature have intertwined themselves with mine.

In A Reader's Guide to the Short Stories of Nathaniel Hawthorne *(1975),*
Lea Bertani Vozar Newman offers the following historical information about
"Young Goodman Brown."

A Reader's Guide to *"Young Goodman Brown"*
LEA BERTANI VOZAR NEWMAN

PUBLICATION HISTORY

This story was first published in April 1835 in the *New-England*   1
Magazine as the work of the author of "The Gray Champion." . . .
Hawthorne did not include "Young Goodman Brown" in either the 1837
or the 1842 edition of *Twice-Told Tales.* It was collected in *Mosses from*
an Old Manse iun 1846.

CIRCUMSTANCES OF COMPOSITION, SOURCES,
AND INFLUENCES

. . . Many sources and influences have been credited with helping   2
to shape this relatively brief story. The most significant ones establish
Hawthorne's debt to the historical actuality of the Salem witchcraft delusion of 1692 as he came to understand it through a variety of means.
The witch folklore transmitted through oral tradition is difficult to document, yet during the course of growing up in the environs of Salem,
Hawthorne had to have been exposed to some of the local folk beliefs.
The devil's power to change his shape is one such superstition that is
incorporated into the story. Written accounts that reflect the Puritan
community before, during, and after the Salem witch trials provide a more
tangible source for the material that forms the basis for the story. Al-
legedly factual reports of witches' Sabbaths were available to Hawthorne
in the records of Essex County Court. C. W. Upham's book, *Lectures*
on Witchcraft (Boston, 1831), also contains a detailed description, although
Upham's book was published after the earliest conjectured composition
date, discussed above.

Historians such as Thomas Hutchinson (*History of Massachusetts Bay,*   3
1764), with whose work Hawthorne is known to have been familiar,
included the Salem witch trials as a part of the social and political history
of New England. Cotton Mather also describes the trials in *Wonders of*
the Invisible World (1693), providing at the same time the official Puritan
dogma regarding witchcraft. The following excerpt clearly establishes the
concepts from Mather that are subsumed in the structure of "Young
Goodman Brown":

> The *Devil,* exhibiting himself ordinarily as a small *Black Man,* has decoy'd
> a fearful knot of proud, froward, ignorant, envious and malicious Creatures,
> to list themselves in his horrid Service, by entring their Names in a Book
> by him tendred unto them. These Witches . . . have met in Hellish Ren-
> dezvouzes [*sic*], wherein the Confessors do say, they have had their Diabolical
> Sacraments, imitating the Baptism and the Supper of our Lord. . . . But

that which makes this Descent [of the Devil] the more formidable, is the
multitude and *quality* of Persons accused of an Interest in this Witchcraft,
by the Efficacy of the *Spectres* which take their Name and Shape upon them.
. . . That the Devils have obtain'd the power, to take on them the likeness
of harmless people. . . .

The passage in the story that describes one of the witches participating
in the satanic rite as "Martha Carrier, who had received the devil's
promise to be queen of hell" is taken almost verbatim from Mather's
Wonders. An earlier work by Cotton Mather, *Memorable Providences
Relating to Witchcraft and Possessions* (1689), provides similar data and
precepts defining the Puritan belief in witches. His *Wonders*, however,
appears to have been written explicitly to justify the Salem trials and to
convince Mather himself and the public that no defendant had been convicted solely on spectral evidence. In June 1692, a more explicit clarification of the specter question was issued by a group of Puritan clergymen;
in a statement probably written by Cotton Mather himself, the devil is
acknowledged as having the power to impersonate innocent people. The
following year such evidence was ruled as inadmissible in the courts.
Levin makes the point that Brown, in his own mind, convicts the townspeople and Faith on the same kind of spectral evidence admitted in the
earlier trials.

Another work by Mather, *Magnalia Christi Americana* (1702), re-   4
cords an incident during Governor Winthrop's visit at Plymouth in 1632
that might have suggested the ironic overtones in the title Hawthorne
affixes to Brown's name; Mather reports the governor's disapproval of
the use of the term *good-man* to describe an unregenerate man. The
name Deacon Gookin, used for the churchgoer who accompanies the
minister to the witches' Sabbath, has also been traced to Mather's *Magnalia*, while Goody Cory is one of the accused witches in *Wonders*. A
possible analogue for Brown's own name has been located in Samuel
Sewall's *Diary*. Goody Cloyse, the "very pious and exemplary dame"
who taught Brown his catechism, is another of the accused witches whose
name appears in the historical records.

An account of the trials that is bitterly critical of the Puritans is   5
probably another source of the reference to Goody Cory as "that unhanged
witch." Robert Calef's *More Wonders of the Invisible World* (1692) presents a detailed account of the interrogation of Goody Cory by Hawthorne's ancestor, John Hathorne, before she was committed to Salem's
prison. The reference in the story to the affirmation by some "that the
lady of the governor" (the wife of Sir William Phips) was among the Devil
worshippers reflects a specific passage in Calef's book.

Another book, Deodat Lawson's *Christ's Fidelity* (1704), which is   6
known to have been part of the Hawthorne family library, may also have
influenced Hawthorne's portrayal of the psychological aberrations involved
in the Salem witch delusion. The testimony of Joseph Ring, which is
recounted in the appendix of Lawson's book, describes the phenomenon
of forced transport to witch meetings; Ring's testimony, which also appears in Mather's *Wonders* in more pallid terms, could have provided the
journey motif as well as the subjective nature of the experience Brown
goes through during his night in the woods. Lawson's sermon, which

makes up the bulk of the book, emphasizes the power of Satan and could have suggested to Hawthorne the ironies inherent in a theological position that inadvertently minimizes God's authority and strength. Lawson's sermon would have held personal implications for Hawthorne because it was originally delivered in Salem Village on March 24, 1962, when his ancestor, John Hathorne, conducted a vigorous interrogation of accused witches.

The source for the flying ointment "receipt" described by Goody   7 Cloyse and the devil is revealed in a brief article called "Witch Ointment," which appeared in the July 1836 issue of *The American Magazine of Useful and Entertaining Knowledge* while Hawthorne was its editor. The recipe in the article, which is almost identical to the one in the story, is attributed to Lord Bacon and can be found in one of his philosophical works, *Sylva Sylvarum.* The efficacy of the formula has been verified by an experiment conducted in connection with Margaret Murray's *The Witch Cult of Western Europe* (Oxford, 1921); two of the ingredients — smallage, which is hemlock, and wolfsbane, which is aconite — were tested in controlled experiments and did produce the illusion of flight. The apparent substitution of one of Bacon's ingredients, "the fat of children digged out of their graves," with "the fat of a new-born babe" is traced to a tale by Cervantes called "El Cologuio de los Perros," or "The Conversation of the Dogs." In it, a witch discusses the common belief that witches anoint themselves with "the blood of infants which we strangle." Cervantes is referred to specifically in the penultimate sentence of the *American Magazine* article:

> Cervantes, in one of his tales, seems to be of opinion that the ointment cast them into a trance, during which they merely dreamt of holding intercourse with Satan. If so, witchcraft differs little from a nightmare. . . .

The equation of witchcraft with nightmare, a central concept in "Young Goodman Brown," can thus be ascribed to Cervantes. One reader believes that Hawthorne's depiction of the evils of witchcraft bears a closer relation to the creed expressed by La Canizares, the witch in Cervantes's story, than to the New England version; Hawthorne's story is not concerned with the diabolical persecution of neighbors, which was an important element in the Salem witch trials, but rather with secret sin covered up by hypocrisy, which is what La Canizares emphasizes about herself as a full-fledged witch.

Like the rite that Brown witnesses, Cervantes's version of the   8 witches' Sabbath suggests orgies of a sexual nature, an association Hawthorne could also have found in a more famous work in European literature, the *Walpurgisnacht* of Goethe's *Faust.* The prearranged nature of Brown's meeting also suggests a Faustian pact with the devil. . . .

One final influence that has only recently been given attention as   9 operative on Hawthorne's work is the periodical market where Hawthorne knew many of his stories would be introduced to the reading public. Mathews suggests that Hawthorne's choice of subject matter could have been guided by the popularity of witchcraft stories with the magazine audiences. He proposes Whittier's "Powow Hill," a story which appeared in the *New-England Magazine* three years before "Young Goodman Brown," in May 1832, as a possible model; some of the circumstances in Whittier's story — a young man in the woods alone at night, a waiting bride, and a pagan ceremonial — are used by Hawthorne but with a decidedly different effect.

For some background about Puritan culture and beliefs, we offer this compact and critical account by the sociologist Kai T. Erikson, whose Wayward Puritans *(1966) is a study of how Puritan communities defined and dealt with social deviance. The second part of our excerpt is from a later section of Erikson's book that discusses the outbreak of the witchcraft hysteria.*

From *Wayward Puritans*
KAI T. ERIKSON

One of the difficulties with written history is that it describes events far more systematically than they were originally experienced. Often, it is only after the tide of history has swept out a government or changed old ways of thinking that we see any pattern in the events by which change was accomplished, and then we are apt to write as if that pattern had been evident from the beginning. There are times, however, when it is important to recognize that events only assume a distinct shape after they have taken place and that the people who experience them do not sense the outlines which seem so apparent to us later. This is particularly true when we turn to the Puritan "ethos" or "world view." The Puritan reformers in England began an upheaval which changed the face of the modern world, and we naturally look for a logic in that course of events — a *movement* or *cause* to give the drama its motive force. Yet we are likely to misunderstand the underlying strength of Puritanism in its early days if we look too narrowly at its formal structure and overlook its subjective appeal. Puritanism in England was a deep religious mood before it became a creed or platform: indeed, the real failure of Puritanism on both sides of the Atlantic may have been that this mood could not be translated into dogma without losing much of its native force and vigor. When we talk about Puritanism in the years before the Civil Wars, then, we are discussing an emotional tone as well as a body of theory, an ideological stance as well as a political program; and it is important to realize that the tone and the stance were difficult to understand even during the age when they were most profoundly felt.

Originally, "Puritan" seems to have been a term of derision, applied rather loosely to people who expressed some dissatisfaction with the workings of the established Church. Because the scope of these objections was sometimes quite trivial, the term came to suggest an argumentative, stubborn frame of mind, a cheerless concern with technicalities. Elizabeth herself had complained that Puritans "were over-bold with God Almighty, making too many subtle scannings of His blessed will, as lawyers do with human testaments." And another observer noted in 1623:

I find many that are called Puritans; yet few, or none, that will own the name. Whereof the reason sure is this, that 'tis for the most part held a name of infamy; . . . Some I know rejoice in the name; but more sure they be such as least understand it. As he is more generally in these times taken, I suppose we might call him a Church-Rebel, or one that would exclude order that his brain might rule.

To many Englishmen of the period, then, Puritanism represented an   3
annoying exaggeration of conventional values, much like the fundamentalism of our own day. Whatever the particular hue of their discontent, the Puritans seemed to lack an ordinary sense of humor and an ordinary sense of proportion because of their obstinate readiness to challenge the authority of the Church and to "fill the world with brawls about undeterminable tenets."

To the early Stuart Kings, however, these theological eccentricities   4
had a particularly sinister ring. The gentlemen of the coffee houses might scorn the Puritans as a group of cranky, contentious men, but James I and Charles I thought they could see a deep menace in those sober ranks. Puritanism meant to them a religious denomination, a political party, a revolutionary force — in each of these respects a clear danger to the throne. Yet even when royal feeling was most pronounced on the subject, few members of the King's official household, let alone the people of the country generally, could say who the Puritans were or what they were up to. . . .

It is not surprising that James would find it difficult to "define a   5
Puritan," no matter how acutely he sensed a danger to his throne from that quarter, for many of the men who later found themselves caught up in the excitement of the Civil Wars were not sure what brought them there. The Puritan movement was manned by a vast assortment of people: they met together for the first time in the early 1640s, stayed together long enough to take the field against their King, and then began to splinter off into the various directions from which they had come, each of them driven by his own private visions and disciplined by his own private convictions. It was no easy matter for a contemporary observer, nor is it now for a later historian, to understand who these people were or where they eventually went.

The group which emigrated to Massachusetts Bay, however, seems   6
to have been fairly homogeneous in matters of religious doctrine. The thinking of these New England saints has been discussed in a number of excellent works, most notably in the writings of Perry Miller, and thus the notes which follow will be less concerned with the formal content of Puritan theory than with the "world view" this theory helped create.

Although Puritanism was known in its own day as a "dangerous   7
novelty," the original tone of the movement suggested revival far more than it did reform. Generally speaking, the Puritan's faith began with a primitive kind of nostalgia. As a Christian, he longed for an intimate experience of grace, a chance to touch and be touched by God directly; and since he felt frustrated in this design by the strict formalities of the Church, he learned to resent most of the religious institutions invented by society to mediate between God and men. He saw the ritual and ornamentation of the Church service as so much foliage obstructing his

view of God, the intricate hierarchy of the organized Church as little more than an elaborate filter through which his expressions of piety had to be strained. To the extent that he had any policies at all, then, the Puritan wanted to restore the church to the simplicity it had known in the days of the Apostles: he wanted to choose his own words in prayer, to worship in a plain setting, to scrape away the decorations and insignia, the rules and formulae, which had formed like a crust over the primitive core of Christianity. . . .

The Puritans had an instrument of authority to offer which governed   8
their lives as firmly as all the bishops in Christendom — the Holy Writ itself. Perhaps the most important difference between the Puritans and their Anglican countrymen was that they regarded the Bible a complete guide to Christian living, a digest of all the statutes and regulations necessary for human government. The Scriptures not only supplied rules for the broader issues of church polity but for the tiniest details of everyday life as well, and many Puritans were fully capable of demanding that a clergyman remove some emblem from his vestments unless he could justify the extravagance by producing a warrant for it from the pages of the Bible. This, in turn, is what Elizabeth had meant when she likened the Puritans to lawyers and complained of their narrow literality: it often seemed that the Puritans were paying more attention to the footnotes than to the main text of human experience.

Like most revivals, Puritanism did not begin as an organized creed   9
at all. So long as it remained a profound sense of piety shared among a few believers and encouraged by the popular pulpit, Puritanism had a certain freshness and vitality which proved immensely appealing; but when this subjective frame of mind was translated into statements of principle, it became the thorny dogma which James had so much difficulty understanding. The tensions which fed the Puritan's deep longing for grace, the conflicts which sharpened his extraordinary discipline, the anxieties which drove him into a constant fear of sin — all these inner strains looked like so many contradictions when converted into figures of language. It was an emotional and an ideological tone which could not be easily written down on paper.

The first Puritans to reach Massachusetts never saw the contradic-   10
tions in their theory (nor would they have worried about it if they had) and continued to feel that their position was derived from the soundest logic. But it is important to understand that the essential strength of that logic lay in the conviction that truth had been forever discovered in its entirety. Puritan logic was not a method for learning the truth; it was a rhetorical means for communicating it to others. The twentieth-century reader who tries to feel his way through the mists of Puritan argument may sooner or later decide that it is nothing more than a versatile display of sophistry, but he then must remind himself that men who already *know* the truth have scant need for the niceties of inductive reasoning. The truth as seen by the Puritans was wholly clear. God had chosen an elite to represent Him on earth and to join Him in Heaven. People who belonged to this elite learned of their appointment through the agency of a deep conversion experience, giving them a special responsibility and a special competence to control the destinies of others. People who had

never been touched by this moment of grace could have no idea what conversion meant, and thus were simply not qualified to teach the truth or share in the government of men. . . .

Despite the conservatism and intellectualism of so much of their   11
scholarship, the Puritans were sometimes remote from the political drifts of their own age, living in a kind of cultural suspension. To begin with, they had drawn away from many of the cultural landmarks which give each people a sense of their place in human history and human society — the folklore and traditions, the art and literature, the monuments and memories which become a part of their national identity. But beyond this, the Puritans had little interest in or respect for the way in which men ordinarily view their own past. History, as they understood it, was largely a story of religious decline anyway, a weary chronicle of knights and princes, battles and kingdoms, which had no relation at all to the fundamental realities of existence. Reality did not belong to any particular time or place: it originated in the imagination of God, and man's only hope of coming to terms with this truth lay in the devotion of his whole attention to the one document in which God had reviewed His intentions.

The Bible was not just an announcement of God's purpose, however.   12
It was a catalogue of all possible forms of human experience, a digest of history both past and yet to come. Events which occur in the lives of men and give them an illusion that time is passing in some orderly fashion are no more than echoes of thoughts in the mind of God, registered permanently in the Scriptures. And so the Puritan world took its form by analogy rather than by sequence of time. Everything that happens in the present world is only a flickering reproduction of something that has happened before, a repetition of some divine truth, and the Puritans assumed that they could discover the archetypes from which their own experience was derived by careful study of the world around them. In a very real sense, they knew that there is nothing new under the sun.

All of this makes the contradictions of Puritanism seem sharper, and   13
when one considers the various themes that played through the Puritan's mind it becomes easier to understand the conclusion reached by so many of his English contemporaries — that the Puritan approach to life was a fabric woven almost entirely out of paradoxes.

The first paradox becomes apparent when one tries to place the   14
Puritans in the historical context of their own age, for Puritanism seems to be at once a survival from the medieval past and a decided protest against everything that that past had represented. More than any other people of Protestant Europe, the Puritans drew their imagery from late medieval religion, sharing its pervading sense of doom, its desperate piety, and its anxious preoccupation with sin. Yet at the same time, they rejected most of the pageantry and festivity, the color and style, which had once acted to offset the harshness of that cosmology. We find the same fatalism in seventeenth-century Massachusetts as in fifteenth-century France, but nowhere do we see majestic cathedrals to offer sanctuary or joyful bells to soften the terror; nowhere do we see the spirit of a compassionate Virgin. In many ways the Puritans were the most direct descendants of the medieval tradition, but in other ways they were almost the last people in Europe to come to terms with that inheritance.

The second paradox is that the Puritans were able to combine a 15 remarkable degree both of pride and humility in the same general frame. On the one hand, they are unworthy products of this sinful world, base creatures who wallow in greed and act contemptibly before their God. Yet on the other hand, these same creatures are fashioned in the image of angels and have been given a commission from God to convert the heathen, strike down the haughty, punish the sinful, and take upon themselves the authority of acting in His name. And so the Puritan always seems to be exhibiting a double nature. In his confessions he insists that he is worthless and contemptible, but in his professions he declares that it is his special privilege and obligation to challenge all the established traditions in Christendom. Humility is the badge of his sanctity; but sanctity, in turn, is his warrant for converting the whole world to his way of thinking. James I was quite sensitive to this ambivalence when he drew attention to

> the preposterous humility of one of the proud Puritans . . . [who say], "We are all but vile worms, and yet will judge and give Law to our King, but will be judged or controlled by none." Surely there is more pride under such a one's black bonnet, than under Alexander the Great his diadem.

The third paradox is that the Puritan outlook depended for balance 16 upon a constant shift between conviction and uncertainty. The hard logic of their creed required the Puritans always to doubt the evidence of their own senses but never to doubt the fundamental precepts of their religion. Life was a long and often painful search for signs of grace: the seeker had to explore every corner of his own consciousness for signs of conversion, weighing his own thoughts, testing his own moods, probing his every impulse, permitting himself no relief from this self-scrutiny for fear that sin would seep into his soul when his guard was down. At times, the very simplicity of this search can be touching. "I am now forty years old," one mason from Quincy wrote in his diary,

> and cannot but be ashamed to look back and consider how I have spent my lost time; being at a great loss whether any true grace be wrought in my soul or no: corruption in me is very powerful; grace (if any) is very weak and languid. . . .

And at other times the gnawing uncertainty can erupt into a terrible violence, as John Winthrop reports in his journal:

> A woman of the Boston congregation, having been in much trouble of mind about her spiritual estate, at length grew into utter desperation, and could not endure to hear of any comfort, etc., so as one day she took her little infant and threw it into a well, and then came into the house and said, now she was sure she would be damned, for she had drowned her child. . . .

One important effect of this insecurity, however, was to make the 17 Puritan all the surer of the things he did know. The Bible told him the difference between right and wrong, and in his efforts to shape the world to those clear moralities he could be positively ferocious. Massachusetts was a society in which the very idea of intelligent controversy seemed absurd: after all, the truth was as plain as the print on everyone's Bible, and any soul capable of entertaining doubt after this truth had been interpreted for him by the godly clergy must either suffer from a crippling defect or be caught in the snares of Satan himself. If a persuasive argument should jar a Puritan's certitude or a clever line of reasoning confuse him, he had every right to suspect that some devilish mischief was afoot. One day the President of Harvard College, soon to be dismissed for his views on infant baptism, confided his thoughts to one of the leading ministers of the Bay. The latter wrote in his diary:

> That day . . . after I came from him, I had a strange experience: I found hurrying and pressing suggestions against Paedobaptism, and injected scruples and thoughts whether the other way might not be right, and infant baptism an invention of men; and whether I might with good conscience baptise children and the like. And these thoughts were darted in with some impression and left a strange sickliness on my spirit. Yet, methought, it was not hard to discern that they were from the Evil One . . . And it made me fearful to go needlessly to Mr. D[unster]; for methought I found a venom and a poison in his insinuations and discourses against Paedobaptism.

Doubt was indeed a "strange experience" for a Puritan saint, even if, as in the above case, he was one of the finest minds produced in the colony.

In general, then, the Puritan's world was made up of sharpened **18** contrasts on all sides — and this gave him an extraordinary sensitivity to the miraculous. In this respect, too, the Puritans remind us of their medieval forebears. They had the same credulity, the same sense of wonder and mystery, the same ability to see hidden meanings in the rustling of a leaf, a sudden toothache, or some unexpected happening. The voices of God could be heard throughout nature, and the Puritans knew how to listen for them with all the awe of children. . . .

No one really knows how the witchcraft hysteria began, but it orig- **19** inated in the home of the Reverend Samuel Parris, minister of the local church. In early 1692, several girls from the neighborhood began to spend their afternoons in the Parris's kitchen with a slave named Tituba, and it was not long before a mysterious sorority of girls, aged between nine and twenty, became regular visitors to the parsonage. We can only speculate what was going on behind the kitchen door, but we know that Tituba had been brought to Massachusetts from Barbados and enjoyed a reputation in the neighborhood for her skills in the magic arts. As the girls grew closer together, a remarkable change seemed to come over them: perhaps it is not true, as someone later reported, that they went out into the forest to celebrate their own version of a black mass, but it is apparent that they began to live in a state of high tension and shared secrets with one another which were hardly becoming to quiet Puritan maidens.

Before the end of winter, the two youngest girls in the group suc- **20** cumbed to the shrill pitch of their amusements and began to exhibit a most unusual malady. They would scream unaccountably, fall into grotesque convulsions, and sometimes scamper along on their hands and knees making noises like the barking of a dog. No sooner had word gone around about this extraordinary affliction than it began to spread like a contagious disease. All over the community young girls were groveling on the ground in a panic of fear and excitement, and while some of the less credulous townspeople were tempted to reach for their belts in the hopes of strapping a little modesty into them, the rest could only stand by in helpless horror as the girls suffered their torments.

The town's one physician did what he could to stem the epidemic, but he soon exhausted his meager store of remedies and was forced to conclude that the problem lay outside the province of medicine. The Devil had come to Salem Village, he announced; the girls were bewitched. At this disturbing news, ministers from many of the neighboring parishes came to consult with their colleague and offer what advice they might. Among the first to arrive was a thoughtful clergyman named Deodat Lawson, and he had been in town no more than a few hours when he happened upon a frightening exhibition of the devil's handiwork. "In the beginning of the evening," he later recounted of his first day in the village, 21

> I went to give Mr. Parris a visit. When I was there, his kinswoman, Abigail Williams, (about 12 years of age,) had a grievous fit; she was at first hurried with violence to and fro in the room, (though Mrs. Ingersoll endeavored to hold her,) sometimes making as if she would fly, stretching up her arms as high as she could, and crying "whish, whish, whish!" several times. . . . After that, she run to the fire, and began to throw fire brands about the house; and run against the back, as if she would run up the chimney, and, as they said, she had attempted to go into the fire in other fits.

Faced by such clear-cut evidence, the ministers quickly agreed that Satan's new challenge would have to be met with vigorous action, and this meant that the afflicted girls would have to identify the witches who were harassing them.

It is hard to guess what the girls were experiencing during those early days of the commotion. They attracted attention everywhere they went and exercised a degree of power over the adult community which would have been exhilarating under the sanest of circumstances. But whatever else was going on in those young minds, the thought seems to have gradually occurred to the girls that they were indeed bewitched, and after they had been coaxed over and over again to name their tormentors, they finally singled out three women in the village and accused them of witchcraft. 22

Three better candidates could not have been found if all the gossips in New England had met to make the nominations. The first, understandably, was Tituba herself, a woman who had grown up among the rich colors and imaginative legends of Barbados and who was probably acquainted with some form of voodoo. The second, Sarah Good, was a proper hag of a witch if Salem Village had ever seen one. With a pipe clenched in her leathery face she wandered around the countryside neglecting her children and begging from others, and on more than one occasion the old crone had been overheard muttering threats against her neighbors when she was in an unusually sour humor. Sarah Osburne, the third suspect, had a higher social standing than either of her alleged accomplices, but she had been involved in a local scandal a year or two earlier when a man moved into her house some months before becoming her husband. 23

A preliminary hearing was set at once to decide whether the three   24
accused women should be held for trial. The girls were ushered to the
front row of the meeting house, where they took full advantage of the
space afforded them by rolling around in apparent agony whenever some
personal fancy (or the invisible agents of the devil) provoked them to it.
It was a remarkable show. Strange creatures flew about the room pecking
at the girls or taunting them from the rafters, and it was immediately
obvious to everyone that the women on trial were responsible for all the
disorder and suffering. When Sarah Good and Sarah Osburne were called
to the stand and asked why they sent these specters to torment the
girls, they were too appalled to say much in their defense. But when
Tituba took the stand she had a ready answer. A lifetime spent in bondage
is poor training for standing up before a bench of magistrates, and anyway
Tituba was an excitable woman who had breathed the warmer winds of
the Caribbean and knew things about magic her crusty old judges would
never learn. Whatever the reason, Tituba gave her audience one of the
most exuberant confessions ever recorded in a New England courtroom.
She spoke of the creatures who inhabit the invisible world, the dark
rituals which bind them together in the service of Satan; and before she
had ended her astonishing recital she had convinced everyone in Salem
Village that the problem was far worse than they had dared imagine. For
Tituba not only implicated Sarah Good and Sarah Osburne in her own
confession but announced that many other people in the colony were
engaged in the devil's conspiracy against the Bay.

So the hearing that was supposed to bring a speedy end to the affair   25
only stirred up a hidden hornet's nest, and now the girls were urged to
identify other suspects and locate new sources of trouble. Already the
girls had become more than unfortunate victims: in the eyes of the
community they were diviners, prophets, oracles, mediums, for only they
could see the terrible spectres swarming over the countryside and tell
what persons had sent them on their evil errands. As they became caught
up in the enthusiasm of their new work, then, the girls began to reach
into every corner of the community in a search for likely suspects. Martha
Corey was an upstanding woman in the village whose main mistake was
to snort incredulously at the girls' behavior. Dorcas Good, five years old,
was a daughter of the accused Sarah. Rebecca Nurse was a saintly old
woman who had been bedridden at the time of the earlier hearings. Mary
Esty and Sarah Cloyce were Rebecca's younger sisters, themselves accused when they rose in energetic defense of the older woman. And so
it went — John Proctor, Giles Corey, Abigail Hobbs, Bridgit Bishop,
Sarah Wild, Susanna Martin, Dorcas Hoar, the Reverend George Burroughs: as winter turned into spring the list of suspects grew to enormous
length and the Salem jail was choked with people awaiting trial. We know
nothing about conditions of life in prison, but it is easy to imagine the
tensions which must have echoed within those gray walls. Some of the
prisoners had cried out against their relatives and friends in a desperate
effort to divert attention from themselves, others were witless persons
with scarcely a clue as to what had happened to them, and a few (very
few, as it turned out) were accepting their lot with quiet dignity. If we
imagine Sarah Good sitting next to Rebecca Nurse and lighting her rancid

pipe or Tituba sharing views on supernatural phenomena with the Reverend George Burroughs, we may have a rough picture of life in those crowded quarters.

By this time the hysteria had spread well beyond the confines of   26
Salem Village, and as it grew in scope so did the appetites of the young girls. They now began to accuse persons they had never seen from places they had never visited (in the course of which some absurd mistakes were made), yet their word was so little questioned that it was ordinarily warrant enough to put respected people in chains.

The earliest published account of the witchcraft trials was provided by Deodat Lawson, the former minister of Salem mentioned in the preceding selection. Lawson was an interested bystander at the trials; the first "afflictions" occurred in the home of his successor, Reverend Samuel Parris, and some recent gossip had connected the untimely deaths of Lawson's wife and daughter three years earlier to witchcraft. Partly because the charges brought by the purported victims against the accused were so intricate that it was "difficult to draw right Conclusions," Lawson took detailed notes on the proceedings. Then with the encouragement of other citizens and the corrections of the presiding judges, he published A Brief and True Narrative of Some Remarkable Passages Relating to Sundry Persons Afflicted by Witchcraft, at Salem Village Which Happened from the Nineteenth of March to the Fifth of April, 1692. *The following excerpts from the opening of Lawson's narrative introduce three of the accused, Rebecca Nurse ("Goodwife N."), Martha Corey (the first "Goodwife C."), and Sarah Cloyse (the second "Goodwife C."). All three were eventually found guilty; Nurse and Corey were later executed.*

From *A Brief and True Narrative of Persons Afflicted by Witchcraft*
DEODAT LAWSON

On the Nineteenth day of March last I went to Salem Village, and lodged   1
at Nathaniel Ingersols near to the Minister Mr. P's. house, and presently after I came into my Lodging Capt. Walcuts Daughter Mary came to Lieut. Ingersols and spake to me, but, suddenly after as she stood by the door, was bitten, so that she cried out of her Wrist, and looking on it with a Candle, we saw apparently the marks of Teeth both upper and lower set, on each side of her wrist.

In the beginning of the Evening, I went to give Mr. P. a visit. When   2
I was there, his Kins-woman, Abigail Williams, (about 12 years of age,) had a grievous fit; she was at first hurryed with Violence to and fro in the room, (though Mrs. Ingersol endeavoured to hold her,) sometimes makeing as if she would fly, stretching up her arms as high as she could, and crying "Whish, Whish, Whish!" several times; Presently after she

said there was Goodw. N. and said, "Do you not see her? Why there she stands!" And the said Goodw. N. offered her The Book, but she was resolved she would not take it, saying Often, "I wont, I wont, I wont, take it, I do not know what Book it is: I am sure it is none of Gods Book, it is the Divels Book, for ought I know." After that, she run to the Fire, and begun to throw Fire Brands, about the house; and run against the Back, as if she would run up Chimney, and, as they said, she had attempted to go into the Fire in other Fits.

On Lords Day, the Twentieth of March, there were sundry of the afflicted Persons at Meeting, as, Mrs. Pope, and Goodwife Bibber, Abigail Williams, Mary Walcut, Mary Lewes, and Docter Griggs' Maid. There was also at Meeting, Goodwife C.° (who was afterward Examined on suspicion of being a Witch:) They had several Sore Fits, in the time of Publick Worship, which did something interrupt me in my First Prayer; being so unusual. After Psalm was Sung, Abigail Williams said to me, "Now stand up, and Name your Text": And after it was read, she said, "It is a long Text." In the beginning of Sermon, Mrs. Pope, a Woman afflicted, said to me, "Now there is enough of that." And in the afternoon, Abigail Williams upon my referring to my Doctrine said to me, "I know no Doctrine you had, If you did name one, I have forgot it."   3

In Sermon time when Goodw. C was present in the Meetinghouse Ab. W. called out, "Look where Goodw. C sits on the Beam suckling her Yellow bird betwixt her fingers"! Anne Putnam another Girle afflicted said there was a Yellow-bird sat on my hat as it hung on the Pin in the Pulpit: but those that were by, restrained her from speaking aloud about it.   4

On Monday the 21st of March, The Magistrates of Salem appointed to come to Examination of Goodw. C. And about twelve of the Clock, they went into the Meeting-House, which was Thronged with Spectators: Mr. Noyes began with a very pertinent and pathetic Prayer; and Goodwife C. being called to answer to what was Alledged against her, she desired to go to Prayer, which was much wondred at, in the presence of so many hundred people: The Magistrates told her, they would not admit it; they came not there to hear her Pray, but to Examine her, in what was Alledged against her. The Worshipful Mr. Hathorne asked her, Why she Afflicted those Children? she said, she did not Afflict them. He asked her, who did then? she said, "I do not know; How should I know?" The Number of the Afflicted Persons were about that time Ten, *viz.* Four Married Women, Mrs. Pope, Mrs. Putman, Goodw. Bibber, and an Ancient Woman, named Goodall, three Maids, Mary Walcut, Mercy Lewes, at Thomas Putman's, and a Maid at Dr. Griggs's, there were three Girls from 9 to 12 Years of Age, each of them, or thereabouts, *viz.* Elizabeth Parris, Abigail Williams and Ann Putman; these were most of them at G. C's Examination, and did vehemently accuse her in the Assembly of afflicting them, by Biting, Pinching, Strangling, etc. And that they did in their Fit see her Likeness coming to them, and bringing a Book to them, she said, she had no Book; they affirmed, she had a   5

Goodwife C: Martha Corey.

Yellow-Bird, that used to suck betwixt her Fingers, and being asked about it, if she had any Familiar Spirit, that attended her, she said, She had no Familiarity with any such thing. She was a Gospel Woman: which Title she called her self by; and the Afflicted Persons told her, ah! She was, A Gospel Witch. Ann Putman did there affirm, that one day when Lieutenant Fuller was at Prayer at her Fathers House, she saw the shape of Goodw. C. and she thought Goodw. N. Praying at the same time to the Devil, she was not sure it was Goodw. N. she thought it was; but very sure she saw the Shape of G. C. The said C. said, they were poor, distracted Children, and no heed to be given to what they said. Mr. Hathorne and Mr. Noyes replyed, it was the judgment of all that were present, they were Bewitched, and only she, the Accused Person said, they were Distracted. It was observed several times, that if she did but bite her Under lip in time of Examination the persons afflicted were bitten on their armes and wrists and produced the Marks before the Magistrates, Ministers and others. And being watched for that, if she did but Pinch her Fingers, or Graspe one hand hard in another, they were Pinched and produced the Marks before the Magistrates, and Spectators. After that, it was observed, that if she did but lean her Breast against the Seat, in the Meeting House, (being the Barr at which she stood,) they were afflicted. Particularly Mrs. Pope complained of grievous torment in her Bowels as if they were torn out. She vehemently accused said C. as the instrument, and first threw her Muff at her; but that flying not home, she got off her Shoe, and hit Goodwife C. on the head with it. After these postures were watched, if said C. did but stir her feet, they were afflicted in their Feet, and stamped fearfully. The afflicted persons asked her why she did not go to the company of Witches which were before the Meeting house mustering? Did she not hear the Drum beat? They accused her of having Familiarity with the Devil, in the time of Examination, in the shape of a Black man whispering in her ear; they affirmed, that her Yellow-Bird sucked betwixt her Fingers in the Assembly; and order being given to see if there were any sign, the Girl that saw it said, it was too late now; she had removed a Pin, and put it on her head; which was found there sticking upright.

They told her, she had Covenanted with the Devil for ten years, six of them were gone, and four more to come. She was required by the Magistrates to answer that Question in the Catechism, "How many persons be there in the God-Head?" she answered it but oddly, yet was there no great thing to be gathered from it; she denied all that was charged upon her, and said, They could not prove a Witch; she was that Afternoon Committed to Salem-Prison; and after she was in Custody, she did not so appear to them, and afflict them as before. . . . 6

On the 25th of March, (as Capt. Stephen Sewal, of Salem, did afterwards inform me) Eliza. Paris had sore Fits, at his house, which much troubled himself, and his wife, so as he told me they were almost discouraged. She related, that the great Black Man came to her, and told her, if she would be ruled by him, she should have whatsoever she desired, and go to a Golden City. She relating this to Mrs. Sewall, she told the child, it was the Divel, and he was a Lyar from the Beginning, 7 and bid her tell him so, if he came again: which she did accordingly, at the next coming to her, in her fits.

On the 26th of March, Mr. Hathorne, Mr. Corwin, and Mr. Higison were at the Prison-Keepers House, to Examine the Child, and it told them there, it had a little Snake that used to Suck on the lowest Joynt of it[s] Fore-Finger; and when they inquired where, pointing to other places, it told them, not there, but there, pointing on the Lowest point of Fore-Finger; where they Observed a deep Red Spot, about the Bigness of a Flea-bite, they asked who gave it that Snake? whether the great Black man, it said no, its Mother gave it.   **8**

The 31 of March there was a Publick Fast kept at Salem on account of these Afflicted Persons. And Abigail Williams said, that the Witches had a Sacrament that day at an house in the Village, and that they had Red Bread and Red Drink. The first of April, Mercy Lewis, Thomas Putman's Maid, in her fitt, said, 'they did eat Red Bread like Mans Flesh, and would have had her eat some: but she would not; but turned away her head, and Spit at them, and said, "I will not Eat, I will not Drink, it is Blood," etc. She said, "That is not the Bread of Life, that is not the Water of Life; Christ gives the Bread of Life, I will have none of it!" This first of April also Mercy Lewis aforesaid saw in her fitt a White man and was with him in a Glorious Place, which had no Candles nor Sun, yet was full of Light and Brightness; where was a great Multitude in White glittering Robes, and they Sung the Song in the fifth of Revelation the Ninth verse, and the 110 Psalm, and the 149 Psalm; and said with her self, "How long shall I stay here? let me be along with you": She was loth to leave this place, and grieved that she could tarry no longer. This Whiteman hath appeared several times to some of them, and given them notice how long it should be before they had another Fit, which was sometimes a day, or day and half, or more or less: it hath fallen out accordingly.   **9**

The third of April, the Lords-Day, being Sacrament-day, at the Village, Goodw. C.° upon Mr. Parris's naming his Text, John 6, 70, *One of them is a Devil*, the said Goodw. C. went immediately out of the Meeting-House, and flung the door after her violently, to the amazement of the Congregation: She was afterward seen by some in their Fits, who said, "O Goodw. C., I did not think to see you here!" (and being at their Red bread and drink) said to her, "Is this a time to receive the Sacrament, you ran-away on the Lords-Day, and scorned to receive it in the Meeting-House, and, Is this a time to receive it? I wonder at you!" This is the summ of what I either saw my self, or did receive Information from persons of undoubted Reputation and Credit.   **10**

Goodw. C: Sarah Cloyse, sister of Rebecca Nurse.

Cotton Mather (1663–1728) was an eminent clergyman and author, the son of an equally famous clergyman and author, Increase Mather (1639–1723). The Mathers lived in Boston, not Salem, and Cotton Mather observed few, if any, of the trials firsthand. But he had written a tract about witchcraft in 1689, and the new Governor William Phipps asked him to address the ongoing Salem crisis, giving him full access to the court records. The Wonders of the Invisible World *was immediately published in 1693. In it, Mather enthusiastically supported the actions of the Salem authorities, including the executions. Yet indirectly the book also helped put the executions to a stop. For Mather's discussion of "spectral evidence" made it clear that the devil could assume the shape of innocent as well as guilty persons. Once the possibility was admitted that the specter of Goodwife G., and not necessarily Goodwife G. herself, had committed some evil deed, the reliability of most evidence was thrown in doubt. While executions soon stopped, accusations and arrests abated only after the governor's wife was charged and after a Boston man scared off his accusers by suing them for defamation of character.*

We include here several excerpts from Wonders: *first, an early section establishing the existence of devils; next, a conjecture about the role of the Puritans in the devilish wilderness of the new world; and then a description of recent witchly activity, along with Mather's consideration of the problem of "spectral evidence."*

From *The Wonders of the Invisible World*
COTTON MATHER

There is a *little room* for [hope], that the *great wrath* of the Devil, will   1
not prove the present ruine of our poor *New-England* in particular. I
believe, there never was a poor Plantation, more pursued by the *Wrath*
of the *Devil*, than our poor *New-England;* and that which makes our
condition very much the more deplorable is, that the *wrath* of the *great
God* Himself, at the same time also presses hard upon us. It was a rousing
alarm to the Devil, when a great Company of English *Protestants* and
Puritans, came to erect Evangelical Churches, in a corner of the World,
where he had reign'd without any controul for many Ages; and it is a
vexing *Eye-sore* to the Devil, that our Lord Christ should be known, and
own'd, and preached in this *howling Wilderness.* Wherefor he has left no
Stone unturned, that so he might undermine his Plantation, and force us
out of our Country.

First, The Indian *Powawes,* used all their Sorceries to molest the   2
first Planters here; but God said unto them, *Touch them not!* Then,
Seducing Spirits come to *root* in this Vineyard, but God so rated them
off, that they had not prevail'd much farther than the Edges of our Land.
After this, we have had a continuel *blast* upon some of our principal Grain,
annually diminishing a vast part of our *ordinary Food.* Herewithal, wasting
Sicknesses, especially Burning and Mortal Agues, have Shot the Arrows
of Death in at our Windows. Next, we have had many Adversaries of
our own Language, who have been perpetually assaying to deprive us of
those *English Liberties,* in the encouragement whereof these Territories
have been settled. As if this had not been enough; The *Tawnies* among
whom we came, have watered our Soil with the Blood of many Hundreds
of our Inhabitants. Desolating *Fires* also have many times laid the chief

Treasure of the whole Province in Ashes. As for *Losses* by Sea, *they* have been multiply'd upon us: and particularly in the present *French War*, the whole English Nation have observ'd that no part of the Nation has proportionally had so many Vessels taken, as our poor *New-England*. Besides all which, now at last the Devils are (if I may so speak) *in Person* come down upon us with such a *Wrath*, as is justly *much*, and will quickly be *more*, the Astonishment of the World. Alas, I may sigh over *this* Wilderness, as *Moses* did over *his*, in *Psal.* 90.7, 9, *We are consumed by thine Anger, and by thy Wrath we are troubled: All our days are passed away in thy Wrath*. And I may add this unto it, *The Wrath of the Devil too has been troubling and spending of us, all our days.*

But what will become of this poor *New-England* after all? Shall we   3
sink, expire, perish, before the *short time* of the Devil shall be finished? I must confess, That when I consider the lamentable *Unfruitfulness* of men, among us, under as powerful and perspicuous Dispensations of the Gospel, as are in the World; and when I consider the declining state of the *Power of Godliness* in our Churches, with the most horrible Indisposition that perhaps ever was, to recover out of this declension; I cannot but *Fear* lest it comes to this, and lest an *Asiatic* Removal of Candlesticks come upon us. But upon some other Accounts, I would fain *hope* otherwise; and I will give *you* therefore the opportunity to try what Inferences may be drawn from these probable Prognostications.

I say, *First*, That surely, *America's* Fate, must at the long run include   4
New-Englands in it. What was the design of our God, in bringing over so many *Europeans* hither of later years? Of what use or state will *America* be, when the *Kingdom of God* shall come? If it must all be the Devils propriety, while the *saved Nations* of the other Hemisphere shall be *Walking in the Light of the New Jerusalem*, Our *New-England* has then, 'tis likely, done all that it was erected for. But if God have a purpose to make here a seat for any of *those glorious things which are spoken of thee, O thou City of God;* then even thou, *O New-England*, art within a very little while of better days than ever yet have dawn'd upon thee. . . .

That the Devil is *come down unto us with great Wrath*, we find, we   5
feel, we now deplore. In many ways, for many years hath the Devil been assaying to Extirpate the Kingdom of our Lord Jesus here. *New-England* may complain of the Devil, as in *Psal.* 129.1, 2, *Many a time have they afflicted me, from my Youth, may* New-England *now say; Many a time have they afflicted me from my Youth; yet they have not prevailed against me.* But now there is a more than ordinary *affliction*, with which the *Devil* is Galling of us: and such an one as is indeed Unparallelable. The things confessed by *Witches*, and the things endured by *Others*, laid together, amount unto this account of our Affliction. The *Devil*, Exhibiting himself ordinarily as a small *Black man*, has decoy'd a fearful knot of proud, froward, ignorant, envious and malicious creatures, to lift themselves in his horrid Service, by entring their Names in a *Book* by him tendred unto them. These *Witches*, whereof above a Score have now *Confessed*, and *shown their Deeds*, and some are now tormented by the Devils, for *Confessing*, have met in Hellish *Randezvouzes*, wherein the Confessors do say, they have had their Diabolical Sacraments, imitating the *Baptism*

and the *Supper* of our Lord. In these hellish meetings, these Monsters have associated themselves to do no less a thing than, *To destroy the Kingdom of our Lord Jesus Christ, in these parts of the World;* and in order hereunto, First they each of them have their *Spectres,* or Devils, commission'd by them, & representing of them, to be the Engines of their Malice. By these wicked *Spectres,* they seize poor people about the Country, with various & bloudy *Torments;* and of those evidently Preternatural torments there are some have dy'd. They have bewitched some, even so far as to make *Self-destroyers:* and others are in many Towns here and there languishing under their *Evil hands.* The people thus afflicted, are miserably scratched and bitten, so that the Marks are most visible to all the World, but the causes utterly invisible; and the same Invisible Furies do most visibly stick Pins into the bodies of the afflicted, and *scale* them, and hideously distort, and disjoint all their members, besides a thousand other sorts of Plagues beyond these of any natural diseases which they give unto them. Yea, they sometimes drag the poor people out of their chambers, and carry them over Trees and Hills, for divers miles together. A large part of the persons tortured by these Diabolical *Spectres,* are horribly tempted by them, sometimes with fair promises, and sometimes with hard threatnings, but always with felt miseries, to sign the *Devils Laws* in a Spectral Book laid before them; which two or three of these poor Sufferers, being by their tiresome sufferings overcome to do, they have immediately been released from all their miseries, and they appear'd in *Spectre* then to Torture those that were before their Fellow-Sufferers. The *Witches* which by their covenant with the Devil, are become Owners of *Spectres,* are oftentimes by their own *Spectres* required and compelled to give their consent, for the molestation of some, which they had no mind otherwise to fall upon; and cruel depredations are then made upon the Vicinage. In the Prosecution of these Witchcrafts, among a thousand other unaccountable things, the *Spectres* have an odd faculty of cloathing the most substantial and corporeal Instruments of Torture, with Invisibility, while the wounds thereby given have been the most palpable things in the World; so that the Sufferers assaulted with Instruments of Iron, wholly unseen to the standers by, though, to their cost, seen by themselves, have, upon snatching, wrested the Instruments out of the *Spectres* hands, and every one has then immediately not only *beheld,* but *handled,* an Iron Instrument taken by a Devil from a Neighbour. These wicked *Spectres* have proceeded so far, as to steal several quantities of Mony from divers people, part of which Money, has, before sufficient Spectators, been dropt out of the Air into the Hands of the Sufferers, while the *Spectres* have been urging them to subscribe their *Covenant with Death.* In such extravagant ways have these Wretches propounded, the *Dragooning* of as many as they can, in their own Combination, and the *Destroying* of others, with lingring, spreading, deadly diseases; till our Countrey should at last become too hot for us. Among the Ghastly Instances of the *success* which those Bloody Witches have had, we have seen even some of their own Children, so dedicated unto the Devil, that in their Infancy, it is found, the *Imps* have sucked them, and rendred them Venemous to a Prodigy. We have also seen the Devils first batteries upon the Town, where the first Church of our Lord in this Colony was gathered, producing those distractions, which have almost ruin'd the Town. We have seen likewise the *Plague* reaching afterwards into other Towns far and near, where the Houses of good Men have the Devils filling of them with terrible Vexations!

This is the Descent, which, it seems, the Devil has now made upon us. But that which makes this Descent the more formidable, is; The *multitude* and *quality* of Persons accused of an interest in this *Witchcraft,* by the Efficacy of the *Spectres* which take their Name and shape upon them; causing very many good and wise Men to fear, That many *innocent,* yea, and some *vertuous* persons, are by the Devils in this matter, imposed upon; That the Devils have obtain'd the power, to take on them the likeness of harmless people, and in that likeness to afflict other people, and be so abused by Prestigious *Demons,* that upon their look or touch, the afflicted shall be odly affected. Arguments from the *Providence of God,* on the one side, and from our *Charity* towards *Man* on the other side, have made this now to become a most agitated Controversie among us. There is an *Agony* produced in the Minds of Men, lest the Devil should sham us with *Devices,* of perhaps a finer Thred, than was ever yet practised upon the World. The whole business is become hereupon so *Snarled,* and the determination of the Question one way or another, so *dismal,* that our Honourable Judges have a Room for *Jehoshaphat's* Exclamation, *We know not what to do!* They have used, as Judges have heretofore done, the *Spectral Evidences,* to introduce their further En-quiries into the *Lives* of the persons accused; and they have thereupon, by the wonderful Providence of God, been so strengthened with *other evidences,* that some of the *Witch Gang* have been fairly Executed. But what shall be done, as to those against whom the *evidence* is chiefly founded in the *dark world?* Here they do solemnly demand our Addresses to the *Father of Lights,* on their behalf. But in the mean time, the Devil improves the *Darkness* of this Affair, to push us into a *Blind Mans Buffet,* and we are even ready to be *sinfully,* yea, hotly, and madly, mauling one another in the *dark.*

6

Here are some opinions offered by scholars and critics about Nathaniel Haw-thorne or "Young Goodman Brown." Judge which opinions seem most interesting or persuasive to you, and think about how you might make use of one or more of them in a well-argued essay.

■ A Sampling of Critical Responses

ÉMILE MONTEGUT, 1879

This marked love of cases of conscience; this taciturn, scornful cast of mind; this habit of seeing sin everywhere, and hell always gaping open; this dusky gaze bent always upon a damned world, and a nature draped in mourning; these lonely conversations of the imagination with the conscience; this pitiless analysis resulting from a perpetual examination of one's self, and from the tortures of a heart closed before men and open to God — all these elements of the Puritan character have passed into Mr. Hawthorne, or, to speak more justly, have filtered into him, through a long succession of generations.

> — Émile Montegut, a French critic quoted by Henry James
> in *Hawthorne* (1879)

HENRY JAMES, 1879

Nothing is more curious and interesting than this almost exclusively *imported* character of the sense of sin in Hawthorne's mind; it seems to exist there merely for an artistic or literary purpose. He had ample cognizance of the Puritan conscience; it was his natural heritage; it was reproduced in him; looking into his soul, he found it there. But his relation to it was only, as one may say, intellectual; it was not moral and theological. He played with it, and used it as a pigment; he treated it, as the metaphysicians say, objectively. He was not discomposed, disturbed, haunted by it, in the manner of its usual and regular victims, who had not the little postern door of fancy to slip through, to the other side of the wall. . . . It was a necessary condition for a man of Hawthorne's stock that if his imagination should take license to amuse itself, it should at least select this grim precinct of the Puritan morality for its playground. He speaks of the dark disapproval with which his old ancestors, in the case of their coming to life, would see him trifling himself away as a story-teller. But how far more darkly would they have frowned could they have understood that he had converted the very principle of their own being into one of his toys!

> — Henry James, *Hawthorne* (1879)

D. H. LAWRENCE, 1923

1   You *must* look through the surface of American art, and see the inner diabolism of the symbolic meaning. Otherwise it is all mere childishness.

2   That blue-eyed darling Nathaniel knew disagreeable things in his inner soul. He was careful to send them out in disguise.

3   Always the same. The deliberate consciousness of Americans so fair and smooth-spoken, and the under-consciousness so devilish. *Destroy! destroy! destroy!* hums the under-consciousness. *Love and produce! Love and produce!* cackles the upper consciousness. And the world hears only the Love-and-produce cackle. Refuses to hear the hum of destruction underneath. Until such time as it will *have* to hear.

4   The American has got to destroy. It is his destiny. It is his destiny to destroy the whole corpus of the white psyche, the white consciousness. And he's got to do it secretly. As the growing of a dragon-fly inside a chrysalis or cocoon destroys the larva grub, secretly.

> — D. H. Lawrence, *Studies in Classic American Literature* (1923)

RICHARD HARTER FOGLE, 1952

"Young Goodman Brown" is generally felt to be one of Hawthorne's more difficult tales, from the ambiguity of the conclusions which may be drawn from it. Its hero, a naive young man who accepts both society in general and his fellow men as individuals at their own valuation, is in one terrible night confronted with the vision of human evil, and is ever afterwards "a stern, a sad, a darkly meditative, a distrustful, if not a desperate man . . ." whose "dying hour was gloom." So far we are clear enough, but there are confusing factors. In the first place, are the events of the night merely subjective, a dream, or do they actually occur? Again, at the crucial point in his ordeal Goodman Brown summons the strength to cry to his wife Faith, "look up to heaven, and resist the evil one." It would appear from this that he had successfully resisted the supreme temptation — but evidently he is not therefore saved. Henceforth, "on the Sabbath day, when the congregation were singing a holy psalm, he could not listen because an anthem of sin rushed loudly upon his ear and drowned all the blessed strain." On the other hand he is not wholly lost, for he is only at intervals estranged from "the bosom of Faith." Has Hawthorne failed to control the implications of his allegory?

— Richard Harter Fogle, *Hawthorne's Fiction:*
The Light and the Dark (1964)

HARRY LEVIN, 1958

Hawthorne, like his story-teller, did not altogether put the ministry behind him when he rejected it as a possible calling; the possibility often rearises; and if it does not break up his entertainment, it gives his stories their homiletic undertone.

— Harry Levin, *The Power of Blackness* (1958)

PAUL W. MILLER, 1959

In "Young Goodman Brown," then, Hawthorne, as well as "explaining" the Salem witch trials, is pleading that what survives of Puritan rigorism in society be sloughed off, and replaced by a striving for virtue starting from the confession of common human weakness. Such a society would be based upon the firm foundation of humility and honesty rather than upon the sinking sands of human pride and the hypocrisy that accompanies it.

— Paul W. Miller, "Hawthorne's 'Young Goodman Brown':
Cynicism or Meliorism?" (1959)

MELVIN W. ASKEW, 1962

In a great number of his best short stories and tales . . . Hawthorne deals with a man who stands on the threshold of loss of innocence. . . . When the protagonist appears in each of these stories, he has just begun to love, or he is soon to be married, or he has only recently been married. Each character, then, is faced with the prospect of assuming mature responsibilities, and each story is an account of how he responds to this crucial psychological situation. . . .

Although the fall is the central theme in Hawthorne's fiction, even in most of those works which do not precisely imitate the matter of Eden or Adam, Hawthorne's characters obviously do not fall from God's grace, or into a theologically conceived hell or heaven. Nor is their "sin" always a theological sin, or their "guilt" theologically construed. They fall, rather, into the worldly, humanistic, and realistic equivalent of these; that is to say, they fall into inhumanity or humanity. If they do not accept the conditions of their fall, the facts of the fallen world, or the knowledge by which their fall was accomplished, they live disoriented in a temporal, dark, and human hell.

— Melvin W. Askew, "Hawthorne, the Fall, and the Psychology
of Maturity" (1962)

FREDERICK C. CREWS, 1966

Was Hawthorne's temperament that of a dogmatic moralist? Everything we hear about him suggests the opposite: he was peculiarly diffident, and rarely held to the same opinion for very long. Presumably, then, the doubting habit itself might be given prominence in a fair account of Hawthorne's mind. And indeed, once we have ceased trying to make him into a source of oracular wisdom, we perceive that Hawthorne's keynote was neither piety nor impiety, but ambivalence. There is in his writings, as Philip Rahv observed long ago, "a submerged intensity and passion — a tangled imagery of unrest and longing for experience and regret at its loss. . . . He was haunted not only by the guilt of his desires but also by the guilt of his denial of them" ("The Dark Lady of Salem," *Image and Idea: Fourteen Essays on Literary Themes*, 1949). In short, Hawthorne was emotionally engaged in his fiction, and the emotions he displays are those of a self-divided, self-tormented man.

— Frederick C. Crews, *The Sins of the Fathers: Hawthorne's*
Psychological Themes (1966)

LEO B. LEVY, 1975

For Hawthorne, the loss of faith is always imminent, a danger that increases in proportion to our involvement in a moral reality that is always more unsettling than we like to believe. His concern in "Young Goodman Brown," apart from describing the terrors of the Puritan struggle for faith, is with our inability to foresee the consequences of our choices or to judge the nature of the moral forces that press upon us. We can easily move past the point of return, and, like Goodman Brown, find that it is too late for what we want and need. Brown's last cry for Faith is the most poignant moment of the story, expressing his need to assimilate the experiences through which he has passed, and even his capacity to do so. . . . The reader is not less stunned than Brown himself, since he cannot easily resolve the paradox into which he has been led. He saw Brown at the outset abandon Faith; if that were all that he is meant to see, the tale would be very simple. But now the reader finds that Faith has deserted Brown — a distinction that may seem elusive but is nevertheless the crux upon which everything turns. . . .

Faith (or faith) becomes unresponsive, it disappears, and when it reappears it stands in the midst of all that it dreads. If, awaking at midnight, Goodman Brown shrinks from the bosom of Faith, it is because he has taken the full measure of her duplicity. "Such loss of faith is ever one of the saddest results of sin," Hawthorne says of Hester Prynne, and in *The Scarlet Letter* he castigates "the Fiend" for leaving nothing "for this poor sinner to revere." But in "Young Goodman Brown" it is Faith, not Satan or the sinner, whose defection is at issue.

> — Leo B. Levy, "The Problem of Faith in 'Young
> Goodman Brown' " (1975)

JAMES L. WILLIAMSON, 1981

Going to the devil, in "Young Goodman Brown," means not just encountering certain unsettling insights into the terrible and the grotesque in human experience, but also confronting a mocking, satiric attitude toward such revelations. The devils who haunt Brown's woods know how to laugh; and there is a kernel of devilish wisdom in the first figure's words to Brown during "a fit of irrepressible mirth": " 'Ha!ha!ha!' shouted he, again and again; then composing himself, 'Well, go on, Goodman Brown, go on; but pr'y thee, don't kill me with laughing!' " Could Brown learn to laugh, that is, could he learn to take an ironic view toward his experience in the Salem woods, then he might well begin to exorcise his tormenting devils. He will never be able to dismiss their words, but he might learn to live with them. . . .

Brown's complacent faith in saintly ancestors and angelic wives, as well as a moral order that reflects a clear-cut segregation between good and evil, makes him an inviting target for the devils' satire.

> — James L. Williamson, " 'Young Goodman Brown': Hawthorne's
> 'Devil in Manuscript' " (1981)

AGNES McNEILL DONOHUE, 1985

The structure of "Young Goodman Brown" is apparently quite simple and circular — from town to forest to town — but a deeper structure, one dictating the gloomy ending, consists of a series of Calvinist principles which Young Goodman Brown acknowledges for everyone but himself. He believes that he, but no one else, can spend one night in the forest consorting with the devil and then return the next day, unblemished, to cling to the skirts of Faith " 'and follow her to Heaven.' " After he accompanies the devil into the wilderness — the forest — Goodman Brown is unable to stop because of "the instinct that guides mortal man to evil"; here he admits that his will is not free. Goodman Brown casually assumes the election of all those "good people" whom he knows — Goody Cloyse, Deacon Gookin, the minister — but as Calvin warns, Goodman Brown learns they are hypocrites, whited sepulchres. Laughing in despair, Goodman says: " 'Come, devil! for to thee is this world given' "; here he admits his total lack of faith. When Goodman Brown returns from the forest, he is a "desperate man," which in Calvinist terms tells us that he had been deluded about having faith; his consenting to diabolism in the forest makes clear his reprobation. He returns to the clearing — i.e., the village — in despondency, terrified of every one else's sin: "he shrank from the bosom of Faith, and at morning or eventide, when the family knelt down at prayer, he scowled, and muttered to himself, and gazed sternly at his wife, and turned away." At his death, "they carved no hopeful verse upon his tomb-stone; for his dying hour was gloom." According to Calvin, only the reprobate, men unelected and without faith, can so despair. Thus, this remarkable story set in Puritan Salem is Hawthorne's study of the most contemptible of men: the hypocrite reprobate who says he will put off his faith for one night of evil and then resume it, who gives himself over to the devil and resulting despair, and who then saturninely judges as damned all those around him except himself. Hawthorne's Calvinism (which is the only explanation of his grave and solemn treatment of the darkling evil of witchcraft) ordains this story's ironic structure and tone.

— Agnes McNeill Donohue, *Hawthorne:*
Calvin's Ironic Stepchild (1985)

MICHAEL COLACURCIO, 1984

Hawthorne's deepest interest and intentions really were in some fundamental way historical. Thus my own view of Hawthorne as "moral historian."

"Historian" not in any sense so literalistic as to suggest that his primary concern was to re-tell or to re-discover the actual events of some memorable or significant but forgotten occasion — even though Hawthorne himself turns out to have been astonishingly learned in exactly this literal way, and even though the properly disposed reader is often forced to make himself knowledgeable in order to appreciate some of Hawthorne's most telling ironies. . . . But "historian" primarily in the sense that the intention which reveals itself in the best of the early tales is the wish to recover the affective quality of human lives lived under conditions or assumptions different from those which prevailed in his own later and more liberal age. Or, alternatively, the desire to re-enact the subtle process by which a solid but often unlovely past had thrown its long and often darkening shadow upon an equally solid and apparently sunnier present. Others may argue whether or not such intentions discover an interest in "history *as history*." What Hawthorne tells us, however, enough times for us to consider believing him, is that imaginative literature is properly competent and perhaps ideally suited to assist us in just such a civilizing and humanizing procedure.

— Michael Colacurcio, *The Province of Piety* (1984)

Questions for Argument

1. Employing any of the chapter's materials that you find helpful, develop an argument that "Young Goodman Brown" reveals Nathaniel Hawthorne's concerns as a "moral historian."

2. Richard Fogle raises a basic uncertainty about the outcome of the story, namely that it's hard to say whether Goodman Brown is "saved" or "damned." Consider the possible evidence on both sides of this question and then write an essay arguing for whichever side you find more persuasive. Use both sets of evidence by introducing the weaker side first and then letting the stronger evidence overcome it. If you find both sides equally persuasive, balance the two sets of evidence and admit your indecision.

3. Contrast the views of Émile Montegut and Paul W. Miller on Hawthorne's attitude toward Puritanism. After articulating the difference between their perspectives, write an essay analyzing the story as each critic might do. Organize your essay so as to favor the view that you find more persuasive.

4. Many readers have felt, as Miller does, that "Young Goodman Brown" is Hawthorne's way of "explaining" the Salem witch trials. You might find this puzzling, since nowhere in the story does Hawthorne explicitly refer to the trials. Reread the selections by Deodat Lawson and Cotton Mather that touch on the trials, then develop an argument about whether or not "Young Goodman Brown" explains anything about the witchcraft episode.

5. Kai T. Erikson claims to find several paradoxes, or contradictions, at the heart of "the Puritan approach to life." By trying out this historical perspective on "Young Goodman Brown" argue whether or not Hawthorne treats Puritanism as something paradoxical.

6. Melvin Askew makes reference to the Garden of Eden story. After consulting the relevant passage in the Bible (see Genesis 2:15–3:24), argue for its applicability, inapplicability, or partial applicability to "Young Goodman Brown."

7. Several of the critics stress sexuality in reading "Young Goodman Brown." Construct your own sexual interpretation of the story, basing your view on specific passages in the text. Is sex at the heart of the story?

8. After looking at the passage by Louise DeSalvo, offer a feminist interpretation of "Young Goodman Brown." Consider the images of women offered by the story and the roles available to women in Salem society. For a broader perspective, you might look back at the readings in Chapter 8, specifically those by Constance Cronin and Jane Margold and Donna Bellorado.

9. D. H. Lawrence's mention of the "white psyche" seems to emerge from nowhere. But let it prompt you to think about possible racial overtones in "Young Goodman Brown." Do you find any evidence of racism in Hawthorne, Brown, or the Salem community? Evaluate that evidence

and argue whether it has a significant shaping effect on the way we should read the story.

10. Several critics speak of Hawthorne's use of "symbols." But *symbolism* is a very slippery word in literary criticism and not everyone seems to mean the same thing by it. After rereading the story and the critical comments, classify some of the possible symbols in "Young Goodman Brown." Which of these symbols in your opinion, are crucial to a meaningful interpretation of the story?

11. Harry Levin claims that Hawthorne's tales are like sermons, at least in their "homiletic undertone." Do you find this true of "Young Goodman Brown"? Argue for or against an interpretation of the story as a sermon, a lecture on moral conduct.

12. Elsewhere in their books, both Frederick C. Crews and Richard Fogle make observations about Hawthorne's style. Here is what Fogle says:

> The deliberate haziness and multiple implications of its meaning are counterbalanced by the firm clarity of its technique, in structure and in style.
>
> This clarity is embodied in the lucid simplicity of the basic action; in the skillful foreshadowing by which the plot is bound together; in the balance of episode and scene; in the continuous use of contrast; in the firmness and selectivity of Hawthorne's pictorial composition; in the carefully arranged climactic order of incident and tone; in the detachment and irony of Hawthorne's attitude; and finally in the purity, the grave formality, and the rhetorical balance of the style. (p. 22)

Here is what Crews says:

> Hawthorne's balance between confession and evasion is reflected in his style, whose distance and abstraction are often confused with Augustan serenity. The meditative poise, the polite irony, the antitheses, the formal diction, and the continual appeal to sentiments that are generally shared, all serve to neutralize the dangerous knowledge that lies at the bottom of his plots. (p. 12)

After wrestling with these general descriptions as best you can, offer your own analysis of Hawthorne's style in "Young Goodman Brown." Decide what you mean by style and illustrate with specific passages from the text. Make your observations serve a central interpretive purpose.

13. If Hawthorne read Cotton Mather, what do you think he felt about him? Develop an argument that "Young Goodman Brown" implies Hawthorne's attitude toward that earlier American writer.

14. Develop the argument that "Young Goodman Brown" expresses Hawthorne's personal sense of guilt. Make sure to define what you mean by "personal" and "guilt."

15. Frederick C. Crews's reading of Hawthorne's fiction is psychoanalytic in approach. Psychoanalytic interpretations can vary a good deal, but we

can offer a few generalizations about them. Psychoanalytic readings stress the pressure of unconscious feelings, including fantasies and dreams, and their capacity for distorting and confusing everyday life. They also stress submerged sexual feelings, often finding sexual symbolism in apparently innocent conversations or in incidental details, such as the descriptions of landscapes. They are not overly concerned about distinguishing between the feelings of a character and the character's author, often finding a strong identification between the two. They tend to see key characters as infantilized, that is to say, stuck at some stage of emotional development short of healthy, well-adjusted adulthood. They often call attention to deeply divided feelings toward figures of authority, particularly parent figures.

Try constructing a psychoanalytic interpretation of "Young Goodman Brown." Here are two provocative further quotes from Crews to help fuel the fire:

> Here and everywhere in Hawthorne's writing, Puritans stand in censorship of imagination. They personify a primitive, unreasonable conscience which is none the less tyrannical for being despised and ridiculed. Indeed, Hawthorne's practice of disparaging, placating, and half-heartedly joking with them is evidence that he cannot ignore the threat of their disapproval — a disapproval which must of course emanate from his own mind. In a word, then, "Puritans" are the repressive side of Hawthorne himself. (p. 31)

> If Brown's sexual attitude is that of a young boy rather than a normal bridegroom, we may be permitted to wonder if parental, not wifely, sexuality is not the true object of his prurience. (p. 103)

16. Read the two final quotations by critics — Agnes Donohue and Michael Colacurcio — as if they are in conversation with each other. What fundamental disagreement about Hawthorne do you see them reenacting? Develop your argument with reference to other critics.

17. After consulting Chapter 10 in this book, develop the argument that "Young Goodman Brown" dramatizes a schizophrenic experience.

18. *Research Project.* In *A Reader's Guide to the Short Stories of Nathaniel Hawthorne,* Lea Bertani Vozar Newman complains that little critical attention has been given to a Hawthorne short story called "The Wives of the Dead." In particular she criticizes Crews for omitting it from *Sins of the Fathers,* "a lamentable oversight considering the ease with which the story lends itself to a psychoanalytic interpretation" (p. 331). After locating both the short story and Crews's study, analyze "The Wives of the Dead" as Crews might do.

CHAPTER 10

Schizophrenia: Causes and Treatments

Framing the Issues

Each year many thousands of people in the United States and Great Britain are diagnosed as "schizophrenic." Schizophrenia accounts for approximately half of the extreme mental disorders (psychoses) diagnosed in this country. But what is schizophrenia? What are its causes? How is it best treated? The materials in this chapter will suggest some possible answers to these questions and will encourage you to form some tentative conclusions of your own. But they may also provoke you to rethink the way we have framed the questions, questions that presume an entity recognizable as schizophrenia. As you will see, problems of definition, classification, and interpretation are crucial to any effort to develop a sustained argument about schizophrenia.

The chapter begins with a poem written by a young woman diagnosed as schizophrenic and is followed by a scholarly overview, published in 1981, describing the nineteenth-century conceptions of schizophrenia and the major approaches developed so far in this century. Next an excerpt from the *Diagnostic and Statistical Manual of Mental Disorders* (*DSM-IIIR,* 1987), the diagnostic manual used by most American psychiatrists and psychologists, outlines the current professional criteria for diagnosing schizophrenia. Then llow four case histories, reports on a range of people diagnosed as schizophrenic. These reports were written by professionals within the past two decades, but the last also includes excerpts from the diary of a disturbed young man who was later diagnosed as schizophrenic. Each report is poignant in its own way, and together all the reports give you the opportunity to begin thinking about issues of definition, understanding, and treatment. The list of preliminary questions is designed to aid your understanding of and reflection on the definition and characteristics of schizophrenia.

The remaining selections are pieces advocating particular theories about causes and treatments of schizophrenia. The first six contribute to the general debate on whether the causes of schizophrenia are primarily biological or environmental. The closing pieces describe specific treatments, including drug therapy, psychotherapy, behavior therapy, and family systems therapy. The chapter closes with suggestions for argument topics.

The following poem was written by a schizophrenic patient during the course of her therapy. It was reprinted in Psychotherapy of Schizophrenia *(1987) by Gaetano Benedetti.*

Poem

ANONYMOUS SCHIZOPHRENIC PATIENT

They understood nothing, nothing,
And so, therefore, I became filled with hatred.
I wanted to spit out my hatred
but they forced me,   4
Spoonful by spoonful,
To swallow what I had vomited.
Then my body enlarged
In all directions.   8
The hatred in me swelled my body.
I became misformed.
Why are you so fat?
You aren't like the other children.   12
They put a corset on me,
Bound my body,
And the hatred pressed itself together,
Atom into atom,   16
Till it fit into the corset.
But the mass of hatred
Had not changed
Neither its weight.   20
In your house there is no air,
Oxygen is missing;
Lack of breath oppresses me.

Fists are hanging in the air,   24
The dead eyes,
The screaming eyes,
Into whose whirlwind one is sucked,
Don't they see   28
That their owner is suffocating,
Even if the mouths
No longer speak
And have not, for ages?   32
This house
Is like blows upon the head.
Despair thrusts itself
Mockingly laughing   36
Out of the nooks and crannies.
You do not see the ghosts
Who, with drawn knives
Crawl up my legs.   40
There,
A millimeter away,
Hell is laughing.
Who will murder me?   44
Am I a murderer?
The light in the house is cold.
Upon my return
Glittering gloom races toward me.   48
Where is my head
Where are my feet
The hands
Which are still carrying the milk pail?   52
Darkness inside and out
Surrounds my senses.
Inside the house
The mother of horror is waiting.   56
Stinking,
The unconscious hatred
Of a family
Ripping itself to shreds   60
For hundreds of years
Spreads
With the ringing of the bell.
I, however, was struck with fear   64
And knew
That the ghosts
Were hanging behind me.
The light   68
Became a bad omen.
I became a murderer.
The corpse,
Which I could only see,   72

Lay there.
I screamed,
And no one understood
What I had seen.   76
Horror shook me
And I cursed the day
On which I had come upon the world.
They called it sickness   80
And gave it an ugly name
Madness!
The grating of the door
Is eternal damnation.   84
A color
Which is no color
A sound and a smell
A swallow of everything   88
But not describable
And in everything
An endless feeling
Where I, who determine   92
No longer exist.
Below
Fear is hanging
Like a giant drop   96
Encompassing the world
And the monstrous depths
Of nothingness
Into which I am falling   100
On the way down
Accompanied by multicolored rage
And the loss of solidity
And the decay into undefined gravel.   104
Always and again this hated presence
While the rage
Like a transparent bomb
Ticks on.   108

History of the Concept of Schizophrenia

SUE A. SHAPIRO

The increased interest in the history and course of illnesses led to the   1
work of Kraepelin and Bleuler, the masters of descriptive psychiatry.
Although Kraepelin is easily criticized for his "callous" questioning of
patients on display in the great amphitheaters of medical schools, his
descriptions and classifications of dementia praecox remain instructive.
It should be recalled that he was not trying to be therapeutic in these

demonstrations. His intention was to point out general characteristics of the disorder and he did so in the style of medical training then current.

In the hundred years before Kraepelin, a number of terms were used to describe what were thought to be different mental illnesses. Vogel used the term "paranoia" in 1764, Kahlbaum described catatonia in 1868, and Hecker coined the term "hebephrenia" in 1870. Kraepelin (1896) was the first to bring these clinical entities together under the general term "dementia praecox." The fundamental characteristic of this group of psychoses was its morbid prognosis — the patient's condition would deteriorate. The syndrome received its name because of its resemblance to dementia; however, its onset was considerably earlier.

In keeping with the spirit of the times, Kraepelin stressed specific symptoms: hallucinations (especially auditory ones), delusions, thought broadcasting and influencing, poor judgment, disturbances of emotional expression, bizarre and stereotyped behavior, and negativism. In his descriptions of patients' premorbid functioning he was sometimes amusingly overinclusive, failing to distinguish between cause, effect, and mere coincidence. Like the witch-hunters of the Middle Ages, Kraepelin was struck by the heightened sexuality of his patients.

Kraepelin distinguished dementia praecox from the organic psychoses by the absence of delirium or gross deficits of intelligence. Orientation, memory, and comprehension remained intact. He subdivided dementia praecox into three types: catatonia, hebephrenia, and paranoid, eventually adding a fourth type — simple. Kraepelin believed that an organic, probably metabolic, disease process was at the root of dementia praecox. A major criticism of his work is that he used the outcome of the illness as a main criterion for diagnosis — a procedure incompatible with the practical need for knowing the diagnosis in order to determine the treatment.

For the contemporary reader, Kraepelin's vivid descriptions of symptoms are flawed by his judgmental, moralistic tone, as illustrated in this typical statement: "The patients have lost every independent inclination for work and action; they sit about idle, trouble themselves about nothing." This statement follows a thorough description of frightening hallucinations and delusions. In later editions of his work, Kraepelin hypothesized that a disorder of will is central to one form of dementia praecox. The other type is marked by what Stransky called the "loss of the inner unity of the activities of intellect, emotion and volition in themselves and among one another." Stransky's description corresponds to Bleuler's "split personality."

The main body of Kraepelin's work is descriptive; he made no distinction between primary and secondary symptoms (a distinction that preoccupied later researchers). The first edition of his book stressed the morbid outcome of dementia praecox to differentiate it from manic-depression. It is for this that Kraepelin is remembered. By 1919, however, in the eighth edition, he had acknowledged that 9 to 14 percent of dementia praecox patients eventually improved. Kraepelin believed that dementia praecox had an organic base, citing as evidence autopsy reports of nerve cell damage in the temporal and frontal lobes and in the higher layers of the cortex. From his description we may infer that some of his patients were probably suffering from syphilis, alcoholism, epilepsy, or physical trauma. But he did not report the cause of death, so his organic findings are highly questionable. He did, however, identify a hereditary predisposition toward dementia praecox and thus paved the way for later studies.

Toward the end of his life, Kraepelin was convinced that dementia 7 praecox had a metabolic basis. He hypothesized that the body becomes autointoxicated, although he did not specify how the process occurred. In this he anticipated some current biochemical research that has investigated possible endogenous hallucinogens.

Bleuler and Freud were also committed to an organic or constitutional 8 explanation of schizophrenia, but they added a new dimension: concern with the meaning and organization of symptoms. Freud's discovery of the psychogenic nature and meaning of hysterical symptoms caused a revolution in psychiatric thinking, and his influence can be seen in Bleuler's work.

Bleuler preferred to call dementia praecox "schizophrenia" to reflect 9 his theory that there is an underlying personality split in the patient, a loss of harmony between various groups of mental functions. He rejected Kraepelin's idea of necessary, progressive deterioration and stated:

> By the term "dementia praecox" or schizophrenia we designate a group of psychoses whose course is at times chronic, at times marked by intermittent attacks, and which can stop or retrograde at any stage, but does not permit a full *restitutio a integruo*.

Bleuler sought to understand the symptoms of schizophrenia in terms 10 of their basic components. He stated:

> The fundamental symptoms consist of disturbances of association and affectivity, the predilection for fantasy as against reality, and the inclination to divorce oneself from reality. Furthermore, we can add the absence of those very symptoms which play such a great role in certain other diseases, such as primary disturbances of perception, orientation and memory.

These fundamental symptoms have been called "the four A's": affect, autism, associations, and ambivalence. Disturbances of affect refer to the peculiar ways in which the schizophrenic's emotional tone seems strikingly at odds with the content of speech, either through general flatness or excessive lability. Typically, the schizophrenic can tell gruesome tales of torture while laughing or appearing to be indifferent.

Autism refers to the predominance of internal life or fantasy over 11 reality. Thus external events take on highly personal meanings — the world becomes a stage for the realization of highly personal fears and desires, with a loss of the ability to test reality. For example, a young woman admitted to the hospital described how she had been walking along when a red street light came on, which meant that she had to turn right. Then she came upon a green light, which meant that she was getting close to her destination . . . and so on, until she wound up at the docks where she was later found, having been raped and beaten.

Loosening of associations is a key aspect of what has become known 12
as a "formal thought disorder," the primary feature of schizophrenia.
Loosening of associations occurs when the person abandons the normal
linguistic constraints on the potential number of words that can be used
at a specific point in a sentence and allows personal, nonconsensual
meanings into the flow of speech. Thus, for example, the sound qualities
of a word will be responded to independently of its meaning, and the
schizophrenic may start rhyming. The train of thought is no longer governed by a sense of purpose.

Psychotic ambivalence refers to a juxtaposition of opposite feelings 13
and desires so extreme as to interfere with volition and action. An example
can be seen in the behavior of a hospitalized teenage girl who first told
me to "fuck off," then kissed me, and finally attacked me with a sliver
of glass.

Bleuler believed that delusions and hallucinations were secondary to 14
and derived from these four fundamental symptoms. He introduced the
notion of ambulatory and latent schizophrenia, believing that people so
diagnosed showed the fundamental signs, whereas delusions and hallucinations were more frequently encountered in hospitalized schizophrenics. These latter phenomena are the flashier, more obvious manifestations
of the underlying loosening of associations and split in the personality.

Bleuler did not explain the origin of these fundamental disturbances, 15
nor did he adequately explain the derivation of hallucinations from the
fundamental symptoms. He did, however, begin to integrate the work
of Freud in his assumption that delusions and hallucinations are meaningful
expressions of wishes. His major contribution lies in the thoroughness
of his descriptions and in his effort to construct a hierarchy of symptoms.

While Kraepelin actively searched for, and others awaited, evidence 16
of somatic damage in brain autopsies of patients, Jung believed that the
toxin which produced schizophrenia was caused by psychological conflicts
and their associated intense affects. According to Jung, the complexes
in hysteria and the other neuroses did not generate a toxin, whereas the
complexes in the psychoses did. The toxin was psychogenic and caused
psychotic symptoms, but it could be inhibited through psychoanalytic
work. Jung, the first to formulate a fully psychological theory of schizophrenia, was more optimistic about treating psychotics than was Freud.

Freud and his followers excited the intellectual community, totally 17
altering the way people view themselves. A great many people now
believe that somatic symptoms, memory failures, and so forth, are psychological or psychogenic until proved otherwise. The positive effect of
this view has been an increased effort to understand, know, and help
schizophrenics, but the negative result has been the reinforcement of the
mind-body split that has characterized humanity's view of itself throughout
history and a consequent inattention to biochemical and genetic findings.

While the psychoanalytic movement was gaining momentum, the rest 18
of the scientific community was entering a golden age of discovery and
specialization. In 1906, the spirochete was discovered to be the cause
of syphilis, and the course of the illness thus became understood. The

similarity in appearance and symptoms of general paresis and schizophrenia led to speculation about the origin of schizophrenia. In 1934, phenylketonuria (PKU), a form of mental retardation, was found to be the result of a single autosomal recessive gene. This gene caused faulty metabolism of an amino acid, which then led to faulty brain development. The discovery of the cause of PKU spurred the search for a genetic basis for schizophrenia. Four years later, Kallmann published the first of his studies on concordance rates in families of schizophrenics.

The work of Sullivan and Fromm-Reichmann at Chestnut Lodge in the 1930s and 1940s sparked a renewed psychoanalytic interest in schizophrenia. Freud's conviction that schizophrenia was an untreatable narcissistic disorder had led to a relative paucity of interest in this syndrome during the first three decades of the twentieth century. Sullivan's "interpersonal theory of psychiatry," and increased work with hospitalized schizophrenics, initiated an interest in the family's role in the genesis of schizophrenia. Fromm-Reichmann coined the term "schizophrenogenic." Simultaneously, English psychoanalysts were becoming more interested in understanding early child development and the psychological experience of infants. Melanie Klein's theory, derived from child analysis, provided a metapsychology for exploring psychotic states. At this same time, Freudian analysts were continuing their efforts to understand the function of the ego. Since Freud never completed a revised view of psychosis from the vantage point of his structural model, that task devolved upon the ego psychologists.   19

Concurrently, academic and experimental psychologists in the first half of the twentieth century carried on the empirical tradition, seeking to know specifically how schizophrenics were different from normal people. Their studies began to fall into broad categories concerning such functions as attention, perception, and memory, which are similar to the categories that Bellak identified as critical ego functions.   20

The increased specialization characteristic of this period eventually led to an identification of basic organismic functions such as attention and perception. Since these are more easily reduced to physiological and biochemical mechanisms than are intrapsychic functions, a beginning interdisciplinary bridge was found. Various familial studies were undertaken, some examining communication patterns, others focusing on concordance rates and the effects of adoption on the children of schizophrenics. In the 1960s, biochemical research aimed at finding a body-made hallucinogen; transmethylation and several other key biochemical theories owe their birth to the discovery of lysergic acid diethylamide (LSD). At the same time, LSD had a profound effect on the way an entire generation viewed "madness." Laing's brilliant early work was obscured by a cult worship that oversimplified his insights into the belief that sanity was madness, that madness was the only true sanity, and that one could learn from psychotic experiences. Social and political conditions in the United States and other countries led to a politicization of Laing's view, exemplified in some sociological theories of madness — for example, Szasz's *The Myth of Mental Illness.*   21

Work proliferated, and the number of journal articles on schizophrenia   22 grew at an enormous pace. In the last five years, several publications devoted solely to this topic have been established, among them the *Schizophrenia Bulletin* (a publication of the National Institute of Mental Health) and Cancro's *Annual Review of the Schizophrenic Syndrome*.

During the late 1960s and 1970s, the pendulum swung once again. 23 A variety of social, economic, and scientific factors contributed to a trend away from theoretical speculation and back to a more cautious empiricism. Several longitudinal projects are currently attempting to identify factors that define vulnerability in people at high risk for schizophrenia. These studies are interdisciplinary and often international in scope. Technological advances in computer design have made broader data collection feasible. And, increasingly, the need for standardized diagnostic criteria and definitions of terms becomes more acute.

Description of and Diagnostic Criteria for Schizophrenia
AMERICAN PSYCHIATRIC ASSOCIATION

The essential features of this disorder are the presence of characteristic 1 psychotic symptoms during the active phase of the illness and functioning below the highest level previously achieved (in children or adolescents, failure to achieve the expected level of social development), and a duration of at least six months that may include characteristic prodromal or residual symptoms. At some phase of the illness schizophrenia always involves delusions, hallucinations, or certain characteristic disturbances in affect and the form of thought. The diagnosis is made only when it cannot be established that an organic factor initiated and maintained the disturbance. . . .

FUNCTIONING BELOW HIGHEST LEVEL
PREVIOUSLY ACHIEVED

During the course of the disturbance, functioning in such areas as 2 work, social relations, and self-care is markedly below the highest level achieved before onset of the disorder. If the onset is in childhood or adolescence, there is failure to achieve the expected level of social development. This diagnostic requirement is included so that people with an isolated symptom, such as an encapsulated delusion, but without a reduction in social or work functioning, are not given the diagnosis of schizophrenia, which typically involves impairment in more than one area of functioning.

CHARACTERISTIC SYMPTOMS INVOLVING
MULTIPLE PSYCHOLOGICAL PROCESSES

Invariably there are characteristic disturbances in several of the fol- 3 lowing areas: content and form of thought, perception, affect, sense of self, volition, relationship to the external world, and psychomotor behavior. It should be noted that no single feature is invariably present or seen only in schizophrenia.

Content of Thought.   The major disturbance in the content of thought involves delusions that are often multiple, fragmented, or bizarre (i.e., involving a phenomenon that in the person's culture would be regarded as totally implausible, e.g., thought broadcasting, or being controlled by a dead person). Simple persecutory delusions involving the belief that others are spying on, spreading false rumors about, or planning to harm the person are common. Delusions of reference, in which events, objects, or other people are given particular and unusual significance, usually of a negative or pejorative nature, are also common. For example, the person may be convinced that a television commentator is mocking him.   4

Certain delusions are observed far more frequently in schizophrenia than in other psychotic disorders. These include, for instance, the belief or experience that one's thoughts, as they occur, are broadcast from one's head to the external world so that others can hear them (thought broadcasting); that thoughts that are not one's own are inserted into one's mind (thought insertion); that thoughts have been removed from one's head (thought withdrawal); or that one's feelings, impulses, thoughts, or actions are not one's own, but are imposed by some external force (delusions of being controlled). Less commonly, somatic, grandiose, religious, and nihilistic delusions are observed.   5

Form of Thought.   A disturbance in the form of thought is often present. This has been referred to as "formal thought disorder," and is different from a disorder in the content of thought. The most common example of this is loosening of associations, in which ideas shift from one subject to another, completely unrelated or only obliquely related subject, without the speaker's displaying any awareness that the topics are unconnected. Statements that lack a meaningful relationship may be juxtaposed, or the person may shift idiosyncratically from one frame of reference to another. When loosening of associations is severe, the person may become incoherent; that is, his or her speech may become incomprehensible.   6

There may be poverty of content of speech, in which speech is adequate in amount, but conveys little information because it is vague, overly abstract, or overly concrete, repetitive, or stereotyped. The listener can recognize this disturbance by noting that little if any information has been conveyed although the person has spoken at some length. Less common disturbances include neologisms, perseveration, clanging, and blocking.   7

Perception.   The major disturbances in perception are various forms of hallucinations. Although these occur in all modalities, the most common are auditory hallucinations, which frequently involve many voices the person perceives as coming from outside his or her head. The voices may be familiar, and often make insulting remarks; they may be single   8 or multiple. Voices speaking directly to the person or commenting on his or her ongoing behavior are particularly characteristic. Command hallucinations may be obeyed, which sometimes creates danger for the person or others. Occasionally, the auditory hallucinations are of sounds rather than voices.

Tactile hallucinations may be present, and typically involve electrical, tingling, or burning sensations. Somatic hallucinations, such as the sensation of snakes crawling inside the abdomen, are occasionally experienced. Visual, gustatory, and olfactory hallucinations also occur, but with less frequency, and, in the absence of auditory hallucinations, always raise the possibility of an organic mental disorder. Other perceptual abnormalities include sensations of bodily change; hypersensitivity to sound, sight, and smell; illusions; and synesthesias.

Affect. The disturbance often involves flat or inappropriate affect. In flat affect, there are virtually no signs of affective expression; the voice is usually monotonous and the face, immobile. The person may complain that he or she no longer responds with normal emotional intensity or, in extreme cases, no longer has feelings. In inappropriate affect, the affect is clearly discordant with the content of the person's speech or ideation. For example, while discussing being tortured by electrical shocks, a person with schizophrenia, disorganized type, may laugh or smile. Sudden and unpredictable changes in affect involving inexplicable outbursts of anger may occur.

Although these affective disturbances are almost invariably part of the clinical picture, their presence is often difficult to detect except when they are in an extreme form. Furthermore, antipsychotic drugs have effects that may appear similar to the affective flattening seen in schizophrenia.

Sense of Self. The sense of self that gives the normal person a feeling of individuality, uniqueness, and self-direction is frequently disturbed in schizophrenia. This is sometimes referred to as a loss of ego boundaries, and frequently is evidenced by extreme perplexity about one's own identity and the meaning of existence, or by some of the specific delusions described above, particularly those involving control by an outside force.

Volition. The characteristic disturbances in volition are most readily observed in the residual phase. There is nearly always some disturbance in self-initiated, goal-directed activity, which may grossly impair work or other role functioning. This may take the form of inadequate interest, drive, or ability to follow a course of action to its logical conclusion. Marked ambivalence regarding alternative courses of action can lead to near-cessation of goal-directed activity.

Impaired Interpersonal Functioning and Relationship to the External World. Difficulty in interpersonal relationships is almost invariably present. Often this takes the form of social withdrawal and emotional detachment. When the person is severely preoccupied with egocentric and illogical ideas and fantasies and distorts or excludes the external world, the condition has been referred to as "autism." Some with the disorder, during a phase of the illness, cling to other people, intrude upon strangers, and fail to recognize that excessive closeness makes other people uncomfortable and likely to pull away.

Psychomotor Behavior.   Various disturbances in psychomotor be- **15** havior are observed, particularly in the chronically severe and acutely florid forms of the disorder. There may be a marked decrease in reactivity to the environment, with a reduction in spontaneous movements and activity. In extreme cases the person appears unaware of the nature of the environment (as in catatonic stupor); may maintain a rigid posture and resist efforts to be moved (as in catatonic rigidity); may make apparently purposeless and stereotyped, excited motor movements not influenced by external stimuli (as in catatonic excitement); may voluntarily assume inappropriate or bizarre postures (as in catatonic posturing); or may resist and actively counteract instructions or attempts to be moved (as in catatonic negativism). In addition, odd mannerisms, grimacing, or waxy flexibility may be present.

ASSOCIATED FEATURES

Almost any symptom can occur as an associated feature. The person **16** may appear perplexed, disheveled, or eccentrically groomed or dressed. Abnormalities of psychomotor activity — e.g., pacing, rocking, or apathetic immobility — are common. Frequently there is poverty of speech, that is, a restriction in the amount of spontaneous speech, so that replies to questions tend to be brief, concrete, and unelaborated. Ritualistic or stereotyped behavior associated with magical thinking often occurs. Dysphoric mood is common, and may take the form of depression, anxiety, anger, or a mixture of these. Depersonalization, derealization, ideas of reference, and illusions are often present, as are hypochondriacal concerns, which may or may not be delusional. Typically, no disturbance in the sensorium is evident, although during a period of exacerbation of the disorder, the person may be confused or even disoriented, or have memory impairment.

AGE AT ONSET

Onset is usually during adolescence or early adulthood, but the dis- **17** order may begin in middle or late adult life. Many studies indicate a somewhat earlier onset in males than in females.

COURSE

As noted previously, the diagnosis of schizophrenia requires that **18** continuous signs of the illness have been present for at least six months, which always includes an active phase with psychotic symptoms. When active or positive symptoms are prominent, negative symptoms, such as social withdrawal and lack of initiative, may be present, but difficult to identify. If the active phase lasts more than six months, it is not necessary to identify a distinct prodromal or residual phase, even though prodromal/residual symptoms have usually been present.

The development of the active phase of the illness is generally preceded by a *prodromal phase* in which there is a clear deterioration from a previous level of functioning. This phase is characterized by social withdrawal, impairment in role functioning, peculiar behavior, neglect of personal hygiene and grooming, blunted or inappropriate affect, disturbances in communication, bizarre ideation, unusual perceptual experiences, and lack of initiative, interests, or energy. Friends and relatives often describe the onset of prodromal symptoms as a change in personality or as no longer "being the same person." The length of this prodromal phase is extremely variable, and its onset may be difficult to date accurately. The prognosis is especially poor when the prodromal phase has taken an insidious, downhill course over many years.

During the *active phase,* psychotic symptoms — e.g., delusions, hallucinations, loosening of associations, incoherence, and catatonic behavior — are prominent. . . . In order to make the diagnosis, the psychotic symptoms must persist for at least one week, unless they are successfully treated. Onset of the active phase, either initially or as an exacerbation of a preexisting active phase, may be associated with a psychosocial stressor.

Usually a *residual phase* follows the active phase of the illness. The clinical picture of this phase is similar to that of the prodromal phase, except that affective blunting or flattening and impairment in role functioning tend to be more common in the residual phase. During this phase some of the psychotic symptoms, such as delusions or hallucinations, may persist, but may no longer be accompanied by strong affect.

A return to full premorbid functioning in this disorder is not common. Full remissions do occur, but their frequency is currently a subject of controversy. The most common course is probably one of acute exacerbations with residual impairment between episodes. Residual impairment often increases between episodes during the initial years of the disorder. There is some evidence, however, that in many people with the disorder, the residual symptoms become attenuated in the later phases of the illness.

Numerous studies have indicated a group of factors associated with good prognosis, including absence of premorbid personality disturbance, adequate premorbid social functioning, precipitating events, abrupt onset, onset in mid-life, a clinical picture that involves confusion, and a family history of mood disorder. . . .

IMPAIRMENT

Invariably, at some point in the disorder as described above, there is impairment in several areas of routine daily functioning, such as work, social relations, and self-care. Supervision may be required to ensure that nutritional and hygienic needs are met and to protect the person from the consequences of poor judgment, cognitive impairment, or actions based on delusions or in response to hallucinations. Between episodes of illness the extent of disability may range from none to disability so severe that institutional care is required.

COMPLICATIONS

Although violent acts performed by people with this disorder often attract public attention, whether their frequency is actually greater than in the general population is not known. What is known is that the life expectancy of people with schizophrenia is shorter than that of the general population because of an increased suicide rate and death from a variety of other causes. 25

PREMORBID PERSONALITY

The premorbid personalities of people who develop schizophrenia are often described as suspicious, introverted, withdrawn, eccentric, or impulsive. . . . 26

PREDISPOSING FACTORS

The diagnosis is made more commonly among the lower socioeconomic groups. The reasons for this are unclear, but may involve downward social drift, lack of upward socioeconomic mobility, and high stress. 27

Certain patterns of family interaction have been hypothesized to predispose to the development, onset, relapse, or chronicity of schizophrenia; but interpretations of the evidence supporting these hypotheses are controversial. 28

PREVALENCE

Studies in Europe and Asia, using a relatively narrow concept of schizophrenia, have reported a lifetime prevalence rate of from 0.2% to almost 1%. Studies in the United States that have used broader criteria and surveyed urban populations have reported higher rates. 29

SEX RATIO

The disorder is apparently equally common in both sexes. 30

FAMILIAL PATTERN

All investigators have found a higher prevalence of the disorder in first-degree biologic relatives of people with schizophrenia than would be expected in the general population. Included are studies in which the adopted offspring of people with schizophrenia have been reared by parents who do not have the disorder. Twin studies consistently show a higher concordance rate of schizophrenia in monozygotic than in dizygotic 31 twins. However, the experience of being a monozygotic twin does not in itself appear to predispose to the development of schizophrenia. Although genetic factors have been proven to be involved in the development of the illness, the existence of a substantial discordance rate, even in monozygotic twins, indicates the importance of nongenetic factors. . . .

DIAGNOSTIC CRITERIA FOR SCHIZOPHRENIA

A. Presence of characteristic psychotic symptoms in the active phase: either (1), (2), or (3) for at least one week (unless the symptoms are successfully treated):

   (1) two of the following:

      (a) delusions
      (b) prominent hallucinations (throughout the day for several days or several times a week for several weeks, each hallucinatory experience not being limited to a few brief moments)
      (c) incoherence or marked loosening of associations
      (d) catatonic behavior
      (e) flat or grossly inappropriate affect

   (2) bizarre delusions (i.e., involving a phenomenon that the person's culture would regard as totally implausible; e.g., thought broadcasting, being controlled by a dead person)
   (3) prominent hallucinations [as defined in (1b) above] of a voice with content having no apparent relation to depression or elation, or a voice keeping up a running commentary on the person's behavior or thoughts, or two or more voices conversing with each other

B. During the course of the disturbance, functioning in such areas as work, social relations, and self-care is markedly below the highest level achieved before onset of the disturbance (or, when the onset is in childhood or adolescence, failure to achieve expected level of social development).

C. Schizoaffective disorder and mood disorder with psychotic features have been ruled out; i.e., if a major depressive or manic syndrome has ever been present during an active phase of the disturbance, the total duration of all episodes of a mood syndrome has been brief relative to the total duration of the active and residual phases of the disturbance.

D. Continuous signs of the disturbance for at least six months. The six-month period must include an active phase (of at least one week, or less if symptoms have been successfully treated) during which there were psychotic symptoms characteristic of schizophrenia (symptoms in A), with or without a prodromal or residual phase, as defined below.

Prodromal phase: A clear deterioration in functioning before the active phase of the disturbance that is not due to a disturbance in mood or to a psychoactive substance use disorder and that involves at least two of the symptoms listed below.

Residual phase: Following the active phase of the disturbance, persistence of at least two of the symptoms noted below, these not being due to a disturbance in mood or to a psychoactive substance use disorder.

Prodromal or residual symptoms:

(1) marked social isolation or withdrawal
(2) marked impairment in role functioning as wage-earner, student, or homemaker
(3) markedly peculiar behavior (e.g., collecting garbage, talking to self in public, hoarding food)
(4) marked impairment in personal hygiene and grooming
(5) blunted or inappropriate affect
(6) digressive, vague, overelaborate, or circumstantial speech, or poverty of speech, or poverty of content of speech
(7) odd beliefs or magical thinking, influencing behavior and inconsistent with cultural norms; e.g., superstitiousness, belief in clairvoyance, telepathy, "sixth sense," "others can feel my feelings," overvalued ideas, ideas of reference
(8) unusual perceptual experiences; e.g., recurrent illusions, sensing the presence of a force or person not actually present
(9) marked lack of initiative, interests, or energy

Examples: Six months of prodromal symptoms with one week of symptoms from A; no prodromal symptoms with six months of symptoms from A; no prodromal symptoms with one week of symptoms from A and six months of residual symptoms.

E. It cannot be established that an organic factor initiated and maintained the disturbance.
F. If there is a history of autistic disorder, the additional diagnosis of schizophrenia is made only if prominent delusions or hallucinations are also present. . . .

TYPES

The types are defined by the cross-sectional clinical picture. Some   32
are less stable over time than others, and their prognostic and treatment implications are variable. The diagnosis of a particular type should be based on the predominant clinical picture that occasioned the most recent evaluation or admission to clinical care.

CATATONIC TYPE

The essential feature of this type is marked psychomotor disturbance,   33
which may involve stupor, negativism, rigidity, excitement, or posturing. Sometimes there is rapid alternation between the extremes of excitement

and stupor. Associated features include stereotypes, mannerisms, and waxy flexibility. Mutism is particularly common.

During catatonic stupor or excitement, the person needs careful supervision to avoid hurting himself or herself or others. Medical care may be needed because of malnutrition, exhaustion, hyperpyrexia, or self-inflicted injury. 34

Although this type was very common several decades ago, it is now rare in Europe and North America. 35

DIAGNOSTIC CRITERIA FOR CATATONIC TYPE

A type of schizophrenia in which the clinical picture is dominated by any of the following: 36

(1) catatonic stupor (marked decrease in reactivity to the environment and/or reduction in spontaneous movements and activity) or mutism
(2) catatonic negativism (an apparently motiveless resistance to all instructions or attempts to be moved)
(3) catatonic rigidity (maintenance of a rigid posture against efforts to be moved)
(4) catatonic excitement (excited motor activity, apparently purposeless and not influenced by external stimuli)
(5) catatonic posturing (voluntary assumption of inappropriate or bizarre postures)

DISORGANIZED TYPE

The essential features of this type are incoherence, marked loosening of associations, or grossly disorganized behavior, and, in addition, flat or grossly inappropriate affect. There are no systematized delusions (as in paranoid type), although fragmentary delusions or hallucinations, in which the content is not organized into a coherent theme, are common. 37

Associated features include grimaces, mannerisms, hypochondriacal complaints, extreme social withdrawal, and other oddities of behavior. 38

This clinical picture is usually associated with extreme social impairment, poor premorbid personality, an early and insidious onset, and a chronic course without significant remissions. 39

In other classifications this type is termed hebephrenic. 40

DIAGNOSTIC CRITERIA FOR DISORGANIZED TYPE

A type of schizophrenia in which the following criteria are met: 41

A. Incoherence, marked loosening of associations, or grossly disorganized behavior.
B. Flat or grossly inappropriate affect.
C. Does not meet the criteria for catatonic type.

PARANOID TYPE

The essential feature of this type of schizophrenia is preoccupation with one or more systematized delusions or with frequent auditory hallucinations related to a single theme. In addition, symptoms characteristic 42 of the disorganized and catatonic types, such as incoherence, flat or grossly inappropriate affect, catatonic behavior, or grossly disorganized behavior, are absent. When all exacerbations of the disorder meet the criteria for paranoid type, the clinician should specify *stable type*.

Associated features include unfocused anxiety, anger, argumentativeness, and violence. Often a stilted, formal quality or extreme intensity in interpersonal interactions is noted. [43]

The impairment in functioning may be minimal if the delusional material is not acted upon. Onset tends to be later in life than the other types, and the distinguishing characteristics may be more stable over time. Some evidence suggests that the prognosis for the paranoid type, particularly with regard to occupational functioning and capacity for independent living, may be considerably better than for the other types of schizophrenia. [44]

DIAGNOSTIC CRITERIA FOR PARANOID TYPE

A type of schizophrenia in which there are: [45]

A. Preoccupation with one or more systematized delusions or with frequent auditory hallucinations related to a single theme.
B. *None* of the following: incoherence, marked loosening of associations, flat or grossly inappropriate affect, catatonic behavior, grossly disorganized behavior.

Specify stable type if criteria A and B have been met during all past and present active phases of the illness. [46]

UNDIFFERENTIATED TYPE

The essential features of the undifferentiated type of schizophrenia are prominent psychotic symptoms (i.e., delusions, hallucinations, incoherence, or grossly disorganized behavior) that cannot be classified in any category previously listed or that meet the criteria for more than one category. [47]

DIAGNOSTIC CRITERIA FOR UNDIFFERENTIATED TYPE

A type of schizophrenia in which there are: [48]

A. Prominent delusions, hallucinations, incoherence, or grossly disorganized behavior.
B. Does not meet the criteria for paranoid, catatonic, or disorganized type.

RESIDUAL TYPE

This category should be used when there has been at least one episode of schizophrenia, but the clinical picture that occasioned the evaluation or admission to clinical care is without prominent psychotic symptoms, though signs of the illness persist. Emotional blunting, social withdrawal, eccentric behavior, illogical thinking, and mild loosening of [49] associations are common. If delusions or hallucinations are present, they are not prominent, and are not accompanied by strong affect. . . .

DIAGNOSTIC CRITERIA FOR RESIDUAL TYPE

A type of schizophrenia in which there are:

A. Absence of prominent delusions, hallucinations, incoherence, or grossly disorganized behavior.
B. Continuing evidence of the disturbance, as indicated by two or more of the residual symptoms listed in criterion D of schizophrenia.

The Case of Diane Franklin
GLORIA RAKITA LEON

A young woman appeared one evening at a walk-in crisis intervention center and told the person interviewing her that she had come to the center because "I've been feeling really weird. I can't think or talk straight, and it's really a scary feeling. . . . It seems like everything is falling apart in my head. I hear voices telling me I'm 'no good.' " The woman's appearance was disheveled; her long brown hair hung down to her shoulders and was uncombed and matted. She looked at the interviewer with an open-eyed, fixed stare and, throughout the discussion, her gaze never moved from the interviewer's face. She indicated that she had heard of the center from the staff and fellow residents of a half-way treatment house she had recently been in.

The young woman's name was Diane Franklin; she was 22 years old. She revealed that she had been in a number of psychiatric treatment facilities since the age of 14, and she had learned to seek help of some type whenever she felt that she could not cope with life on her own. Diane indicated that her family lived in the same city, but she had been trying to be somewhat independent of them. She currently shared a small apartment with another young woman whom she had met at the half-way house.

Diane was the youngest in a family of three children; her 29-year-old sister, a college graduate, was married and had two children; Diane's brother was 26, also a college graduate, and employed as an accountant. Diane's mother had been hospitalized periodically over the past 20 years and was diagnosed as paranoid schizophrenic. Mr. Franklin divorced his wife 11 years previously and subsequently remarried. The family was white, of middle-class, Protestant background.

The counselor at the walk-in clinic suggested that Diane sign herself into an acute psychiatric care facility associated with the center. Diane readily agreed to do so and she was hospitalized on a psychiatric inpatient ward of the hospital.

FAMILY BACKGROUND

Diane was interviewed by a psychiatry resident. She described her childhood as unhappy and sometimes scary, and recalled the many arguments her parents had had. She indicated that often the heated verbal exchanges between her parents escalated to the point where her mother would grab her father by the shoulders and begin shaking him until her father would have to forcefully push his wife away from him. Diane remembered her mother as being extremely unpredictable, one moment calm and conversing quietly, the next moment becoming quite angry and shouting. Diane felt that her mother had almost always provoked the arguments with her father, often for no reason apparent to Diane.

Diane recalled that during her childhood, her mother was periodically away from home for varying periods of time. Something was always mysterious about these absences; her father typically would only state that Mrs. Franklin had gone for "a rest," and was vague about where his wife had gone to or how long she would be away. These absences increased in frequency and length during the time Diane was in elementary school. Generally, Mr. Franklin's sister came to the house and helped with the family chores when Mrs. Franklin was away. However, she usually did not come to visit when Mrs. Franklin was at home.

Diane indicated that the other members of her family generally "babied" her. She described her father as quite warm and indulgent with her during her childhood when he was not preoccupied with personal problems relating to his wife. She remembered that her older sister made sure that Diane ate properly and she also helped Diane prepare her clothes for school the next day. She felt that her sister and brother generally made extra efforts to be nice to her. They often let her get her way and even took care of some of the household tasks that she was supposed to do, if Diane did not feel like doing them. She said that her aunt also tended to give in to her whims.

The family situation became even more confusing to Diane around the time of her tenth birthday. She recalled that her mother had been particularly argumentative and suspicious, and her parents had engaged in a series of intense arguments. Diane's maternal grandparents, whom she had not seen in several months, came to the house unexpectedly one day. More arguments ensued, and then her parents left with them. Her father returned home later in the day and told Diane and the other children that their mother had been hospitalized for her "nerves" and would be in the hospital for some time. Diane stated that, as it turned out, her mother did not come back to live with them. Mr. Franklin's sister and his parents became more involved in caring for the family, but the children rarely saw their maternal grandparents.

Several months after Mrs. Franklin left the house, Mr. Franklin told his children that he and their mother were getting a divorce. Diane recalled this period of time as an extremely bewildering one for her. She became even more confused when a number of months later her father brought a woman named Betty Sanders to the house, and told the children that he would like them to meet her. Diane said that Betty seemed rather distant and uncomfortable with her, and Diane felt the same way. This mutual feeling did not change as Betty visited the home more frequently. Diane recalled that when her father told the children that he and Betty were going to be married, she quietly accepted this announcement. However, she felt very frightened and perplexed because she had not seen her mother since she had been hospitalized, and Diane did not know what was going to happen to her mother.

Diane was around 13 years old when she saw her mother for the 10
first time since her hospitalization. Diane described this visit as extremely
upsetting because her mother had seemed very distant and uninterested
in being with her children. The visit took place at some sort of boarding
home, and Diane remembered that a number of the other persons there
had stared at her and her sister and brother but had not attempted to
converse with them. Diane had felt frightened and uncomfortable for
several weeks following this visit, and none of the children had gone out
of their way to see their mother after that time. Further, Mr. Franklin
discouraged these visits because he felt that they were too upsetting for
everyone involved. Their mother rarely called them or made overtures
to be with her children.

A social worker conducted several interviews with Mr. Franklin while 11
Diane was hospitalized. Diane's father indicated that living with his first
wife had become impossible. For the children's benefit as well as his, he
had obtained a divorce and custody of the children. Their mother has
continued to alternate between the hospital and being maintained on
medications in community treatment settings. She apparently was having
increasing difficulty communicating with others, and at the time of the
evaluation, the Franklin children had not seen their mother in some time.
Mr. Franklin revealed that he was content in his second marriage, but
wished that his second wife could have been more affectionate and less
strict with the children.

Mr. Franklin could recall nothing unusual in Diane's birth or early 12
development, nor had she ever had any unusual medical diseases or
significant injuries. Mr. Franklin appeared to be genuinely concerned about
his daughter and frustrated and uncertain about how he could help her.
He expressed the fear that Diane had fallen into the same pattern of
repeated hospitalizations that her mother exhibited. Mr. Franklin stated
that his two eldest children were happy and functioning quite adequately,
and did not manifest the emotional instability that Diane did. Mr. Franklin
confirmed that Diane had been treated as the baby of the family and had
not been encouraged to be as independent and self-reliant as she might
have been. He recalled that he always was somewhat bewildered by
Diane's behavior and had difficulty deciding how to deal with her. As a
child, she seemed especially sensitive and hurt by criticism or verbal
reprimands, while as an adolescent she sometimes seemed impervious
to reprimands or the loss of privileges. Diane and her stepmother argued
frequently, and the latter accused Mr. Franklin of being too lenient with
his daughter. In retrospect, Mr. Franklin felt that the family pattern
that had developed in dealing with Diane was one of inconsistency and
indulgence.

SCHOOL AND PEER RELATIONSHIPS

Mr. Franklin indicated that Diane did fairly well in school, although 13
she occasionally went through periods when she appeared confused and
"didn't seem to have her two feet on the ground." Her several hospitalizations during adolescence interfered with her school progress, but
she nonetheless graduated from high school and had taken some further

course work. However, she generally lost interest in her college courses about half-way through the semester, and often did not appear for the final examination.

Diane had a number of male and female friends during high school and she seemed to enjoy being with them. However, Mr. Franklin felt that Diane often did not take a stand about her own wishes and ideas, and she sometimes followed the poor judgment of the persons she was with. In addition, she seemed to go through periods of confusion and inefficiency that often required some type of professional help. During these periods, she seemed to lose interest in her friends and surroundings. **14**

Diane also mentioned that she had enjoyed interacting with other teenagers "when my head was straight." She said that during adolescence she had used marijuana in group settings with her friends and had tried some "downers," but these experiences usually made her feel "weird" afterwards. Her first heterosexual experience occurred when she was 16. She had intercourse on a number of occasions with a boy she had known and liked for some time. These experiences were satisfying, and Diane did not feel guilty about sexual relationships before marriage as long as there was affection involved in the relationship. She has occasionally had sexual relationships with other young men since that time. **15**

SYMPTOM HISTORY

The information gained from Diane and her father indicated a long-standing pattern dating back to the period of elementary school in which Diane exhibited poorly organized thinking and behavior, confusion, and inefficiency. Diane periodically experienced difficulties in concentrating and completing her school assignments, and she was evaluated a number of times by a school psychologist. These several evaluations were consistent in finding that Diane was of above average intelligence, but her responses to the test material were often quite unusual and bizarre in comparison to the ideas and associations exhibited by most persons her age. Her uneven concentration on the tasks she was working on also interfered with her performance on the tests. **16**

At 14, Diane saw a psychologist for several months because her complaints of feeling "weird," her forgetfulness, and her confusion about recent events had become quite noticeable. For example, she had taken a test in school the previous week and had received a C− on this examination. Diane later told her father that she could not compete academically with her classmates and she was certain she was not going to pass. She said that the test she had taken was a college entrance examination, and her failing grade would prevent her from continuing in school. However, the teacher indicated to Mr. Franklin that the examination had only involved a class assignment. **17**

The weekly sessions with the psychologist did not improve Diane's behavior and her confusion continued to intensify. Diane was then hospitalized for six weeks in a psychiatric hospital. Under a structured schedule including daily classroom activities, her confusion and feelings of un- **18** reality gradually decreased and she was able to return to her regular school.

A similar episode of confusion and concentration difficulties occurred 19 when Diane was 16, and she was hospitalized again. Mr. Franklin was told that Diane was exhibiting many signs of a schizophrenic process. She again complained that she could not think straight, that she had difficulty following through on tasks she was involved in, and that she felt extreme anxiety because it seemed as if she were unable to control the things she said or did. The structured hospital milieu, set up so that events happened on a routine schedule, plus the antipsychotic medication she was placed on, proved helpful. Diane was discharged from the hospital three months later, maintained on the medication. She was enrolled in a different high school and did well for the next year.

After graduating from high school, Diane seemed to drift for a period 20 of over a year. She was involved in activities with her friends from time to time, but she could not decide whether to go to college full-time or get a job. She had stopped taking the antipsychotic medication prescribed for her because she felt the drugs masked her true personality. She again experimented with marijuana and on a number of occasions, cocaine. She was hospitalized at age 20 for several months when her confusion and feelings of unreality intensified again. At this time, she was placed on a different kind of antipsychotic medication. When she had improved to the point where she could be released from the hospital, arrangements were made for her to live in a half-way treatment facility in the community. She stayed at the community facility for a number of months and then moved into an apartment with an acquaintance from the half-way house. She functioned reasonably well in this arrangement for approximately six months, and regularly participated in activities with persons her age. She then stopped taking the prescribed medications, and gradually the confusion and feelings of unreality returned. At this point, she sought help at the walk-in clinic.

The Case of John Fraser
GLORIA RAKITA LEON

John Fraser's high school guidance counselor referred him to a local 1 counseling center because of John's uninterested and shy behavior at school, and because it appeared that he was constantly daydreaming in class. John was 18 years old and in the tenth grade when he was seen.

John was black, and of lower socioeconomic class background. He 2 had a sister Ann, who was three years older than he. Both of his parents were born in southern rural areas and they had only elementary school educations. His parents separated when John was 4 years old, and his mother worked as a hospital orderly for many years. Mr. Fraser was a musician, and, according to Mrs. Fraser, he had never worked steadily because of a drinking problem.

Mrs. Fraser accompanied John to the counseling center. She was 3 interviewed by a social worker, and John was seen by a psychologist.

Mrs. Fraser described John as a good boy who had always been quiet and dreamy. She was surprised that the school now considered his behavior a problem.

DEVELOPMENTAL HISTORY

Mrs. Fraser reported that her pregnancy with John was uneventful. **4** He was born at full term and weighed about 6½ pounds. The period of labor and birth were free of complications, and John did not have any feeding problems during infancy or childhood. He had the measles at age five, but no other childhood diseases.

Mrs. Fraser stated that John was a quiet and generally satisfied baby. **5** He was easy to take care of, and he did not cry very much. Mrs. Fraser indicated that John's development progressed smoothly, but she thought that he was a little slow in talking. He did not say words or phrases until he was almost three years old.

FAMILY HISTORY

John's parents grew up in the South, and they moved to a large city **6** in the Midwest soon after their marriage because Mr. Fraser thought he could find a better job there. John's sister was born a year later. When Ann was three months old, she was taken back to the South to live with her maternal grandmother so that Mrs. Fraser could go back to working full time. Ann continued to live with her grandmother and saw her parents only infrequently.

The Frasers' marital history was one of numerous separations and **7** reconciliations. Mrs. Fraser stated that she and her husband constantly quarreled because of incidents related to her husband's job as a musician and the persons he met at work. Both Mr. and Mrs. Fraser had received a strict Baptist upbringing, and Mrs. Fraser did not approve of the behavior of her husband's friends or the bars he played in when they came to the North. Mr. Fraser's working hours were irregular, and he was continuously exposed to drugs and alcohol. He frequently got involved with other women, and many times he did not come home for a period of several days.

The Frasers moved from a rooming house to an apartment in a low- **8** income housing project after John was born, and John and his mother still lived there. Mrs. Fraser said that she did not want to send John to live with her mother because she was having severe marital difficulties, and she wanted to have someone near her. She worked on the 3 to 11 P.M. shift at the hospital, and she was able to arrange for one of her neighbors to take care of John while she was at work. Mrs. Fraser said that she could not rely on her husband to watch John, and Mr. Fraser's job also involved evening hours when he was working.

Because John was such a quiet child, he needed only minimal attention **9** when Mrs. Fraser was away at work. After supper, the neighbor took John back to the Frasers' apartment and put him to sleep. She locked the door, and then returned to her own apartment. Mrs. Fraser stated that she did not have to worry about John being left alone, because the walls in the apartment building were so thin that if John started to cry, the neighbor was able to hear him from her own apartment. When John no longer required a neighbor's supervision, Mrs. Fraser made him promise that he would stay in the house by himself whenever she was away at work, and she spanked him if she discovered that he had been out of the apartment while she was gone.

Mrs. Fraser said that she and her husband fought loudly and frequently when John was small, and John often started to cry when his parents began arguing. Mrs. Fraser stated that John had been afraid of his father ever since the violent arguments he witnessed when he was a child. **10**

John's parents separated permanently when John was four years old. Mr. Fraser still lived in the area but he rarely saw his son, and his drinking problem apparently became more severe. Mrs. Fraser indicated that the way of life in the urban area they were living in was drastically different from the life style she knew in the rural South. She said that the city ways were rough and often sinful, but the only alternative was to go back to a poverty-stricken area where there was little one could do to earn a living. **11**

Mrs. Fraser felt that it was especially harmful for a girl to grow up in an urban ghetto environment because of the loose standards of behavior. This was another reason why she sent her daughter Ann to live with her mother. Mrs. Fraser noted that when she decided to have John remain with her, she vowed to shield him as much as possible from the bad influences of the neighborhood. **12**

Mrs. Fraser took John to church with her quite regularly. She indicated that she tried to stress to him the importance of staying on the good path and avoiding bad companions. She was very concerned that John would be exposed to narcotics, and she constantly preached to him about the evils of trying heroin and other drugs. **13**

Mrs. Fraser stated that John was used to being by himself, and he usually did not play with other children or go out of the house while she was at work. John occasionally played with some boys younger than he, when he was about 9 or 10 years old. However, Mrs. Fraser ended these relationships because she said that she did not want other children in the apartment when she was away. She punished John by spanking him with a belt if she noticed that some children had been over. **14**

Since that period, John had not had any friends, either at school or in the neighborhood. Mrs. Fraser indicated that John got used to being either with her or by himself, and they both found this to be a comfortable arrangement. She said that she was not interested in becoming friends with another man, and she was content just to take care of John. Although she and John did not talk to each other very much, she felt they were content in each other's presence. **15**

Mrs. Fraser stated that John had never expressed an interest in girls, nor had he asked questions about sexual matters. She also reported **16** that she had to constantly fuss at John to get him to bathe or change his clothes. She felt that he would continue wearing the same things day after day if she did not keep track of when he had last changed.

Although John was 18 years old when he was seen, he had never **17** expressed any thoughts about what he would like to do when he finished high school. Mrs. Fraser said that she had never brought this topic up either, because she felt there was no use in planning things too far ahead.

Mrs. Fraser noted that as John got older, he became quieter and **18** seemed less interested in what was going on around him. John spent a great deal of time watching television, but sporting events were the only type of program that he seemed to enjoy.

SCHOOL HISTORY

John's school records showed that he did passing work in grammar **19** school, but his performance was becoming progressively poorer each year. He had repeated the ninth grade and was in the process of repeating the tenth grade as well. His high school teachers felt that he was not working up to his capacity and they reported that he appeared to be uninterested in the events in the classroom.

Throughout John's school career, his teachers consistently described **20** him as a shy and nonaggressive child, who seemed to spend a great deal of time daydreaming and never got into trouble. One of his teachers commented that he frequently seemed to be in a world of his own, oblivious to the activities ensuing in the classroom. He was often unresponsive to comments directed to him by his teacher and fellow pupils, and he made no attempt to follow the clothes styles of his peer group.

The school personnel labeled John's behavior as a problem one year **21** prior to his referral. However, the comments about John's behavior from grade school on made it evident that he had been detached and withdrawn ever since he started school. During the previous year, there was a noticeable increase in the frequency of incidents where other youngsters made fun of John and called him odd. These incidents served to focus greater teacher attention on John's behavior.

PSYCHOLOGICAL EVALUATION

Mr. S., the psychologist, entered the waiting room and introduced **22** himself to John and Mrs. Fraser. John got up readily from his chair and followed the psychologist to the interview room. As they walked down the corridor, John responded to the examiner's comments with either a "yes" or "no" answer, or else he did not reply at all.

John was of average height and slightly overweight. He was neatly **23** dressed, but he made no attempt to maintain an orderly appearance. For example, when a shirt tail pulled out of his pants as he was reaching for something, he did not tuck his shirt back in. After he took a handkerchief from his pocket, he rather haphazardly stuffed the handkerchief back in his pocket and left it, half in and half out.

John never looked directly at the psychologist, even when he was answering questions. He tended to look down at his hands or off to one side of the room. He gave short answer responses in a flat tone of voice, and he stared silently at the floor after each response. John did not gaze around the room or look at any of the objects on the desk in front of him. His facial features rarely changed, and he maintained a blank, expressionless look throughout the testing sessions.   24

Mr. S. asked the client if he had any special interests or if there was something he especially enjoyed doing. John's response was "nothing." The psychologist inquired about what John did after school each day, and John's reply was "not much." John affirmed that he liked school, and when asked whether he had any problems there, he said "no."   25

The test results indicated that John was able to perform within the dull normal range of intelligence, and there was evidence that he had the capacity for higher intellectual functioning. The client scored relatively poorer on those questions measuring social awareness and social judgment, and he scored equally as poor on items measuring the ability to think abstractly.   26

The client gave one word responses to many of the Rorschach ink blots, and he said that he did not see anything on several of the cards presented. Some of the perceptions that he verbalized were quite different from those of most persons taking the test. These unusual responses were not indicative of the use of imagination or creativity, and they were not bizarre in nature. They suggested, rather, an impoverishment of cognitive processes reflecting a limited response to one's environment.   27

The descriptions to the TAT cards [Thematic Apperception Test, another projective test] were also quite short, and represented a very superficial account of the interactions that could be depicted. An example of the type of story the client gave is the following: "Two people. Just there." There was no description of conversation or emotional expression, nor was there any suggestion that the persons might be engaging in unusual thoughts or behavior.   28

The general impression gained from the testing and interviews was that the client typically responded in a minimal way to his social environment. There were indications that at times his behavior might appear unusual or peculiar to other persons. The test material showed no evidence of organic brain damage.   29

The Case of Ruby Eden

R. D. LAING AND A. ESTERSON

CLINICAL PERSPECTIVE

When Ruby, aged seventeen, was admitted to the hospital she was in an inaccessible catatonic stupor. At first she refused to eat, but gradually she was coaxed to do so. After a few days she began to talk.   1

She rambled in a vague and woolly way, often contradicting herself   2
so that we could get no consistent story from her of her relationship
with her family or with others. One moment she would say her mother
loved her and the next that she was trying to poison her. She would say
that her family disliked her and wanted to get rid of her and abandon her
in hospital and then she would say that they were good and kind to her.

In clinical psychiatric terms there was shallowness of affect and in-   3
congruity of thought and affect. For example, sometimes when she spoke
of her recent pregnancy and miscarriage she laughed while at other times
she discussed it indifferently.

She complained of bangings in her head, and of voices outside her   4
head calling her "slut," "dirty," "prostitute." She thought that "people"
disliked her and were talking disparagingly about her. She said she was
the Virgin Mary and Cliff Richard's wife. She feared crowds and "people."
When she was in a crowd she felt the ground would open up under her
feet. At night "people" were lying on top of her having sexual intercourse
with her: she had given birth to a rat after she was admitted to hospital:
she believed she saw herself on television.

It was clear that the fabric of this girl's "sense of reality," of what   5
is the case and what is not the case, was in shreds. . . .

THE FAMILY SITUATION

In order to spare the reader the initial confusion of the investigators,   6
not to say of this girl, we shall tabulate her family nexus.

BIOLOGICAL STATUS	TITLES RUBY WAS TAUGHT TO USE
Father	Uncle
Mother	Mummy
Aunt (mother's sister)	Mother
Uncle (mother's sister's husband)	Daddy — later Uncle
Cousin	Brother

For the sake of clarity the names of her biological relatives will be   7
printed in roman type and the names by which she called them, and/or
by which they referred to themselves, in italics.

Her mother and she lived with her mother's married sister, this   8
sister's husband (*daddy* or uncle) and their son (her cousin). Her father
(*uncle*) who was married, with another family elsewhere, visited them
occasionally.

Her family violently disagreed about whether Ruby had grown up   9
knowing who she was. Her mother (*mummy*) and her aunt (*mother*)
strongly maintained that she had no inkling of the real state of affairs,
but her cousin (*brother*) insisted that she must have known for years.
They (mother, aunt, and uncle) argued also that no one in the district
knew of this, but they admitted finally that, of course, everyone knew

she was an illegitimate child, but no one would hold it against her. The most intricate splits and denials in her perception of herself and others were simultaneously expected of this girl and practiced by the others.

She fell pregnant six months before admission to hospital and had a   10
miscarriage at four months.

Like all these families, this one was haunted by the specters of scandal   11
and gossip, with what people were saying or thinking, and so on. Ruby's pregnancy intensified all this. Ruby thought people were talking about her, and her family knew that in fact they were, but when she told them about this they tried to reassure her by telling her not to be silly, not to imagine things, of course no one was talking about her.

This was just one of the many mystifications surrounding this girl.   12
Here are a few of the others.   13
In her distracted paranoid state she said that she thought her mother,   14
aunt, uncle, and cousin disliked her, picked on her, mocked her, and despised her. As she got "well" again, she felt very remorseful about having thought such terrible things, and said that her family had been "really good" to her, and that she had a "lovely family."

They in fact gave her every reason to feel guilty for seeing them in   15
this way, expressing dismay and horror that she should think that they did not love her.

They told us, however, with vehemence and intensity, that she was   16
a slut and no better than a prostitute. They tried to make her feel bad or mad for perceiving their real feelings.

She guiltily suspected that they did not want her at home and accused   17
them, in sudden outbursts, of wanting to get rid of her. They asked her how she could think such things. Yet they were extremely reluctant to have her at home. They tried to make her think they wanted her at home, and to make her feel mad or bad if she perceived that they did not want her home, when in fact they did not want her home.

Extraordinarily confused attitudes were brought into play when she   18
became pregnant.

As soon as they could after hearing about it from Ruby, *mummy* and   19
mother got her on the sitting-room divan, and while trying to pump hot soapy water into her uterus, told her with tears, reproaches, pityingly and vindictively at once, what a fool she was, what a slut she was, what a terrible mess she was in (just like her *mummy*), what a swine the boy was (just like her father), what a disgrace, history was repeating itself, how could one expect anything else. . . .

This was the first time her true parentage had ever been explicitly   20
made known to her.

Subsequently, Ruby's feeling that "people" were talking about her   21
disparagingly began to develop in earnest. As we have noted, she was told this was nonsense. They told us that everyone was "very kind" to her "considering." Her cousin was the most honest. "Yes, most people are kind to her, just as if she were colored."

The whole family was choked with its sense of shame and scandal.   22
While emphasizing this to Ruby again and again, they told her that she was only imagining things when she thought that people were talking

about her. Their lives began to revolve round her. They fussed over her and, at the same time, accused her of being spoiled and pampered. When she tried to reject their pampering they told her that she was ungrateful and that she needed them, she was still a child, and so on.

Ruby was made to feel both that she was mad and bad for thinking   23
that her uncle did not love her, and that he wanted to get rid of her. She was repeatedly told by her mother and aunt how he would do anything for her. Her uncle certainly had intense feelings for her.

Her uncle was first of all represented by her mother and aunt to us   24
as a very good uncle who loved Ruby and who was like a father to her. They assured us that he was willing to do anything he could to throw light on Ruby's problem.[1]

According to the testimony of her uncle, mother, and aunt, this girl   25
had repeatedly been told by him that if she did not "mend her ways" she would have to get out of the house. We know that on two occasions she was actually told by him to go, and she did. But when she said to him that he had told her to get out, he denied it to her though not to us! It was only when his wife and son would not back up his stories to us, although apparently they did in his stories to Ruby, that he admitted that he lost his temper with her, that he called her names when he was angry, but that he did not really mean it.

Her uncle told us tremblingly how she had pawed him, run her hands   26
over his trousers, and how he was sickened by it.

His wife said coolly that he did not give the impression of having   27
been sickened at the time.

Ruby had apparently no idea that her uncle did not like being cuddled   28
and petted. She thought he liked it — she did it to please him.

Not just in one area, but in all aspects of her life, in respect of her   29
clothes, her speech, her work, her friends — this girl was subject to multiple mystifications.

The following summary of a home visit reveals some of them.   30

The family lives in a small working-class street where everyone   31
knows everyone else.

First, mother was seen alone: she reported that things were all right,   32
Ruby was very well, and so on. There was no trouble.

Her uncle was then seen alone. He let out a flood of invective.   33

Uncle: That girl — what I've done for her — her ingratitude. I've a good   34
    mind to turn her out. What is she doing? She's always swearing —
    the foul language is terrible.
Us: What does she say?   35
Uncle: "Bollocks" (mouthed) — because I tell her to stop stroking me.   36
    The language — I've no idea where she gets it from. She won't
    leave me in peace — she's always stroking me, just like that, pawing

---

[1] However, at no time was it possible to see him for a prearranged interview. Six mutually convenient appointments were made during the period of the investigation and every one was broken, and broken either without any notice at all, or at no more than twenty-four hours' notice. He was seen only once by us and that was when we called at his house without notice.

me. She knows it gets on my nerves, but she does it deliberately. I won't pamper her like her mother and aunt. She's got them running round her in circles. They give her everything, tea in bed, everything. She's been spoiled. She's been given everything. She thinks she can get away with everything. If I pampered her she'd stop pawing me but I don't.

Us: Her mother says everything is all right.   37

Uncle: Her mother says everything is all right? — I'll be frank, you can't   38
take any notice of what she or her aunt say. She's always been spoiled and disobedient, contrary. Even when she was being toilet trained, for months they tried to sit her on the pot, but as soon as they let her off she'd go and do it somewhere else. I'll give you another example; when she was small I used to take her and my son out together. We'd get on a bus and I'd say, "Come and sit here beside your dad," but not her. She'd go and sit on the other side, just to be awkward. Another thing she'd get away with was examinations. She'd never sit an examination, instead she'd go to bed the day before. She'd say she was ill and she'd vomit, to get out of the examination.

Us: What about her pregnancy?   39

Uncle: The pregnancy? That was a shock to me. I nearly went gray   40
overnight. It was the last thing I expected of her. I always said that she'd scratch out any man's eyes who tried that sort of thing on her. I used to take her photo to work — she used to be very pretty, she looks terrible now. I used to be proud of her looks. I'd take her photo to work and show it, and my mates would say: "That's a fine bit of stuff there," and I'd say, "Just watch it, she'd scratch out the eyes of any man that tried that sort of thing." It was a terrible business. There's no excuse for it.

Mother and uncle were then seen together. We reported to mother   41
what uncle had just said. She pitched into him.

Mother: It's not true she's spoiled. You're the one that's spoiled, you   42
and Alistair. We're always doing things for you, Peggie and me. You're pampered more than she is.

Moreover, she accused him of being more nervy and tense than Ruby   43
was. Uncle was quite taken aback by this and at a loss for words.

Uncle: Mmmm . . . Me tense? — Not me, I've got nerves of steel. Yes,   44
a bit edgy, maybe that's it — edgy (trembling all over).

We asked her mother about the issue of Ruby's stroking her uncle,   45
an issue that so incensed him.

Mother: Stroking? Yes, she's always stroking her uncle. Very irritating   46
but she doesn't mean any harm. She's always doing it to her dad. He was playful.

Uncle: Yes, she used to stroke him and slap his leg. I've seen her slap   47
his legs till they were red and he just sat there and laughed. He seemed to enjoy it. It irritates me. I'm not the playful type, not even with my son.

Mother: Oh but you play sometimes with me and Peggie. She's a good   **48**
girl Ruby. . . .

[The cousin, Alistair, joined the interview session.] At this point,   **49**
with an apparently firm alliance between uncle and cousin in full swing,
and mother looking decidedly crushed, we were joined by Ruby's aunt
(uncle's wife, mother's sister, cousin's mother, alias *mother*).

Alistair began to become more expansive, and to get somewhat out   **50**
of hand. He started to develop criticisms of the ways Ruby was handled
by his mother and aunt, which, in a curious way, they agreed with.

Cousin: She should be left to do things for herself. She's indecisive.   **51**
She's not allowed to make a decision. It's put on her plate for her.
If she's not allowed to make a decision in small things she won't
learn to make them in big things.

Aunt: Yes, she won't make any decision. Do you remember when she   **52**
left that job? I thought she should do this, and you thought she should
do that?

Mother: Yes, I thought she should do that, but you were right, Peggie.   **53**

Aunt: Yes, so I told her but she wouldn't do it. I couldn't get her across   **54**
the doorstep.

Uncle: That's right. She expects others to do it for her.   **55**

Cousin: She won't sit any examinations. She gets ill before examinations.   **56**
She won't make a decision.

Aunt: Yet after the examination she's able to do the things all right. Do   **57**
you remember her dancing? Mrs. Smith said, "Isn't that funny, she
wouldn't do the examination, and yet she's doing it lovely now." That
time she couldn't write for the exam, but afterwards she wrote and
wrote all things that she should have written.

Uncle: No, I couldn't have expressed myself properly. She doesn't put   **58**
it on being ill before the examination. She works herself up to a pitch
so she's ill. Oh I wouldn't say she did it deliberately.

We asked Alistair whether he thought Ruby was made a "favorite."   **59**

Cousin: Favoritism? I think she felt I was being favored. Well I'll be   **60**
frank. I think it's fair to say I was the apple of my grandmother's
eye and I think Ruby felt it.

Uncle: I treated them equal, no difference.   **61**

Aunt: What one got the other got.   **62**

Mother: Yes.   **63**

We asked how he felt about her pregnancy.   **64**

Cousin: Pregnancy? I've got nothing against her for that. It could happen   **65**
to anybody, nice people, respectable people, one of my friends. No,
it wasn't being pregnant, it was her attitude — casual, couldn't care
less — that shocked me.

Uncle: Yes.   **66**

Mother: It was a shock. I'd just had a letter from her father and I said,   **67**
"Ruby, I've got a shock for you," and she said "I've got one for you,
I'm in trouble" — Oh it was terrible.

Aunt: Yes I was there. I said, "Don't joke, Ruby, it's serious, how can   68
you say that at a time like this?" And she said, "I'm not joking."
What a shock. We rushed her off to the doctor to make sure.

Uncle: Yes I took her. We had to know.   69

Mother: Yes.   70

Cousin: I wasn't surprised. My cousin Edith was at that party and a   71
couple of days after she said to me, "You should have seen Ruby."
I hushed her up because there was someone else there at the time.
I didn't tell anyone because I didn't know if it was true. Edith's a
trouble-maker. But as I say it could happen to anyone, but it was
her attitude. The chap wasn't up to much. He was as much to blame.
He came round and said he would marry her but he asked us not
to tell his father. I believe he knocked her around too.

Mother: Yes, she used to show me the bruises.   72

Uncle: He was a bad one.   73

Mother: But she said she liked him for all that.   74

Aunt: It's often like that. They treat them badly, and they're still liked.   75

Uncle: Yes.   76

We asked about the neighbors — one of the most important issues   77
to clarify — since much of Ruby's "illness" was her supposed delusions
of reference that "the whole district" knew about her, talked about her,
and pretended to her they did not.

Mother: Neighbors, no. Nobody said anything.   78

Aunt: Yes the neighbors are so helpful. They're so sweet. Mrs. Smith   79
says, "No need to leave Ruby alone, I'll always look after her for
you." We talked over about a job for Ruby. We're a close community
here, everyone helps everyone else. They are so kind to her. They're
all interested in her welfare. No one has said a word to her about
it or going into the hospital, not a word, there's no gossip. I don't
know why Ruby should think the neighbors are talking about her.

Uncle: No.   80

Mother: No.   81

Aunt: Ruby once asked if I thought the neighbors talked about her, if   82
they knew she was in the hospital, and I said, "Of course not." Ruby
is the one who can't keep things to herself. She'll tell everyone her
business, but she will do it.

Mother: Yes.   83

Uncle: Yes.   84

Aunt: Remember that time she was going on a visit to Auntie Joan. She   85
went to the hairdresser and told the hairdresser, and the next I heard
from Mrs. Williams — "I heard Ruby's gone to her Auntie Joan" —
No she won't keep anything to herself. But the neighbors don't gossip.
They're so sweet. Whenever she comes home on leave from the
hospital, they greet her, "Hello Ruby, home again?" — Nobody's
ever been unkind to her.

Cousin: They don't talk in front of her. They're sweet to her, but they   86
talk about her all right in private. It's like a colored person coming
to stay here. Nobody will say a word against her to her face, but

they'll have plenty to say when she's not there. They talk about her all right.

The Case of David G.
MALCOLM B. BOWERS, JR.

David G., at the time of his hospitalization, was a 21-year-old senior at   **1**
a Western university. He was approaching the end of his college career with a great deal of concern about his future. Though he had already been accepted by a prominent law school, David was not certain about his choice of vocation, and had also given some consideration to medicine and writing. David knew that his father, a lawyer, had also encountered difficulty in choosing a vocation and had taken a kind of moratorium after college by going abroad to participate in a foreign civil war. The experience had been disillusioning, however, and Mr. G. had given up his idealism completely, directing his attention to making money. In many ways, Mr. G. considered himself a failure, and though he made a good living for his family, he was unhappy with his accomplishments. He had managed to purchase a very expensive home, though there always seemed to be outstanding debts.

Mrs. G., long intimidated by her husband, sought psychiatric as-   **2**
sistance for intractable asthma two years before David's hospitalization. As a result she became more assertive toward her husband in ways that frequently took the form of undercutting his authority in the home and belittling his sexual ability. Mr. G. was usually very passive toward his wife, dealing with her aggression with a kind of sarcastic banter. However, following bouts of drinking he would engage in violent outbursts, and on such occasions David, his 18-year-old sister, and his 13-year-old brother were often witnesses to the abusive arguments of their parents. Mrs. G. held the threat of divorce constantly over the heads of other family members.

David had a special girlfriend, Laura, who had been in psychotherapy   **3**
for two years. Their relationship was characterized by a great deal of sexual experimentation, with David frequently doubting his own sexual ability. Separations and reconciliations were violent, highly charged experiences, much in the fashion of the relationship between David's parents. In mid-February Laura had dated a boy in another city and refused to tell David the details. He immediately fantasied that Laura had engaged in intercourse with her date and wrote a very vindictive poem to her, calling her a whore. Having mailed the poem, he felt angry and guilty. A trip to another city, where he visited friends, served only to assure David that they had their own troubles. Following his return, he wrote a short story entitled "Test to Be a Man" in which the storyteller finds that his best friend has stolen his sweetheart. He became even more overwrought when he learned that a lifelong friend, Nathan, sided with Laura in her quarrel with David. This discovery prompted him to write Nathan a "hate letter," accusing him of betraying their friendship. At this

point, David essentially confined himself to his room at college, attended a few classes, but spent most of his time — day and night — at the typewriter attempting to get his thoughts on paper. At one point, he seemed to view this process as a self-analysis. He recorded the progress of events in calendar form as follows:

Sunday, Feb. 22 — wrote letter to Laura, severing.

Weekend, Feb. 28 — fled to Cleveland, no good.

Monday, March 2 — wrote story "Test to Be a Man."

Friday, March 6 — found Nathan sympathetic to Laura, story comes true.

Sunday & Monday, March 8 & 9 — two hate letters to Nathan.

Monday & Tuesday, March 9 & 10 — intense anxiety.

Wednesday, March 11 — partial solution (intuitive) in letter to Nathan.

Friday, March 13 — ended diary.

Saturday, March 14 — began self-analysis.

March 17 — case closed.

The following day he found his way to the hospital emergency room where he presented a picture of intense fright, pressure of speech, ideas of influence and reference, and autistic thinking. The diagnosis, based on clinical data and psychological tests, was acute, undifferentiated schizophrenic reaction. Later, when his parents visited his room at school, they found the typed account that is reprinted below. There has been some deletion and condensation where certain sections were repetitive, but otherwise the account has not been altered in any way. The stream-of-consciousness style has been left as written by the patient, who has given his consent for the publication of this material. Brief explanatory footnotes have been included where they seem indicated.

4

SLIGHT DEPRESSION
OR
WATCHING YOURSELF LIVE
OR
JUST A WEEK LIKE ANY OTHER

Monday, March 9, 1964. She had said she loved me (bopping off to Providence in between protests I suppose I could swallow that though) but I don't think if it were ever true, that she still does. (N told me that, told me just like that and the reason he hadn't called was cause he was playing pickup sticks with her date he's so charmingly forthright I puke).

5

His logic is so good he can laugh at his own [girl] having her insides torn out he's so positive and rational and knows just how everything works including one divorce, one abortion that he's undoubtedly reassured her everything's all right such a good friend midwife to disasters a cool guy that's what so even if she does still love me (she was so cold on

6

the phone) anyway so cold her voice on the phone she wanted to chat I fantasied suicide for twenty-four hours . . . twenty-four hours you begin to scare yourself like that wanted to chat bragged she'd burned "everything" (I wanted to ask if that everything included thirty dollar cashmeres doubt it) chat about her date etc. If he had been alone I would have killed I promise if I believe anything is left in myself I promise I would have killed but he was only there as a friend so that solution would have been disproportionate honor among friends (I had asked him not to meddle asked him as a friend ha ha) being outdated anyhow no one not even me would have understood not being able to kill him and less able to kill myself I just got drunk alone in Harlem. If she still loves me if then still I can't see her talk to her until I am worthy if I can ever be of her of anything until at least say (stinking symbolism runs my life) even then if I see her at all it must be to propose to say here I am me at last me I respect myself can respect love marry you can bolt myself onto life and ride ride ride we'll ride together some say it's a good thing I'd like to give it a try when I trust myself and what I am when that time comes I shall say I love you.

I have a right I do have a right to hold that bastard responsible . . .   7
my game wasn't pretty perhaps; I wanted her to relent first, that's all, just relent first that much of the double standard I hold by if that means double standard but she bore the burden she ran off on me I had a right . . . she made no attempt at apology that night none none so we're both prideful but all I wanted was an I'm sorry even to the letter I wrote, horrible letter designed to humble and that's all just asking an emotional sacrifice an ego sacrifice on her part something she had been as little willing to make as I was . . . but she couldn't do it with that snake whispering in her ear someone for her anyone for her to talk to excuse herself to but me.[1] . . .

March 10, 5 P.M.   I'm becoming a monomaniac it's incredible it just   8
doesn't stop there are moments when I can do no more than tear up matchbooks futile futile things and others of greater lucidity when I can see so clearly what went wrong why we were unable to commit ourselves each coming to the brink at different moments I came to her that evening at her house felt my insides dissolve with wanting, expecting to burst free she put me off good put me off and put me off and then 12 hours later when the thing lay sticky like bile inside me then only then we went to bed together and she had her orgasm and I did crossword puzzles. Did she ever come at me yes I suppose, at the beginning, too fast too desperately when she knew there was no chance and was doing it on her doctor's advice and I kept telling her I was no therapist that wasn't my job not my job. But that letter should have been a test it was a test I wanted her to make it on her own without help confronting everything but she dragged in a surrogate she dragged in my lily-livered friend and he came galloping to the rescue in all the accoutrements of maiden rescue

---

[1] The foregoing passage deals with his presumed betrayal by Laura and Nathan's willingness to be Laura's confidant in the argument.

and good will. There are moments of lucidity when I see how close hate and love can lie, back to back, moment to moment I could kill I could love I lie here tearing up matchbooks. My story was rejected and I think I mucked an English test this morning. Will do the same for a French test tomorrow. The big test is still ahead or behind I tear up matchbooks. First a tragedy then a comedy I keep trying to laugh. Someone said you can refuse a man a loan you can refuse him your sympathy but you can't refuse him a fight if he wants to fight. I'll beat him on the streets I'll beat him in front of Laura or before his parents. He'll fight. Anyhow at last that second self is returning the one that wants to turn his life into a work of art it's returning a little in writing momentary sweet breaths of sanity in the end perhaps it's the only way I must write even poorly. . . .

Tuesday, March 10, 11 P.M.   It's silly to stop now, I've got a good   9
rhythm going. I type for twenty minutes and then read back over the past two months for forty. That makes an hour. Then I begin again. Pretty soon I'll get sleepy from all this banging down on the keys and then I'll go to sleep and start fresh in the morning. I ought to entitle this to my future headshrinker cause Mr. White says this is about the age when the snap occurs . . . he says anything can set it off if it's there to begin with (what that means, of course, he's not sure . . . I am) any drop in (get this) "esteem income" occasioned by test situations or symbolic maturity crises like graduation, or tests or even a love affair (what a bland term!) So I'm waiting. Where and when does it begin? Do you at some point decide to go crouch in a corner talking to yourself unable to shit? Except maybe I'm pulling myself out of it, kind of reeling out the intestines of it diseased inch by inch . . . sublimating in otherwords. My concerns are once again pretentiously self-conscious, I notice in my rereadings an increasing number of quotes and witticisms . . . I'm showing off again, what a good thing: Like the eighty-year old women in the asylum to whom the scientists gave estrogen just to see what would happen . . . sure enough, they began combing their hair and fixing their dresses and primping, in short preparing like mad to go out and have their hymens busted again. Everybody, doctors and relatives and other patients thought Oh what a good thing that they're taking a renewed interest in life! I thought it was a rather touching thing myself. So I'm taking a renewed interest in life . . . I even began criticizing certain turns of construction in the pages just written . . . hot diggity, pretty soon I'll be sitting around in a pile of writing up to my ears and simply tickled pink! Like feces I'll play with the paper make gliders and little sailor hats and be innocent again.[2]

Rereading this time, I just noticed a terrible thing . . . I'm such a   10
short sighted misanthrope that I will never be able (in a particularly severe paroxysm of self pity of course) to give this to any of my friends . . . There isn't a single one I've spared much less said a good word of! I'm

---

[2] Here, as in other places, he seems to flirt with the idea of going insane even to the point of addressing, in a sense, his future psychiatrist.

sorry really. The obvious solution is to send it to Laura and then blow my brains in (I'd prefer to fall on a sword but I'd probably take it through the forearm) that way she'd feel bad about burning it. Egotism the bosom serpent, I need a good priest. . . .

Midnight, Tuesday–Wednesday.   But jesus I feel that I've changed **11** I really do I've never felt this way before I'm even beginning to trust it a little bit . . . so if you are introspective then BE introspective . . . all the way . . . you come through the bottom and out the other side and there's a world out there just waiting to be eaten played on lived with worked for jumped up and down upon made love to sung about man I'm six years old.

I could be simply overawed but in rereading this I see an incredible, **12** an astonishing structure . . . automatic writing but there is development, there is almost an internal plot . . . the hand of god? Or of the subconscious? Or of both at the same time? Grace and peace and inner peace. Or have I gone mad? Am I talking rationally . . . skip the french paper I've got to get out of this room this typewriter and find out no . . . I'm okay. . . .

You go in and out deeper and shallower and you come back you **13** always come back it's like a drug but without the excuse of being drugged drugs do do that they make you think you're going to know yourself and then make you forget yourself so they promise and then they take away promise and take away someone promised and took her the bitch Laura my mother my mother promised to love me and then took it away and gave it back to him and kept doing that taking it away and giving it back to him you can't trust them they're not to be trusted they give and then take back and they make you cry and leave you frightened and crying and watching from your crib as they walk away walk away back to their room bedroom her room they don't rock you anymore they always stop rocking you and leave you there in the dark to cry and cry and cry boy I must have cried like hell as a baby . . . my mother said I cried a lot . . . post nasal drip or something she said, the bitch she was lying I knew what they were doing she was covering up hiding it from me she was scared and guilty about it and I knew and cried coming out . . . I'm trembling also smoking a lot cause it hurts it hurts to know this but I MUST MUST MUST know this I don't want any more secrets I've had enough secrets secrets kept me from my beautiful lovely Laura in the purple velvet dress no more secrets cause of that bitch my mother whip out the happiness kit its your key your safety valve your proof it can be done you did it you saw that morning sometime that morning when it rained stars it will rain stars again no question about it so I figured I'd do it to my sister to get him back cause he liked my sister too come to think of it I kind of did it with my mother with her her her (oh go on say it we'll burn the thing) with her panties a fetish that's all it was no it wasn't. Like my grandfather said my penis would fall off if I played with it so I played with it and played with it and am still playing with it and I suppose I'm still waiting for it to fall off . . . suppose who are you kidding buster . . . you want it to fall off want it to wish it would you hate it because because because it did all those things what things things with mother and father and freddie and sister and brother that's enough.

———— *Preliminary Questions* ————

1. In your own words, what are the main features of schizophrenic behavior? Write a paragraph describing them.
2. After reading Sue A. Shapiro's "History of the Concept of Schizophrenia," compare Bleuler's and Kraepelin's views of schizophrenia.
3. Compare Shapiro's overview and the discussion in "Description of and Diagnostic Criteria for Schizophrenia." What differences in emphasis can you note?
4. According to Shapiro, how did Sigmund Freud influence the treatment of schizophrenia? Write a paragraph explaining Shapiro's interpretation.
5. After reading all four case histories, construct a definition of schizophrenia, using illustrative examples.
6. Write a short essay diagnosing each of the four cases in relation to the diagnostic criteria described by the American Psychiatric Association.
7. Choose two cases in which you find close parallels. Analyze the structure of circumstances that may have contributed to the schizophrenic behavior of the two subjects.
8. Choose the two cases that seem the most dissimilar. Use them to illustrate the breadth of a possible definition for the term *schizophrenia.*
9. Can you offer any generalizations about stages in the development of schizophrenia? Offer a serial account. Or, if you find no single pattern of development, write a short essay contrasting two or more patterns.
10. Explain the distinction between chronic and acute schizophrenia with reference to two or more of the cases.
11. Would you hesitate to classify any of the subjects in these cases as schizophrenic? If so, write a short essay explaining why.
12. Consider the ways in which the people reporting these cases help shape your responses to them. Which of the reports seems most objective? Write a short essay defending your opinion.
13. All cases of schizophrenia are not alike. From the point of view of someone trying to respond as humanely as possible to schizophrenic behavior, what do you think are the most important differences to keep in mind?
14. What role does school seem to play in the development of schizophrenia? Assemble your evidence in a short essay.
15. People sometimes misuse the term *schizophrenia* to refer to "split personality." What misunderstanding does this use reveal, and why do you think it may have arisen?

Complicating the Issues

The following six pieces contribute to the general debate on whether the causes of schizophrenia are primarily biological or environmental. The first selection consists of excerpts from a landmark study published in 1958. August B. Hollingshead and Frederick C. Redlich argue for an environmentalist position from a sociological perspective.

From *Social Class and Mental Illness*
AUGUST B. HOLLINGSHEAD AND FREDERICK C. REDLICH

TWO RESEARCH QUESTIONS

After several months of preliminary work, the central questions of this research emerged, namely: (1) Is mental illness related to class in our society? (2) Does a psychiatric patient's position in the status system affect how he is treated for his illness?   1

The first query is related to the etiology of mental illnesses. The psychodynamic concept of unconscious conflict between instinctual forces and the demands of the environment is crucial for many attempts at explanation of most neurotic and psychotic illnesses. Knowing that the different social classes exhibit different ways of life, we conjectured that emotional problems of individuals might be related to the patterns of life characteristic of their class positions.   2

The second question is focused on treatment. Our observations and experiences with psychiatric treatment led us to think that the kind of treatment a patient receives is not a function solely of the state of medical knowledge which is embodied in the art and science of making a diagnosis and prescribing treatment. Subtle and powerful psychological and social processes appear to be important determinants in the choice of treatment and its implementation. We are interested particularly in finding out whether the various psychiatric treatments patients receive are affected by class status.   3

WORKING HYPOTHESES

The third major step in the formulation of our research plans was taken when we crystallized our thoughts on these questions around a series of tentative hypotheses. Eventually, five working hypotheses were written into the research design. Each hypothesis connected the two major concepts of the research, namely, social class and mental illness, in such a way that the resulting proposition could be tested empirically. The several hypotheses were phrased thus: 4

> *Hypothesis 1.* The prevalence of treated mental illness is related significantly to an individual's position in the class structure.

Hypothesis 2. The types of diagnosed psychiatric disorders are connected significantly to the class structure.

Hypothesis 3. The kind of psychiatric treatment administered by psychiatrists is associated with the patient's position in the class structure.

Hypothesis 4. Social and psychodynamic factors in the development of psychiatric disorders are correlative to an individual's position in the class structure.

Hypothesis 5. Mobility in the class structure is associated with the development of psychiatric difficulties.

ASSUMPTIONS

Several assumptions are implied in these hypotheses: First, the social   5
structure of our society is characterized by a system of stratification.
Second, individuals living in a given class are subjected to problems of
living that are expressed in emotional and psychological reactions and
disorders different in quantity and quality from those expressed by persons in other classes. Third, psychiatrists, who are responsible for diagnosing and treating mental illness, are controlled, as members of the
society, by its value system. This presumption implies that psychiatrists
work with phenomena that are essentially social in origin, and they cope
with them in ways that are prescribed, on the one hand, by the professional subculture of psychiatry as a medical specialty and, on the other,
by the expectancies, working rules, and values that impinge upon them
in their day-to-day professional and lay activities. Fourth, the working
rules of psychiatry are practiced in ways that are connected implicitly
with class status. Fifth, mental illness is defined socially; that is, whatever
a psychiatrist treats or is expected to treat must be viewed as mental
illness. This position is based upon the fact that in our society psychiatrists
treat individuals whose behavior would be ignored in a second society,
punished by the criminal courts in a third, and in still others given over
to priests. We agree with Romano that "the conventional conceptual
scheme of disease is not applicable to mental disease." Sixth, the class
status of individuals in the society is viewed as the independent or *antecedent* variable; the diagnosis of a patient's illness and the treatment
prescribed for him by a psychiatrist are considered to be dependent or
consequent variables. Demonstration of the validity of these assumptions
rests upon a systematic examination of the five hypotheses. . . .

TESTS OF THE WORKING HYPOTHESES

Each hypothesis was tested with different kinds of data and different   6
research methods. The first three utilize data drawn from the entire
community of New Haven, Connecticut. One might call this a "macro-
scopic" or survey approach. *Hypotheses 4* and *5* are investigated by the
detailed study of fifty psychiatric patients and their families who live in
this community; one might refer to this as a "microscopic" or clinical

approach. The two approaches supplement one another: The survey approach furnishes well-defined quantitative data on a cross section of the community, whereas the clinical approach gives a close view of fine details on individuals and families and permits insights into the origins of maladjusted behavior and responses to treatment under sharply different social conditions. . . .

The data we have gathered may be used as a base line for the accumulation of comparable data in other, but similar, communities. Cross-community comparisons of social structure and the distribution and treatment of psychiatric patients should contribute to the solution of some of the theoretical and practical problems highlighted in this research. Without encroaching upon our findings we may ask: Why is the age- and sex-adjusted rate per 100,000 for schizophrenic patients in psychiatric treatment from the New Haven community over nine times higher in the lowest social class than in the highest one? Why do "lower" class psychiatric patients drop out of treatment after one, two, or three visits to clinics? If similar questions are asked and similar findings are reported from other urbanized communities, social science and medical researchers will have factual data upon which they may base theories and plan procedures for coping with mental health problems. . . .

7

THE FINDINGS IN BRIEF

The many systematic tests we made of [our] hypotheses demonstrate that our original assumptions are correct. Highly significant associations do exist between class status and (a) the prevalence of psychiatric patients in the population, (b) the types of disorders mentally ill individuals present to psychiatrists, and (c) the kinds of treatment psychiatrists administer to their patients. These hypotheses are clearly tenable in the setting described in this book. However, many readers may ask: Does the same situation prevail in my community or any other community? It may, but only additional research can give a meaningful answer.

8

Seymour Kety, a psychiatrist, presents cross-cultural research to support the theory that there is a genetic contribution to schizophrenia. His article was published in 1978.

Heredity and Environment
SEYMOUR KETY

In psychiatry there has always been evidence to suggest the operation of genetic factors in the major mental illnesses, evidence which had many shortcomings but which was nevertheless difficult to ignore. Schizophrenia and manic depressive psychosis was observed to run in families. There is a ten percent risk for schizophrenia in the first-degree relatives of schizophrenics and a one percent risk for schizophrenia in the general

1

population. Then there were the twin studies in which it was shown repeatedly (in more than twelve studies) that the monozygotic twin of a schizophrenic or manic depressive patient is much more likely to have the same illness than is a dizygotic twin. In fact, the risk for schizophrenia in the co-twin of a dizygotic schizophrenic is about ten percent, the same as for other siblings. In a monozygotic twin, on the other hand, the risk is fifty percent.

Such evidence, however, was not accepted as proof that genetic factors are important in these illnesses, and for good reasons. There were fairly large loopholes in this evidence — large enough for whole schools of psychiatry to march through them. What was the difficulty? Even though schizophrenia runs in families, many things run in families. Poverty runs in families, wealth runs in families, pellagra runs in families. That is hardly good evidence that these are genetically determined, since families share not only genetic endowment but also environment and life experience. Therefore, showing that something runs in families proves very little about its origins.

Twin studies are a more compelling form of genetic data, but even twin studies depend on the assumption that the only thing that differentiates monozygotic from dizygotic twins is their genetic relatedness, and that environmental factors are somehow canceled out or randomized. But that is not the case. Monozygotic twins share much of their environment as well as their genetic endowment. They live together; they sleep together; they are dressed alike by their parents; they are paraded in a double parambulator as infants; their friends cannot distinguish one from the other. In short, they develop a certain ego identification with each other that is very hard to dissociate from the purely genetic identity with which they were born.

It was interpretive difficulties such as these that in 1961 stimulated several of us at the National Institute of Mental Health — David Rosenthal, Paul Wender, and myself — to decide independently that there was another approach to the problem of dissociating genetic from environmental variables in schizophrenia. We reasoned that although an adopted person derives his genetic endowment from one family, his life experience and environment occur with another family. This occurred to me because I noticed a rather interesting peculiarity of adoptive parents. Such parents notice various characteristics in their adopted child and have a tendency to attribute to genetic factors the qualities they do not like about the child; on the other hand, if the child does things of which they approve, they attribute them to their environment. That, of course, is wishful thinking, but it did suggest the possibility of separating the two influences by a more scientific process. We also realized that to avoid selective bias, it would be necessary to start with a total population of adoptive individuals and then identify those who were schizophrenic rather than to start with schizophrenics and try to find those who were adopted. To avoid subjective bias all diagnoses would have to be made in ignorance of the relationship of one individual to another.

After trying in the United States to pull together a total sample, we gave up and went to Denmark. We were given access, on the basis of complete confidentiality, to the remarkably accurate records that Denmark keeps on its inhabitants. An adoption file has all of the country's legally adopted individuals going back for a number of generations. Because we were interested only in adoptees who were adults at the time of the study and therefore old enough to have acquired schizophrenia, we searched for mental illness among the 14,500 people in Denmark who are now between twenty-five and fifty years of age and who were legally adopted at an early age by people other than their biological relatives. Because Denmark has a system of national health insurance, there is also a central register that lists the names of all people who have been seen in any psychiatric facility in Denmark, with the exception of one hospital, which for a long time refused to report. We therefore made a search through the psychiatric register and, separately, through the records of that one hospital. We found that the psychiatric register was quite complete; by going through the hospital records individually we found that only five percent of the people ever admitted to a mental hospital were not listed in the register. We therefore searched through the register for any one of those 14,500 adoptees who had ever been seen in a psychiatric facility. Ten percent of them had — about what one would expect in the general population in Denmark.

The difficult problem then arose of picking out those who could be   6
called schizophrenic, since schizophrenia means different things in different places. In Denmark, schizophrenia is what Kraepelin thought it was, that is, chronic process schizophrenia. But in America other subgroups have been added to the original syndrome. There is a category of latent, ambulatory, or borderline schizophrenia that has many of the characteristics of chronic schizophrenia except that it usually does not have the psychotic features. Another category, called acute schizophrenic reaction, is simply an acute psychotic reaction that in Denmark would be called schizophreniform psychosis or psychogenic psychosis but would not be called schizophrenia. We decided that since American psychiatry calls all three categories schizophrenia we would, for the purpose of our study, accept all three, but would define each category appropriately and use the diagnoses carefully in the hope that we might find out not only whether genetic factors operate but also what different factors operate in these different categories of schizophrenia.

We read the psychiatric records or abstracts, translated into English,   7
of those adoptees who had been seen in a psychiatric facility. By this time the three of us had established a collaboration with Fini Schulsinger, who is Chief of Psychiatry at the Kommunehospital and through whose good offices we had been introduced to the record system in Denmark and to the authorities. Schulsinger organized a team in Denmark to collect the data that we required.

If the three of us in America and Schulsinger independently agreed   8
that someone was schizophrenic in one of the three categories, then that person became an index case. If we all four independently decided he was not schizophrenic, then he was rejected. If one or another of us suggested schizophrenia, then we would hold a conference on that particular case and if as a result of that conference we could all agree on

schizophrenia, then he would become an index case. In this way, we selected seventy-four persons whom we all finally diagnosed as schizophrenic. What we wanted to do was to examine their biological and adoptive relatives; if schizophrenia runs in the family because of shared environmental factors, it should run in the adoptive families, whereas if the familial tendency in schizophrenia is the result of heredity, it would appear in the biological relatives. In Denmark it is not difficult to identify the relatives of adoptive persons: The adoption records themselves are quite complete, giving the names of biological parents and adoptive parents, and there is a register listing the name of anyone who has lived in Denmark more than three weeks, his birthdate, all addresses he has had since birth, the names of every child in the household, name of spouse, and so forth. By going through this register with the names of the parents, biological and adoptive, we could identify all the other children the parents had. These children would then be full siblings or half siblings of the adoptee, depending upon whether they shared both parents or only one. In this manner we assembled the relatives of the seventy-four index adoptees with schizophrenia, as well as the relatives of seventy-four adopted controls, each matched with an index case in terms of age, sex, socioeconomic class of the rearing family, and length of time spent with the biological mother.

We then shuffled these names together and from then on we identified relatives and made diagnoses without knowing the relationship of one person to another or whether the person was related to an index case or control. The total of index cases and controls gave us more than 1,100 relatives. The names of these relatives were then searched through the psychiatric register as well as other registers — for example, military records and records compiled by the Department of Justice from psychiatric examinations of prisoners. In all such sources we looked for relatives who had had any experience with a psychiatrist or a psychiatric institution. That information was abstracted, translated into English, and edited to remove any clues that would permit a sophisticated reader to guess whether this was a biological relative, an adoptive relative, an index or control relative. Then each of us independently read these records and made a psychiatric diagnosis using the three types of schizophrenia that we were tentatively accepting: chronic, borderline or latent, and acute. We quickly decided that we needed to create another category, questionable or uncertain schizophrenia. In picking the index cases, we had excluded those in which the schizophrenia was uncertain, but with the relatives we had to make a diagnosis, even if we were not sure. Thus, "uncertain schizophrenia" included those cases in which the symptoms were too mild or atypical for a diagnosis or in which for some reason or another we thought schizophrenia was the most likely diagnosis but could not be sure. As a result, we were testing the hypothesis that genetic factors in schizophrenia might be manifested not only in the three kinds of schizophrenia we had labeled but also in cases of uncertain schizophrenia. For some time there has been the notion that "schizoid" or "inadequate" personality disorder is also a *forme fruste* of schizophrenia. We speculated that there might be a schizophrenic spectrum of disorders that ranged from definite schizophrenia through these types of uncertain schizophrenia. If we could get enough information, we hoped that we would be able to test this hypothesis.

When we had diagnosed all relatives on whom we had any information, **10** we broke the code and allocated the relatives to their respective populations. What we found was as follows: Among the index cases, 24 out of 405 biological relatives exhibited a schizophrenic spectrum disorder, whereas 2 out of 173 adoptive relatives exhibited these disorders. Among the control cases, 4 out of 387 biological relatives and 4 out of 194 adoptive relatives exhibited a schizophrenic spectrum disorder. The difference in schizophrenic spectrum disorders between index and control biologic relatives is highly significant ($p = 0.0001$). The number of schizophrenic spectrum disorders in the biologic and adoptive relatives of the controls and in the adoptive relatives of the index cases are the one or two percent that one would expect in the population as a whole. On the other hand, the biological relatives of index cases show a significant concentration of spectrum disorders, nearly six percent. . . .

Now what about environmental factors? All that we could say was **11** that the data suggested the operation of genetic factors, but that did not exclude environmental factors, even though the adoptive relatives did not show any more schizophrenia than the adoptive relatives of controls. We therefore thought that it would be useful if we could carry out intensive psychiatric interviews with these relatives. This might give us a great deal more information about their mental status, personalities, and environmental influences. Such interviews might also make possible psychiatric diagnoses on people who had never been seen by a psychiatrist. It was clearly impractical to conduct interviews on all 1,100 relatives. However, we felt that we could do such a study on a subgroup of this population, the subgroup that were adopted in greater Copenhagen. Of the 14,500 adoptees, 5,500 were adopted through the courts of Copenhagen, and of these 5,500, 33 were among our index cases and 33 were among the controls. These individuals had given us 512 of the 1,100 relatives.

We were very fortunate to enlist the collaboration of Bjørn Jacobsen, **12** a young psychiatrist who spent two years carrying out these interviews. There were, of course, some ethical considerations in such an enterprise. We had agreed with the authorities that we would keep all the information confidential, even from people whom it might concern. And we did not think it was ethical to go up to a middle-aged housewife in Denmark and say, "Mrs. Hansen, we would like to interview you because at the age of eighteen you had an illegitimate child who now has schizophrenia." On the other hand, we felt that it was necessary to inform prospective subjects regarding the nature of the interview but without discussing adoption, the hypothesis that was being tested, or how they were selected. So we wrote to all the relatives in the greater Copenhagen sample that we were interested in doing a study on factors concerning health and requesting their participation in an interview by a physician regarding their life history and its medical-psychological aspects. They were assured that the interview would be protected by the Danish laws of confidentiality for information given to physicians. These interviews have been used only for research and are not available to the Danish system of records.

About half the people immediately responded, giving a time when [13] the interview could take place. Those that did not respond got a telephone call from the secretary first and then from Jacobsen, who tried to persuade them. For those who still had not responded, Jacobsen would knock on their door and try to persuade them to have an interview. In this way ninety percent of the relatives alive and residing in Denmark, Sweden, or Norway agreed to an interview.

The interviews were exhaustive, averaging thirty-five pages in tran- [14] script. They elicited a great deal of medical, psychological, and sociological information on the individual from birth, as well as providing a complete mental status examination. The interviews were dictated by Jacobsen in English and edited to remove any clues identifying the biological or adoptive relationship of the person to our index or control cases. Rosenthal, Wender, and myself then again read and classified each interview. Schulsinger did not participate in this step because we thought he might know some of the people in the Copenhagen sample.

First, there was a very significant increase in deaths among the [15] biological relatives of the index group, thirty-five as compared to thirteen in the control group. We tracked down the causes of death in most of these cases through death certificates and hospital records and found that the excess of death was accounted for by suicide or probable suicide and a few other kinds of sudden death. When we counted only natural deaths or medical illnesses, the numbers in each group were comparable. In fact, all of the eight suicides in the total population of relatives were biological relatives of the index group. Since suicide is an unfortunate outcome in many instances of schizophrenia, it is possible that some schizophrenics had removed themselves from our sample before they were ever diagnosed as such.

. . . There were fewer index biological relatives interviewed because [16] of the higher death rate among them. . . . We considered about forty percent of the relatives to be normal, or at least without a psychiatric diagnosis, and these were distributed randomly. In about fifty percent of the relatives we made some type of psychiatric diagnosis, and these diagnoses also seemed to be randomly distributed.

For schizophrenia diagnoses, however, the situation is different: Eight [17] percent of the biological relatives of the index group were given the diagnosis of definite schizophrenia, and one to three percent of the control relatives, a highly significant difference. If we add to that the people we called uncertain schizophrenics, we simply get an exaggeration of the same phenomenon: Now we have definite or uncertain schizophrenia in sixteen percent of those who are genetically related to the index cases. Thus, uncertain schizophrenics also cluster in the biological relatives of the index cases. . . .

There is a major loophole in all of this evidence, however. Adoption [18] does not separate genetic from environmental factors completely, because even an adopted child shares an environment *in utero* with his biological mother and receives a certain amount of early mothering at her hands.

It is not impossible that during perinatal period some environmental factors could be transmitted from the mother to the child which, twenty years later, might result in schizophrenia. We approached this problem in the following way: There are a lot of biological half siblings in this sample because the biological parents usually were not married at the time they had the child they put up for adoption, and many subsequently had other children with their partners. And since a man can have more children in a given period of time than a woman can, we found as expected that the fathers had substantial numbers of children with other partners; these would be the biological paternal half siblings of our adoptees, of whom there were 127 — more than any other type of relative in the sample. Paternal half siblings help us with this problem because they have the same father but different mothers, that is, they do not share the same uterine environment or the same early mothering experience. [Table 1] shows data for these paternal half siblings. There are a nearly equal number in each group, sixty-three biological paternal half siblings of the index cases, sixty-four of the controls. The amount of schizophrenia, however, is very heavily concentrated in the index relatives. In the case of definite or uncertain schizophrenia, twenty-two percent of the biological paternal half siblings of the schizophrenic adoptees have this diagnosis, versus three percent of the controls; if we restrict ourselves to definite schizophrenia, it is thirteen percent versus two percent — differences that are highly significant.

We have concluded from these findings that genetic factors must be   19
operating in schizophrenia. But what is the nature of these genetic factors? When we inspected individual families closely, we found some other interesting information. The relatives with chronic schizophrenia were nearly always in the biological families of the chronic schizophrenic adopt- ees. Secondly, the adoptees with borderline schizophrenia never have biological relatives with schizophrenia more severe than borderline. More- over, no schizophrenia-like illness appeared in the biological relatives of half of the adoptees. This suggests that we may be dealing not with a single illness but with a heterogeneous cluster of illnesses that have different etiologies.

TABLE 1.   Schizophrenia in the Biological Paternal Half Siblings of the Index and Control Adoptees

ADOPTEE	IDENTIFIED	HAVING DEFINITE OR UNCERTAIN SCHIZOPHRENIA[1]	%	HAVING DEFINITE SCHIZOPHRENIA[2]	%
Index	63	14	22.0	8	13.0
Control	64	2	3.0	1	1.6

[1] Difference is significant at $p = 0.001$.
[2] Difference is significant at $p = 0.015$.

We also have to recognize the possibility that there are forms of 20 schizophrenia in which genetic loading is very important and forms of schizophrenia in which environmental factors probably play the important role. The best evidence that environmental factors are important comes from twin studies, which show that the concordance rate among monozygotic twins is only fifty percent. Clearly, genetic factors cannot account for the whole story. How, then, to get at the environmental factors? Certainly there has been a great emphasis for the past twenty-five years on intrafamily psychological factors, schizophrenogenic mothers, schizophrenogenic parents, the communication of irrationality, and the like. Theodore Lidz has been a major proponent of this position, which he based on observation and psychoanalytic interviews with the parents of schizophrenics at the Yale Psychiatric Institute. Lidz finds a high incidence of psychopathology in parents of schizophrenic patients, to which he attributes an etiological role in the schizophrenia of the children. It seems to me, however, that there are a number of loopholes in his evidence regarding schizophrenogenic parents, as sensitive and perceptive as it is. There are no controls, for example, and the interviewers were not blind. It is difficult to see how an interviewer could avoid finding what he expected to find, given the complexity and the enormous amount of data in a series of psychoanalytic interviews.

Alanen, recognizing the need for controls, compared the parents of 21 schizophrenics with those of neurotics and normal individuals. Alanen was not entirely blind, and therefore his observations suffer from a certain amount of subjective bias. Nonetheless, he found much more psychopathology in the parents of schizophrenics than in the parents of neurotics, who in turn had more psychopathology than the parents of normal individuals. More recently, Wynne and Singer have been carrying out a number of studies in which a great effort is made to control the observations. Their studies depend largely on projective tests, especially the Rorschach. Rorschach testing is done with parents by an observer who may or may not be blind, but then the tapes of these interviews are sent to Margaret Singer, who analyzes them without knowing whether the subjects are related to schizophrenics or controls. Using this method, Wynne and Singer report not so much frank psychopathology as consistent "communication deviance."

There are, however, three alternative hypotheses that such studies 22 have not ruled out. One possibility is that parental differences, including deviant communication, could be a reflection of genetic factors that the parents share with their schizophrenic offspring. A second hypothesis is that the problems associated with rearing a schizophrenic child do something to parents — change them psychologically, alter their pattern of communication in some way. A third alternative is that there is some artifact in the testing situation: someone who has reared a schizophrenic may react differently during psychological testing from someone who has not had that experience. That hypothesis has some interesting support from work by Shopler and Loftin. They tested one group of parents of psychotic children after telling them that they were doing so to learn more about the illness in their child. Another group of parents were tested after being told that they had reared a normal child (which they had); the fact that they had also reared a psychotic child was ignored. The parents presumably took the test situation with the two different sets; only one group had a feeling that they were being studied because of the schizophrenia in their child. More psychopathology was found in the parents who were told that the test's purpose was to learn about their psychotic child. So it is quite possible that the guilt feelings and anxieties of parents of schizophrenics might cause differences that a sophisticated observer could detect in the parents' responses to projective tests.

Wender thought it was possible to test some of these hypotheses   23
by using the adoption model, so he pulled together a population of adopted schizophrenics in Bethesda. This was a sample of Americans whose adoptive parents were alive and would stay at the Clinical Center in Bethesda long enough for them and their schizophrenic sons or daughters to be studied. Psychiatric evaluation, Rorschach tests, and other kinds of projective tests were performed. Similar assessments were carried out on a group of adoptive parents of normal children and on a group of natural parents of schizophrenics who had reared their own children. When psychopathology in the parents was classified according to Alanen's system, as much psychopathology was found in the natural parents of schizophrenics as Alanen had found. On the other hand, the adoptive parents of schizophrenics had less psychopathology, about as much as Alanen had found in the parents of neurotics. This is similar to our finding in the Danish sample that the adoptive parents of schizophrenics consistently showed no more schizophrenia and no more psychopathology in general than do the adoptive parents of controls.

Wender sent the Rorschach tapes of these parents to Margaret Singer   24
for her blind analysis. She came up with a very interesting result. With one hundred percent accuracy she could differentiate parents who had reared a schizophrenic from those who had reared a normal individual, whether or not the schizophrenic was genetically related to the parents. In other words, she found some kind of communication deviance in all of the people who had reared a schizophrenic. Now that excludes one hypothesis — the hypothesis that what Wynne and Singer have been measuring is simply a reflection of the genetic overlap between the parents and the offspring. But what does it really mean? One interpretation is that now at last one has proven that communication deviance is of etiologic significance in schizophrenia. A more precise conclusion, however, would be that people who have reared a schizophrenic give different responses in a Rorschach test than do those who have not. The possibility that having reared a schizophrenic affects the psychology of the parents or their response to a test situation has still not been ruled out.

Wender has gone on to do another Rorschach study comparing the   25
adopted parents of schizophrenics, the biological parents of schizophrenics, and the parents of children with a nongenetic form of mental retardation. In this comparison it was not possible to differentiate the parents of schizophrenics from the parents of mentally retarded individuals, although both groups were different from the normals. This is compatible

with the thesis that rearing any seriously disturbed child may change the response of a parent to a projective test and make it possible for sophisticated observers to differentiate them from parents who have not had that experience. The possibility that rearing or particular aspects of rearing are etiologically important in schizophrenia is viable and certainly worth examining further, but it is a hypothesis to be tested rather than an established fact.

What other factors might be operating in the environmental sphere?   26
In our Danish interviews we obtained much information about the background of the relatives that has now been coded, and John Rimmer has been carrying out an extensive computer analysis of the data. He is seeking to define some factors that distinguish adoptive relatives of schizophrenics from adoptive relatives of the controls. No consistent feature has as yet been distinguished, but this approach may be relatively insensitive. Psychoanalytic interviews probably obtain more information than Jacobsen did in his psychiatric examination of only a few hours. The mere fact that we have been unable to find a systematic pattern of differences does not rule out the possibility of their existence.

A couple of years ago Dennis Kinney asked me whether he could   27
work on our adoption data with a very ingenious approach. Recalling that half of the schizophrenic adoptees had schizophrenic biological relatives while half did not, he pointed out that those adoptees who became schizophrenic with relatively little genetic predisposition would constitute a good sample in which to look for important environmental factors. In fact, by comparing the two groups of schizophrenic adoptees, those environmental variables might emerge. Kinney therefore studied these adoptees and their relatives without knowing which adoptee had a genetic load and which did not.

Among the schizophrenic adoptees with a low genetic risk he found   28
a significantly higher incidence of brain injury, either at birth or postnatally. Furthermore, Herbert Barry reported some years ago the interesting finding that there was an excess of schizophrenics born in the cold winter months. This prompted other studies, and eventually Dalen, reviewing all the studies in the literature and his own findings in Sweden, concluded that there was a consistent but slight excess of schizophrenics born in winter. Interestingly enough, in our Copenhagen sample of only thirty-three schizophrenics, Kinney has found that eighty percent of the adoptees with low genetic risk were born in the January to April period; the adoptees with medium to high genetic risk showed the normal expectancy of approximately thirty percent of births in the January to April period. Between brain injury and being born in the cold winter months, he can account for every one of the schizophrenic adoptees with a low genetic risk except one, this one being the only adoptee who had an adoptive sibling with chronic schizophrenia.

What does all this mean? Dalen finds that the cold winter months   29
are associated with greater birth trauma. It is also true, however, that there are peaks of certain virus infections during that time as well as in the summer months, which would represent the first trimester of the pregnancies. Kinney concludes that of these thirty-three schizophrenics,

all but one are associated with some crucial biological factor, be it genetic predisposition, brain injury, or a seasonal factor that may be a birth injury, a viral infection, or something as yet unidentified.

Still there is so much we do not know. We do not know the mode 30 of genetic transmission. We do not know the biochemical mechanisms by which the genes express themselves. We do not know the environmental factors that are also necessary for schizophrenia. Certainly we have many interesting hypotheses for all these questions, but none of these hypotheses has really been proven. But we are fortunate today in having plausible, heuristic hypotheses and a generation of young investigators motivated and competent to test them.

Nancy C. Andreasen, Gladwin Hill, and Heinz E. Lehmann all approach schizophrenia from the perspective of biomedical science. Andreasen and Lehmann are both medical doctors; Hill is a journalist. All three selections were published in 1985.

What Is Schizophrenia?
NANCY C. ANDREASEN

While we are accustomed to referring to [schizophrenia] with a single 1 word, thereby implying that it may be a single disease, the possibility of course exists that it may instead be several different diseases. Whether one sees schizophrenia as unitary or as multiple disorders will dramatically affect how one formulates research questions about it. Since the brain itself is composed of many different highly specialized regions, one's underlying assumptions about the unitary or diverse nature of schizophrenia will particularly affect the way one attempts to relate the pathophysiology of the disorder to brain structure.

Schizophrenia is a puzzling illness because its manifestations are so 2 diverse. Anyone who works on a clinical service and sees large numbers of schizophrenic patients cannot help being impressed at how different individual patients referred to as schizophrenic may be. Indeed, if one works in a teaching center and must try to explain schizophrenia to medical students and residents, one is often hard pressed to show exactly what it is that these diverse patients have in common. On a single day only a few weeks ago I saw three schizophrenic patients who differed markedly in nearly all their clinical manifestations. The first was a 57-year-old woman who looked as if she had stepped from the pages of *Vogue* magazine. She became ill in her late 20s, had been treated more or less continuously with medications and had been repeatedly hospitalized, suffered primarily from delusions but had some social withdrawal, and yet had been able to rear a family of four children to normal adulthood. She was a relatively typical late-onset, high-functioning paranoid. The second was a 17-year-old young woman who giggled inappropriately and spoke so vaguely and incoherently that it was difficult to obtain a history. Nevertheless, she did admit to auditory hallucinations. She had never been treated, but it was apparent that she had been steadily deteriorating for the past three years. The third was a 26-year-old man who had had symptoms since age 21. These consisted primarily of both visual and auditory hallucinations that were persistent and refractory to treatment. He also had episodic outbursts of violent behavior both toward himself and toward others. His affect was normal and responsive; in fact, he was highly aware of his symptoms and troubled by them. As these three patients illustrate, people suffering from schizophrenia may differ markedly in their premorbid history, the nature of their onset, the type of symptoms that they have, the course of their illness, their response to treatment, and their degree of impairment. If one attempts to relate this variable phenomenology to underlying brain pathology, it is indeed difficult to think of a single explanation for such diverse patterns.

We of course do not yet understand the pathophysiology of schizophrenia. Looking at the matter simply, one might say there are two different possibilities. One possibility is that schizophrenia is a single illness — that it has a single pathophysiology. For example, one modern investigator, T. J. Crow, has hypothesized that schizophrenia is due to some type of viral illness that may affect different regions of the brain and may even wax and wane, thereby accounting for the variable symptoms and variable course. A second possibility is that schizophrenia is indeed several different illnesses due to several different pathophysiologies or etiologies. These might be multifactorial with a number of different necessary but not sufficient causes, such as prenatal and perinatal factors, head injuries, infectious illnesses, genetic predispositions, and a wide range of social and environmental influences. These different illnesses might be due to different causes, and they might be due to causes that in fact affect different brain regions or brain functions. Recent research on structural brain abnormalities in schizophrenia has implicated such diverse areas as the frontal system, the limbic system, the basal ganglia, and the hypothalamus.

Where Schizophrenia Comes From
GLADWIN HILL

The woman behaved normally most of the time. But occasionally she had spells when she would suddenly start mouthing gutter profanities, tear off her clothes, and go through the motions of leaning on a saloon bar, emulating a rough, tough character. Oddly enough, this behavior was not too mysterious. It was a textbook ailment called temporal lobe epilepsy, which causes strange conduct rather than the convulsions usually associated with epilepsy. It has been traced to an abnormality in a part of the brain called the hippocampus.

The woman was a patient of Dr. Arnold Scheibel, a professor of anatomy and psychiatry at the University of California Medical School in

West Los Angeles. Dr. Scheibel was duly sympathetic but not wildly intrigued, because the woman's ailment was a well-documented, quite specialized syndrome. His big interest was in another malady, schizophrenia, the most widespread of all mental disorders, whose origin has always been a mystery. Its forms range from odd behavior to murderous impulses.

"I had been looking at temporal lobe epilepsy, along with schizophrenia, for fifteen years," Dr. Scheibel related recently. "For some time I had been struck by similarities in behavior patterns between this epilepsy, a known physical disorder, and symptoms we see in schizophrenia. As I observed this woman's aberrations, the idea that there might be some similarity of cause in the two ailments took on a certain inevitability." 3

Was it possible that schizophrenia, the mystery disease, likewise stemmed from something wrong in the hippocampal area of the brain? Dr. Scheibel, a pleasant, soft-spoken man of 61 who looks like actor James Whitmore, set out nearly a decade ago to test the idea by examining the brains of deceased schizophrenics. The first phase of his research, completed only in recent months, supports the theory that schizophrenia, the great mental crippler, results from a physical abnormality — probably one that the victims are born with. This in turn raises the possibility — although Dr. Scheibel emphasizes that it is a distant possibility — that schizophrenic vulnerability *might be detected even before birth.* Schizophrenia, while it fluctuates in severity from case to case, has no known cure. But pinpointing its source is obviously a basic step in combating the disease. And prenatal detection could open the way for a variety of conceivable measures to ameliorate its woeful impacts. 4

Schizophrenia afflicts probably more than a million and a half individuals in the United States. Estimates of its incidence range from three persons to ten persons in every thousand, among both men and women. It is responsible for half the admissions to mental hospitals. Contrary to a popular notion, the name "schizophrenia" does not connote a split personality in the Jekyll-Hyde sense. It means an impairment, or rift, in the normal association of ideas and emotions. A schizophrenic may simply become withdrawn from life. He may have paranoid delusions, such as the notion that a spouse is a Russian spy, or hallucinations, such as an impression that a giraffe is sitting on the sofa. Occasionally a schizophrenic may become catatonic, a trancelike state of bodily rigidity. 5

"A lot of people go around with peculiarities similar to schizophrenic symptoms, and we just call them strange," Dr. Scheibel says. "Thoreau's reclusiveness could be viewed as withdrawal. Extreme fatigue may cause people to see things that aren't there. But these are superficial, passing states. It's when chronic symptoms interfere with a person's leading a normal life, or endanger themselves or others, that it becomes clinical schizophrenia. 6

"If a person has schizophrenic tendencies," he continues, "it often is some sort of challenge or occasion of stress that sends them over the edge. With young people, it may be something as common as the onset of puberty, or going away to college, or entering military service — experiences other people handle without trouble. These pressures might 7 seem to be environmental — of external causation. But schizophrenia is found all over the world, among people who don't have stresses like college or military service. This universality suggests some sort of physical predisposition or vulnerability."

There is a lot of evidence that schizophrenia, or susceptibility to it, is genetic in origin. It tends to run in families. Researchers have formulated some precise tables of probability: a 13 percent chance that a sibling of a schizophrenic will also develop the malady — rising to 50 percent in the case of identical twins; a 46 percent chance that a child of two schizophrenic parents likewise will be schizophrenic. 8

The three main lines of treatment of schizophrenia have been psychiatric counseling, electric or medicinal shock, and drug therapy. Each has had palliative effects in some cases; none has been effective always, or, with any certainty, permanently. "As with someone who's had a heart attack," Dr. Scheibel says, "there's always the possibility of recurrence." . . . 9

As Dr. Scheibel embarked on his quest in 1975, prior studies had suggested some link between schizophrenia and certain abnormal conditions in the brain. But the linkage was quite imprecise. The same brain conditions sometimes related not to schizophrenia but to such quite different maladies as Huntington's disease (the genetic nerve ailment that killed Woody Guthrie) and Alzheimer's disease. A specific root of schizophrenia had not been sorted out from the roots of other ailments. 10

Dr. Scheibel set out to see if this cryptic root was not in the hippocampus. The hippocampus is an oddly coiled element, about the size of a little finger, in each hemisphere of the brain. "Hippo" is Greek for horse, and the name is thought to have derived from the curvature of a sea horse or a racetrack. Like other parts of the brain, the two hippocampi are composed of millions of cells that have taken up their positions and roles, by genetic "programming," soon after conception. 11

Hanging casually from the ceiling in Dr. Scheibel's laboratory office, like a mobile, is a bunch of what look like desiccated bare-root rosebushes. The branches in each case converge in a small lump. The lump represents a single hippocampal cell enlarged several thousand times. The wispy branches are called dendrites — tendrils the brain cells put out as their functions become more ramified. These tendrils seem to have roles in perception, memory, correlation, and resulting behavior. 12

Dr. Scheibel wanted to see if there was anything peculiar about certain hippocampal cells of schizophrenics. From the state mental hospital at Camarillo he got eighteen brains preserved from autopsies. Ten were from individuals who had schizophrenia; eight, for comparison, were from people who had different mental ills. From each brain he took cross sections of the hippocampus and several other brain structures and examined them. 13

It soon appeared that his suspicions were correct. In the hippocampal specimens from the schizophrenics, many of the cells did not have normal dendritic structure. The microscopic bare-root rosebushes, instead of standing up straight, were bent over at their bases as much as 90 degrees, 14 like saplings felled by a windstorm. They had grown, but in the wrong direction. His previous studies of brain cells, consistent with the findings of many other researchers, made it highly likely that this bent-over malformation *was in place when the individuals were born.*

"By the time of birth," he says, "the fundamental plan of brain   15
structure is essentially as it will be through life, even though a great increase in complexity continues for some years."

But scientific notions that might affect the lives of millions in the   16
future cannot be left to surmise. They have to be exhaustively tested and documented to stand up under the rigorous scrutiny of scientific peers. Preoccupied with other matters, Dr. Scheibel had to back-burner his schizophrenia inquiry at UCLA's Brain Research Institute for several years. Then he and one of his graduate students, Joyce Kovelman, agreed that comprehensive verification of his findings would be a good topic for her doctoral thesis.

They started back at square one, this time obtaining eighteen brains   17
from the veterans' hospital in West Los Angeles. Ten were from schizophrenics, eight (unlike the Camarillo specimens) from individuals with no history of mental illness. From each brain they took slices of precisely defined areas of the left hippocampus. They cut these into tissue-thin cross sections, stained them to highlight their structures, and microphotographed them magnified 500 times, enlarging cell images to about a quarter of an inch. A colleague uninvolved in the study was enlisted to give the pictures code numbers so the researchers would not know which samples came from which brain specimens. Then came an elaborate analytical procedure, in which five-by-seven-inch photoenlargements were marked off in sections containing precise numbers of cells, and the cells measured minutely in respect to their shapes, axial orientation, and spatial relationships. The process could be compared to taking satellite pictures of far-distant crowds and classifying the configuration of people's faces and the direction in which they were looking. This procedure was carried out 13,000 times, over a period of two-and-a-half years. The observations were reduced to figures and tabulated. Only after the tabulations were correlated statistically against the original codings could Dr. Scheibel and Ms. Kovelman be sure of the results. Then the answer was unmistakable. Translated from complex scientific terminology, it was: the cell structure and arrangement in the schizophrenic specimens were measurably distorted and higgledy-piggledy; in the others they were not.

"The functional significance of the cell disarray isn't yet clear," Dr.   18
Scheibel says. "It may be an anatomical basis for clinical schizophrenia. On the other hand, it may be just an indicator of vulnerability to the disorder."

The "disorganized" state of the cells, the researchers theorize, may   19
affect the linkage of synapses, the junction points where nervous-system messages are relayed, leading to "altered information processing."

"Because of the disarray of nerve cells and dendrites," Dr. Scheibel   20
says, "the order of incoming signals may even be reversed. This may be related to the hallucinations and paranoia in schizophrenics."

While the schizophrenic specimens were quite distinct statistically   21

and qualitatively in their cell abnormality from the nonschizophrenic specimens, small degrees of cell disorganization were found in the supposedly
normal brains.

"This suggests," Drs. Scheibel and Kovelman say in a forthcoming   22
report, "a spectrum of disorientation patterns ranging from the clinically
nonpsychotic individual, through borderline states, to the intractable, long-
term psychotic." In other words, it might account for individuals considered a little "strange," who never become social problems.

"Our interpretation of the data," Dr. Scheibel summarizes with   23
professional conservatism, "suggests that there is an embryological fault,
occurring at the time the cells originally are migrating into the hippocampus. We feel this happens at the end of the first trimester of pregnancy."

The implications of the Scheibel-Kovelman findings are far-reaching.   24
If a brain abnormality conducive to schizophrenia is prenatal, it raises
two obvious questions: What causes the abnormality, and what can be
done about it? Possible causes are myriad. During the early fetal period,
cells migrate and divide at rates of as much as 30,000 per minute. The
purely mathematical chances of misalignment and faulty connections are
obvious.

"It's possible," Dr. Scheibel acknowledges, "that hippocampal mal-   25
formation is not genetic, but is caused by some accident at the time of
conception or soon thereafter, such as an early-pregnancy virus infection."

In either case, it might be possible at some future time to detect   26
the abnormality by a prenatal test such as amniocentesis. In this procedure, some cells of an unborn baby are extracted from womb fluid. A
cell contains the complete array of gene-bearing chromosomes that "blue-
print" the human body. An abnormal array of chromosomes can point to
such postnatal defects as Down's syndrome.

A big question for the future is, if the hippocampal malformation   27
is detected, does it presage a prospective institutional case — or just
an individual who may go quite happily through life being just a little
"strange"?

"We need to assess further the different levels of cell disorganization   28
we have observed — those that don't really represent significant hippocampal abnormality and those that constitute the threshold of psychotic
behavior," Dr. Scheibel says.

The findings suggest some legal enigmas. If an instance of criminal   29
behavior is traceable to schizophrenia, and the ailment is established as
congenital, how morally responsible is the offender? Conversely, given
that no cure for schizophrenia is known, if such an offender were to be
imprisoned, how could he ever logically be released? Another question
is, given genetic susceptibility to schizophrenia, what measures might be
taken, as with epilepsy, to cushion an individual's passage through life,
to avoid those stresses that tip the scales of stability? Should schizo-
phrenically susceptible individuals be cautioned against marrying, or having
children? If schizophrenic clues were detected during pregnancy, Dr.
Scheibel comments, "it is obvious that we would have to counsel the
parents." What that counsel might be he leaves open.

But such contingencies are, for better or for worse, some distance   30 down the road. Drs. Scheibel and Kovelman already have a sizable agenda ahead of them to round out their findings. "One direction our research will be going in the months ahead," Dr. Scheibel says, "is a study of some of the molecules on brain nerve surfaces — molecules recognized as playing key roles in guidance and alignment of cells during development of the nervous system soon after conception.

"Also, abnormalities in the hippocampus may indicate wider problems 31
in the embryo, such as chemical peculiarities. In the last few years, CAT scans of the brains of schizophrenics have suggested subnormal size in the cerebellum, the portion of the brain right on top of the spinal column. That could be due to lack of cell development. Other studies have hinted at abnormalities in red blood cells in schizophrenics. It's possible that schizophrenia is a body-wide process. But we feel we've pinpointed one specific area of abnormality."

The Scheibel-Kovelman findings are due to get their first professional 32
airing this winter, in the prestigious *Journal of Biological Psychiatry*. If, as often happens in scientific pioneering, many other researchers pounce on the findings to pursue their many implications, further significant advances in combating schizophrenia, the great mental crippler, may not be too far off.

The following article by Heinz E. Lehmann contains a number of anatomical and physiological terms, and those of you with a life science background will have an easier time with this piece than those lacking such background. But we encourage everyone to give Lehmann's article a try, for he defines some terms in context and frequently summarizes the meanings of a technical discussion. You won't need a scientist's vocabulary to get a sense of his argument.

We provide a glossary of some of the terms that figure in Lehmann's discussion. You will also find a few of the definitions handy when reading the other biologically oriented excerpts that follow this piece.

Glossary of Technical Terms

adrenocortical Of, relating to, or derived from the cortex of the adrenal glands.

CAT or CT scans/PET/NMR/RCBF Various computerized radiological methods for gaining cross-sectional, three-dimensional images of body structures or metabolism.

dopamine A neurotransmitter.

dopaminergic Relating to, participating in, or activated by the neurotransmitter activity of dopamine.

ECT or electroconvulsive therapy Electroshock treatments — the induction of unconsciousness and convulsions through electric shock.

EEG or electroencephalograph A machine for detecting and recording brain waves. The actual recording itself is called an *electroencephalogram*.

EEG *(cont.)* Three characteristic waves are: *alpha,* usually associated with relaxation; *beta,* usually associated with conscious activity and arousal; and *delta,* which occurs in deep sleep, infancy, and many diseased conditions of the brain.

frontal lobe The anterior or forward division of each cerebral hemisphere, encased in large part by the forehead and temples.

ganglia (singular ganglion) A mass of nerve tissue containing nerve cells.

gliosis Excessive development of supporting tissues that is intermingled with essential elements of nervous tissue, especially in the brain and spinal cord.

histology (and histologic), neurohistology, neurohistopathology Histology is that branch of anatomy concerned with the minute structure of animal and plant tissues, structures discernible only with a microscope. Neurohistology is the subdivision of histology concerned with the nervous system.

hyperplasia Unusual increase in the number of cells in an organ or tissue.

hypertrophy Excessive development of an organ or part of an organ.

hypoxemia Condition characterized by insufficient supply of oxygen in the blood.

hypoxia Condition characterized by insufficient supply of oxygen reaching the tissues of the body.

laterality (or lateralization) The functional differentiation of the two cerebral hemispheres. For example, certain areas of the left hemisphere seem necessary for the production and comprehension of language while certain areas of the right hemisphere seem necessary for spatial perception and orientation.

limbic region or system A group of structures below the cortex that are involved with emotion and motivation.

MAO inhibitor A drug used for depression.

monoamine A substance important for neural transmission. A deficiency of monoamines is thought to contribute to depression.

neurotransmitter A substance that enables nerve impulses to be transmitted across neurons.

ventricle One of the communicating cavities in the brain that form a system joined to the central canal of the spinal cord.

Current Perspectives on the Biology of Schizophrenia
HEINZ E. LEHMANN

In the 1899 edition of his *Textbook of Psychiatry,* Emil Kraepelin wrote that the nature of dementia praecox almost certainly involved heredity and a tangible affection of the brain, probably damage or destruction of cortical cells due to autointoxication, which was the result of chemical disturbances that in some way may be associated with a disorder of the gonads. And in 1916 Eugen Bleuler had this to say about the etiology of schizophrenia: "One must acknowledge that at least the great majority of clinical pictures which are now collected under the name of dementia praecox rests on some toxic action or anatomical process which arises independently of psychic influences. . . . The principal group, in my opinion, is certainly caused by organic changes." Thus the two key figures in the history of the dementia praecox/schizophrenia concept felt convinced of the biopathologic or organic nature of the disease although they had no evidence for it and had, of course, dealt mainly with its psychopathologic aspects. But, in contrast to Kraepelin, who perceived dementia praecox as a unitary disease, Bleuler saw it as a group of clinical pictures. In doing so he added two other questions to the one implied by Kraepelin about the biologic mechanisms that are responsible for its manifestations, namely: Which of the various clinical pictures, subsumed under the name of dementia praecox or schizophrenia, is the principal group with an organic pathology, and how can it be detected?

The same assumptions and questions still dominate today's perspective of schizophrenia. Although we have made tremendous progress in our research into the biologic background of schizophrenia, it is remarkable that few recent theories or ideas have been advanced that had not been considered as potential physical explanations of schizophrenia almost at the time of its first description. One major exception is the dopaminergic theory of schizophrenia, which is based on the relatively recent discovery of neurotransmitters and their important role in regulating affects and behavior. Most of the progress in our scientific understanding of the biopathology of schizophrenia is not the result of original conceptualizations but has come about because of several surprising breakthroughs in high-technology instrumentation and sophisticated laboratory techniques.   2

In order to gain a state-of-the-art perspective on the biologic nature of schizophrenia it is not only useful, but probably essential, to review the historical phases of the notions that were held about schizophrenia as these notions have been presenting themselves in changing organic theories and physical treatments over the years. It will then become apparent that history has repeated itself more than once in this field, and that the eventual solution to the biologic puzzle of schizophrenia may possibly lie either in the proof of one of the old theories or in the synthesis of a number of them.   3

PROPOSED BIOLOGIC CAUSES AND TREATMENTS
OF SCHIZOPHRENIA

A brief survey of the proposed causes of schizophrenia in roughly the chronologic order in which they were announced in important publications, divided into constitutional and environmental theories, is presented in Table 1. Table 2 reviews in the same manner the various biologic treatment methods, unspecific and specific ones, that have notably influenced the therapeutic management of schizophrenia at one time or another. A neuropathologic theory had already been proposed, at least speculatively, by both Kraepelin and Bleuler. Both had also assumed that heredity was causally involved, and Kraepelin, in his 1899 textbook, had speculated about metabolic (chemical autointoxication) and endocrine (gonadal) factors.   4

TABLE 1. Proposed Biologic Causes of Schizophrenia

CONSTITUTIONAL

Neurohistopathology	(Alzheimer, 1913)
Endocrine disorder	(Mott, 1919)
Cardiovascular Hypoplasia	(Lewis, 1925)
Altered brain macrostructure and metabolism	(Jacobi and Winkler, 1927)
Metabolic disorder	(Gjessing, 1935)
Heredity	(Kallman, 1938)
Electrophysiological dysfunction	(Heath, 1954)
Protein factors	(Heath, 1957)

ENVIRONMENTAL

Seasonal factors	(Tramer, 1929)
Infection	(Loewenstein, 1933)
Perinatal factors	(Pollin, 1966)

CONSTITUTIONAL FACTORS

Neurohistopathology. A neuropathologic bias had prevailed in German psychiatry since the time of Wernicke at the end of the last century, and Alzheimer lent strong support to it in 1913 when he published his neuropathologic findings in the brains of 55 dementia praecox patients. He described gliosis and disorganization of ganglion cells associated with lipid degeneration, which were most pronounced in the second and third layers of the cerebral cortex; he thought that these changes were specific and could be diagnostic of dementia praecox, although they could not be correlated with the clinical type of the disease.

During the next 10 years several other investigators came to the same conclusion that there were no specific histologic changes in the brains of schizophrenic patients, although Adolph Meyer had called for

TABLE 2. Biologic Treatments of Schizophrenia

UNSPECIFIC

Continuous sleep	(Kläsi, 1922)
Convulsions	(von Meduna, 1935)
Coma	(Sakel and Dussik, 1936)
Psychosurgery	(Moniz, 1936)
Hemodialysis	(Wagemaker and Cade, 1977)

SPECIFIC

Hormones	(Danziger and Kindwall, 1953)
Pharmacotherapy (neurotransmitters-receptors)	(Delay and Deniker, 1952)
Megavitamins	(Hoffer et al., 1957)

caution before accepting these pathologic findings uncritically, pointing out that few clinicians would dare to make a diagnosis on such a basis.

7

In 1923 Dunlap set up a study with careful selection criteria and matched controls. From his findings he concluded that there was no basis for the statement, or even for a suspicion, that an organic brain disease was the basis for schizophrenia.

8

But in 1930 Spielmeyer again asserted that, even though he did not find any abnormal changes in many of his own cases, destructive changes could usually be seen in the acute stages of the disease. He believed that dementia praecox was an organic brain disease, albeit without a specifically determined pathology.

9

An interesting and novel approach to the problem of cerebral changes in functional psychoses was taken by Elvidge and Reed in 1933 when they obtained biopsies from the brains of patients diagnosed as suffering from schizophrenia and manic-depressive psychosis. They observed swelling of oligodendroglial cells in the material from both types of patients. There was also often some hypertrophy of astrocytes, and these changes seemed to be persistent and were most pronounced in the subcortical white matter. Elvidge and Reed hypothesized that these phenomena had resulted from toxic metabolic factors. It is not likely that a similar, invasive study could be repeated today or in the near future.

10

The period of neuropathologic studies of schizophrenia, covering the first half of the century, came to a controversial close at the First International Congress of Neuropathology held in Rome in 1952. By that time more than 250 studies on the neuropathology of schizophrenia had been published. However, the opinions differed between the delegates from Continental Europe, whose research supported neuropathologic changes in schizophrenia, and the investigators from the United States and Great Britain, who claimed that the observed changes had occurred in terminal stages of postmortem. At the Congress, the Vogts had reported numerous changes in 35 brains studied by serial section. Later studies have reported degenerative changes in diencephalic regions and the brainstems of schizophrenic patients. In recent years the limbic region has received particular attention from neuropathologists. . . .

11

Many of these studies, some of which were carried out on brains of the Vogt collection, that is, on material that was obtained before the advent of the neuroleptic drugs, could confirm the findings of the early authors about the presence of neuropathologic abnormalities in the brains of many schizophrenic patients. However, these abnormalities were non-specific, inconsistent, and nondiagnostic. Moreover, it is impossible to ascertain to what extent these changes were causal, coincidental, or due to secondary alterations that were unrelated to the pathogenesis of schizophrenia. It is well known that schizophrenia-like symptoms can follow organic lesions of almost any brain region. The evidence of neurohistopathologic findings today suggests that in the majority of schizophrenic patients there are physical changes of brain cells of the kind that point to degenerative phenomena and that the limbic region is most critically affected.

We should note that the opinions that we hold on this subject today have come full circle, back to Kraepelin's belief at the turn of the century, after having passed through a period of marked scepticism, even scornful contempt, when brain pathology in schizophrenia for years was referred to as "brain mythology" by many influential psychiatrists on the international scene. 12

Endocrine Disorder. Unlike the intense, controversial, and sustained story of the neuropathologic theory of schizophrenia, the endocrine hypothesis has had a much simpler development. Its origin also goes back to Kraepelin, but endocrinology as a scientific discipline did not yet exist when he formulated the concept of dementia praecox, and very little was known about the nature of specific hormones. The first major report on atrophy of the testicles in schizophrenia appeared in 1919, and others published similar findings in the following years, as well as reports on ovarian dysfunction. However, a systematic study on biopsies of testicles of the entire population of the research ward in Worcester State Hospital in Massachusetts in 1952 could not confirm any of the previous claims, and seems to have refuted the gonadal hypothesis of schizophrenia. In addition to gonadal pathology, thyroid and adrenal disorders were also reported in a major study by Lewis in 1923 but never confirmed. Following the exciting discovery of the adrenocortical steroids, adrenocortical hypofunction was thought by Hoagland and Pincus to be involved in the pathogenesis of schizophrenia, but this too was a short-lived hypothesis. Finally, in the last few years Horrobin, on entirely speculative grounds, has evolved a theory about a role of prostaglandins in the pathogenesis of schizophrenia without any significant evidence for this idea until now. 13

Cardiovascular Hypoplasia. In 1923 and 1925 Lewis published some interesting reports on 4,800 autopsies performed on mental patients, of whom 601 had been given a certain diagnosis of dementia praecox. Based on these autopsies and a smaller number of detailed postmortem findings in dementia praecox patients, he announced that dementia praecox was characterized by a primary hypoplasia of the cardiovascular system. Dementia praecox patients, Lewis claimed, had small hearts and aplastic aortae with narrow luminae, and this hypoplasia extended throughout the vascular tree and was responsible for a relative cerebral hypoxemia. During the next 15 years others reported similar findings that supported the vascular theory but since the 1940s little interest has been shown in this approach. 14

Altered Brain Macrostructure and Metabolism. The fascination with imaging of the living brain that so greatly dominates today's investigations and theories had its beginnings in psychiatry in 1927 when two German authors reported on pneumoencephalographic findings in chronic schizophrenics. They found hydrocephalus in 18 of 19 patients. This publication was followed by more than 30 similar studies, although many 15 of them, like the first one, were marred by inadequate diagnostic criteria, questionable procedures, and lack of controls. Nevertheless, most of the best studies on pneumoencephalographic imaging of brains of schizophrenic patients between 1935 and 1967 agreed on one finding: enlarged ventricles. One study reported no statistical differences between schizophrenics and neurologic controls, but also found abnormal pneumoencephalograms in more than one-third of the schizophrenic patients.

With its greatly improved instrumentation and consequent reliability, **16** computerized tomography (CT) scanning has become one of the most popular noninvasive procedures in schizophrenia research ever since Johnstone et al. and Weinberger et al. observed that the CT scans of a group of schizophrenic patients had abnormally large ventricles. Since then several other studies have confirmed the finding that many schizophrenic patients show signs of cerebral atrophy, in the form of either enlarged ventricles or wider fissures and sulci. Atrophy of the cerebellar vermis was also seen in schizophrenic patients. Other brain image abnormalities that were observed more frequently in schizophrenics than in controls were reversals of the normal hemispheric asymmetries and reduced density of the brain matter. There have also been two careful recent studies that could not confirm the lobar asymmetries, and it should be remembered that atrophy of the cerebellar vermis has been seen in only a relatively small number of schizophrenics. Clinically it was found that the patients with the largest ventricles showed the poorest response to treatment, had the greatest cognitive deficiencies, and were most likely to manifest negative rather than positive symptoms. In a more recent publication the Weinberger group have stressed that CT changes seen in schizophrenic patients are not specific, that such changes correlate best with age, and that abnormalities in CT measures should not be ascribed to any one psychiatric disorder.

Regional cerebral blood flow (RCBF) can now be measured without **17** much time lag, in real time, by injecting intraarterially a solution with the inactive, radioactively labeled gas xenon-133 and then recording the RCBF from outside the resting subject's skull. In 1974 Ingvar and Franzen reported that normal controls show hyperfrontality, a higher distribution of blood flow in the frontal than in the posterior regions of the brain, while schizophrenic patients are characterized by hypofrontality, with blood flow concentrated away from the frontal regions. The authors also established that there is a good correlation between cortical metabolism and RCBF, and therefore imaging the distribution of blood flow in the brain can serve indirectly as an immediate indicator of regional brain metabolism. The procedure has been made less invasive by having the patient simply breathe the xenon gas, and other workers have confirmed the earlier investigators' findings.

A more direct measure of regional brain metabolism can be obtained **18** through positron emission tomography (PET), although this method is more invasive, slower, and much more expensive. Findings with this method not only confirmed the cortical hypofrontality of schizophrenic patients but, for the first time, also demonstrated in vivo a basal ganglia dysfunction.

Indirectly related to these imaged changes of structures and metabolic   19
distributions in the brains of schizophrenic patients are the recent functional studies on laterality of cerebral functioning in schizophrenia. On
the basis of the frequency of lateral eye movements, performance, and
perceptual tests, several workers have argued that there is overarousal
of the left hemisphere and a disadvantaged right hemisphere, or left
hemisphere dysfunction, or bilateral dysfunction of the frontal and temporal lobes in schizophrenic patients.

Metabolic Disorder. A metabolic disorder in the form of biochem-   20
ical (e.g., autointoxicating) factors had also been suspected in the etiology
of schizophrenia by Kraepelin and Bleuler. In their time neither the
instruments nor the techniques for in-depth studies of this hypothesis
were available. In the context of the present broad survey, only a few
of the most significant, relevant hypotheses can be mentioned in the
chronologic sequence in which they were produced and tested. Some of
them were short-lived but caused considerable excitement while they
prevailed; others linger on in uncertain limbo. One hypothesis is currently
the most widely accepted theory of schizophrenia. As will become evident
from the various subheadings in this section, metabolic disorder can serve
as a catchall for many things.

Nitrogen Metabolism Disorder. In the 1930s and 1940s the Nor-   21
wegian psychiatrist Gjessing investigated the metabolism of certain schizophrenic patients as comprehensively as was possible at that time with
extraordinary perseverance and attention to detail. He had chosen to
study a rare and somewhat atypical category of schizophrenia, periodic
catatonia, and while his findings were later confirmed by others, his
findings could not be generalized to other types of schizophrenia. The
core finding of his research, which extended over many years, was that
the affected patients suffered from a primary disturbance of nitrogen
metabolism that caused them periodically to switch to-and-from between
positive and negative nitrogen balance. He found that he could block or
prevent these metabolic changes with the therapeutic administration of
thyroxin. Although Gjessing's discovery could be applied only to the small
subgroup of patients suffering from periodic catatonia, and seemed to
have little relevance to the main field of schizophrenia, it was nevertheless
the first reliable scientific foundation for a theory of specific pathogenesis
in schizophrenia, and it led to a rational and effective treatment for this
condition.

Transmethylation Disorder. In 1952 Osmond and Smythies evolved   22
a theory that schizophrenia was caused by a toxic hallucinogenic substance.
. . . This theory was later elaborated by Hoffer, who claimed that this
substance was adrenochrome. However, adrenochrome could never be
demonstrated in the body fluids of schizophrenic patients. Nor could
others confirm Hoffer's description of a subtype of schizophrenia that he
called "malvaria," which was characterized by a "mauve factor."

In 1963, Friedhoff and van Winkle reported the presence of a "pink   23
spot" in the chromatograms of the urines of schizophrenic patients. The
pink spot was dimethoxyphenylethylamine (DMPEA), a transmethylation

product, but its specific relation to schizophrenia could not be confirmed. Finally, a review of the whole transmethylation theory left little support for it.

Ceruloplasmin/Copper Disorder. A stir was created for a short time 24 in the psychiatric community by a theory that an increased plasma level of the copper-containing substance ceruloplasmin might be causally related to schizophrenia. In 1957 Akerfeld developed a simple test for ceruloplasmin that he thought was diagnostic of mental disorders. However, the hopes for an easy biologic marker for schizophrenia were soon dashed, when it was shown that the ceruloplasmin level depended on the ascorbic acid blood level and that institutionalized schizophrenic patients often have low ascorbic acid levels.

Neurotransmitter Disorder. At the same time the biochemist Woolley 25 published his hypothesis that schizophrenia was causally related to a decrease in the then still relatively new neurotransmitter serotonin. One of the reasons given was that the hallucinogen LSD was thought to be a powerful serotonin antagonist, and that the LSD-induced model psychosis resembled schizophrenia.

This hypothesis did not survive very long. Another hypothesis in- 26 volving a different neurotransmitter was first proposed by Carlsson and Lindqvist in 1963. This hypothesis developed into the theory, widely accepted at this time, of an overactive dopaminergic system as a physical substrate of schizophrenia. Since there is no direct evidence of dopamine increase in the brain, most of the key research into the dopamine hypothesis has centered on dopamine receptors. . . .

Enzyme Disorder. In 1968 Meltzer published a series of papers on 27 the enzyme creatine-phosphokinase, which he found to be increased in most acute psychotics but not specifically in schizophrenic patients. Three years later Murphy and Wyatt released a flurry of papers on monoamine oxidase (MAO) in the platelets of psychiatric patients. As early as 1941 Birkhauser had reported a decrease of this enzyme in the brains of schizophrenic patients. While a decrease of MAO is found in the platelets of many, especially chronic, schizophrenic patients, it is not a specific marker but seems to represent a genetic indicator of vulnerability for a variety of psychiatric disorders. However, a recent study has found that schizophrenic patients with low platelet MAO have a better prognosis than those with higher MAO activity.

It has been claimed that dopamine-β-hydroxylase (DBH) is decreased 28 in autopsied brains of schizophrenic patients. Others have found this enzyme to be decreased in the serum and in the spinal fluid of those schizophrenic patients who respond to pharmacotherapy. While some investigators have not been able to confirm these findings, it does seem that there is a subgroup of schizophrenic patients who show decreased DBH activity.

Other neurotransmitters . . . have been investigated as potential 29 etiologic factors in schizophrenia. Peptides too, particularly the endorphins, have received their share of speculation in this connection. In fact, the whole field of metabolic (i.e., biochemical, neurochemical, and neuroendocrinologic) research, including an array of neuroenzymes, neurohormones, neuropeptides, and their metabolites has, since the 1970s, been the most active in the century-old search for the biological nature of schizophrenia. . . .

Electrophysiologic Dysfunction.   For a short time in the 1930s 30 the electroencephalogram (EEG) was hoped to be the royal road to psychiatry, until it was discovered that its value was much greater for neurology and that the diagnostic usefulness of the EEG in psychiatry was very limited. For years most studies were unable to reveal any EEG abnormalities that were specific for schizophrenia, although a higher proportion of abnormalities seemed to occur in schizophrenic patients than in controls. In 1954 Heath and his coworkers reported that in schizophrenic patients with implanted intracerebral electrodes, characteristic spiking could be observed in the septal and neighboring hippocampal and amygdala regions. Because for ethical reasons, such invasive procedures cannot be easily repeated, there has been no substantial confirmation of these specific abnormalities by others.

Using modern sophisticated electrophysiologic methods, such as 31 power spectral analysis and event-related potentials (ERP), several research groups have found that many schizophrenic patients show some characteristic abnormalities. There is good agreement, for instance, that the EEG of schizophrenic patients exhibits excessive slow delta waves and also increased fast beta activity, as well as reduced alpha activity and increased amplitude variability. The prevailing theory regarding the electrophysiologic mechanisms in schizophrenia assumes that there is an impairment in the subcortical gating and filtering processes in this disease. . . . [But] none of these electrophysiologic abnormalities in schizophrenia is sufficiently consistent and specific to serve by itself as a diagnostic indicator.

Protein Factors and Immune Disorder.   The idea of a blood-borne 32 schizophrenia factor goes back to Kraepelin's time. Numerous reports have been published describing toxic substances in the blood or urine of schizophrenic patients that caused changes in the behavior of cells, plants, and animals, from spiders to rats and monkeys. These substances were often assumed to be protein factors, but they were difficult to identify.

Immune Disorder. Between 1960 and 1970 there was particular in- 33 terest in protein factors in schizophrenia, with a resulting rush of papers on the subject. In 1957 Heath and coworkers had published a report on an abnormal blood protein they called Taraxein, isolated from the serum of schizophrenic patients. When injected into monkeys, Taraxein produced behavioral changes and septal spiking in the EEG. In normal human volunteers, Heath claimed, the substance induced a temporary psychotic state that greatly resembled schizophrenia. Heath determined that Taraxein was present in gamma immunoglobulin (IgG) taken from schizophrenics, and . . . , he theorized, it would interfere with brain function and produce schizophrenic manifestations. In summary, he contended, schizophrenia may be considered an autoimmune disease. This was an elegant theory and it has never been completely repudiated, but Heath's fundamental experimental findings could not be replicated.

Protein Factors. In 1960 Frohman and his coworkers announced the   34
presence of a factor in the serum of schizophrenic patients identified as an alpha globulin with a molecular weight of about 400,000. This factor seemed to alter the anaerobic metabolism of chicken red blood cells, produced rope-climbing delay in rats, and was thought to be identical to a plasma factor that had been isolated by Russian workers and possibly associated with some immunologic abnormalities in schizophrenic patients. These studies overlap to some extent with more recent work on an infectious-agent etiology of schizophrenia, which will be discussed further on.

Most of the recent work in the field of schizophrenia as an immu-   35
nologic disease has been concerned with HLA antigens, the quantitative determination of immunoglobins, and the autoimmune model of schizophrenia. One interesting suggestion has been that autoantibodies, possibly virus-induced, might overstimulate dopaminergic receptors. Although there are no experimental data to support this hypothesis, it does represent an ingenious attempt to integrate with autoimmune theory of schizophrenia with a virus hypothesis and with the dopamine theory.

ENVIRONMENTAL FACTORS

Seasonal Factors.   Since the 1920s the season of birth has been   36
considered a factor in the births of children who would later be diagnosed as schizophrenic. Almost all studies concur on the finding that children born during the winter months are at somewhat higher risks to develop schizophrenia than children born during other seasons. This was found to be true for different geographic regions.

The most recent work on seasonal factors has avoided statistical   37
pitfalls and has investigated the interaction of genetic high risk for schizophrenia, urban environment, and winter months as a complex of risk factors. It was argued that genetic vulnerability would be increased due to the higher risk of viral infection during the winter season and the higher risk of transmission in an urban setting. At the present time the hypothesis of a virus infection is felt to be the most reasonable explanation for the epidemiologic observation of an association between winter births and schizophrenia.

Infection.   Tuberculosis was suspected to be responsible for schizo-   38
phrenia for a few years after Loewenstein described a procedure to establish the diagnosis of tuberculosis in occult cases. He claimed that his procedure was more sensitive and reliable than the traditional laboratory methods for the detection of Koch's bacillus. He also suggested, on the basis of his own findings, that tuberculosis might be the cause of certain mental diseases, in particular schizophrenia. However, nobody was able to confirm his theory, and since that time tuberculosis has been no longer suspected as a causal factor in schizophrenia.

Earlier, gastroenteritis has been blamed for schizophrenia by some **39**
physicians, and some destructive surgery had been performed in the
mistaken belief that the removal of focal infections would be therapeutic.
However, no bacterial infection is now seriously considered an etiologic
factor in schizophrenia.

Viruses that were mentioned as early as 1951 by Papez and Bateman **40**
as a possible etiologic factor for certain histopathologic changes seen in
the postmortem brains of some schizophrenic patients, are more often
discussed in current research on schizophrenia. Crow has recently combined his theory of two types of schizophrenia, characterized respectively
by the presence of positive or negative symptoms, with a virus hypothesis. He argues that, according to genetic specific predisposition, a virus
might produce a neurohumoral (dopamine) disorder in one individual,
resulting in positive symptoms, and a more treatment-resistant, structural
disorder with negative symptoms, in another.

Perinatal Factors. Related to two other environmental factors, **41**
seasonality and infection, are perinatal factors. Pollin and his coworkers
were among the first to discuss this issue systematically in the middle
1960s, and others have followed their lead. The mother's nutritional state
at the birth of the child, complications arising during delivery, intracranial
hemorrhages, postnatal apnea and hypoxia of the newborn, as well as
potential exposure to infectious agents, which may depend on the season
of birth and on the immediate postnatal living conditions (e.g., crowded
family) of the infant, are the main factors that have been considered. It
has, for instance, been observed that of monozygotic twins who are
discordant for schizophrenia, the twin who remains normal is regularly
the one who weighed more at birth and, in most cases, is the first-born.

BIOLOGIC TREATMENTS: UNSPECIFIC

Continuous Sleep. In the early 1920s the Swiss psychiatrist Kläsi **42**
devised the first physical treatment for schizophrenia. He used barbiturates to induce and sustain sleep for one week or longer in schizophrenic
patients, who were allowed to wake only for their meals and bodily
functions. Although he could report some promising therapeutic results,
the treatment did not find wide acceptance, because the hypnotic drugs
available then were too toxic and the respiratory complications, including
pneumonias, which often supervened during the prolonged sleep treatment, could not be effectively managed at the time. Kläsi might have
been inspired to use an altered physiological state of the organism as an
unspecific treatment by the dramatic results Wagner-Jauregg had achieved
a few years earlier with the malaria fever therapy for general paresis,
for which he is the only psychiatrist to have received the Nobel prize.

Convulsions. The Hungarian psychiatrist von Meduna believed that **43**
schizophrenia and epilepsy were diseases that are biologically incompatible
and, based on this assumption for which no valid evidence was ever
produced, he reasoned that convulsions should have a therapeutic effect

on schizophrenic patients. This unfounded conclusion, nevertheless, led to successful results that he reported in 1935. However, almost all his schizophrenic patients who had shown immediate dramatic remissions following camphor and metrazol-induced convulsions relapsed within a few weeks. Convulsive treatment eventually was found to be much more effective in affective disorders than in schizophrenia. Furthermore, convulsions induced by camphor or metrazol injections subjected patients to almost cruelly stressful experiences.

Three years later Cerletti and Bini introduced electroconvulsive therapy (ECT), which caused little discomfort to patients, and which could be administered with greater precision than the pharmacologic treatment. Today, ECT is still an important treatment for patients suffering from affective disorders, but it is seldom used as the first treatment for schizophrenia. The action mechanism of this unspecific, global procedure still remains a mystery after almost a half century of clinical use. **44**

Coma. At the same time that convulsive therapy was first tried in Hungary, Sakel in Austria, was developing insulin coma therapy for schizophrenia. He had observed that some schizophrenic drug addicts treated with small doses of insulin for their addiction had accidentally gone into deep hypoglycemic coma and, on emerging from it, had shown great improvement of their psychotic symptoms. Proceeding from this observation, he developed a technique for systematically inducing hypoglycemic come as a "shock treatment" for schizophrenia. The treatment was not without hazard. It required specially trained personnel and lasted for several months, during which the patient had to be hospitalized. The procedure was effective in a significant proportion of schizophrenic patients, particularly when it was given during the first six months following the onset of symptoms. It was, in fact, the first treatment for schizophrenia that had ever given consistent therapeutic results. Other coma treatments for schizophrenia produced cerebral hypoxia by having the patient breathe pure nitrogen or induced a toxic state with atropine injections. These were soon abandoned in favor of hypoglycemic coma therapy, which became the standard treatment for nearly two decades, until it was replaced by pharmacotherapy. **45**

Psychosurgery. The late 1930s was a fertile period for the conception and introduction of aggressive physical treatments for schizophrenia. In 1936, the same year Sakel had published his first results with insulin coma therapy, Moniz, a Portuguese neurologist, announced his results with frontal lobotomy in schizophrenic patients. He conceived of this type of intervention after he heard the neurophysiologist Fulton report on the behavioral changes in monkeys resulting from similar surgery. Frontal lobotomy (or leucotomy) for schizophrenic patients was first received with great optimism by the psychiatric community. Special large-scale projects were set up to test its efficacy, and many modifications of the original procedure were devised, some of them so simple ("ice pick operation") that they led to excessive use of the treatment in the 1940s. It was later agreed that psychosurgery had a place in certain functional **46** psychiatric conditions under special circumstances, but certainly not as a routine treatment for schizophrenia.

Hemodialysis.   Not until 40 years later, in 1977, was another un-   **47**
specific somatic treatment for schizophrenia proposed by Wagemaker and Cade. Cade had observed unexpected improvement of psychotic symptoms following hemodialysis in a paranoid schizophrenic patient who required this treatment because of kidney disease. Speculating that the dialysis may have removed a noxious blood factor that was responsible for the psychotic manifestations, Wagemaker and Cade applied hemodialysis to a group of schizophrenic patients who had no kidney disease, and observed promising results. Again, the international psychiatric community and the public responded with excitement. Various modifications of the original procedure were developed, and since this treatment required expensive equipment, there was a danger the treatment would be abused in profitable business ventures before its efficacy and safety had been properly determined.

A number of carefully controlled clinical trials produced only equivocal   **48**
or negative results. A recent clinical team, on the basis of a double-blind controlled trial with 15 patients, has again found that dialysis was not an effective treatment for schizophrenia. Since the number of patients treated under controlled conditions is still small, further trials will be required to draw firm conclusions. Until now no specific noxious substance has been found to be consistently present in the dialysate of schizophrenic patients.

BIOLOGICAL TREATMENTS: SPECIFIC

Thyroid Treatment.   In the 1920s Lewis had reported hypotrophy   **49**
of the thyroid gland in many autopsied schizophrenics. In the 1930s and 1940s Gjessing had shown that treatment with thyroxine could modify the cycles of periodic catatonia; and for years, following the introduction of coma and convulsive treatments, the leading hypothesis of their mechanisms of action postulated that it was the rebound action of increased oxygenation of the brain, induced by temporary hypoxia, that produced the therapeutic effect in schizophrenic patients.

In this climate of theoretic orientation toward disturbed oxygen me-   **50**
tabolism in schizophrenia, Danziger and Kindwall conducted a clinical trial with large doses of thyroid extract in schizophrenic patients, with the aim of increasing cerebral oxygen metabolism. They reported good therapeutic results, but the trial had been uncontrolled and others could not confirm their findings. The thyroid treatment of general schizophrenia was short-lived. Nevertheless, it should be recognized that this was the first specific, physical treatment for schizophrenia that was conceived as the result of a biologic theory and put to clinical trial. All other physical treatments until then had been unspecific and were the pragmatic results of clinical observations, rather than rational consequences of explicit hypotheses, with the exception of Gjessing's thyroxine treatment for pe-

riodic catatonia, which could be applied only to a subgroup comprising not more than 3 percent of all schizophrenic patients.

Pharmacotherapy (Neurotransmitters-Receptors). It is a psy-   51
chiatric curiosity that the most successful physical treatment for schizo-phrenia, namely pharmacotherapy, has a mechanism of action closely related to the most popular hypothesis about the nature of this disorder, but the treatment is not the rational result of the hypothesis. Rather, the treatment gave rise to the dopamine hypothesis through deductive reasoning after the treatment had already been in general clinical use for a full decade.

Chlorpromazine was originally produced on the request of the surgeon   52
Laborit who had asked a pharmacologic laboratory for a phenothiazine with minimal antihistamine and maximal sedative properties for clinical use in anesthesia. The antipsychotic (neuroleptic) action of the drug was discovered by the clinical psychiatrists Delay and Deniker in 1952, simply through trial and error, when they used chlorpromazine in the treatment of a group of excited schizophrenic patients. The dramatic and specific antipsychotic effects of the drug came as a surprise to the international psychiatric community that, by that time, had almost given up hope of finding a satisfactory biologic explanation or treatment for schizophrenia, and were orienting themselves more toward a psychosocial concept of the disorder.

Thus the most specific biologic treatment for schizophrenia remained   53
for many years another unspecific and unexplained therapeutic approach. It was only when Carlsson and Lindqvist in 1963 discovered that all drugs with antipsychotic properties, regardless of their different chemical struc-tures, were potent blockers of dopaminergic neurons that they deduced that some kind of dopaminergic hyperactivity must lie at the basis of schizophrenia or, more precisely, of psychotic disorders. It should be understood that neuroleptic drugs have antipsychotic but not antischi-zophrenic properties, and are a specific treatment modality only to the extent that schizophrenia is by far the most frequent and important psy-chotic disorder.

Since there is no direct evidence of increased dopamine in the brain,   54
blood, or spinal fluid of schizophrenic patients, much interest has been focused on a reported increase of dopamine receptors in the autopsied brains of schizophrenic patients. This research, however, is somewhat hampered by the fact that few schizophrenic patients die today without having received antipsychotic drug therapy, and this may have interfered with the number of dopamine receptors. . . .

In 1972 Atsmon and his coworkers reported favorable therapeutic   55
results with the beta-blocker propranolol in schizophrenic patients. Many other publications on this subject have appeared since then, with a ratio of roughly two to one reporting positive versus negative results.

Another pharmacologic treatment of schizophrenia, using very large   56
doses of diazepam [Valium] — up to 400 milligrams per day — has been proposed recently. This therapy aims at GABA receptors in the brain, since it has been assumed that increased dopaminergic activity in the brain may be counterbalanced by decreased GABA activity, and this may

be corrected by the GABA-agonist effects of diazepam. Results of this treatment have so far been equivocal. . . .

Megavitamins. Megavitamin therapy was introduced into psychia-   57
try by Hoffer and his coworkers in 1957. On the basis of Osmond and Smythies's theory of faulty transmethylation in schizophrenia, Hoffer reasoned that a toxic metabolic product of adrenaline was produced in schizophrenic patients, but that the excessive methyl groups responsible for this toxic metabolite could be captured by megadoses, from 3,000 to 9,000 milligrams per day, of nicotinic acid or nicotinamide and thus prevented from producing their noxious effects. Later he increased the doses of niacin further and combined megavitamin treatment with pharmacotherapy, ECT, and orthomolecular treatment. The literature on megavitamin treatment is very extensive and highly controversial. Most of the favorable results were observed in uncontrolled studies and most of the negative results in controlled studies.

The term "orthomolecular therapy" was coined in 1968 by Linus   58
Pauling, a Nobel laureate in chemistry. Pauling discussed in a theoretical paper his conviction that some mental illnesses are the result of chemical imbalances in the brain which could be corrected by proper nutrition to create an "orthomolecular environment of the mind." It is difficult, if not impossible, to find criteria for treating individual patients specifically, since, according to orthomolecular theory, every living organism has its own idiosyncratic needs for vitamins, metals, and various trace substances. For this reason, orthomolecular therapy is probably more an unspecific than a specific treatment. There is little clear evidence of its efficacy. Although some schizophrenic patients, and many other people, could probably benefit from it, no reliable criteria exist by which such individuals could be identified.

DISCUSSION

Starting with Kraepelin, and covering a span of almost 90 years, I   59
have sketched a brief survey of the comings and goings of 19 different biologic approaches to schizophrenia — 11 conceptualizations and 8 treatment modalities. What then is the current perspective on the biology of schizophrenia? Of the 11 biologic theories, only two have been discarded today, those of endocrine disorder and cardiovascular hypoplasia. Eight others have received sufficient factual support to remain viable, and one, that of virus infection, while lacking direct evidence, is nonetheless gaining momentum today. Of the eight biologic treatment modalities, five have become obsolete or partly so (ECT); one, i.e., pharmacotherapy, is effective and generally accepted; and for two, hemodialysis and megavitamins, the jury is still out.

We have seen that the various working hypotheses and theories have   60
been arrived at by various modes of reasoning — for example, by analogy (toxic substance like a hallucinogen), by deduction (the dopamine hypothesis), by faulty assumption (convulsive treatment), by free speculation (prostaglandin theory), or by clinical observation (genetic theory).

It is tempting to gather all the biologic factors and ideas related to   61
schizophrenia that have survived until today, and integrate them into
some cohesive pattern. If this is tried, two different models emerge: the
genetic and the environmental. While it is generally agreed today that
the two dimensions of heredity and environment are always intertwined
and interacting at many points, they still represent two primary structures
with different causalities — one programmed, the other random.

Within the genetic model there are two configurations. One is con-   62
stituted by assuming that in schizophrenic patients there is an inborn
error of metabolism that produces abnormal protein factors, which are
responsible for a disorder of the immune system that either renders the
subject highly vulnerable to minor stresses, or evolves into an autoimmune
disease that produces neurohistopathologic changes and finally morphologic changes in the brain. Somewhere along the line, cerebral pathways
and projections are disturbed in such a way that a dopaminergic disorder
appears as the final common path and the physical substrate underlying
the psychotic manifestations. In the chronic stages of the disease, the
destructive histopathologic changes in the brain supervene, and the dopaminergic disturbance fades. This is reflected in a decrease of positive
and an increase of negative symptoms. In certain subgroups of schizophrenics the genetic disorder may directly affect the dopaminergic system
without producing destructive changes in the brain, and such patients
would have only acute psychotic symptoms without negative symptoms
and personality deficits.

The environmental model of schizophrenia might assume a slow virus   63
as the causative factor instead of an inborn error of metabolism. The
causal chain would lead from the virus through antibodies to a dopaminergic disturbance with or without destructive neuronal changes, gliosis,
and atrophic morphologic changes in the brain.

The various morphologic (macrostructural) changes in the brains of   64
schizophrenic patients, as well as their different regional distributions and
autonomous strategies of cerebral metabolism and blood flow, as determined by modern imaging, will probably serve the clinician as biologic
markers in the future. They might allow him to distinguish objectively
between different groups of patients and to ascertain the optimal therapeutic approach in an individual case.

The enigma of schizophrenia is far from being solved today. Its   65
challenge will undoubtedly continue to haunt us for many years. There
was, in this discussion, no mention made of the myriad of psychosocial
problems that surround schizophrenia and constitute some of its core
features. However, we may again safely conclude that Kraepelin and
Bleuler were right when they believed that schizophrenia, or the groups
of schizophrenias, are biologic disorders.

*R. C. Lewontin, Steven Rose, and Leon J. Kamin are, respectively, a geneticist,
a biologist, and an experimental psychologist. In their book* Not in Our Genes
*(1984), they take issue with the hereditarian position, focusing on the work
presented by Seymour Kety (see p. 590).*

Schizophrenia: The Clash of Determinisms
R. C. LEWONTIN, STEVEN ROSE, AND **LEON J. KAMIN**

THE CASE OF SCHIZOPHRENIA

The diagnosis and treatment of schizophrenia are paradigms of the determinist mode of thinking, for this is the mental disorder on which more biochemical and genetic research has been lavished than any other, the one in which claims to have discovered *the* cause in a particular molecule or gene have been made most extensively. It is now so widely believed that psychiatry has proved the disorder to be biological that if the case fails here, where it is strongest, it must be even weaker elsewhere. But schizophrenia is interesting from another point of view as well, for in opposition to the biologizing tendencies of medical psychiatry there has grown up a strong countermovement in recent years. Antipsychiatry, in the hands of practitioners like R. D. Laing and theorists like Michel Foucault, has gone far in the opposite direction, almost to the point of denying the existence of a disorder or group of disorders diagnosable as schizophrenia at all. Thus in the case of schizophrenia we find precisely that clash of determinisms, on the one hand biological and on the other cultural, which it is one of [our] purposes . . . to transcend.

1

If the bulk of our effort here is directed toward the biochemical and particularly the genetic explanations offered for schizophrenia, this is because at the present time these explanations are so strongly entrenched in establishment psychiatry and medicine. We emphatically do not wish in this emphasis to be tipped over into an uncritical resuscitation of dualism, or cultural determinism like that of Laing or Foucault.

2

What Is Schizophrenia? Schizophrenia literally means "split mind." The classic picture of a schizophrenic is of a person who feels in some fundamental way cut off from the rest of humanity. Unable to express emotion or interact normally or express themselves verbally in a way that is rational to most others, schizophrenics appear blank, apathetic, dull. They may complain that their thoughts are not their own or that they are being controlled by some outside force. According to the textbooks, dramatically ill schizophrenics appear not to be able to or wish to do anything for themselves — they take little interest in food, sexual activity, or exercise; they experience auditory hallucinations; and their speech seems rambling, incoherent, and disconnected to the casual listener. Some psychiatrists doubt whether schizophrenia is a single entity at all, or speak of core schizophrenia and a wider range of schizophrenia-like symptoms.

3

The idea of a single disease of schizophrenia may be a hangover from the nineteenth-century definition of madness — so-called dementia praecox — which preceded it. The diagnosis of schizophrenia in a patient with a given set of symptoms can vary between doctor and doctor and culture and culture. It is true that when matched and carefully controlled transnational surveys are done there is some concordance of diagnosis; however, in real life the diagnostic and prescribing practices of doctors and psychiatrists differ sharply from the more controlled procedures of

4

clinical trials. Comparisons of figures in different countries have shown that the most frequent use of the diagnosis of schizophrenia occurs in the United States and the Soviet Union. Nonetheless, even in Britain, where it is defined in a somewhat narrower sense, up to 1 percent of the population is said to suffer from schizophrenia; and 28,000 — or 16 percent — of the admissions to hospital for mental illness in 1978 were for a diagnosis of schizophrenia or its related disorders.

Faced with the complex phenomena that result in a diagnosis of schizophrenia, the biological determinist has a simple question: What is it about the biology of the individual schizophrenic that predisposes him or her toward the disorder? If no obvious gross brain difference can be found, predisposition must lie in some subtle biochemical abnormality — perhaps affecting the connections between individual nerve cells. And the thrust of the determinist argument is that the causes for these abnormalities, although they might have been environmental, are most likely to lie in the genes.

THE DRUG INDUSTRY AND MENTAL ILLNESS

Hence the enthusiastic hunt, over many decades now, for the biochemically abnormal component in schizophrenia. How should this search be conducted? A standard pattern in the biologizing of human medicine has been to seek for experimental animals that show what appear to be analogous symptoms. Or the animals can be induced to manifest similar symptoms by damaging them in some way, infecting them, or treating them with drugs. In the case of mental disorders this approach is problematic. How could one recognize a schizophrenic cat or dog, even if the term had any meaning anyhow? Such difficulties have not entirely chilled the enthusiasm of the researchers. Experimental animals have been treated with drugs such as LSD and have been shown to become disoriented, to show abnormal fear reactions, or whatever. These may be interpreted as analogous to hallucination, and hence the effect of the drug is argued to be analogous to the assumed biochemical dysfunction in schizophrenia.

But such evidence is not very convincing, and most research is directed to a study of the biochemistry of the schizophrenic subjects themselves. Brain samples are rarely obtainable except postmortem, and so more readily accessible body materials — urine, blood, or cerebrospinal fluid — from certified schizophrenics are compared with those from control "normal" people with all the assiduity that the Roman augurs used to apply to the examination of animals' entrails. It is assumed that any biochemical abnormality in the brain will reflect itself in the production of abnormal metabolites in the blood, ultimately to be excreted in the urine.

When such approaches were first adopted several decades ago they soon began to show up large differences in the biochemistry of hospitalized schizophrenic patients from those of normals matched for sex, age, and so forth. But these differences turned out to be artifactual; nonschizophrenic hospitalized patients showed similar differences from the normal.

The differences were eventually traced to the effects of long periods of eating poor hospital diets, or to the chemical-breakdown products of drugs that had been administered to the patients — or even to excessive coffee-drinking by hospitalized patients.

Even when proper care is taken to circumvent this problem by ensuring that the subjects studied have been kept off drugs for a period, that they have the same diet as their matched controls, and so forth, there remains a general methodological problem that cannot be avoided. Even if an abnormal chemical is found in the body fluids of a diagnosed schizophrenic compared with the best-matched of controls, one cannot infer that the observed substance is the cause of schizophrenia; it might instead be a consequence. The causal argument assumes that the substance is present, and, as a result, the disorder begins. A consequential argument says that first the disorder occurs and then as a result the substance accumulates. If an individual suffers an infection from a flu virus there is a considerable increase in the antibodies present in the blood and mucus of the nose — they are the body's defense mechanisms against the virus. The antibodies and the mucus haven't caused the infection, and one cannot readily deduce the actual causes simply by observing such consequences.

Such problems have made yet another approach more attractive to reductionist thinking: to observe the effects of pharmacological agents — drugs — on human behavior. If a drug induces schizophrenia-like behavior — for example, auditory hallucinations — then attempts will be made to conclude that the drug interferes with a biochemical process in the normal person which is damaged in the schizophrenic. Hence, for example, there was a period in the 1960s in which attempts were made to find links between LSD and schizophrenia on the grounds that users of LSD experienced hallucinations that might be seen as analogous to those of the schizophrenic. This logic, which argues backwards from the effect of a drug to the cause of a disease (*ex juvantibus* logic), is plainly a risky procedure, both for the logician and for the patient. . . . No drug has a single site of action. Foreign chemicals introduced into the body are not magic bullets.

Yet such thinking has dominated more than thirty years of research on the biochemistry of schizophrenia, generated endless research papers, made scientific and medical reputations, and brought incidental substantial profit to the big drug firms. The history of thinking among biochemists about schizophrenia over the period is inextricably intertwined with that of the pharmaceutical industry, for which psychotropic drugs have been one of the biggest money spinners. One in five of drugs issued in the British National Health Service in 1979 was for a drug acting on the central nervous system. Hoffmann–La Roche earns nearly $1 billion a year worldwide from its sales of Valium. It is estimated that chlorpromazine, introduced in 1952 for the control of long-stay hospitalized schizophrenics and related patients, had been administered to 50 million people worldwide within the first ten years of its use.

There is still another twist to the spiral of interdependence of the drug industry and the diagnosis of mental illness. With prolonged use of drugs, a whole new range of disorders has become apparent. Substances intended to cure one problem generate another, and the growth in such iatrogenic (medically induced) disorders is serious and disturbing. This is particularly the case for the major tranquilizers like chlorpromazine. There has been a slow recognition in the last decade or so of the disorder category known as tardive dyskinesia, apparent particularly among hospitalized patients who have been long users of chlorpromazine. The symptoms, which include characteristic motor disabilities and uncontrollable gestures (for instance, movements of the mouth), do not necessarily disappear when the patient is taken off the drug. There are reports that between 10 and 40 percent of those who regularly use major tranquilizers may suffer from tardive dyskinesia, and about 50 percent of those who get the disorder will have some irreversible consequential brain damage. Nor are there at present any drugs to combat these effects, though tardive dyskinesia has become a prolific spin-off area for neurobiological research.

It would be wearisome and unnecessary to recount in detail the history of research into the biochemistry of schizophrenia over the past thirty years. Almost every biochemical substance known to be present in the brain has, within two or three years of its introduction into the biochemical dictionary, been studied for possible involvement in schizophrenia by clinical scientists with the hope of a breakthrough in their hearts and with grant money (often from drug companies) burning holes in their pockets. **13**

We do not in any way wish to minimize the enormous difficulties faced in clinical research. The desire for a solution to the problem of schizophrenia is real and great, and the insistence on a biological mode of explanation that will enable effective drugs to be developed is part of a pressurizing culture to which clinical research is responding. Drugs that alleviate symptoms, like the use of aspirin for toothache, may be worth developing even if they tell nothing about the causes of the disorder. The multiplicity of drugs (and formulations of drugs) is an aspect of the way the pharmaceutical companies work in a field where knowledge of patent law is as important as clinical skills. The problem is that of confounding the effect of a drug with the offer of an explanation, the alleviation of suffering with a cure for the disease. **14**

Among the claims for causative factors in schizophrenia made since the 1950s we may point to: abnormal substances secreted in the sweat of schizophrenics; injection of the blood serum of schizophrenics into other, normal subjects inducing abnormal behavior; and the presence of abnormal enzymes in red blood cells and blood proteins. Between 1955 and the present day, conflicting research reports have claimed that schizophrenia is caused by disorders in serotonin metabolism (1955); noradrenaline metabolism (1971); dopamine metabolism (1972); acetylcholine metabolism (1973); endorphin metabolism (1976); and prostaglandin metabolism (1977). Some molecules, such as the amino acids glutamate and gamma-amino-butyric acid, came into fashion in the late 1950s, fell into neglect, and now, in the 1980s, have come back into fashion once more. **15**

Most of the substances referred to above are brain chemicals known   16
to play a part in the transmission of nerve impulses between cells. This
points to the main idea running through all such research. The notion is
that in some way, in schizophrenia, messages between cells in those
regions of the brain concerned with information processing and with affect
become scrambled, resulting in inappropriate responses. The evidence
for any and all of the various molecular disorders is based on a combination
of the types of methodologies and logic described earlier. Rarely have
results obtained by one group of researchers been confirmed by another
group of researchers in a different group of patients. Rarely has any
resolution of conflicting claims been attempted. Rarely has any concern
been expressed by the enthusiastic clinical researchers that schizophrenia
might be associated with many different biochemical effects, or indeed
that many different types of biochemical change might lead to or be
generated by the same behavioral outcomes.

THE GENETICS OF SCHIZOPHRENIA

The statement that the brain of a person manifesting schizophrenia   17
shows biochemical changes compared with that of a normal person may
be no more than a reaffirmation of a proper materialism that insists on
the unity of mind and brain. But the ideology of biological determinism
goes much deeper than this. It is, as we have reiterated, linked to an
insistence that biological events are ontologically prior to and cause the
behavioral or existential events, and hence to a claim that if brain biochemistry is altered in schizophrenia, then underlying this altered biochemistry must be some type of genetic predisposition to the disorder.
By 1981 psychologists were claiming to be able to detect potential schizophrenics when they are only three years old — up to fifty years before
the disease manifests itself. The claim, made by Venables to a meeting
of the British Association for the Advancement of Science, is based on
a survey of three-year-olds in Mauritius; "potentially abnormal" children
were said to show "abnormal autonomic responses."

Push the diagnosis back beyond the three-year-old and we are soon   18
with embryo or gene. But the hunt for a genetic basis for schizophrenia
goes far beyond an interest in therapy, as there is no way in which the
mere demonstration of a genetic basis for the disorder would aid in its
treatment. . . . The lineage of the effort to find genetic predispositions
runs back through the eugenic thinking of the 1930s and 1920s, with its
belief in genes for criminal degeneracy, sexual profligacy, alcoholism, and
every other type of activity disapproved of by bourgeois society. It is
deeply embedded in today's determinist ideology. Only thus can we account for the extraordinary repetitive perseverance and uncritical nature
of research into the genetics of schizophrenia. Whatever such research
may say about the disorder it proposes to explain, an examination of the
claims of its protagonists says a very great deal about the intellectual
history of our contemporary determinist society, and hence is worth
analyzing in some detail.

The belief that schizophrenia has a clear and important genetic basis   19
is now very widely held. The father of psychiatric genetics, Ernst Rüdin,
was so convinced of this that, arguing on the basis of statistics collected
by his co-workers, he advocated the eugenic sterilization of schizophrenics. When Hitler came to power in 1933, Rüdin's advocacy was no longer
merely academic. Professor Rüdin served on a panel, with Heinrich Himm-
ler as head, of the Task Force of Heredity Experts who drew up the
German sterilization law of 1933.

Perhaps the most influential psychiatric geneticist in the English-   20
speaking world was a student of Rüdin's, the late Franz Kallmann. The
blizzard of statistics published by Kallmann seemed to indicate conclusively
that schizophrenia was a genetic phenomenon. From his study of a thousand pairs of affected twins, Kallmann concluded that if one member of
a pair of identical twins was schizophrenic there was an 86.2 percent
chance that the other would be also. Further, if two schizophrenic parents
produced a child, there was a 68.1 percent chance that the child would
be schizophrenic. These figures led Kallmann to argue that schizophrenia
could be attributed to a single recessive gene.

The particular genetic theory espoused by Kallmann has made it   21
possible for latter-day psychiatric geneticists to attempt a spectacular
rewriting of their history. Thus, in a recent textbook the following note
appears: "Kallmann's [theory] was apparently not based solely on his
data. His widow has indicated that Kallmann advocated a recessive model
because he could then argue convincingly against the use of sterilization
to eliminate the gene. As a Jewish refugee, Kallmann was very sensitive
to this issue and afraid of the possible social consequences of his own
research." The point here is that if a disease such as schizophrenia is
caused by a recessive gene, many carriers of the gene will not themselves
display symptoms. Thus, sterilization merely of those who do show symptoms would be inefficient and would fail to eliminate the disease.

The picture of Kallmann as a bleeding-heart protector of schizo-   22
phrenics, adjusting his scientific theories to mirror his compassion, is
grotesquely false. The first Kallmann publication on schizophrenia is in a
German volume edited by Harmsen and Lohse that contains the proceedings of the frankly Nazi International Congress for Population Science.
There, in Berlin, Kallmann argued vigorously for the sterilization of the
apparently healthy relatives of schizophrenics, as well as of schizophrenics
themselves. This was necessary, according to Kallmann, precisely because his data indicated that schizophrenia was a genetically recessive
disease. Two Nazi geneticists, Lenz and Reichel, rose to argue that there
were simply too many apparently healthy relatives of schizophrenics to
make their sterilization feasible.

The eugenicist views of Kallmann were not confined to obscure Nazi   23
publications but were also made widely available in English after his arrival
in the United States in 1936. In 1938 he wrote of schizophrenics as a
"source of maladjusted crooks, asocial eccentrics, and the lowest type
of criminal offenders. Even the faithful believer in . . . liberty would be
much happier without those. . . . I am reluctant to admit the necessity
of different eugenic programs for democratic and fascistic communities

. . . there are neither biological nor sociological differences between a democratic and a totalitarian schizophrenic."

The extremity of Kallmann's totalitarian passion for eugenic sterilization was clearly indicated in his major 1938 text. Precisely because of the recessivity of the illness, it was above all necessary to prevent the reproduction of the apparently healthy children and siblings of schizophrenics. Further, the apparently healthy marriage partner of a schizophrenic "should be prevented from remarrying" if any child of the earlier marriage is even a suspected schizophrenic, and even if the second marriage is with a normal individual. 24

These views of the future president of the American Society for Human Genetics are so bloodcurdling that one can sympathize with the efforts of present-day geneticists to misrepresent or to suppress them. They have not, however, suppressed the mountains of published statistics with which Kallmann attempted to prove that schizophrenia . . . was a hereditary form of degeneracy. Those figures are presented to students in today's textbooks as the fruits of impartial science. . . . 25

TYPES OF STUDIES

Family Studies. There are basically three kinds of inquiries that attempt to demonstrate a genetic basis for schizophrenia: family studies, twin studies, and adoption studies. There is no need to spend much time on the first. The simple idea behind them is that if schizophrenia is inherited, the relatives of schizophrenics are likely to display the disease as well. Further, the more closely related a person is to a schizophrenic, the more likely it should be that the person will be affected. The problem is, of course, that these predictions would also follow from a theory that maintained that schizophrenia was environmentally produced. There is an obvious tendency for close relatives to share similar environments. 26

For what such data are worth, the major compilation of family studies seems to have been made by Zerbin-Rüdin. The compilation was presented to English-readers in "simplified form" by Slater and Cowie. Their table indicates, e.g., that fourteen separate studies yield a 4.38 percent expectation of schizophrenia among the parents of schizophrenic index cases. The expectation among sibs, in ten studies, was 8.24 percent; and among children, 12.31 percent in five studies. For uncles and aunts, grandchildren, and cousins the figures were all under 3 percent, but still higher than the expected 1 percent. 27

The exactness of these figures, however, is more apparent than real. The same basic set of studies was also summarized by Rosenthal in 1970. The relatives diagnosed in these studies, Rosenthal noted, had often been dead for many years. The studies are quite old, and methods of diagnosis and of sampling are not always spelled out. The combined figures are dominated by Kallmann's massive samples and by data gathered by other members of Rüdin's "Munich school." The Rosenthal tables make clear a fact that is obscured by the Slater and Cowie summary. There are vast differences in the rates of schizophrenia reported in different studies. For parents of index cases, reported risks range from 0.2 percent (lower 28 than in the population at large) to 12.0 percent. For sibs, the range is between 3.3 and 14.3 percent. The risk for sibs is in one study twenty-nine times larger than that for parents; but in another the risk for parents is 1½ times larger than that for sibs. These studies at best demonstrate what nobody would have contested. There is at least a rough tendency for diagnosed schizophrenia to "run in families." [1]

Twin Studies.   The basic logic of twin studies depends upon the   29
fact that while MZ twins are genetically identical, DZ [dizygotic] twins on average share (like ordinary siblings) only half their genes. Thus, if a trait is genetically determined, one would obviously expect MZs [monozygotic twins] to be concordant for that trait more often than DZs. The major logical problem with twin studies is that MZ twins, who typically resemble one another strikingly in appearance, are treated much more similarly than are DZs by parents and peers. There is abundant evidence . . . that the environments of MZs are very much more similar than those of DZs. (Twin studies typically compare concordance rates among MZs, who are always of the same sex, with concordance rates among same-sexed DZs.) The demonstration that concordance is higher among MZs does not necessarily establish a genetic basis for the trait in question. Perhaps the difference is due to the greater environmental similarity of MZs. We shall soon discuss evidence which indicates that this possibility is not at all farfetched.

Well-designed twin studies should take as their index cases all schizo-   30
phrenic twins admitted to a particular hospital during a particular time period. The alternative — feasible in small Scandinavian countries, which maintain population registers — is to start with the entire population of twins and to locate index schizophrenic cases. With either technique, a number of procedural problems are inevitable. The co-twins of index cases are often dead or unavailable for personal examination. Thus, informed guesses often must be made both about whether a given pair is MZ or DZ, and whether or not the co-twin is schizophrenic. The guesses are typically made by the same person, opening the way for contaminated diagnoses. There is sometimes an effort to have blind diagnoses made of individual cases by independent judges, working from written case histories.

The case histories, however, contain selective material gathered and   31
prepared by investigators who were not themselves "blind." Further, the case records of those twins who have in fact been hospitalized — and their diagnoses — had been written up by doctors who questioned the ill twins in detail about possible taint in their family lines. The diagnosis of schizophrenia, as should by now be clear, is by no means a cut-and-dried affair. The fact that a person's relative may have suffered from schizophrenia is often used to help doctors make a diagnosis.

---

[1] Even this modest conclusion is not unchallenged in the literature. Two studies in the United States found rates of schizophrenia among the first-degree relatives of schizophrenics which were scarcely above the rate in the general population.

The biases that contaminate twin studies stand out clearly from an   32
attentive reading of the published case history materials. The very first
case described by Slater in 1953 is the story of Eileen, a hospitalized
schizophrenic, and of her identical twin, Fanny. Eileen had been hospitalized in 1899, "suffering from acute mania," and died in the hospital in
1946. With Eileen as the index case, Slater's task was to investigate the
mental status of Fanny, who died, aged seventy-one, in 1938. We are
told by Slater:

> While still in the twenties she had a mental illness, of which no details are
> available. . . . Fanny in [1936] proved very difficult to examine . . . so that
> only the barest details were obtainable. She suppressed all mention of her
> own mental illness in early years, which fact was obtained from the history
> of her twin sister given at the time of her admission to hospital. Though
> there was no sign of any present schizophrenic symptoms, this suspicion
> and reserve are such as are commonly found as sequelae of a schizophrenic
> psychosis. Unfortunately, no facts are obtainable about the nature of her
> past mental illness, but the probabilities are very greatly in favour of it having
> been a schizophrenic one . . . she made a fairly complete and permanent
> recovery . . . though psychologically her reserve and lack of frankness sug-
> gest that the schizophrenia was not entirely without permanent after-effect.
> . . . According to her daughter-in-law, who had not heard of her mental
> illness, she led a hard life. Neither her family nor the neighbours noticed
> anything odd about her.

These MZ twins, according to Slater, were concordant for schizo-   33
phrenia. The only evidence that Fanny had once suffered from schizophrenia was her twin's assertion — while "suffering from acute mania"
in 1899 — that Fanny had had some kind of mental illness. Fanny herself,
in 1936, was difficult and suppressed all mention of her illness. That lack
of frankness, Slater noted, was typical of recovered schizophrenics, who
otherwise appear normal. Fanny's dead identical twin had clearly been
schizophrenic. For Slater this made it obvious that Fanny's supposed
mental illness fifty years earlier had been schizophrenia. Fanny's neighbors
and family, unlike Slater and other students of the Munich school, had
not the wit to detect Fanny's schizophrenia.

Consider now the first pair of discordant DZ twins described by   34
Gottesman and Shields in their 1972 study. Twin A was a hospitalized
schizophrenic. What about Twin B? "No psychiatric history. Family unwilling for him to be contacted for Twin Investigation. . . . The pair differs
from most in that neither twin was seen by us." The investigators concluded that Twin B was normal; and six blind judges, pondering a case
study summary prepared by the investigators, unanimously agreed that
Twin B was free of psychopathology. With DZ Pair 16 of the same study,
all judges again agreed that the co-twin was normal, making the pair
discordant. The diagnosis of the co-twin had not been made under ideal
conditions: "He refused to be seen for the Twin Investigation, remaining
upstairs out of sight, but his wife was seen at the door. . . . He was
regarded as a healthy, levelheaded, solid happy person." That might in
fact be the case — but few will agree that diagnoses of co-twins made
in this way are solid or levelheaded. . . .

Those who perform [twin] studies still claim, however, that the higher   35
concordance observed among MZs — a unanimous finding — demonstrates at least some genetic basis for schizophrenia. We have already
noted that MZs not only are genetically more similar than DZs but also
experience much more similar environments than do DZs. The environmental similarity, no less than the genetic similarity, might plausibly
account for the higher concordance of MZs.

There are in fact some simple and critical tests that can be made of   36
this environmental hypothesis. There is no doubt that DZ twins experience more similar environments than do ordinary siblings. The DZ twins,
however, are genetically no more alike than are ordinary siblings — they
are only siblings who happen to have been born at the same time. Thus,
from an environmental viewpoint — and only from such a viewpoint —
we would expect concordance among DZs to be higher than among ordinary sibs. There have been a number of studies that reported rates of
schizophrenia concordance among DZ twins, as well as rates among
siblings of the twins. . . .

Though the reported differences are very small in the early studies,   37
all studies agree in showing a higher concordance rate among DZs than
among sibs. Within more modern studies, the difference is often statistically significant, with the risk for DZs reported as two or three times
that for sibs. When we note that similarity of environment can double or
triple the concordance of DZs above that of sibs, it seems entirely plausible
to attribute the still higher concordance of MZs to their still greater
environmental similarity.

The same kind of point can be demonstrated by comparing the con-   38
cordance rates of same-sexed and of opposite-sexed DZs. Though both
types of DZ twins are equally similar genetically, it is obvious that same-
sexed pairs experience more similar environments than do opposite-sexed
pairs. The available data . . . again support the environmentalist expectation. There have been statistically significant differences reported by
several investigators, always indicating a higher concordance among same-
sexed twins. . . .

There is little wonder in the fact that even psychiatric geneticists   39
have not found twin studies to be wholly convincing, and have turned to
studies of adoption. The adoption studies, in theory at least, might be
able to disentangle genetic from environmental effects in a way that twin
studies cannot.

Adoption Studies.   The basic procedure of adoption studies is to   40
begin with a set of schizophrenic index cases, and then to study the
biological relatives from whom they have been separated by the process
of adoption. Thus — at least in theory — the index case and his or her
biological relatives have only genes, and not environment, in common.
The question of interest is whether the biological relatives of the index
cases, despite the lack of shared environments, display an increased
incidence of schizophrenia. To answer that question it is necessary to

compare the rate of schizophrenia among the biological relatives with the rate observed in some appropriate control group.

The adoption studies carried out in Denmark in recent years by a collaborative team of American and Danish investigators have had enormous impact. To some critics who could detect the methodological weaknesses of twin studies, the Danish adoption studies appeared to establish the genetic basis of schizophrenia beyond any doubt. The eminent neuroscientist Solomon Snyder referred to these studies as a landmark "in the history of biological psychiatry. It's the best work that's been done. They take out all the artifacts in the nature vs. nurture argument." . . . The Danish studies have been universally accepted as an unequivocal demonstration of an important genetic basis for schizophrenia. Clearly these studies require detailed critical examination. **41**

Though they have been described in many separate publications, there are basically two major Danish adoption studies. The first [which will be dealt with here], with Kety as senior investigator, starts with adoptees as the schizophrenic index cases and examines their relatives. . . . **42**

The study that began with adoptees as index cases was first reported by Kety in 1968. Based on Copenhagen records, the investigators located thirty-four adoptees who had been admitted to psychiatric hospitals as adults and who could be diagnosed from the records as schizophrenics. For each schizophrenic adoptee a control adoptee who had never received psychiatric care was selected. The control was matched to the index case for sex, age, age at transfer to the adoptive parents, and socioeconomic status (SES) of the adoptive family. **43**

The next step was to search the records of psychiatric treatment for all Denmark, looking for relatives of both the index and control cases. Those who searched the records did not know which were the relatives of index cases and which were the relatives of controls. Whenever a psychiatric record was found, it was summarized and then diagnosed blindly by a team of researchers who came to a consensus. The relatives were not at this stage personally examined. **44**

The researchers traced 150 biological relatives (parents, sibs, or half-sibs) of the index cases, and 156 biological relatives of the controls. The first point to note is one not stressed by the authors: There were virtually no clear cases of schizophrenia among the relatives either of the index or of the control cases. To be precise, there was one chronic schizophrenic among the index relatives and one among the controls. To obtain apparently significant results the authors had to pool together a "schizophrenic spectrum of disorders." The spectrum concept lumps into a single category such diagnoses as chronic schizophrenia, "borderline state," "inadequate personality," "uncertain schizophrenia," and "uncertain borderline state." With such a broad concept, 8.7 percent of the biological relatives of index cases and 1.9 percent of the biological relatives of controls were diagnosed as displaying spectrum disorders. There were nine biological families of index cases in which at least one spectrum diagnosis had been made, compared to only two such families among the **45** controls. That difference is the supposed evidence for the genetic basis of schizophrenia. Without the inclusion of such vague diagnoses as "inadequate personality" and "uncertain borderline schizophrenia" there would be no significant results in the Kety study.

From the Kety data of 1968 it is possible to demonstrate that such vague diagnoses — falling within the "soft spectrum" — are not in fact associated with schizophrenia. Among the sixty-six biological families reported on in 1968 there were a total of six in which at least one "soft" diagnosis had been made. There was *no* tendency for such diagnoses to occur any more frequently in families in which definite schizophrenia had been diagnosed than in other families. However, the "soft spectrum" diagnoses very definitely tended to occur in the same families in which "outside the spectrum" psychiatric diagnoses had been made — that is, such clearly nonschizophrenic diagnoses as alcoholism, psychopathy, syphilitic psychosis, etc. There were "outside the spectrum" diagnoses in 83 percent of the families containing "soft spectrum" diagnoses, and in only 30 percent of the remaining families — a statistically significant difference. Thus it appears that the Kety et al. results depend upon their labeling as schizophrenia vaguely defined behaviors that tend to run in the same families as do alcoholism and criminality — but which do not tend to run in the same families as does genuine schizophrenia. However, it remains the case that these frowned-upon behaviors did occur more frequently among the biological relatives of adopted schizophrenics than among the biological relatives of adopted controls. What might account for such a finding? **46**

The most obvious possibility is that of selective placement, a universal phenomenon in the real world in which adoptions in fact occur, and a phenomenon that undermines the theoretical separation of genetic and environmental variables claimed for adoption studies. The children placed into homes by adoption agencies are never placed randomly. For example, it is well known that biological children of college-educated mothers, when put up for adoption, are placed selectively into the homes of adoptive parents with higher socioeconomic and educational status. The biological children of mothers who are grade-school dropouts are usually placed into much lower status adoptive homes. Thus it seems reasonable to ask: Into what kinds of adoptive homes are infants born into families shattered by alcoholism, criminality, and syphilitic psychosis likely to be placed? Further, might not the adoptive environment into which such children are placed cause them to develop schizophrenia? **47**

From raw data kindly made available to one of us by Dr. Kety, we have been able to demonstrate a clear selective placement effect. Whenever a record of psychiatric treatment of a relative was located by Kety's team, notation was made about whether the relative had been in a mental hospital, in the psychiatric department of a general hospital, or in some other facility. When we check the adoptive families of the schizophrenic adoptees, we discover that in eight of the families (24 percent) an adoptive parent had been in a mental hospital. That was not true of a single adoptive parent of a control adoptee. That, of course, is a statistically significant difference — and it suggests as a credible interpretation of the Kety et **48** al. results that the schizophrenic adoptees, who indeed had been born into shattered and disreputable families, acquired their schizophrenia as a result of the poor adoptive environments into which they were placed. The fact that one's adoptive parent goes into a mental hospital clearly does not bode well for the psychological health of the environment in which one is reared. There is, by the way, no indication that the biological parents of the schizophrenic adoptees have been in mental hospitals at an excessive rate. That occurred in only two families (6 percent), a rate in fact lower than that observed in the biological families of the control adoptees.

The same set of subjects has also been reported on in a later paper by Kety et al. For this later work as many as possible of the relatives of index and control adoptees had been traced down personally and interviewed by a psychiatrist. The interviews were edited, and consensus diagnoses were then made blindly by the investigators. The basic picture did not change much. There were more spectrum diagnoses among relatives of index cases than among relatives of controls, although the interview procedure greatly increased the overall frequency of such diagnoses. This time, however, diagnoses of inadequate personality had to be excluded from the spectrum, since they occurred with equal frequency in both sets of relatives. The significance of the 1968 results, based on records rather than interviews, had depended upon including inadequate personality in the elastic spectrum.   49

Personal correspondence with the psychiatrist who conducted the interviews with relatives has revealed a few interesting details. The 1975 paper speaks only of "interviews," but it turns out that in several cases, when relatives were dead or unavailable, the psychiatrist "prepared a so-called pseudo interview from the existing hospital records." That is, the psychiatrist filled out the interview form in the way in which he guessed the relative would have answered. These pseudo interviews were sometimes diagnosed with remarkable sensitivity by the team of American investigators. The case of the biological mother of S-11, a schizophrenic adoptee, is one particularly instructive example.   50

The woman's mental hospital records had been edited and then diagnosed blindly by the investigators in 1968. The diagnosis was inadequate personality — at that time, inside the spectrum. The 1975 paper — by which time inadequate personality is outside the spectrum — indicates that, upon personal interview, the woman had been diagnosed as a case of uncertain borderline schizophrenia — again inside the spectrum. But personal correspondence has revealed that the woman was never in fact interviewed; she had committed suicide long before the psychiatrist attempted to locate her, and so — from the original hospital records — she was "pseudo interviewed." Perhaps the most remarkable aspect of the story, also revealed by personal correspondence, is that the woman had been hospitalized twice — and each time had been diagnosed as manic-depressive by the psychiatrists who actually saw and treated her. That is, she had been diagnosed as suffering from a mental illness unrelated to schizophrenia, and very clearly outside the schizophrenia spectrum. We can only marvel at the fact that the American diagnosticians,   51 analyzing abstracts of these same records, were twice able to detect — without ever seeing her — that she really belonged within the shifting boundaries of the spectrum. . . .

SCHIZOPHRENIA AS SOCIALLY DETERMINED

To reveal, as we have tried, the theoretical and empirical impov-   52
erishment of the conventional wisdom of biological determinism in relationship to schizophrenia does not then argue that there is nothing relevant
to be said about the biology of the disorder, and still less does it deny
that schizophrenia exists. The problem of understanding the etiology of
schizophrenia and a rational investigation of its treatment and prevention
is made vastly more difficult, perhaps even hopelessly tangled, by the
extraordinary latitude and naiveté of diagnostic criteria. Certainly one may
wonder about the relevance of biology to the diagnosis of schizophrenia
either by the forensic psychiatrists of the Soviet Union or by the British
psychiatrist who diagnoses a young black as schizophrenic on the basis
of his use of the religious language of Rastafarianism.

Misgivings are not eased when one recalls a well-known study by   53
Rosenhan and his colleagues in California in 1973. Rosenhan's group of
experimenters presented themselves individually at mental hospitals complaining of hearing voices. Many were hospitalized. Once inside the hospital, according to the strategy of the experiment, they declared that
their symptoms had ceased. However, it did not prove so easy to achieve
release. The experimenters' claims to normality were disregarded, and
most found themselves treated as mere objects by nurses and doctors
and released only after considerable periods of time. A pseudo patient
who took notes in one of the hospitals, for instance, was described by
nurses as showing "compulsive writing behavior."

Even more revealing, perhaps, was the drop in hospital admissions   54
for schizophrenia in the area after Rosenhan circulated the results of the
first experiment among doctors and indicated that they might be visited
by further pseudo patients in the future, although none were actually
sent.

It is this sort of experience that lies behind the argument, developed   55
in its most extreme form by Michel Foucault and his school over the last
two decades, that the entire category of psychological disorders is to be
seen as a historical invention, an expression of power relationships within
society manifested within particular families. To simplify Foucault's intricate argument, he claims that all societies require a category of individuals who can be dominated or scapegoated, and over the centuries
since the rise of science — and particularly since the industrial revolution
of the nineteenth century — the mad have come to fill this category. In
medieval times, he says, houses of confinement were built for lepers,
and madness was often explained in terms of possession by demons or
spirits. According to Foucault the idea of institutionalizing the mad developed during the eighteenth and nineteenth centuries after the clearing
of the leper houses left a gap for new scapegoats to replace the old ones.

In this view madness is a matter of labeling; it is not a property of   56 the individual but merely a social definition wished by society on a proportion of its population. To look for correlates of madness in the brain or the genes is therefore a meaningless task, for it is not located in the brain or the individual at all. To dismiss the suffering and the deranged behavior of the schizophrenic merely as a problem of social labeling by those who have power over those who have not seems a quite inadequate response to a complex social and medical problem. Despite Foucault's historiography and the enthusiasm of its reception in Britain and France at the crest of the wave of antipsychiatry of the 1960s and 1970s, the actual historical account he gives of when and how asylums for the insane arose has been called into question. And by cutting the phenomenon of schizophrenia completely away from biology and locating it entirely in the social world of labeling, Foucault and his followers arrive, from a very different starting point, back in the dualist Cartesian camp, which . . . preceded the full-blown materialism of the nineteenth century. So much has Foucault retreated that at certain points in his argument he even seems to be ambiguous as to whether "physical" quite apart from "mental" illness exists except in the social context that proclaims it.

More modest than Foucault's grand theorizing but nonetheless culturally determinist are the social and familial theories of schizophrenia developed by R. D. Laing. For Laing — at least the Laing of the sixties and early seventies — schizophrenia is essentially a family disorder, not a product of a sick individual but of the interactions of the members of a sick family. Within this family, locked together by the nuclear style of living of contemporary society, one particular child comes to be picked upon, always at fault, never able to live up to parental demands or expectations. Thus the child is in what Laing calls (in a term derived from Gregory Bateson) a double bind; whatever he or she does is wrong. Under such circumstances the retreat into a world of private fantasy becomes the only logical response to the intolerable pressures of existence. Schizophrenia is thus a rational, adaptive response of individuals to the constraints of their life. Treatment of the schizophrenic by hospitalization or by drugs is therefore not seen as liberation from the disease but as part of that person's oppression.

Family context may be crucial in the development of mental illnesses such as schizophrenia, but it is clear that a larger social context is also involved. The diagnosis is made most often of working-class, inner-city dwellers, least often of middle- and upper-class suburban dwellers. To a social theorist, the argument about the social context that determines the diagnosis is clear. An example of the class nature of the diagnosis of mental illness comes from the studies of depression by Brown and Harris in 1978 in Camberwell, an inner-city, largely working-class area of London, with some pockets of middle-class infiltration. They showed that about a quarter of working-class women with children living in Camberwell were suffering from what they defined as a definite neurosis, mainly severe depression, whereas the incidence among comparable middle-class women was only some 6 percent. A large proportion of these depressed individuals, who if they had attended psychiatric clinics would have been diagnosed as ill and medicalized or hospitalized, had suffered severe threatening events in their lives within the past year, such as loss of husband or economic insecurity. The use of drugs — mainly tranquilizers — among such groups of women is clearly very high.

Biological determinism faces such social evidence with arguments [59] that, for example, people with genotypes predisposing toward schizophrenia may drift downward in occupation and living accommodation until they find a niche most suited to their genotype. But it would be a brave biological determinist who would want to argue that in the case of the depressed housewives of Camberwell it was their genes that were at fault.

An adequate theory of schizophrenia must understand what it is about [60] the social and cultural environment that pushes some categories of people toward manifesting schizophrenic symptoms; it must understand that such cultural and social environments themselves profoundly affect the biology of the individuals concerned and that some of these biological changes, if we could measure them, might be the reflections or correspondents of that schizophrenia with the brain. It may well be that, in our present society, people with certain genotypes are more likely than others to suffer from schizophrenia — although the evidence is at present entirely inadequate to allow one to come to that conclusion. This says nothing about the future of "schizophrenia" in a different type of society, nor does it help us build a theory of schizophrenia in the present. Neither biological nor cultural determinism, nor some sort of dualistic agnosticism, is adequate to the task of developing such a theory. For that, we must look to a more dialectical understanding of the relationship between the biological and the social.

The rest of this chapter focuses on specific treatments of schizophrenia. The first three selections, all published within the past ten years, discuss drug therapies. J. Joel Jeffries and Judy Levene, in an excerpt from an educational pamphlet, describe the major drugs used to treat schizophrenia. Then David L. Rosenhan and Martin E. P. Seligman offer a second overview of drug therapies. Finally, David, Derald, and Stanley Sue focus on one specific line of biochemical treatment: the dopamine hypothesis.

Drug Treatments for Schizophrenia
J. JOEL JEFFRIES AND JUDY LEVENE

Q. What drugs are useful for the treatment of schizophrenia?   [1]
A. The most important drugs in the treatment of schizophrenia are those [2] that are called "neuroleptics," though other types of drugs are used in addition.
Q. What are the neuroleptics that are used in schizophrenia? [3]
A. They will be listed one by one with some comments about each. [4]

Chlorpromazine.   This is sold under a variety of trade names, the [5] most popular of which is Largactil. It is taken in daily dosages, as high as 5,000 mg. It commonly causes drowsiness early in treatment, though this tends to disappear after a while: If it persists, it is often reduced by taking the medication in one dose at bedtime. It may also cause blurring of vision and dryness of mouth. Some people have constipation. Parkinsonism, which is described later, occurs fairly often. In many people chlorpromazine produces a sensitivity to sunlight, and people taking this drug should either stay out of the sun or else use protective clothing or barrier cream.

Thioridazine. Although cheaper copies are now available, this drug was originally sold as Mellaril. It is used in dosages up to 800 mg a day. It tends to have less side effects than chlorpromazine, particularly in women. The problem with men is that it may sometimes cause temporary impotence. Drowsiness is fairly common as are lightheadedness, difficulty in focusing and dry mouth. Parkinsonism is rare. 6

Trifluoperazine. Although cheaper copies are now available, this drug was originally sold as Stelazine. It is used in dosages up to 120 mg a day. It does not tend to cause drowsiness but has quite marked effects on muscles, leading to parkinsonism and often also quite severe muscular restlessness or severe spasms, which require the use of other drugs to control them. 7

Piperacetazine (Quide). This drug is somewhat less potent than the ones mentioned above but tends to have relatively few side effects, the most significant of which are mild drowsiness and temporary impotence in men. It is used in doses up to 400 mg a day. It was due to be withdrawn from the market in 1984. 8

Fluphenazine Decanoate (Modecate). This is a long-acting intramuscular injection. Usual maximum dosage for this drug is about 150 mg by injection every week, though some people are maintained on as little as 12.5 mg every four weeks. It may cause quite marked parkinsonism and muscular restlessness. These side effects are worse in the four days following the injection. Generally, it has been found that people taking this drug stay healthy longer than those who take oral medications and this is not because the drug is any better in itself but because it is much more likely that people will continue to take the medication when it is given by injection than when they have to take it daily by mouth. 9

Haloperidol (Haldol). Quite different chemically from the drugs mentioned above, this is a very potent medication which is usually used in dosages up to 80 mg a day (in some settings as high as 300 mg a day). It tends to have side effects very similar to trifluoperazine's. 10

Haloperidol Decanoate (Haldol LA). This is a recently introduced depot injection, a long-acting version of Haloperidol. Usual doses are up to 400 mg, and injections may last four weeks. 11

Pimozide (Orap). This is a newer drug which appears to have   12
mild side effects. It is normally used for people with mild illness or those
whose symptoms are already controlled, but who are continuing to have
troublesome side effects. It is used often for paranoid disorder. It is used
in dosages up to 40 mg a day.

Q. What is Parkinsonism?   13
A. A condition caused by neuroleptics. It involves tension in the muscles   14
   with loss of facial expression, loss of arm motion when walking,
   shuffling gait and, occasionally, drooling.
Q. What drugs are used for the Parkinsonism side effects of neuro-   15
   leptics?
A. There a number of such available. The ones commonly used include: 16

Kemadrin (Procyclidine)   Disipal, Norflex (Orphenadrine)
Artane (Trihexyphenidyl)   Parsitan (Ethopropazine)
Cogentin (Benztropine)   Amantadine (Symmetrel)

Often these drugs are prescribed to be taken regularly two, three,
or four times a day. However, it is probably best to take them
whenever one starts to feel side effects of the neuroleptic. Side
effects from these drugs are relatively minor unless they are abused:
They can produce constipation, dry mouth, blurred vision.
Q. What is akathisia?   17
A. This is a physical restlessness produced by neuroleptics. The patient   18
   may be unable to sit still and often feels quite uncomfortable. Anti-
   parkinsonisms are often used for this condition, but diazepam (Valium)
   or propanolol (Inderal) may work better.
Q. What is tardive dyskinesia?   19
A. This is a serious reaction to neuroleptic medication that usually occurs   20
   in older patients after prolonged treatment though it may occur fairly
   quickly. It usually consists of involuntary movements of the tongue,
   face, eyes, mouth, or jaw that the patient may not be aware of.
   Other people may be aware of it, as a most obvious component is
   facial grimacing. Another form of the condition affects limb and trunk
   muscles. The best treatment of this condition is not yet clear and
   the neuroleptic may need to be changed or discontinued.
Q. What other drugs are commonly used in schizophrenia?   21
A. Antidepressants are often used for people who are depressed. An-   22
   tianxiety drugs are used for people who are anxious but they also
   seem to have a useful effect on some who develop muscular restlessness (akathisia) with the neuroleptics.

The Treatment of Schizophrenia

DAVID L. ROSENHAN AND MARTIN E. P. SELIGMAN

Until the mid-1950s, treatment of schizophrenia was primarily custodial.   1
Patients were warehoused for long periods of time in environments that
were both boring and hopeless. Often their disorder and the hospital
environment interacted to bring about behavior that required physical

restraint. In 1952, however, a lucky accident changed this bleak situation, and led to a revolution in the treatment of schizophrenia.

DRUG THERAPY

While synthesizing new drugs called *antihistamines* that benefit asthmatics and those with allergies, researchers noticed the strong calming effects of these drugs. In fact, one of the drugs, promethazine, was so tranquilizing that the French surgeon Henri Laborit gave it to his patients as a prelude to anesthesia. Using a close relative of promethazine with even stronger sedative effects, French psychiatrists Jean Delay and Pierre Deniker treated various mentally disordered patients with varying results. Those who improved had a common diagnosis: schizophrenia. The drug they took was chlorpromazine. Now a prominent member of a class of drugs variously called *neuroleptics, psychotropics,* or *tranquilizing agents,* chlorpromazine revolutionized the treatment schizophrenia. In 1955, there were about 560,000 patients in American psychiatric hospitals. One out of every two hospital beds was devoted to psychiatric care. It was then estimated that, by 1971, 750,000 beds would be required to care for growing psychiatric populations. In fact, there were only 308,000 patients in psychiatric hospitals in 1971, less than half the projected estimate, and about 40 percent fewer than were hospitalized in 1955. And by 1977, the patient census had declined to less than 160,000. Such is the power of the major tranquilizers.

Anti-Psychotic Effects of Drug Therapy. Of the major tranquilizers, Thorazine and Haldol, whose generic names are respectively chlorpromazine and haloperidol, are two of the most commonly used. Their most striking effect is the degree to which they "tranquilize," make peaceful, even sedate. Could it be that these phenothiazines are no different from barbiturates, whose sedative action produces no greater improvements for schizophrenics than placebos? Some evidence suggests that this is not the case. The phenothiazines seem to have specific ameliorating effects on schizophrenic symptoms, beyond their sedative effects and even beyond their impact on anxiety. Thought disorder, hallucinations, affect, and withdrawal, all these are affected by the phenothiazines. Equally important, these drugs have virtually no effect on psychiatric symptoms that are not associated with schizophrenia. Subjective emotional experiences, such as guilt and depression, continue unabated despite a course of drug treatment.

Just how the phenothiazines achieve their effects on schizophrenic symptoms is not yet clear. Regardless, the average hospital stay for a schizophrenic patient has declined to fewer than thirteen days, when formerly it was months, years, even a lifetime. Phenothiazines have, nearly alone, been responsible for a revolution in psychiatric care.

Side Effects of Drug Therapy. The antipsychotic drugs have a variety of unpleasant side effects that often lead patients to discontinue using them. Side effects of chlorpromazine (Thorazine), for example, frequently include dryness of mouth and throat, drowsiness, visual disturbances, weight gain or loss, menstrual disturbances, constipation, and depression. For most patients, these are relatively minor problems, but annoying enough to induce them to discontinue medications on discharge.

One class of more serious side effects, called extra-pyramidal or   **6**
Parkinson-like effects, appears to arise because, as we have seen, anti-psychotic medications affect the dopamine receptors, which are in turn implicated in Parkinson's disease. These drugs do not cause Parkinson's disease, but they do induce analogous symptoms. These symptoms include stiffness of muscles and difficulty in moving, freezing of facial muscles which results in a glum or sour look as well as an inability to smile, tremors at the extremities as well as spasms of limbs and body, and *akathesia* — a peculiar "itchiness" in the muscles which results in an inability to sit still, and an urge to pace the halls continuously and energetically. Other drugs can control these side effects, but interestingly, no phenothiazine has yet been produced which avoids them.

Even more serious is a neurological disorder called *tardive dyskinesia.*   **7**
Its symptoms consist of sucking, lip-smacking, and tongue movements that seem like fly-catching. Tardive dyskinesia is not reversible. Conservatively, it affects 18 percent of hospitalized schizophrenics, a figure that rises with the patients' age and length of time they have been on anti-psychotic medication.

The Revolving Door Phenomenon.   The widespread use of psy-   **8**
chotropic drugs promised a virtual revolution in the treatment of schizophrenia. Even if the disorder could not be cured, it seemed certain that it could be contained. No longer would thousands spend their lives in back wards. No longer would families and society be deprived of their contribution. And no longer would massive economic resources be wasted on custodial care. But the pharmaceutical revolution fell short of its promise. For, while the hospital population of schizophrenics has declined radically since 1955, the readmission rates for schizophrenics have soared. In 1972, for example, 72 percent of the schizophrenics admitted to hospitals had been there before. It is estimated that between 40 percent and 60 percent of schizophrenic patients will be rehospitalized within two years of discharge; 65 percent to 75 percent by the end of five years. One likely reason for rehospitalization is that only 15 to 40 percent of them are able to work or care for themselves. Another is that they return to aversive environments and to communities that are less than welcoming. Third, they lack work skills and social skills. Finally, they often stop taking medications on discharge because of the drugs' aversive side effects.

One can interpret this "revolving-door" aspect of psychiatric hospitals   **9**
both negatively and positively. On the negative side, the readmission rates are discouraging; they suggest that the attempt to treat schizophrenics is futile. But on the positive side, is it not better for a patient to be readmitted, than never to have been discharged at all? This latter situation characterized the plight of many patients before the advent of the phenothiazines.

Even if one opts for the more positive response to the high read-   **10**
mission rate, the task of understanding its cause and of eventually reducing

it remains. One thing is clear: Anti-psychotic drugs help ameliorate the symptoms of schizophrenia, but the symptoms of schizophrenia are by no means the entire problem. Indeed, the very fact that these drugs alter symptoms and only symptoms raises profound questions about what is meant by treatment, recovery, and cure.

Biochemistry: The Dopamine Hypothesis
DAVID SUE, DERALD SUE, AND STANLEY SUE

Biochemical explanations of schizophrenia have a long history. A century   1
ago, for example, Emil Kraepelin suggested that these disorders result from a chemical imbalance that develops due to abnormal secretion by the sex glands. Since then, a number of studies have been undertaken to demonstrate that body chemistry is involved in schizophrenia. Most have led only to dead ends.

What generally happens is that a researcher finds a particular chemical   2
substance in schizophrenic subjects and does not find it in "normal" controls, but other researchers cannot replicate those findings. This was the case with a substance called *taraxein,* which was isolated from the blood serum of schizophrenics. The problem generally arises because schizophrenic patients differ from normals in lifestyle and in food and medication intake, all of which affect body chemistry and tend to confound research results.

One promising line of biochemical research has focused on one of   3
the neurotransmitters, *dopamine,* and its involvement in schizophrenia. According to the *dopamine hypothesis,* . . . schizophrenia may result from an excess of dopamine activity at certain synaptic sites. This high level of activity is due either to the release of excess dopamine by presynaptic neurons or to the oversensitivity of dopamine receptors.

Support for the dopamine hypothesis has come from research with   4
three types of drugs. The first is the *phenothiazines,* which are anti-psychotic drugs that decrease the severity of thought disorders, alleviate withdrawal and hallucinations, and improve the mood of schizophrenics. Their effectiveness is not due to a generalized sedating effect (pheno-barbital, a depressant with sedative properties, is not nearly so effective against schizophrenic symptoms). Rather, there is increasing evidence that the phenothiazines reduce dopamine activity in the brain by blocking dopamine receptor sites in postsynaptic neurons.

Another drug, *L-Dopa,* is generally used to treat such symptoms of   5
Parkinson's disease as muscle and limb rigidity and tremors. The body converts L-Dopa to dopamine, and the drug sometimes produces schizo-phrenic-like symptoms. (By contrast, the phenothiazines, which reduce dopamine activity, can produce side effects that are similar to the symptoms of Parkinson's disease.)

Finally, there is research on the effects of the *amphetamines,* stim-   6
ulants that increase the availability of dopamine and norepinephrine (an-other neurotransmitter) in the brain. When nonschizophrenic subjects are given continual doses of amphetamines, they exhibit symptoms very much

like those found in acute paranoid schizophrenia. Continual low dosages of these drugs also produce psychotic-like symptoms in monkeys. And very small doses may increase the severity of symptoms in diagnosed schizophrenics. Other stimulants, such as caffeine, do not produce these effects.

Thus a drug that is believed to block dopamine reception has the effect of reducing the severity of schizophrenic symptoms, whereas two drugs that increase dopamine availability either produce or worsen these symptoms. Such evidence supports the idea that excess dopamine may cause schizophrenic symptoms. 7

The evidence is not all positive, however. For example, on the basis of the dopamine hypothesis, one would expect that the treatment of schizophrenia with phenothiazines would be effective in the vast majority of cases. Yet approximately one-fourth of schizophrenic patients were found to be minimally responsive or unresponsive to antipsychotic medication. In fact, in one study of 65 schizophrenics who were treated with antipsychotic medications, 25 percent reported that the medication had *negative* effects on them. In addition, a group of schizophrenics who were given amphetamines, one-third did not experience a worsening of their symptoms. Such results point to the involvement of something other than excess dopamine. 8

Schizophrenia may very well be a group of disorders with differing etiologies; such an explanation could account for the variable course of the disorders and the unevenness of schizophrenics' responses to the phenothiazines. Moreover, researchers may be looking for too simple an explanation by focusing on dopamine alone, without considering the interactive functioning of the brain and the biochemical system as a whole. Or perhaps dopamine blockers can influence the symptoms of schizophrenia but not the course of the illness. Obviously, much more remains to be discovered. 9

In the next two selections, published in 1961 and 1973, therapists Otto Will and Theodore Lidz each present their views on the role of psychotherapy in treating schizophrenia.

Process, Psychotherapy, and Schizophrenia
OTTO WILL

Miss X and I worked in therapy for four and a half years, the first eighteen months of which she lived in the hospital. During the first two years we met five to seven days each week, usually spending an hour together; but on some occasions the session was extended to two hours or longer. I frequently (usually each day) discussed the course of treatment with the nurses and others concerned with the patient's care, and the collaborative nature of this work deserves much greater attention 1 than I am able to devote to it here. Although I had a regular schedule for my meetings with Miss X, I also saw her at unscheduled times at her request, or because she was disturbed, or because I thought that therapy would be advanced by so doing. In the last three years of treatment we met regularly three to four hours weekly.

In the first few months of therapy Miss X was frequently disturbed, and I made an effort to be consistent in my attitudes, to present a clear picture to myself, to avoid making verbal statements that conflicted with my nonverbal operations, and to set clear-cut and firm limits to any destructive behavior. During this period I usually met Miss X in her room because she was too frightened and unpredictably violent to come to my office. I emphasized tangible aspects of the situation available to observation by both of us, avoided "pushing" for information about obviously distressing subjects, and did not attempt to interpret the content of dreams and hallucinations, although I listened to her accounts of these as I did to any other communication — without excessive interest or surprise. One of my goals during this time was to identify a need of the patient, respond to it quickly when possible, help her recognize her own need and express it more clearly, and encourage her to accept the help of others in meeting her needs as well as to discover ways of more effectively meeting them herself.

During the first year Miss X's anxiety subsided somewhat. I was more acceptable to her; we were consistently identified as therapist and patient (although she was frequently anything but in agreement with many of my ideas); hallucinations appeared only at times of intense anxiety; and we were able to meet in my office.

After the reduction of the major disturbance Miss X spoke of me as a therapist, but made many observations about me that I did not attempt to interpret but observed as slowly forming a picture of me not entirely in keeping with the usual view of myself. I was described as some twenty years older than my actual age, harsh, cold, unsympathetic, controlling, and seductive, and she feared that my only concern with her would be to satisfy my own ambitions. With the experience of much anxiety and recurrent outbursts of rage Miss X noted that in her description of me she was telling me about her attitudes toward her father and men in general, and something of life in her home. We were able to discriminate realistic and accurate (sometimes painfully so) observations of me from those that were more exaggerated and to a greater extent influenced by her past.

With increasing clarification of her relationship to her father Miss X seemed more at ease, and for a couple of months she talked with relative freedom about many current and past events, but had very little to say of her mother. The sessions then became marked by increasing anxiety, the source of which we could not at first identify. Miss X became more suspicious of me and her anger increased, with the result that she would suddenly attack me. I was now described as something loathsome, filthy, disgusting, and essentially evil that would destroy the young woman. Any interpretations I made were met with denial, silence, or increases of anxiety, and I realized that I was being dealt with by Miss X in terms of experience that possibly had occurred early in life, had been dissociated, and could not be expressed readily in words. When her anxiety was very intense and her behavior unpredictable she would be admitted to the hospital for periods of one to three or four days. During this time of the recurrent intense anxiety accompanying the coming into awareness of symbols of very troublesome aspects of important interpersonal experiences, we slowly learned something of her relationship with her mother. I personally felt considerable anxiety while we worked on these problems, and was disturbed by the intensity of the patient's emotions, by my own anger and fear aroused in response to them, and by the vagueness and lack of organization that characterized the communication. At times I found myself strongly moved by feelings whose origins I could not at first discover; but later I noted that they were apparently in response to the multitude of nonverbal cues presented by the patient, not clearly observed in my awareness, but nonetheless reacted to by me in an empathic fashion.

With increased comprehension of Miss X's relationship to her mother, anxiety again was reduced. She visited her parents (which she had not wished to do for about two years), and the therapy continued in a more conventional manner. We sat in chairs about six feet apart, and I listened while she attempted to note and express verbally whatever "came to mind." Evidences of psychosis were no longer present and for the last two years we explored her current and past relationships (including the one between us), and she took part in activities which she had previously avoided. Her physical symptoms — fatigue, diarrhea, vomiting — were increased at intervals during the first three years of therapy, but subsided without our attempting to "explain" their possible connection to obscure referents. She took pride in her obviously increasing attractiveness, gained tolerance of competitive situations, began to date with young men, and completed her college studies. We terminated our work together when she was well on the way to gaining increased satisfaction in her living, related to people without excessive anxiety, had a reasonably accurate and confirmable view of herself (and of me), and was no longer so fearful of her self-identity. **6**

In this case so briefly presented (and with others in my experience) the initial problem is to establish a working relationship characterized by some durability, a lessening of anxiety, and increasing clarity as to the identity of the participants. When this has been accomplished the various transference or parataxic distortions can be observed and eventually recognized. The more easily identified and less anxiety-ridden relationships are dealt with first — in this instance that of the father. Early life relationships characterized by great obscurity and anxiety can be dealt with adequately later in therapy after a considerable definition of the therapeutic field has been achieved and it has been proven to be dependable and somewhat secure. **7**

An important and common aspect of the therapeutic relationship with the schizophrenic person is his need for and his fear of relatedness, accompanied by the feeling that his attainment of greater self-identity will be destructive to himself or someone close to him. In the therapeutic situation Miss X often expressed the feeling that "something dreadful is **8** going to happen if I do something," but the nature of the "something" was unclear. She then said that she feared that I would die, or that she would kill me, or that somehow I would be destroyed by association with the evil that she felt to be so much a part of her, and she tried to terminate treatment. I persisted in meeting with her, making it clear that I appreciated her apprehension, but did not share it, and should be able to survive any "evil" in the relationship. As the security of our relationship increased Miss X expressed the fear that progress in therapy would be hurtful to someone in her family. Of this she said: "It's as if the price for my getting well is someone else dying." Her parents had been consulting regularly with a psychiatrist and it became clear to Miss X that I was not going to resist or suffer from changes in her, and that her parents were increasingly able to tolerate her growth. She then observed that she feared her own development and was anxious at her further self-identification, clinging, as it were, to the old ways of living, and mourning for the fading distortions of interpersonal relationships. Throughout the years of treatment we dealt repeatedly and in varying contexts with Miss X's need for relatedness, the anxiety aroused in her by relationship, and her fear of what seemed to be an alternative — isolation, loneliness, and self-destruction. In the work the anxiety of relationship was reduced, and she slowly learned that relatedness and self-identity are not incompatible — that there can be no true closeness to another unless there is also distance and the maintenance of a sense of self. All of her problems were not resolved and she would continue to be subject to anxiety; but she now knew a fair amount about herself in relationship to her past, her family, and her culture, and she was more free than she had been to let herself be known to others and to grow in the process.

Modifications of Psychoanalytic Techniques
THEODORE LIDZ

Therapeutic tasks require an approach that differs in many ways from conventional psychoanalytically oriented therapy. Most, if not all, psychoanalysts who treat schizophrenic patients with reasonable success have greatly modified psychoanalytic techniques, often developing therapies that are psychoanalytic only in . . . utilizing certain psychoanalytic insights, and in expecting the patient to take as much initiative as seems feasible at any given time. An understanding of the nature and origins of schizophrenic disorders and how they differ from the various neuroses provides guidance to the therapist in adapting his techniques to treating schizophrenic patients.   1

Free association is not encouraged. The patient, who is already apt to be flooded by extraneous associations, primary process material, and preoperational cognition, needs to be guided into sharper conceptualization and to use shared meanings and syntax. We wish to have him regain the filtering function of categories rather than remain in the nebulous realm   2 of the egocentric presentation of ruminations. Placing the patient on the couch not only loosens associations by lessening perceptual contact, but can also foster delusions based on transference to the therapist of a parent's incestuous behavior. The therapist seeks to strengthen ego functions rather than have the patient set them aside for the purpose of associating freely. For similar reasons, we do not foster anxiety to achieve therapeutic movement, for anxiety, through stimulating the sympathetic nervous system which lowers the stimulus barrier, can increase cognitive disorganization. Indeed, it is for such reasons that the phenothiazines which counter the impact of anxiety on physiological functioning and raise the stimulus barrier can, when used moderately, help make it possible for the patient to work in psychotherapy. In general, emphasis is not placed on the analysis of distortions of understanding arising from mechanisms of defense of the ego as much as on the distortions imposed by the parents' needs to defend their own tenuous egos. We seek to imbue in the patient trust in his own feelings and ideas while we question those that are essentially his parents' feelings and perceptions offered as his own; and the patient is usually sensitive to the therapist's ability to differentiate the two. The therapist fosters the patient's self-esteem, his ideas, and his feelings that he had long been taught to distrust in favor of what the parents projected onto him. By eschewing any pretence of omniscience, the psychotherapist counters the patient's tendencies to believe that others know the way and why of living that have been concealed from him, and rather seeks to help the patient clarify and understand his own ideas and emotions.

The psychotherapist has the critical task of reestablishing sufficient trust and hope in the patient to enable him to brook once again the danger of shattering disillusionment and to dare to seek a meaningful relationship. It is a very personal function that cannot be filled by assuming the classic position of the analyst as a blank screen upon which the patient's transferences, projections, and other defenses can be examined. The schizophrenic patient develops a therapeutic relationship when he can trust; and he trusts when he feels understood and begins to believe that the therapist will neither use him nor abandon him when the angry, dark, and covetous sides of his ambivalences emerge. Communication is of the essence, and the patient is weaned from his autistic preoccupations and his idiosyncratic communications by the therapist's ability to hear and understand what the patient wishes to say even while he seeks to conceal through the use of idiosyncratic metaphor and cryptic associations.

Familiarity with the common dilemmas in the lives of schizophrenic patients gained from direct family studies and hunches derived from theoretic concepts can be particularly important in helping the therapist appreciate what the patient is communicating in his covert and strange ways. Thus, when a young woman who became psychotic during her first year in college told her therapist that when she had first left her home to go to college she had locked herself in her railroad compartment, stripped off her clothes, thrown them out the window and then dressed in a new outfit, he quietly mused, "At last, you could become yourself

. . . leave at home the person your mother needed you to be." When, on a later occasion, she puzzled about why, for a period during the college year, she had secretly taken another girl's overcoat each night, slept in it, and replaced it early in the morning, her therapist queried, "You found someone you wished to be like?" The patient must come to trust and utilize verbal communication, and does so by learning that the therapist listens to what he says and seeks to understand, and does not impose his own ideas upon the patient.

The therapeutic relationship long remains a tenuous thread, its strength repeatedly tested by the patient before it becomes a means of reliving and reevaluating childhood experiences. It is fraught with the actual dangers of the patient's childhood intrafamilial experiences. Often just as the patient feels himself becoming attached to his therapist, he flees — flees from the therapist, or into psychosis. The therapist, who was beginning to become hopeful, can become profoundly discouraged at the results of his efforts and give up — in actuality, through falling back on physical therapies or through losing his commitment to the patient. If, however, he expects the setback, understands why the patient feels endangered, and perseveres, a firmer working relationship follows. The patient has equated the therapist's interest, concern, and attention with his parents' intrusiveness and envelopment, and with their imperviousness to his needs and feelings. In brief, a major requirement for the therapist concerns the ability to care and refuse to give up while not needing the patient or his devotion. The therapist seeks to convey that even though he wants very much for the patient to improve and will go a long way and make personal sacrifices to foster such improvement, he pursues this goal neither for the parents' sake nor because he needs a therapeutic success. . . .

I also wish to emphasize the importance of the traditional role of the mental institution as a "retreat" from the life stresses that have contributed to the psychosis, or even precipitated it. The youthful patient who has not been able to find an ego identity or manage as a reasonably autonomous individual is granted a moratorium during which he can marshal his inner resources and utilize therapeutic guidance. Even more specifically, the moratorium counters the tendency of the patient, who has suffered an acute psychotic disorganization and is frantically searching for meaning and direction, to find a delusional resolution of his difficulties, reconstitute around them, and move into a chronic schizophrenic state.

The following article (1986) provides an overview of research on behavioral modification programs for chronic schizophrenic patients. There are differences in the way various token economy programs are set up, but the essential notion is this: Behavior can be encouraged, reduced, or shaped by positive or negative reinforcers. So, for example, patients might be rewarded with candy or cigarettes (or tokens they can redeem for such goods) for cooperating with others or keeping themselves groomed or decreasing the frequency of bizarre movements.

Token Economies and Schizophrenia: A Review

JOHN HALL AND ROGER BAKER

There is . . . fairly clear evidence that it is possible to modify almost   1
any schizophrenic symptom, including the experience and behavioral con-
comitants of auditory hallucinations. However, the degree of modification
found from one patient to another is extremely variable. In the study by
Wincze et al., seven of ten chronic paranoid schizophrenic patients showed
decreases of at least 20 percent in delusional speech in response to token
contingencies, one of the seven showing complete suppression of delusions and another near complete. As with many studies, there was little
spontaneous generalization of improvement outside the ward setting,
although subsequent special generalization training with eight of the patients effectively reduced delusional speech in four patients. A handful of
studies have reported the appearance of aberrant behaviors following
modification of symptoms, but florid symptoms such as hallucinations have
been totally eradicated without any apparent "symptom substitution."
Some studies have reported suppression of all the major symptoms demonstrated by an individual. While it has often been said that such patients
have simply been trained to talk less about their symptoms, others see
no reason why the modification of behavior should not affect subjective
states.

Florid symptoms are only one aspect of schizophrenia. There has   2
been renewed interest in the negative and positive symptoms of schizophrenia. The assessment of negative symptoms, such as social withdrawal and apathy, does pose problems, but the "social withdrawal" and
"socially embarrassing" factors of the Wing Ward Behaviour Rating Scale
are measures of some validity. Five separate British studies of chronic
schizophrenic patients showed that token economy programs improve the
"social withdrawal" factor. This includes behavior such as self-care,
speed of movement, and speech. Changes in socially embarrassing behavior in the five studies were more variable, . . . There is a wealth of
other evidence, using a range of assessment methods, that different
aspects of social withdrawal can be modified. A consistent finding has
also been that behavior change has failed to generalize outside the treatment setting in which it has developed. This may be overcome by special
generalization training, by moving the token economy into the community,
or by implementing behavior modification programs in the homes of
chronic schizophrenic patients by their families.

OTHER FACTORS IN TOKEN ECONOMIES

Although there has been increasing concern to assess symptomatic   3
change in token economies, a number of other aspects of token economy
programs have been investigated, such as individual variations in response
to token programs. . . . Richard Butler analyzed 51 individual treatment
programs carried out on a token ward, and found that the less withdrawn

patients did best on the program, and the non-responsiveness to token programs was reduced by individualizing programs very carefully. Woods et al. examined data from six patients exposed to a token program for five years, suggesting that the program had a specific therapeutic effect for only three of the patients. . . .

WHY DO TOKEN ECONOMIES WORK?

In 1977 Paul and Lentz were able to state confidently that: "The overall comparative results on the relative effectiveness of the programs in the current project could not be clearer. The social learning (token) program was significantly more effective than either the milieu program or the traditional hospital program. Its greater effectiveness was consistent across all classes of functioning in the intramural setting." However, this statement does not indicate *why* token economy programs are effective. [In recent years,] considerable doubt has arisen as to whether contingent token reinforcement is the main therapeutic ingredient in a token economy. A token program involves the introduction of a systematic goal-setting and monitoring system, as well as the use of verbal reinforcement and informational feedback, so the contribution of these factors may outweigh the effect of any material reinforcement available via the tokens. Since the tokens presumably acquire their value to patients by systematic linking to the availability of desired backup or primary reinforcers, it should be demonstrable that the back-up reinforcers alone can produce systematic change. In none of the quoted studies has this been demonstrated for the group of patients used in the main experimental study. Many of the chronic patients used in token programs display high levels of anhedonia, i.e., low levels of motivation to experience pleasure. Coupled with the very low cash purchasing power of most token schemes, the incentive to earn tokens is not high, so the level of anhedonia of patients and its relationship to symptom patterns, may be a characteristic on which patients should be selected for token economies. For all of these reasons, there have been a number of changes in the way in which token economy programs are now designed and in the way in which they are conceptualized.

One major change is that the ward-wide standard token packages have been superseded in Britain by more differentiated behavioral regimes, within which tokens may be used for some, but not for all patients. This change has been stimulated partly because of the evidence of the studies already quoted, but partly because of the continuing reduction in size of the large psychiatric hospitals by the discharge of the least handicapped patients. The wards, formerly full of patients who were relatively similar to each other, are now half-empty and contain a more varied and usually more actively disturbed group of patients, less suitable for "package" programs. Other treatment approaches have been introduced, such as social skills training and problem-solving techniques, and their use in combination with other behavioral techniques means that a "pure" token economy is now hard to find. Indeed, it is now difficult to imagine that a ward-wide token program, with tokens as the main therapeutic element for all patients, would be a regime of choice in most psychiatric hospitals in Britain.

Alongside changes in technique have come changes in interpretation. **6** As long ago as 1973 Stoffelmayr found that a token regime was superior to social therapy on all accounts, but noted that nurses on the token economy interacted more frequently with patients and prompted and ordered patients less often than nurses in the control social therapy regime. This might suggest that the nature of staff-patient interaction is the main therapeutic factor. Studies by Fraser have drawn attention to the role of instructions as the most potent variable in training long-stay patients. This view has also been taken by Lowe and Higson, who point out how verbal self-control methods have been explored relatively little with chronic patients. . . .

Another way of conceptualizing some of the information derived from **7** token programs involves the application of environmental psychology, or "ward ecology." Careful examination of the behavior of chronic patients suggests that their behavior can be greatly affected by the physical environment within which they live. Studies such as that of Polsky and Chance, examining the patterns of use of space by chronic patients in a ward setting, or of Holahan, looking at the effects of seating arrangements on communication between psychiatric patients, illustrate this trend. . . .

One must still ask precisely *what* variable is responsible for the **8** improvements that have resulted from token economies. Our own studies led us to conclude that contingent token reinforcement was *not* responsible, speaking of the token economy as a total environment, rather than as a technique for individual patients or programs. The work of Fernandez and Fraser . . . attempted to address this question. Fernandez indicated that some target behaviors show greatest change when instructions and prompting are combined with verbal reinforcement, and that some behaviors can be changed using instruction alone. Fraser used an impressive multiple baseline design, and suggested that instructions about expected behavior made the most significant contribution to behavior change. Unfortunately, both these sets of studies used very short experimental phases (two to six weeks), whereas our own, using a 12-month experimental phase, shows that the long-term effectiveness of a token economy program is confused by the immediate but short-lived effects of contingent token reinforcement. Nonetheless, the evidence that instructions are perhaps the main therapeutic factor is strong. Fraser clearly thinks so: "The token economy is therefore seen to achieve its effects solely through the elaborate social information system which is embodied in its application and the conditioning theory of its operation must, as a result, surrender to Occam's razor since there has been no reliable evidence to date that contingent token presentation is a critical therapeutic variable." This view has considerable practical implications, since, if comparable results can be achieved without exchangeable tokens, it is no longer necessary to bother to exchange tokens for goods, nor indeed ethically defensible to restrict access to rights and privileges. There would still remain the need to retain a complex goal-setting and monitoring system, together with the information about what behavior is acceptable, as implied by the elaborate social information system view.

Wing has advocated on many occasions a three-fold classification of the causation of chronic handicap in schizophrenic patients. He conceives of (a) primary handicaps, arising directly from the psychiatric condition; (b) secondary handicaps relating to the changed reaction or attitude of the patient and relatives to the patient himself; and (c) premorbid handicaps. Only since it has been possible to study schizophrenic patients at home in their family has it been possible to identify more carefully those handicaps due solely to institutional living. Recent studies have also pointed to the high proportion of patients with a physical disability or untreated medical condition, which further complicates their treatment. This type of analysis suggests that intervention at several different levels is required to meet the full range of needs of the chronic schizophrenic patient. Quite apart from the contingencies which operate in a ward, for example, the appropriate level of social and environmental stimulation still needs to be determined.

Perhaps one test of the influence of token economy methods is to compare the state of the art of psychiatric rehabilitation before the advent of token economies with the present time. General professional views of rehabilitation and the nature of the identified clinical problems, have changed considerably over those 15 years. In 1970 continued discharge of chronic patients was accepted relatively uncritically and most large psychiatric hospitals contained perhaps hundreds of patients who could not immediately be discharged, but for whom a goal-directed social learning regime seemed appropriate. In 1985 the deinstitutionalization movement is proceeding much more cautiously, and those chronic patients remaining within hospital present a much more differentiated and in general more severe range of problems. One of the requirements of token economy methods is that they need a degree of staff control over patients which is incompatible with the general service move towards greater patient freedom and community alternatives to psychiatric hospitals.

It may seem paradoxical that only as the numbers of chronic patients in hospital have fallen, have important British books on psychiatric rehabilitation been published. . . . A careful reading of these books indicates the major contribution of behavioral methods to present day psychiatric rehabilitation, in four respects. Firstly, an increased emphasis on careful and comprehensive assessment of the patient and his environment, using behavioral methods and relating to regular monitoring procedures. Secondly, a broadening range of behavioral treatment procedures which *may* use individual or group token programs. Thirdly, a clearer formation of the significance of patient-staff and patient-patient interaction for ward milieus. Fourthly, better guidance on the design of both patient treatment programs and staff training programs so that positive results of the program generalize to the real world. All four of these developments owe much to the token economy practice and research of the last fifteen years, although the token economy itself, in its original "pure" form, has fallen into abeyance.

9

10

11

Jay Haley is a leading proponent of a "family systems" approach to the origin and treatment of schizophrenia. This influential theory suggests that schizophrenia is a reaction to complex conflicts within a person's family: "It is assumed," writes Haley in this article published in 1980, "that the members of the family are in conflict, and that the child is expressing that." This assumption leads Haley to propose a treatment that has the entire family assessing and changing its pattern of communication and the way it organizes itself.

A Family Orientation
JAY HALEY

FAILURE TO DISENGAGE FROM THE FAMILY

1   At one time, it was theorized that a young person behaved bizarrely at the moment of success because of his or her fragile nature and inability to tolerate responsibility. It was also postulated that there was an inner fear, perhaps carried over from childhood, that terrified the young person when confronted by self-sufficiency and autonomy. Failure was thought to be caused by inner anxiety. Such an explanation was the only one available, because causes were assumed to reside inside the person rather than in the social context, which was not observed. In the 1950s, when whole families were brought together and observed within a concept of systems, it was noticed that a young person who behaved in a bizarre way could be described as responding adaptively to peculiar communication within his family. For the first time, it was suggested that the thought processes and inner anxiety of a person were responses to the kind of communication system in which he was embedded. When people communicate in deviant ways, their thought processes are deviant.

2   As observation of families continued, it was noted that people communicate in deviant ways in response to an organizational structure of a deviant type. A special organization leads to special communication behavior, which leads to peculiar inner thought processes.

3   Today, when clinicians and researchers look at a young person behaving in a bizarre way, they tend to conceptualize the problem in different ways:

1. Some clinicians assume the issue is peculiar thought processes. These thoughts cause peculiar communicative behavior, and the person forms relationships which make a deviant organization. The therapy focuses on correcting disordered thinking and misperceptions.
2. Other clinicians assume that the disordered, deviant communicative behavior of the people intimate with the problem person causes the bizarre behavior and thought processes. Their therapeutic endeavor is therefore to clarify and change communication among intimates in the family.
3. Still other clinicians assume that the problem is a malfunctioning and deviant organization. That organization requires peculiar communicative behavior and therefore peculiar thought processes.

It is the argument of this work that the most effective therapeutic   4
intervention is directed at the basic organizational structure. As that
changes, so do other factors. In fact, if one thinks in organizational terms,
a therapist cannot avoid being part of the family organization. As a therapist talks to a young person about his thought processes, he is an outsider
dealing with a family member, and the organization has rules for dealing
with outsiders. If he clarifies family communication, by that act he has
become an authority in the family hierarchy. To overlook the organizational situation can lead to naive interventions which prevent change or
even make matters worse. In fact, families will make use of a naive
clinician to stabilize and avoid change.

The importance of the social situation has been overlooked in the   5
clinical field for a number of reasons. For centuries, individual character
and personality had been emphasized; the scientific task was to classify
individuals, not social situations, into types. In addition, cultural institutions are based on the idea of the individual as the unit of responsibility.
To allow the social situation to be causal would lead to the jailing or
hospitalization of families and friends rather than individuals. Many facets
of the culture depend on the fact, or myth, of the individual as a unit.

Until the concept of systems, there was no adequate theory of social   6
situations. To describe behavior which keeps repeating, and so forms an
organizational structure of habitual responses, is a new way of thinking
about people. The concept of a self-correcting system of relationships is
difficult for many people to grasp, much less to take for granted. It is
easier to say a particular person caused a difficulty than it is to think
of the difficulty as one step in a repeating cycle in which everyone
participates.

Another problem in accepting the social situation as a unit is the   7
simple idea that people live in social situations, and so they take them
for granted. Ordinary situations, like stages of family life, seemed so
obvious that they were not considered a subject of scientific concern.
Everyone knew there was a family life-stage when young people leave
home, but it was not thought important, so no one noticed the conjunction
of malfunctioning people and that life-stage. It is now appearing that, in
any organization, the time of greatest change occurs when someone is
entering the organization or leaving it.

When a young person succeeds outside the home, it is not merely   8
a matter of individual success. He is simultaneously disengaging from a
family, which can lead to consequences for the whole organization. A
young person's success or failure is inextricably part of the reorganization
of a family, as new hierarchical arrangements are made and new communication pathways develop.

In the normal course of family living, young people graduate from   9
school and begin to work and support themselves while still living at
home. Sometimes they physically move out of the home when they go
to work. When they become self-supporting, they are in a position to
marry and establish homes for themselves. Usually parents are involved
in the approval of a mate and in helping their children set up their own
homes. As the young people have children, the parents become grand-

parents and continue to be involved as the family changes its organization over the years. In many families, the children's leaving home appears to cause only a mild disruption. Parents can even find it a relief to have the children off their hands and to be free to do the things they would like to do together.

When a person in the late teens or early twenties begins to behave in strange and failing ways, it should be assumed that the stage of leaving home is malfunctioning and that the organization is in trouble. The trouble will take different forms depending on the structure of the organization. In single-parent families a mother often lives with her own mother and raises children. As the children disengage, mother and grandmother are left as only a dyad and face a reorganization. Sometimes the mother is a lonely single parent, and if the only members of her organization are herself and her child, the child's leaving is a major disruption. 10

In two-parent families, the parents are faced with only each other, after many years of functioning in a many-person organization. Sometimes parents have communicated with each other primarily through a particular child and have great difficulty dealing with each other more directly. When the child leaves home, the parents become unable to function as a viable organization. Sometimes they threaten divorce or separation. The emphasis in this work is on problems in the offspring, but at this stage of family life problems can appear in one or both parents. When divorce occurs, or a middle-aged parent develops a depression or other symptom, it often coincides with the children leaving, and the problem is a response to an organizational change. 11

Sometimes the difficulty in the family becomes extreme when the first child leaves; sometimes not until the last one is leaving; and at times, it is a middle child who is in some way special to the parents. The problem is a triangle between the parents and a special child who is the bridge between them; when that child begins to leave home, the family becomes unstable. The issues that the parents did not deal with because of the children must now be faced. All the marital themes that were communicated about in terms of the child must be dealt with differently when the child is no longer going to be active in the triangle. 12

When a family is in real trouble because a child is leaving home, there is one way the trouble can be resolved and the family stabilized — the child can stay at home. Yet, as young people reach their late teens and early twenties, the social forces of the community, as well as physiological changes, exert pressure on the family to disengage the young person. School or work is expected, as well as social life outside the family. The young person may stay at home for months or even years, but the expectation increases that the offspring will have a life outside the family and the parents will be left facing each other. 13

A SOLUTION

One way the young person can stabilize the family is to develop some incapacitating problem that makes him or her a failure, so that he or she continues to need the parents. The function of the failure is to let the 14 parents continue to communicate through and about the young person, with the organization remaining the same. Once the young person and parents fail to disengage, the triangular stability can continue for many years, independent of the offspring's age, though the onset of the problem began at the age of leaving home. The "child" can be forty years old, and the parents in their seventies, still taking their crazy son or daughter from hospital to hospital and doctor to doctor.

There are two ways the family can stabilize: The parents can use 15 an official institution to restrain their offspring, so that he or she does not become independent and self-supporting. By placing the young person in a mental hospital or other social control institution, or by arranging that a doctor heavily medicate the offspring, the parents keep the family stable. The professional community can become an arm of the family to restrain the offspring and maintain them in a handicapped state. For example, I can recall that, years ago, when electric shock was more popular, a mother would threaten a daughter that if she did not behave she would be taken down to the doctor for shock treatments. With rich families, the offspring is sometimes placed in a private institution for years, and the family is stable as long as the incarceration continues. A naive therapist talking to a young person in an institution can believe that he is an agent of change, when he has actually been hired by a family to stabilize the organization so that change does not occur. The parents can visit the institution regularly and keep involved with the offspring, without the inconvenience of actually living with and taking care of him or her.

The other way the family can stabilize by means of a failing offspring 16 is for the young person to wander about in a failing life. He can be a vagrant on the road and serve as a stabilizing agent in the family, as long as he regularly lets the parents know that he is continuing to fail. He can do this by writing to them regularly and asking for money, by letting them know he is in jail, or through some other unfortunate circumstance.

There are borderline situations, where the young person is failing in 17 one sense and not another. He can live on a commune as a deviant and be a failure in the eyes of the parents. Or, a more common situation these days, he can join a deviant religious cult. Within the cult he may be a success at begging or recruiting new members, but as far as the parents are concerned he is still a failure. Often they not only commiserate with each other for their unfortunate offspring but even hire people to kidnap them from the cult and deprogram them. The focus continues to be on the offspring.

Whether dependent on an institution arranged by the family or com- 18 munity, or on an institution sought out by the young person, the offspring is defined as a failure by the parents, and they communicate about him as if he has not left home. For example, the parents can blame each other for causing the problem or argue about what still might be done. The offspring cannot be left out of their plans as could a successful offspring earning a living. The parents also do not change their relationship with each other; it continues frozen, as if they cannot move to the next stage of family life any more than the dependent offspring can. Their difficulties with each other do not get resolved because when an issue between them comes up, the child is introduced into it just as if he were in the room. For example, a father can complain that his wife did something that irritated him and he didn't mention it to her. When asked why he did nothing about it, he will say, "Well, I know my wife is worried about our son." The concern and preoccupation with the young person prevents an organizational change because the triangle persists unchanged.

Although the family crisis and failure of the young person usually occur in the late teens or early twenties, it can occur later. Sometimes a child who has left home collapses back when his youngest sibling leaves the parent's home. For example, a woman in her late thirties had been out of the home for several years. She began to behave bizarrely, and her parents set out to help her by hospitalizing her and planning her return home to be cared for. This event coincided with the family's youngest child leaving home for college. Because of the older daughter's failure and return home, the family continued to be an organization with a child at home. **19**

When one approaches a mad young person with an interest in organizational change, it is evident that such change does not occur with institutionalization but rather with normal behavior in the community. Therapeutic change therefore occurs most rapidly when the family is encouraged to push the child into normal activities immediately — that is when action in the family happens. **20**

THE CYCLE

One of the ways to describe the situation is in terms of a recurring cycle. As the young person reaches the age of leaving home, he or she begins to succeed in work or school or in forming intimate relations outside the family. At that point the family becomes unstable, and the young person begins to manifest strange and troublesome behavior. All family members seem upset and behaving in deviant ways, but when the offspring is selected as the problem his behavior appears more extreme, and the other family members stabilize and appear to be reacting to him. The parents, who are divided over many issues, become so divided that they cannot deal with the young person, who begins to take charge and have power over the family. If the parents begin to pull together to deal with their child, it is not unusual for him or her to gain support from more distant relatives, such as the father's mother, against the parents. As the wider kin system comes into conflict with the parents over the young person, the parents become more unable to control him or her, and the behavior escalates. Outside experts are turned to for help, and the expert typically is used by the parents to restrain the offspring with medication or custody; the family stabilizes itself by such restraints. Conflict often increases, however, as family members blame each other for what has happened. The expert then typically attempts to rescue the young person from the parents and so joins him or her in a cross-generational coalition against them, thereby undermining their executive **21** position. This mad situation becomes clinical when the young person is released from restraint and begins once again to function in the community. As he or she begins to take preliminary steps to succeed in work or school or in forming intimate relations outside the family, the conflict and instability appear again. The young person begins to behave eccentrically, the family says it cannot deal with him, and experts are called. The young person is sent back to the place he was sent before. The second time, everyone knows where he belongs — the place he went the first time. Once again in the institution, the young person is treated for a period and then sent home. The situation is stable until the young person starts to succeed in work or school, the parents threaten separation, the family becomes unstable, and the cycle repeats. The goal of the therapy proposed here is to end that cycle, to get the young person past that eccentric episode and successfully functioning outside the family, with the family reorganized to survive that change.

THE ISSUE OF RESPONSIBILITY

Where there is madness, there is irresponsible behavior, by defini- 22 tion. People are not doing what they should do, or are doing what they should not do, according to accepted rules of social conduct. What differentiates mad and eccentric behavior from other behavior is not only its extreme form but the indication that the person cannot help himself and is not responsible for his actions. This inability to help oneself is also communicated by the ways the continuing acts lead to repeated failure and misery. It is characteristic of problem young people that they do something that breaks social rules and then qualify the act with an indication that it is not their fault. The drug addict lives a deviant life and indicates that his compulsion forces him to these acts. It is not his responsibility because he cannot help himself. Similarly, the girl starving herself says she is not responsible because she has no appetite or is repelled by food. The eccentric thief steals what he does not need, indicating that he is helpless to stop.

The truly mad are most expert at doing something and qualifying it 23 in a way that indicates they are not responsible for the act. Sometimes they indicate that they are not really themselves but someone else, or that the place and time are not what others say they are, and therefore the act is not their doing. A young person can refuse to get a job and say it is because he has millions of dollars in funds hidden away; in this way he indicates that he does not know what he is doing.

For the therapist, it is important to acknowledge that a problem 24 young person is behaving irresponsibly and must be required to take responsibility for his actions. It is equally important to note that the people around the eccentric are behaving irresponsibly. When there is nutty behavior, the eccentric will say it is not his fault because a voice from another planet told him to do it. The parents will each say they are not responsible because it is the fault of the other parent, or the influence of evil companions, or drugs, or heredity. The experts who are called in often blame the parents, or "illness," or genetics. They do not acknowledge that their interventions compound the problem. When the young person is locked up, the psychiatrist will deny responsibility for committing him, saying it is the judge who did it. The judge will say he is not responsible for giving a person an indefinite sentence because he must depend on the advice of the experts on mental illness. So no one takes responsibility for what has happened or for doing something about it.

When no one takes charge or assumes responsibility, it means that an organization is in confusion, with no hierarchy marking clear lines of authority. When the hierarchy of an organization is in confusion, mad and eccentric behavior occurs and is adaptive. The mad behavior will tend to stabilize the organization and clarify the hierarchy. When normality returns, the organization again enters confusion. To correct the mad behavior, it is necessary to correct the hierarchy of the organization so that the eccentric behavior is not necessary or appropriate.   25

STAGES OF THERAPY

Given this view of the problem, the therapy of young eccentrics can be outlined in the following stages: 26

1. When the young person comes to community attention, the experts must organize themselves in such a way that one therapist takes responsibility for the case. It is better not to have multiple therapists and modes of therapy. The therapist *must* be in charge of dosage of medication and, if possible, of institutionalization.

2. The therapist needs to gather the family for a first meeting. If the young person is living separately, even with a wife, he should be brought together with the family of origin. No blame should be placed on the parents. Instead, the parents (or mother and grandmother, or whoever it might be) should be put in charge of solving the young person's problem. They must be persuaded that they are the best therapists for the problem offspring. It is assumed that the members of the family are in conflict, and the child is expressing that. By being required to take charge and set the rules for the young person, the family members are communicating about the young person as usual, but in a positive way. Certain issues need to be clear:

   a. The focus should be on the problem person and his behavior, not on a discussion of family relations. If the offspring is an addict, the family should focus on what is to happen if he ever takes the drug again; if mad and misbehaving, what they will do if he misbehaves again in the way that led to the hospital before.

   b. The past, and past causes of the problem, are ignored, not explored. The focus is on what to do now.

   c. It is assumed that the hierarchy in the family is in confusion. Therefore if the therapist, with his expert status, crosses the generation line and sides with the young person against the parents, he will make the problem worse. The therapist should side with the parents against the problem young person, even if this seems to be depriving him or her of individual choices and rights, and even if he or she seems too old to be made that dependent. If the young person does not like the situation, he or she can leave and become self-supporting. After the person is behaving normally, his or her rights can be considered.

d. Conflicts between the parents or among other family members are ignored and minimized, even if those involved bring them up, until the young person is getting back to normal. If the parents say they need help too, the therapist should say that that can be dealt with after their son or daughter is back to normal.

e. Everyone should expect the problem person to become normal and not excuse failure. The experts should indicate to the family that there is nothing wrong with the child and that he or she should behave like others of the same age. Medication should be eliminated as rapidly as possible. Going to work or school immediately should be expected, with no delay for day hospitalization or long-term therapy. It is going back to normal that brings about family crisis and change. It is the continuation of an abnormal situation that stabilizes the family in misery.

f. It is to be expected that as the young person becomes normal by going successfully to work or school or by making friends, the family will become unstable. The parents may threaten separation or divorce, and one or both may become disturbed. One of the reasons for the therapist fully siding with the parents at the first stage of therapy, even to the point of joining them against the child, is to be in a position to help them at this stage. If the therapist cannot help the parents, the problem young person will commit some mad act, and the family will stabilize around the young person and his eccentricity once again. Institutionalization needs to be prevented at this point to keep the cycle of home-to-institution-to-home from continuing. One way to put it is that the therapist replaces the young eccentric in the family, and the young person is then free to become normal and go about his business. The therapist must then either resolve the family conflict or move the young person out of that conflict so it will continue more directly and not through him. At that point the young person can continue to be normal.

3. The therapy should be an intense involvement and a rapid disengagement rather than regular interviews spanning years. As soon as change occurs, the therapist can begin to recess and plan termination. The task is not to resolve all family problems, only the organizational ones around the problem young person, unless the family wants to make a new contract for other problems.

4. The therapist should occasionally check with the family to follow up what has happened and ensure that positive change continues.

In essence, the therapy approach is like an initiation ceremony. The 27 procedure helps parents and offspring disengage from each other so that the family does not need the young person as a communication vehicle, and the young person establishes a life of his or her own. Two extremes have often failed. Blaming the parents as a noxious influence and sending the young person away from his family typically fails. The young person collapses and comes back home. The opposite extreme — keeping the young person at home and attempting to bring about harmony between child and parents — also fails. This is not a time of coming together but a time of disengagement. The art of the therapy is to bring the young person back within the family as a way of disengaging him or her for a more independent life.

Questions for Argument

1. Which make more sense, the biological or the environmental explanations for schizophrenia? Consider the evidence and take a position.
2. It becomes clear as you read the articles in this chapter that "environmental causes" can refer to a wide range of things — from viruses and toxins to family dynamics to socioeconomic class. Argue for the importance of some environmental factors over others *or* argue that the environmentalist position is best understood as an interconnected system of causes.
3. Is "schizophrenia" too loose a diagnostic label? After considering the charge that the term is imprecise, either suggest an alternative procedure of classification or defend the present one.
4. What are the economic issues in the treatment of schizophrenia? After assembling economic considerations, write a speculative essay about how they might influence treatment. You won't be able to argue from actual dollar figures, but don't be afraid to estimate relative costs.
5. Argue for or against the "medical model" of schizophrenia.
6. Develop and critically examine the argument that we as a society should be more concerned with controlling schizophrenia than with curing it.
7. Several of the pieces in this section report on research. Which research seems to you the most scientific? Make sure you define what you mean by "scientific," and make specific comparisons.
8. Develop the argument that the various therapeutic methods can best be distinguished, not on how scientific they are but on how humane they are. Be sure to define and illustrate what you mean by "humane."
9. Develop the argument that it is important to see schizophrenia as a process, and distinguish among several stages in that process.
10. Argue for the importance of distinguishing between acute and chronic schizophrenia. After explaining the differences, connect those differences to issues of treatment.
11. What is the best role for the therapist in dealing with schizophrenia, or is there no single best role? Consider the full range of possibilities, and take a clear position.

12. Develop the argument that schizophrenia is an illness not of individuals but of families. If you disagree with this argument, refute it.

13. Heinz E. Lehmann concludes his article on the biology of schizophrenia by saying that "Kraepelin and Bleuler were right when they believed that schizophrenia, or the groups of schizophrenias, are biologic disorders." Do you think Lehmann's own summary of past research supports his conclusion? Do the conclusions of the other writers on the biology of schizophrenia support that conclusion? Write a paper using the findings that Lehmann and the other biologically oriented writers present to challenge Lehmann's conclusion.

14. Having read a variety of discussions of schizophrenia, write an interpretation of the poem that prefaces this argument packet. Cite particular authors or theories or cases to support your interpretation.

15. *Research Project.* Several readings in this chapter refer to the double bind theory developed by Gregory Bateson and D. D. Jackson. Look up the original article and argue for or against its applicability to the case histories in this chapter. (The original article, by Gregory Bateson, Don D. Jackson, Jay Haley, and John H. Weakland, "Toward a Theory of Schizophrenia," appeared in *Behavioral Science*, Vol. 1, No. 4 [1956], pp. 251–264. It was also reprinted in Gregory Bateson's book *Steps to an Ecology of Mind* [New York: Chandler, 1972].)

CHAPTER 11

What's Funny?
Investigating the Comic

Framing the Issues

Arguments about what's funny aren't funny. In fact, coming to some reasoned point of view about what you or others find funny can be a sobering experience. But it's a topic well worth thinking about, if only because comic moments exert so strong, and unexamined, a presence in most of our lives. As you think about the materials in this section, comic and otherwise, we hope that your sense of humor remains intact.

The subject of humor is notoriously difficult to grasp. How do we define what we are talking about when we discuss humor? Certainly, jokes, as deliberate efforts to elicit laughter, are part of the territory. So are comedy acts, comic movies and plays, TV situation comedies, the columns of syndicated humorists like Erma Bombeck and Russell Baker, and the many comic strips that pack the pages of most daily newspapers. Comedy in most of these forms has become a kind of commodity in our society. Even if we do not quite know what it is, we know where to find it and can expect it to be delivered on demand. But comedy is also interwoven more subtly as part of our day-to-day and face-to-face experience. And it can erupt at times and in places where we least expect it — like a not quite unexpected visitor to whom the door is always open.

This chapter begins with an assemblage of comic materials. First you'll find a joke collection and rating scale that may tell you something about your own humor preferences. Following after is a brief anthology of American comic strips spanning almost a century of cartooning. Then we present three pieces of comic fiction: a representative piece by James Thurber from a 1930s *New Yorker*; an excerpt from Joseph Heller's comic novel about World War II, *Catch-22* (1955); and an episode from Rita Mae Brown's *Rubyfruit Jungle* (1980), a feminist novel of the 1970s. Next follows a Native American folktale anthologized by Richard Erdoes and Alfonso Ortiz in 1984. Then comes reporter Steve Emmons's investigation of the contemporary phenomenon of sick jokes. We close this part of "What's Funny?" with a set of preliminary questions designed to get you thinking reflectively about comic material.

The chapter then moves on with a series of theoretical pieces by philosopher Henri Bergson, researcher Gershon Legman, and social critic and novelist Arthur Koestler. Next, two anthropologists, Thomas R. Shultz and Mary Douglas offer interpretations of the universality of humor. Then folklorists Lawrence W. Levine and José E. Limón analyze ethnic jokes, and essayist Annie Dillard reflects on the art of joke-telling. Finally psychologist Harvey Mindess asserts a relation between a comic attitude and psychic well-being. The chapter closes with suggestions for argument topics.

Psychologist Harvey Mindess provides the following jokes in his book Laughter and Liberation *(1971), which is about the value of a comic attitude to psychic well-being. You can use the jokes and the scale to rate your own reactions to humor.*

Rating Jokes
HARVEY MINDESS

1. Love is a disease that creates its own antibody: marriage.

   very funny |__|__|__|__|__| not funny

2. Q: What does a 500-lb. canary say?
   A: CHURP!

   very funny |__|__|__|__|__| not funny

3. A famous actor is accosted by a whore. He spends the night at her place. When he is leaving, she says, "But you didn't give me anything." So he gives her two tickets to a matinee. She objects, "I don't want to see a show. I'm hungry. I need bread." To which he replies, "If you need bread, screw the baker. From me you get tickets to the theater."

   very funny |__|__|__|__|__| not funny

4. "Mama, Mama — daddy's on fire!"
   "Okay, honey — get the marsh-mallows."

   very funny |_|_|_|_|_| not funny

5. Q: What's red and white and goes, "putt-putt-putt"?
   A: An outboard radish.

   very funny |_|_|_|_|_| not funny

6. When two politicians accuse each other of lying, both of them are telling the truth.

   very funny |_|_|_|_|_| not funny

7. Sign on a brothel door:
   OUT TO LUNCH
   GO F—K YOURSELF

   very funny |_|_|_|_|_| not funny

8. A philosopher, in the throes of death, moans, "What's the answer? What's the answer?
   His colleague, who is attending to his needs, shrugs his shoulders and replies, "What's the question?"

   very funny |_|_|_|_|_| not funny

9. Patient: Please help me, doctor. I'm afraid I'm losing my memory.
   Doctor: Mmm — mmm. And how long have you had this problem?
   Patient: What problem?

   very funny |_|_|_|_|_| not funny

10. A farmer is showing a beautiful lady visitor around his farm. They watch a bull lustily mating a cow. Putting his arm around the lady's waist, the farmer says, "Boy, I'd sure like to do something like that." "Well, why don't you?" she replies. "It's your cow."

    very funny |_|_|_|_|_| not funny

11. Advice to the overweight: Want to lose ten pounds of ugly, useless fat? Cut off your head.

    very funny |_|_|_|_|_| not funny

12. A group of scientists developed the ultimate computer. They decide, therefore, to ask it the ultimate question: "Is there a god?" The computer whirrs and clicks, its lights blink, and finally its message appears. It reads: "Now there is."

    very funny |_|_|_|_|_| not funny

RUDOLPH DIRKS. 1898.

THE KATZENJAMMER KIDS CHANGE GRANDPA'S GLASSES.
Everything seems bigger through these spectacles until Grandpa discovers the joke.

THEN THINGS BEGIN TO LOOK LIVELY FOR THE KIDS.

C. H. SYKES. From *Life* Magazine, 1927.

© 1943 by Thomas Craven. Reprinted by permission of Simon & Schuster, Inc.

CHICAGO COP: *What've you got in that car?*
GANGSTER: *Nothin' but booze, Officer.*
COP: *I beg your pardon — I thought it might be history books.*

JAMES THURBER. From *The New Yorker*, 1932.

"I Don't Know. George Got It Somewhere."

*"Now read me the part again where
I disinherit everybody."*

PETER ARNO.
From *The New Yorker*, 1940.

669

CHARLES ADDAMS. From *The New Yorker,* 1942.

Drawing by Charles Addams; © 1942, 1970 The New Yorker Magazine, Inc.

"Are you unhappy, darling?"
"Oh, yes, yes! Completely."

AL CAPP. *The Shmoo,* 1948.

WALT KELLY. *Pogo,* 1950.

ERNIE BUSHMILLER. *Nancy,* 1958.

671

GAHAN WILSON. From *Gahan Wilson's America,* 1985.

© 1985 by Gahan Wilson. Reprinted by permission of Simon & Schuster, Inc.

"You'd think over the years one or two of them would catch on."

BILL WATTERSON. *Calvin and Hobbes,* 1987.

The Night the Bed Fell
JAMES THURBER

I suppose that the high-water mark of my youth in Columbus, Ohio, was the night the bed fell on my father. It makes a better recitation (unless, as some friends of mine have said, one has heard it five or six times) than it does a piece of writing, for it is almost necessary to throw furniture around, shake doors, and bark like a dog, to lend the proper atmosphere and verisimilitude to what is admittedly a somewhat incredible tale. Still, it did take place.

It happened, then, that my father had decided to sleep in the attic one night, to be away where he could think. My mother opposed the notion strongly because, she said, the old wooden bed up there was unsafe: It was wobbly and the heavy headboard would crash down on father's head in case the bed fell, and kill him. There was no dissuading him, however, and at a quarter past ten he closed the attic door behind him and went up the narrow twisting stairs. We later heard ominous creakings as he crawled into bed. Grandfather, who usually slept in the attic bed when he was with us, had disappeared some days before. (On these occasions he was usually gone six or eight days and returned growling and out of temper, with the news that the federal Union was run by a passel of blockheads and that the Army of the Potomac didn't have any more chance than a fiddler's bitch.)

We had visiting us at this time a nervous first cousin of mine named Briggs Beall, who believed that he was likely to cease breathing when he was asleep. It was his feeling that if he were not awakened every hour during the night, he might die of suffocation. He had been accustomed to setting an alarm clock to ring at intervals until morning, but I persuaded him to abandon this. He slept in my room and I told him that I was such a light sleeper that if anybody quit breathing in the same room with me, I would wake instantly. He tested me the first night — which I had suspected he would — by holding his breath after my regular breathing had convinced him I was asleep. I was not asleep, however, and called to him. This seemed to allay his fears a little, but he took the precaution of putting a glass of spirits of camphor on a little table at the head of his bed. In case I didn't arouse him until he was almost gone, he said, he would sniff the camphor, a powerful reviver. Briggs was not the only member of his family who had his crotchets. Old Aunt Melissa Beall (who could whistle like a man, with two fingers in her mouth) suffered under the premonition that she was destined to die on South High Street, because she had been born on South High Street and married on South High Street. Then there was Aunt Sarah Shoaf, who never went to bed at night without the fear that a burglar was going to get in and blow chloroform under her door through a tube. To avert this calamity — for she was in greater dread of anesthetics than of losing her household goods — she always piled her money, silverware, and other valuables in a neat stack just outside her bedroom, with a note reading: "This is all I have. Please take it and do not use your chloroform, as this is all I have." Aunt Gracie Shoaf also had a burglar phobia, but she met it with more fortitude. She was confident that burglars had been getting into her house every night for forty years. The fact that she never missed anything was to her no proof to the contrary. She always claimed that she scared them off before they could take anything, by throwing shoes down the hallway. When she went to bed she piled, where she could get at them handily, all the shoes there were about her house. Five minutes after she had turned off the light, she would sit up in bed and say "Hark!" Her husband, who had learned to ignore the whole situation as long ago as 1903, would either be sound asleep or pretend to be sound asleep. In either case he would not respond to her tugging and pulling, so that presently she would arise, tiptoe to the door, open it slightly, and heave a shoe down the hall in one direction and its mate down the hall in the other direction. Some nights she threw them all, some nights only a couple of pair.

But I am straying from the remarkable incidents that took place during the night that the bed fell on father. By midnight we were all in bed. The layout of the rooms and the disposition of their occupants is important to an understanding of what later occurred. In the front room upstairs (just under father's attic bedroom) were my mother and my brother Herman, who sometimes sang in his sleep, usually "Marching Through Georgia" or "Onward, Christian Soldiers." Briggs Beall and myself were in a room adjoining this one. My brother Roy was in a room across the hall from ours. Our bull terrier, Rex, slept in the hall.   **4**

My bed was an army cot, one of those affairs which are made wide enough to sleep on comfortably only by putting up, flat with the middle section, the two sides which ordinarily hang down like the sideboards of a drop-leaf table. When these sides are up, it is perilous to roll too far toward the edge, for then the cot is likely to tip completely over, bringing the whole bed down on top of one with a tremendous banging crash. This, in fact, is precisely what happened, about two o'clock in the morning. (It was my mother who, in recalling the scene later, first referred to it as "the night the bed fell on your father.")

Always a deep sleeper, slow to arouse (I had lied to Briggs), I was at first unconscious of what had happened when the iron cot rolled me onto the floor and toppled over on me. It left me still warmly bundled up and unhurt, for the bed rested above me like a canopy. Hence I did not wake up, only reached the edge of consciousness and went back. The racket, however, instantly awakened my mother, in the next room, who came to the immediate conclusion that her worst dread was realized: the big wooden bed upstairs had fallen on father. She therefore screamed, "Let's go to your poor father!" It was this shout, rather than the noise of my cot falling, that awakened my brother Herman, in the same room with her. He thought that mother had become, for no apparent reason, hysterical. "You're all right, mamma!" he shouted, trying to calm her.

They exchanged shout for shout for perhaps ten seconds: "Let's go to your poor father!" and "You're all right!" That woke up Briggs. By this time I was conscious of what was going on, in a vague way, but did not yet realize that I was under my bed instead of on it. Briggs, awakening in the midst of loud shouts of fear and apprehension, came to the quick conclusion that he was suffocating and that we were all trying to "bring him out." With a low moan, he grasped the glass of camphor at the head of his bed and instead of sniffing it poured it over himself. The room reeked of camphor. "Ugf, ahfg!" choked Briggs, like a drowning man, for he had almost succeeded in stopping his breath under the deluge of pungent spirits. He leaped out of bed and groped toward the open window, but he came up against one that was closed. With his hand, he beat out the glass, and I could hear it crash and tinkle in the alleyway below. It was at this juncture that I, in trying to get up, had the uncanny sensation of feeling my bed above me! Foggy with sleep, I now suspected, in my turn, that the whole uproar was being made in a frantic endeavor to extricate me from what must be an unheard-of and perilous situation. "Get me out of this!" I bawled. "Get me out!" I think I had the nightmarish belief that I was entombed in a mine. "Gugh!" gasped Briggs, floundering in his camphor.

By this time my mother, still shouting, pursued by Herman, still shouting, was trying to open the door to the attic, in order to go up and get my father's body out of the wreckage. The door was stuck, however, and wouldn't yield. Her frantic pulls on it only added to the general banging and confusion. Roy and the dog were now up, the one shouting questions, the other barking.

Father, farthest away and soundest sleeper of all, had by this time   **8** been awakened by the battering on the attic door. He decided that the house was on fire. "I'm coming, I'm coming!" he wailed in a slow, sleepy voice — it took him many minutes to regain full consciousness. My mother, still believing he was caught under the bed, detected in his "I'm coming!" the mournful, resigned note of one who is preparing to meet his Maker. "He's dying!" she shouted.

"I'm all right!" Briggs yelled, to reassure her. "I'm all right!" He still believed that it was his own closeness to death that was worrying mother. I found at last the light switch in my room, unlocked the door, and Briggs and I joined the others at the attic door. The dog, who never did like Briggs, jumped for him — assuming that he was the culprit in whatever was going on — and Roy had to throw Rex and hold him. We could hear father crawling out of bed upstairs. Roy pulled the attic door open, with a mighty jerk, and father came down the stairs, sleepy and irritable but safe and sound. My mother began to weep when she saw him. Rex began to howl. "What in the name of God is going on here?" asked father.

The situation was finally put together like a gigantic jigsaw puzzle. Father caught a cold from prowling around in his bare feet but there were no other bad results. "I'm glad," said mother, who always looked on the bright side of things, "that your grandfather wasn't here."

From *Catch-22*

JOSEPH HELLER

Doc Daneeka lived in a splotched gray tent with Chief White Halfoat, whom he feared and despised.

"I can just picture his liver," Doc Daneeka grumbled.

"Picture my liver," Yossarian advised him.

"There's nothing wrong with your liver." 4

"That shows how much you don't know," Yossarian bluffed, and told Doc Daneeka about the troublesome pain in his liver that had troubled Nurse Duckett and Nurse Cramer and all the doctors in the hospital because it wouldn't become jaundice and wouldn't go away.

Doc Daneeka wasn't interested. "You think you've got troubles?" he wanted to know. "What about me? You should've been in my office the day those newlyweds walked in."

"What newlyweds?"

"Those newlyweds that walked into my office one day. Didn't I ever 8 tell you about them? She was lovely."

So was Doc Daneeka's office. He had decorated his waiting room with goldfish and one of the finest suites of cheap furniture. Whatever he could he bought on credit, even the goldfish. For the rest, he obtained money from greedy relatives in exchange for shares of the profits. His office was in Staten Island in a two-family firetrap just four blocks away from the ferry stop and only one block south of a supermarket, three beauty parlors, and two corrupt druggists. It was a corner location, but nothing helped. Population turnover was small, and people clung through habit to the same physicians they had been doing business with for years. Bills piled up rapidly, and he was soon faced with the loss of his most precious medical instruments: his adding machine was repossessed, and then his typewriter. The goldfish died. Fortunately, just when things were blackest, the war broke out.

"It was a godsend," Doc Daneeka confessed solemnly. "Most of the other doctors were soon in the service, and things picked up overnight. The corner location really started paying off, and I soon found myself handling more patients than I could handle competently. I upped my kickback fee with those two drugstores. The beauty parlors were good for two, three abortions a week. Things couldn't have been better, and then look what happened. They had to send a guy from the draft board around to look me over. I was Four-F. I had examined myself pretty thoroughly and discovered that I was unfit for military service. You'd think my word would be enough, wouldn't you, since I was a doctor in good standing with my county medical society and with my local Better Business Bureau. But no, it wasn't, and they sent this guy around just to make sure I really did have one leg amputated at the hip and was helplessly bedridden with incurable rheumatoid arthritis. Yossarian, we live in an age of distrust and deteriorating spiritual values. It's a terrible thing," Doc Daneeka protested in a voice quavering with strong emotion.

"It's a terrible thing when even the word of a licensed physician is suspected by the country he loves."

Doc Daneeka had been drafted and shipped to Pianosa as a flight surgeon, even though he was terrified of flying.

"I don't have to go looking for trouble in an airplane," he noted, blinking his beady, brown, offended eyes myopically. "It comes looking for me. Like that virgin I'm telling you about that couldn't have a baby."

"What virgin?" Yossarian asked. "I thought you were telling me about some newlyweds."

"That's the virgin I'm telling you about. They were just a couple of young kids, and they'd been married, oh, a little over a year when they came walking into my office without an appointment. You should have seen her. She was so sweet and young and pretty. She even blushed when I asked about her periods. I don't think I'll ever stop loving that girl. She was built like a dream and wore a chain around her neck with a medal of Saint Anthony hanging down inside the most beautiful bosom I never saw. 'It must be a terrible temptation for Saint Anthony,' I joked — just to put her at ease, you know. 'Saint Anthony?' her husband said. 'Who's Saint Anthony?' 'Ask your wife,' I told him. 'She can tell you who Saint Anthony is.' 'Who is Saint Anthony?' he asked her. 'Who?' she wanted to know. 'Saint Anthony,' he told her. 'Saint Anthony?' she said. 'Who's Saint Anthony?' When I got a good look at her inside my examination room I found she was still a virgin. I spoke to her husband alone while she was pulling her girdle back on and hooking it onto her stockings. 'Every night,' he boasted. A real wise guy, you know. 'I never miss a night,' he boasted. He meant it, too. 'I even been puttin' it to her mornings before the breakfasts she makes me before we go to work,' he boasted. There was only one explanation. When I had them both together again I gave them a demonstration of intercourse with the rubber models I've got in my office. I've got these rubber models in my office with all the reproductive organs of both sexes that I keep locked up in separate cabinets to avoid a scandal. I mean I used to have them. I don't have anything any more, not even a practice. The only thing I have now is this low temperature that I'm really starting to worry about. Those two kids I've got working for me in the medical tent aren't worth a damn as diagnosticians. All they know how to do is complain. They think they've got troubles? What about me? They should have been in my office that day with those two newlyweds looking at me as though I were telling them something nobody'd ever heard of before. You never saw anybody so interested. 'You mean like this?' he asked me, and worked the models for himself awhile. You know, I can see where a certain type of person might get a big kick out of doing just that. 'That's it,' I told him. 'Now, you go home and try it my way for a few months and see what happens. Okay?' 'Okay,' they said, and paid me in cash without any argument. 'Have a good time,' I told them, and they thanked me and walked out together. He had his arm around her waist as though he couldn't wait to get her home and put it to her again. A few days later he came back all by himself and told my nurse he had to see me right away. As soon as we were alone, he punched me in the nose."

12

"He did what?"

"He called me a wise guy and punched me in the nose. 'What are you, a wise guy?' he said, and knocked me flat on my ass. Pow! Just like that. I'm not kidding."

"I know you're not kidding," Yossarian said. "But why did he do it?"

"How should I know why he did it?" Doc Daneeka retorted with annoyance.

"Maybe it had something to do with Saint Anthony?"

Doc Daneeka looked at Yossarian blankly. "Saint Anthony?" he asked with astonishment. "Who's Saint Anthony?"

"How should I know?" answered Chief White Halfoat, staggering inside the tent just then with a bottle of whiskey cradled in his arm and sitting himself down pugnaciously between the two of them.

Doc Daneeka rose without a word and moved his chair outside the tent, his back bowed by the compact kit of injustices that was his perpetual burden. He could not bear the company of his roommate.

Chief White Halfoat thought he was crazy. "I don't know what's the matter with that guy," he observed reproachfully. "He's got no brains, that's what's the matter with him. If he had any brains he'd grab a shovel and start digging. Right here in the tent, he'd start digging, right under my cot. He'd strike oil in no time. Don't he know how that enlisted man struck oil with a shovel back in the States? Didn't he ever hear what happened to that kid — what was the name of that rotten rat bastard pimp of a snotnose back in Colorado?"

"Wintergreen."

"Wintergreen."

"He's afraid," Yossarian explained.

"Oh, no. Not Wintergreen." Chief White Halfoat shook his head with undisguised admiration. "That stinking little punk wise-guy son of a bitch ain't afraid of nobody."

"Doc Daneeka's afraid. That's what's the matter with him."

"What's he afraid of?"

"He's afraid of you," Yossarian said. "He's afraid you're going to die of pneumonia."

"He'd *better* be afraid," Chief White Halfoat said. A deep, low laugh rumbled through his massive chest. "I will, too, the first chance I get. You just wait and see."

Chief White Halfoat was a handsome, swarthy Indian from Oklahoma with a heavy, hard-boned face and tousled black hair, a half-blooded Creek from Enid who, for occult reasons of his own, had made up his mind to die of pneumonia. He was a glowering, vengeful, disillusioned Indian who hated foreigners with names like Cathcart, Korn, Black, and Havermeyer and wished they'd all go back to where their lousy ancestors had come from.

"You wouldn't believe it, Yossarian," he ruminated, raising his voice deliberately to bait Doc Daneeka, "but this used to be a pretty good country to live in before they loused it up with their goddam piety."

Chief White Halfoat was out to revenge himself upon the white man. He could barely read or write and had been assigned to Captain Black as assistant intelligence officer.

"How could I learn to read or write?" Chief White Halfoat demanded with simulated belligerence, raising his voice again so that Doc Daneeka would hear. "Every place we pitched our tent, they sank an oil well. Every time they sank a well, they hit oil. And every time they hit oil, they made us pack up our tent and go someplace else. We were human divining rods. Our whole family had a natural affinity for petroleum deposits, and soon every oil company in the world had technicians chasing us around. We were always on the move. It was one hell of a way to bring a child up, I can tell you. I don't think I ever spent more than a week in one place."

His earliest memory was of a geologist.   36

"Every time another White Halfoat was born," he continued, "the stock market turned bullish. Soon whole drilling crews were following us around with all their equipment just to get the jump on each other. Companies began to merge just so they could cut down on the number of people they had to assign to us. But the crowd in back of us kept growing. We never got a good night's sleep. When we stopped, they stopped. When we moved, they moved, chuckwagons, bulldozers, derricks, generators. We were a walking business boom, and we began to receive invitations from some of the best hotels just for the amount of business we would drag into town with us. Some of those invitations were mighty generous, but we couldn't accept any because we were Indians and all the best hotels that were inviting us wouldn't accept Indians as guests. Racial prejudice is a terrible thing, Yossarian. It really is. It's a terrible thing to treat a decent, loyal Indian like a nigger, kike, wop, or spic." Chief White Halfoat nodded slowly with conviction.

"Then, Yossarian, it finally happened — the beginning of the end. They began to follow us around from in front. They would try to guess where we were going to stop next and would begin drilling before we even got there, so we couldn't even stop. As soon as we'd begin to unroll our blankets, they would kick us off. They had confidence in us. They wouldn't even wait to strike oil before they kicked us off. We were so tired we almost didn't care the day our time ran out. One morning we found ourselves completely surrounded by oilmen waiting for us to come their way so they could kick us off. Everywhere you looked there was an oilman on a ridge, waiting there like Indians getting ready to attack. It was the end. We couldn't stay where we were because we had just been kicked off. And there was no place left for us to go. Only the Army saved me. Luckily, the war broke out just in the nick of time, and a draft board picked me right up out of the middle and put me down safely in Lowery Field, Colorado. I was the only survivor."

Yossarian knew he was lying, but did not interrupt as Chief White Halfoat went on to claim that he had never heard from his parents again. That didn't bother him too much, though, for he had only their word for it that they were his parents, and since they had lied to him about so many other things, they could just as well have been lying to him about that too. He was much better acquainted with the fate of a tribe of first cousins who had wandered away north in a diversionary movement and pushed inadvertently into Canada. When they tried to return, they were stopped at the border by American immigration authorities who would not let them back into the country. They could not come back in because they were red.

It was a horrible joke, but Doc Daneeka didn't laugh until Yossarian   **40** came to him one mission later and pleaded again, without any real expectation of success, to be grounded. Doc Daneeka snickered once and was soon immersed in problems of his own, which included Chief White Halfoat, who had been challenging him all that morning to Indian wrestle, and Yossarian, who decided right then and there to go crazy.

"You're wasting your time," Doc Daneeka was forced to tell him.

"Can't you ground someone who's crazy?"

"Oh, sure. I have to. There's a rule saying I have to ground anyone who's crazy."

"Then why don't you ground me? I'm crazy. Ask Clevinger."   **44**

"Clevinger? Where *is* Clevinger? You find Clevinger and I'll ask him."

"Then ask any of the others. They'll tell you how crazy I am."

"They're crazy."

"Then why don't you ground them?"   **48**

"Why don't they ask me to ground them?"

"Because they're crazy, that's why."

"Of course they're crazy," Doc Daneeka replied. "I just told you they're crazy, didn't I? And you can't let crazy people decide whether you're crazy or not, can you?"

Yossarian looked at him soberly and tried another approach. "Is Orr   **52** crazy?"

"He sure is," Doc Daneeka said.

"Can you ground him?"

"I sure can. But first he has to ask me to. That's part of the rule."

"Then why doesn't he ask you to?"   **56**

"Because he's crazy," Doc Daneeka said. "He has to be crazy to keep flying combat missions after all the close calls he's had. Sure, I can ground Orr. But first he has to ask me to."

"That's all he has to do to be grounded?"

"That's all. Let him ask me."

"And then you can ground him?" Yossarian asked.   **60**

"No. Then I can't ground him."

"You mean there's a catch?"

"Sure there's a catch," Doc Daneeka replied. "Catch-22. Anyone who wants to get out of combat duty isn't really crazy."

There was only one catch and that was Catch-22, which specified   **64** that a concern for one's own safety in the face of dangers that were real and immediate was the process of a rational mind. Orr was crazy and could be grounded. All he had to do was ask; and as soon as he did, he would no longer be crazy and would have to fly more missions. Orr would be crazy to fly more missions and sane if he didn't, but if he was sane he had to fly them. If he flew them he was crazy and didn't have to; but if he didn't want to he was sane and had to. Yossarian was moved very deeply by the absolute simplicity of this clause of Catch-22 and let out a respectful whistle.

"That's some catch, that Catch-22," he observed.

"It's the best there is," Doc Daneeka agreed.

From *Rubyfruit Jungle*
RITA MAE BROWN

The Christmas pageant was an enormous production. All the mothers came, and it was so important that they even took off work. Cheryl's father was sitting right in the front row in the seat of honor. Carrie and Florence showed up to marvel at me being Virgin Mary and at Leroy in robes. Leroy and I were so excited we could barely stand it, and we got to wear makeup, rouge and red lipstick. Getting painted was so much fun that Leroy confessed he liked it too, although boys aren't supposed to, of course. I told him not to worry about it, because he had a beard and if you had a beard, it must be all right to wear lipstick if you wanted to because everyone will know you're a man. He thought that sounded reasonable and we made a pact to run away as soon as we were old enough and go be famous actors. Then we could wear pretty clothes all the time, never pick potato bugs, and wear lipstick whenever we felt like it. We vowed to be so wonderful in this show that our fame would spread to the people who run theaters.

Cheryl overheard our plans and sneered, "You can do all you please, but everyone is going to look at me because I have the most beautiful blue cloak in the whole show."

"Nobody's gonna know it's you because you're playing Joseph and that'll throw them off. Ha," Leroy gloated.

"That's just why they'll all notice me, because I'll have to be specially skilled to be a good Joseph. Anyway, who is going to notice Virgin Mary, all she does is sit by the crib and rock Baby Jesus. She doesn't say much. Any dumb person can be Virgin Mary, all you have to do is put a halo over her head. It takes real talent to be Joseph, especially when you're a girl." 4

The conversation didn't get finished because Miss Potter bustled backstage. "Hush, children, curtain's almost ready to go up. Molly, Cheryl, get in your places."

When the curtain was raised there was a rustle of anticipation in the maternal audience. Megaphone Mouth said above all the whispers, "Isn't she dear up there?"

And dear I was. I looked at Baby Jesus with the tenderest looks I could manufacture and all the while my antagonist, Cheryl, had her hand on my shoulder digging me with her fingernails and a staff in her right hand. A record went on the phonograph and "Noel" began to play. The Wise Men came in most solemnly. Leroy carried a big gold box and presented it to me. I said, "Thank you, O King, for you have traveled far." And Cheryl, that rat, says, "And traveled far," as loud as she could. She wasn't supposed to say that. She started saying whatever came in her head that sounded religious. Leroy was choking in his beard and I was rocking the cradle so hard that the Jesus doll fell on the floor. So I decided two can play this game. I leaned over the doll and said in my most gentle voice, "O, dearest babe, I hope you have not hurt yourself. Come let Mother put you back to bed." Well, Leroy was near to dying of perplexity and he started to say something too, but Cheryl cut him off with, "Don't worry, Mary, babies fall out of the cradle all the time." That wasn't enough for greedy-guts, she then goes on about how she was a carpenter in a foreign land and how we had to travel many miles just so I could have my baby. She rattled on and on. All that time she spent in Sunday School was paying off because she had one story after another. I couldn't stand it any longer so I blurted out in the middle of her tale about the tax-collectors, "Joseph, you shut up or you'll wake the baby." Miss Potter was aghast in the wings, and the shepherds didn't know what to do because they were back there waiting to come on. As soon as I told Joseph to shut up, Miss Potter pushed the shepherds on the stage. "We saw a star from afar," Robert Prather warbled, "and we came to worship the newborn Prince." Just then Barry Aldridge, another shepherd, peed right there on the stage he was so scared. Joseph saw her chance and said in an imperious voice, "You can't pee in front of little Lord Jesus, go back to the hills." That made me mad. "He can pee where he wants to, this is a stable, ain't it?" Joseph stretched to her full height, and began to push Barry off the stage with her staff. I jumped off my chair, and wrenched the staff out of her hand. She grabbed it back. "Go sit down, you're supposed to watch out for the baby. What kind of mother are you?"

"I ain't sittin' nowhere until you button your fat lip and do this right."   **8**

We struggled and pushed each other, until I caught her off balance and she tripped on her long cloak. As she started to fall, I gave her a shove and she flew off the stage into the audience. Miss Potter zoomed out on the stage, took my hand and said in a calm voice, "Now ladies and gentlemen, let's sing songs appropriate to the season." Miss Martin at the piano struck up "O Come All Ye Faithful."

A Tale of the White River Sioux
ANONYMOUS

Iktome, the wicked Spider Man, and Shunk-Manitou, Coyote, are two no-good loafers. They lie, they steal, they are greedy, they are always after women. Maybe because they are so very much alike, they are friends, except when they try to trick each other.

One day Iktome invited Coyote for dinner at his lodge. Ikto told his wife: "Old Woman, here are two fine, big buffalo livers for my friend Coyote and myself. Fry them up nicely, the way I like them. And get some *timpsila,* some wild turnips, on the side, and afterwards serve us up some *wojapi,* some berry soup. Use chokecherries for that. Coyote always likes something sweet after his meal."

"Is that all?" asked Iktome's wife.

"I guess so; I can't think of anything else."   **4**

"There's no third liver for me?" the wife inquired.

"You can have what's left after my friend Coyote and I have eaten," said Iktome. "Well, I'll go out for a while; maybe I can shoot a fine, plump duck too. Coyote always stuffs himself, so one liver may not be enough for him. But watch this good friend of mine; don't let him stick his hands under your robe. He likes to do that. Well, I go now. Have everything ready for us; Coyote never likes to wait."

Iktome left and his old woman got busy cooking. "I know who's always stuffing himself," she thought. "I know whose hands are always busy feeling under some girl's robe. I know who can't wait — it's that no-good husband of mine."

The fried livers smelled so wonderful that the wife said to herself: "Those greedy, stingy, overbearing men! I know them; they'll feast on these fine livers, and a few turnips will be all they leave for me. They have no consideration for a poor woman. Oh, that liver here looks so good, smells so good; I know it tastes good. Maybe I'll try a little piece, just a tiny one. They won't notice." 8

So the wife tasted a bit of the liver, and then another bit, and then another, and in no time at all that liver was gone. "I might as well eat the other one too," the wife said to herself, and she did.

"What will I do now?" she thought. "When Iktome finds out, he'll surely beat me. But it was worth it!"

Just then Coyote arrived. He had dressed himself up in a fine beaded outfit with fringed sleeves. "Where is my good friend Iktome?" he asked. "What's he up to? Probably nothing good."

"How are you, friend?" said the woman, "My husband, Iktome, is out taking care of some business. He'll be back soon. Sit down; be comfortable." 12

"Out on business — you don't say!" remarked Coyote, quickly sticking his hand under the woman's robe and between her legs.

"Iktome told me you'd try to do that. He told me not to let you."

"Oh, Iktome and I are such good friends," said Coyote, "we share everything." He joked, he chucked the woman under the chin, he tickled her under the arms, and pretty soon he was all the way in her; way, way up inside her.

"It feels good," said the woman, "but be quick about it. Iktome could be back any time now." 16

"You think he'd mind, seeing we are such good friends?"

"I'm sure he would. You'd better stop now."

"Well, all right. It smells very good here, but I see no meat cooking, just some *timpsila*. Meat is what I like."

"And meat is what you'll get. One sees this is the first time that you've come here for dinner; otherwise you'd know what you'll get. We always serve a guest the same thing. Everybody likes it." 20

"Is it really good?"

"It's more than good. It's *lila washtay*, very good."

Coyote smacked his lips, his mouth watering. "I can't wait. What is it? Tell me!"

"Why, your *itka*, your *susu*, your eggs, your balls, your big hairy balls! We always have the balls of our guests for dinner." 24

"Oh my! This must be a joke, a very bad joke."

"It's no joke at all. And I'd better cut them off right now with my big skinning knife, because it's getting late. Ikto gets mad when I don't have his food ready — he'll beat me. And there I was, fooling around with you instead of doing my cooking. I'll do it right now; drop your breechcloth. You won't feel a thing, I do this so fast. I have practice."

The woman came after Coyote with the knife in her hand.

"Wait a bit," said Coyote. "Before you do this, let me go out and make some water. I'll be right back," and saying this, he ran out of the lodge. But he didn't come back. He ran and ran as fast as his feet would carry him.   28

Just then Iktome came back without any ducks; he had caught nothing. He saw Coyote running away and asked, "Old Woman, what's the matter with that crazy friend of mine? Why is he running off like that?"

"Your good friend is very greedy. He doesn't have the sharing spirit," his wife told Iktome. "Never invite him again. He has no manners. He doesn't know how to behave. He saw those two fine buffalo livers, which I cooked just as you like them, and didn't want to share them with you. He grabbed both and made off with them. Some friend!"

Iktome rushed out of the lodge in a frenzy, running after Coyote as fast as he could, shouting: "Coyote! *Kola!* Friend! Leave me at least one! Leave one for me! For your old friend Iktome!"

Coyote didn't stop. He ran even faster than Ikto. Running, running, he looked back over his shoulder and shouted: "Cousin, if you catch me, you can have both of them!"   32

"Sick" Jokes: Coping with the Horror
STEVE EMMONS

One day after news broke of the nuclear power plant disaster in the Ukraine, Prof. Alan Dundes's anthropology students at UC Berkeley were jotting down the radiation jokes already making the rounds.   1

What has feathers and glows in the dark? (Chicken Kiev.)   2

What do you serve with chicken Kiev? (A black Russian.)   3

What's the weather report from Kiev? (Overcast and 10,000 degrees.)   4

"You know it's sick and disgusting when you tell these," said Dundes, a folk humor specialist. "But the fact that these are all over the country suggests it's not any one group telling them."   5

Next-day joking about the nuclear disaster was hardly a speed record in the United States. Within ninety minutes after the space shuttle *Challenger* exploded, Joseph Boskin, a Boston University history professor specializing in contemporary humor, had received calls from friends in New York who told him five dead-astronaut jokes.   6

"ABSOLUTELY AMAZING"

"Some people from the West Coast called at the end of the same day, and they told me the *same* jokes. It's absolutely amazing," Boskin said.   7

Amazing, he said, not because of the apparent callousness of the   8 jokes but because of the lightning speed with which they appear and spread.

They are neither published nor broadcast by mass media, yet they   9
are transmitted throughout the nation within hours of a disaster — apparently passed along by middle-class office workers and commercial travelers whose long-distance telephoning is a routine part of the business day. "It's the middle class that largely determines what humor is in America," Boskin said. Once planted in a community, the joking spreads. One week after the nuclear disaster, the joke being told by pupils at Chandler Elementary School in Van Nuys was "What do you call a man exiled to Siberia two weeks ago?" (Answer: Mr. Lucky.)

DEATH, DEFORMITY, SUFFERING

Almost all such jokes and wisecracks are "sick" humor, Dundes said   10
— that is, they are part of the longstanding "sick" genre that deals with death, deformity, and suffering.

But few of these jokes are sick in the psychological sense, said Dr.   11
William F. Fry, a psychiatrist at the Stanford University Medical School who specializes in the implications of humor.

A crack made as horrible news is pouring from the TV screen is   12
merely the way that person is "trying to cope with the horror. He's saying it for himself, not necessarily for the others around him," Fry said.

"Maybe the person is more horrified than you are," Fry said. "We   13
shouldn't be alarmed by these jokes; they're perfectly natural in our human functioning."

Yet even psychologists concede that these jokes can be social dy-   14
namite, depending on the circumstances in which they are told.

Alleen Pace Nilsen, assistant dean of Arizona State University's grad-   15
uate college and co-editor of *English Journal* magazine, attended the Fifth International Conference on Humour in Ireland last year and said that "more psychologists than anyone" were in attendance.

"It just amused me that they were telling these jokes over cocktails   16
but that nobody got up and formally talked about it," she said.

They refrained, perhaps, with good reason.   17

"I've given lectures on sick humor," said Harvey Q. Mindess, director   18
of the graduate psychology department at Antioch University West in Venice, Calif. "When I say it has a legitimate function in helping people cope with anxieties, some are so offended that they will get up and be very angry."

When Dundes wrote a scholarly article recounting and analyzing the   19
"Auschwitz jokes" recently being told in West Germany, he provoked an avalanche of criticism and demands for his dismissal. "They blame *me* for the jokes," Dundes said.

"I don't think you should print them," he warned. "What you can   20
say, you can't write. You have to know who you're telling them to."

There is nearly unanimous agreement, even among the people who   21 tell them, that the disaster jokes are "not nice" and should be told only among friends, Boskin said.

"But why, really? The humor is funny. Otherwise, people wouldn't 22 laugh. It's when you think about it — '*Should* I laugh?' — that you gasp. And that's taste, which is entirely different.

"The problem here, I think, is we don't understand humor in America, 23 and we don't want to. Of all the European-based cultures that I know, we treat humor as if it makes no sense."

A Southern California advertising executive, returning after a year's 24 stay in Mexico, said that after the Mexico City earthquake, Baja Californians were joking openly about it on buses. "Something like: 'How do you make a Mexican sandwich? With one Mexican and two slices of concrete,' " she said.

Dominique Moisi, deputy director of the French Institute of Inter- 25 national Relations in Paris, said the same strain of seemingly callous humor has been practiced in Europe for generations. "The more you're scared, the more you have to create jokes," he said.

"Eastern Europe survived with jokes. Really. Whenever you arrive 26 in the Soviet Union or, more so, a country of Eastern Europe, jokes are mentioned to you. It's a way of confronting a reality that you can't modify."

He said one current pun, which does not translate well into English, 27 is "We thought the Communists had promised us a radiant future, but they meant an irradiated one."

In some cases, however, the catastrophe is not a single disaster but 28 a prolonged misery, such as political repression, Moisi said.

He cited a joke that made the rounds in Poland in recent years. In 29 it, a fairy godmother descends to grant a Pole three wishes. He uses all three to wish that the Chinese would invade Poland — because they'd have to march through the Soviet Union to get there.

"It's interesting," Moisi said. "American history, by comparison, has 30 not been tragic. With Vietnam, you entered into the path of historical normalcy.

"We in Europe know that history can be sad, bad, collectivized by 31 humiliation. You didn't know that. That may be a reason why you're surprised by the arrival of these jokes. For you, the shuttle was the new frontier that knew no defeat, no tragedy."

Dundes disputes that point of view. He insists that virtually every 32 American event that "hit the national nerve" — from the death of a President to a Hollywood scandal — has prompted such jokes.

"They are unique only in one sense: that TV and perhaps newspapers 33 make everyone a witness," Dundes said.

"In the old days, by the time the news spread it was already old 34 news. Now you are essentially an unwilling eyewitness.

"How many times did you see that damned shuttle explode? Some 35 people actually saw it happen. They show the damned thing again and again. A press conference, and they show it blowing up. Recovering the bodies, and they show it again. You're an eyewitness whether you like it or not.

"We all saw those smiling people getting aboard — including one of 36
us, a civilian, a nonprofessional. That's what makes it different now. We
all share, and we share immediately. It has sped up the normal process.
It has increased the number of people involved."

The joking emerges because people are confronted with a disaster 37
that "makes things appear to be out of control," said Walter E. O'Connell,
a psychologist for the Veterans Administration in Houston who has published articles and taught courses on the relationship of humor and death.

"We want to think we have absolute control, but when we find 38
out we don't, we're shocked. . . . Joking is a healthy reaction for people
who are overwhelmed. It's a far better way than to get all the psycho-
physiological problems and breakdowns that can happen."

By macabre coincidence, O'Connell's class on the implications of death 39
and dying convened in Clear Lake City, Tex., only a few hours after the
space shuttle exploded.

The Johnson Space Center is in Clear Lake City, and nearly all of 40
O'Connell's students were either employees of the National Aeronautics
and Space Administration or relatives of employees. One woman was the
wife of an early astronaut. Some knew the astronauts who had just died.

"I had them do psychodramas in which they talked to the [dead] 41
astronauts. Some of them played the astronauts. They did a lot of crying
and a lot of feeling better. They could see something more than the
immediate tragedy," O'Connell said.

"They had to go through the grief first. That class worked it out. 42
Even afterward, I never heard any of the students getting into those
jokes.

"That was for two reasons: First, the people in the classes worked 43
out their anxiety, so there was no need for the jokes. And second, the
community as a whole had *too much* anxiety, so the jokes weren't funny.
It's really a small-town atmosphere. Most of the astronauts lived there
at one time or another.

"This is probably the big fact we've discovered in humor research," 44
O'Connell said. "Too much tension — or no tension — and there's no
laughter." But if there is no other way to work off the anxiety, physical
breakdowns can result, O'Connell said. He cited the classic case of Plainfield, Wis., whose story was recounted in the "Bulletin of Menninger
Clinic."

In November 1957, police in the small farming community discovered 45
that Edward Gein, the 51-year-old "town fool," had for several years
been stealing female bodies from fresh graves and had killed at least two
local women.

He had strung their bodies up by their heels in his barn and had 46
mutilated and dismembered them. The ghoulish details horrified the
townsfolk.

According to the article, jokes known as "Gein-ers" sprung up state- 47
wide and were "gleefully recited by young and old alike. . . . The joking
was so common that it could be considered a mass repetition compulsion."

But not in Plainfield, where the horror was too great to permit joking. 48
Instead, the tension persisted, and local physicians reported an outbreak

of gastrointestinal complaints. Even the patients connected the ailments to the grisly discoveries.

"Humor is the ability to override the really negative things, to let go of hostility and guilt and to be able to play with them," O'Connell said. "They [the jokes] are really not the sickest reaction. The sickest is to have the breakdown." 49

Dundes said such jokes run in cycles, "but they're always with us, because you never know when the next catastrophe will be. I have my students alerted: Write them down and write down what day you hear them." 50

He said he tries to teach his students that humor always works the same: "The more horrible things are, the more you need these things. 51

"All humor is based on tragedy. Every joke always has to be at someone's expense. It's no fun for the guy slipping on the banana peel. In most humor, somebody's in trouble, making a fool of himself. 52

"Once you realize that comedy and tragedy are two sides of the same coin, it begins to make sense." 53

Preliminary Questions

1. After filling out the rating scales for the twelve jokes on pages 665–666, can you make any generalizations about the jokes or your responses to them? Can you classify the jokes? Do you think your preferences say anything about your own personality? Do you think the rating scale itself is slanted in any particular way?
2. The psychologist who presented these jokes thinks that a person's responses to the rating scale reveal something about his or her personality. But do you think there is a possibility that some of these jokes are simply better than others? If so, try to define what makes them so.
3. Start afresh and assemble your own group of jokes and rating scale. Make the jokes as varied as possible but also make sure to include subgroups of jokes that resemble one another. Have your classmates or assorted acquaintances rate the jokes. What conclusions can you draw?
4. Do you think people are honest in responding to surveys like the one offered here? What circumstances might skew the responses?
5. Stand-up comic Adrianne Tolsch has said that dealing with people who heckle her act is "all about control." Do you think her observation is applicable to comedy in general? Write a summary of one or more of the preceding pieces, shaping it around the idea that comedy is "all about control."
6. Classify stand-up comics. Try to provide at least two examples for each of the categories you come up with. Here, in alphabetical order, are some suggestions, but don't be limited by them: Roseanne Barr, Andrew Dice Clay, Rodney Dangerfield, Whoopie Goldberg, Bobcat Goldthwait,

Sam Kinison, Jay Leno, Eddie Murphy, Richard Pryor, Paul Rodriguez, Lily Tomlin, Tracy Ullman, Robin Williams.

7. Compare the routines of two stand-up comedians. (Refer to the list in question 6 to get you started.) What common features do they share? Does their appeal spring from different sources, or do they differ only superficially?

8. Take into consideration the publication date of each cartoon. Do you see any particular pattern in the series of cartoons presented in the cartoon anthology? Present an interpretation of that sequence.

9. Classify the cartoons. What conclusions can you draw from the categories you come up with?

10. Choose a daily newspaper with a comics page and classify its cartoons. What conclusions can you draw?

11. Contemplate the phenomenon of animal cartoons. Why do so many exist? Do they subdivide into types? If so, what different purposes do the types fulfill?

12. Choose at least five comic strips (either from this book or from any newspaper or magazine) and do a serial interpretation of the way comic effects develop as you move through the frames of a strip. Do you see a common pattern among the strips?

13. If you see a common pattern in the structure of comic strips, do you find that pattern similar to the pattern of jokes? If not, what varieties of sequential pattern do you see?

14. In a short essay, analyze the structure of the Thurber story. Do you find that structure related to why you did or didn't find it funny?

15. Compare the Thurber story and the Thurber cartoon. Do you see any underlying similarities, or are the two forms of comedy quite different?

16. What do you see as the sources of comedy in the excerpt from *Catch-22*? Does it share any of the features of the jokes you looked at earlier?

17. What do you see as the sources of comedy in the excerpt from *Rubyfruit Jungle*? Does the humor conform to the conception of humor you've developed thus far, or does it expand it in some way?

18. Can you find any evidence for the "sick joke" phenomenon described by Steve Emmons? Taking the most recent catastrophe that has earned national publicity, see if you can uncover among friends and acquaintances any signs of a national network for such jokes.

19. Are the joke experts consulted by Emmons in agreement about sick jokes? Based on the evidence in this article, does joke scholarship seem to be a unified field, or are there crucial differences in point of view?

20. Joke networks, or for that matter joke preferences, may move along cultural lines — passed on among people of particular ethnicities, for example, or professions, or age groups. Test this possibility by collecting a sample of jokes current among college freshmen and comparing it with a sample of jokes compiled from some other group. Design your method of compiling samples as carefully as you can. Analyze your data. What conclusions can you draw?

21. After considering some or all of the material in this preliminary section, try constructing a definition of one of the following terms: *humor, comic, funny, comedy.* Elaborate your definition with pertinent illustrative examples.

Complicating the Issues

The rest of this chapter is devoted to theoretical pieces about humor. The first of these is by the French philosopher Henri Bergson, whose influential book Laughter *(1900) first directed serious attention to the topic of humor.*

From *Laughter*
HENRI BERGSON

I

The first point to which attention should be called is that the comic does not exist outside the pale of what is strictly *human*. A landscape may be beautiful, charming and sublime, or insignificant and ugly; it will never be laughable. You may laugh at an animal, but only because you have detected in it some human attitude or expression. You may laugh at a hat, but what you are making fun of, in this case, is not the piece of felt or straw, but the shape that men have given it, — the human caprice whose mold it has assumed. It is strange that so important a fact, and such a simple one too, has not attracted to a greater degree the attention of philosophers. Several have defined man as "an animal which laughs." They might equally well have defined him as an animal which is laughed at; for if any other animal, or some lifeless object, produces the same effect, it is always because of some resemblance to man, of the stamp he gives it or the use he puts it to. 1

Here I would point out, as a symptom equally worthy of notice, the *absence of feeling* which usually accompanies laughter. . . . Laughter has no greater foe than emotion. I do not mean that we could not laugh at a person who inspires us with pity, for instance, or even with affection, but in such a case we must, for the moment, put our affection out of court and impose silence upon our pity. In a society composed of pure intelligences there would probably be no more tears, though perhaps there would still be laughter; whereas highly emotional souls, in tune and unison with life, in whom every event would be sentimentally prolonged and re-echoed, would neither know nor understand laughter. . . . To produce the whole of its effect, then, the comic demands something like a momentary anesthesia of the heart. Its appeal is to intelligence, pure and simple. 2

This intelligence, however, must always remain in touch with other intelligences. And here is the third fact to which attention should be 3 drawn. You would hardly appreciate the comic if you felt yourself isolated from others. Laughter appears to stand in need of an echo. Listen to it carefully: It is not an articulate, clear, well-defined sound; it is something which would fain be prolonged by reverberating from one to another, something beginning with a crash, to continue in successive rumblings, like thunder in a mountain. Still, this reverberation cannot go on for ever. It can travel within as wide a circle as you please: The circle remains, nonetheless, a closed one. Our laughter is always the laughter of a group. It may, perchance, have happened to you, when seated in a railway carriage or at *table d'hôte,* to hear travelers relating to one another stories which must have been comic to them, for they laughed heartily. Had you been one of their company, you would have laughed like them, but, as you were not, you had no desire whatever to do so. A man who was once asked why he did not weep at a sermon when everybody else was shedding tears replied: "I don't belong to the parish!" What that man thought of tears would be still more true of laughter. However spontaneous it seems, laughter always implies a kind of secret freemasonry, or even complicity, with other laughters, real or imaginary. How often has it been said that the fuller the theater, the more uncontrolled the laughter of the audience! . . . To understand laughter, we must put it back into its natural environment, which is society, and above all must we determine the utility of its function, which is a social one. Such, let us say at once, will be the leading idea of all our investigations. Laughter must answer to certain requirements of life in common. It must have a *social* signification.

Let us clearly mark the point towards which our three preliminary   4
observations are converging. The comic will come into being, it appears, whenever a group of men concentrate their attention on one of their number, imposing silence on their emotions and calling into play nothing but their intelligence. What, now, is the particular point on which their attention will have to be concentrated, and what will here be the function of intelligence? To reply to these questions will be at once to come to closer grips with the problem. But here a few examples have become indispensable.

II

A man, running along the street, stumbles and falls; the passers-by   5
burst out laughing. They would not laugh at him, I imagine, could they suppose that the whim had suddenly seized him to sit down on the ground. They laugh because his sitting down is involuntary. Consequently, it is not his sudden change of attitude that raises a laugh, but rather the involuntary element in this change, — his clumsiness, in fact. Perhaps there was a stone on the road. He should have altered his pace or avoided the obstacle. Instead of that, through lack of elasticity, through absent-mindedness and a kind of physical obstinacy, *as a result, in fact, of rigidity or of momentum,* the muscles continued to perform the same movement when the circumstances of the case called for something else. That is the reason of the man's fall, and also of the people's laughter.

Now, take the case of a person who attends to the petty occupations   6
of his everyday life with mathematical precision. The objects around him,
however, have all been tampered with by a mischievous wag, the result
being that when he dips his pen into the inkstand he draws it out all
covered with mud, when he fancies he is sitting down on a solid chair
he finds himself sprawling on the floor, in a word his actions are all topsy-
turvy or mere beating the air, while in every case the effect is invariably
one of momentum. Habit has given the impulse: What was wanted was
to check the movement or deflect it. He did nothing of the sort, but
continued like a machine in the same straight line. The victim, then, of
a practical joke is in a position similar to that of a runner who falls, —
he is comic for the same reason. The laughable element in both cases
consists of a certain *mechanical inelasticity,* just where one would expect
to find the wideawake adaptability and the living pliableness of a human
being. The only difference in the two cases is that the former happened
of itself, whilst the latter was obtained artificially. In the first instance,
the passer-by does nothing but look on, but in the second the mischievous
wag intervenes.

All the same, in both cases the result has been brought about by an   7
external circumstance. The comic is therefore accidental: It remains, so
to speak, in superficial contact with the person. How is it to penetrate
within? The necessary conditions will be fulfilled when mechanical rigidity
no longer requires for its manifestation a stumbling-block which either
the hazard of circumstance or human knavery has set in its way, but
extracts by natural processes, from its own store, an inexhaustible series
of opportunities for externally revealing its presence. Suppose, then, we
imagine a mind always thinking of what it has just done and never of
what it is doing, like a song which lags behind its accompaniment. Let
us try to picture to ourselves a certain inborn lack of elasticity of both
senses and intelligence, which brings it to pass that we continue to see
what is no longer visible, to hear what is no longer audible, to say what
is no longer to the point: in short, to adapt ourselves to a past and
therefore imaginary situation, when we ought to be shaping our conduct
in accordance with the reality which is present. This time the comic will
take up its abode in the person himself; it is the person who will supply
it with everything — matter and form, cause and opportunity. Is it then
surprising that the absentminded individual — for this is the character
we have just been describing — has usually fired the imagination of comic
authors? . . . Absentmindedness, indeed, is not perhaps the actual fountain-head of the comic, but surely it is contiguous to a certain stream of
facts and fancies which flows straight from the fountain-head. It is situated,
so to say, on one of the great natural watersheds of laughter.

Now, the effect of absentmindedness may gather strength in its turn.   8
There is a general law, the first example of which we have just encountered, and which we will formulate in the following terms: When a certain
comic effect has its origin in a certain cause, the more natural we regard
the cause to be, the more comic shall we find the effect. . . . To choose
a definite example: Suppose a man has taken to reading nothing but
romances of love and chivalry. Attracted and fascinated by his heroes,

his thoughts and intentions gradually turn more and more towards them, till one fine day we find him walking among us like a somnambulist. His actions are distractions. But then his distractions can be traced back to a definite, positive cause. They are no longer cases of *absence* of mind, pure and simple; they find their explanation in the *presence* of the individual in quite definite, though imaginary, surroundings. Doubtless a fall is always a fall, but it is one thing to tumble into a well because you were looking anywhere but in front of you, it is quite another thing to fall into it because you were intent upon a star. It was certainly a star at which Don Quixote was gazing. How profound is the comic element in the over-romantic, Utopian bent of mind! . . .

Now, let us go a little further. Might not certain vices have the same **9** relation to character that the rigidity of a fixed idea has to intellect? Whether as a moral kink or a crooked twist given to the will, vice has often the appearance of a curvature of the soul. . . . Here, too, it is really a kind of automatism that makes us laugh — an automatism, as we have already remarked, closely akin to mere absentmindedness. To realize this more fully, it need only be noted that a comic character is generally comic in proportion to his ignorance of himself. The comic person is unconscious. . . . He becomes invisible to himself while remaining visible to all the world. . . .

It is unnecessary to carry this analysis any further. From the runner **10** who falls to the simpleton who is hoaxed, from a state of being hoaxed to one of absentmindedness, from absentmindedness to wild enthusiasm, from wild enthusiasm to various distortions of character and will, we have followed the line of progress along which the comic becomes more and more deeply embedded in the person, yet without ceasing, in its subtler manifestations, to recall to us some trace of what we noticed in its grosser forms, an effect of automatism and of inelasticity. Now we can obtain a first glimpse — a distant one, it is true, and still hazy and confused — of the laughable side of human nature and of the ordinary function of laughter.

What life and society require of each of us is a constantly alert **11** attention that discerns the outlines of the present situation, together with a certain elasticity of mind and body to enable us to adapt ourselves in consequence. *Tension* and *elasticity* are two forces, mutually complementary, which life brings into play. If these two forces are lacking in the body to any considerable extent, we have sickness and infirmity and accidents of every kind. If they are lacking in the mind, we find every degree of mental deficiency, every variety of insanity. Finally, if they are lacking in the character, we have cases of the gravest inadaptability to social life, which are the sources of misery and at times the causes of crime. Once these elements of inferiority that affect the serious side of existence are removed — and they tend to eliminate themselves in what has been called the struggle for life — the person can live, and that in common with other persons. But society asks for something more; it is not satisfied with simply living, it insists on living well. What it now has to dread is that each one of us, content with paying attention to what affects the essentials of life, will, so far as the rest is concerned, give way to the easy automatism of acquired habits. . . . Society will therefore be suspicious of all *inelasticity* of character, of mind and even of body, because it is the possible sign of a slumbering activity as well as of an activity with separatist tendencies, that inclines to swerve from the common center round which society gravitates: in short, because it is the sign of an eccentricity. And yet, society cannot intervene at this stage by material repression, since it is not affected in a material fashion. It is confronted with something that makes it uneasy, but only as a symptom — scarcely a threat, at the very most a gesture. A gesture, therefore, will be its reply. Laughter must be something of this kind, a sort of *social gesture.* By the fear which it inspires, it restrains eccentricity. . . . [There is, then,] a certain rigidity of body, mind, and character that society would still like to get rid of in order to obtain from its members the greatest possible degree of elasticity and sociability. This rigidity is the comic, and laughter is its corrective.

Gershon Legman writes about the sociology, folklore, and literature of sex. In Rationale of the Dirty Joke *(1968), he has compiled and classified a staggering number of sexual jokes. Here in an introductory section much influenced by the perspective of Sigmund Freud, Legman discusses the relationship between joke tellers and their audiences.*

From *Rationale of the Dirty Joke*
GERSHON LEGMAN

It is the ambiguity of purpose of the "dirty" dirty joke, as well as its   1
tellers' openly compulsive need for it, that is disquieting. Far more so than its crude directness and purposely ugly images, lolloping up & down with screams of pretended pleasure and horror, as it so often does, in shit, snot, vomit, maggots, scabs, smegma, toe-punk, pus, dead and putrefying bodies, and cut-off parts of the body: all frequent motifs, as also in the identical but for some reason more respectable folktale format of the "ghost" or horror-story. In the jokes certainly, the ambiguity or contradiction that is so difficult to endure, especially for the unwarned listener, is that the "dirty" dirty joke apparently enjoys and offers as entertainment precisely those objects and images that both teller and listener really fear and are repelled by. . . .

One is disgusted and yet one laughs, and one is disgusted with oneself   2
for laughing. Yet, as the whole mud-bath has been entered into under the name of humor and under the mask of jokes and good-fellowship, there can be no end until one does laugh. The wild laughter overriding, that is one's only escape. . . .

Certainly such jokes are not thought of by anyone as being "funny   3
ha-ha," nor do they ever raise a really enjoyable laugh, though the laughers may collapse to the floor "in stitches," in their partly simulated hysterical enjoyment. Most often the laughter really expresses relief that the story

is at last *over,* as with horror-stories about ghosts and clanking chains, or theoretically non-sexual tortures. . . . Or the story may be brought to an end by the welcome punctuation of the laughter itself, as by the pressing of a button, while the teller desperately tries to outshout the laughter with his best "super-topper" punchline of degradation and filth. Sometimes the ambiguous backing & filling — or even stuttering — of an occasional teller of jokes on these themes also expresses his own fear and excitement in connection with his "favorite" themes, a fear he is trying to share with or slough off on the essentially unwilling listener, who generally realizes just under the level of consciousness that he is being soiled and used. Dirty-talking professional entertainers in nightclubs and burlesque shows often visibly belong to this Nervous Nelly group. Their whole inner idea is to press as far as possible the limits of what they can "get away with," without receiving the punishment (from fathers, audience, police) that they almost consciously believe they deserve.

For jokes are essentially an unveiling of the joke-teller's own neuroses   4
and compulsions, and his guilts about these, which he hopes to drive off and nullify by means of the magical release of exciting the listener's laughter. Thus forcing him to *forgive* the teller for having told the joke, and also to act as its butt and scapegoat. The laughter forgives and relieves the teller of his fears and guilt, through the listener's apparently agreeing and siding with him, and driving off the teller's fears by means of the format of "humorous" presentation and the culminating laughter. If there is no laughter there is no forgiveness. That is why most tellers can be "driven up the wall" in an almost visible anxiety crisis if the listeners refuse to laugh. And why members of the audience who — rejection of all rejections! — attempt to *get up and leave* are reserved the most violent and insulting Parthian shots of which tellers are capable.

Jokes are, not least, a disguised aggression or verbal assault directed   5
against the listener, who is always really the butt, and whose natural response, in some matching aggression, it is attempted to evade or preempt by means of the humorous disguise. The unmasking of the jokester's insincere humor is expressed perfectly by Owen Wister in the character of *The Virginian* (1902), who, when asked to accept without reaching for a knife or gun the insulting term "son-of-a-bitch," replies grimly: *"When you call me that, SMILE!"* Jokes originate as hostile impulses of free-floating aggression in the tellers of jokes, as a response to or an expression of social and sexual anxieties they are otherwise unable to absorb or express. The laughter created (which the teller generally does not share, though he may pretend to do so, and did laugh on hearing the same joke originally) depends on the listener's willingness to accept the hostility basic to the joke, in return for the satisfaction he feels in sloughing off, by means of laughter, the specific anxieties he shares with the teller — especially when struck suddenly in the face with them by the teller's *joke.* If there is no sharing of anxieties, and instead the listener feels the teller has "gone too far," there will be no laugh: The joke is "stupid." The social format of joke-telling, and the teller's accustomed art, are intended to prevent just such fiascos, but do not by

any means always succeed. The listener's laughter, rising as it does from hidden springs, is therefore essentially uncontrollable, though the joke-teller's whole conscious effort is to create and control such laughter. . . .

It is seldom consciously realized that the laughter which greets the 6
"punchline" of jokes is really an expression of the anxiety of all concerned over the taboos that are being broken, both in the story and in its telling, and by both the teller and his listeners. Anxieties as to cruelty, hostility, "dirt," or sexuality. If this were understood there would seldom be any laughter.

The following selection is excerpted from Arthur Koestler's wide-ranging study The Act of Creation *(1964). Koestler proposes that creative acts stem from the association of normally incompatible frames of reference. In the excerpt, Koestler speculates on those characteristics that make jokes original and effective.*

The Logic of Laughter
ARTHUR KOESTLER

Some of the stories that follow, including the first, I owe to my late friend 1
John von Neumann, who had all the makings of a humorist: He was a mathematical genius and he came from Budapest.

> Two women meet while shopping at the supermarket in the Bronx. One looks cheerful, the other depressed. The cheerful one inquires:
> "What's eating you?"
> "Nothing's eating me."
> "Death in the family?"
> "No, God forbid!"
> "Worried about money?"
> "No . . . nothing like that."
> "Trouble with the kids?"
> "Well, if you must know, it's my little Jimmy."
> "What's wrong with him, then?"
> "Nothing is wrong. His teacher said he must see a psychiatrist."
> Pause. "Well, well, what's wrong with seeing a psychiatrist?"
> "Nothing is wrong. The psychiatrist said he's got an Oedipus complex."
> Pause. "Well, well, Oedipus or Shmoedipus, I wouldn't worry so long as he's a good boy and loves his mamma."

The next one is quoted in Freud's essay on the comic. 2

> Chamfort tells a story of a Marquis at the court of Louis XIV who, on entering his wife's boudoir and finding her in the arms of a Bishop, walked calmly to the window and went through the motions of blessing the people in the street.
> "What are you doing?" cried the anguished wife.
> "Monseigneur is performing my functions," replied the Marquis, "so I am performing his."

Both stories, though apparently quite different and in their origin   **3**
more than a century apart, follow in fact the same pattern. The Chamfort
anecdote concerns adultery; let us compare it with a tragic treatment of
that subject — say, in the Moor of Venice. In the tragedy the tension
increases until the climax is reached: Othello smothers Desdemona; then
it ebbs away in a gradual catharsis, as (to quote Aristotle) "horror and
pity accomplish the purgation of the emotions."

In the Chamfort anecdote, too, the tension mounts as the story   **4**
progresses, but it never reaches its expected climax. The ascending curve
is brought to an abrupt end by the Marquis's unexpected reaction,
which debunks our dramatic expectations; it comes like a bolt out of the
blue, which, so to speak, decapitates the logical development of the
situation. . . .

I said that this effect was brought about by the Marquis's unexpected   **5**
reaction. However, unexpectedness alone is not enough to produce a
comic effect. The crucial point about the Marquis's behavior is that it is
both unexpected and perfectly logical — but of a logic not usually applied
to this type of situation. It is the logic of the division of labor, the *quid
pro quo,* the give and take; but our expectation was that the Marquis's
actions would be governed by a different logic or code of behavior. It is
the clash of the two mutually incompatible codes, or associative contexts,
which explodes the tension.

In the Oedipus story we find a similar clash. The cheerful woman's   **6**
statement is ruled by the logic of common sense: If Jimmy is a good boy
and loves his mamma there can't be much wrong. But in the context of
Freudian psychiatry the relationship to the mother carries entirely different associations.

The pattern underlying both stories is *the perceiving of a situation or*   **7**
idea, L, in two self-consistent but habitually incompatible frames of ref-
erence, M_1 and M_2 [see Figure 1]. The event L, in which the two intersect,
is made to vibrate simultaneously on two different wavelengths, as it
were. While this unusual situation lasts, L is not merely linked to one
associative context, but *bisociated* with two.

I have coined the term "bisociation" in order to make a distinction   **8**
between the routine skills of thinking on a single "plane," as it were, and
the creative act, which . . . always operates on more than one plane.
The former may be called single-minded, the latter a double-minded,
transitory state of unstable equilibrium where the balance of both emotion
and thought is disturbed. . . . [Let us] test the validity of these generalizations in other fields of the comic.

At the time when John Wilkes was the hero of the poor and lonely, an
ill-wisher informed him gleefully: "It seems that some of your faithful supporters have turned their coats." "Impossible," Wilkes answered. "Not one
of them has a coat to turn."

In the happy days of *La Ronde,* a dashing but penniless young Austrian
officer tried to obtain the favors of a fashionable courtesan. To shake off
this unwanted suitor, she explained to him that her heart was, alas, no longer
free. He replied politely: "Mademoiselle, I never aimed as high as that."

"High" is bisociated with a metaphorical and with a topographical 9
context. The coat is turned first metaphorically, then literally. In both
stories the literal context evokes visual images which sharpen the clash.

> A convict was playing cards with his [jailers]. On discovering that he
> cheated they kicked him out of [jail].

This venerable chestnut was first quoted by Schopenhauer and has 10
since been roasted over and again in the literature of the comic. It can
be analyzed in a single sentence: two conventional rules ("offenders are
punished by being locked up" and "cheats are punished by being kicked
out"), each of them self-consistent, collide in a given situation — as the
ethics of the *quid pro quo* and of matrimony collide in the Chamfort story.
But let us note that the conflicting rules were merely *implied* in the text;
by making them explicit I have destroyed the story's comic effect.

Shortly after the end of the war a memorable statement appeared 11
in a fashion article in the magazine *Vogue*:

> Belsen and Buchenwald have put a stop to the too-thin woman age, to
> the cult of undernourishment.

It makes one shudder, yet it is funny in a ghastly way, foreshadowing 12
the "sick jokes" of a later decade. The idea of starvation is bisociated
with one tragic, and another, utterly trivial context. The following quotation from *Time* magazine strikes a related chord: .

REVISED VERSION

> Across the first page of the Christmas issue of the *Catholic Universe
> Bulletin*, Cleveland's official Catholic diocesan newspaper, ran this eight-
> column banner head:
> "It's a boy in Bethlehem.
> Congratulations God — congratulations Mary — congratulations Joseph."

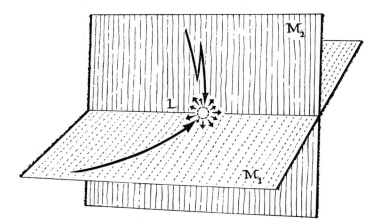

FIGURE 1

Here the frames of reference are the sacred and the vulgarly profane.   13
A technically neater version — if we have to dwell on blasphemy — is
the riposte which appeared, if I remember rightly, in the *New Yorker*:
"We wanted a girl."

ORIGINALITY, EMPHASIS, ECONOMY

I have discussed the logic of humor and its emotive dynamics, and   14
have tried to indicate how to analyze a joke. But nothing has been said
so far about the criteria which decide whether it is a good, bad, or
indifferent joke. These are, of course, partly a matter of personal taste,
partly dependent on the technique of the humorist; only the second is
our concern.

There are, I shall suggest, three main criteria of comic technique: 15
originality, emphasis, and economy. . . .

> An art dealer (this story is authentic) bought a canvas signed "Picasso"
> and traveled all the way to Cannes to discover whether it was genuine.
> Picasso was working in his studio. He cast a single look at the canvas and
> said: "It's a fake."
>
> A few months later the dealer bought another canvas signed Picasso.
> Again he traveled to Cannes and again Picasso, after a single glance, grunted:
> "It's a fake."
>
> "But *cher maître*," expostulated the dealer, "it so happens that I saw
> you with my own eyes working on this very picture several years ago."
>
> Picasso shrugged: "I often paint fakes."

One measure of originality is its surprise effect. Picasso's reply —   16
as the Marquis's in the Chamfort story — is truly unexpected; with its
perverse logic, it cuts through the narrative like the blade of the guillotine.

But creative originality is not so often met with either in art or in   17
humor. One substitute for it is suggestiveness through *emphasis*. The
cheap comedian piles it on; the competent craftsman plays in a subtler
way on our memories and habits of thought. Whenever in the *Contes
Drolatiques* Balzac introduces an abbé or a monk, our associations race
ahead of the narrative in the delectable expectation of some venal sin to
be committed; yet when the point of the story is reached we still smile,
sharing the narrator's mock-indignation and pretended surprise. In other
words, anticipations of the type of joke or point to come do not entirely
destroy the comic effect, provided that we do not know when and how
exactly it will strike home. It is rather like a game: Cover my eyes and
I shall pretend to be surprised. Besides, the laughter provoked by spicy
jokes is . . . only partly genuine, partly a cloak to cover publicly less
demonstrable emotions — regardless whether the story in itself is comic
or not. . . .

However, except in the coarsest type of humor and the trashiest   18
forms of art, suggestion through emphasis is not enough; and it can defeat
its own purpose. It must be compensated by the opposite kind of virtue:
the exercise of *economy*, or, more precisely: the technique of *implication*.

Picasso's "I often paint fakes" is at the same time original, emphatic,   19 and implicit. He does not say: "Sometimes, like other painters, I do something second-rate, repetitive, an uninspired variation on a theme, which after a while looks to me as if somebody had imitated my technique. It is true that this somebody happened to be myself, but that makes no difference to the quality of the picture, which is no better than if it were a fake; in fact you could call it that — an uninspired Picasso apeing the style of the true Picasso."

None of this was said; all of it was implied. But the listener has to 20 work out by himself what is implied in the laconic hint; he has to make an imaginative effort to solve the riddle. If the answer were explicitly given, on the lines indicated in the previous paragraph, the listener would be both spared the effort and deprived of its reward; there would be no anecdote to tell.

To a sophisticated audience any joke sounds stale if it is entirely 21 explicit. If this is the case the listener's thoughts will move faster than the narrator's tale or the unfolding of the plot; instead of tension it will generate boredom. "Economy" in this sense means the use of hints in lieu of statements; instead of moving steadily on, the narrative jumps ahead, leaving logical gaps which the listener has to bridge by his own effort: He is forced to co-operate. . . .

Economy, in humor as in art, does not mean mechanical brevity but 22 implications. "Implicit" is derived from the Latin word for "folded in." To make a joke like Picasso's "unfold," the listener must fill in the gaps, complete the hints, trace the hidden analogies. Every good joke contains an element of the riddle — it may be childishly simple, or subtle and challenging — which the listener must solve. By doing so, he is lifted out of his passive role and compelled to cooperate, to repeat to some extent the process of inventing the joke, to re-create it in his imagination. The type of entertainment dished out by the mass media makes one apt to forget that true recreation is re-creation.

Emphasis and implication are complementary techniques. The first 23 bullies the audience into acceptance; the second entices it into mental collaboration; the first forces the offer down the consumer's throat; the second tantalizes, to whet his appetite.

In fact, both techniques have their roots in the basic mechanisms of 24 communicating thoughts by word or sign. Language itself is never completely explicit. Words have suggestive, evocative powers; but at the same time they are merely stepping stones for thought. Economy means spacing them at intervals just wide enough to require a significant effort from the receiver of the message; the artist rules his subjects by turning them into accomplices.

In the next two selections, social scientists Thomas R. Shultz and Mary Douglas present their views on the universality of humor. Shultz is a psychologist who finds a simple but powerful pattern at work in the humor of all cultures, while Douglas, an anthropologist, stresses how cultural contexts determine what is considered funny. Shultz's article was published in 1977. Douglas's analysis appears in her book Implicit Meanings *(1975).*

A Cross-Cultural Study of the Structure of Humor
THOMAS R. SHULTZ

One of the enduring issues in humor research has been the structure of   1
humor and its relation to cognitive processing. It is often assumed that
jokes, regardless of their particular content, share some underlying structure and that a person's cognitive processes must somehow match this
structure in order for him to appreciate a joke. Recent analyses of the
structure of humor have specified two structural features: incongruity
and resolution. The concept of "incongruity" reflects the idea that the
joke contains something which is surprising, unusual, or misexpected.
The concept of "resolution" further specifies that the joke contains information which serves to resolve, explain, or make sense of the incongruity.

The incongruity and resolution theory has generated a fair amount   2
of empirical research on various aspects of the comprehension and appreciation of humor. Until now, this body of research has been restricted
to English speaking, North American samples. In this sense, it constitutes
a cognitive-structural account of the humor existing in a particular cultural-
linguistic context. Although it is generally assumed that humor is prevalent
in all cultural groups, possible cultural variations in the cognitive-structural
features of humor have not been systematically studied. This question
can be viewed as part of the general problem of the relation between
culture and thinking, an issue which has generated a wide range of opinions. There are those who have proposed that the basic functions of
thought are common to all of humanity as well as those who have postulated substantial differences in culturally imposed thought structures.

The focus of the present research was to investigate cultural vari-   3
ations in the structural features of humor. English translations of verbal
humor were collected from the folklore literature of cultures vastly different from that of Western technological society. These instances of
humor were subjected to a structural analysis similar to that performed
on Western humorous materials. The analyses are discussed under four
different headings: Chinese jokes, riddles from nonliterate cultures, Japanese riddles, and folktales.

CHINESE JOKES

The only substantial collection of non-Western jokes the author was   4
able to find was from China. Of these 242 jokes, 210 were found to
possess a structure of incongruity and resolution; 6 did not appear to
have this structure; and 20 others remained inscrutable. Understanding
the substance of a joke was, of course, a prerequisite for determining
whether it fitted within the theoretical model. There were striking similarities between the resolutions employed in the Chinese jokes and those
employed in Western jokes. A number were resolved on the basis of
either lexical or phonological ambiguity. For example, one joke resolved
on the basis of phonological ambiguity concerned a Buddhist priest, a

Taoist priest, and a man with a beard who were crossing the Yangtsze together when a bad squall suddenly came on. The two priests threw their prayer book overboard and called on their Gods to save them. The other man, not having any religious articles, pulled a hair out of his beard and threw that into the river. When the priests asked him why he did that, he answered, "I thought it was time to drop my mao." The author explains that the words for "hair" and "anchor" are both expressed by the same sound, "mao." In terms of the theory, the incongruity in this joke is that the man reacts to the storm by throwing a hair of his beard into the river. The resolution is based on the phonological ambiguity of the words for "hair" and "anchor."

Resolutions by means other than linguistic ambiguity were common among the Chinese jokes as they are among Western jokes. An example is a joke about a father and a son who were chopping firewood together. When the father accidentally wounded the son's fingers with the hatchet, the son cried, "You old pimp, are you blind?" The grandson, who was standing by, hearing his grandfather cursed in this very disrespectful way, turned to his father and said, "You son of a bitch! Do you curse your own father?" The incongruity in this joke is that the grandson, despite his intention to protest the disrespect shown by his father to his grandfather, in fact curses his father and his grandmother, thereby showing even more disrespect than he was protesting. The precise form of the resolution depends on how much knowledge is attributed to the grandson. Either he inadvertently insults his elders in his anger over his father's action or he intentionally insults them under the guise of criticizing his father's disrespect. 5

RIDDLES FROM NONLITERATE CULTURES

The riddle is a form of humor which is found in many cultures, particularly those with a high level of institutional interrogation. Children between about seven years and adolescence seem to be the most typical users of riddles; adults apparently prefer more complex forms such as tales and anecdotes. Riddles may be somewhat better suited to children because they are relatively easy to tell and remember. Sutton-Smith asked American children to relate their favorite jokes and found that the younger children tended to contribute riddles while the older ones told jokes. The particular context for riddling varies somewhat from culture to culture but wakes, harvest times, courtships, and puberty initiation ceremonies are often cited as occasions for riddling. Riddle games and contests are also quite common and, in many cultures, riddling is restricted to the evening hours. It is sometimes held that, if riddles are asked in the daytime (during working hours), they may be answered by evil spirits or otherwise bring bad luck. 6

An important structural analysis of the riddle was undertaken by Georges and Dundes. Utilizing Taylor's extensive collection of traditional English riddles, they defined three principal riddle types: literal, metaphorical, and oppositional. In the literal riddle, the referent or answer is identical to the topic of the descriptive elements in the question: "Got 7 somet'in yeller inside an' green outside. (Pumpkin.)" In the literal riddle, the question is given a straightforward, rational answer. There is no incongruity and, consequently, no need for resolution. In contrast, the answer to a metaphorical riddle is incongruous or surprising. This is because the referent is different than the topic of the descriptive elements: "Two rows of white horses on a red hill. (Teeth.)" The resolution is provided by the metaphorical relation between the referent and the descriptive elements. In an oppositional riddle, the incongruity is contained within the question itself and the answer or referent provides the resolution. The question expresses an opposition between at least one pair of descriptive elements: "What turns and never moves? (A road.)" Oppositional riddles are almost always metaphorical or have some combination of metaphorical and literal descriptions.

Collections of riddles from six nonliterate cultures (two Asian, two   8 African, and two American) were analyzed and classified as literal, metaphorical, or oppositional. An example of a literal riddle is taken from the Makua: "What thing flourishes in the dry season? (The nfangwi tree, which blossoms only in the dry season.)" An example of a metaphorical riddle is from Burma: "A cup of milk spilled over the whole countryside. (The moon.)" And an example of an oppositional riddle is from the Bisayans: "Always taking shelter but forever wet. (Tongue.)" All riddles of the metaphorical and oppositional types were considered to possess a structure of incongruity and resolution while literal riddles were not considered to have this structure. The numbers of riddles of each type are presented in Table 1 for each of the six cultures.

The results of the classification indicate that the vast majority of the   9 riddles in each culture were characterized by the incongruity and resolution structure. The only notable exceptions were the literal riddles found in the Bisayan, Burmese, Nyanja, Makua, and Ten'a cultures. Although literal riddles were in the minority in each of these cultures, they existed in sufficient numbers to constitute a substantial exception and were also present in Taylor's sample of English riddles. Their presence may perhaps be explained in terms of Rapp's interesting theory of the phylogenesis of humor. He viewed the riddle as a direct descendant of the "duel of mental skill" in which pairs of primitive people would stage an intense nonphysical competition. While the winner of such a duel might well have

TABLE 1.   Classification of Riddles by Type

	LITERAL	METAPHORICAL	OPPOSITIONAL
Bisayan (Filipino)	19	54	28
Burmese	5	13	5
Nyanja (Eastern Bantu)	10	102	11
Makua (Bantu)	13	104	18
Amuzgo (Mexican)	0	32	13
Ten'a (Yukon)	27	73	2

laughed at the climactic outcome, Rapp claimed that it was only much later in history that the verbal exchanges per se became humorous. Literal riddles could be considered as vestiges from these primitive wit duels. If so, it should be possible to demonstrate that they are gradually being replaced by the funnier metaphorical and oppositional riddles. This seems to be true in Western culture as the author has been unable to locate a single literal riddle in any current English publications of riddles for children. Recent studies in which American children have been asked to relate their favorite riddles also suggest that literal riddles are relatively primitive. Park and Sutton-Smith both found that literal riddles (or what they called "preriddles") were common among very young children but were extremely rare among older children. It would be interesting to determine if these findings could be extended to non-Western cultures and to test the hypothesis that, where literal riddles exist, they are less funny than metaphorical and oppositional riddles.

JAPANESE RIDDLES

Japanese riddles are discussed separately because it was found that   10 many of them do not fit the structural scheme of Georges and Dundes. Three different forms of Japanese riddles have been identified: kangae-mono, nazo, and children's nazo. Polivanov described the kangaemono (kangae = "think," mono = "object") as a question consisting of two sentences with a consistently occurring antithesis. Of the seven kangae-mono collected by Preston, two appeared to be metaphorical, four oppositional, and one was difficult to understand. Both of the metaphorical kangaemono and three of the four oppositional kangaemono were resolved by phonological ambiguity. An example of the latter is the following: "Everybody likes pie but everyone dislikes a certain pie. What (what kind of) pie is it? (Worry.) (Note — the wordplay involves pai "pie" as a constituent sequence of sinpai worry.)"

Polivanov described the nazo (riddle) as a question-and-answer for-   11 mally united into a whole which includes three sentences: (1) the question, "What can such-and-such be compared with?," (2) the answer, "It may be compared with such-and-such," and (3) the explanation of the comparison. Although the nazo does not at all fit the scheme of Georges and Dundes, it surely can be understood in terms of incongruity and resolution. The first two sentences constitute an incongruous comparison which is resolved by the third sentence. Many of their resolutions are based on the types of linguistic ambiguity common to Western riddles. Of the 189 nazo contained in two published collections, 133 were resolved on the basis of lexical ambiguity, 32 on the basis of phonological ambiguity, 2 on the basis of a combination of lexical and phonological ambiguities, and 21 were resolved by nonlinguistic means (the remaining nazo was difficult to interpret). An example of the last category is the following: "What can you compare a bride from the aristocracy with? With a hundred yen banknote. That's because neither the one nor the other is obtained by the poor man."

The structure of the children's nazo is quite different from that of   12
the nazo proper. Children's nazo consist of two parts rather than three.
The first part describes an unknown object which is to be guessed; the
second part is the answer to the riddle. Although they are considered
rather inferior to true nazo, they appear to be quite similar to Western
riddles and thus can be analyzed according to the Georges and Dundes
system. Of the thirteen children's nazo collected by Starr, four were
metaphorical, five were oppositional, and four were difficult to understand.
One of the metaphorical type was resolved by a lexical ambiguity and
one of the oppositional type was resolved by phonological ambiguity. The
remainder were resolved by nonlinguistic means. An example of this last
category is the following: "Having six feet, it walks with four. What is
that? (Man on horseback.)" . . .

FOLKTALES

Folktales are somewhat more complicated than riddles or simple   13
jokes. They are considerably longer and thus more difficult to remember.
Recitation of folktales is often quite dramatic being supplemented with
expressive gestures, mimicry, and other devices. Rather than searching
through the vast literature on folktales, it was decided to analyze a fairly
representative set of fourteen humorous tales which were collected by
Bowman. These tales are from a variety of cultures; most of them are
archetypal in the sense that different versions of the same story can be
found in other cultures. The main point of each of the fourteen tales was
found to have a definite structure of incongruity and resolution. Two
examples follow. A fairly common type of humorous tale is that in which
one character outwits the others by pitting them against each other. "In
an African story, for example, the rabbit challenges first the hippopotamus
and then the elephant to a tug of war. He arranges that they pull against
each other, each thinking, of course, that his opponent is the rabbit. The
huge beasts pull and strain, baffled at the 'rabbit's' strength, until they
are exhausted, whereupon the crafty rabbit goes to each separately and
claims the victory, which the stupid and unsuspecting pachyderms are
forced to concede." In this tale it is, of course, incongruous that the
hippopotamus and the elephant are defeated in a tug of war by the much
smaller rabbit. The resolution is that the rabbit has cleverly arranged for
the two larger animals to unknowingly pull against each other.

"Tales of the hare-and-tortoise type, in which the slower animal wins   14
the race, are common, although the victory is achieved more often by
trickery than by perseverance. In a Bondei story the tortoise and the
falcon compete for the hand of the chief's daughter. The tortoise, knowing
that he has no chance to win unless he resorts to trickery, consults the
hare, who evolves a plan. In accordance with this, the tortoise enlists
the cooperation of a number of his tortoise friends, all of whom look alike
to the falcon. One of them hides at each resting place along the route.
The race begins and the falcon reaches the first resting place confident
that he has left his competitor far behind, only to find that the 'tortoise'
is already there. This is repeated at each stop and again at the finish line

in the village, where the tortoise himself is hiding. When the falcon comes flying into the village, crying that he has beaten the tortoise, the latter emerges out of hiding, claims the victory, and wins the hand of the chief's daughter. In an Ikon version the frog races with the bushbuck and wins by stationing other frogs along the route. In a Benga tale the tortoise defeats the antelope by the same kind of plot, and a similar version is told by the Wakweli." In these tales it is incongruous for the slower animal to win a race over the faster one; the resolution is that the slower animal only appears to win through the trick of stationing his relatives along the route.

DISCUSSION

An answer to the question of cultural variation in humor depends   15
very much on the level at which humor is analyzed. On the most abstract level, it seems to be the case that all cultures possess humor in some form. At least there are no reports of a culture in which instances of humor are absent. On the most concrete level, it is equally obvious that different cultures joke about different things. The Chinese jokes were generally concerned with problems in social relationships. In contrast, humor in the Bisayan, Burmese, Nyanja, Makua, Amuzgo, and Ten'a cultures was more often focused on aspects of the immediate physical environment. As Freud pointed out, Western humor deals principally with the twin preoccupations of sex and aggression.

Intermediate levels of analysis must be explored to answer questions   16
of cultural variation in the structure of humor. There is a great deal of cultural variation in specific structural and stylistic techniques. Roberts and Forman found that certain forms of humor, such as the riddle, are prevalent in some cultures but nonexistent in others. In the present study, it was noted that lexical and phonological ambiguities were commonly used to resolve incongruities in the literate cultures but were rare in the nonliterate cultures sampled. Similarly, syntactic ambiguity is employed as a resolution device in a small number of Western jokes and riddles but was not observed in any of the present non-Western samples. Certain stylistic forms, such as the tripartite Japanese nazo, also appeared to be culturally idiosyncratic.

At a more basic level, however, there was a striking commonality   17
across cultures in the use of incongruity and resolution. This structure was found in the vast majority of the jokes, riddles, and humorous tales of every culture sampled. As such, the results of the present study offer considerable support for the "psychic-unity" hypothesis proposed many years ago by Boas. This is the idea that the most basic structures of mind are common to all of humanity. But why should the structure of incongruity and resolution be a universal feature of humor? This is not too mysterious when one considers the incongruity and resolution structure in terms of its relation to pleasure and arousal. It has been hypothesized that the cognitive experience of incongruity and resolution has physiological correlates in terms of momentary fluctuations in arousal. It may be that the discovery of the incongruity in a joke arouses the listener

and the construction of a resolution returns the arousal to its baseline level. The pleasure-giving potential of arousal induction and reduction in man and animals has been well documented in experimental psychology. Since this sequence is compressed into an extremely short time interval in most jokes, the pleasure associated with humor could be expected to be quite intense.

Jokes
MARY DOUGLAS

A joke is a play upon form. It brings into relation disparate elements in   1
such a way that one accepted pattern is challenged by the appearance of another which in some way was hidden in the first. I confess that I find Freud's definition of the joke highly satisfactory. The joke is an image of the relaxation of conscious control in favor of the subconscious. For the rest of this article I shall be assuming that any recognizable joke falls into this joke pattern which needs two elements, the juxtaposition of a control against that which is controlled, this juxtaposition being such that the latter triumphs. Needless to say, a successful subversion of one form by another completes or ends the joke, for it changes the balance of power. It is implicit in the Freudian model that the unconscious does not take over the control system. The wise sayings of lunatics, talking animals, children, and drunkards are funny because they are not in control; otherwise they would not be an image of the subconscious. The joke merely affords opportunity for realizing that an accepted pattern has no necessity. Its excitement lies in the suggestion that any particular ordering of experience may be arbitrary and subjective. It is frivolous in that it produces no real alternative, only an exhilarating sense of freedom from form in general.

SOCIAL CONTROL OF PERCEPTION

While hailing this joke pattern as authentic, it is a very different   2
matter to use it for identifying jokes. First we should distinguish standardized jokes, which are set in a conventional context, from spontaneous jokes. Freud's claim to have found the same joke pattern in all joking situations hides an important shift in levels of analysis. The standard joke, starting for instance with "Have you heard this one?" or "There were three men, an Irishman, etc.," contains the whole joke pattern within its verbal form. So does the pun. The joke pattern can easily be identified within the verbal form of standard jokes and puns. But the spontaneous joke organizes the total situation in its joke pattern. Thus we get into difficulties in trying to recognize the essence of a spontaneous joke if we only have the utterance or the gesture and not the full pattern of relationships. If the Kaguru think it witty to throw excrement at certain cousins or the Lodagaba to dance grotesquely at funerals or the Dogon to refer to the parents' sexual organs when they meet a friend, then to

recognize the joke that sends all present into huge enjoyment we need not retreat into cultural relativism and give up a claim to interpret. The problem has merely shifted to the relation between joking and the social structure.

The social dimension enters at all levels into the perception of a joke. 3 Even its typical patterning depends on a social valuation of the elements. A twentieth-century audience finds the Beaumarchais comedy weak because it one-sidedly presents the aristocrats' manners as live and their servants' manners as lifeless imitations. But to an eighteenth-century audience of French aristocrats any dramatist presenting both lords and commoners as equally lively in their own right would have had, not a comedy, but a theme of social reform to tempt only a Bernard Shaw in his most tendentious vein. In every period there is a pile of submerged jokes, unperceived because they are irrelevant or wrongly balanced for the perspective of the day. . . .

So much for the social control of perception. As to the permitting 4 of a joke, there are jokes which can be perceived clearly enough by all present but which are rejected at once. Here again the social dimension is at work. Social requirements may judge a joke to be in bad taste, risky, too near the bone, improper, or irrelevant. Such controls are exerted either on behalf of hierarchy as such, or on behalf of values which are judged too precious and too precarious to be exposed to challenge. Whatever the joke, however remote its subject, the telling of it is potentially subversive. Since its form consists of a victorious tilting of uncontrol against control, it is an image of the leveling of hierarchy, the triumph of intimacy over formality, of unofficial values over official ones. Our question is now much clearer. We must ask what are the social conditions for a joke to be both perceived and permitted. . . .

THE JOKER

Now we should turn to the role of the joker. He appears to be a 5 privileged person who can say certain things in a certain way which confers immunity. He is by no means anything like a taboo breaker whose polluting act is a real offense to society. . . . He has a firm hold on his own position in the structure and the disruptive comments which he makes upon it are in a sense the comments of the social group upon itself. He merely expresses consensus. Safe within the permitted range of attack, he lightens for everyone the oppressiveness of social reality, demonstrates its arbitrariness by making light of formality in general, and expresses the creative possibilities of the situation.

From this we can see the appropriateness of the joker as ritual 6 purifier. Among the Kaguru, certain common sexual offenses such as sexual intercourse between affines are thought to bring illness, sterility, or death on the kin of the two offenders. There are other graver sexual offenses, but these relatively minor ones can be ritually cleansed by the joking partners of the transgressors. . . . Now I suggest that the relevance of joking to purification emerges as another elaborate ritual pun. These rites make a double play on the joke experience: Laughter itself is cathartic at the level of emotions; the joke consists in challenging a dominant structure and belittling it; the joker who provokes the laughter is chosen to challenge the relevance of the dominant structure and to perform with immunity the act which wipes out the venial offense. . . .

Perhaps the joker should be classed as a kind of minor mystic. Though only a mundane and border-line type, he is one of those people who pass beyond the bounds of reason and society and give glimpses of a truth which escapes through the mesh of structured concepts. Naturally he is only a humble, poor brother of the true mystic, for his insights are given by accident. They do not combine to form a whole new vision of life, but remain disorganized as a result of the technique which produces them. He is distinctly gimmicky. . . .

It is much easier now to see the role of the joker at a funeral. By restraining excessive grief he asserts the demands of the living. I would expect joking at funerals to be more possible and more required the more the community is confident that it will turn the mourner's desolation into a temporary phase. Then the question is: Who must joke and what should be his precise degree of relationship with the bereaved and the dead? The central African joking partner is a friend cultivated by gifts and hospitality, and is by definition not a close kinsman: His role at a funeral is to cheer the bereaved and to relieve them of the polluting duties of burial. There are here the elements of another ritual pun; for it is the kin who are ritually endangered by contact with the dead, the kin who are involved in the social structure of inheritance and succession, and it is the personal friend, the joking partner, who is uninvolved in the social structure and is the person who is immune from pollution of death.

There are many ways in which it can be appropriate to joke at a funeral. When a man dies his friends fall to reviewing his life. They try to see in it some artistic pattern, some fulfillment which can comfort him and them. At this moment obvious inconsistencies and disharmonies are distressing. If he is a great man, a national figure, of course his achievements are cited, but it seems important to be able to say that in his private life he also had fulfilled his family roles. If he is an ordinary citizen then the assessment of his success goes on entirely at the level of family and community. He is judged as a man, not as an item of social structure.

The role of the joker at the funeral could call attention to his individual personality. Indeed, in the Jewish *shib'ah,* a week of mourning after burial, the friends who come in to comfort the bereaved and praise the departed, invariably find themselves joking at his expense. Thus they affirm that he was an individual, not only a father or brother in a series of descending generations, but a man. So much for the social symbolism.

On the subject of funeral joking it is tempting to consider some metaphysical implications. A joke symbolizes leveling, dissolution and recreation. As a symbol of social relations it is destructive (somewhat like fire?) and regenerative (somewhat like water?). The joke, working on its own materials, mimics a kind of death. Its form in itself suggests the theme of rebirth. It is no coincidence that practical jokes are common in initiation rites, along with more concrete expressions of dying and being reborn.

Jokes can reflect the social order. In the two passages that follow, folklorists Lawrence W. Levine and José E. Limón analyze certain kinds of ethnic jokes within the context of race relations in the United States. Levine's analysis, published in 1977, is more historical in nature while the excerpt from Limón's article, published in 1982, focuses on the exchanges of contemporary college students. As you read these materials, think about the ethnic jokes you've heard. What do they suggest about the current state of race relations in the United States?

From *Black Culture and Black Consciousness*
LAWRENCE W. LEVINE

In his important analysis, *Laughter* [see p. 691], Henri Bergson specified   1
what he called "inversion" as one of the prime comic methods: "Picture
to yourself certain characters in a certain situation: If you reverse the
situation and invert the roles, you obtain a comic scene. . . . Thus, we
laugh at the prisoner at the bar lecturing the magistrate; at a child
presuming to teach its parents; in a word at everything that comes under
the heading of 'topsyturvydom.' " Other students of humor have called
this comic principle by other names: "universe-changing," "deviations
from institutionalized meaning structures," and perhaps most commonly,
"incongruity." All describe the same process: the trivialization or degradation of ideas or personages normally held to be lofty or noble, and
the advancement of those normally consigned to an inferior or inconse-
quential position.

The British actor and comedian John Bernard, who lived in the United   2
States between 1797 and 1819, would have found these analyses particularly applicable to the slaves in whose culture he was so interested. After
calling the slaves "the great humorists of the Union," Bernard characterized
their humor as that "which lowered the most dignified subjects into
ludicrous lights and elevated the most trivial into importance." We have
already observed [earlier in this book] this element at work in the slave
trickster tales which induced laughter through a sudden reversal of roles
or fortunes. However temporarily, the venerated were vanquished or at
least made to look foolish by the lowly. Reversal of roles remained one
of the chief mechanisms of black laughter long after slavery, not only in
the trickster tales which continued to be popular but in the entire body
of jokes which the freedmen and their descendants told one another.

One of the oldest and most persistent cycles of jokes in Afro-American   3
lore focused upon the numskull doings of immigrant Irishmen. Jokes
ridiculing the Irish became popular in the United States following the
large-scale migrations from Ireland in the mid-nineteenth century. Negroes, who came into hostile contact with the Irish immigrants in the
South and the North, learned the current anecdotes and undoubtedly
created many of their own. These jokes were probably known to the
slaves and were certainly widely disseminated among the freedmen. They
were collected as early as the 1870s; Joel Chandler Harris included one
in the first volume of his Uncle Remus tales; and by the end of the

century they had become so ubiquitous that the *Southern Workman* noted in 1899, "Irishmen stories form as widespread a part of the American Negro folklore as do the animal stories." The jokes were evidently told with great style. In 1876 Lafcadio Hearn noted that the Negro stevedores along the Cincinnati levee "can mimic the Irish accent to a degree of perfection which an American, Englishman, or German could not hope to acquire."

The Irishman remained a central butt of black humor throughout the   4
twentieth century. In her 1917 collection of black lore from Guilford County, North Carolina, Elsie Clews Parsons reported that "Anecdotes about Irishmen have a distinct vogue. Indeed, the Archman [Irishman] has become as much of a stock character as Rabbit or Hant." In 1923 the Negro folklorist Arthur Huff Fauset collected jokes about the Irish from Philadelphia blacks and two years later, after ranging widely through Alabama, Mississippi, and Louisiana, he concluded that left to themselves Negroes were even more apt to relate a story about the Irish than about Brer Rabbit: "It is curious to hear a native-born southern Negro, nearly full-blooded, telling a story about Pat and Mike with all the spirit and even the inflection of voice that one might expect of an Irishman." A generation later Richard Dorson found jokes and anecdotes ridiculing the Irish still quite common, South and North.

Jokes at the expense of the immigrant Irish who were themselves   5
at the lower reaches of the American society and economy may hardly seem a good example of incongruity in black humor. Yet I think they are. Humor about the Irish functioned in several ways. Most obviously, these jokes allowed Negroes to join the white majority in looking down upon and feeling superior to the strange folkways of an alien group. For once black Americans could feel part of the mainstream as they ridiculed the awkward actions of unassimilated immigrants. (Just as for their part European immigrants could quickly feel at one with their new country by identifying themselves with the white majority.) Thus on the one hand these jokes permitted a reversal of roles by elevating blacks and allowing them to identify with and share the superior feelings of the groups at the center of American society. But they also reversed roles in the more traditional sense, for no matter how marginal the Irish may have been, they remained white, and as part of the racial majority they had made the Negro suffer at their hands, as in the New York Draft Riots in 1863. Irish jokes became a means of taking revenge upon these newcomers who had learned to hate Negroes so quickly and efficiently. Perhaps more importantly, they allowed Negroes to openly ridicule and express contempt for white people. The Irish characters of black jokelore became surrogates for all the other whites against whom it could be dangerous to speak openly. This may well account for the ease with which folklorists were able to collect these anecdotes and for the fact that they remained a central part of Afro-American expressive culture for at least a century.

The tone of most of these jokes was captured in the nineteenth-   6
century story of the visitor to Hell who saw Germans, English, Japanese, and Negroes burning in torment, but no Irish. When he asked why, the Devil took him into a warm room filled with Irish. "We are just drying

them here," the Devil informed his guest, "they are too green to burn now." Irishmen in Afro-American lore were pictured as the quintessential greenhorn immigrants bumbling their way through an environment with which they were in no way prepared to cope. Discovering pumpkins for the first time, an Irishman is told they are mule's eggs. He pays an exhorbitant price for one, tries to hatch it by sitting on it, and when it rolls out from under him into the brush below frightening a rabbit which scampers off, he is convinced his egg has hatched and runs after the rabbit calling, "Koop Colie! Koop Colie! Here's your mammy." Buying their first watermelon, two Irishmen give the heart of it away to some nearby Negroes and keep only the rind for themselves saying, "Guts is good enough for Naygurs." The Irish that march through [such] anecdotes mistake turtles for pocket watches, wear them between their breeches, and respond to queries about the time by saying things like "eleven-thirty, and scratching like hell for twelve"; they mistake mosquitoes for squirrels, frogs for deer, deer for railroad trains, a black slave for the Devil, and his fiddle for a squalling baby. One Irishman finds a pocket watch, listens to it go "tick, tick," is convinced that it is the mother of all the ticks in the world, and smashes it with a club; others do the same thing when they mistake a watch for a rattlesnake. Pat and Mike see a gun for the first time, buy it from its black owner, and Mike immediately kills Pat by trying to shoot a grasshopper off his chest. Death by drowning is the fate of two Irishmen who decide that the water in which they have dropped their watch is shallow enough to wade into when they hear some frogs singing what sounds like "Knee deep, knee deep, knee deep." Asked which way a road goes, an Irishman answers, "Faith, I've been living here twenty years, and it's never gone anywhere yet."

Nor were the Irishmen in these tales going anywhere, hampered as they were by their great disabilities. The Irish immigrants with whom Negroes often came into economic competition were pictured in black humor as invariably incompetent and lazy. In one anecdote a recent Irish migrant gets a job as a hod carrier and writes to his brother in the Old Country, "Come at once, I've got a good easy job, a dollar and nine cents an hour carrying brick and mortar on the second floor. The other fellow does all the work, so come at once. Your brother Pat." In a nineteenth-century anecdote an Irish orator cries out, "Who puts up all the fine buildings? — The Irish. And who puts up the court-houses? — The Irish. And who builds the State penitentiaries? — The Irish. And who fills them? — The Irish, begobs!" When they became tired of lampooning Irish stupidity, indolence, and dishonesty, black storytellers could and did turn to Irish religion. Walking through the woods Pat comes across a panther, kills it with a club, and then continues to beat it into a bloody pulp. A passer-by asks him why he is doing that, "Can't you see it's dead?" "Yes," responds Pat. "But I want to show him that there's punishment after death." Two Irishmen in a boat are caught in rough seas and conclude, "Be fait' an' be Chris'! I believe we better pray." Pat prays, "O Gawd, Gawd! If you help me across dis time, I'll give you a big pertater. De 'tater will be as big as a peck tub." His partner remonstrates, "You know you ain't got no 'tater like dat." Pat responds,

7

"Hush, hush, hush! I jes' foolin' him. I jes' want him to get me 'cross de river." In an identical situation, another Irishman prays vulgarly, "O Gawd, Gawd! If you help me cross dis bloody river, I wouldn't worry you no damn mo'."

Black attitudes toward the Irish were not as unambiguous as the   8
general tone of these jokes implies. No matter how great the animosity between the two groups, they shared a lowly position in American society which created a certain empathy among Negroes for their Irish protagonists. This sympathy was manifest in the commonly told story of the Irishman and Englishman who go hunting and kill a turkey and a turkey buzzard: "When the hunt was over, of course the Englishman thought he was the smartest man. He suggested how the game ought to be divided. He said, 'Pat, I killed both the real turkey and the buzzard; but you may take the turkey-buzzard, and I the turkey; or I'll take the turkey, and you the buzzard.' — 'Say that again,' said Pat to Joe; and he said it again the same way. 'You haven't said turkey to me the first nor the last, now I'll take the real turkey,' said Pat to Joe, 'and leave the smart Englishman very sorrowful." In another joke a sea captain has some fun with one of his Irish sailors by telling him he might marry the most beautiful of his daughters if he can find three ends to a piece of rope. Pat studies the problem for several days and finally calls the captain over to the ship's side. He shows the captain both ends of the rope and then throws it overboard, saying, "Faith, and there's the other end!" In a South Carolina story an Irishman is condemned to be hung alongside a black man and a Dutchman. Allowed to pick the tree they would be hung on, the black chooses an oak, the Dutchman a pine tree, and the Irishman a gooseberry bush. Informed it would not be large enough the latter replies, "By Jesus! Me will wait till it grow." The sensitive identification that occasionally marked Irish stories was reflected too in the strangely moving anecdote concerning three Irish greenhorns who knew only three phrases in English. Through a series of comic misadventures these three expressions lead them to confess to a murder they did not commit. "They knew too much after all," the storyteller concluded. "They knew just enough about America to get hung."

History, Chicano Joking, and the Varieties of Higher Education

JOSÉ E. LIMÓN

Some years ago Professor Américo Paredes identified two important   1
ethnic joking traditions involving Anglos and Mexican Americans in Texas and perhaps elsewhere. In one of these joke cycles, a wily, trickster-like Mexican figure takes advantage of an Anglo-American — the butt of the joke — often through a misunderstanding of language. Paredes calls this cycle the "Stupid American" joke. In the other, the self-satirical joke, Mexican Americans actually make fun of themselves and their inability to manage American culture, particularly in its technological dimensions. Both forms circulate among Mexican Americans. . . .

The general purpose of . . . [my] study is to explore the continuation **2**
of these traditions among contemporary Mexican-American students at
the University of Texas at Austin (hereafter UT-A). . . . I shall argue
for an . . . interpretation of these traditions which emphasizes their socially critical . . . significance. . . .

A late night gathering at a student apartment; twelve Chicano males **3**
are present; all of us are drinking beer. A number of jokes have already
been narrated when I begin to take notes on this ethnic joke cycle.

> Pepito was in school and the *gringa*° teacher didn't want him to talk
> because he was always saying crazy things. One day the teacher was teaching
> the word *rat,* and she asked, "Who can do a sentence with the word *rat?*"
> And, Pepito raised his hand quickly, "Teacher, teacher, I can, I can!" And
> the teacher thought to herself, "Well, what can he do wrong with *rat?*"
> "Alright, Pepito, go ahead." And Pepito said, "I have a rat!" "Very good,
> Pepito," says the teacher, but Pepito keeps going . . . "A big fucking rat!"

[A few more minutes elapse before three jokes are narrated in quick
succession by three different narrators.]

> There was this mentally crazy Chicano in an insane asylum and through
> the fence he was watching a *gringo* who had a flat tire . . . and the *gringo*
> was really pissed because he had kicked the hubcap where he had the tire
> bolts and they had fallen into the sewer. And he was really angry because
> he didn't know what to do. And the crazy Chicano calls him, "Hey, mister,
> come here." The *gringo* came close and the crazy guy says, "Why don't
> you take one bolt from each of the other tires and you can have enough to
> put on the spare, until you can get to an auto supply house?" And, the *gringo*
> said, "Hey, that's pretty smart! Listen, what's a smart guy like you doing
> in an insane asylum?" And the crazy Chicano says, "Well, mister, I'm crazy,
> but I'm not stupid!"

The second narrator adds this:

> "Now that we're talking about stupid *gringos,* do you know the one
> about the Chicano who was pissing in the restroom. . . .

He is momentarily interrupted by another participant who says, "Yeah,
the one about 'pretty chilly' . . . everyone knows that one!" The narrator
continues,

> No man, not that one . . . this Chicano had just finished pissing and
> was leaving when this *gringo* says, "Hey Mex, don't Meskins ever wash
> their hands when they piss?" And the Chicano replied, "Well, it's just that
> Mexicans don't piss in their hands!"

The third narrator immediately continues:

> It's like the one about the Mexican who walks into a bar and sits down
> next to a *gringo* who had a big dog. The Chicano wants to be real friendly
> so he asks the *gabacho,*° "That's a nice dog you have there, mister; what
> kind is it?" And the *gringo* answered, "He's half Meskin and half sonofabitch!"
> "Oh," said the Mexican, "he is related to both of us!"

gringa/gringo: Foreigner, especially Anglo-American.
gabacho: Anglo-American.

In this narrative sequence, jokes that are often nonethnic in character   4
have been converted into variants of the Stupid American joke. Among
the general Texas-Mexican population, such . . . jokes always attach and
dupe institutional and authority figures, but these are not defined in ethnic
terms. . . .

Such jokes may be converted into ethnic jokes in the University of   5
Texas scene; [the jokes just narrated] definitely have become ethnic jokes
of the Stupid American subgenre. . . . In this [UT-A] Anglo-dominated
educational context, [the jokes serve as] . . . an implicit criticism of
teachers and presumptuous Anglos in general, especially those that think
they are educationally superior. . . .

These Chicano joke texts seem to symbolically challenge and subvert   6
the accepted social order, that is, the hegemony of the dominant class
and cultural interests of Texans. Anglo-Americans are brought down from
their towers of power; oppressive institutional representations like teachers, waitresses, and rich customers are subverted; and the subversion
is often carried out by proletarian folk heroes.

*In this autobiographical reflection, published in 1986, the essayist and poet
Annie Dillard recalls her family's style of telling jokes and considers the performative aspect of joke telling, the art of delivery.*

The Leg in the Christmas Stocking: What We Learned from Jokes
ANNIE DILLARD

Our parents would have sooner left us out of Christmas than leave us   1
out of a joke. They explained a joke to us while they were still laughing
at it; they tore a still-kicking joke apart so we could see how it worked.
When we got the first Tom Lehrer album in 1954, when I was 9, Mother
went through it with me, cut by cut, explaining.

Our father kept in his breast pocket a black notebook. There he   2
noted jokes he wanted to remember. Remembering jokes was a moral
obligation. People who said "I can never remember jokes" were like
people who said, obliviously, "I can never remember names" or "I don't
bathe."

"No one tells jokes like your father," Mother said. Telling a good   3
joke well — successfully, perfectly — was the highest art. It was an art
because it was up to you. If you did not get the laugh, you had told it
wrong. Work on it, and do better next time. It would have been reprehensible to blame the joke or, worse, the audience.

As we children got older, our parents discussed with us every tech-   4
nical, theoretical, and moral aspect of the art. We tinkered with a joke's
narrative structure: "Maybe you should begin with the Indians." We
polished the wording. There is a Julia Randall story set in Baltimore that
we smoothed together for years. Must the man say, "Folks generally
call me Bominitious?" No, he can just say, "They call me Bominitious."

We analyzed many kinds of pacing. We admired with Father the   5
leisurely meanders of the shaggy dog story. "Fellow went to Juilliard,"
one story of his began, "studied composition" and ended, to a blizzard
of thrown napkins ". . . known as the Moron Tab and Apple Choir."
"Frog goes into a bank," another story began, to my enduring pleasure.
The joke was not great, but with what a sweet light splash you could
launch it!

And so my sisters and I learned to love it all, all that any joke-teller   6
needs, and a good bit of what any writer needs. We learned to love
thinking about narration — about the imaginative power in its manipulable
segments. We learned to calculate and guide a narration's effects on an
audience at every stage. We learned to love careful, controlled language.
We learned to love paradox, incongruity and surprise.

Father was fond of stories set in bars that starred zoo animals or   7
insects. These creatures apparently came into bars all over America,
either accompanied or alone, and sat down to face incredulous, sarcastic
bartenders. (It was a wonder the bartenders were always so surprised
to see talking dogs or drinking monkeys or performing ants, so surprised
year after year, when clearly this sort of thing was the very essence of
bar life.) In the few years he had been loose, before he married, Father
had frequented bars in New York, listening to jazz. His bar jokes — "and
there were the regulars, all sitting around" — gave him the raffish air
of a man who was at home anywhere.

Our mother favored a staccato, stand-up style; if our father could   8
perorate, she could condense. Fellow goes to a psychiatrist. "You're
crazy." "I want a second opinion!" "You're ugly."

What else in life so required, and so rewarded, such care?   9
"Tell the girls the one about the four-by-twos, Frank."   10
"Let's see. Let's see."   11
"Fellow goes into a lumberyard. . . ."   12
"Yes, but it's tricky. It's a matter of point of view." And Father left   13
the dining room, rubbing his face in concentration, or as if he were
smearing on greasepaint, and returned when he was ready.

"Ready with the four-by-twos?" Mother said.   14
Our father hung his hands in his pockets and regarded the far ceiling   15
with fond reminiscence.

"Fellow comes into a lumberyard," he began.   16
"Says to the guy, 'I need some four-by-twos.' 'You mean two-by-   17
fours?' 'Just a minute. I'll find out.' He walks out to the parking lot where
his buddies are waiting in the car. They roll down the car window. He
confers with them awhile and comes back across the parking lot and says
to the lumberyard guy, 'Yes. I mean two-by-fours.'

"Lumberyard guy says, 'How long do you want them?' 'Just a minute,'   18
fellow says, 'I'll find out.' He goes out across the parking lot and confers
with the people in the car and comes back across the parking lot to
the lumberyard and says to the guy, 'A long time. We're building a
house.' "

After any performance Father rubbed the top of his face with both   19
hands, as if it had all been a dream. "And when you tell a joke," Mother
said to my sisters and me, "laugh. It's mean not to."

We were brought up on the classics. Our parents told us all the great   20
old American jokes, practically by number. They collaborated on, and for
our benefit specialized in, like paleontologists, the painstaking reconstruction of vanished jokes from extant tag lines. They could vivify old New
Yorker cartoons, source of many tag lines. The lines themselves — "Back
to the old drawing board" and "I say it's spinach and I say the hell with
it" and "A simple yes or no will be sufficient" — were no longer funny;
they were instead something better, they were a fixture in the language.
The tag lines of old jokes were the most powerful expressions we learned
at our parents' knees.

There was one complicated joke, in a select category, which required   21
a long weekend with tolerant friends. You had to tell a joke that was not
funny. It was a long, pointless story about a construction job that ended
with someone throwing away a brick. There was nothing funny about it
at all, and when your friends did not laugh, you had to pretend you'd
muffed it. (Your husband in the crowd could shill for you: " 'Tain't funny,
Pam. You told it all wrong.")

A few days later, if you could contrive another occasion for joke-   22
telling, and if your friends still permitted you to speak, you set forth on
another joke, this one a 19th-century chestnut about angry passengers
on a train. The lady plucks the lighted, smelly cigar from the man's mouth
and flings it from the moving train's window. The man seizes the little
black poodle from her lap and hurls the poor dog from the same window.
When at last the passengers draw unspeaking into the station, what do
they see coming down the platform but the black poodle, and guess what
it has in its mouth? "The cigar," say your friends, bored sick and vowing
never to spend another weekend with you. "No," you say triumphant,
"the brick." This was Mother's kind of joke. Its very riskiness excited
her. It wasn't funny, but it was interesting to set up, and it elicited from
her friends a grudging admiration.

How long, I wondered, could you stretch this out? How boldly could   23
you push an audience — not to, in Mother's terms, "slay them," but to
please them in some grand way? How can you convince the listeners
that you know what you are doing, that the payoff will come? Or conversely, how long could you lead them to think you are stupid, a dumb
blonde, to enhance their surprise at the punch line and heighten their
pleasure in the story you have controlled all along? Alone, energetic and
trying to fall asleep, walking the residential streets long distances every
day, I pondered these things. You've got to think about something.

Our parents were both sympathetic to what professional comedians   24
call flop sweat. Boldness was all at our house, and of course you would
lose some. Anyone could be misled by poor judgment into telling a "woulda
hadda been there." Telling a funny story was harder than telling a joke;
it was trying out, as a tidy unit, some raveling shred of the day's fabric.
You learned to gauge what sorts of thing would "tell." You learned that
some people, notably your parents, could rescue some things by careful
narration from the category "woulda hadda been there" to the category
"it tells."

At the heart of originating a funny story was recognizing it as it   25
floated by. You scooped the potentially solid tale from the flux of history.

Once I overheard my parents arguing over a 30-year-old story's credit line. "It was my mother who said that," Mother said. "Yes, but" — Father was downright smug — "I was the one who noticed she said that."

My parents favored practical jokes of the sort you set up and then **26** retire from, much as one writes books, possibly because imagining people's reactions beats witnessing them. They procured a live hen and "hypnotized" it by setting it on the sink before the bathroom mirror in a friend's cottage by the New Jersey shore. They spent weeks constructing a 10-foot sea monster — from truck inner tubes, cement blocks, broomsticks, lumber, pillows — and set it afloat in a friend's pond. I woke one Christmas morning to find in my stocking a leg. Mother had charmed a department store display manager into lending her one.

When I visited my friends, I was well advised to rise when their **27** parents entered the room. When my friends visited me, they were well advised to duck.

Central in the orders of merit, and the very bread and butter of **28** everyday life, was the crack. Our mother excelled at making cracks. We learned early to feed her lines just to watch her speed to the draw. If someone else fired a crack simultaneously, we compared their concision and pointedness and declared a winner.

Naturally my younger sisters and I prized the ability to make good **29** cracks the way Sioux girls prized the ability to take tiny stitches — or, more aptly, the way Sioux boys prized the ability to take scalps. I remember well the occasion of the first crack I made that people laughed at, and the second. My parents were apparently modestly — but actually deliriously — proud.

Feeding our mother lines, we were training as straight men. The **30** straight man's was an honorable calling, a bit like that of the rodeo clown: despised by the ignorant masses, perhaps, but revered among experts who understood the skills required and the risks run. We children mastered the deliberate misunderstanding, the planted pun, the Gracie Allen remark that can make of any interlocutor an instant hero.

How very gracious is the straight man! — or, in this case, the straight **31** woman. She spreads before her friend a gift-wrapped, beribboned gag line he can claim for his own, if only he has the sense to pick it up, instead of — as happens nauseatingly often — pausing to contemplate what a nitwit he's talking to. Those men who recognize the ability for what it is, on the other hand, usually propose marriage on the spot.

In this second excerpt from his book Laughter and Liberation (1971), *Harvey Mindess writes about the integral connection between humor and psychological health and, specifically, about the role humor can play in psychotherapy.*

Humor as Therapy
HARVEY MINDESS

Catharsis, insight, self-acceptance, reconditioning, and emotional open-   1
ness: these experiences, by and large, have been the classical agents of
psychotherapy. By fostering one or more of them, psychologists and
psychiatrists have attempted — and sometimes even managed — to help
their patients cope with their distress. The field, however, has been
limited to variations on these themes. It is time, therefore, to propose
an addition to their ranks. In these days, in particular, when clinical
inspiration is restricted to the ecstasies of the existentialists and the
banalities of the behaviorists, we are ripe for a new therapeutic gambit.
We stand in need of an agent that can help us when the traditional forms
of treatment falter.

Such an agent exists. It has, in fact, been part of our human equipment   2
since time immemorial. Its name — no joke — is humor. Humor not in
its superficial, merely entertaining manifestations, but in its deepest, most
genuine essence. We all agree that when a person — patient, therapist,
or normal human being — exercises this faculty, he becomes more re-
silient to the stresses of living. What we need to understand, however,
is the process by which the faculty can be brought into play and, for
those in the business, the role the psychotherapist can perform in acti-
vating it.

Let us be clear now on what we are talking about. Humor in its   3
deepest essence: What does the phrase denote? Is it the ability to tell
jokes and make people laugh? No. Delightful as they may be, jokes and
comic routines are contrived, artificial products. They bear about the
same relation to genuine humor as painting pretty pictures does to art.
Is it then the ability to deliver spontaneous witticisms? Not quite. Such
a talent comes closer to humor's core, but it does not encompass it.
Deep, genuine humor — the humor that deserves to be called therapeutic,
that can be instrumental in our lives — extends beyond jokes, beyond
wit, beyond laughter itself to a peculiar frame of mind. It is an inner
condition, a stance, a point of view, or in the largest sense an attitude
to life.

A cluster of qualities characterize it. Flexibility, spontaneity, uncon-   4
ventionality combined with shrewdness, playfulness, and humility: they
each play their part in the drama of the humorous outlook. For that drama
to unfold, therefore, each one of these qualities must be called upon.
The starring role, however, is reserved for a specific characteristic. We
may call it enjoyment of the ironies that run through all human affairs.
To command a deep sense of humor, a person must become acutely,
vividly, aware of the anomalies and paradoxes that embroider our behavior. He must come to know, not theoretically but practically, with all
his being, that the happiest relationships are larded with suffering, that
the greatest accomplishments are anticlimactic, that rational acts are
motivated by irrational drives, that psychotic thinking makes excellent
sense, that the most altruistic gestures are selfish at their core. He must
know these things and enjoy them — enjoy them because they are true
and because they give three, if not four, dimensions to human beings.

The peculiarities of our characters make us the infuriating, fascinating   5
creatures we are. It is not by accident that man is the only animal who
has a sense of humor. He is also the only animal who wears clothing,
denies himself sex, worships nonexistent deities, starves in order to
create, kills and dies for his country, slaves and cheats for his bank
balance. Clearly, he is the only animal who *needs* a sense of humor.

An ancient folktale illustrates these observations succinctly. It tells   6
of a morose young man who met a kind fairy in the woods.

> "What ails thee?" asked the fairy.
> "I would be happy," the young man replied, "if only I were handsome."
> So the fairy instructed him in the application of certain salves and
> ointments, and lo and behold, in a short while the young man was very
> handsome.
> He remained, however, despondent. Once again the fairy asked, "What
> ails thee?"
> "I would be happy," said the handsome young man, "if only I were
> rich."
> So the fairy taught him how to find precious jewels in hidden caves in
> the mountains, and in no time at all the young man became exceedingly
> wealthy.
> He remained, nevertheless, downcast. And yet again the fairy asked,
> "What ails thee?"
> "I would be happy," said the rich and handsome young man, "if only I
> were loved."
> So the fairy introduced him to the subtle art of winning fair maidens'
> affections, and soon he was well beloved by many charming girls. Despite
> his success, however, he remained dejected. One last time, therefore, the
> fairy inquired, "What ails thee?"
> And the rich and handsome and well-beloved young man replied, "I
> would be happy, really happy, if only I had something to strive for."

Like the hero of this simple tale, we are all more impossible than   7
we acknowledge. We yearn for whatever we do not have and, when
allowed to do everything exactly as we wish, we end up painting ourselves
into corners. We make life difficult for ourselves and we make it difficult
for each other. . . .

One way or another, we are both the perpetrators and the victims   8
of this kind of maneuver. We create, for ourselves and others, intolerable
predicaments from which there is no escape. Life can be pleasant, we
all know that; but somehow or other we always manage to screw it up.
That, in short, is the vein of truth that genuine humor mines. What makes
it a liberating rather than a depressing discovery, however, is the particular manner in which it is unearthed. To our sense of humor, even
the brutal truth is curious, a source of amusement, because we are not
completely identified with it. We see our irrationality, our stupidity, our
immorality as facts of life, but not the ultimate facts, for infuriating as
we may be, we know that we are also lovable, and ridiculous as we may
behave, we know that we are also sensible.

When we operate out of our sense of humor, we train a widened   9
perspective on ourselves. We see ourselves and our lives from a certain
distance, and that distance makes all the difference in the world. . . .

If my description is apt, if the suggestion that genuine humor involves   **10**
both a widened perspective on ourselves and an appreciation of the ironies
on which our lives are built is to the point, the question that faces me
as a psychotherapist is How can I encourage it in my patients? . . .

Directly? No. I am convinced of that because, whenever I am feeling   **11**
troubled, my friends are apt to say, "Well, you're the big humor expert.
Why don't you laugh it off?" — a piece of advice that rarely pastes a
smile on my face. No; as with love or faith or courage, it avails little to
advise a patient to exercise his sense of humor. I might just as well write
out a prescription — "One teaspoonful of wit before every meal and at
bedtime" — for all the good it will do.

Nor does it do much good to try to make a patient laugh. It might   **12**
be possible, for a therapist whose wit was sharp enough, to ridicule or
chide his patients into seeing the ludicrous side of their complaints, but
I doubt that his efforts would be appreciated. More than likely, he would
receive a few wallops for his trouble, which might make the whole procedure more comical to the onlooker but which would hardly win him the
analyst-of-the-year award.[1]

The problem is, to say the least, perplexing. How does one encourage   **13**
an outlook which, to be genuine, must be spontaneous? It seems like a
contradiction in terms, and yet it is precisely such contradictions on which
humor thrives. From personal experience, I think it can be done, and I
even think I can indicate how. The process is analogous to growing plants
or flowers, in the sense that we can provide the conditions conducive to
their growth, though it would be folly to grab them by the stems and
try to yank them up.

The conditions conducive to the growth of genuine humor are those   **14**
I mentioned earlier. Flexibility: in this case, a willingness to examine
every side of every issue and every side of every side. Spontaneity: the
ability to leap instantaneously from one mood or mode of thought to
another. Unconventionality: freedom from the values of time, place, and
even profession. Shrewdness: the refusal to believe that anyone — least
of all one's self — is what he seems to be. Playfulness: the grasp of life
as a game, a tragicomic game which nobody wins but which does not
have to be won to be enjoyed. And humility: that elusive simpleness that
disappears whenever we are conscious of having attained it.

The point is that to encourage a humorous outlook in his patients   **15**

---

[1] Since writing this chapter, I have changed my mind on this score. I have become
so bold that I have tried, now and then, to "kid" a patient out of his or her desperation,
and the reactions have not all been negative. Once, for example, a woman I had been
seeing for several months threatened to commit suicide. She had made some messy and
abortive suicidal gestures in the past, so now, when she wailed that her life was so miserable
that she thought she might kill herself, I said, "Oh yeah. That's the great solution you
came up with before!" and, instead of telling me to go to hell, she laughed, saw her
foolishness and relinquished that particular gambit — at least for that particular day.

But it is a risky game to make fun of someone else's anguish, even with the best of
intentions. You can never be sure your humor won't be interpreted as derision. In fact,
you can be sure it will — unless, and this is the key, the patient unequivocally perceives
you as his or her ally. The safest course, I think, is to watch for any sign that the patient
himself has an inkling of the ridiculousness of his behavior or the irony of his predicament
and then jump in and reinforce it by agreeing with him and praising him for seeing it that
way.

the therapist must keep the dimension alive in himself. If he can perceive the irony in their predicaments and in his own as well, his perception will permeate his interviews and will, when his patients are supple enough to take it, enlarge their comprehension of themselves.

But there — I'm afraid we must confess — 's the rub. A glance at   16
any professional journal, a visit to any professional meeting, make it apparent that psychotherapists take themselves too seriously. We really believe — and the more renowned among us believe it the more — that the theories we propound and the techniques we apply are cogent, valid, and beneficial. Not only *do* we believe it; we *must* believe it to be effective. And yet, as long as the belief is maintained, a deep and genuine sense of humor cannot be achieved and therefore promoted. As long as we fail to contemplate the likelihood that our professional activities are useless, that psychotherapy of any sort is absurd in the larger scale of things, we remain bound to the very outlook from which we need to free our patients.

We could do worse than take a cue from a former patient of mine.   17
An attractive, intelligent young woman, she was suffering from obesity. She had tried every method of reducing but had had no success to speak of. One day, however, she composed the following paragraphs. They did not, let me hasten to add, enable her immediately to lose weight, but they did, I believe, mark the opening of a new perspective on her plight:

> I just got the most beautiful insight about how to solve a vexing social problem in what I might modestly term a completely original way. It is simply to make being obese against the law. My thinking on it is this. Many things in this world are exceedingly tempting, but society has coped by making them illegal. Other people's wives, property, possessions, little goodies like these have tempted malefactors through the ages. How to discourage them? Everything from social ostracism to capital punishment has been tried to more or less effect. In this light it is clear to me and to others of my ilk, or should I say bulk, that some motivation beyond self-disgust and the oy-veys of husband and family must become operational. You take your average chubby housewife who has caught a nice husband and is raising a family and coping with Life. She often eats as an outlet, less dangerous to everyone's well-being than, say, flirting with the Helm's man or sniffing glue with the high school dropout across the street. But now this can change. If you confront her with the prospect of being hauled into court on an obesity charge, sentenced by a judge and fined or imprisoned, I think you would be well on your way to a permanent solution of this disgraceful problem. But why should such drastic measures be applied to these unfortunates, you may be asking. Well, fat people take up too much of the earth's precious room and air, they crowd you on the bus and they crush you on the elevator, and for their own good they have to take the strain off their feet, their hearts, and their consciences.
>
> In case you're wondering, yes, this is a personal problem. I admit I'm desperate. I've tried everything, now I'm yelling for help. The government has stepped in everywhere else, so why not here? Please. Somebody! Stop me before I eat again. Where is the relentless arm of the law? Where are the measures for girth control? All interested senators and congressmen please contact me. I can usually be found in the back booth of Kantor's Delicatessen. Just look for a large, guilty-looking woman eating an Eddie Cantor Special (turkey, ham, roast beef, and chopped liver on rye).

When a person begins to see his own predicament in a humorous light, he is on his way to overcoming it. Not necessarily to eliminating it — our central dilemmas, we must know by now, can never be eliminated anyway — but to overcoming its debilitating influence on his well-being.

Because it raises us above our usual level of comprehension and allows us to accept what would ordinarily be unacceptable, spontaneous, genuine humor is a coping mechanism of the very highest caliber. It should, therefore, be one of the psychotherapist's goals to further its development. He is, in fact, in an excellent position to do so, since his own calling is nothing if not ridiculous. Every day of his life, patients come to him expecting what he cannot give but must give, so that, in the process, they can discover in themselves what they mistakenly, but necessarily, had hoped he possessed.

In the framework of such an admittedly ironic outlook, I have tried to indicate how humor can be cultivated in psychotherapy. My suggestions themselves may seem a joke. Perhaps they are. But if so — in all seriousness — I don't think that would be so bad.

Questions for Argument

1. Develop the argument that Henri Bergson's theory does or does not apply to contemporary forms of comedy.
2. Does what Gershon Legman says about dirty jokes hold for most other forms of humor too? Develop an argument pro or con, using varied examples.
3. Are Bergson's and Legman's theories of the comic, despite some differences of emphasis, fundamentally in agreement? Or are their differences fundamental?
4. Using Emmons's piece on the sick joke, Legman's on the dirty joke, and any other articles that seem helpful, develop the argument that there's really very little that's lighthearted or pleasing about comedy.
5. What, in your opinion, differentiates other forms of humor from jokes? Make your case in a well-developed argument using numerous examples.
6. Compare the pattern discerned cross-culturally by Thomas R. Shultz — incongruity and resolution — with the pattern seen by either Bergson, Legman or Koestler. Do you find Shultz's explanation adequate for how comedy works?
7. Do cartoons have the same features as jokes, or are they a very different form of comedy? Develop an argument that defends your opinion.
8. Develop the argument that what Mary Douglas says about "the joker" in various societies applies to the comedian in ours. Does it apply to all comedians equally, or do some seem to fit this role better than others?
9. Mary Douglas makes the claim that some social situations are themselves structured like jokes and that such situations seem to create jokes almost

automatically. Can this be true? After coming up with an assortment of examples to adequately test her idea, argue for or against it.

10. Do you see a relationship between comedy and racism? If so, develop an argument expressing your point of view.

11. Argue, with examples, that ethnic jokes serve different psychological and social functions depending on whether they're told by and for members of a particular ethnic group or by others outside that ethnic group.

12. Lawrence Levine, José Limón, Annie Dillard, and Arthur Koestler all stress, in one way or another, the performative or creative aspects of joke telling. Synthesizing their observations and incorporating your own, argue that the art of joke telling involves more than the act of telling jokes.

13. "All laughter is aggression. Comedy is cruel." Support or dispute this claim with a well-developed argument.

14. Compare the anthropological analyses of Douglas and Shultz. What makes them seem so different? Argue for your preference.

15. Using Legman as a representative Freudian, argue whether psychologist Harvey Mindess seems to share a Freudian view of humor.

16. Is a comic perspective capable of transforming something we ordinarily don't think of as comic? Try developing a comic interpretation of one of the following and evaluate your results: one of the creation stories (pp. 119–123), one of the schizophrenia case studies (pp. 567–587), the short story "Young Goodman Brown" (pp. 494–504).

17. In "Hecklers and Horrors" (a chapter of the book *Comic Lives: Inside the World of Stand-up Comedy*), Betsy Borns discusses the alternating invincibility and vulnerability of the stand-up comic — that is, the fact that the comic has power over the audience at the same time that he or she is vulnerable to indifference or even abuse. Using supporting readings in this chapter, argue that comedy can best be defined and understood as an alternation between invincibility and vulnerability.

18. *Research Project.* Using any of the material in this section to help you, classify situation comedies on television and then proceed to analyze one episode. Are such shows simply vehicles for jokes or something more?

Acknowledgments (continued from p. iv)

Graham T. Allison. "Conceptual Models and the Cuban Missile Crisis." From *The American Political Science Review,* vol. 63, no. 3 (September, 1969). Copyright 1969. Reprinted by permission of The American Political Science Association.

American Psychiatric Association. *Diagnostic and Statistical Manual of Mental Disorders,* 3rd edition, revised. Washington, D.C.: American Psychiatric Association, 1987.

Nancy C. Andreasen, M.D., Ph.D. "Structural Brain Abnormalities in Schizophrenia." Reprinted with permission of Macmillan Publishing Company, a division of Macmillan, Inc., from Nancy C. Andreasen, M.D., Ph.D., "Structural Brain Abnormalities in Schizophrenia" in *New Perspectives in Schizophrenia* by Morton Menuck and Mary Seeman.

Anonymous. A Bantu myth. From *Bantu Myths and Other Tales,* translated by Jan Knappert. Copyright 1977. Reprinted by permission of E. J. Brill, Leiden, the Netherlands.

Anonymous. A tale of the White River Sioux. From *American Indian Myths and Legends,* edited by Richard Erdoes and Alfonso Ortiz. Copyright 1984. Reprinted by permission of Pantheon Books, a division of Random House, Inc.

Anonymous. Reprinted by permission of New York University Press from *Psychotherapy of Schizophrenia* by Gaetano Benedetti. Copyright © 1987 by New York University.

Aristophanes. Extract taken from *The Birds,* translated by Gilbert Murray, reproduced by kind permission of Unwin Hyman Ltd. Copyright 1950 Allen & Unwin, London.

Isaac Asimov. From *The Human Brain,* copyright © by Isaac Asimov. Reprinted by permission of Houghton Mifflin Company.

Rita L. Atkinson, Richard C. Atkinson, and Ernest R. Hilgard. "Alcoholism and Drug Dependence." Excerpt, pages 484–86, from "Alcoholism and Drug Dependence" in *Introduction to Psychology,* 8th edition, by Rita L. Atkinson, Richard C. Atkinson, and Ernest R. Hilgard, copyright © 1983 by Harcourt Brace Jovanovich, Inc., reprinted by permission of the publisher.

Ben H. Bagdikian. From *Caged: Eight Prisoners and Their Keepers.* Copyright © 1976 by Ben H. Bagdikian. Reprinted by permission of Harper & Row, Publishers, Inc.

Walter H. Beale. From *A Pragmatic Theory of Rhetoric.* Copyright 1987. Reprinted by permission of Southern Illinois University Press, Carbondale.

Ann Beattie. "Hale Hardy and the Amazing Animal Woman." From *Distortions* by Ann Beattie. Copyright © 1976 by Ann Beattie. Reprinted by permission of International Creative Management.

William O. Beers. "Contributions of American Industry to the Improvement of American Nutrition." Paper delivered at the Food and Nutrition Conference sponsored by the New York Academy of Sciences in Philadelphia, PA, December 1–3, 1976. Reprinted by permission of William O. Beers.

Yardley Beers. From *Introduction to the Theory of Errors* (Addison-Wesley). Copyright 1953. Reprinted by permission of Yardley Beers.

R. N. Bellah et al. From *Habits of the Heart: Individualism and Commitment in American Life.* Copyright © 1985 by the Regents of the University of California. Reprinted by permission of the University of California Press.

Thomas Bentz. Reprinted by permission of the publisher from *New Immigrants: Portraits in Passage* by Thomas Bentz. Copyright © 1981, the Pilgrim Press, New York.

Henri Bergson. "Laughter." From *Comedy,* edited by Wylie Sypher. © 1956 by Wylie Sypher. Reprinted by permission of Doubleday, a division of Bantam, Doubleday, Dell Publishing Group, Inc.

Paul Berliner. From *Soul of Mbira: Music and Traditions of the Shona People of Zimbabwe,* page xiii, to be used in *Critical Strategies for Academic Writing* (Bedford Books). © 1978 the Regents of the University of California.

J. David Bolter. From *Turing's Man: Western Culture in the Computer Age* by J. David Bolter. © 1984 the University of North Carolina Press. Reprinted by permission.

Malcolm B. Bowers, Jr. "Psychosis Associated with Heterosexual Rejection." From *Retreat from Sanity: The Structure of Emerging Psychosis.* Copyright 1974. Reprinted by permission of Human Sciences Press.

André Breton. "Manifesto of Surrealism" (1924). From *Manifestoes of Surrealism,* translated by Richard Seaver and Helen R. Lane. Copyright 1969.

Pamela J. Brink and Judith M. Saunders, "Cultural Shock: Theoretical and Applied." From Pamela J. Brink, ed., *Transcultural Nursing: A Book of Readings* (Copyright © 1976), reissued with changes 1990 by Waveland Press, Inc., Prospect Heights, Illinois, pp. 129, 131. Reprinted with permission.

William Broad and Nicholas Wade. From *Betrayers of the Truth.* Copyright © 1982 by William Broad and Nicholas Wade. Reprinted by permission of Simon & Schuster, Inc.

Jane Brody. Reprinted from *Jane Brody's Nutrition Book* by Jane Brody, by permission of W. W. Norton & Company, Inc. Copyright © 1981 by Jane E. Brody.

Jacob Bronowski. From *The Ascent of Man* by Jacob Bronowski. Copyright © 1973 by J. Bronowski. By permission of Little, Brown and Company. Also reprinted by permission of BBC Books, London.

Judith K. Brown. "Iroquois Women: An Ethnohistoric Note." From *Toward an Anthropology of Women,* edited by Rayna R. Reiter (Monthly Review Press). Copyright © 1975 by Rayna R. Reiter. Reprinted by permission of Monthly Review Foundation.

Rita Mae Brown. "The Christmas Pageant." From *Rubyfruit Jungle* by Rita Mae Brown. Copyright 1988. Reprinted by permission of Bantam Books, a division of Bantam, Doubleday, Dell Publishing Group, Inc.

Jeremy Campbell. From *Grammatical Man.* Copyright 1982. Reprinted by permission of Simon & Schuster, Inc.

Albert Camus. From *The Stranger,* translated by Stuart Gilbert. Copyright © 1988 by Alfred A. Knopf, Inc. Reprinted by permission of Alfred A. Knopf, Inc.

Raymond Carver. "Preservation." From *Cathedral* by Raymond Carver. Copyright © 1981, 1982, 1983 by Raymond Carver. Reprinted by permission of Random House, Inc.

Alston Chase. "How to Save Our National Parks." From *Atlantic* (July 1987). Copyright 1987. Reprinted by permission of Alston Chase.

Patricia Cline Cohen. From *A Calculating People: The Spread of Numeracy in Early America.* © 1982 the University of Chicago. All rights reserved. Reprinted by permission of the University of Chicago Press.

Michael Colacurcio. From *The Province of Piety.* Copyright 1984. Reprinted by permission of Harvard University Press.

Aaron Copland. "Listening to Music." From *What to Listen for in Music* by Aaron Copland. Copyright 1957. Reprinted by permission of McGraw-Hill Publishing Company.

Fred M. Cox et al. Reproduced by permission of the publisher, F. E. Peacock Publishers, Inc., Itasca, Illinois. From Cox et al., Strategies of Community Organization, copyright 1979, p. 3.

Frederick C. Crews. From *The Sins of the Fathers: Hawthorne's Psychological Themes* by Frederick C. Crews. Copyright © 1966 by Frederick C. Crews. Reprinted by permission of Oxford University Press, Inc.

F. H. C. Crick. "Thinking about the Brain." From *Scientific American* (September 1979). Copyright 1979. Reprinted by permission of Scientific American.

Constance Cronin. "Illusion and Reality in Sicily." From *Sexual Stratification,* edited by Alice Schlegal (Columbia University Press). Copyright 1977. Reprinted by permission of Alice Schlegal.

Helena Curtis. From *Biology.* Copyright 1983. Reprinted by permission of Worth Publishers, Inc.

Robert Dallek. From *The American Style of Foreign Policy.* Copyright 1983. Reprinted by permission of Random House, Inc.

Simone de Beauvoir. From *The Second Sex,* translated by H. M. Parshley. Copyright 1953. Reprinted by permission of Random House, Inc.

Louise DeSalvo. From *Nathaniel Hawthorne and Feminists.* Copyright 1987. Reprinted by permission of Harvester Press, Brighton, England.

Emily Dickinson. "I started Early — Took my Dog —" Reprinted by permission of the publishers and the Trustees of Amherst College from *The Poems of Emily Dickinson,* Thomas H. Johnson, ed. Cambridge, Mass.: The Belknap Press of Harvard University Press. Copyright 1951, © 1955, 1979, 1983 by the President and Fellows of Harvard College.

Annie Dillard. "The Leg in the Christmas Stocking: What We Learned from Jokes." From the *New York Times Book Review* (December 7, 1986). Reprinted by permission of the author and her agent, Blanche C. Gregory, Inc. Copyright © 1986 by Annie Dillard.

John Dollard et al. From *Frustration and Aggression.* Copyright 1939. Reprinted by permission of Yale University Press.

Agnes McNeill Donahue. From *Hawthorne: Calvin's Ironic Stepchild.* Copyright 1985. Reprinted by permission of Kent State University Press.

Charles Doria and Harris Lenowitz. Excerpts from *Origins: Creation Text from the Ancient Mediterranean* by Charles Doria and Harris Lenowitz. Copyright © 1975, 1976 by Charles

Doria and Harris Lenowitz. Reprinted by permission of Doubleday, a division of Bantam, Doubleday, Dell Publishing Group, Inc.

Mary Douglas. "Jokes." From *Implicit Meanings* by Mary Douglas. Copyright 1975. Reprinted by permission of Routledge, International Thomson Publishing.

Patricia Draper. "Kung Women: Contrasts in Sexual Egalitarianism in Foraging and Sedentary Contexts." From *Toward an Anthropology of Women,* edited by Rayna R. Reiter (Monthly Review Press). Copyright © 1975 by Rayna R. Reiter. Reprinted by permission of Monthly Review Foundation.

Emile Durkheim. Reprinted with permission of the Free Press, a division of Macmillan, Inc., from Emile Durkheim, *The Rules of Sociological Method,* translated by Sarah A. Solovay and John H. Mueller. Edited by George E. G. Catlin. Copyright 1938 by George E. G. Catlin, renewed 1966.

Steve Emmons. " 'Sick' Jokes: Coping with the Horror." From the *Los Angeles Times* (May 30, 1986). Copyright, 1986, Los Angeles Times. Reprinted by permission.

Louise Erdrich. "Scales." From *That's What She Said,* edited by Rayna Green. Copyright 1984 by Indiana University Press. Reprinted by permission of Indiana University Press.

Kai T. Erikson. Reprinted with permission of Macmillan Publishing Company from *Wayward Puritans: A Study in the Sociology of Deviance.* Copyright © 1968 by Macmillan Publishing Company.

E. E. Evans-Pritchard. From *The Position of Women in Primitive Societies and Other Essays in Social Anthropology.* Copyright 1965. Reprinted by permission of Faber and Faber Limited, Publishers, London.

David K. Fieldhouse. "The Economic Exploitation of Africa: Some British and French Comparisons." From *France and Britain in Africa,* edited by Prosser Gifford and William Roger Louis. Copyright 1971. Reprinted by permission of Yale University Press.

Richard Harter Fogle. From *Hawthorne's Fiction: The Light and the Dark,* by Richard Harter Fogle. Copyright © 1964 by the University of Oklahoma Press.

Michel Foucault. From *Discipline and Punishment: The Birth of the Prison* by Michel Foucault, translated by Alan Sheridan. Copyright © 1977 by Alan Sheridan. Reprinted by permission of Pantheon Books, a division of Random House, Inc.

John Fowles. From *The Collector* by John Fowles Ltd. Copyright © 1963 by John Fowles Ltd. By permission of Little, Brown and Company.

Benjamin Franklin. *Autobiography.* From *Autobiography and Other Pieces,* edited by Dennis Welland. Copyright 1970. Reprinted by permission of Oxford University Press, Oxford.

Milton Friedman and Rose D. Friedman. Excerpt from the Introduction to *Free to Choose,* copyright © 1980 by Milton Friedman and Rose D. Friedman, reprinted by permission of Harcourt Brace Jovanovich, Inc.

Frank J. Frost. From *Greek Society,* 2nd edition. Copyright 1980. Reprinted by permission of D. C. Heath & Co.

Ann Ruggles Gere. From *Writing Groups: History, Theory, and Implications.* Copyright 1987. Reprinted by permission of Southern Illinois University Press, Carbondale.

Ellen Gilchrist. "The Lower Garden District Free Gravity Mule Blight or Rhoda, a Fable." From *Victory over Japan* by Ellen Gilchrist. Copyright 1984.

Nikki Giovanni. "The Women's Alliance." Excerpt from "The Women's Alliance," p. 85 of *Sacred Cows . . . and Other Edibles* by Nikki Giovanni. Copyright © 1988 by Nikki Giovanni. Reprinted by permission of William Morrow and Company, Inc.

Erving Goffman. Excerpts from *The Presentation of Self in Everyday Life* by Erving Goffman. Copyright © 1959 by Erving Goffman. Reprinted by permission of Doubleday, a division of Bantam, Doubleday, Dell Publishing Group, Inc.

Patrick Goldstein. "Violence Sneaks into Punk Scene." From the *Los Angeles Times* (June 29, 1980). Copyright 1980. Reprinted by permission of Patrick Goldstein.

David M. Gordon. "Class and the Economics of Crime." From *Review of Radical Political Economics* 3:3 (Summer 1971). Copyright, *Review of Radical Political Economics.* Reprinted by permission of the Union for Radical Political Economics.

André Gorz. From *Ecology as Politics* by André Gorz, translated by Patsy Vigderman and Jonathan Cloud (Boston: South End Press, 1980).

Stephen Jay Gould. Reprinted from *The Panda's Thumb: More Reflections in Natural History,* by Stephen Jay Gould, by permission of W. W. Norton & Company, Inc. Copyright © 1980 by Stephen Jay Gould.

Harvey J. Graff. From *The Literacy Myth: Literacy and Social Structure in the Nineteenth Century City.* Copyright 1979. Reprinted by permission of Academic Press, Inc., Orlando, FL, and the author.

The Brothers Grimm. "The Singing Bone." From *Complete Brothers Grimm Fairy Tales,* edited by Lily Owens. Copyright © 1981 by Crown Publishers, Inc. Reprinted by permission of the publisher.

Thom Gunn. "Flying above California." From *My Sad Captains* by Thom Gunn. Copyright © 1961, 1971, 1973 by Thom Gunn. Reprinted by permission of Farrar, Straus and Giroux, Inc. Also reprinted by permission of Faber and Faber Ltd. from *My Sad Captains* by Thom Gunn.

Sally Hacker with Clara Elcorobairutia. "Women Workers in the Mondragon System of Industrial Cooperatives." From *Gender and Society* 1:4, pp. 358–79. Copyright 1987 by Sage Publications, Inc. Reprinted by permission of Sage Publications, Inc.

Jay Haley. From *Leaving Home: The Therapy of Disturbed Young People.* © 1980. Reprinted by permission of McGraw-Hill Publishing Company.

John Hall and Roger Baker. "Token Economics and Schizophrenia: A Review." From *Contemporary Issues in Schizophrenia,* edited by Alan Kerr and Philip Snaith (London: Gaskell). Copyright 1986. Reprinted by permission of The Royal College of Psychiatrists.

Martin A. Haskell and Lewis Yablonsky. Excerpt from *Criminology: Crime and Criminality,* 3rd edition, by Martin A. Haskell and Lewis Yablonsky. Copyright © 1983 Harper & Row, Publishers, Inc. Reprinted by permission of Harper & Row, Publishers, Inc.

Nathaniel Hawthorne. Material from Nathaniel Hawthorne, *The Scarlet Letter,* is reprinted by permission. © 1962 by the Ohio State University Press. All rights reserved.

L. S. Hearnshaw. Reprinted from L. S. Hearnshaw, *Cyril Burt, Psychologist.* Copyright © 1979 L. S. Hearnshaw. Used by permission of the publisher, Cornell University Press.

Shirley Brice Heath. From *Ways with Words.* Copyright 1983. Reprinted by permission of Cambridge University Press.

Robert L. Heilbroner. Reprinted from *Beyond Boom and Crash* by Robert L. Heilbroner, by permission of W. W. Norton & Company, Inc. Copyright © 1978 by W. W. Norton & Company, Inc.

Joseph Heller. From *Catch-22.* Copyright © 1955, 1961, 1989 by Joseph Heller. Reprinted by permission of Simon & Schuster, Inc.

Judith Herman and Lisa Hirschman. "Father-Daughter Incest." From *The Signs Reader: Women, Gender, and Scholarship,* edited by Elizabeth Abel and Emily K. Abel. Copyright © 1983 by the University of Chicago. All rights reserved. Reprinted by permission of the University of Chicago Press.

Hesiod. "Theogony." From *Hesiod and Theognis,* translated by Dorothea Wender (London: Penguin Classics, 1973), p. 27. Translation copyright © Dorothea Wender, 1973. Reproduced by permission of Penguin Books Ltd.

Ernest R. Hilgard, Richard C. Atkinson, and Rita L. Atkinson. Excerpt, pages 225–26, from *Introduction to Psychology,* 5th edition, by Ernest R. Hilgard, Richard C. Atkinson, and Rita L. Atkinson, copyright © 1971 by Harcourt Brace Jovanovich, Inc., reprinted by permission of the publisher.

Gladwin Hill. "Where Schizophrenia Comes From." From *California Magazine* (February, 1985). Reprinted by permission of Gladwin Hill.

Linda Hogan. "Death, Etc." Reprinted from *Seeing through the Sun* by Linda Hogan (Amherst: University of Massachusetts Press, 1985), copyright © 1985 by Linda Hogan.

August B. Hollingshead and Frederick C. Redlich. From *Social Class and Mental Illness.* Copyright © 1958. Reprinted by permission of John Wiley & Sons, Inc.

Garret Kaoru Hongo. "And Your Soul Shall Dance." Copyright © 1982 by Garret Kaoru Hongo. Reprinted from *Yellow Light* by permission of Wesleyan University Press.

J. Edgar Hoover. "The Faith of Free Men." From *Vital Speeches of the Day* 23:3 (November 15, 1965). Reprinted by permission of Vital Speeches of the Day.

Ted Howard and Jeremy Rifkin. From *Who Should Play God?* by Ted Howard and Jeremy Rifkin. Copyright © 1977 by Center for Urban Education. Reprinted by permission of Dell Publishing, a division of Bantam, Doubleday, Dell Publishing Group, Inc.

Karl Jaspers. From *Man in the Modern Age,* translated by Eden and Cedar Paul. Copyright 1959. Reprinted by permission of Routledge, London.

J. Joel Jeffries and Judy Levene. "All about Schizophrenia." Reprinted with permission of Macmillan

Publishing Company, a division of Macmillan, Inc., from J. Joel Jeffries and Judy Levene, "All about Schizophrenia" in *New Perspectives in Schizophrenia* by Morton Menuck and Mary Seeman.

Horace Freeland Judson. From *The Eighth Day of Creation.* Copyright © 1979 by Horace Freeland Judson. Reprinted by permission of Simon & Schuster, Inc.

C. G. Jung. From *Memories, Dreams, Reflections,* translated by Richard Winston and Clara Winston, edited by Aniela Jaffe. Copyright 1963. Reprinted by permission of Pantheon Books, a Division of Random House, Inc.

Herman Kahn. From *The Coming Boom.* Copyright © 1982 by the Hudson Institute, Inc. Reprinted by permission of Simon & Schuster, Inc.

Alfred Kazin. "The Jew as Modern American Writer." From *The Commentary Reader,* edited by Norman Podhoretz. Copyright © 1966 by American Jewish Committee. Reprinted by permission of Alfred Kazin.

Rhoda Kellogg. *Analyzing Children's Art.* © 1969, 1970 by Rhoda Kellogg.

Seymour Kety. "Heredity and Environment." *Schizophrenia: Science and Practice,* ed. John C. Shershow, pp. 47–65. Copyright © 1978 by the President and Fellows of Harvard College. Adapted by permission of Harvard University Press.

Maxine Hong Kingston. From *The Woman Warrior: Memoirs of a Girlhood among Ghosts* by Maxine Hong Kingston. Copyright © 1975, 1976 by Maxine Hong Kingston. Reprinted by permission of Alfred A. Knopf, Inc.

Arthur Koestler. From *The Act of Creation* (London: Hutchinson). Copyright 1964. Reprinted by permission of the Peters Fraser & Dunlop Group Ltd.

Conrad Phillip Kottak. From *Cultural Anthropology,* 3rd edition. Copyright 1982. Reprinted by permission of McGraw-Hill Publishing Company.

R. D. Laing. "The Politics of Experience" from *The Politics of Experience and the Bird of Paradise* by R. D. Laing (Penguin Books, 1967). Copyright © 1967 by R. D. Laing.

R. D. Laing and A. Esterson. From *Sanity, Madness, and the Family.* Copyright 1972. Reprinted by permission of Tavistock Publications, Northway, England.

Deodat Lawson. "A Brief and True Narrative." Reprinted with permission of Charles Scribner's Sons, an imprint of Macmillan Publishing Company from *Narratives of the Witchcraft Cases, 1648–1706,* George Lincoln Burr, editor. Copyright 1914 by Charles Scribner's Sons, renewed 1942.

Eleanor Burke Leacock. From the Introduction to *Origins of the Family, Private Property, and the State* by Friedrich Engels. © 1972 by International Publishers, N.Y. Reprinted by permission of International Publishers.

Li-Young Lee. "Persimmons." Copyright © 1986 by Li-Young Lee and reprinted from *Rose* by Li-Young Lee with the permission of BOA Editions, Ltd., 92 Park Avenue, Brockport, NY 14420.

G. Gershon Legman. From *No Laughing Matter.* Copyright 1968. Reprinted by permission of Indiana University Press.

Heinz E. Lehmann, M.D. "Current Perspectives on the Biology of Schizophrenia." Reprinted with permission of Macmillan Publishing Company, a division of Macmillan, Inc., from Nancy C. Andreasen, M.D., Ph.D., "Structural Brain Abnormalities in Schizophrenia" in *New Perspectives in Schizophrenia,* edited by Morton Menuck and Mary Seeman. (Macmillan, New York, 1985.)

Gloria Rakita Leon. From Gloria Rakita Leon, *Case Histories of Deviant Behavior,* 3rd edition. Copyright © 1984 by Allyn and Bacon. Reprinted with permission.

Harry Levin. From *The Power of Blackness.* Copyright 1958 by Harry Levin. Reprinted by permission of Alfred A. Knopf, Inc.

Lawrence W. Levine. From *Black Culture and Black Consciousness: Afro-American Folk Thought From Slavery to Freedom,* by Lawrence W. Levine. Copyright © 1977 by Oxford University Press, Inc. Reprinted by permission.

Leo B. Levy. "The Problem of Faith in Young Goodman Brown." From *Journal of English and Germanic Philology* 74:3, pp. 375–87. © 1975 by the Board of Trustees of the University of Illinois. Reprinted by permission of the University of Illinois Press.

R. C. Lewontin, Steven Rose, and Leon J. Kamin. From *Not in Our Genes: Pathology, Ideology, and Human Nature.* Copyright © 1984 by R. C. Lewontin, Steven Rose, and Leon J. Kamin. Reprinted by permission of Pantheon Books, a division of Random House, Inc.

Theodore Lidz. From *The Origin and Treatment of Schizophrenic Disorders* by Theodore Lidz.

Copyright © 1973 by Theodore Lidz. Reprinted by permission of Basic Books, Inc., Publishers.

Sara Lawrence Lightfoot. From *The Good High School: Portraits of Character and Culture* by Sara Lawrence Lightfoot. Copyright © 1983 by Basic Books, Inc. Reprinted by permission of Basic Books, Inc., Publishers.

José E. Limón. "History, Chicano Joking, and the Varieties of Higher Education." From *Journal of the Folklore Institute* 19:2–3 (Bloomington: Folklore Institute of the University of Indiana). Copyright 1982. Reprinted by permission of José E. Limón.

K. Lincoln with A. L. Slagle. From *The Good Red Road: Passages into Native America.* Copyright © 1987 by Kenneth Lincoln and Al Logan Slagle. Reprinted by permission of Harper & Row, Publishers, Inc.

John C. Livingston. From *Fair Game? Inequality and Affirmative Action* (San Francisco: Freeman). Copyright 1979. Reprinted by permission of Ethel M. Livingston.

Konrad Lorenz. Excerpt, pages 252–53, from *On Aggression* by Konrad Lorenz, copyright © 1963 by Dr. G. Borotha-Schoeler Verlag, Wien; English translation copyright © 1966 by Konrad Lorenz; copyright © 1983 by Deutscher Taschenbuch Verlag GmbH & Co. KG, München, reprinted by permission of Harcourt Brace Jovanovich, Inc.

McGraw-Hill Dictionary of Scientific and Technical Terms, 3rd edition. Edited by Sybil P. Parker. Copyright © 1984 by McGraw-Hill.

Reginald McKnight. "Uncle Moustapha's Eclipse." Reprinted from *Moustapha's Eclipse,* by Reginald McKnight, by permission of the University of Pittsburgh Press. © 1988 by Reginald McKnight.

Larry McMurtry. Excerpts from *The Last Picture Show* by Larry McMurtry. Copyright © 1966 by Larry McMurtry. Reprinted by permission of Doubleday, a division of Bantam, Doubleday, Dell Publishing Group, Inc.

Cary McWilliams. *Southern California: An Island on the Land* (Salt Lake City: Gibbs Smith, Publisher/Peregrine Smith Books, 1983), p. 3. Reprinted by permission of the publisher.

Ed Magnuson. "The Curse of Violent Crime." From *Time* (March 23, 1981). Copyright 1981 Time Inc. Reprinted by permission.

Bernard Malamud. "Idiots First." Excerpt from "Idiots First" from *Idiots First* by Bernard Malamud. Copyright © 1961, 1963 by Bernard Malamud. Reprinted by permission of Farrar, Straus and Giroux, Inc.

Jane Margold and Donna Bellorado. "Matrilinear Heritage: A Look at the Power of Contemporary Micronesian Women." From *Women in Asia and the Pacific,* edited by Madeleine J. Goodman (University of Hawaii Press). Copyright 1985. Reprinted by permission of Madeleine J. Goodman.

William F. Marsh and Jeff Dozier. From *An Introduction to Physical Geography* (Addison-Wesley). Copyright © 1981. Reprinted by permission of John Wiley & Sons, Inc.

Paule Marshall. "Brooklyn" and "To Da-Duh, in Memoriam." From *Reena and Other Stories* by Paule Marshall. Copyright 1983 by the Feminist Press. Reprinted by permission of the Feminist Press and Paule Marshall. All rights reserved.

Jean Mayer. From *U.S. Nutrition Policies in the Seventies.* Copyright 1973. Reprinted by permission of W. H. Freeman and Company.

Margaret Mead. Excerpt from *Male and Female* by Margaret Mead. Copyright © renewed 1976, 1977 by Margaret Mead. By permission of William Morrow and Company, Inc.

James R. Mellow. Excerpts from *Nathaniel Hawthorne in His Times* by James R. Mellow. Copyright © 1980 by James R. Mellow. Reprinted by permission of Houghton Mifflin Company.

John Chester Miller. Excerpt from *Alexander Hamilton: Portrait in Paradox* by John C. Miller. Copyright © 1959 by John C. Miller. Reprinted by permission of Harper & Row, Publishers, Inc. Excerpt from *The Wolf by the Ears: Thomas Jefferson and Slavery* by John Chester Miller. Copyright © 1977 by the Free Press. Reprinted with permission of the Free Press, a division of Macmillan, Inc.

Paul W. Miller. "Hawthorne's 'Young Goodman Brown': Cynicism or Meliorism?" Reprinted from *Nineteenth Century Fiction* 14:2 (September 1959): 264. © 1959 by the Regents of the University of California. Reprinted by permission of the University of California Press.

Marvin Minsky. From *Society of Mind.* Copyright 1986. Reprinted by permission of Simon & Schuster, Inc.

Joan Moore. Excerpt from *Homeboys: Gangs, Drugs, and Prison in the Barrios of Los Angeles* by Joan Moore. Copyright © 1978. Reprinted by permission of Temple University Press.

Edmund S. Morgan. From *The Birth of the Republic, 1776–83,* revised edition. Copyright © 1956, 1977 by the University of Chicago. All rights reserved. Published 1956. Revised edition 1977. Reprinted by permission of the University of Chicago Press and Edmund S. Morgan.

Vladimir Nabokov. From *Ada* by Vladimir Nabokov. Copyright © 1969 by Article 3C Trust under will of Vladimir Nabokov. Reprinted by permission of Random House, Inc. and the Estate of Vladimir Nabokov.

Maria Nagy. "Interviews by Maria Nagy." From *The Meaning of Death,* edited by Herman Feifel. Reprinted by permission of McGraw-Hill Publishing Company.

Gloria Naylor. From *The Women of Brewster Place* by Gloria Nagy. Copyright © 1980, 1982 by Gloria Naylor. Reprinted by permission of Viking Penguin, a division of Penguin Books USA, Inc.

Lea Newman. From *A Reader's Guide to the Short Stories of Nathaniel Hawthorne.* Copyright 1979 and reprinted with the permission of G. K. Hall & Co., Boston.

Kwame Nkrumah. From *Neo-colonialism: The Last Stage of Imperialism.* Copyright 1965. Reprinted by permission of International Publishers.

Lewis Nordan. "Sugar Among the Freaks." From *Welcome to the Arrowcatcher Fair.* Copyright © 1983 by Lewis Nordan. Reprinted by permission of Louisiana State University Press.

Douglass C. North and Roger L. Miller. Excerpt from *The Economics of Public Issues,* 6th edition, by Douglass C. North and Roger L. Miller. Copyright © 1983 by Harper & Row, Publishers, Inc. Reprinted by permission of the publisher.

C. P. Oberndorf. "The Psychoanalytic Insight of Nathaniel Hawthorne." From *The Psychoanalytic Review* (October 1942). Copyright 1942. Reprinted by permission of *The Psychoanalytic Review.*

Sherry B. Ortner. "Is Female to Male as Nature Is to Culture?" From *Women, Culture, and Society,* edited by Michelle Zimbalist Rosaldo and Louise Lamphere (Stanford: Stanford University Press, 1974).

David Owen. From *None of the Above* by David Owen. Copyright © 1985 by David Owen. Reprinted by permission of Houghton Mifflin Company.

Oxford English Dictionary, selections. Reprinted from the *Oxford English Dictionary,* 2nd edition, 1989, by permission of Oxford University Press, London.

Grace Paley. "Living." Excerpt from "Living" from *Enormous Changes at the Last Minute* by Grace Paley. Copyright © 1965, 1974 by Grace Paley. Reprinted by permission of Farrar, Straus and Giroux, Inc.

Talcott Parsons. "Social Systems." Reprinted with permission of the Free Press, a division of Macmillan, Inc. From *Structure and Process in Modern Societies* by Talcott Parsons.

Linda Perrin. "A Brief History of U.S. Immigration Laws." From *Coming to America: Immigrants from Southern Europe* by Gladys Nadler Rips. Copyright © 1981 by Visual Education Corporation. Reprinted by permission of Visual Education Corporation.

Opal Lee Popkes. "Zuma Chowt's Cave." From "Zuma Chowt's Cave" by Opal Lee Popkes, in *The Man to Send Rain Clouds,* edited by Kenneth Rosen. Copyright 1985 by Kenneth Rosen. Reprinted by permission of Viking Penguin, a division of Penguin Books USA, Inc.

James Purdy. *Malcolm.* From *Malcolm and Color of Darkness* (Garden City, NY: Doubleday, 1974). Copyright 1974. Reprinted by permission of William Morris Agency.

Thomas Pynchon. From *Gravity's Rainbow* by Thomas Pynchon. Copyright © 1973 by Thomas Pynchon. Reprinted by permission of Viking Penguin, a division of Penguin Books USA, Inc.

David Randolph. "Five Basic Elements of Music." From *This Is Music: A Guide to the Pleasures of Listening* (New York: McGraw-Hill, 1964). Reprinted by permission of David Randolph.

Random House College Dictionary definition of *model.* Reprinted by permission from *The Random House College Dictionary,* revised edition. Copyright © 1988 by Random House, Inc.

Robert Redfield. From *The Little Community.* All rights reserved. Published 1955. Reprinted by permission of the University of Chicago Press.

Ishmael Reed. From *Yellow Back Radio Broke Down* by Ishmael Reed. Copyright © 1969 Ishmael Reed. Reprinted with permission of Atheneum Publishers, an imprint of Macmillan Publishing Co.

David Reisman. From *The Lonely Crowd.* Copyright 1950. Reprinted by permission of Yale University Press.

Adrienne Rich, "Diving into the Wreck" is reprinted from *The Fact of a Doorframe: Poems Selected and New, 1950–1984* by Adrienne Rich, by permission of W. W. Norton & Company, Inc. Copyright © 1984 by Adrienne Rich. Copyright © 1975, 1978 by W. W. Norton & Company, Inc. Copyright © 1981 by Adrienne Rich.

Richard C. Richardson, Jr., Elizabeth C. Fisk, and Morris A. Okun. From *Literacy in the Open-access College.* Copyright 1983. Reprinted by permission of Jossey-Bass, Inc., Publishers.

Thomas P. Rohlen. *Japan's High Schools,* pages 154–155, to be used in *Critical Strategies for Academic Writing* (Bedford Books). © 1983 the Regents of the University of California.

Mike Rose. From *Writer's Block: The Cognitive Dimension,* by Mike Rose, © 1983. Reprinted by permission of Southern Illinois University Press.

Mike Rose. From *Writing Around Rules* (Little, Brown). Copyright 1985. Reprinted by permission of Scott, Foresman and Company.

David L. Rosenhan and Martin E. P. Seligman. Reprinted from *Abnormal Psychology* by David L. Rosenhan and Martin E. P. Seligman, by permission of W. W. Norton & Company, Inc. Copyright © 1984 by W. W. Norton & Company, Inc.

Philip Roth. From *Goodbye, Columbus* by Philip Roth. Copyright © 1959 by Philip Roth. Reprinted by permission of Houghton Mifflin Company.

Cornelius Ryan. From *The Last Battle.* Copyright © 1966 by Cornelius Ryan. Reprinted by permission of Simon & Schuster, Inc.

Karen Sacks. "Engels Revisited." From *Toward an Anthropology of Women,* edited by Rayna R. Reiter (Monthly Review Press). Copyright © 1975 by Rayna R. Reiter. Reprinted by permission of Monthly Review Foundation.

Marta Sanchez. *Contemporary Chicana Poetry: A Critical Approach to an Emerging Literature,* page 1, to be used in *Critical Strategies for Academic Writing* (Bedford Books). © 1985 the Regents of the University of California. Reprinted by permission of the University of California Press.

John Sayles. "Tan." Excerpt from page 257. From *The Anarchists' Convention and Other Stories* by John Sayles. © 1975, 1976, 1977, 1978, 1979 by John Sayles. By permission of Little, Brown and Company.

Maggie Scarf. Excerpts from *Unfinished Business: Pressure Points in the Lives of Women* by Maggie Scarf. Copyright © 1975, 1976, 1980 by Maggie Scarf. Reprinted by permission of Doubleday, a division of Bantam, Doubleday, Dell Publishing Group, Inc.

Jonathan Schell. From *The Fate of the Earth* by Jonathan Schell. Copyright © 1982 by Jonathan Schell. Reprinted by permission of Alfred A. Knopf, Inc. Originally appeared in *The New Yorker.*

Robert Scholes and Eric S. Rabkin. From *Science Fiction: History, Science, Vision* by Robert Scholes and Eric S. Rabkin. Copyright © 1977 by Oxford University Press, Inc. Reprinted by permission.

E. F. Schumacher. Excerpt from *Small Is Beautiful* by E. F. Schumacher. Copyright © 1973 by E. F. Schumacher. Reprinted by permission of Harper & Row, Publishers, Inc.

Edwin M. Schur. From *Labeling Deviant Behavior.* Copyright © 1971 by Edwin M. Schur. Reprinted by permission of Harper & Row, Publishers, Inc.

Martin E. P. Seligman. From *Helplessness: On Depression, Development, and Death.* Copyright 1975. Reprinted by permission of W. H. Freeman and Co.

Sue A. Shapiro. From *Contemporary Theories of Schizophrenia.* Copyright 1981. Reprinted by permission of McGraw-Hill Publishing Company.

Thomas R. Shultz. "A Cross-Cultural Study of the Structure of Humor." From *It's a Funny Thing, Humour* (Pergamon Press, 1977). Selection reprinted by permission of Thomas R. Shultz.

Leonard Silk. "Why Experts Don't Agree." From the *New York Times* (March 26, 1980). Copyright © 1980 by the New York Times Company. Reprinted by permission.

Peter Singer. Excerpt from *The Expanding Circle* by Peter Singer. Copyright © 1981 by Peter Singer. Reprinted by permission of Farrar, Straus and Giroux, Inc.

L. C. Solomon. *Microeconomics,* © 1980, Addison-Wesley Publishing Co., Inc., Reading, Massachusetts. Reprinted with permission of the publisher.

Nancy Sommers. "Revision Strategies of Student Writers and Experienced Adult Writers." From *College Composition and Communication* (December 1980). Copyright 1980 by the National Council of Teachers of English. Reprinted with permission.

Gary Soto. "Cruel Boys" and "Oranges." Reprinted from *Black Hair* by Gary Soto, by permission of the University of Pittsburgh Press. © 1985 by Gary Soto.

James P. Spradley and Brenda J. Mann. From *The Cocktail Waitress.* Copyright 1975. Reprinted by permission of McGraw-Hill Publishing Company.

Margaret O'Brien Steinfels. "Of Tubes and Motherhood: Hatching Better Babies." From the *Los Angeles Times* (January 3, 1982). Copyright 1982. Reprinted by permission of Margaret O'Brien Steinfels.

Randall Stewart. From *Nathaniel Hawthorne: A Biography.* Copyright 1948. Reprinted by permission of Yale University Press.

Steven Strasser et al., "Showdown in Asia." From *Newsweek* (March 5, 1979). © 1979, Newsweek, Inc. All rights reserved. Reprinted by permission.

T. G. H. Strehlow. From *Aranda Traditions* (Johnson Reprint, 1968). Reprinted by permission of Strehlow Research Foundation. Copyright owner D. K. S. Strehlow.

David Sue, Derald Sue, and Stanley Sue. *Understanding Abnormal Behavior,* 2nd edition. Copyright © 1986 by Houghton Mifflin Company. Used with permission.

Gresham M. Sykes. From *The Society of Captives: A Study of a Maximum Security Prison.* Copyright © 1958 by Princeton University Press. Excerpt, pp. 9–12, reprinted with permission of Princeton University Press.

Mary Tall Mountain. "Naaholooyah." From *That's What She Said,* edited by Rayna Green. Copyright 1984 by Indiana University Press. Reprinted by permission of Indiana University Press.

Studs Terkel. "Barbara Herrick." From *Working* by Studs Terkel. Copyright © 1972, 1974 by Studs Terkel. Reprinted by permission of Pantheon Books, a division of Random House, Inc.

Lewis Thomas. From "On Embryology," *The Medusa and the Snail* by Lewis Thomas. Copyright © 1978 by Lewis Thomas. All rights reserved. Reprinted by permission of Viking Penguin, a division of Penguin Books USA, Inc.

James Thurber. "The Night the Bed Fell." Copyright © 1933, 1961 James Thurber. From *My Life and Hard Times,* published by Harper & Row. Reprinted by permission of Rosemary A. Thurber.

Barbara Tomlinson. From *The Buried Life of the Mind* (to be published). Used by permission of Barbara Tomlinson.

Jane Tompkins. "'Indians': Textualism, Morality, and the Problem of History." From *"Race," Writing and Difference,* edited by Henry Louis Gates. Copyright 1986. Reprinted by permission of the University of Chicago Press and Jane Tompkins.

Estela Portillo Trambley. From *Rain of Scorpions* (Tonatiuh Publications). Copyright 1975. Reprinted by permission of Estela Portillo Trambley.

James S. Trefil. "How the Universe Will End." From *Smithsonian* (June 1983). Copyright 1983. Reprinted by permission of James S. Trefil.

G. M. Trevelyan. From *A Shortened History of England.* Copyright 1942. Reprinted by permission of Longman, England.

Gordon Tullock. "Does Punishment Deter Crime?" Reprinted with permission of the author from *The Public Interest* 36 (Summer, 1974), pp. 103–11. © 1988 by National Affairs, Inc.

John Updike. "Your Lover Just Called." From *Museums and Women.* Copyright © 1960, 1965, 1967, 1968, 1969, 1970, 1971, 1972 by John Updike. This story first appeared in *Harper's* magazine (1966). Reprinted by permission of Random House, Inc.

José Antonio Villerreal. Excerpts from *Pocho* by José Antonio Villerreal. Copyright © 1959 by José Antonio Villerreal. Reprinted by permisson of Doubleday, a division of Bantam, Doubleday, Dell Publishing Group, Inc.

Kurt Vonnegut, Jr. From *Slaughterhouse Five* by Kurt Vonnegut, Jr. Copyright © 1969 by Kurt Vonnegut, Jr. Reprinted by permission of Delacorte Press/Seymour Lawrence, a division of Bantam, Doubleday, Dell Publishing Group, Inc.

Nicholas Wade. "IQ and Heredity: Suspicion of Fraud Beclouds Classic Experiment." From *Science* 194 (November 26, 1976): 916–19. Copyright 1976 by AAAS.

Charles P. Wallace and Tim Waters. "Gunman Kills Himself after Hostage Drama." From the *Los Angeles Times* (May 10, 1981). Copyright, 1981, Los Angeles Times. Reprinted by permission.

G. M. Wickens. "The Middle East as a World Centre of Science and Medicine." From *Introduction to Islamic Civilization,* edited by R. M. Savory. Copyright 1976. Reprinted by permission of Cambridge University Press.

Norbert Wiener. Excerpt from *The Human Use of Human Beings* by Norbert Wiener. Copyright 1950, 1954 by Norbert Wiener. Copyright © renewed 1977 by Margaret Wiener. Reprinted by permission of Houghton Mifflin Company.

Otto Will. "Process, Psychotherapy, and Schizophrenia." From *Psychotherapy of the Psychoses,* edited by Arthur Burton. © 1961 by Basic Books, Inc. Reprinted by permission of Basic Books, Inc., Publishers.

James L. Williamson. " 'Young Goodman Brown': Hawthorne's 'devil in manuscript.' " From *Studies in Short Fiction* 18. Copyright 1981. Reprinted by permission of Newberry College, Newberry, SC.

Charles Wright. Excerpt from *The Wig* by Charles Wright. Copyright © 1966 by Charles Wright. Reprinted by permission of Farrar, Straus and Giroux, Inc.

Malcolm X. From *The Autobiography of Malcolm X,* with the assistance of Alex Haley. Copyright © 1964 by Alex Haley and Malcolm X. Copyright © 1965 by Alex Haley and Betty Shabazz. Reprinted by permission of Random House, Inc.

Hisaye Yamamoto. "Las Vegas Charley." From *Asian American Heritage,* edited by David Wand. Copyright 1974. Reprinted by permission of Hisaye Yamamoto DeSoto.

Patricia Zavella. Reprinted from Patricia Zavella, *Women's Work and Chicano Families: Cannery Workers of the Santa Clara Valley.* Copyright © 1987 by Cornell University. Used by permission of the publisher, Cornell University Press.

Index of
Authors and Titles

Selections are indexed both by author and title. Following each entry, the academic discipline represented appears in brackets.